Torrington Project

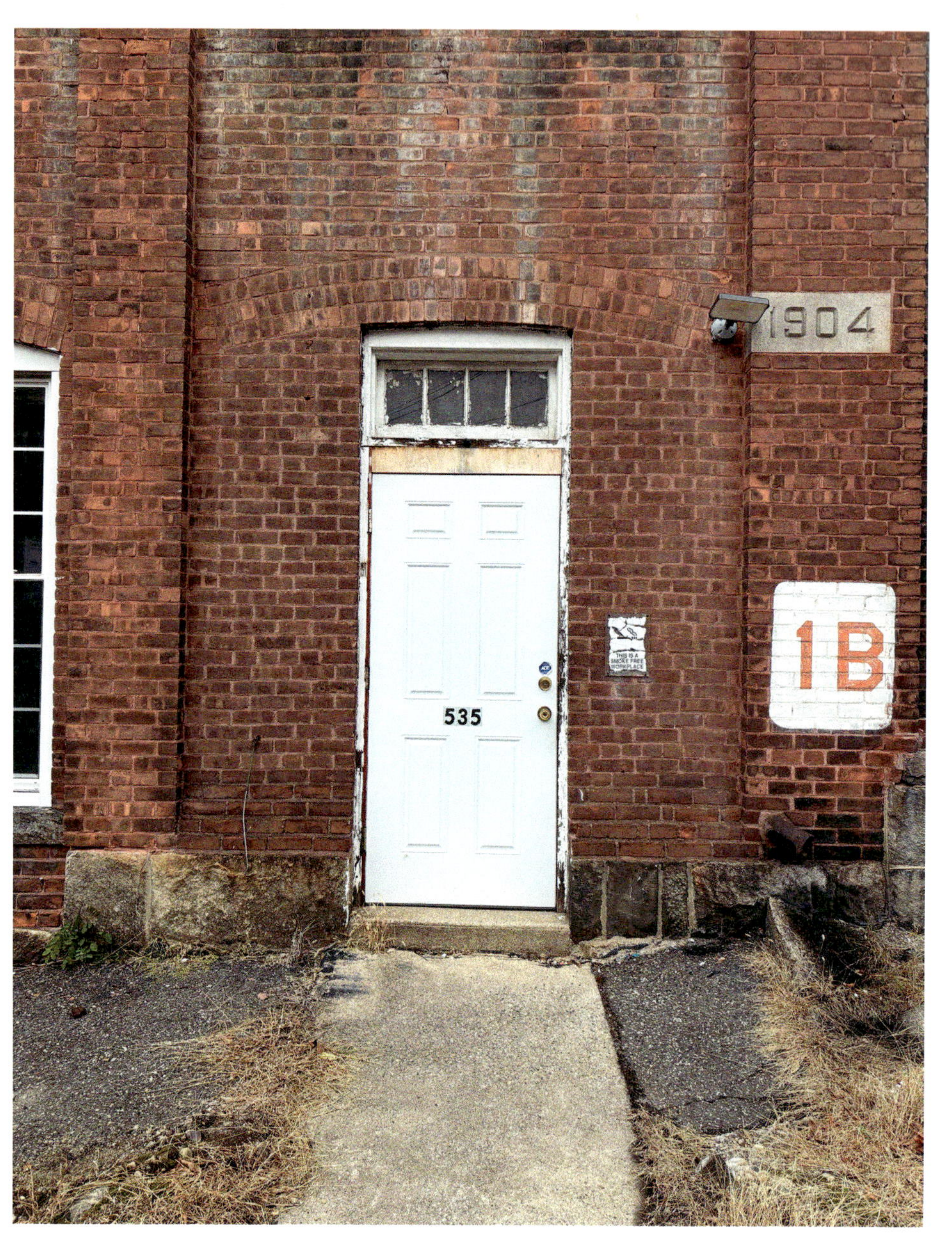

PRIMARY INFORMATION

Tom Burr

Edited by Blake Oetting

Torrington Project

Aria Dean   Christine Messineo   David Joselit
George Baker   Humberto Moro   Jody Graf   Jordan Carter
Renée Green   Maria Hassabi   Gordon Hall   Nick Mauss

I wanted to find space—to find a physical place to make and arrange work that had a vastness to it, a sort of boundlessness, yet still with clear boundaries in place—physical, architectural boundaries, but also temporal limitations. I didn't want this to go on indefinitely.

I wanted to find a space that could operate on multiple levels at once, to play with my own, and others', notions of a studio and what that could possibly mean, and give that space, that studio, a past, a present, and a future tense. It needed to look backward and forward. Backward to what I've done—and what some others have done before me—and forward, to speculate and imagine. To dream a bit, even. But I also wanted to delve deeply into the present, my own physical present, and feel seemingly endless hours and days pass through me, as slowly as possible. It felt to me that this issue of speed, and of slowness, was particularly key to discovering certain things about how I work and also why I work, which were nagging at me and couldn't be examined in the sort of operational rush of deadlines and commitments I found myself in, one where time trudges on all around, creating its own momentum, not listening or pausing or ever drawing a blank, answering noise with noise.

The sort of space mattered. It needed to have its own character apart from what I would do to it and within it. I wanted to find a space that had a compelling set of conditions that already existed, a sort of found object that I could then play with and against, that had the qualities of a vacated theater or an empty movie set. I tried to find exactly that type of abandoned theatrical space, but when I failed, I broadened my search. I imagined one kind of building character from the beginning and ended up with another altogether. When I set out to search in earnest, I gravitated toward storefronts and malls, places where commerce had been on display to the street. I wanted to prop my work up in salesrooms made for other types of merchandise. But none of these properties panned out. They either commanded higher rents than I was willing to pay, or in one way or another fell flat.

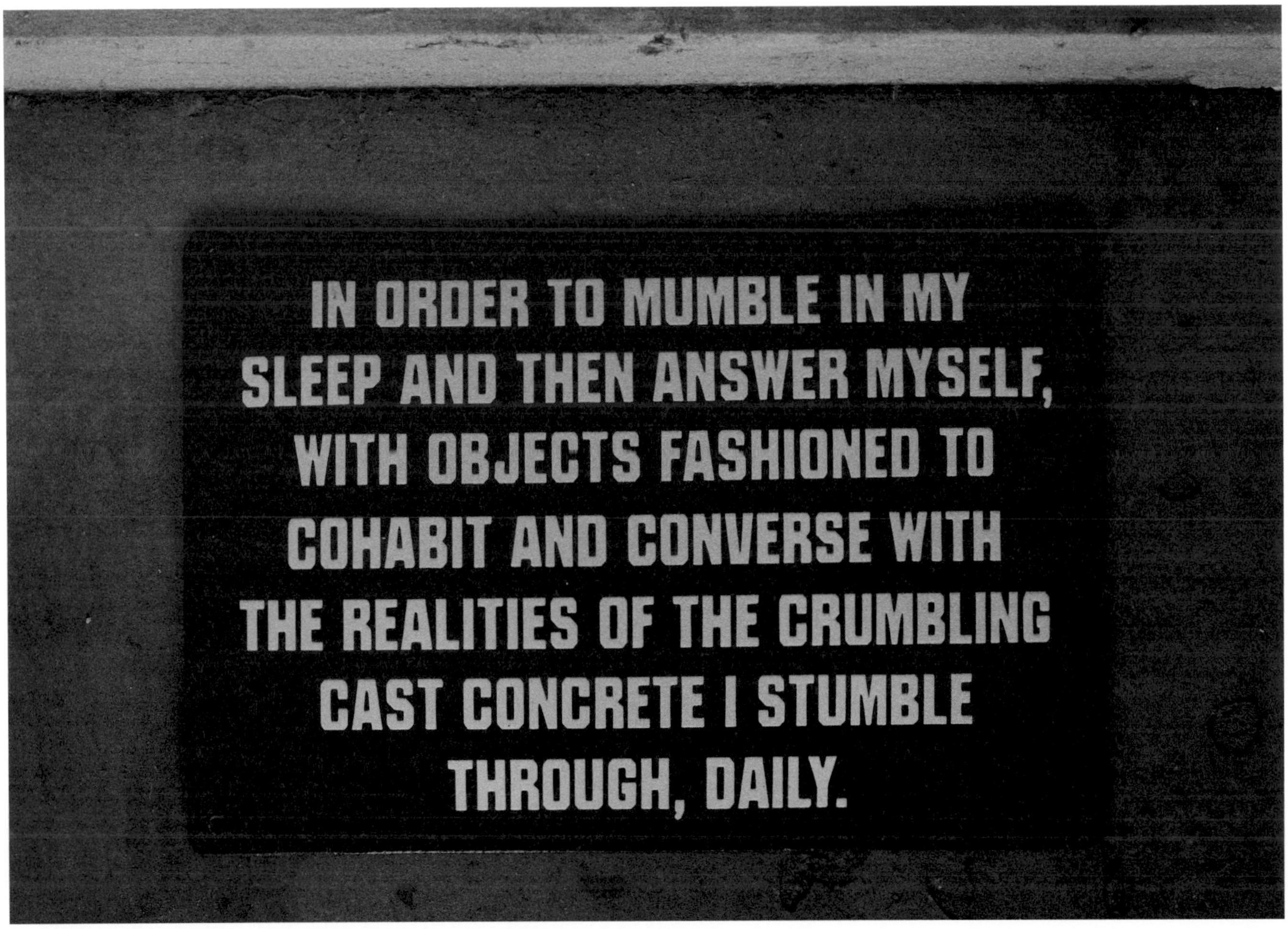

IN ORDER TO MUMBLE IN MY
SLEEP AND THEN ANSWER MYSELF,
WITH OBJECTS FASHIONED TO
COHABIT AND CONVERSE WITH
THE REALITIES OF THE CRUMBLING
CAST CONCRETE I STUMBLE
THROUGH, DAILY.

During his 2019 exhibition at *auroras*, São Paulo, *Hélio-Centricities*, Tom Burr made a series of enamel plaques, each one sequentially emblazoned with a segment of an untitled poem he had written in 2010. Writing in poetic as well as more art-critical vernaculars has been a consistent feature of Burr's practice, a way of grappling with and mapping the stances, affects, and conditions undergirding his work from the late 1980s onward. At this particular, relatively advanced juncture in his career, Burr's poem stuck out to him as a text to concretize—to place in literal relief—as an elliptical treatise on what exactly that "work" entails, namely ruminating, drafting, casting, and handling his eclectic array of sculptural materials. One of the plaques in question reads thus: "In order to mumble in my sleep and then answer myself, with objects fashioned to cohabit and converse with the realities of the crumbling cast concrete I stumble through, daily." While *Torrington Project* (2021–24) would not begin for another two years, this excerpt proleptically summarized that multi-pronged enterprise to come, the labyrinthine archive qua studio qua escape route that motivates the present publication.

My journey to Torrington and to drafting this text began in the fall of 2018, when I contacted Burr about a paper I was writing on his exhibition, *42nd Street Structures*, which took place at American Fine Arts, Co. in 1995. Our conversation eventually led me to his archive in New York City, many visits to the archive of American Fine Arts, Co. at Bard College, interviews with him about his work in the 1990s, and other excavations of Burr's thematic triangulation of Minimalism, cruising, and gentrification, one he choreographed with a particularly austere elegance in *42nd Street Structures*. In other words, my initial relationship to Burr's work was one shot through with the mixture of retrieval, pleasure, dead ends, and disappointment that encompasses the archival encounter—the sputtering half-baked statements

    Blake Oetting

found throughout file folders, news clippings, photographs, research dossiers, notes, and ephemera. Unbeknownst to me at the time of this initial research into *42nd Street Structures* was that Burr had begun a similar process with his own work, writing, and planning from the early days of his career. With Christine Messineo as his research partner and conceptual co-conspirator (and with financial support from the sale of his 1993 work *An American Garden* to collector Patrick Collins), he initiated *Torrington Project* in a former sports equipment factory at 535 Migeon Avenue in Torrington, Connecticut, about thirty minutes from his home in Norfolk. After installing a series of walls and adopting the factory's office as his own, Burr, along with Messineo, gradually began a parafictional process of institution building, assembling inventory and interlocutors into a nebulous organization somewhere between an estate, studio, museum, and *gesamtkunstwerk*.

Work that had been lost or damaged over the course of Burr's career, like his Prospect Park series from 1989, was reconstituted in *Torrington*, occupying a sunny zone in the northwest corner of the building he referred to as "The Clinic." Other works, like *Sexual Soft Target* (2017), were returned to Burr from his galleries in New York, Berlin, London, and Turin. Still other projects were born in *Torrington*, like Burr's *Journal* series (2024), before being shipped out to shows around the world. Alongside the sculptural work dotting the expansive building, drawings from Burr's archive, cleaning and construction equipment, ladders, computers, gardening supplies, and posters were stored in Torrington's nooks, crannies, bathrooms, and interstitial spaces. Between the reclamation of old work, the centralization of his archive's multiple homes, and the manifestation of new ideas, *Torrington Project* was conceived as a site of import and export—what Burr and I have jokingly and more seriously called "a conceptual loading dock."

This conceptualness—a word that, in this context, signals a critical, parodic, or contemplative distance— emerges from Burr's ambivalence towards studios, the fantasies of the solitary artist they play into, and the private visitations they so often service. Indeed, Burr entered an art world that had already deconstructed the studio; he belonged to a generation of young practitioners who bandied about the term "post-studio" as part of their inherited aesthetic lexicon, a way of designating artwork that eschewed the normative production flows of painting and sculpture to embrace more heterodox, ephemeral forms and strategies, like site-specific intervention, land art, installation, and performance. In the critical spirit of the 1960s and 1970s, the studio was also identified—most famously by Daniel Buren in his 1979 essay "The Function of the Studio"—as an important nodal point within art's financialization, a "commercial depot" for the manufacture of "ready-to-wear" work sent out to museums and galleries.[1] There in the studio, authorship is legitimated and authenticity secured, both of which ratify the value of artworks along their various peregrinations through and across other "frames, envelopes, and limits."[2] With this suspicion towards the traditional notion of the studio well established in the intellectual circles Burr found himself as a young artist (for instance, he read Buren's text while studying under Craig Owens at the School of Visual Arts), Burr never consistently maintained such a space. The time he spent at 535 Migeon Avenue is, in fact, the closest he has come to occupying that mythically monastic zone of artistic production for any extended period of time.

But *Torrington Project* was stranger and more expansive than traditional studio practice. Long fatigued by the "behind-the-scenes" showmanship required for visits from curators, critics, and collectors—and the mix of hope and disappointment they so often elicit—Burr purposefully chose a secluded location

1   Daniel Buren, "The Function of the Studio," trans. Thomas Repensek, *October* 10 (Autumn 1979): 53.

2   Ibid., 51.

Blake Oetting

in which to work. To get to Torrington from New York City, for instance, one either had to drive or take the train to Wassaic, New York, where Burr would pick people up and drive them another forty minutes into Connecticut. Built into the viewing experience of *Torrington Project*, then, was a demonstration of desire—for Burr's work, for Burr, for the pilgrimage itself—which pushed the visit beyond the off-handed, often estranged interactions carried out during studio visits. Furthermore, if one of the assumptions of the studio visit is that artists entertain their guests, upon entering Burr's space in Torrington it was often you, the visitor, who became the subject of analysis. If you were not directly photographed by Elijah Jaquez-Starks (who worked with Burr throughout the project to document every aspect of the activities that took place there) or shown photos of others that came before you, Burr's well-rehearsed description of his ambivalence towards the studio, studio visits, and the prying eyes of others would do the job of sparking self-consciousness about your presence in the space. In other words, as much as visiting Torrington was about viewing the work Burr made across his career, with *Torrington Project* the artist aimed to consider the dynamic of visitation itself. People were certainly invited to the space, and requests for visits were accepted, but what lingered in the air during my own long, ambling, friendly conversations with Burr in *Torrington* was the distinct sense of being folded into the artist's baroque conceptual structure.

Burr's insertion of his visitors into *Torrington Project*'s promiscuous materiality emerges, cheekily at points, in the present publication. Images of individual and group visits appear throughout the book, each one evidence of Burr's inversion of the studio visit's typical focus on the artist. More critical operations also emerge. For instance, in a photo taken during a visit back in 2023, staff from Bortolami are seen posed

Foreword Backward

in front of freshly minted collages that Burr made for his show at the gallery that year, collages that themselves incorporate images of owner Stefania Bortolami from an earlier visit to *Torrington*. While Burr's documentation of the Bortolami photoshoot depicts the gallery's staff members in the context of the slightly grimy post-industrial building, in the gallery's hands the image was reworked so they appear instead within a digitally fabricated white cube. Site-unspecified into the no-place of PDF previews. The tension between these images is but one instance of *Torrington Project*'s function as a stress test on the space between Burr, his work, and the institutional apparatus surrounding him—a way of putting into relief how the autonomy he sought out in Torrington rubbed up against an array of pre-existing contingencies. Rather than a blanket critique, these moments of slippage and negotiation showcase the intimate network of personal and professional relationships that Burr's work moves through, the act of balancing his constant desire for critical distance from art's commercial structure with the forms of support that structure provides. Indeed, while Bortolami was not financially involved in *Torrington Project* (beyond selling work originally made in the space, which of course matrixes the project back through the market), the gallery did help fund the similarly expansive 2017 project *Body/Building* in New Haven.

Burr's self-reflexive consideration of the studio as a space of hosting is indicative of *Torrington Project*'s broader examination of what exactly encompasses artistic practice. While the studio is traditionally the zone in which artwork is made, the activities that took place in *Torrington* redefine what constitutes that production in the first place. For example, the refabrication of certain sculptures like *Container (1-3)*, unexhibited since its creation in 2001, demonstrates the way that the continued maintenance and care of artwork eventually becomes a large part of artistic

          Blake Oetting

labor over the course of one's career. Elsewhere, the prominent office space located in the building's southern flank is a manifestation of the administrative tasks that make up a large part of post-studio practices like Burr's: coordinating with fabricators and art handlers, paying bills, writing texts, and responding to constant communication. The books, personal ephemera, photographs, and notes strewn across tables in the space Burr called "The Studio" (where he made new work) foreground the deep research that defines his process, the way that planning the scale of a sculpture; reading Gregroy Battcock, James Baldwin, and Paul B. Preciado; or poring over images of his family are all part of the work he engages in. Other actions, more imperceptible, more inscrutable, are also electrified through *Torrington Project*'s capacious parameters. Burr's 2023 *Capricornus* series, for instance, shows the artist lounging, leaning, and walking around the space, at times reading, at times simply lost in thought, collectively showcasing what the artist has referred to as "low density performing."[3]

This aesthetic, bureaucratic, and social activity comes together on the conceptual stage of *Torrington Project*, coalescing into a singular mesh of artistic functions. This aspect of the work has always reminded me of Bruce Nauman's photographs and videos from the late 1960s, like *Failing to Levitate in the Studio* (1966) or *Slow Angle Walk (Beckett Walk)* (1968) since, in a similar way, they also frame mundane moments, such as the artist slumped against a chair or getting coffee as performative acts in their own right. One might similarly imagine Burr, as sometimes shown in the *Capricornus* photographs, reading, playing with his dog Agnes, or merely strolling around the space. As Nauman noted about this period in his career, "I was an artist and I was in the studio, then whatever it was I was doing in the studio must be art. And what I was in fact doing was drinking coffee and pacing the floor. It became a question then of how to structure those

3   Tom Burr, email message sent to the author, February 10, 2023.

Foreword Backward

4   Bruce Nauman, "Bruce Nauman Interviewed,
    1979 (October 1978)," interview by Ian
    Wallace and Russell Keziere, in *Please Pay
    Attention Please: Bruce Nauman's Words;
    Writings and Interviews*, ed. Janet Kraynak
    (MIT Press, 2003), 194.

5   Robert Slifkin, *Bruce Nauman Going Solo*
    (Companion Editions, 2012), 25.

activities into being art, or some kind of cohesive unit that could be made available to people. At this point art became more of an activity and less of a product."[4] If studios operate as one of the institutional frames that offer objects the Midas touch of artistic aura, providing them with "markers of aesthetic significance like frames and pedestals," Nauman, auguring Burr's work with *Torrington Project* decades later, exploits that fact in order to radically reconsider what precisely accounts for the work of the artist.[5]

One other part, a crucial one, of how that work manifested in *Torrington* was Burr's arrangement of his sculptures and ephemera throughout the space. Burr is at an inflection point in his career, one in which his early work is increasingly considered "historical" and has subsequently become overloaded with the weight and repetitive invocation of particular descriptions, labels, and associated artists. Burr is, alternatively or all at once, a Minimalist, a queer artist, a second-wave practitioner of Institutional Critique, a former member of the now legendary gallery American Fine Arts, Co., or an artist that engages architecture and the built environment. This complex of ideas and formal tendencies has created a profile for Burr—one that comes with an obvious and welcome prestige, of course—a rhetorical space that he fits neatly into and helps secure him a position within the ongoing narrative of art history. While there is no doubt truth to, and a certain utility in, using these sorts of historical classifications, they also become constraints on how, and even for whom, the work resonates. Renée Green, who has been subject to some of the same formal and historical associations as Burr, and who writes about their overlapping trajectories in this publication, cogently described an awareness of how these discursive walls might easily close around her in 1992, when both artists were just beginning their careers. As she wrote at that early stage, "Designating influences at the moment makes me a bit fearful, primarily

          Blake Oetting

6   Renée Green, "Open Letter #1: On Influence"
in *Other Planes of There: Selected Writings*
(Duke University Press, 2014), 74.

because once this assertion is printed, then the likelihood of definite categorization is inevitable, although of course this is just as likely if one were to keep quiet as not."[6]

Torrington Project offered Burr a chance to both model and intervene into this process of historiographic calcification. One response witnessed Burr creating a stamp out of the logo for American Fine Arts, Co. (with the original font, Friz Quadrata), which he then used near the bottom of the version of *Construction of an American Garden* (1993/2022) made in Torrington. This playful gesture reconfigured Burr's status as a former American Fine Arts, Co. artist—and the subsequent association as someone engaged in anti-market, experimental, and critical work in the 1990s—as a *brand* that literally and symbolically inscribes his practice. Another tactic he employed was the orchestration of his archival offerings. Rather than arrange the space chronologically or thematically in ways that would shore up narratives about his career, Burr paired together works that had never been put in conversation, a reflection of his Broodthaersian inheritance. As I've written elsewhere in regard to *Torrington Project*, perhaps the most effective and poetic example of this curatorial spirit was found in the dynamic established between *Container (1-3)* and *Construction of an American Garden*. The former was made for an exhibition at nGbK in Berlin as part of a show featuring the work of three couples, one member of each of whom having passed away from HIV/AIDS related causes. Burr's large black cubes, a reference to the work of Donald Judd, framed a series of paintings by his former partner Ull Hohn, who died in 1995. The latter work, a similarly minimalist construction containing a section of foliage from the Ramble in Central Park (an area often used for cruising) was shown as part of art historian and curator James Meyer's important 1993 exhibition, *What Happened to the Institutional*

Foreword Backward

Critique?, staged in the midst of and presaging further demolition of queer space in New York City. A relay of desire, HIV/AIDS, loss, intimacy, and Minimalist sculpture ricocheted between these two works in *Torrington*, conjuring a dense relationality punctuated by the fact that Hohn himself watered the plants that made up *Construction of an American Garden* during its first showing. If the terms encompassing this relationship are familiar in regard to Burr's work, in *Torrington Project* they emerged in new and unexpected ways, through the ever-shifting constellation of works the artist chose to display.

Conceived as the final element of *Torrington Project*, meant to appear even after the works themselves had been put back into storage and the lease of 535 Migeon Avenue had ended, this book is an extension of the multiform, at times imperceptible "work" Burr has produced over the past four years. On one hand, we hope the images, text, and notations included in these pages will operate as a comprehensive portrait of Burr's grandiose project. Indeed, throughout the brainstorming and execution of this book, we have referred to it as "*Torrington Project*'s catalogue raisonné." On the other, in addition to documenting the works shown, the events staged—like the closing performances by Maria Hassabi, Nick Mauss, and Gordon Hall—and the people who visited the space, our goal is for the book to replicate *Torrington Project*'s conceptual core, for it to continue to destabilize the presentation of Burr's practice, operating as a translation of the refractive game of mirrors he has been playing the past four years. Can the pages that follow function as satellite spaces of the rooms in Torrington? Can a book contain rather than constrain? Will Burr's critical attention to historicization, the archive, and the relationship between artists, galleries, museums, publishers, and writers take shape through words, photographs, design, and a more permanent form? *Torrington Project* begs the question. ◇

     Blake Oetting

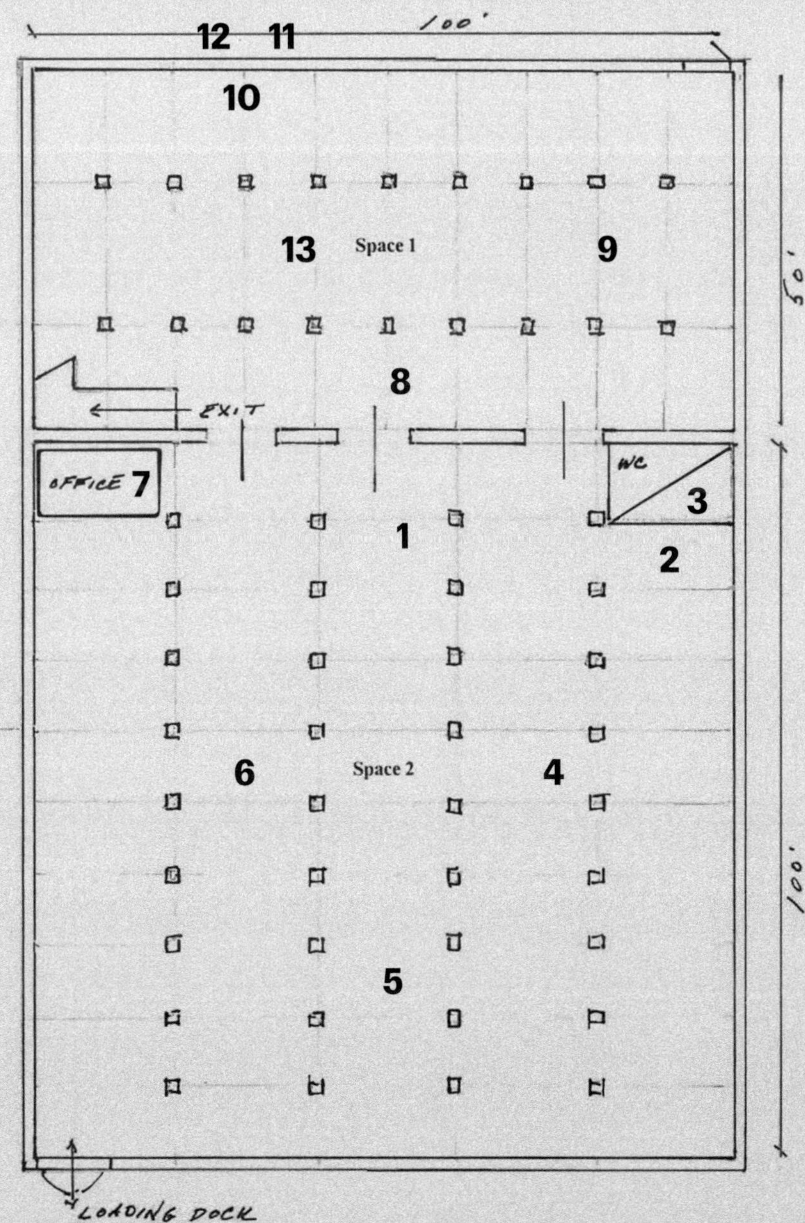

100'
12 11
10
50'
Space 1
13
9
8
EXIT
WC
OFFICE 7
3
1
2
6
Space 2
4
5
100'
LOADING DOCK

1

I visited the building at 535 Migeon Avenue a couple of times, initially dismissing it as all too romantic and familiar: It was a nineteenth-century warehouse building, reminiscent of SoHo, or Marfa, or Dia Beacon, or endless artist studios located in the empty shells of past industrial economies, with artists unconsciously residing there, neither reflecting on the conflation of past and present roles, nor making much of that relationship in their work.

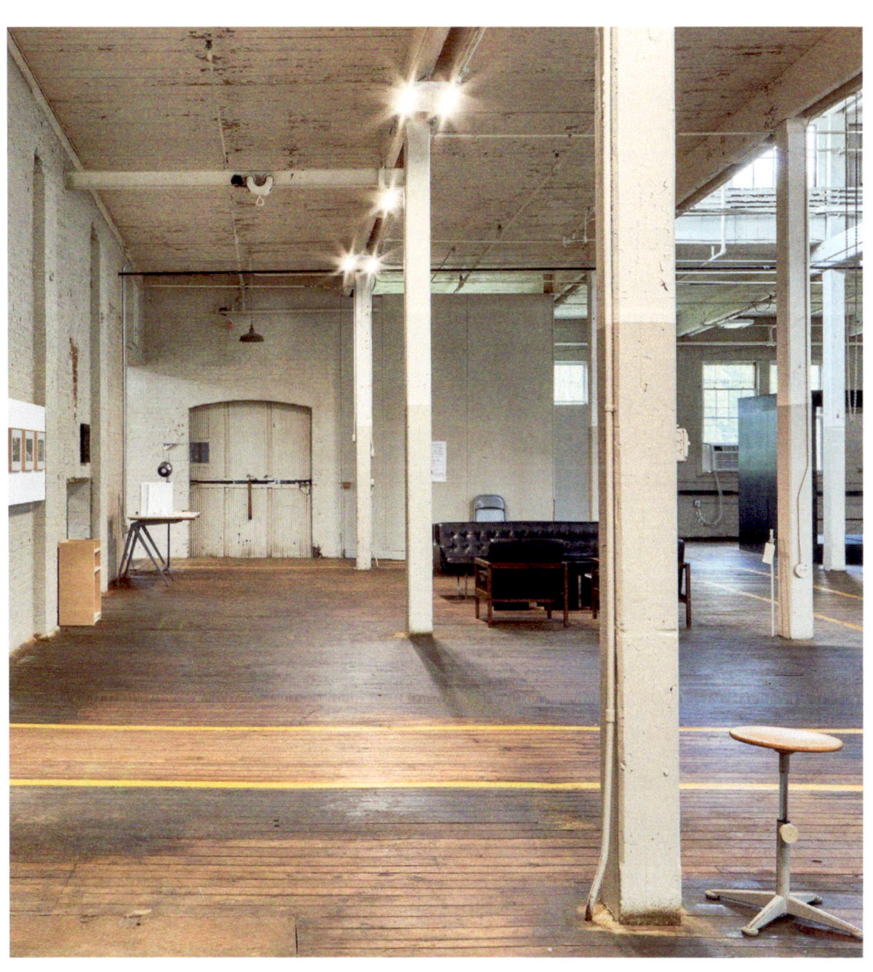

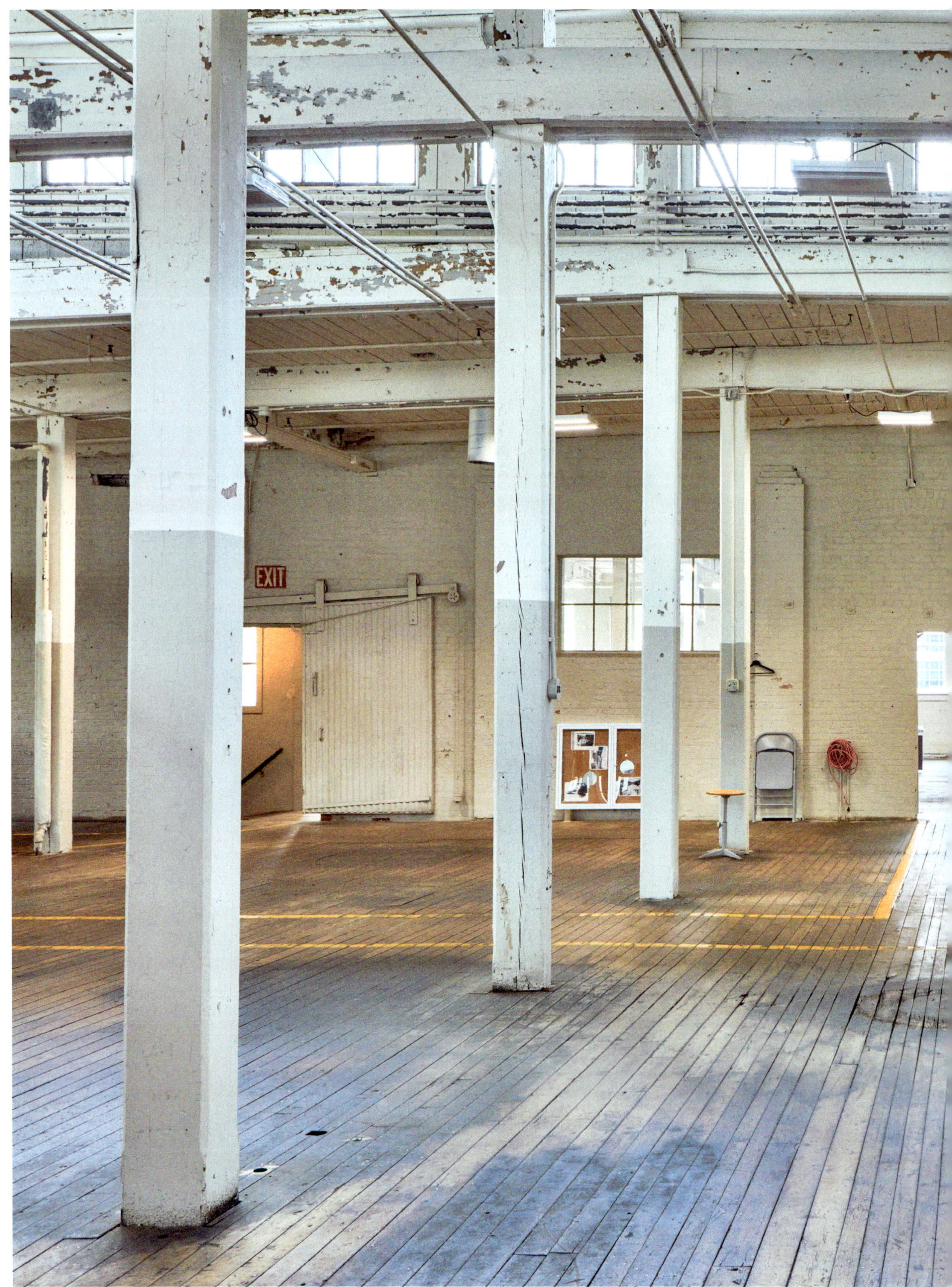

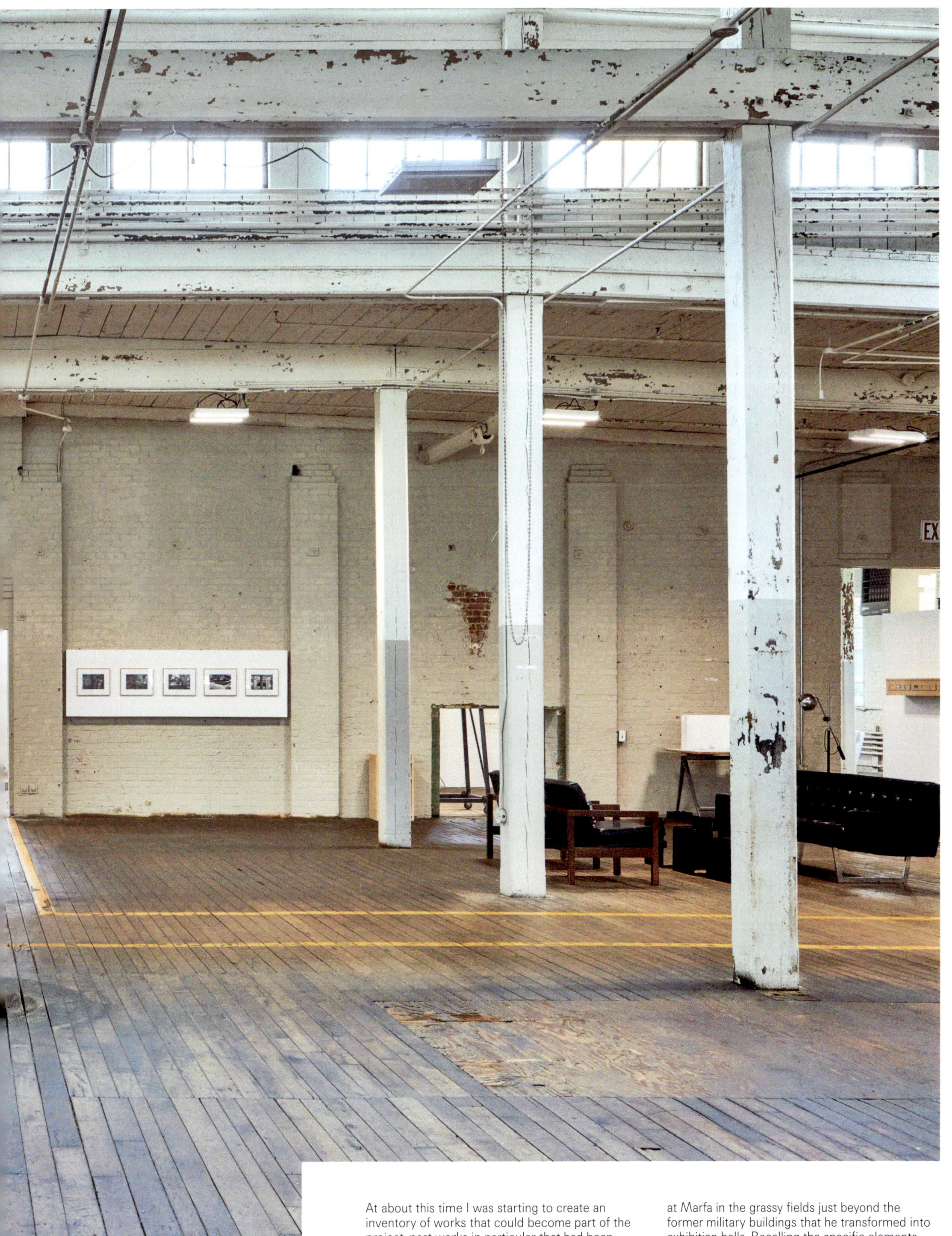

At about this time I was starting to create an inventory of works that could become part of the project, past works in particular that had been damaged or dismantled and would need to be remade on-site. The first of these, *Container (1–3)* is a work from 2001 that had been exhibited once in an exhibition in Berlin, and then a part of it was shown in a Berlin art fair some months later, and then the entire work was dismantled shortly after that. *Container (1–3)* takes on the form of Donald Judd's concrete works which are installed at Marfa in the grassy fields just beyond the former military buildings that he transformed into exhibition halls. Recalling the specific elements of that story started to matter to me. And the idea of bringing my work—which is something of an impersonation of Judd's—indoors and into this particular sort of space as a container, one that reverberates with this SoHo-Marfa-Beacon typology, began to feel like the right move; it made sense to me and to the work itself. So the stage was set, based on this one work as an anchor.

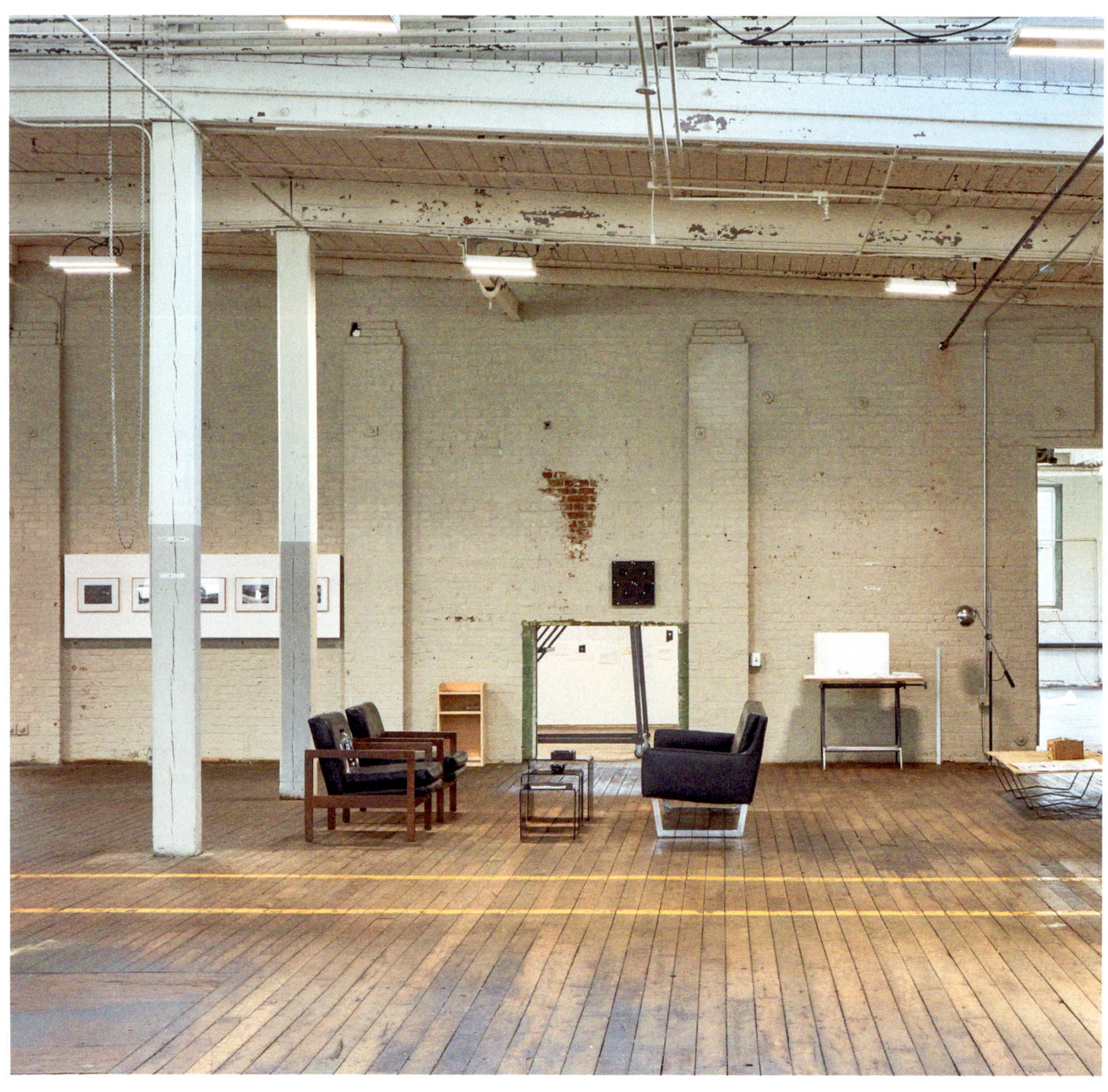

The project was born of different registers of emotions and distinct goals that emanated from those feelings. There were also problems I wanted to solve if possible, logistical problems of shipping and storage that had led to works being considered dead weight, and too much to maintain. There was anxiety I wanted to shift up and out of itself. There were past works I wanted to revisit, and re-present to the world, works that had been lost or destroyed, or packed away for years, lodged in my storage or the storage of the galleries I work with. I wanted particular works to see the light of day again, to mess with the logic of chronology—1993 next to 2001 across from 2010 just beyond 1988—to produce a dizzying series of associations. I also wanted to make new work from within the space of my older work. This part was about pleasure—about restructuring more pleasure into my work patterns and practices as a way of navigating forward while continuously glancing backwards.

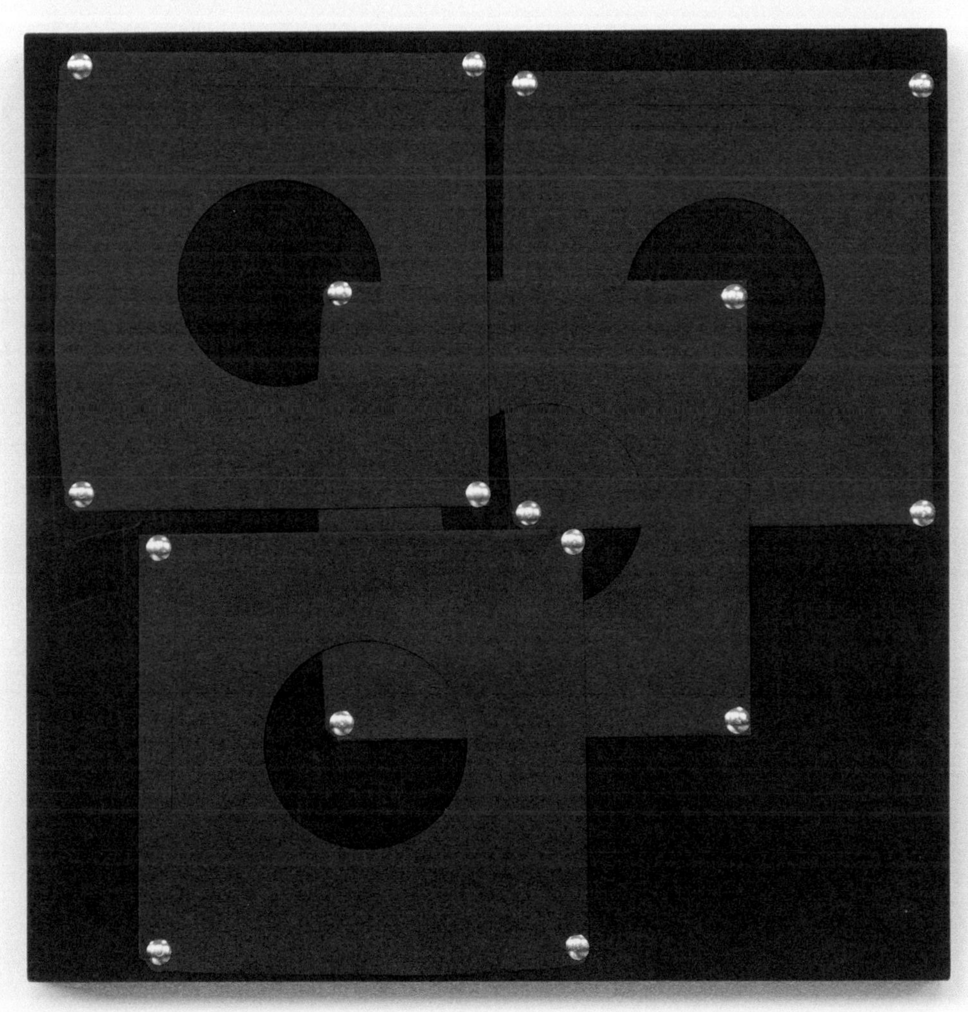

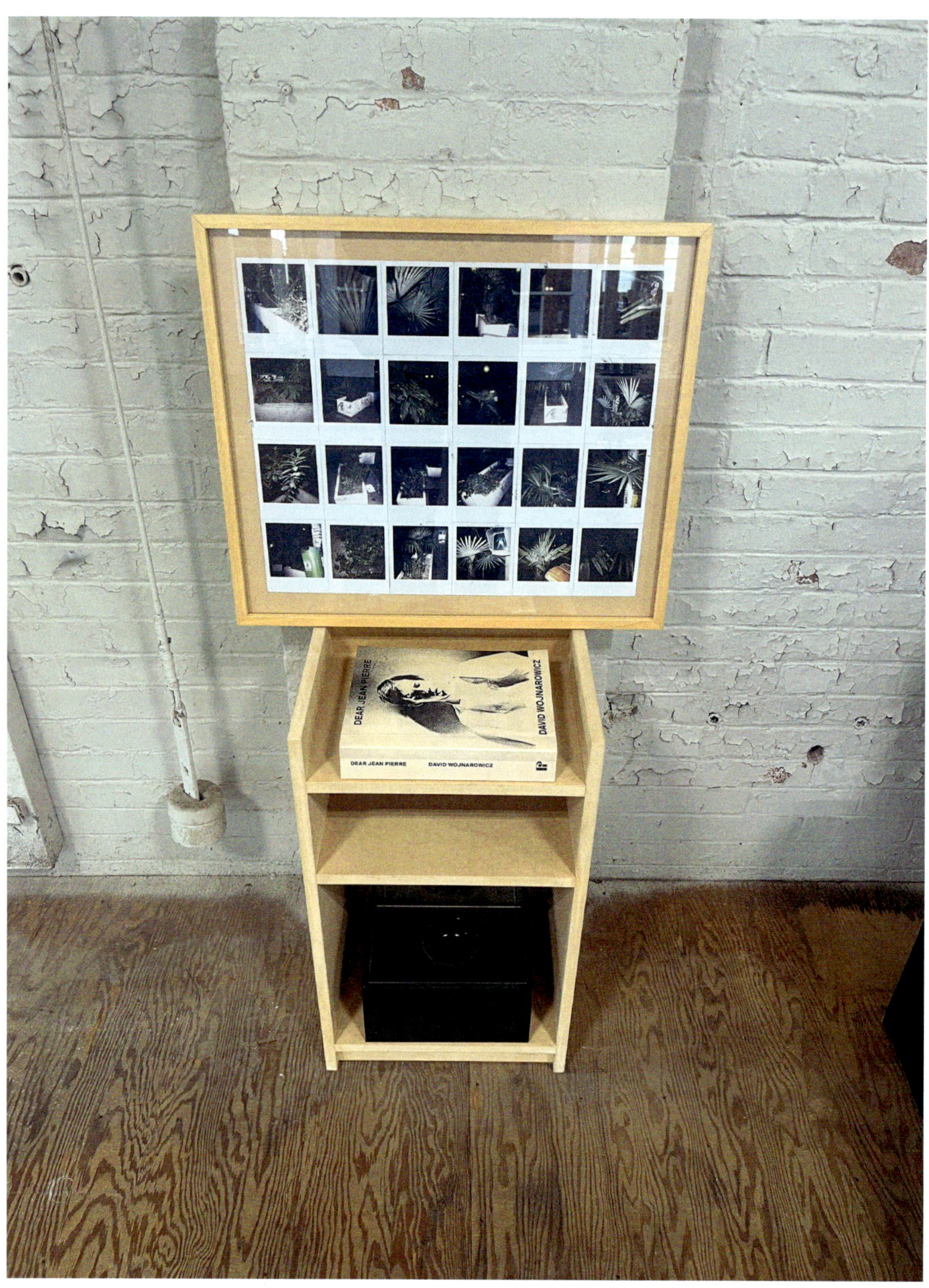

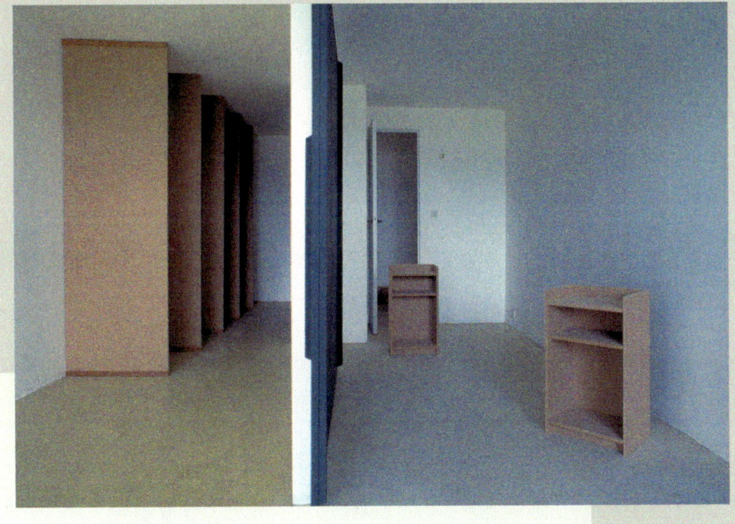

From mobile to immobile and back

A scattered, partial history of domestic storage units could inscribe its way from the realm of furniture and descreet objects, and the age of the cabinetmaker, up to a providing of architecturally based solutions, the built-in closet and storage system. The latter is included within the logic of the architectural scheme, to greater or less degrees, while the earlier furniture examples, the oak chest, the castan, the wardrobe, etc., were tradtional, portable units which made their way from location to location. The furniture solution did not give way to the more architecturally based method of storage, but rather the various solutions have been employed to accomodate the different architectural, economic, and stylistic enviroments they are meant to serve. One could also examine such developments from the perspective of the emergence of
a modernist agenda, where it becomes not so much a matter
of furniture versus architecture, but of an attempted dissolution of these categories. Built-in units extend from the design of architectural surroundings creating an integrated enviroment, theoretically eliminating the need for future furniture choice or further interior design.

Privacy

In a recent "occupants survey" of (U.S.) low and middle income housing projects, two issues were cited as being fundamental factors in determinig a tenant's satisfaction with their given living space. Both of these factors were grouped together in
the development of a single issue: privacy. The first of these, insulation and sound-proofing between the apartments, was discussed primarily in relation to the *outside*, with concerns expressed both about hearing sounds from other apartments, and of being heard themselves by the adjacent apartments.
The second factor, regarding the storage space available within each apartment, began to indicate a concern with privacy *within* each apartment unit of multiple occupants, and suggested the need to view the issue of privacy vis-a-vis the accumulation of objects, and the storage of these objects out of view of the other occupants. It was generally maintaied that there was inadequate storage space available in the apartments under study, leading within these terms, to a lack of sufficient privacy.

Gordon Matta Clark

(In the Firminy project), through the over-articulaton of the storage situation, by means of structural changes, (built-in closets and cabinets which adhere to, but which fail miserably in their attempts to produce a congruous effect within the
given architecture), the storage problem becomes positive space, temporarily removed from its status as hidden.
It is foregrounded within the apartment, as opposed to being concealed within it, and structured as open, and empty, rather than concealing objects and personal effects. In this sense, both the structural untis are exposed, and the space of their potential content revealed. The units are viewed in their various attempts to be seen as contingent with, and ultimately (ideally) invisible within, the existing architecture of the apartment.
The structures may be seen as sculptural and architectural intrusions into the pre-orchestrated scheme of the dwelling unit, not on the original plan, and cutting into the original

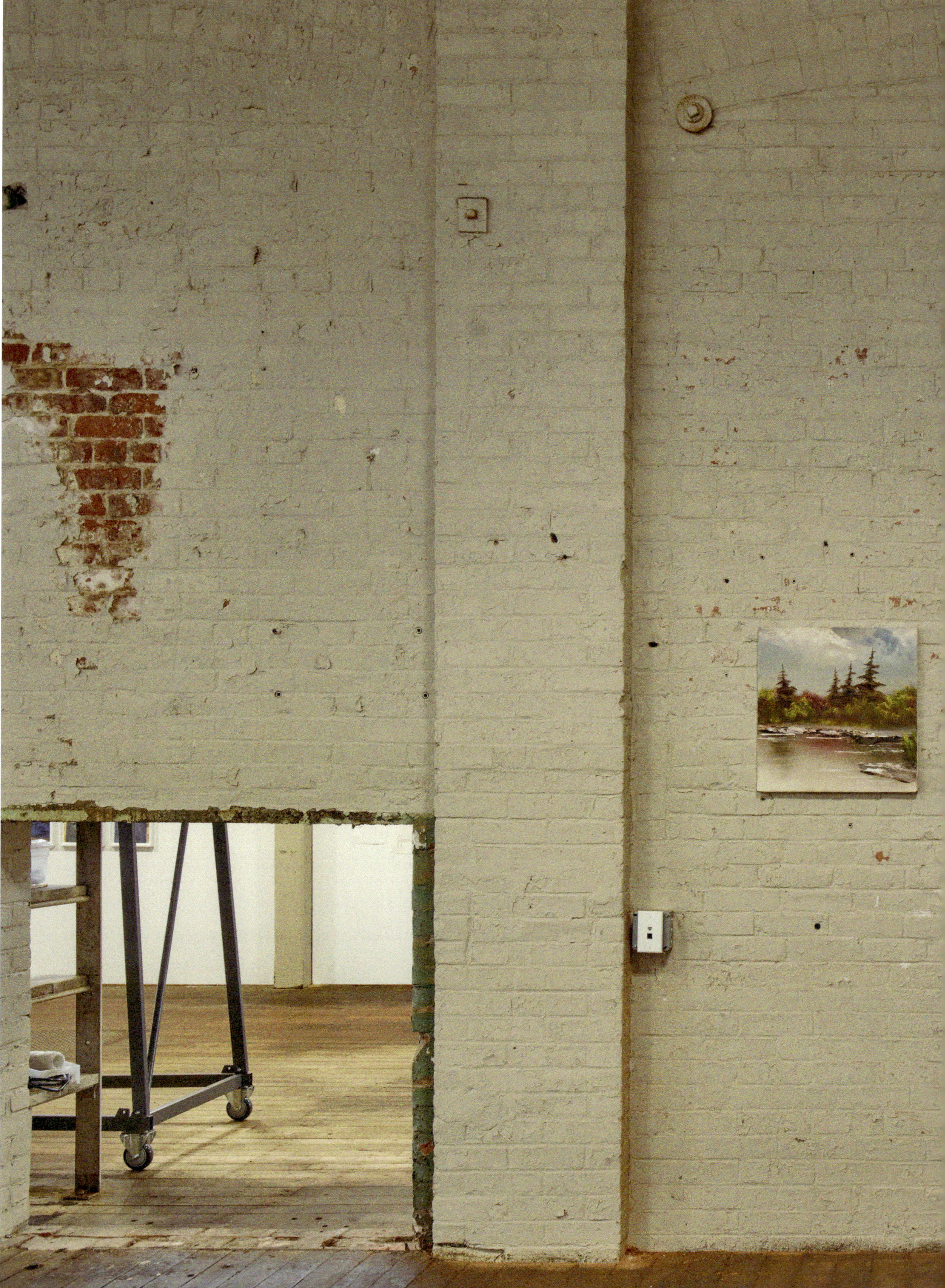

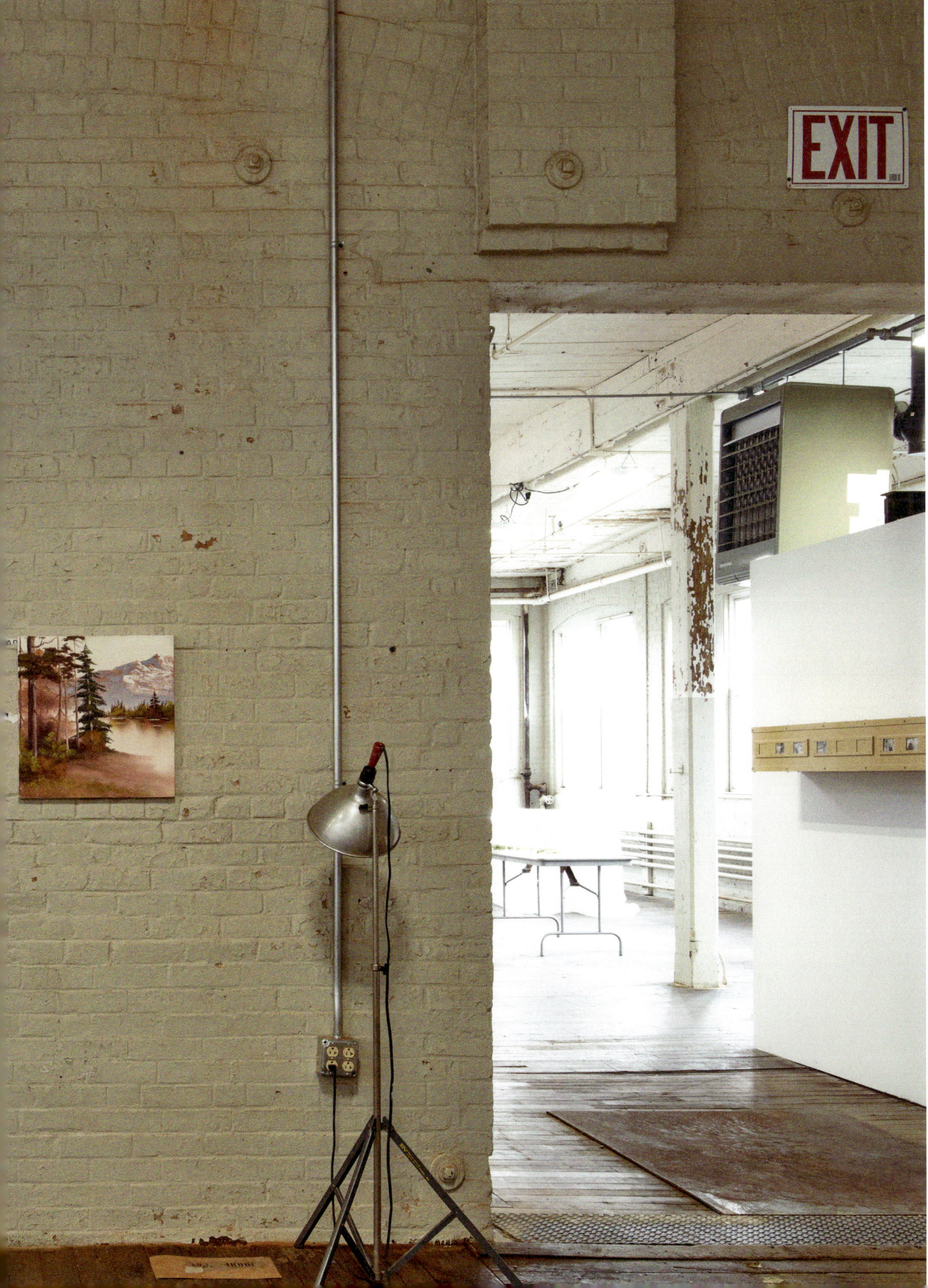
EXIT

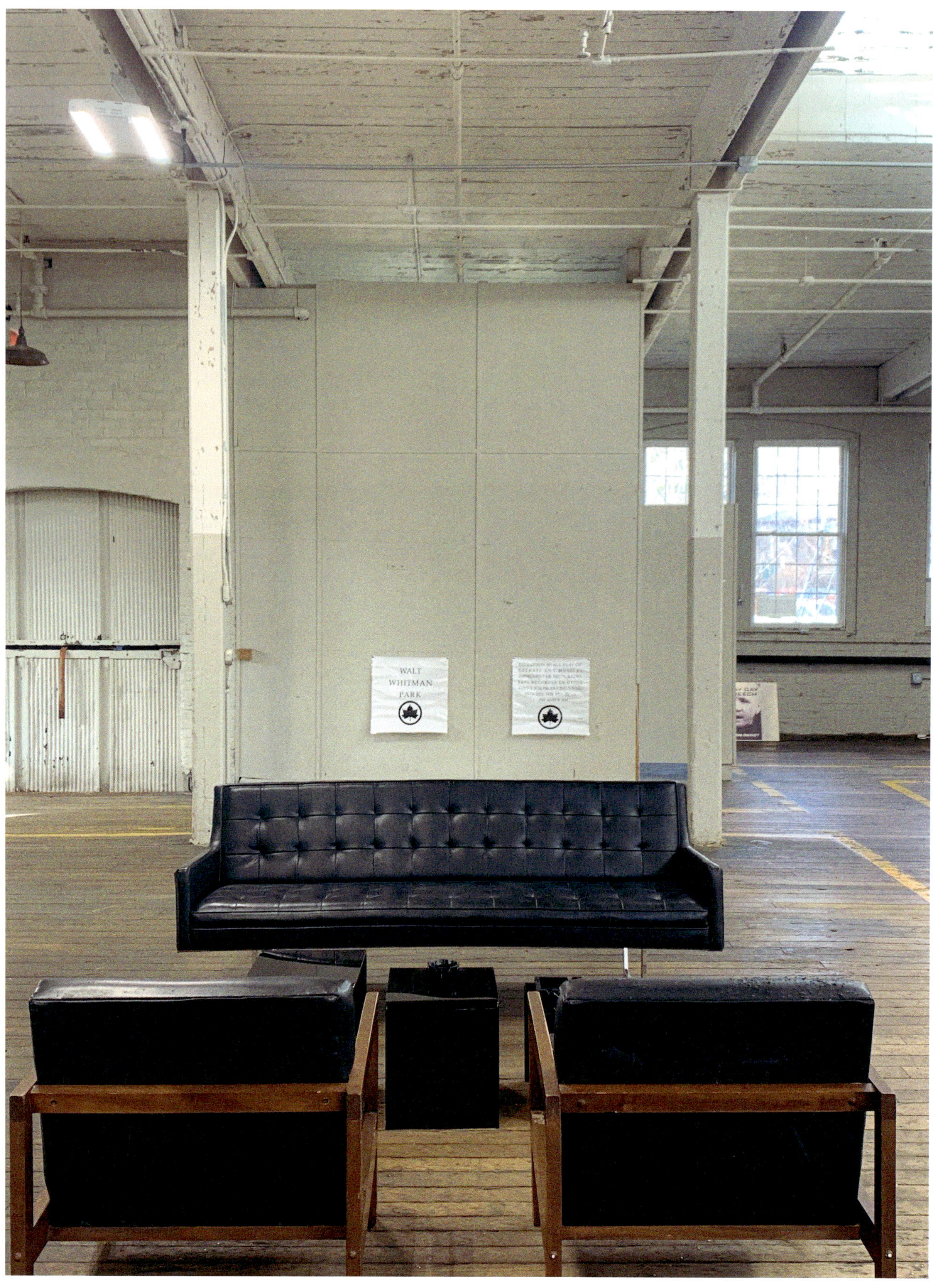
WALT
WHITMAN
PARK

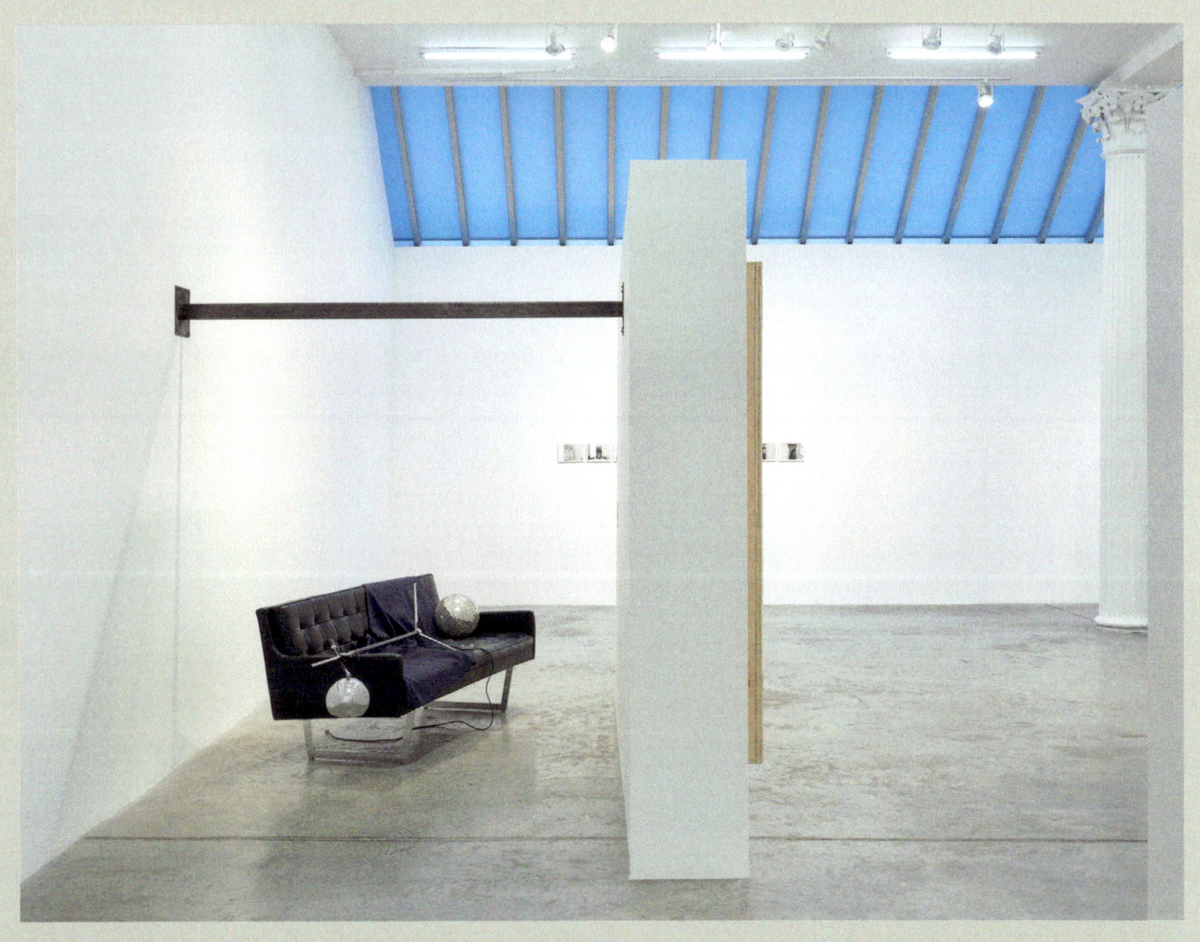

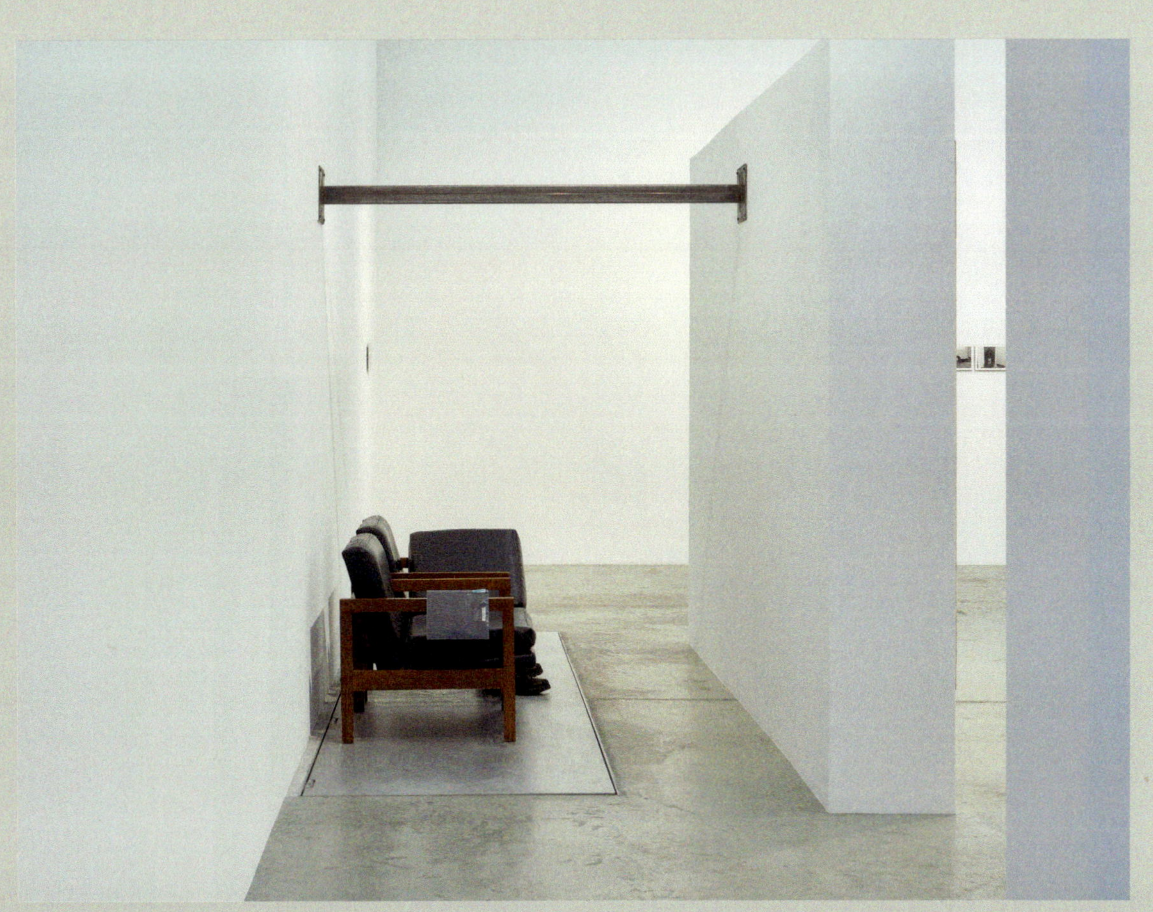

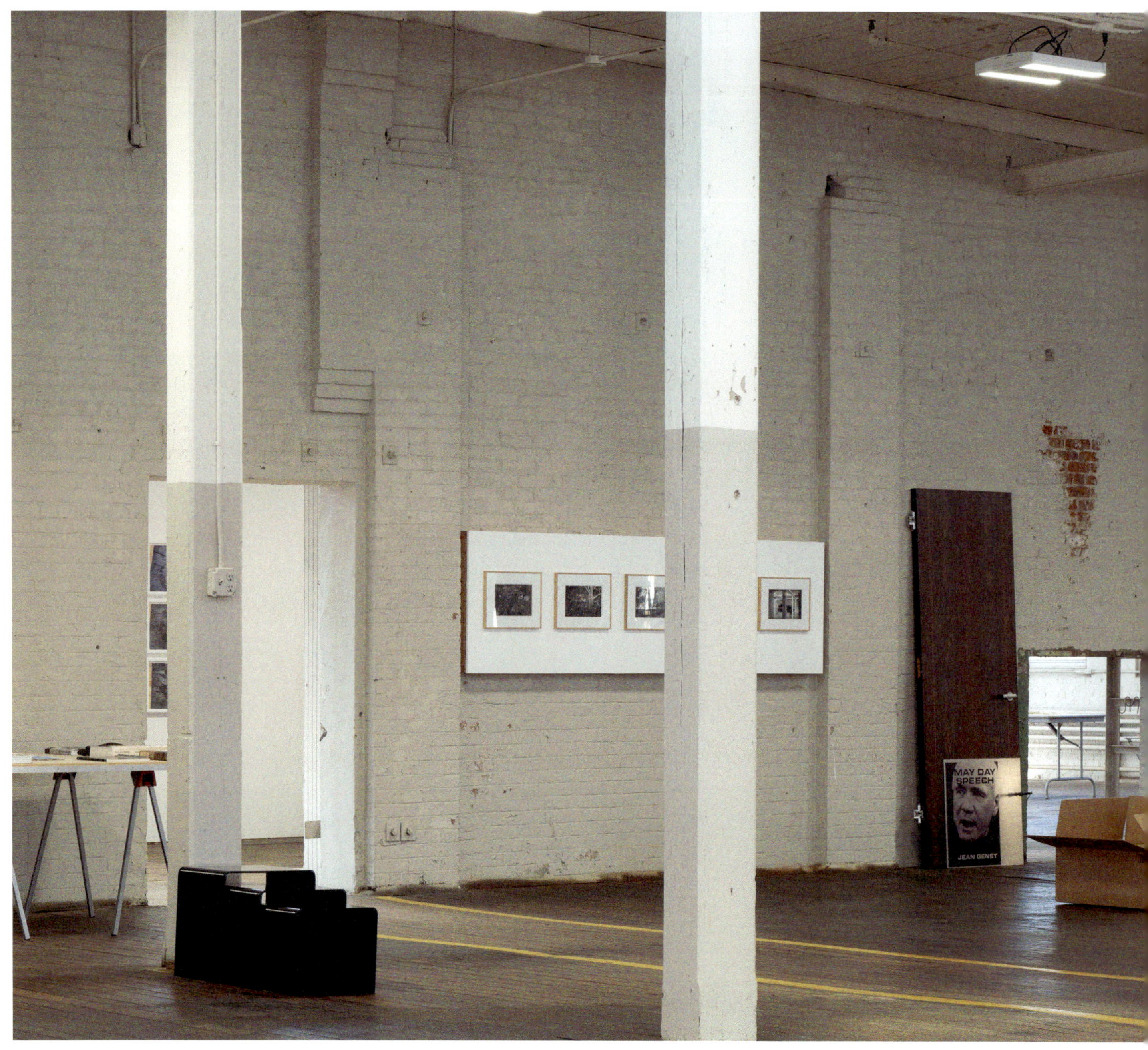

The settings that I make my work in have always been shifting and I like to work, and live, largely under the radar. I don't like studio visits. I don't think I *believe* in them—not as they are currently set up and accepted. They work, they function, they function too well in fact, but not necessarily for the full benefit of artists. There's a kind of rote dumbness to it all—a dog and pony show—an awkward, largely insincere spectacle that leaves me empty and longing. Colin used to tell inquiring curators and collectors that I was the sort of artist who has meetings in "bars, clubs, and cafés." I liked that then and now, and I mourn the disappearance of most of those spaces, though I still have one or two I can depend on. *Torrington Project* faced these irritations and frustrations head-on, and turned them, I think, into a work. Seen from just one perspective, *Torrington Project* was one long, durational studio visit. Three years plus. Exhausting and exhilarating, both, but probably never to be repeated, at least not in this way.

I do have vivid memories of two studio visits from Colin, though, or one at least, and the lead-up to a second. The first visit was also the first time we had met, when Colin came to open studio day at the Whitney ISP in the spring of 1988. He came to see my work, stayed for quite a while and we talked, then said goodbye and he left, only to come back again maybe fifteen or twenty minutes later, saying that he had gotten a few blocks down Broadway and turned around because he wanted to clarify something he had said earlier, which was that he was often attracted to work that reminds him of other artists' work, and in my case it was Richard Prince and Mary Kelly that he was reminded of. He came back to make sure I wasn't dejected by the comment, which I can't remember if I was or not—mostly I was delighted to see him round the corner again into my space, because I found him so charming and smart. The second memory is of the apartment I was sharing with Ull in Park Slope sometime the following year. Colin was coming to see us in the evening after the gallery had closed, but he was delayed and it got later, and later still, and he called and apologized, and then he called a final time and told us Pat Hearn would be joining him, a fact that sent Ull into a frenzy of vacuuming and rearranging of his work and the furniture—Pat burned brightly for him. And for me too. It was after 11 p.m. when they arrived.

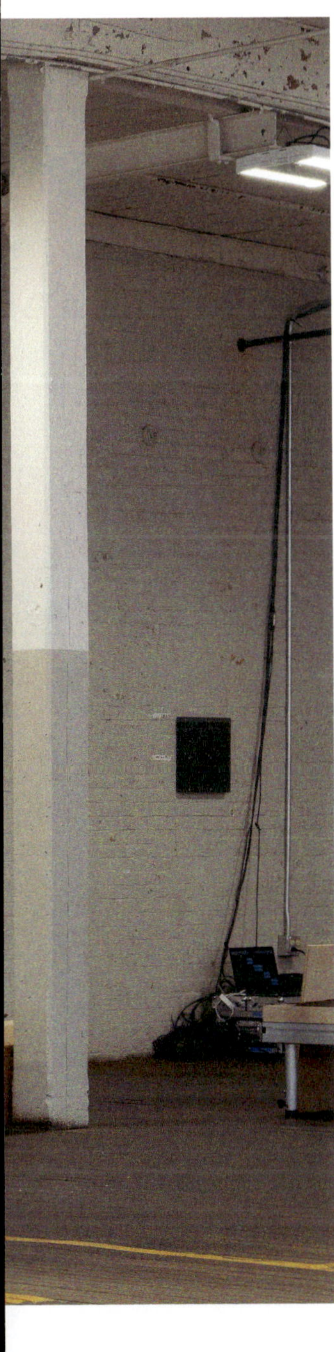

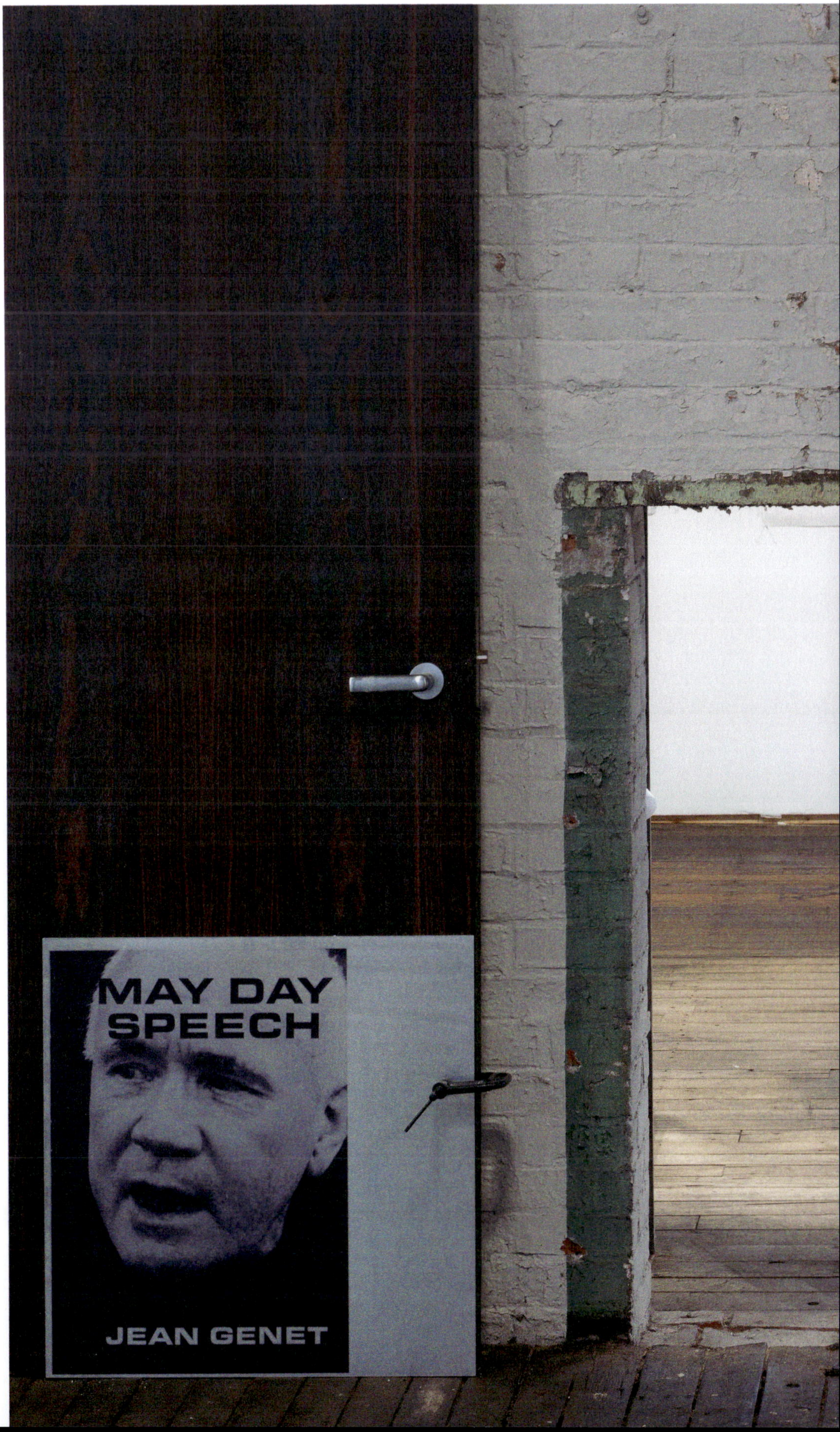

MAY DAY
SPEECH
JEAN GENET

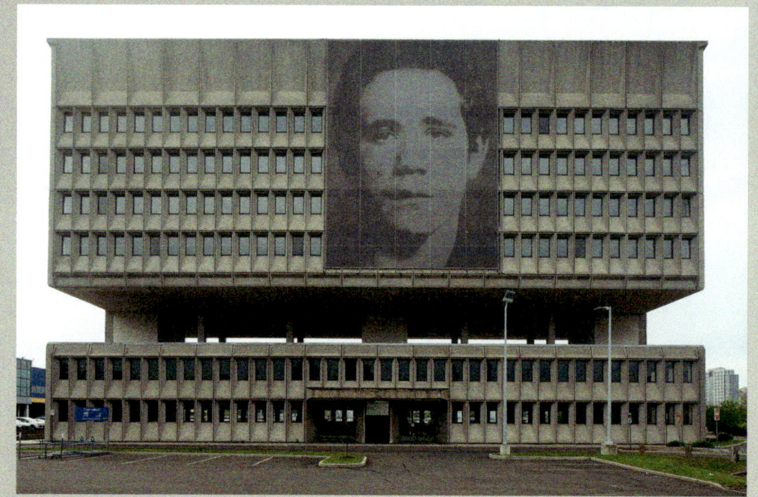 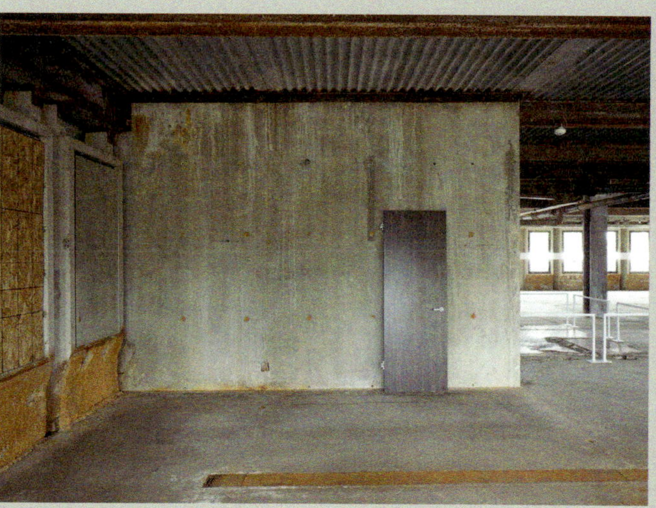

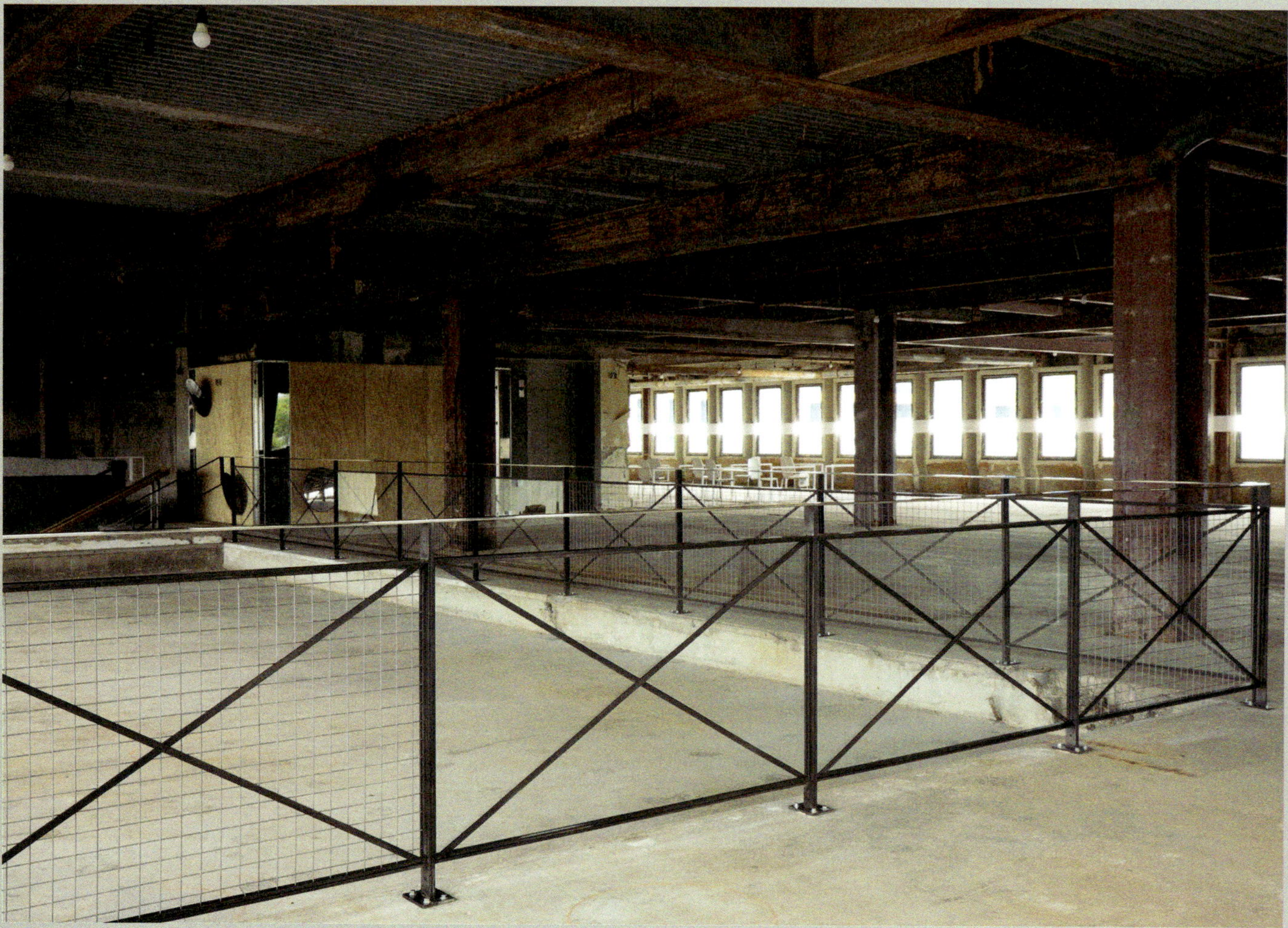

I think the story of Torrington goes back decades, as many as I've lived. There are memories of the many spaces I created when I was a kid, and then as a teenager, both actual and imagined, spaces that were, I think, elaborations of the need for safety and protection, but also a form of grafting myself onto and into structures and spaces as a way to present myself to others: hedges between houses, furniture arrangements in my childhood bedroom, closets, crawlspaces, all of these were venues for refuge from and projection into the world.

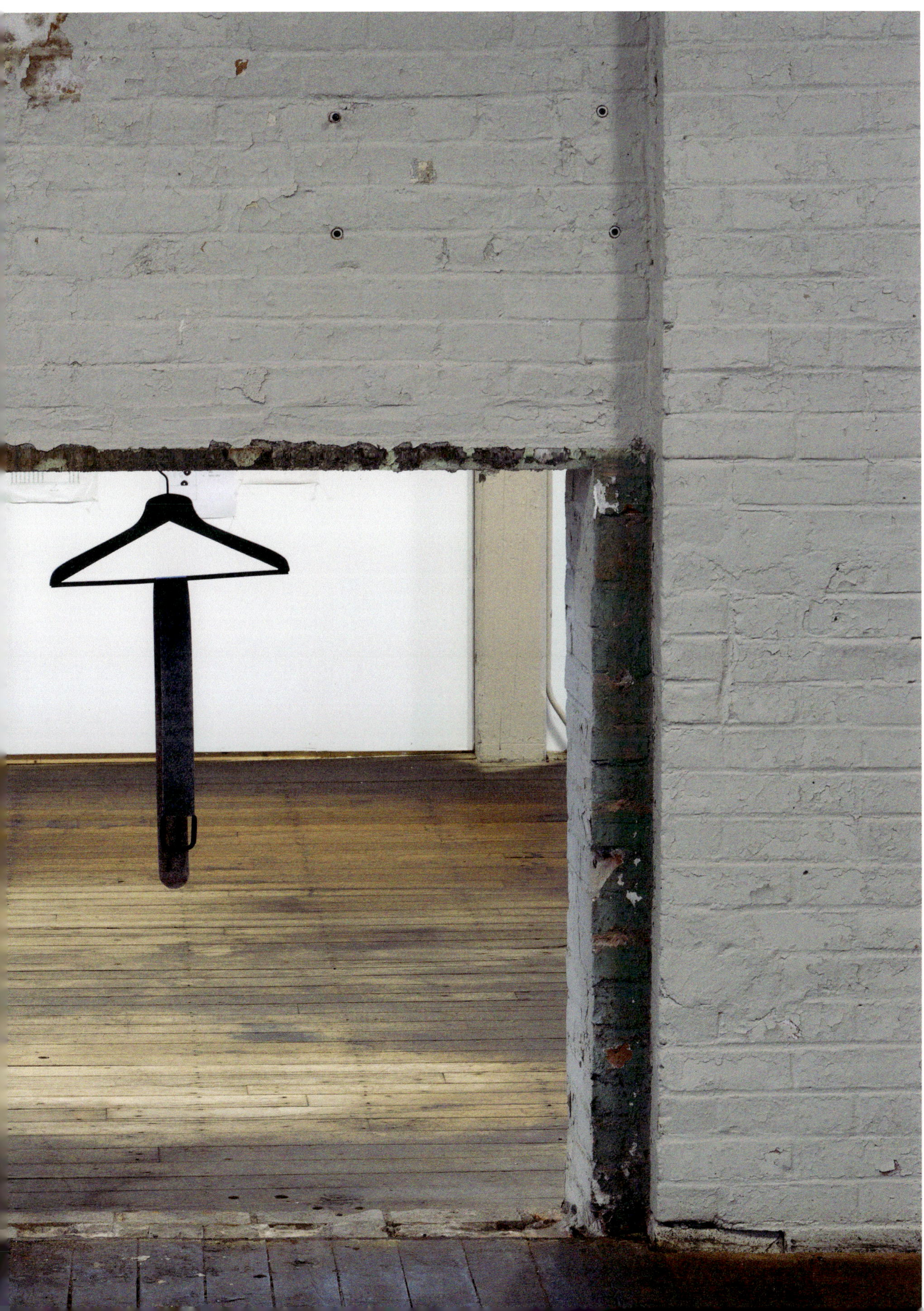

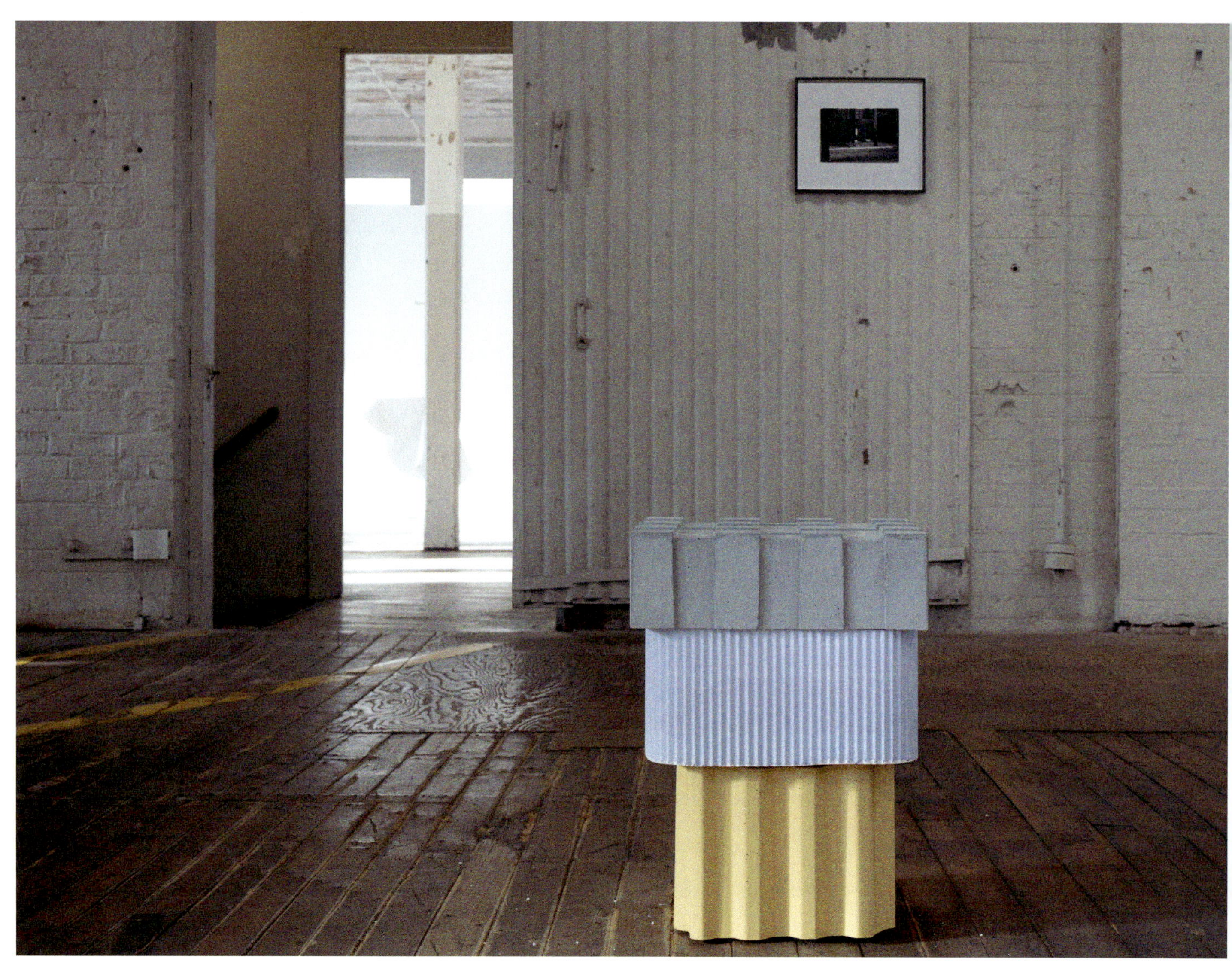

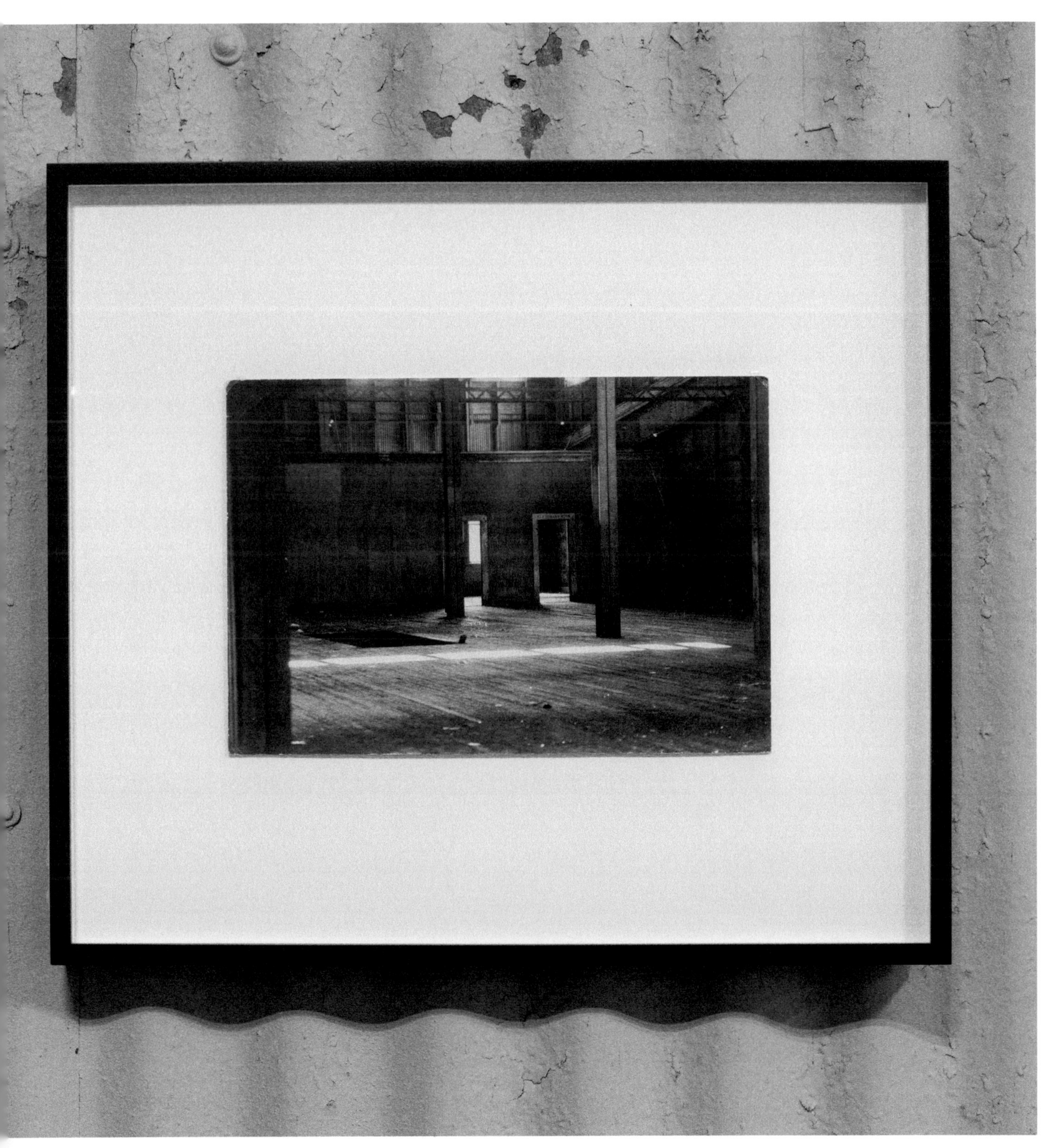

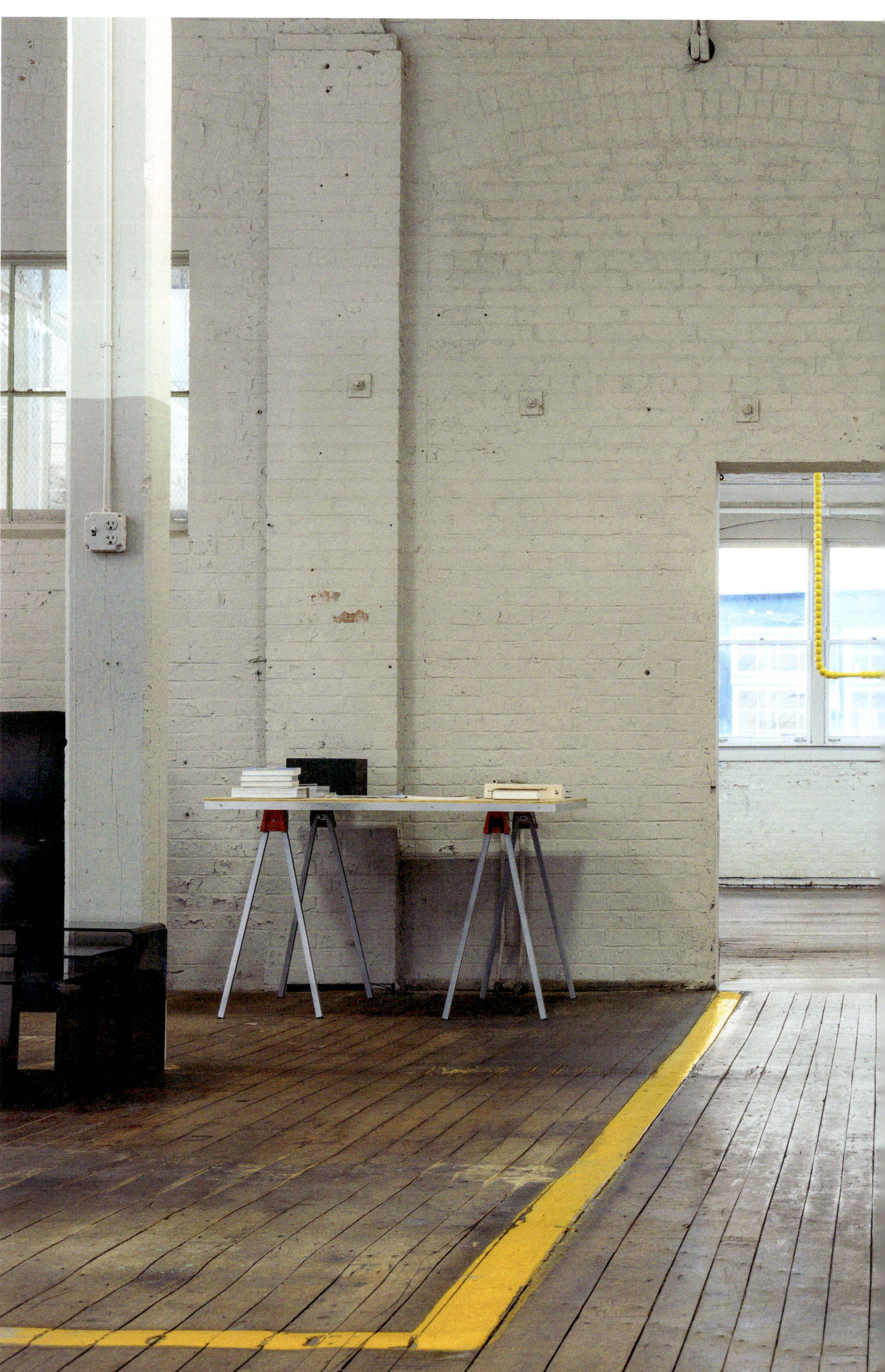

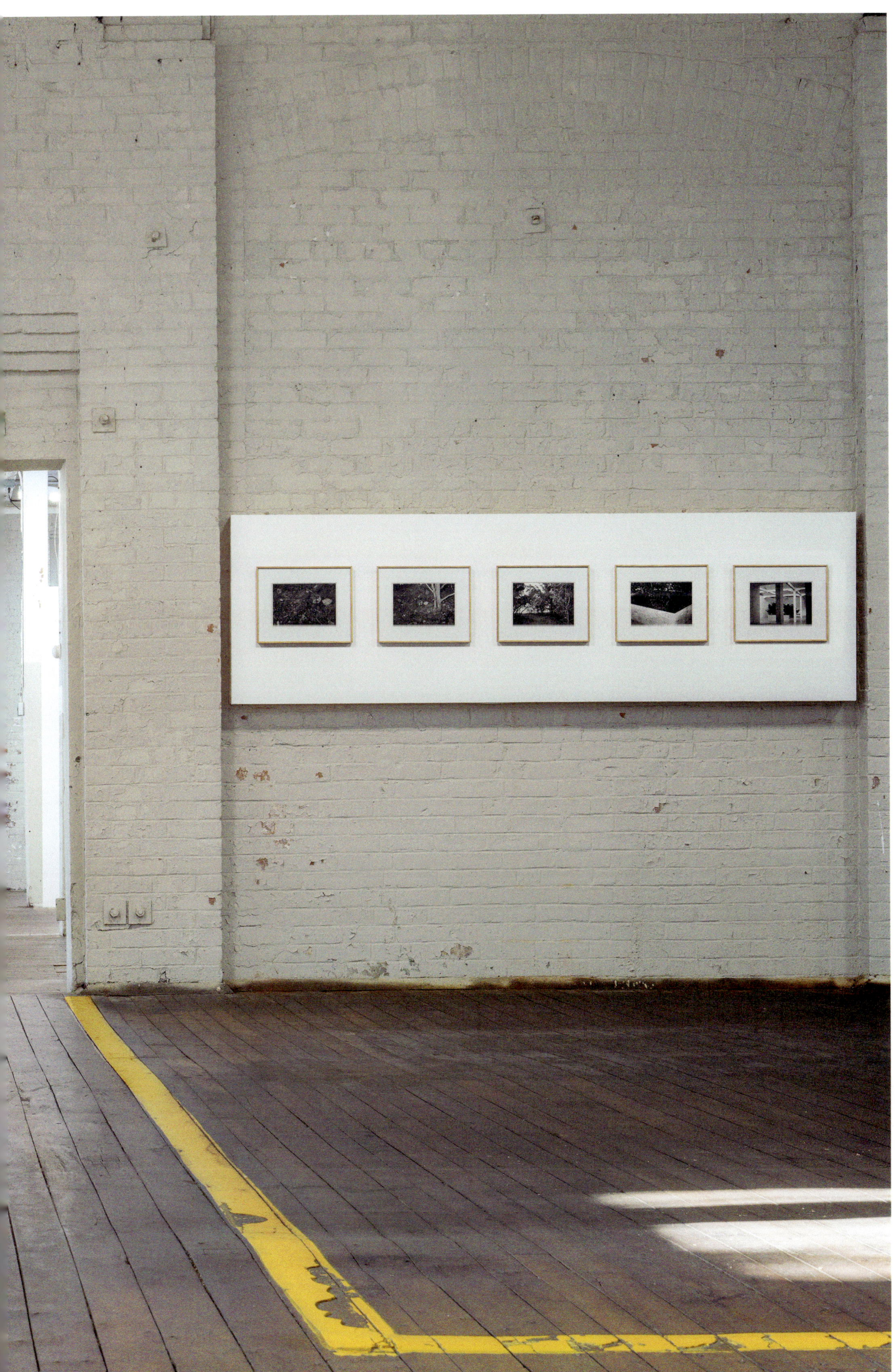

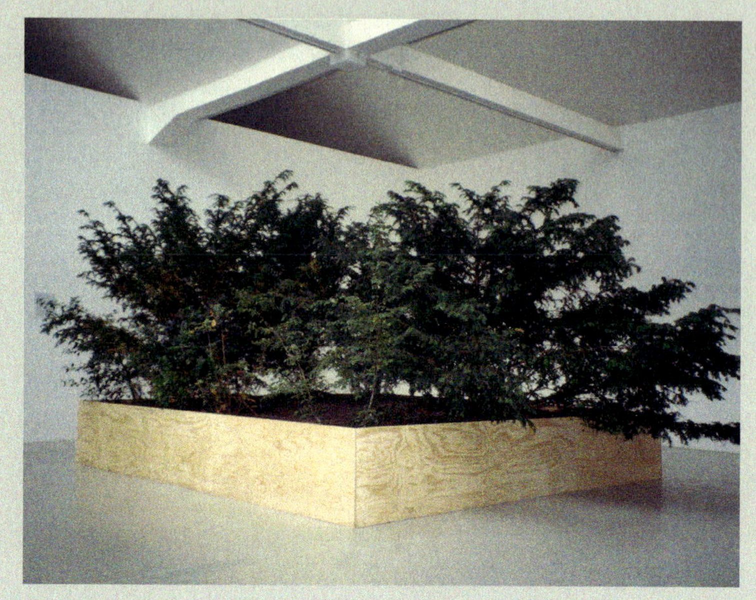

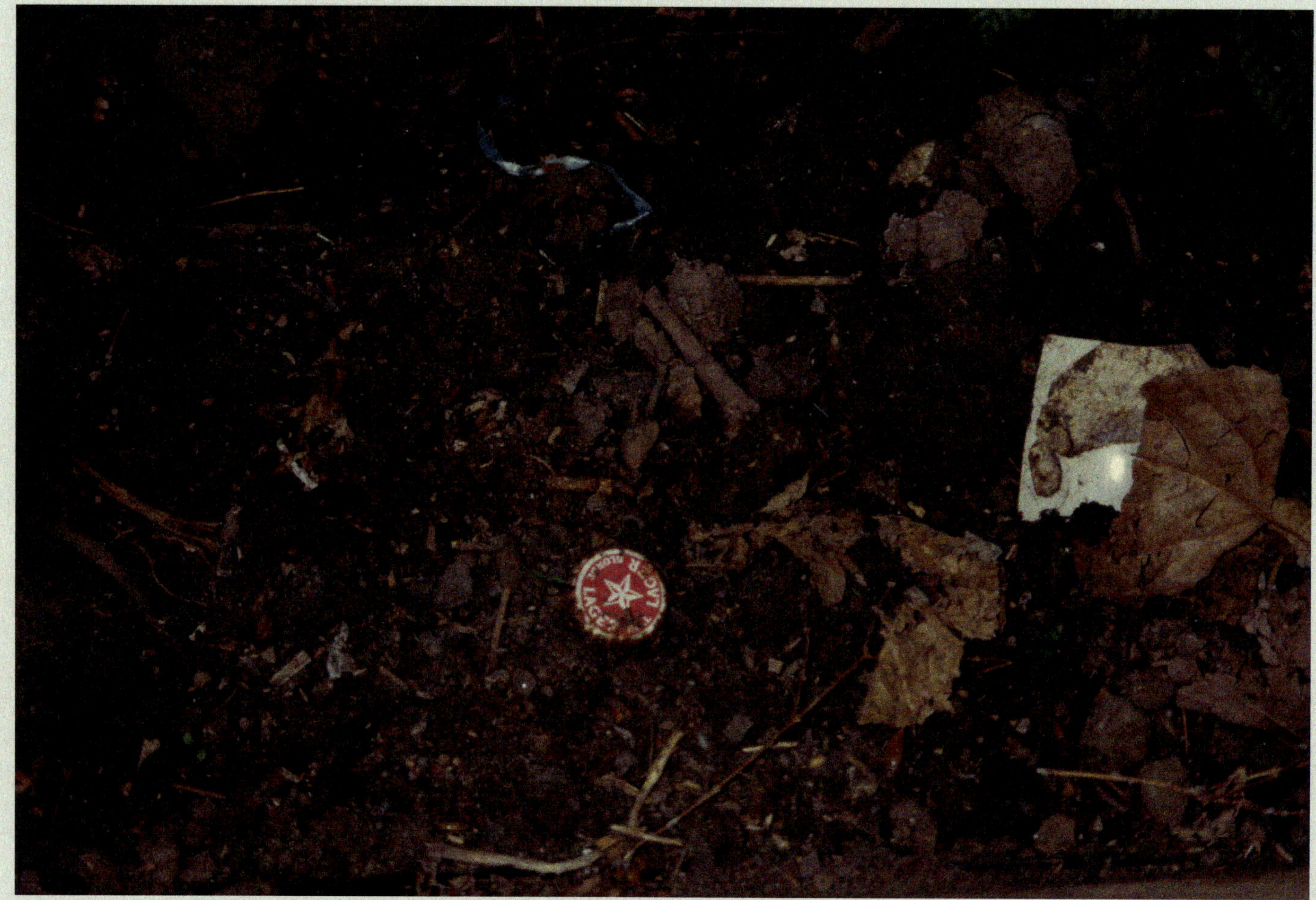

TRASH

Tom Burr

Information ...

Mr. Studhalter makes his way through the park, rapidly spewing our bundles of information spanning developments of the past twenty years, one moment pointing to an expanse of ground cover recently planted, the next to the numerous stumps of 70 year old taxus plants, which have been cut back in the order to create new growth at much lower levels. He indicates what is new to the park, and what was here when he came to the Gartenbauamt in the 1970's. When he arrived on the scene the Platzspitz looked radically different from the way it appears today. Heavy growth was everywhere ... large clusters of taxus, rhododendrons and holly divided the relatively small space of the park into a series of passageways and outside rooms ... beech trees towered over everything, (many still do), and beech saplings had sprung up all over the open areas beneath them, (all since removed) ... Large chestnut trees next to the Landesmuseum further darkened the park, and where the various shrubbery and ground coverings couldn't survive due to a lack of sunlight, the earth remained barren and exposed to the elements and to the inevitable process of erosion. Mr. Studhalter explains that this overgrown enviroment was probably a wrong development, creating too many isolated spaces within the park, very much the opposite of the Platzspitz today where one can look out across the entire space of the park, and sunlight makes its way down into the park, allowing grass and flowers to flourish in large open areas. In the 1970's, Mr. Studhalter notes, the park was unattractive and rarely visited. Workers used the park during lunch time, and people would bring children for short periods during the mid-day, but mainly the Platzspitz served as a passageway from one area of town to another, an easy alternative for crossing from one bridge to the other, rather than walking up around in front of the Landesmuseum and the train station. And at night, Mr. Studhalter adds, the park was home to alcoholics, hustlers and homosexuals, who thrived in the seclusion offered by the dim park lighting, the winding gravel paths and the dense overabundance of rhododendrons, taxus and holly ...

D

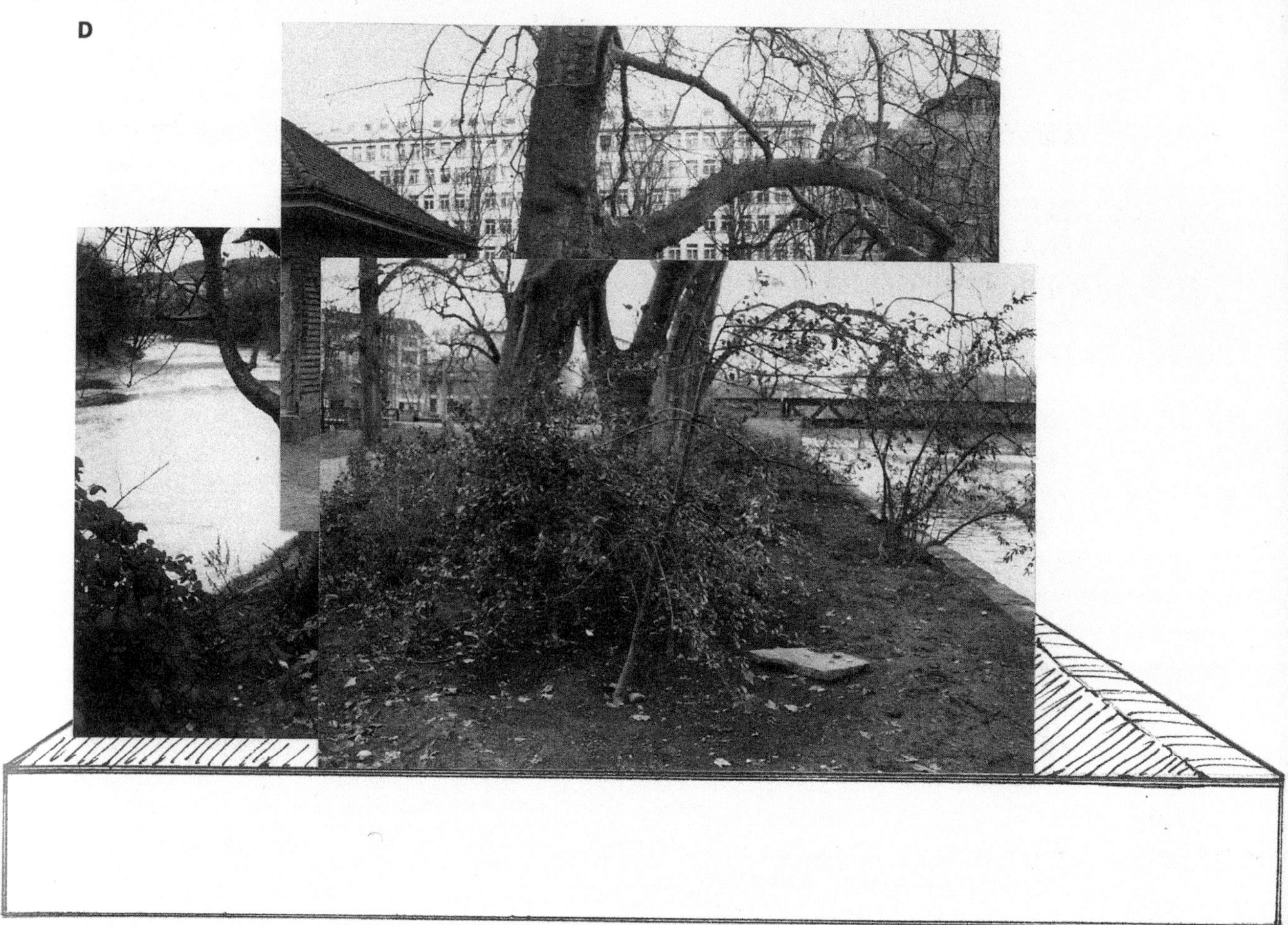

CIRCA 1977. LANDSCAPE DISPLACEMENT FROM THE
PLATZSPITZ, ZURICH TO THE KUNSTHALLE ZURICH.
4 x 4 METERS. PLYWOOD CONTAINER WITH SOIL,
PLANTS, TREES + ROCKS. JUNE 1995.

Plates

A *Joe Dallesandro and Jane Forth in Andy Warhol's film "Trash"*

B *Munich 1971, Andy Warhol, Jane Forth and Joe Dallesandro at Andy Warhol's Trash premiere*

C *Robert Smithson, Partially Buried Wood Shed, Kent State University, Ohio, 1970*

D *Collage for installation at Kunsthalle Zürich*

83

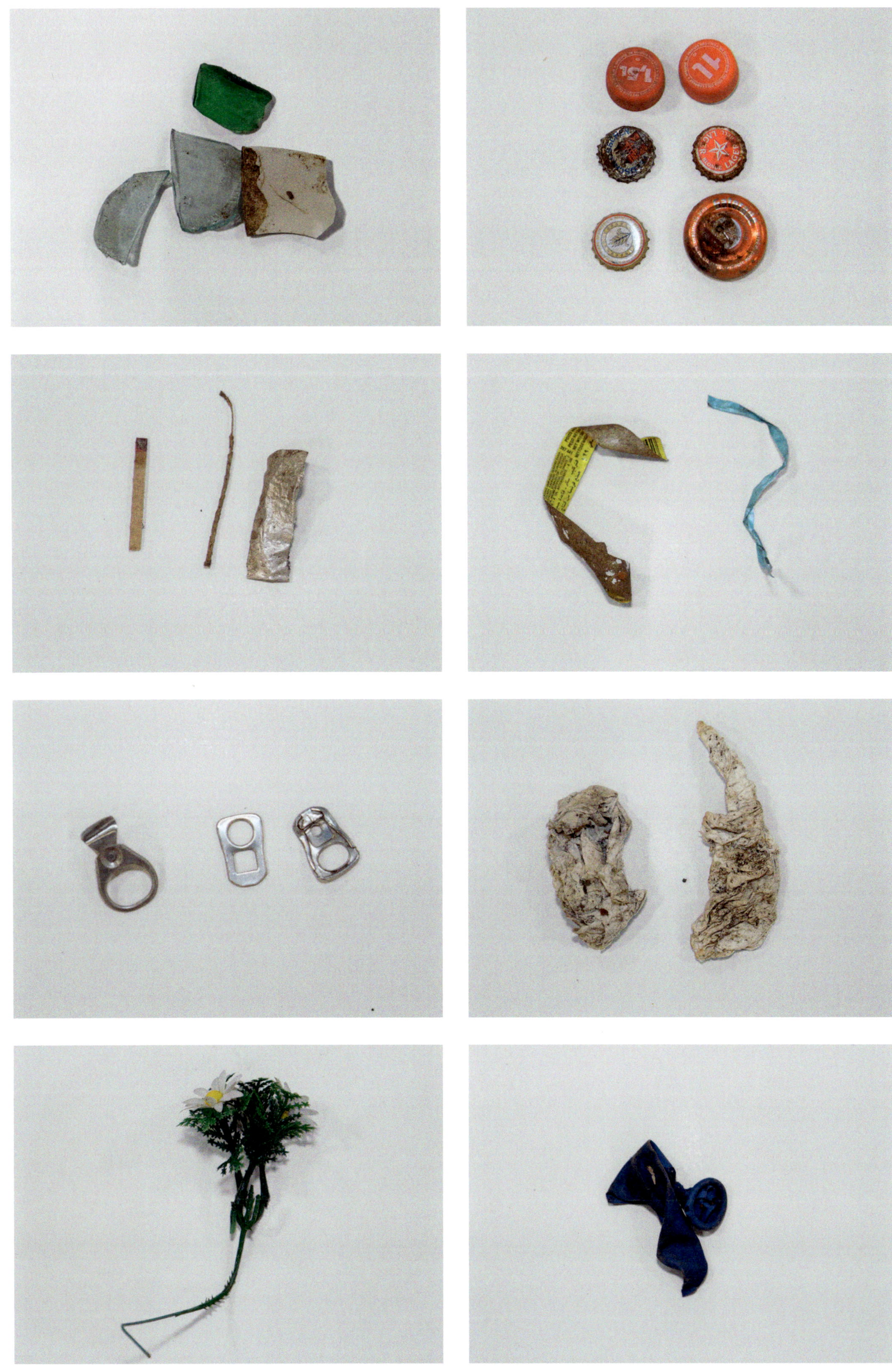

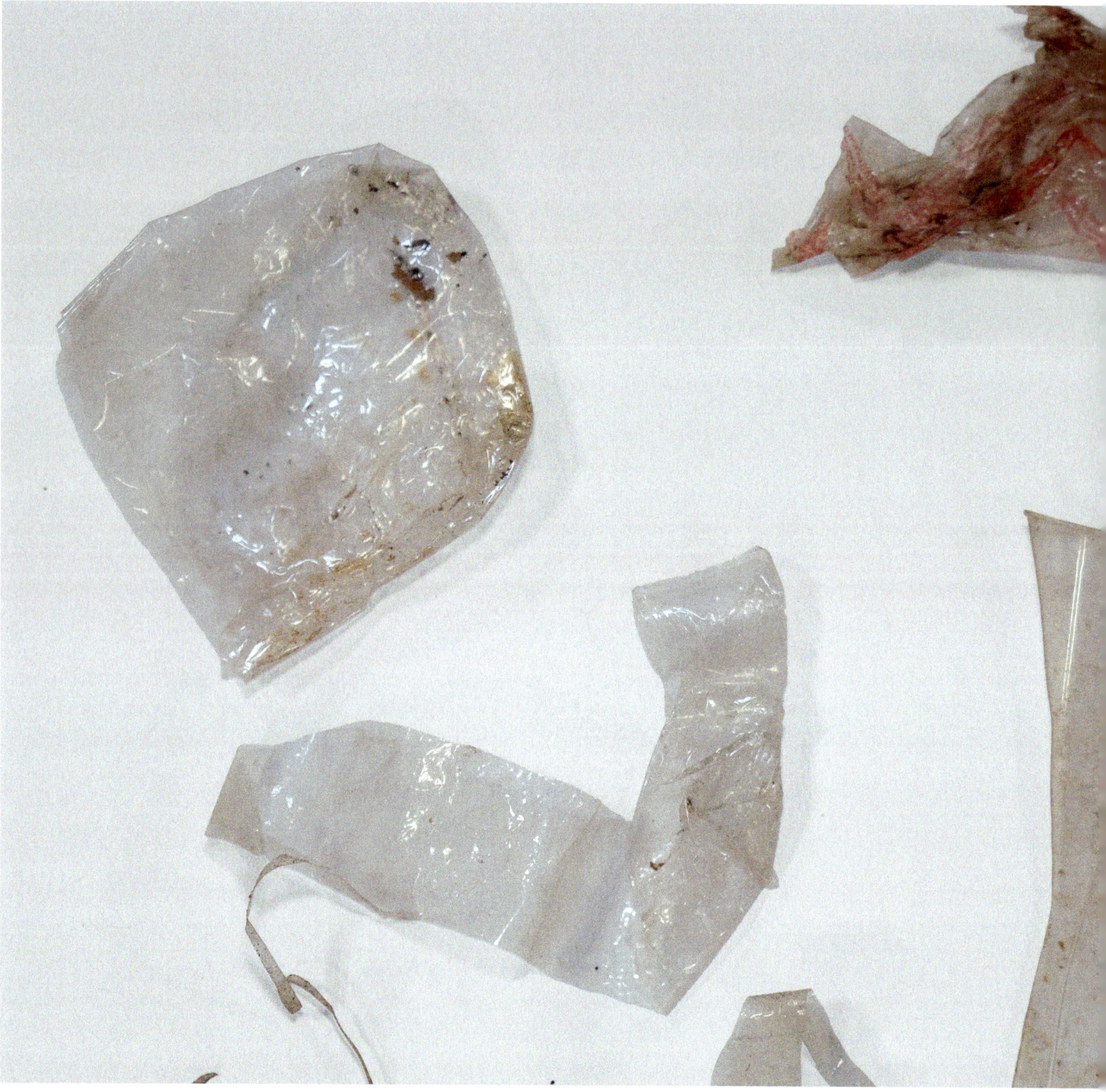

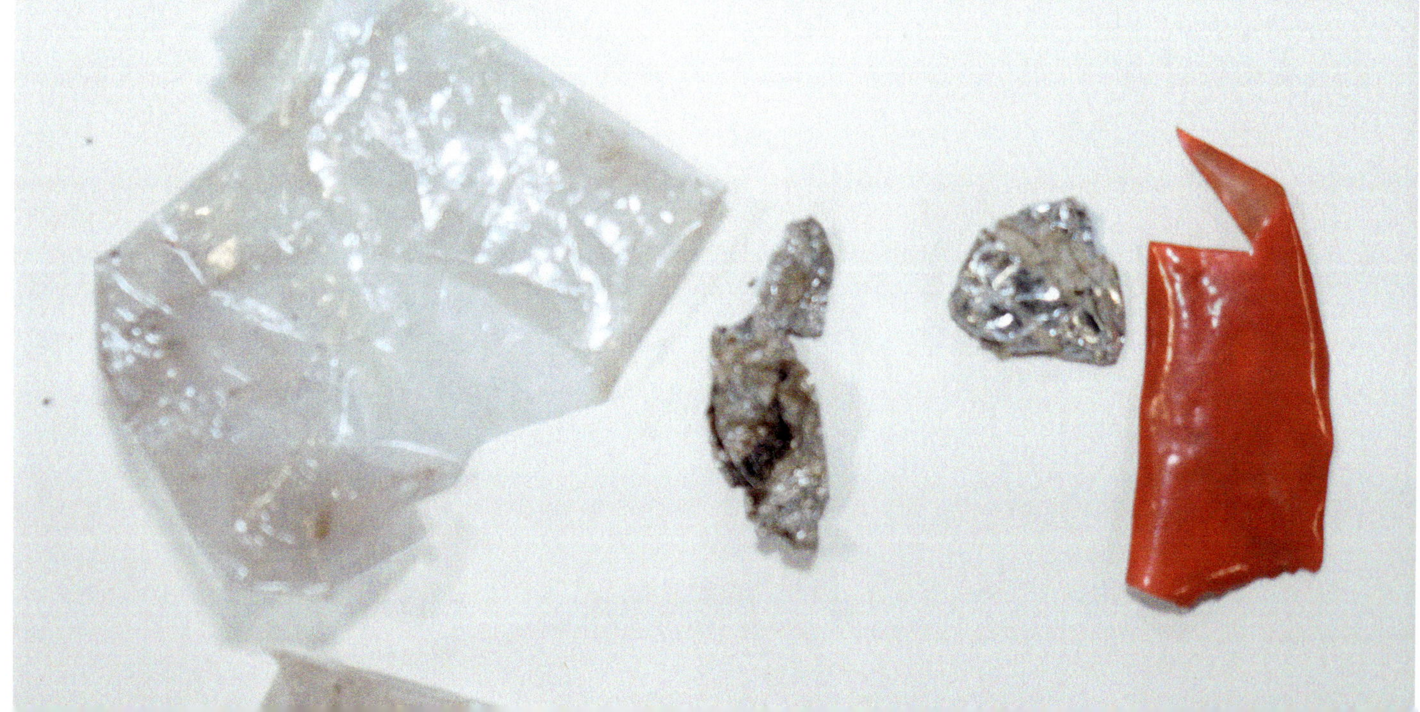

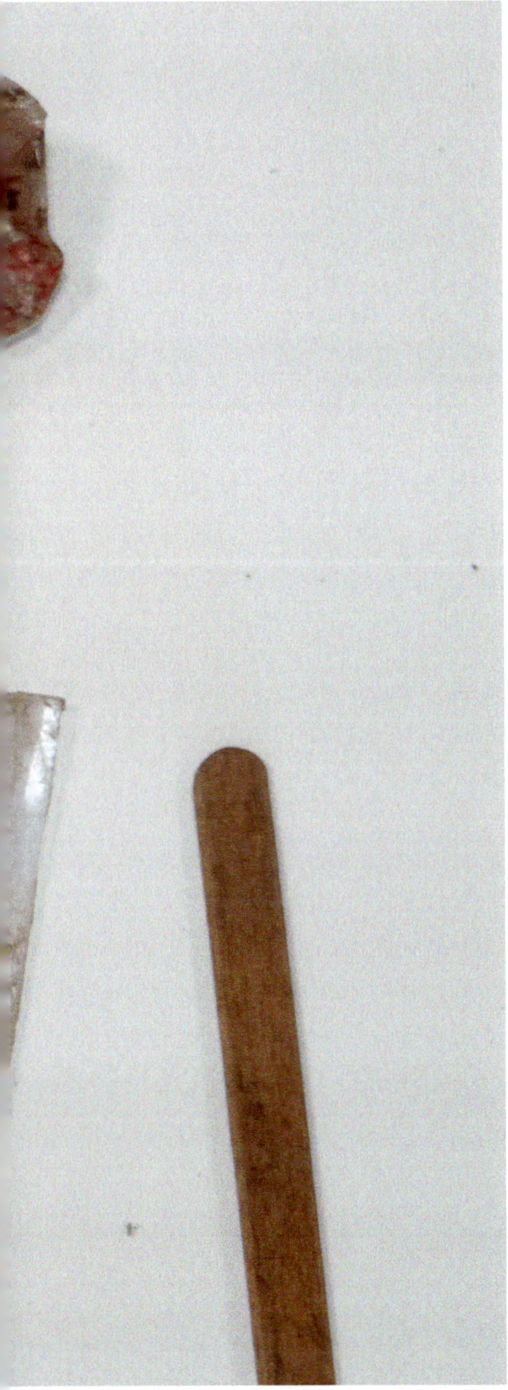

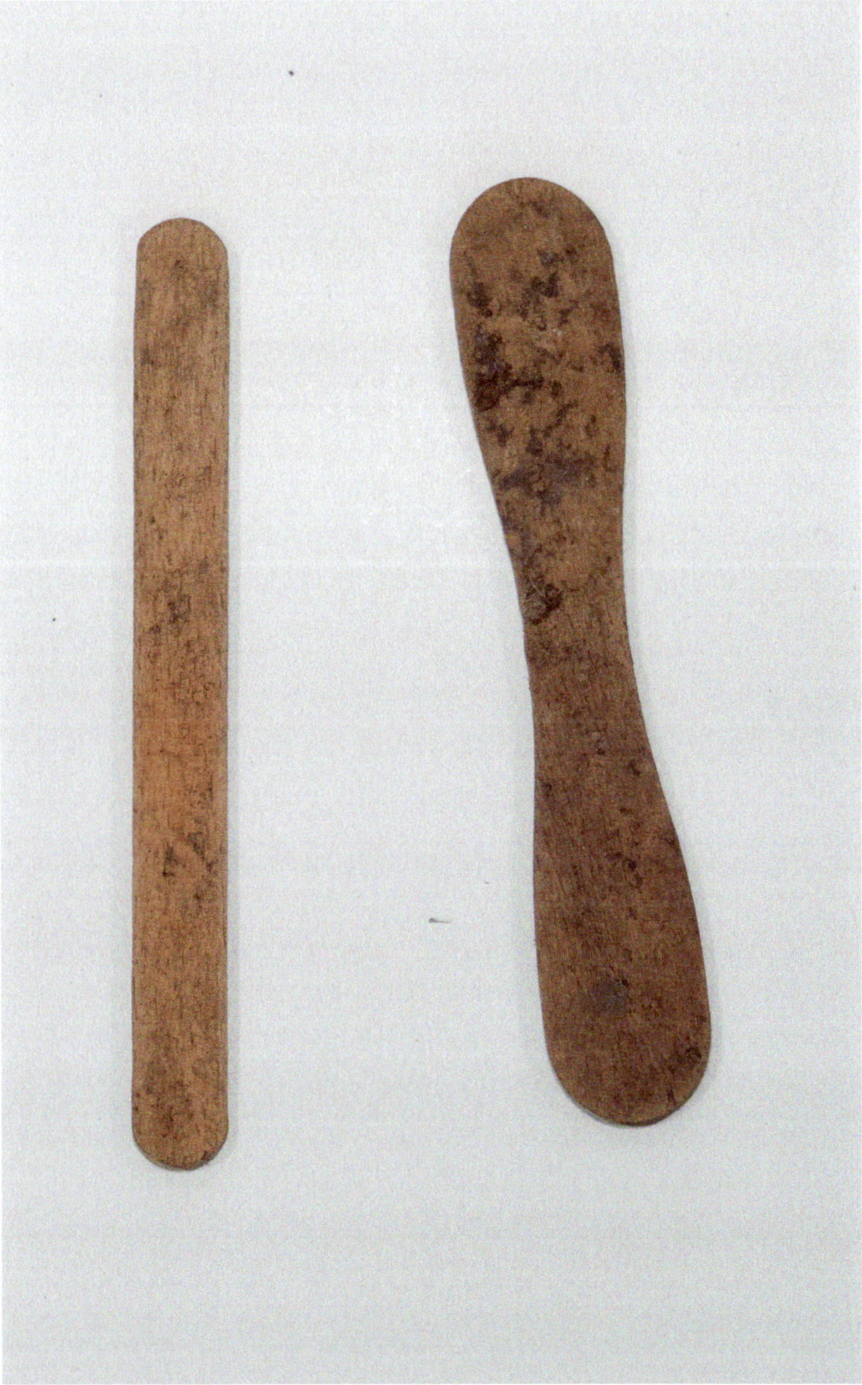

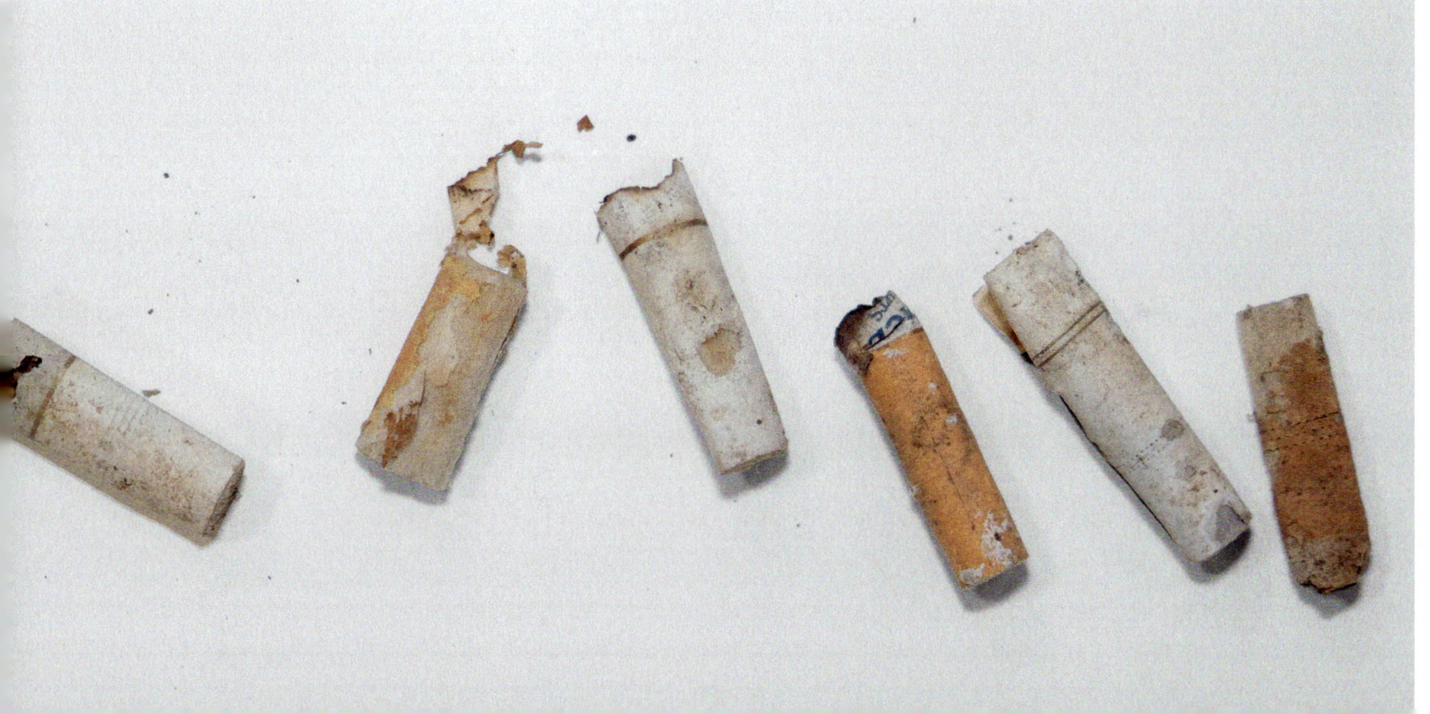

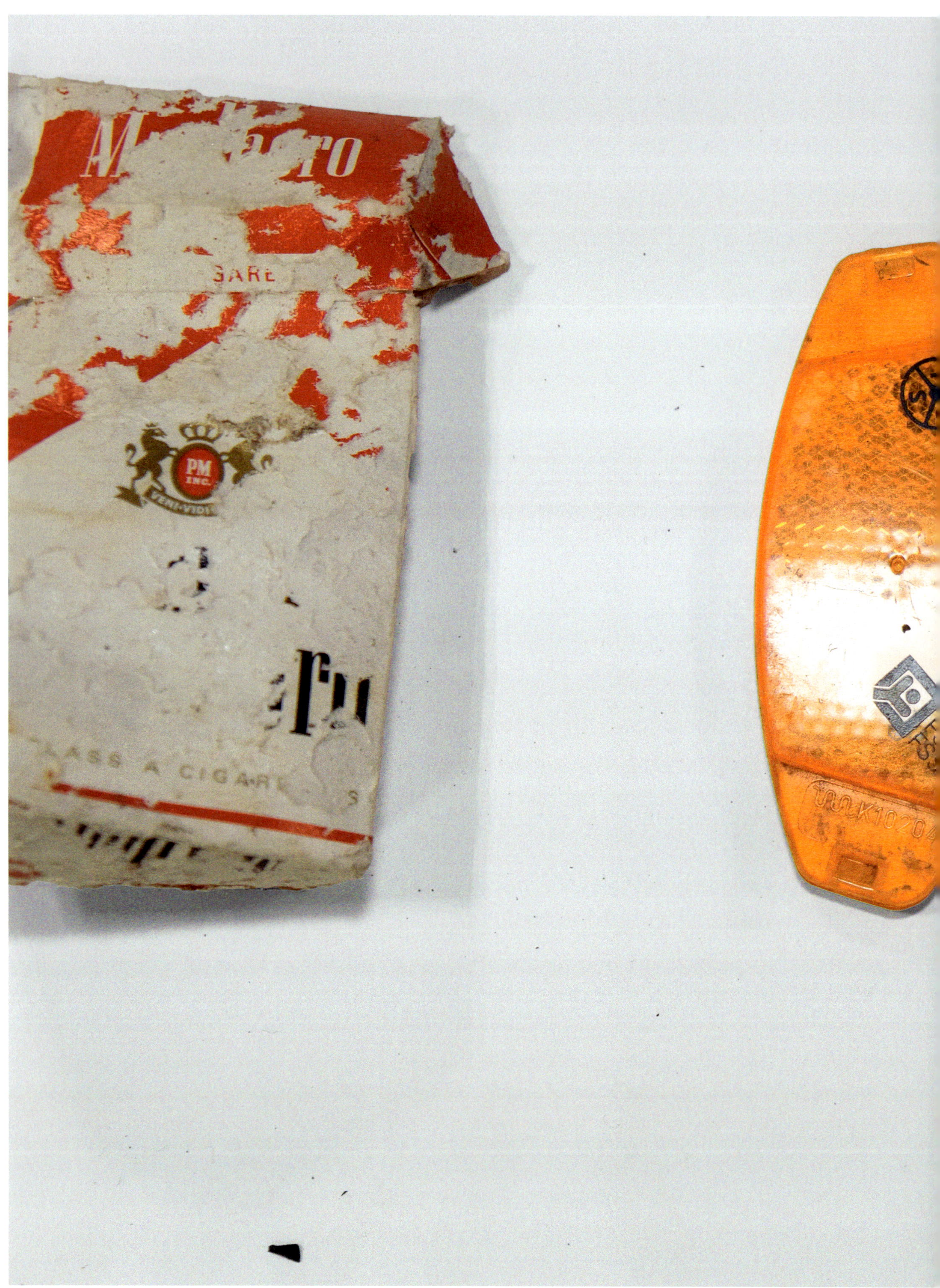

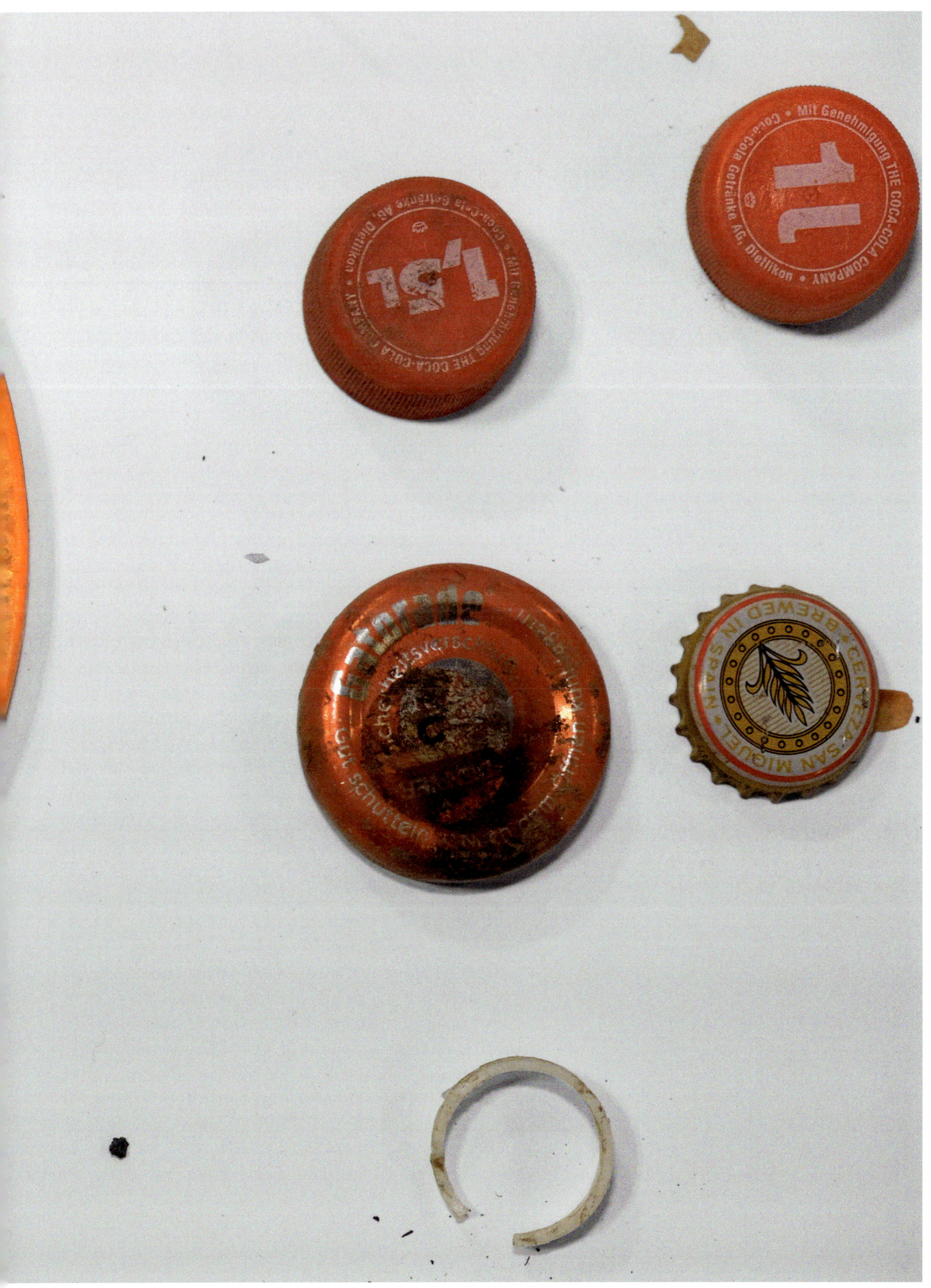

I was living in Los Angeles when Tom invited me to come see him in Norfolk. I took a car to LAX, a plane to JFK, and the train from Grand Central to Wassaic, New York, where Tom picked me up in his Volvo and we drove to his home. The following morning we had an appointment at Bard College, to spend time with the archives of American Fine Arts, Co. Colin de Land's legendary gallery was the first Tom forged a serious relationship with, starting with a group show in 1993 and followed by his first solo exhibition there the following year.

The archives held slides, typed-out checklists, blue-tinted Polaroids, three-by-five-inch photographs from an opening, and pages of faxes that looked as if butter had bled across them, smudging their ink and rendering them translucent. We took a loupe to all of these materials, attempting to magnify structural details: the walls, a sliver of the back office, or an open door to the storage closet. We commented on faces we recognized: "Oh, that's Jutta? Or Christine?" But what we were really hunting for, hungrily, was any documentation of Tom's work. A thirty-year history, without warehouses or a consistent studio, full of the unwieldy, the site-specific, of sculptures and objects that, faced with the concrete cost of storage, had been dismantled, or in some cases destroyed.

On my journey to Norfolk—a backpack in hand packed with chargers, a computer, headphones, a notebook, a few days' medication—I began to think about Tom's peripatetic journey, the one we would soon be mapping together across his archival material. He lived in New York's Chinatown in 1990 with his boyfriend Ull, sharing a working studio before the relationship fell apart, which prompted a 1993 move to Stanton Street on the Lower East Side. He took a top-floor apartment in a tenement, where, in 2005, he staged and hosted

　　　Christine Messineo

Residence, an exhibition space and conceptual precursor to *Torrington Project*, of sorts. Along the way, Tom's museum and gallery exhibition schedule grew, crossing continents and multiplying the venues where he created objects attuned to, responding to, and at times replicating the architecture that housed them. His career might be framed as a prolonged intervention into sites that sit in and outside of the white cube, or an investigation of the idea of "site-specificity" itself.

Going through the archive at Bard, I wondered about the journeys Tom's works had taken. How do these objects live on past the time frame of their initial exhibitions? When a work is shown again—rebuilt according to Tom's tightly written instructions and drawings, informed by memories and photographs—how does it account for its new environment? How does its backstory—how it was shipped from one space to another—influence what it becomes? The permanence implied (or winkingly performed) by Tom's choice of materials—plywood, soil, mirror, and metal—invites the question: Does a sculptor have the responsibility to also be a warehouse? Is it reasonable to expect an artist to store these things? And if not, what will be lost in all the inevitable moves and indefinite transit? This in-betweenness made me think of my own travels, how I moved through the world: without specially designed wood crates, taking up temporary tenancy wherever I went.

Long before that trip to Norfolk, I had made another long journey to be with Tom, this time to see the building that eventually became *Torrington Project*. When I entered the old building, Tom was circling the space in an industrial cleaning machine, a remnant of previous tenants. I had brought my young son with me, and he immediately jumped at the chance to join Tom for a ride. Peeling paint confettied the wood floors.

Treaded

Windows spread out along all sides, creating a surprising banner of natural light. The front door was inconspicuous and lightweight, with a single door handle, clearly repurposed from a suburban home. Tom and I have spent so much time locating his work—scouring documentation, sourcing individual pieces from gallery storage, museum shows, collectors, Tom's own home—all in an attempt to revisit, rebuild, and recapture what might have fallen through the cracks. This may be why, when I looked at the vast, empty, post-industrial space, it seemed to present an infrastructure so ready to hold Tom's ambitious reclamation. That day, we found a tape measure, a couple of black folding chairs randomly situated close to a wall, and got back to work. ◊

Christine Messineo

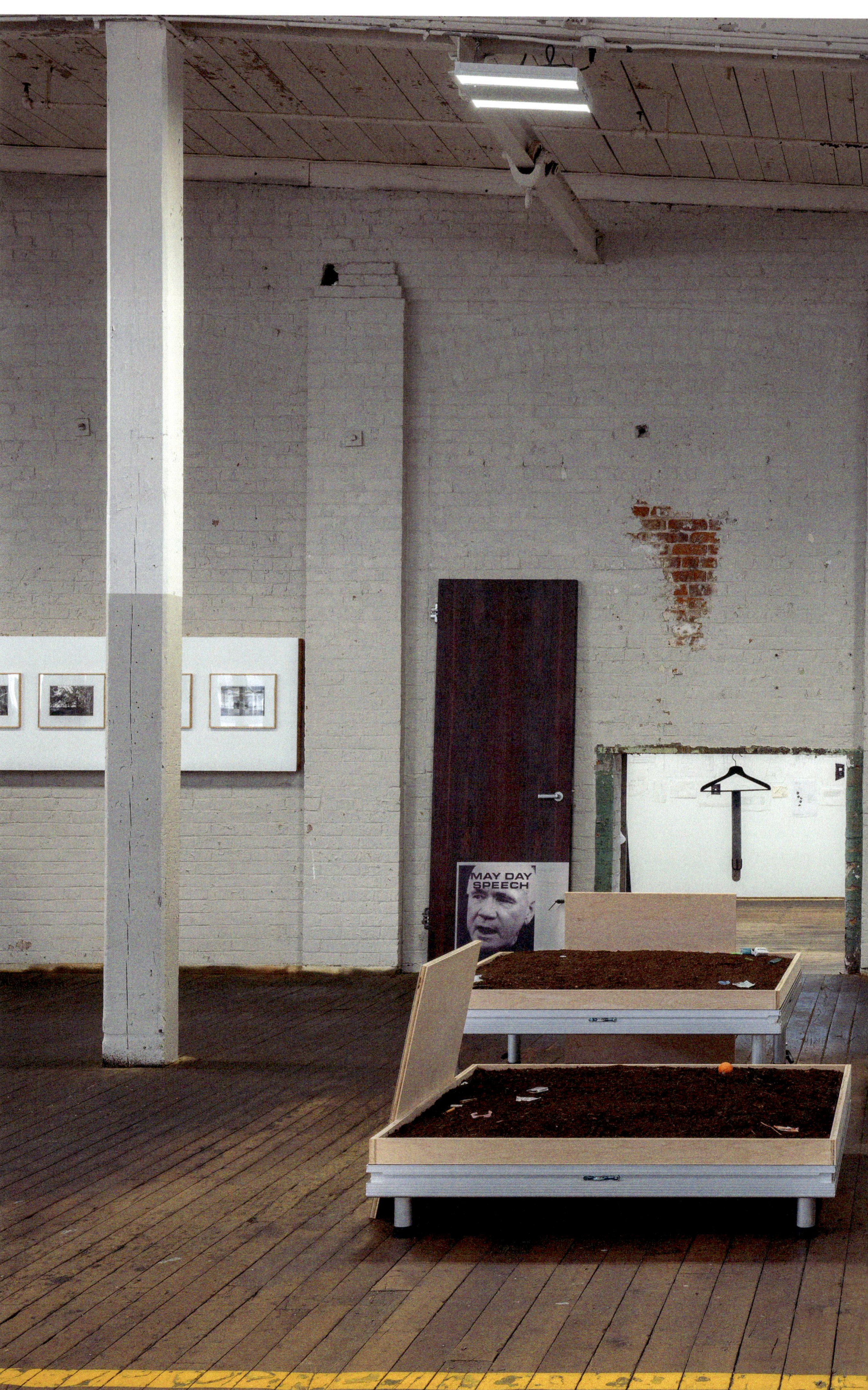
MAY DAY
SPEECH

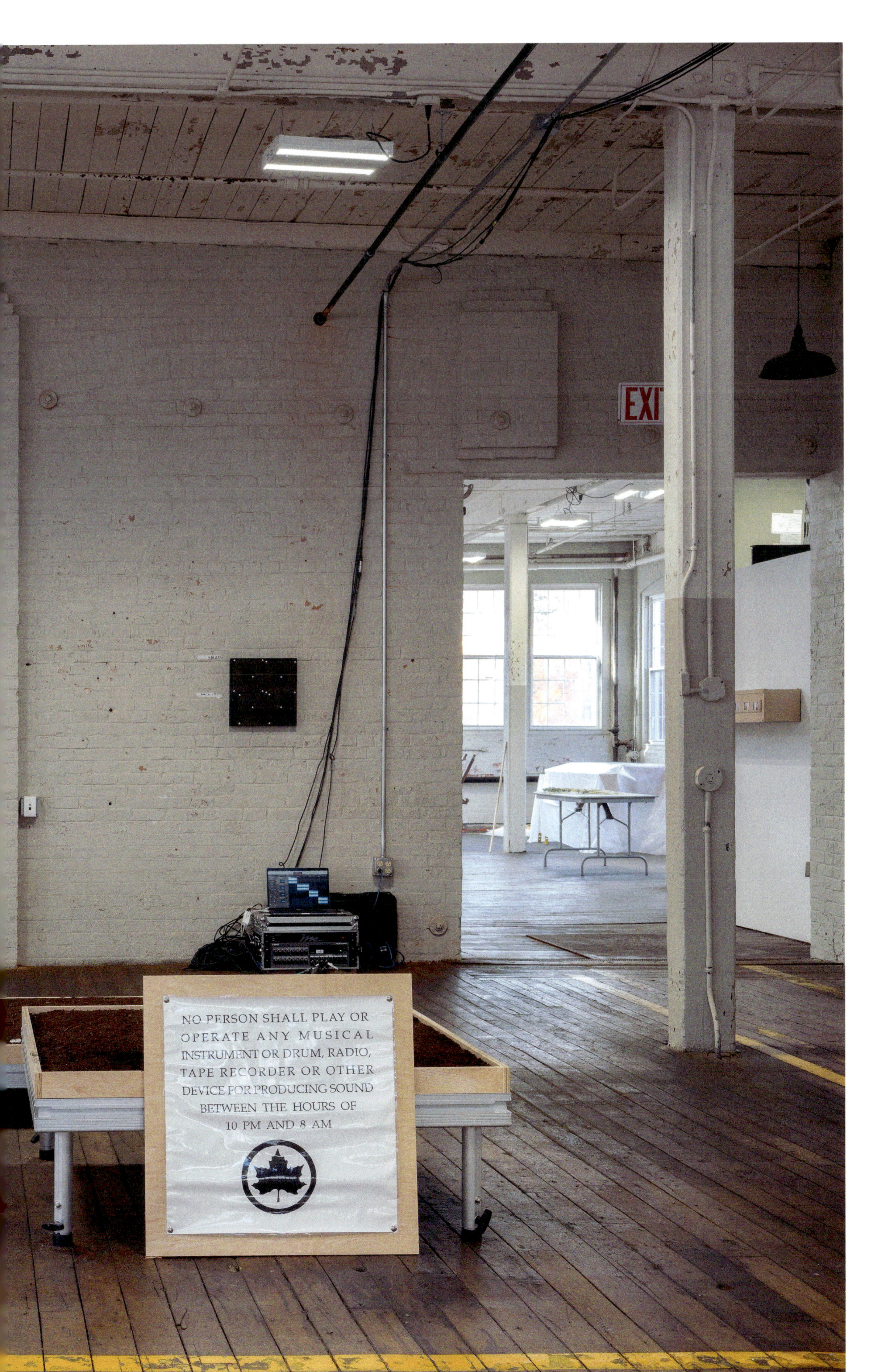
EXIT
NO PERSON SHALL PLAY OR
OPERATE ANY MUSICAL
INSTRUMENT OR DRUM, RADIO,
TAPE RECORDER OR OTHER
DEVICE FOR PRODUCING SOUND
BETWEEN THE HOURS OF
10 PM AND 8 AM

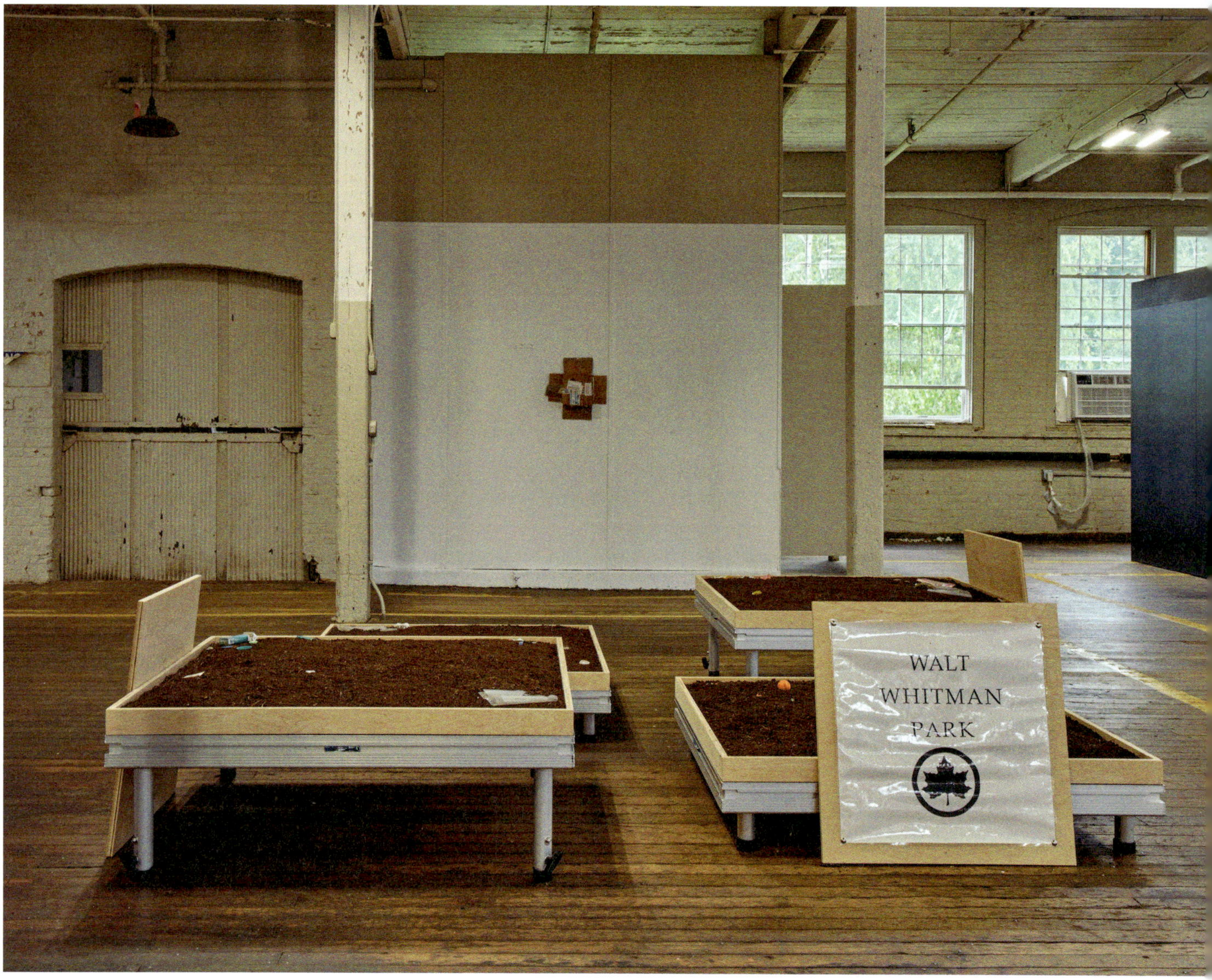

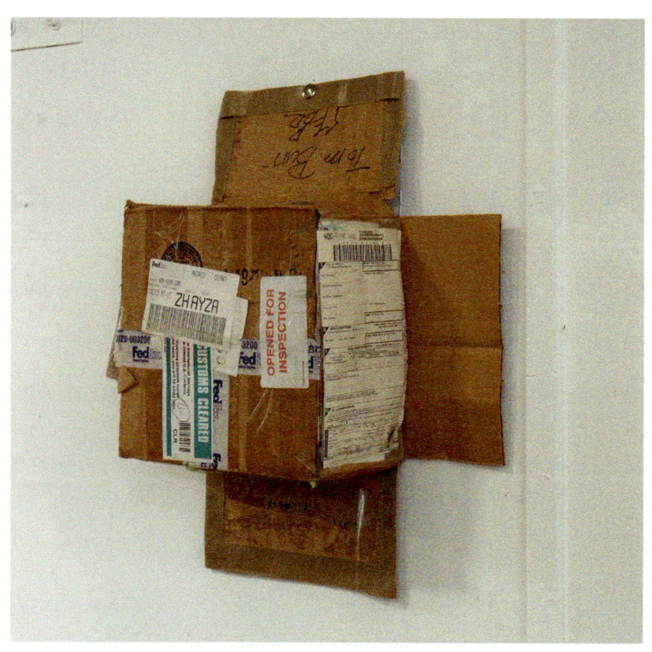

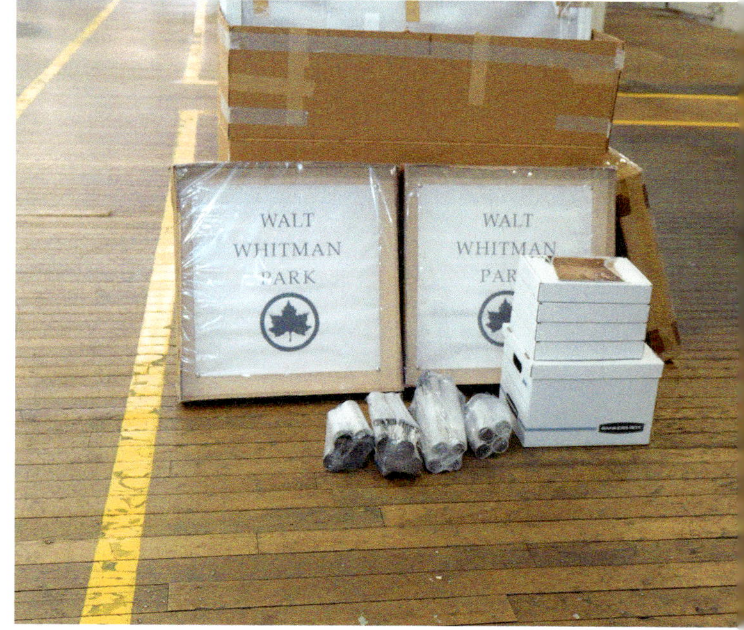
WALT
WHITMAN
PARK

WALT
WHITMAN
PARK

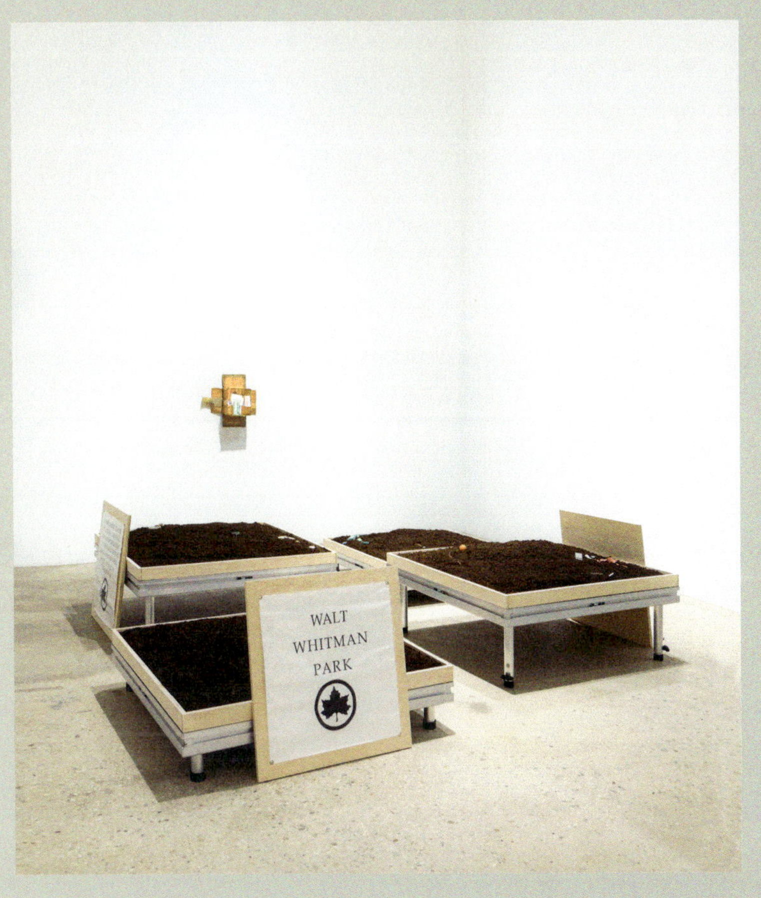
WALT
WHITMAN
PARK

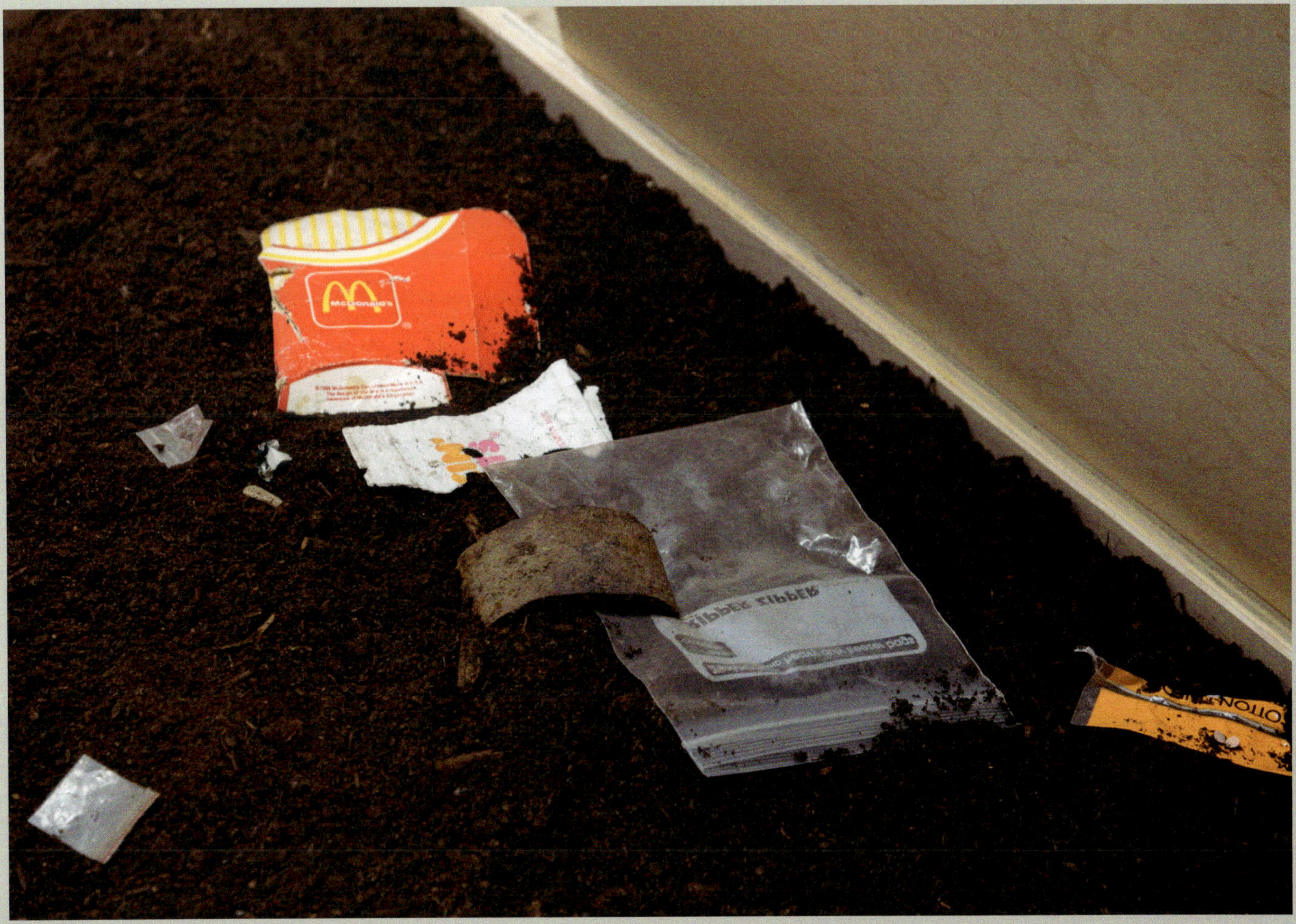

In 1996, for instance, I designed a proposal for a project I called *An Ambient Lounge*, which was meant to occupy the space of a former veterinary practice on 22nd Street, in the middle of Chelsea's emerging gallery district, for a period of three months. Rents had not exploded yet for this type of storefront space. *An Ambient Lounge* had as its mission the contemplation of spaces, places, and locations. It was to be club-like or lounge-like, very still and slow as an experience, and it would serve as ground zero for a mapping of sites across New York City that either figured in my work or in the daily rhythms of my life, which were often the same thing. There wouldn't be images or forms, just a list of sites to ruminate on. I would design couches and tables, and create some sort of soundtrack using my voice or someone else's. We got close to realizing the whole thing, but in the end, only the model I made of the experience still exists.

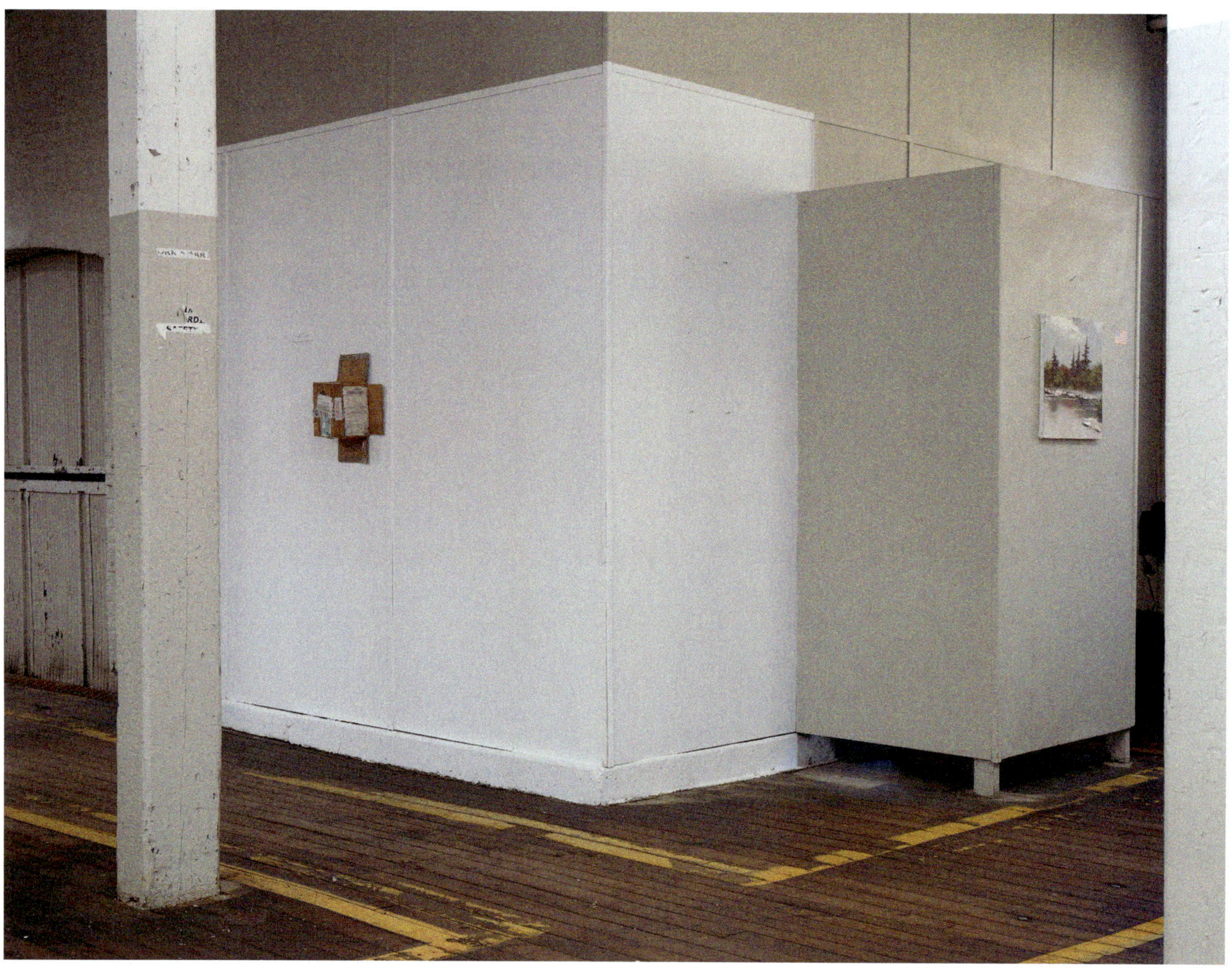

Later, in 2005, Barbara and Howard Morse asked me to create a project as part of their MICA Foundation commissions. Christian had produced the first project for the foundation: a design of MICA's letterhead with a podium for it to sit on. Andrea performed the second, where she greeted visitors to Barbara and Howard's West 86th Street apartment, in an official foundation welcome, as she stripped off her clothes. I was the third. My proposal was to transform my apartment at 150 Stanton Street into a type of salon for the period of a year. I'd call it *Residence*.

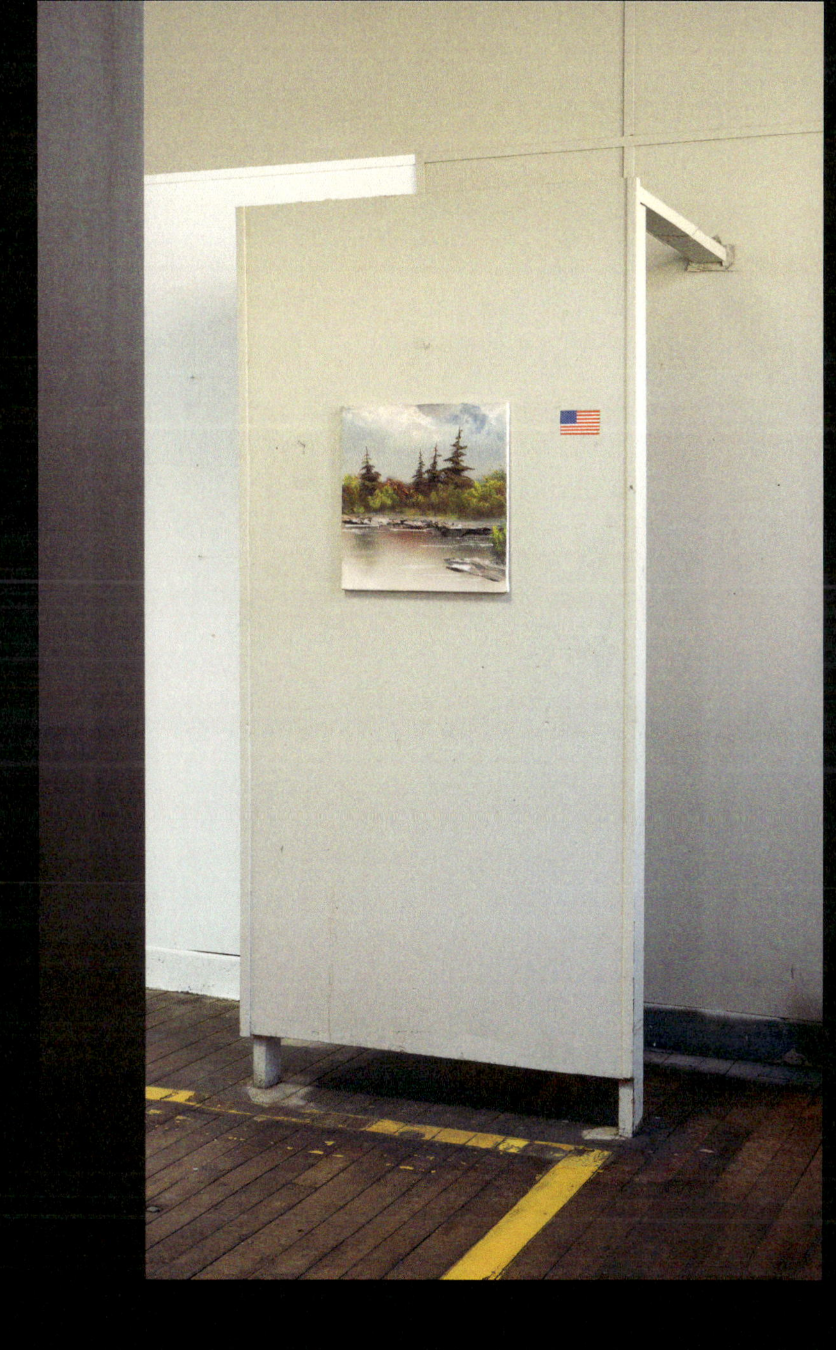

I redesigned the rooms of the railroad apartment with brown velvet curtains, alternating
pale-green and off-white walls, black plywood
floors, clear plastic furniture, and Colin's oak
office desk, which was lent to me after his
passing in 2003. Christian's podium was there
too, at the entrance to the apartment. Over
the course of the year, *Residence* hosted an
eclectic series of presentations and gather-
ings, some that were more formally organized
and many that were impromptu explosions of
people who ended up there after openings or

other events. I was teaching at Cooper Union
at the time and the students created a series
of physical interventions in the space. There
were film screenings and exhibitions, talks, and
many parties. One night Christian and I threw
a cocktail party. Cosima von Bonin came and
took videos throughout the night, including of
the crowd leaving down the fire escape to the
ground floor because the front-door lock had
broken at some point, but the footage was lost
in the Cologne fire I think. *Residence* remains
wildly undocumented.

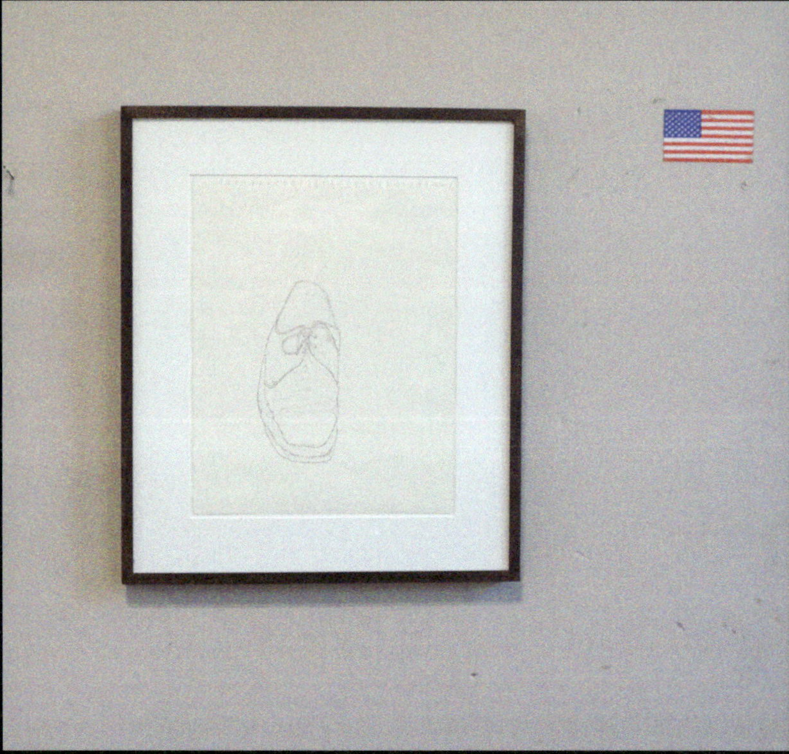

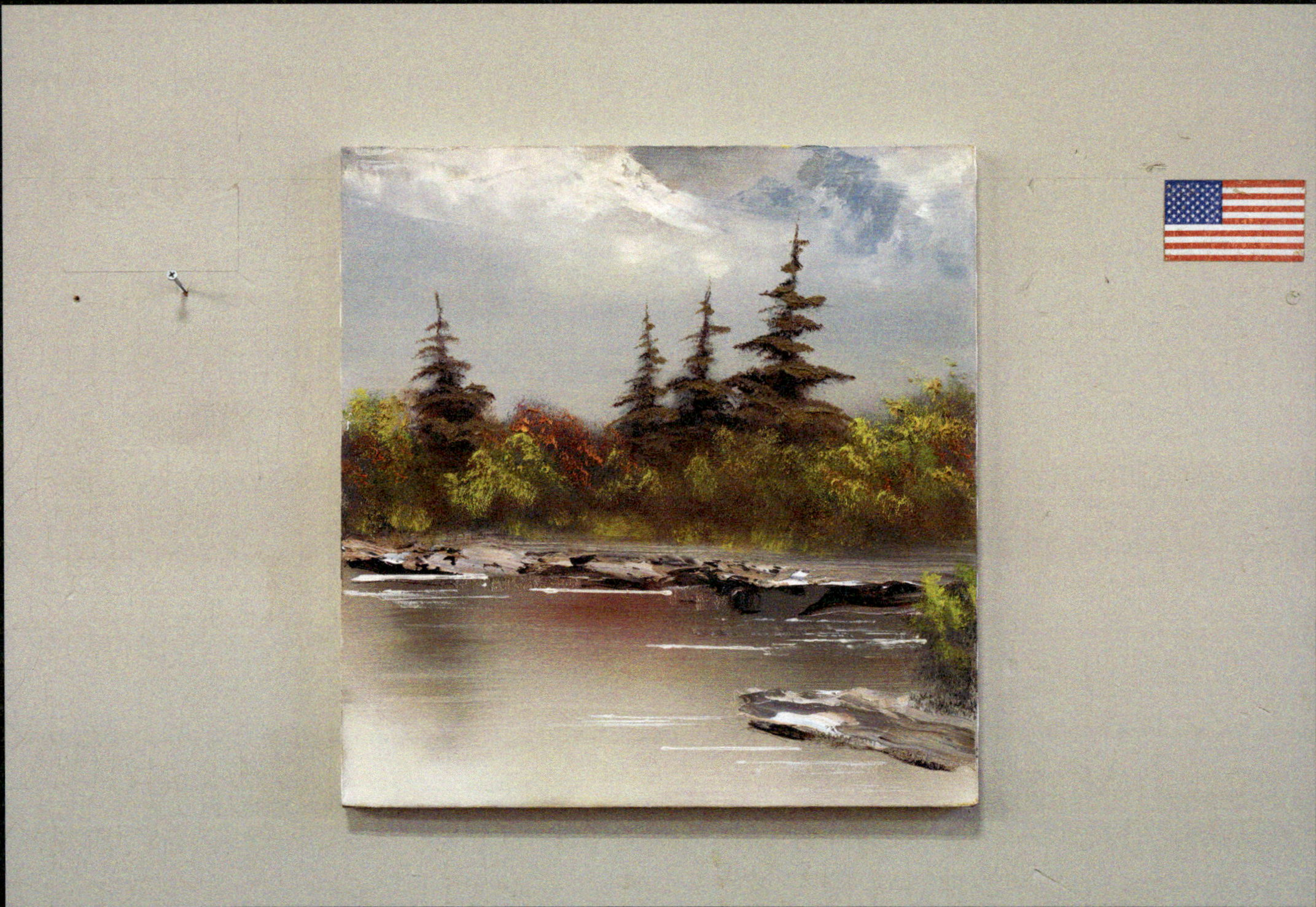

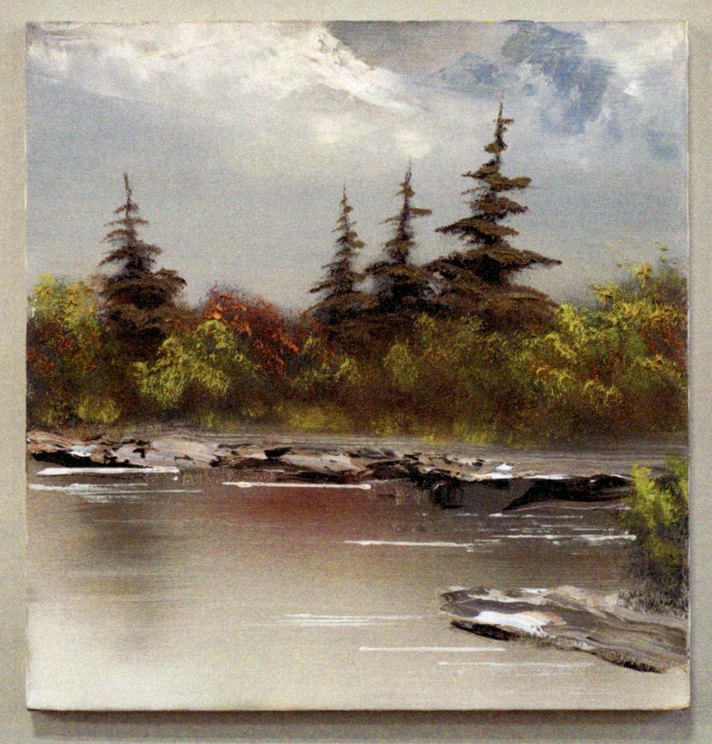
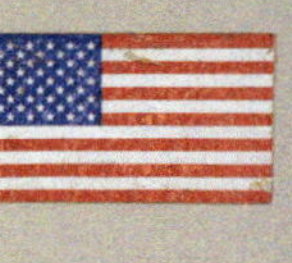

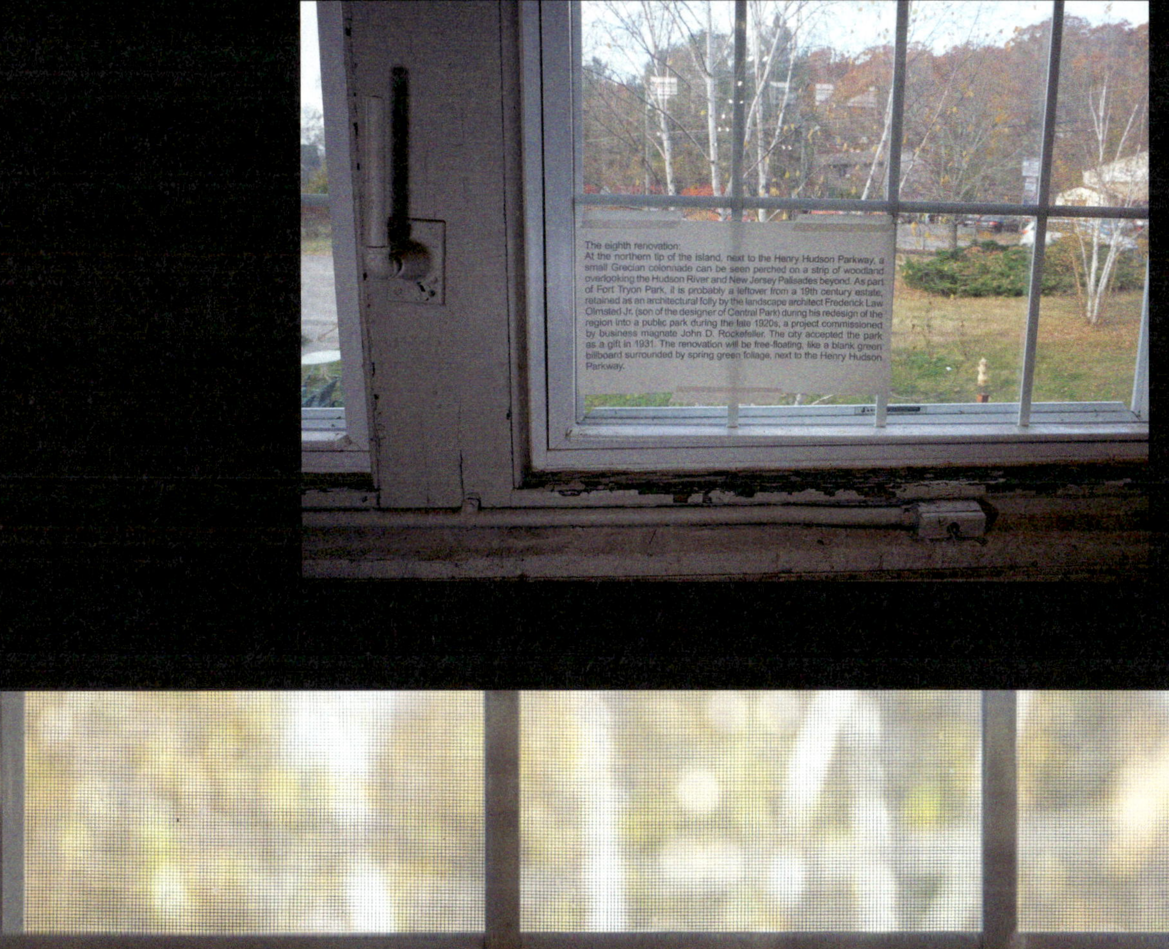

The eighth renovation:
At the northern tip of the island, next to the Henry Hudson Parkway, a small Grecian colonnade can be seen perched on a strip of woodland overlooking the Hudson River and New Jersey Palisades beyond. As part of Fort Tryon Park, it is probably a leftover from a 19th century estate, retained as an architectural folly by the landscape architect Frederick Law Olmsted Jr. (son of the designer of Central Park) during his redesign of the region into a public park during the late 1920s, a project commissioned by business magnate John D. Rockefeller. The city accepted the park as a gift in 1931. The renovation will be free-floating, like a blank green billboard surrounded by spring green foliage, next to the Henry Hudson Parkway.

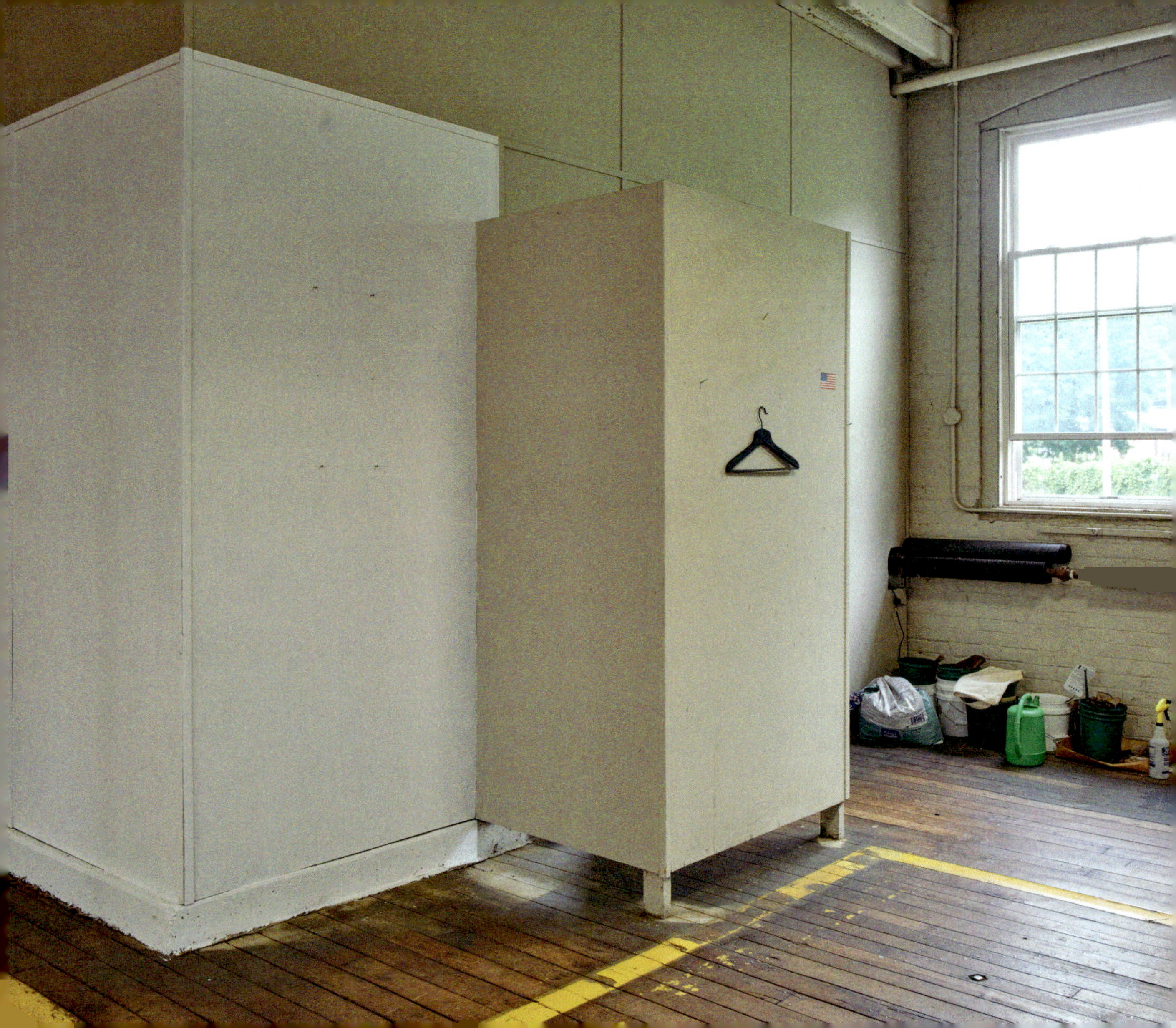

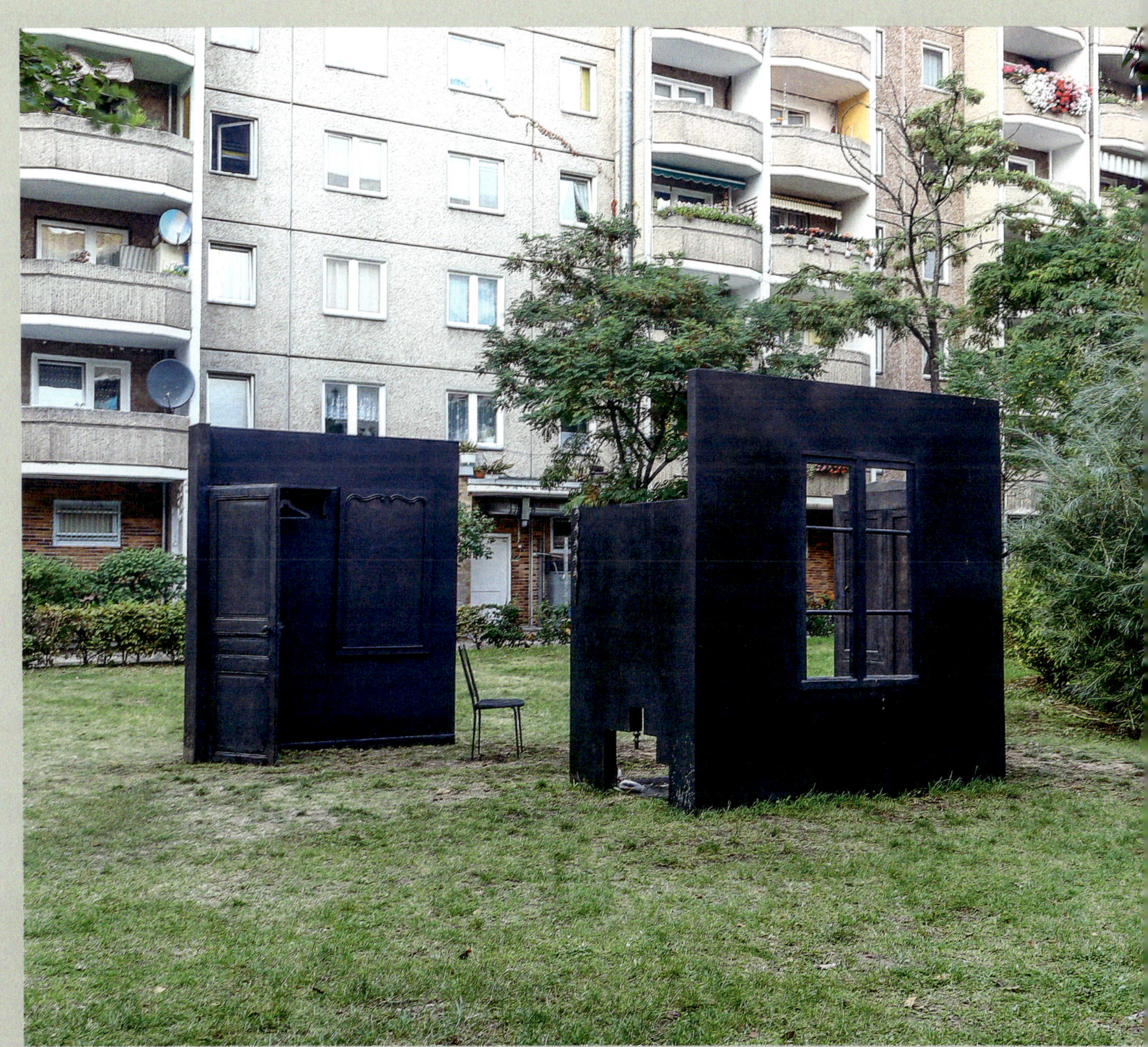

In 2017, I embarked on a project in New Haven. Stefania Bortolami had just started a gallery initiative called *Artist-City*, which paired an artist with a site somewhere—anywhere, really—in the United States for a yearlong exhibition project. The idea of the program was to offer greater creative motivation to artists to make work in new locations, new venues, potentially fostering new audiences, new acquisitions, new possibilities. There had been one example already by the time I was approached—Buren in Miami— and I recall being unsure about what I could do for my project. Without the prompt of an already established location, with its given set of circumstances, there was nothing to react to.

My immediate thought was to go out west, to a desert somewhere, in an echo of the histories of the 1960s and '70s artists that had been critical for me, but this was more of a reflex, and ultimately I rejected this direction, unable to find a way in. I still think about attempting to make a project in the desert somewhere, and I do still want to think about Robert Smithson, but also Georgia O'Keeffe, the two figures who, together, embodied my teenage longing to become some sort of radical landscape artist. O'Keeffe for me was significantly more about her persona than her paintings, more about her clothing and her self-styled figure, and her independence, captured in so many photographs by Alfred Stieglitz early on, and by others later, but well before the moment Calvin Klein got involved sometime in the mid-1980s. I remember a

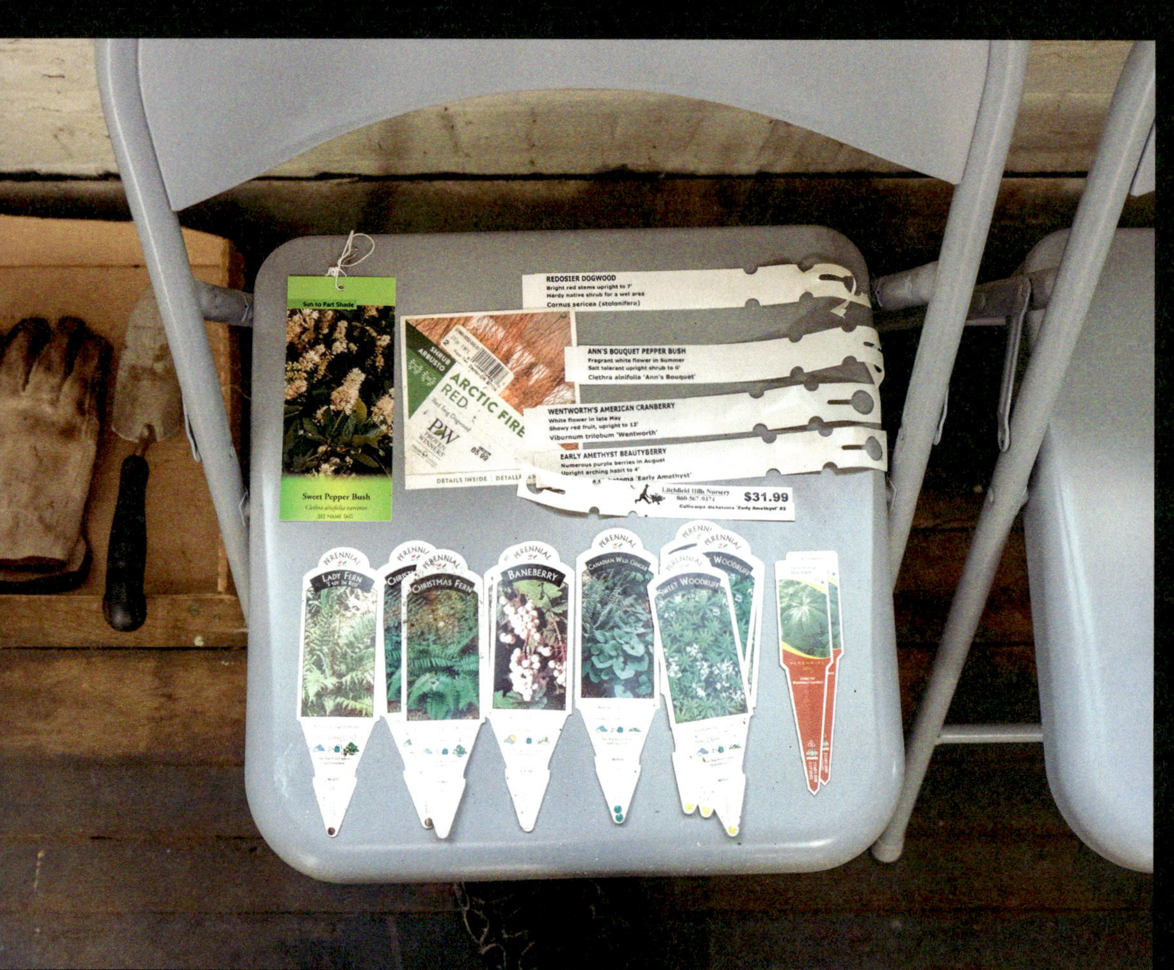

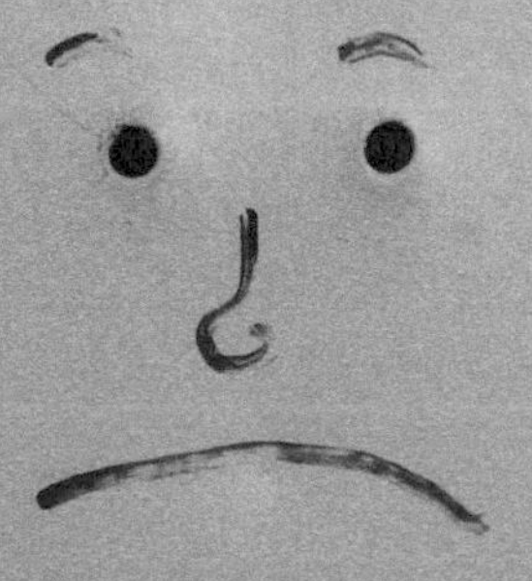

3

fashion shoot at Ghost Ranch with Klein himself modeling his menswear, and wondering how it was that this happened at all and whether or not it was a mutual agreement, a coercion, or some sort of late-in-life publicity move. I suppose Klein's attraction to O'Keeffe wasn't all that different from my own, but we came to different conclusions. He grafted the artist onto his ever more robust commercial retooling of Minimalism, while I found myself in a process of questioning myths as I had known them, including that of Minimalism. But something lingers here. When Riccardo Tisci was the designer for Givenchy, for instance, he voiced his interest in collaborating; for instance, we even made some steps in this direction. I visited the fashion house's archive in Paris multiple times, located in the basement of the headquarters on Avenue Georges V. Fashion has always had a desire to legitimate itself through the supposed seriousness of art, whereas artists understand the unwritten rule that fashion is too flagrantly commercial, that it doesn't submit itself to the puritan restraint required of critical cultural production. *Torrington*, in all its low-grade dramaturgy, was a way of exploring those boundary lines between art, fashion, and the equally performative roles of recluse and celebrity, Georgia and Calvin. There is a one-off ad for Kiko Kostadinov in *Another Man* that shows me standing in Torrington—maybe an ad, the only ad, for *Torrington Project*—where I am shown as being open to and perhaps embodying the ambivalence of these interlocking industries. Blake told me to take the magazine out of the space once. I liked the panic.

After some time, someone who knew me well suggested the possibility of New Haven, my hometown, as a potential site and subject for the Bortolami initiative. The idea made me queasy at first—New Haven was where I grew up, where I discovered the type of artist I wanted to be. But then I thought, instead of distance and expansion, I could contemplate a counter-direction of regression and return, of going nowhere, in a sense. The idea resonated with me—if the site was the right one, I'd have the opportunity to put that subjective development into an architectural, historical, and social context and create something out of it.

If it were to be New Haven, it was important to find a Brutalist building or site. I was drawn to this architecture while growing up, and I wanted to align childhood, and coming of age individually and socially, with different forms and definitions of brutality. I liked that this linguistic slippage had always occurred—between the original notion of an architecture of raw materials, and one that became socially expressive as brutal, and denigrated as such—and I wanted to play with that as well. We explored several venues: Kevin Roche's Knights of Columbus building, Paul Rudolph's Temple Street parking garage, Eero Saarinen's Yale additions, and several others. Then we found that Marcel Breuer's Armstrong/Pirelli building was empty and potentially available for rent. Bortolami approached the owner of the building, Ikea, and negotiated the lease of the ground floor for the period of a year.

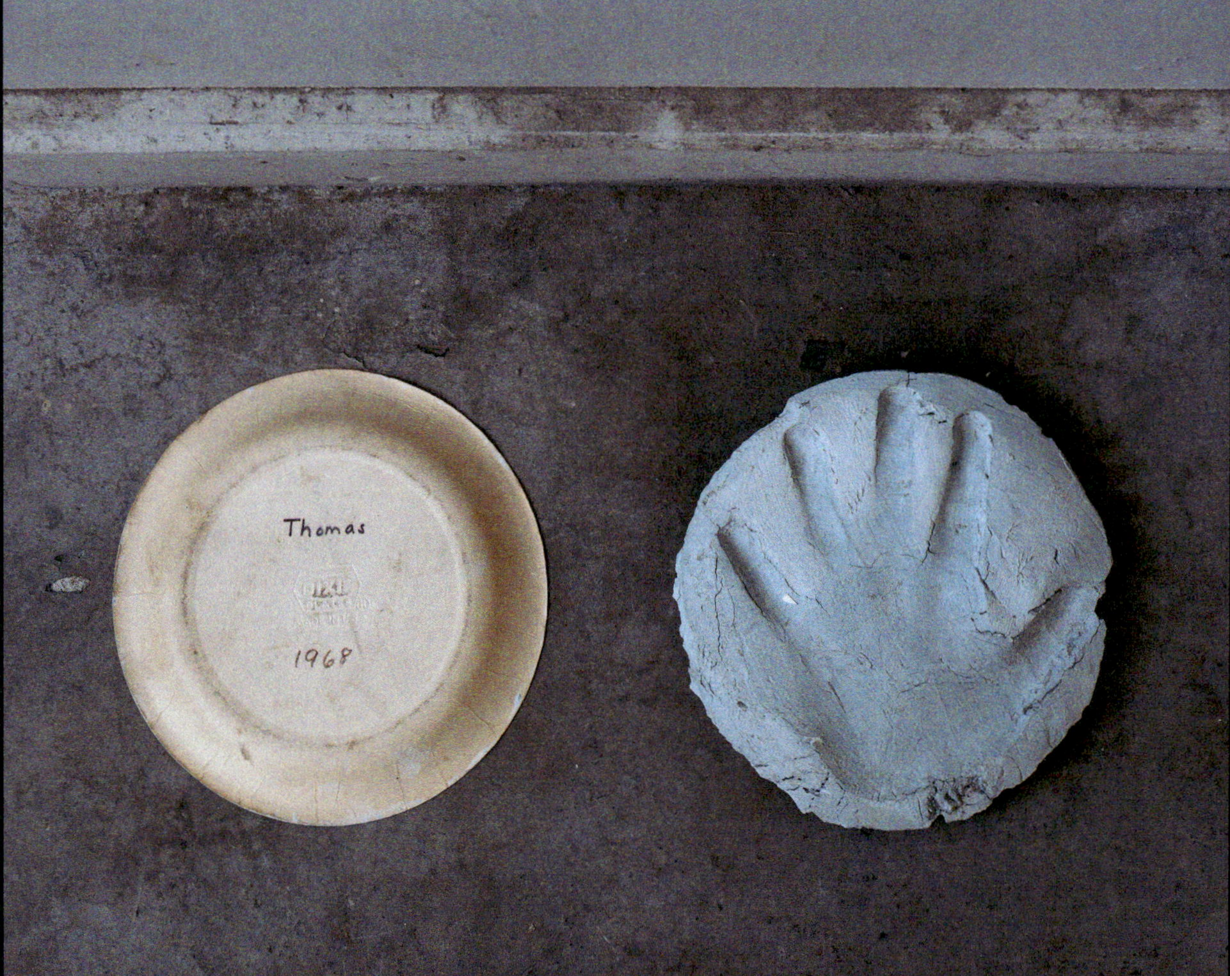

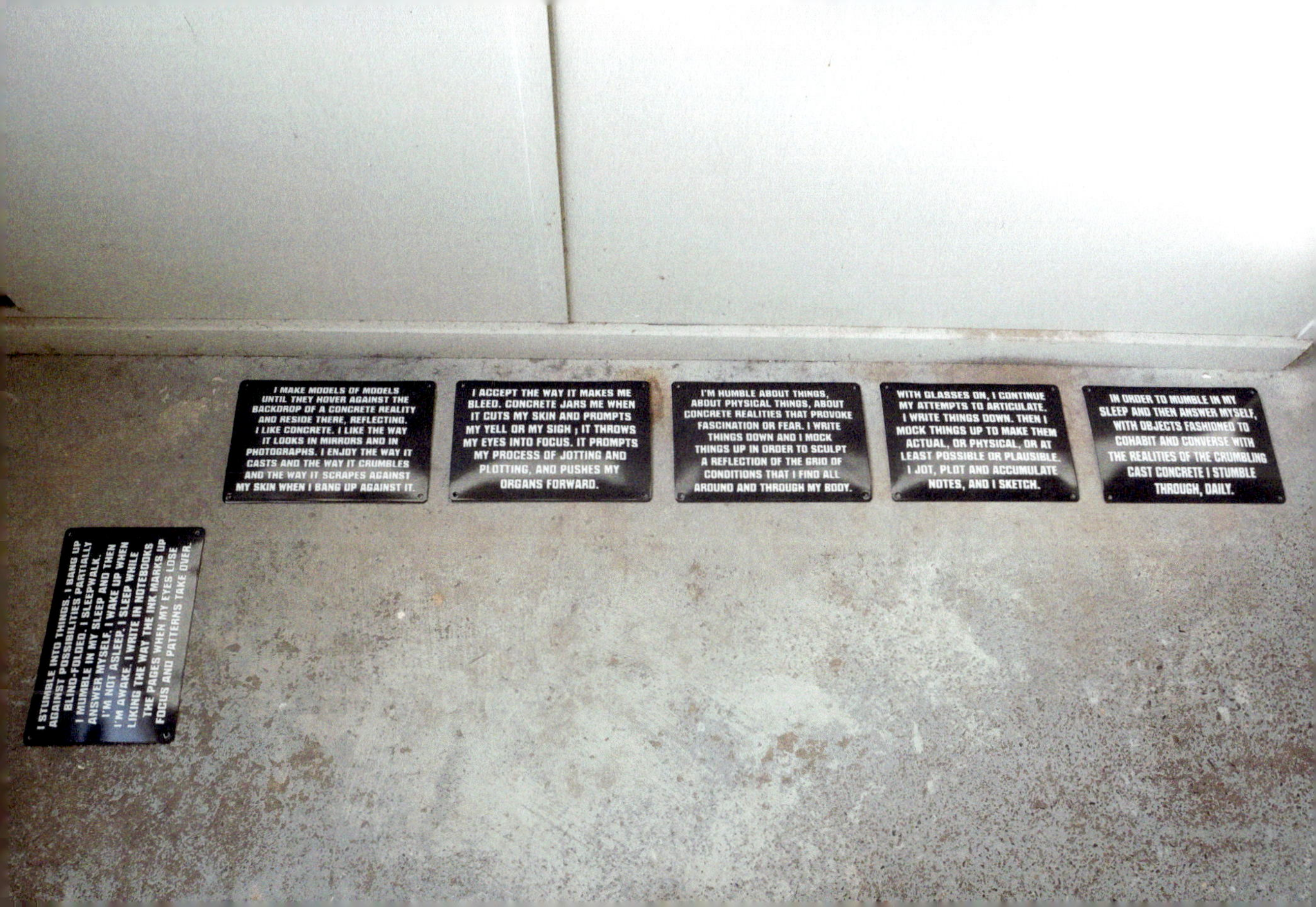
I MAKE MODELS OF MODELS UNTIL THEY HOVER AGAINST THE BACKDROP OF A CONCRETE REALITY AND RESIDE THERE, REFLECTING. I LIKE CONCRETE. I LIKE THE WAY IT LOOKS IN MIRRORS AND IN PHOTOGRAPHS. I ENJOY THE WAY IT CASTS AND THE WAY IT CRUMBLES AND THE WAY IT SCRAPES AGAINST MY SKIN WHEN I BANG UP AGAINST IT.
I ACCEPT THE WAY IT MAKES ME BLEED. CONCRETE JARS ME WHEN IT CUTS MY SKIN AND PROMPTS MY YELL OR MY SIGH ; IT THROWS MY EYES INTO FOCUS. IT PROMPTS MY PROCESS OF JOTTING AND PLOTTING, AND PUSHES MY ORGANS FORWARD.
I'M HUMBLE ABOUT THINGS, ABOUT PHYSICAL THINGS, ABOUT CONCRETE REALITIES THAT PROVOKE FASCINATION OR FEAR. I WRITE THINGS DOWN AND I MOCK THINGS UP IN ORDER TO SCULPT A REFLECTION OF THE GRID OF CONDITIONS THAT I FIND ALL AROUND AND THROUGH MY BODY.
WITH GLASSES ON, I CONTINUE MY ATTEMPTS TO ARTICULATE. I WRITE THINGS DOWN. THEN I MOCK THINGS UP TO MAKE THEM ACTUAL, OR PHYSICAL, OR AT LEAST POSSIBLE OR PLAUSIBLE. I JOT, PLOT AND ACCUMULATE NOTES, AND I SKETCH.
IN ORDER TO MUMBLE IN MY SLEEP AND THEN ANSWER MYSELF, WITH OBJECTS FASHIONED TO COHABIT AND CONVERSE WITH THE REALITIES OF THE CRUMBLING CAST CONCRETE I STUMBLE THROUGH, DAILY.
I STUMBLE INTO THINGS. I BANG UP AGAINST POSSIBILITIES PARTIALLY BLIND-FOLDED. I SLEEPWALK. I MUMBLE IN MY SLEEP AND THEN ANSWER MYSELF. I WAKE UP WHEN I'M NOT ASLEEP. I SLEEP WHILE I'M AWAKE. I WRITE IN NOTEBOOKS LIKING THE WAY THE INK MARKS UP THE PAGES WHEN MY EYES LOSE FOCUS AND PATTERNS TAKE OVER.

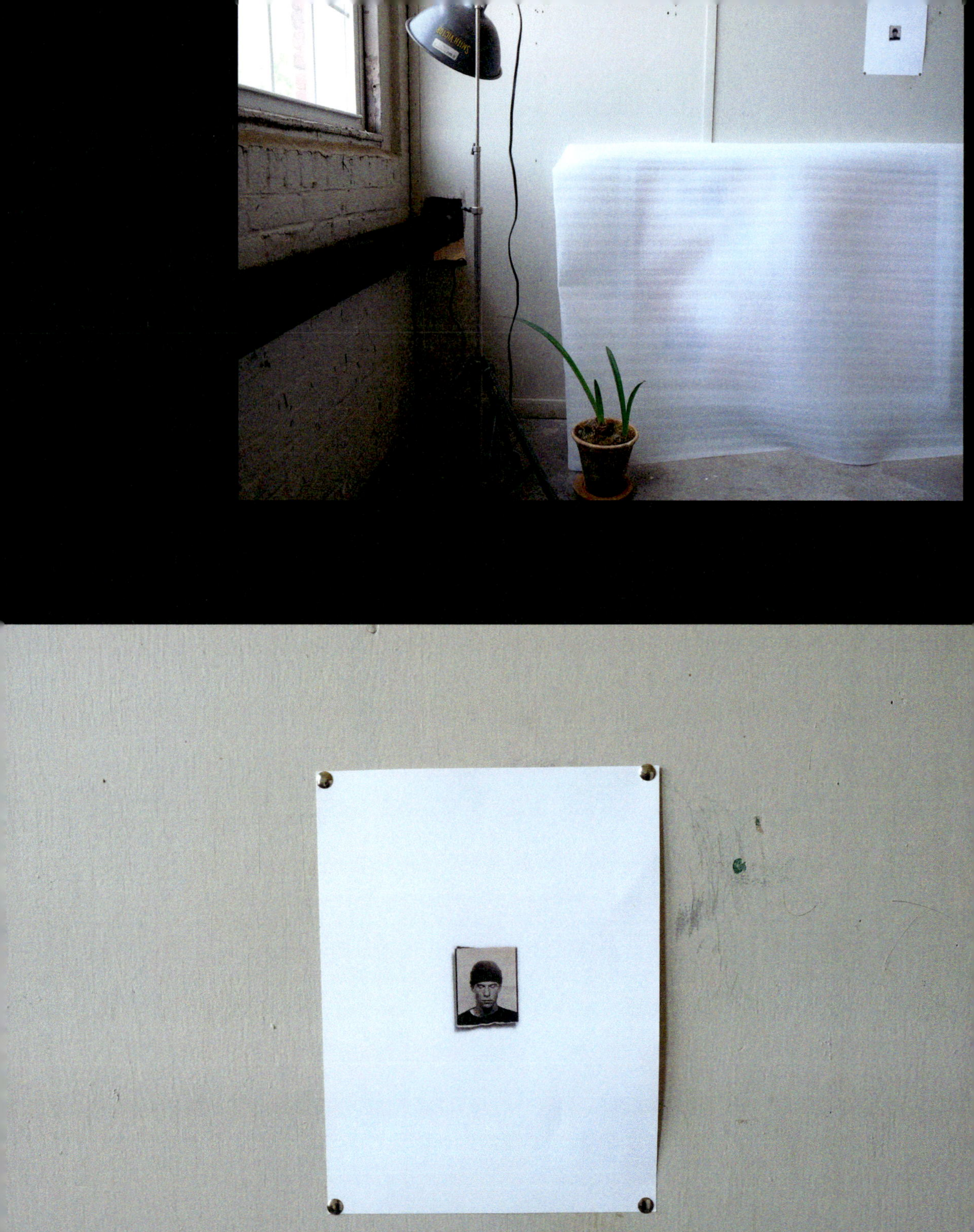

The seventh renovation:
On the northeast corner of 3rd Avenue and 14th Street, partially hidden by construction scaffolding, sits an adult all-male video store. The outside is covered in matte black wood and shiny black glass and Plexiglas, with the word video repeated several times in neon letters near the entrance. The store sits tentatively on its corner, awaiting its displacement by the high-rise apartment building that is scheduled to be erected on the site within the next two years. Inside the store, the front room offers up a supply of videotapes, dildos and lubricants for sale, while the second space holds the individual video booths. The renovation will take place on the outside of the store, in some configuration of interaction with the existing black façade and the adjacent construction scaffolding.

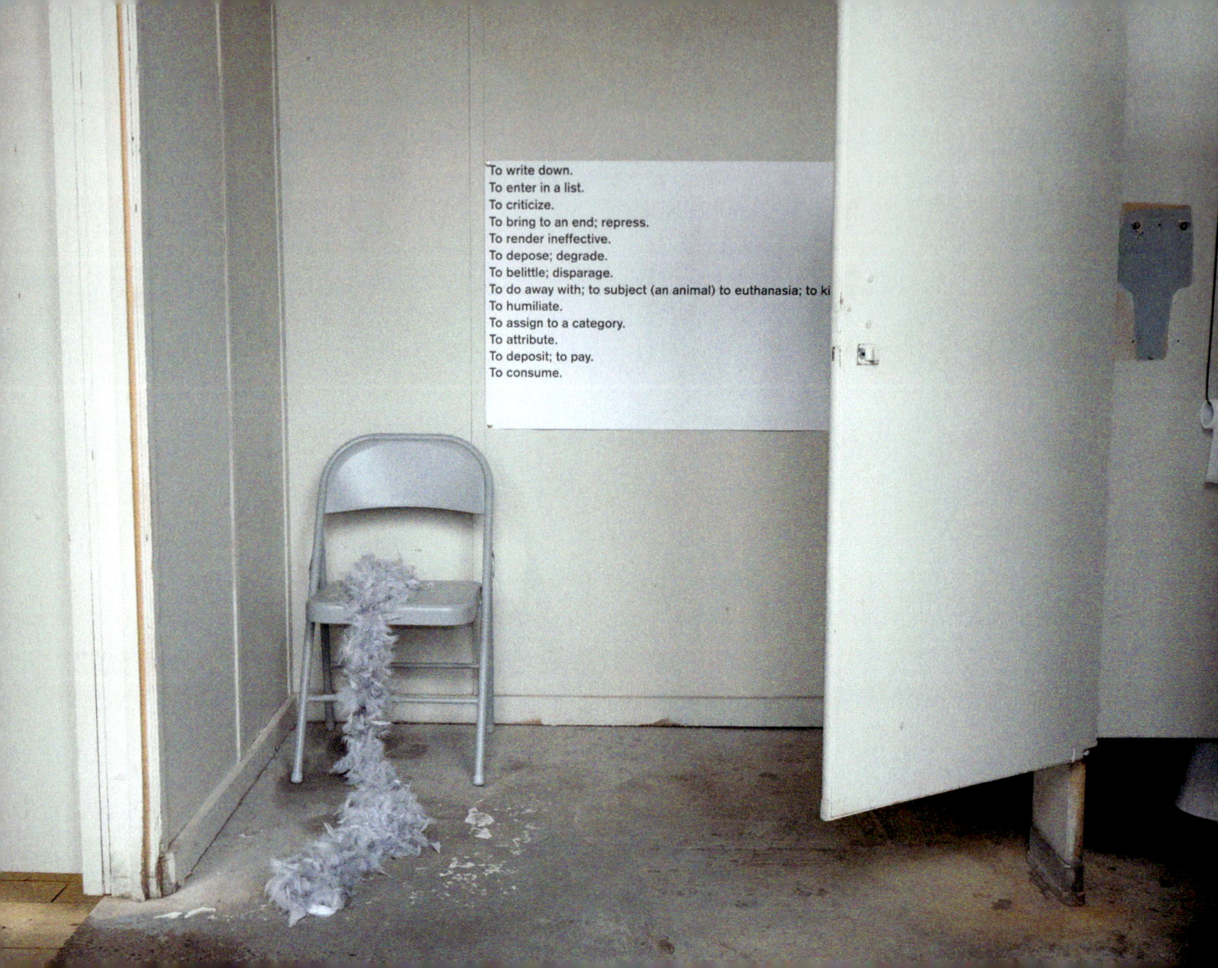
To write down.
To enter in a list.
To criticize.
To bring to an end; repress.
To render ineffective.
To depose; degrade.
To belittle; disparage.
To do away with; to subject (an animal) to euthanasia; to ki
To humiliate.
To assign to a category.
To attribute.
To deposit; to pay.
To consume.

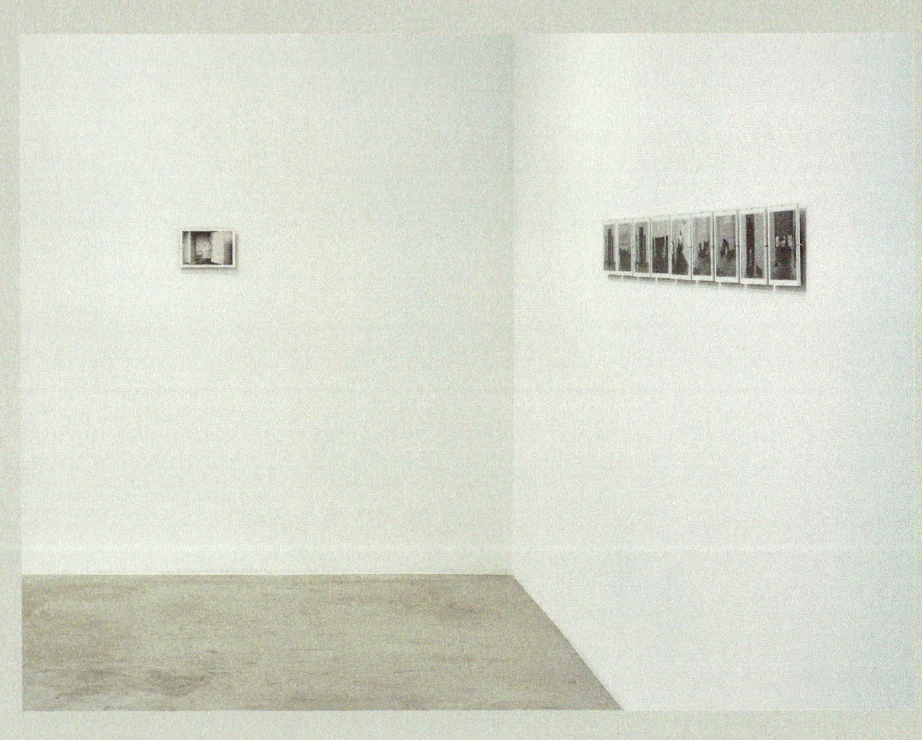

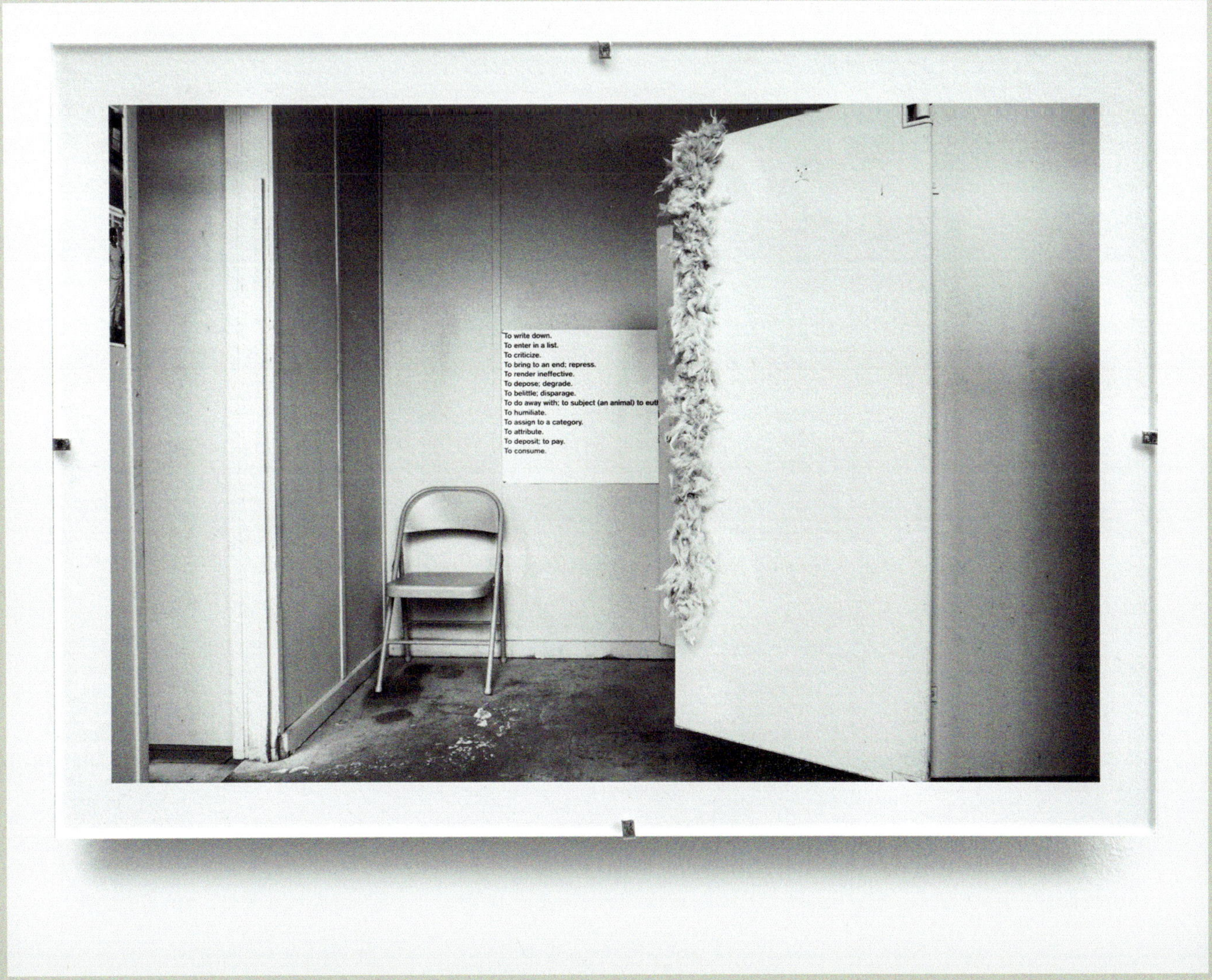

To write down.
To enter in a list.
To criticize.
To bring to an end; repress.
To render ineffective.
To depose; degrade.
To belittle; disparage.
To do away with; to subject (an animal) to euth
To humiliate.
To assign to a category.
To attribute.
To deposit; to pay.
To consume.

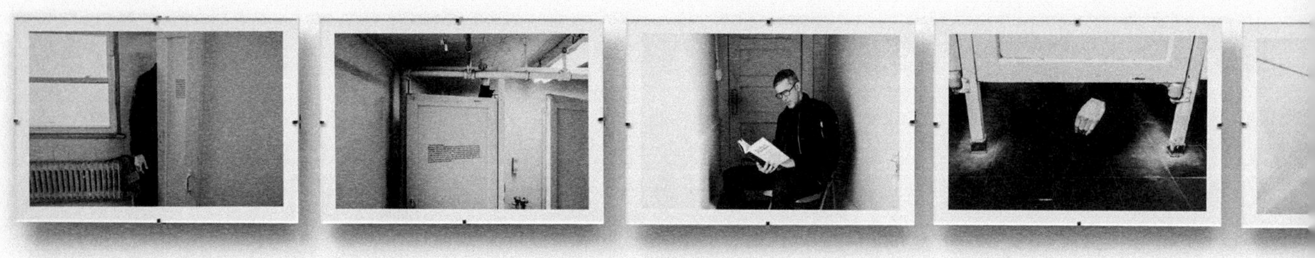

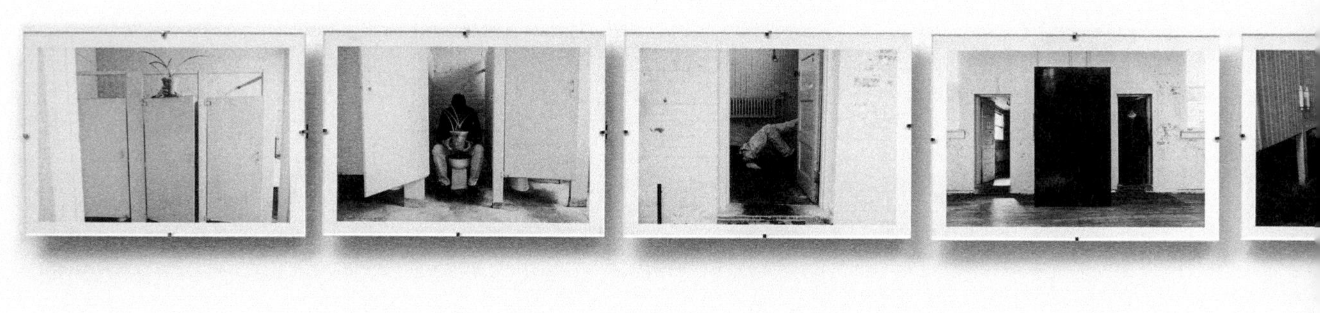

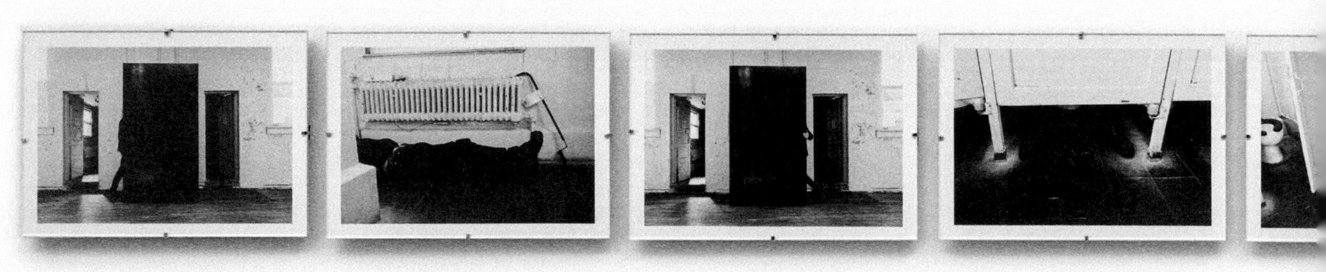

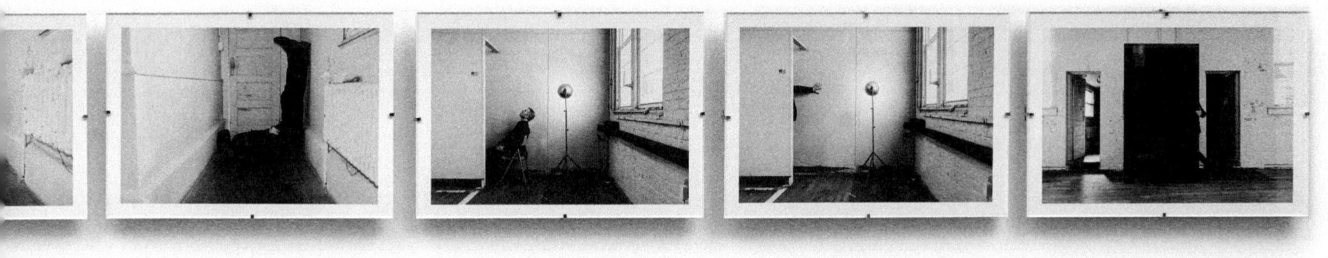

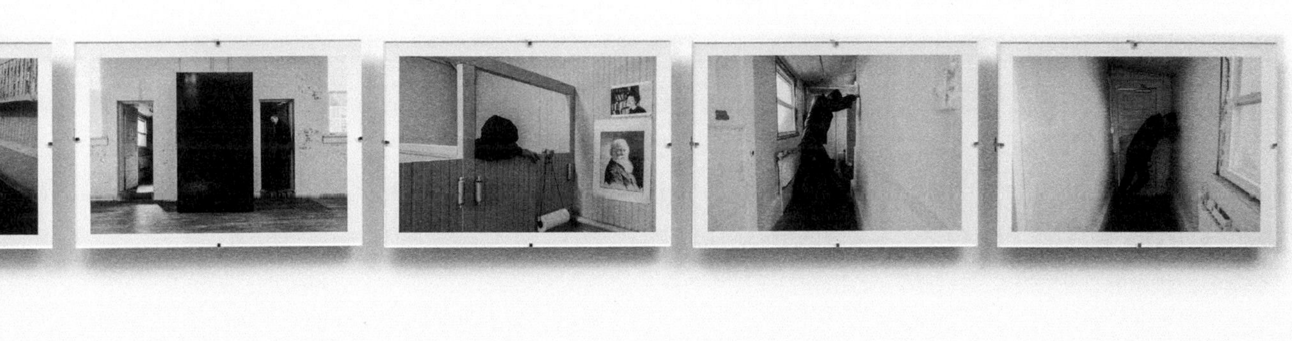

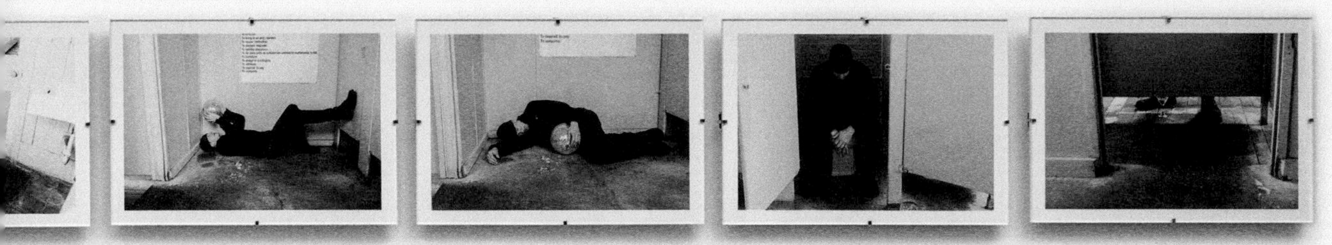

71

4

Sometime around the time of the New Haven project, my conversations with Patrick Collins began to evolve. Patrick had acquired a substantial group of works of mine over several years, many of which were older, historical works, and he had gradually joined a relatively small group of people who are deeply interested in the dynamics embedded in and surrounding the projects I've embarked on, not simply the physical results. I place a high value on these moments with curators, gallerists, writers, and collectors—and with other artists maybe most of all—who recognize the intense dynamics and sheer brutality of the art marketplace, and who can also find a way to think through it, creating counter-models and counter-responses. Such moments have helped to guide many of my efforts to safety when my instincts at times have been toward a mode of self-sabotage.

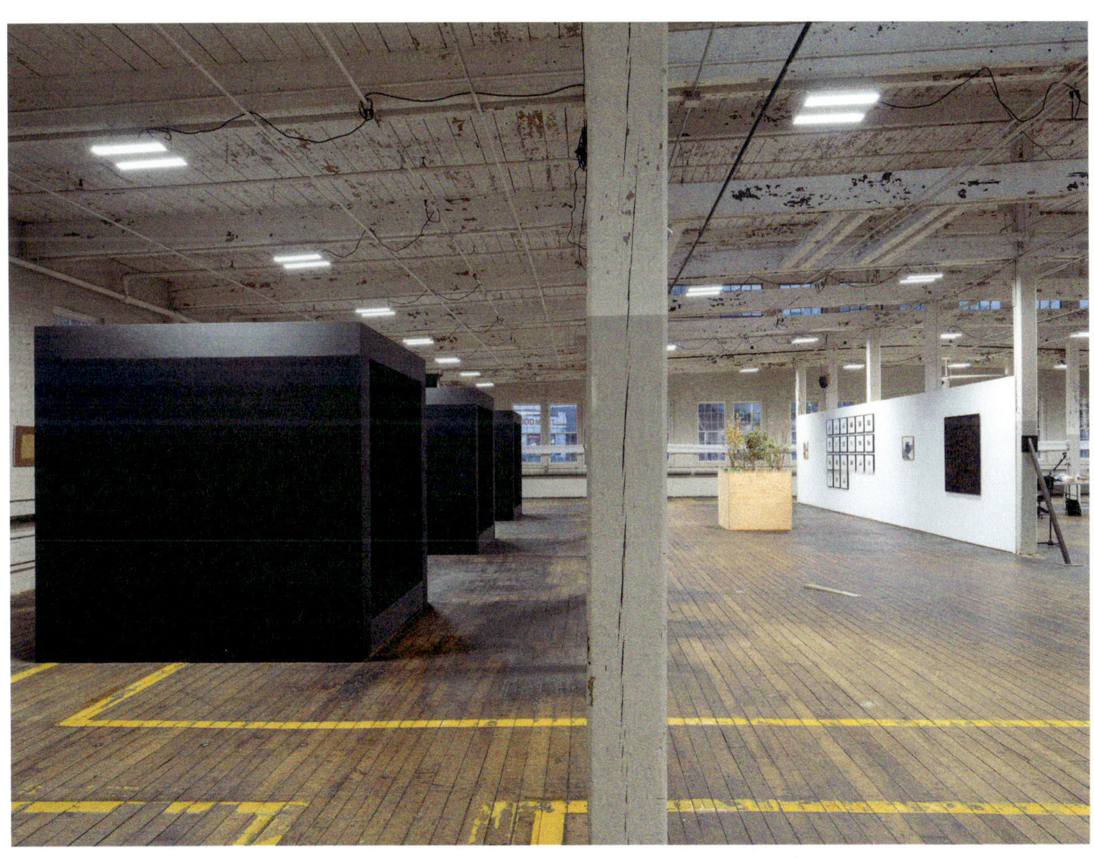

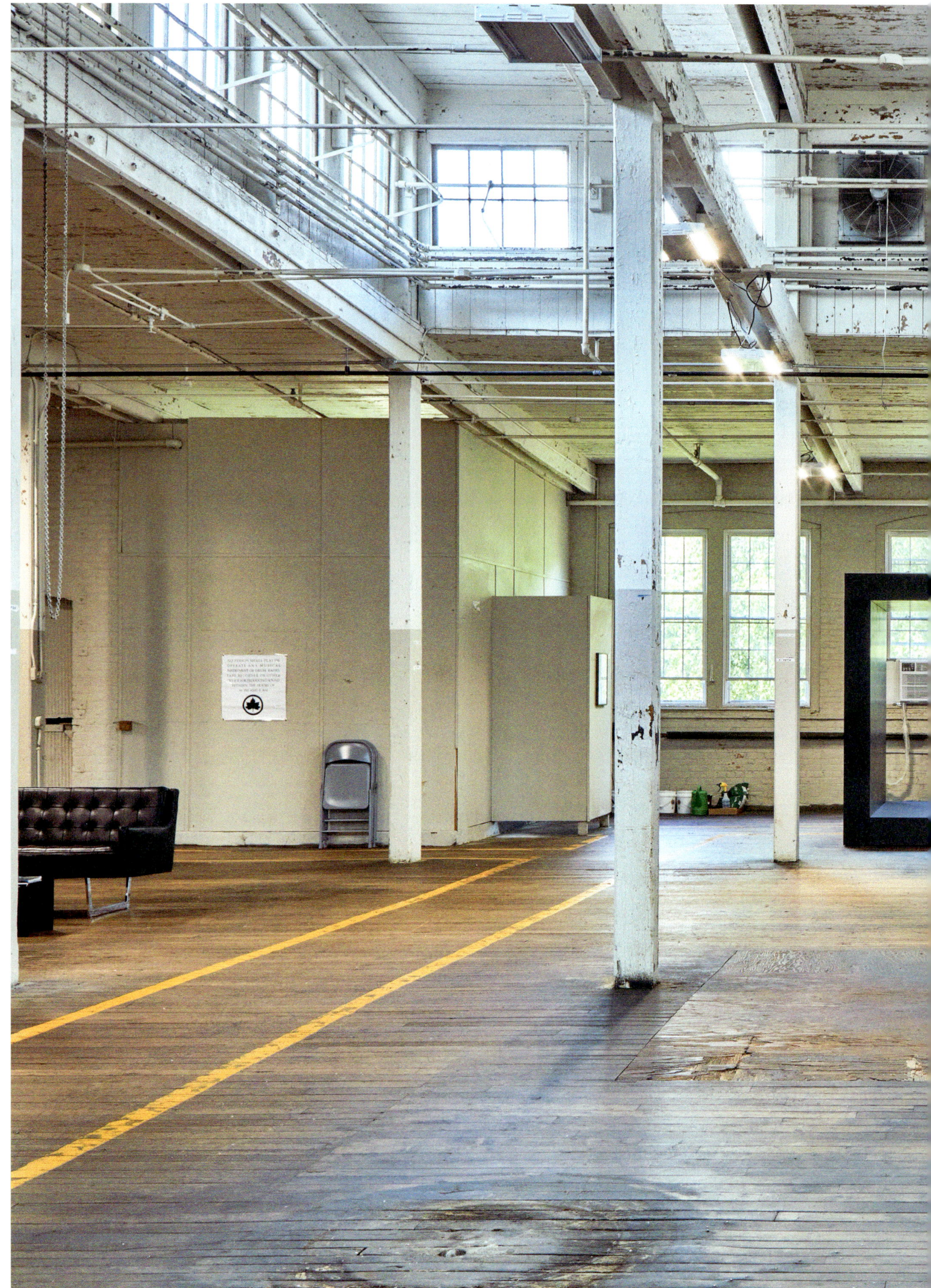

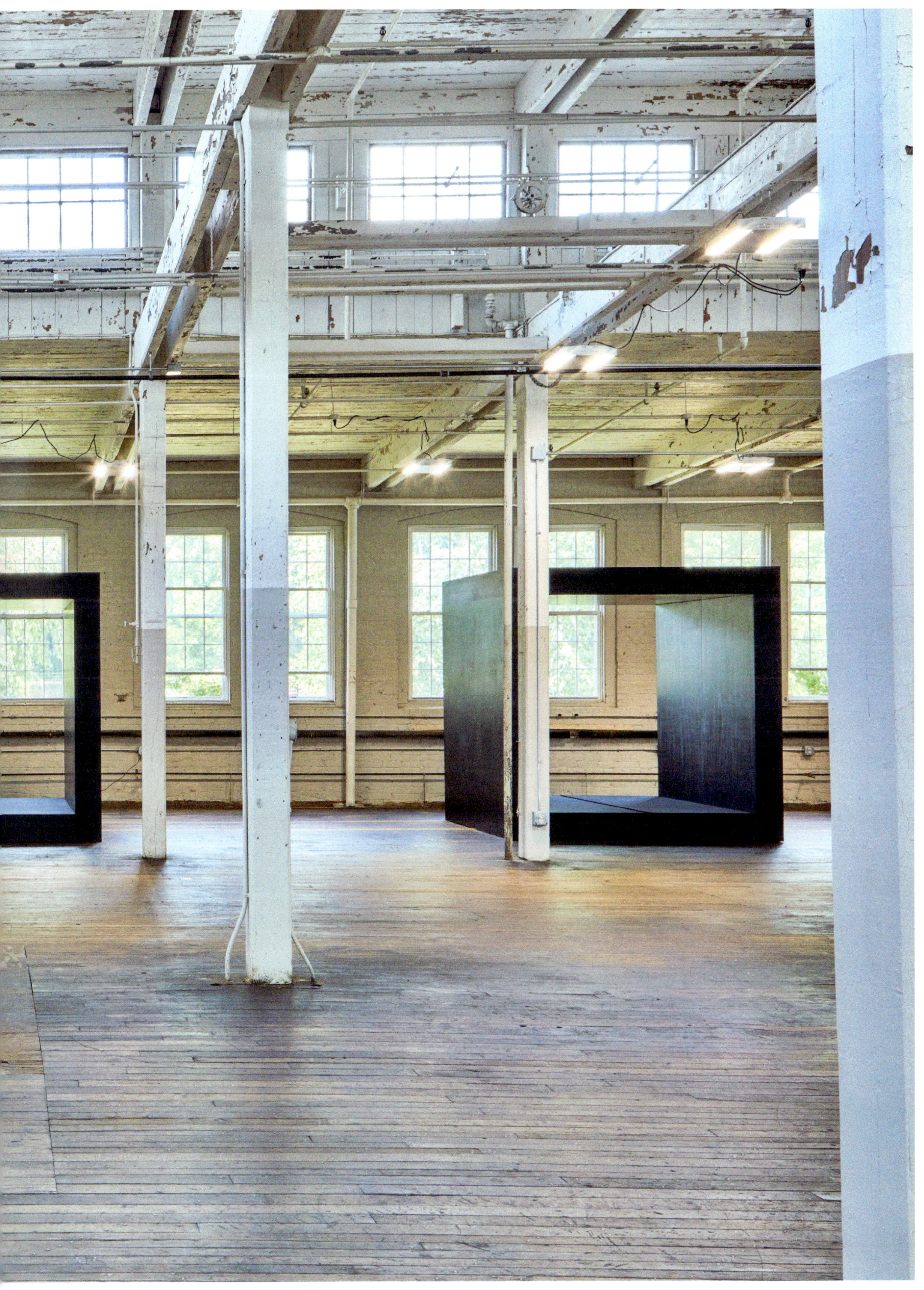

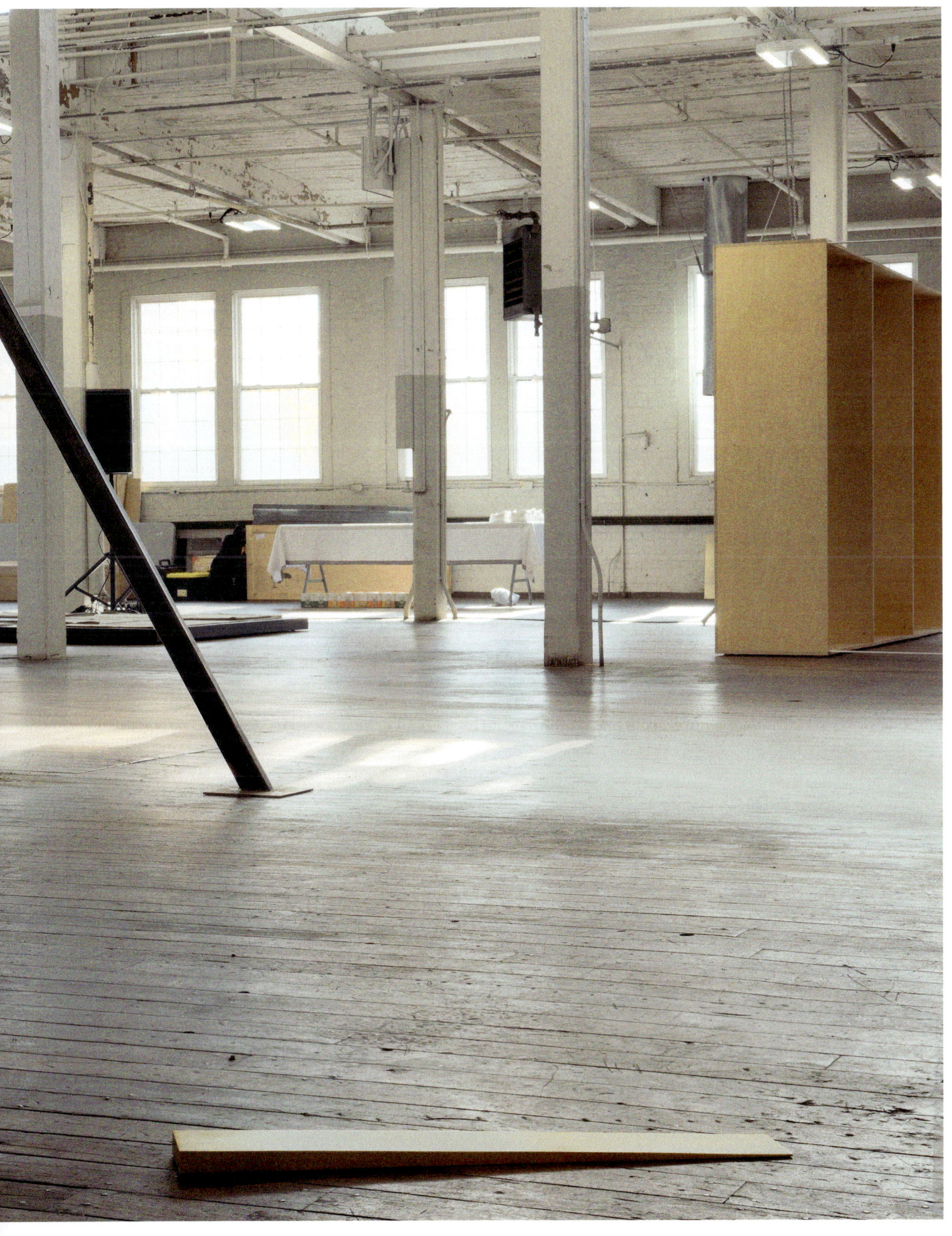

We were at a dinner when Patrick asked me to speak more about my work *Deep Purple* and its different exhibition contexts over the years. Christine Messineo was there too, I remember. Patrick also talked about his desire to work with artists in some way beyond the acquisition model, to engage with artists in *something else*, some other sort of supportive collaboration and exchange. He asked me to think about that, and I did, and when the beginnings of an idea began to develop in my head a few years later, about the thing that would eventually become *Torrington Project*, I thought of Patrick and our conversation that night. And I thought of Christine, who had long been a collaborator in my projects, first in her role at Bortolami, and then independently after her move to the West Coast. She, Patrick, and I had been involved in the planning stages for an outdoor commission in Dallas before the pandemic, so we already had a dialogue in place, which in 2020 I decided to pick up again with this new focus.

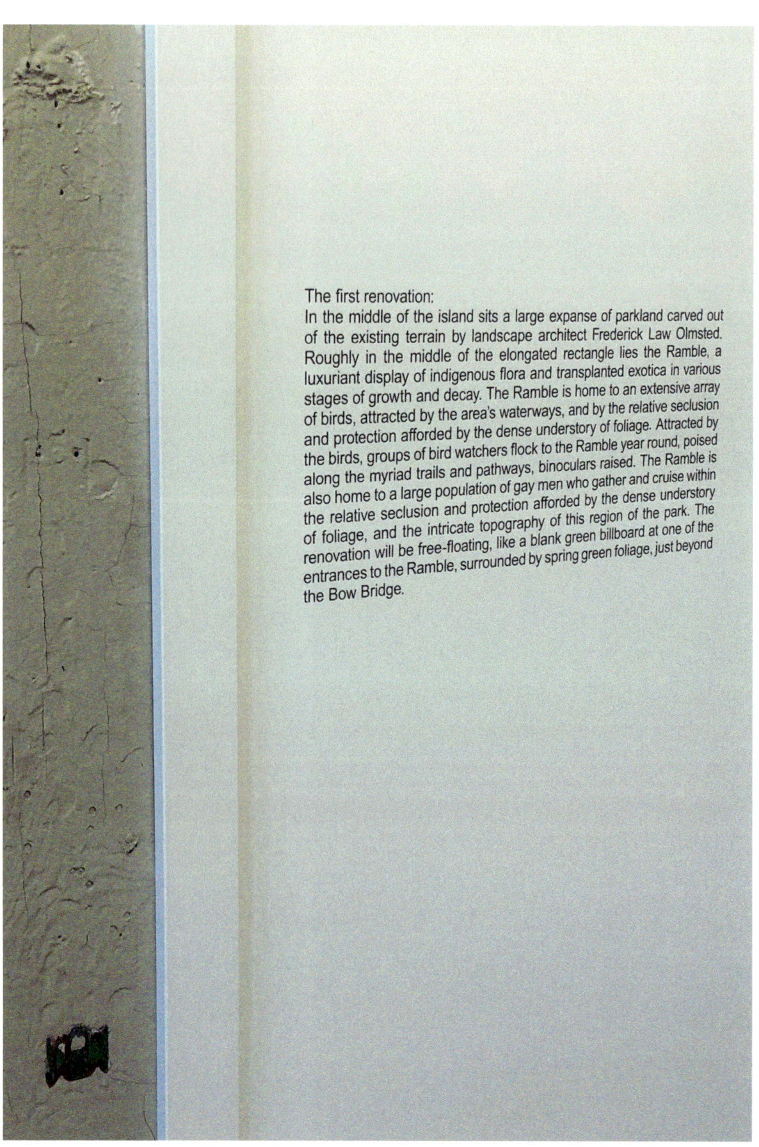

The first renovation:
In the middle of the island sits a large expanse of parkland carved out of the existing terrain by landscape architect Frederick Law Olmsted. Roughly in the middle of the elongated rectangle lies the Ramble, a luxuriant display of indigenous flora and transplanted exotica in various stages of growth and decay. The Ramble is home to an extensive array of birds, attracted by the area's waterways, and by the relative seclusion and protection afforded by the dense understory of foliage. Attracted by the birds, groups of bird watchers flock to the Ramble year round, poised along the myriad trails and pathways, binoculars raised. The Ramble is also home to a large population of gay men who gather and cruise within the relative seclusion and protection afforded by the dense understory of foliage, and the intricate topography of this region of the park. The renovation will be free-floating, like a blank green billboard at one of the entrances to the Ramble, surrounded by spring green foliage, just beyond the Bow Bridge.

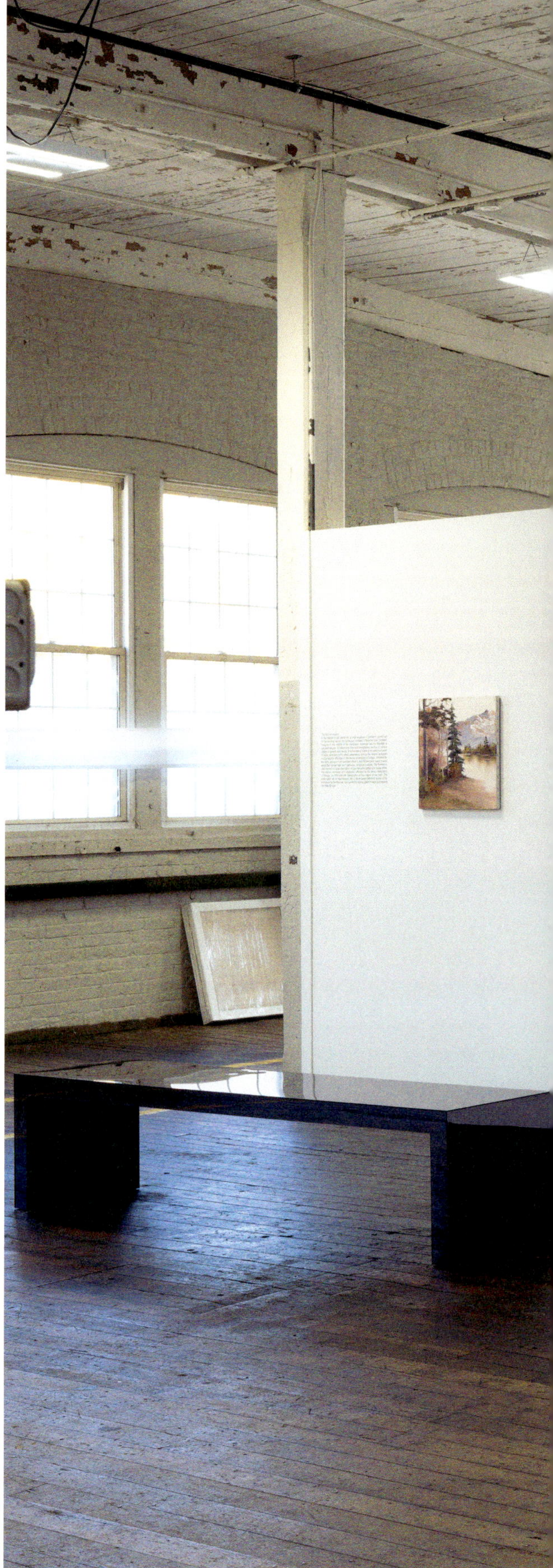

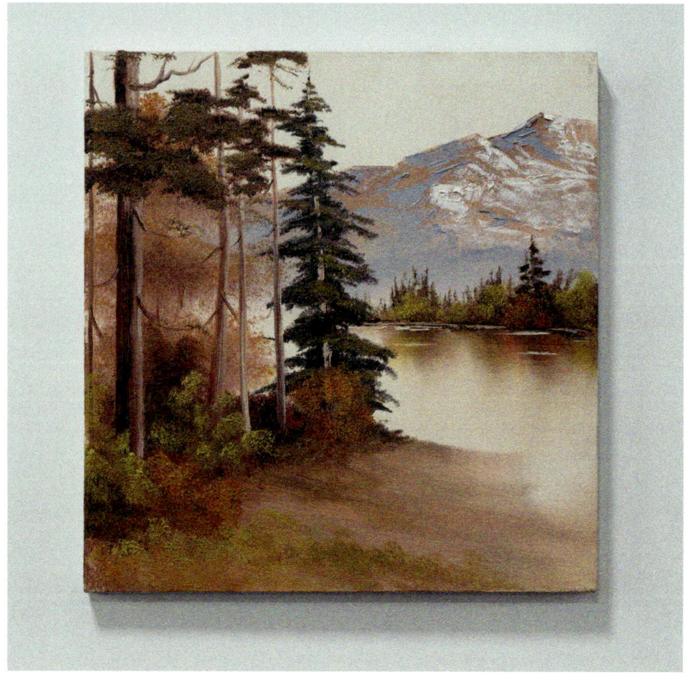

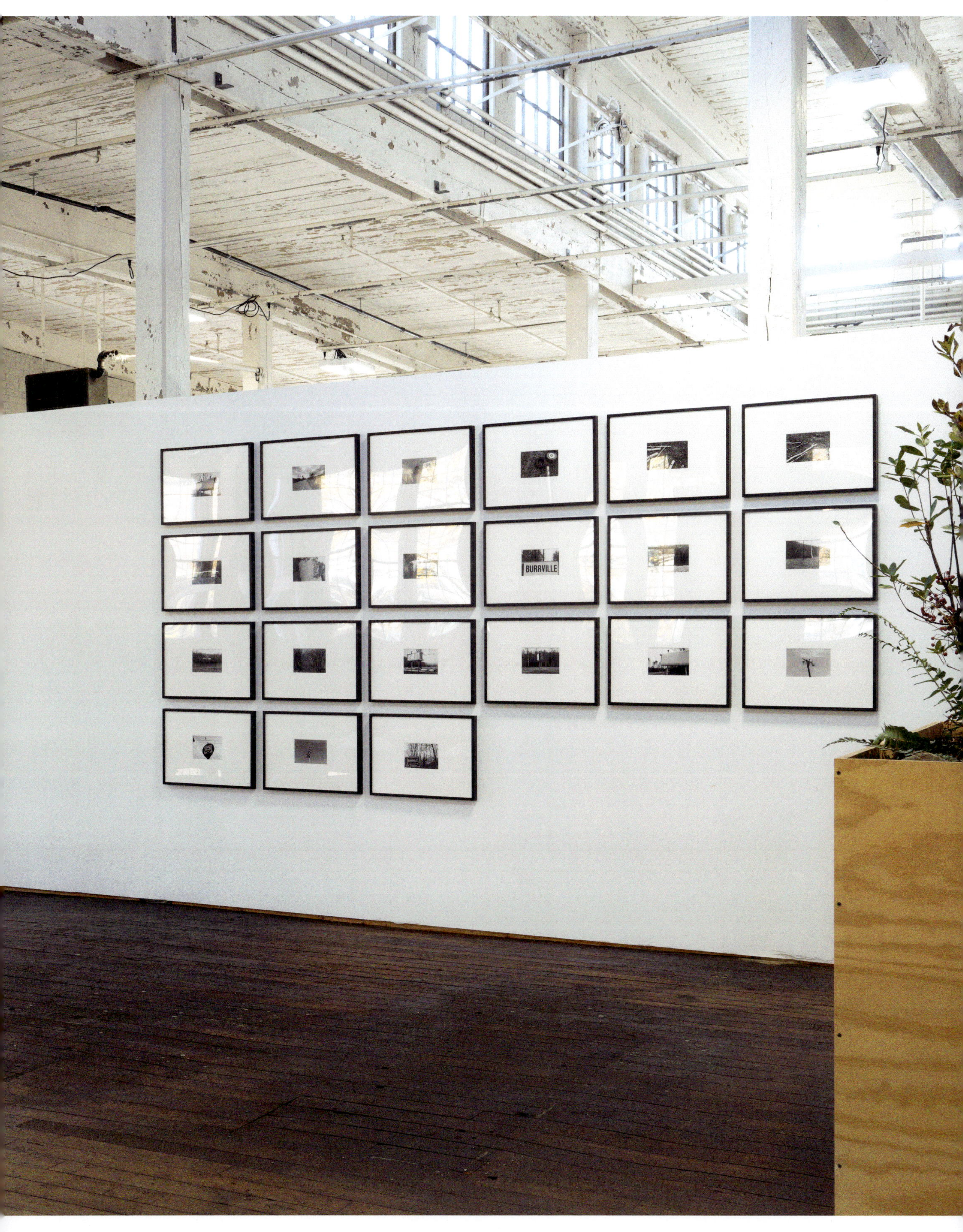

BURRVILLE

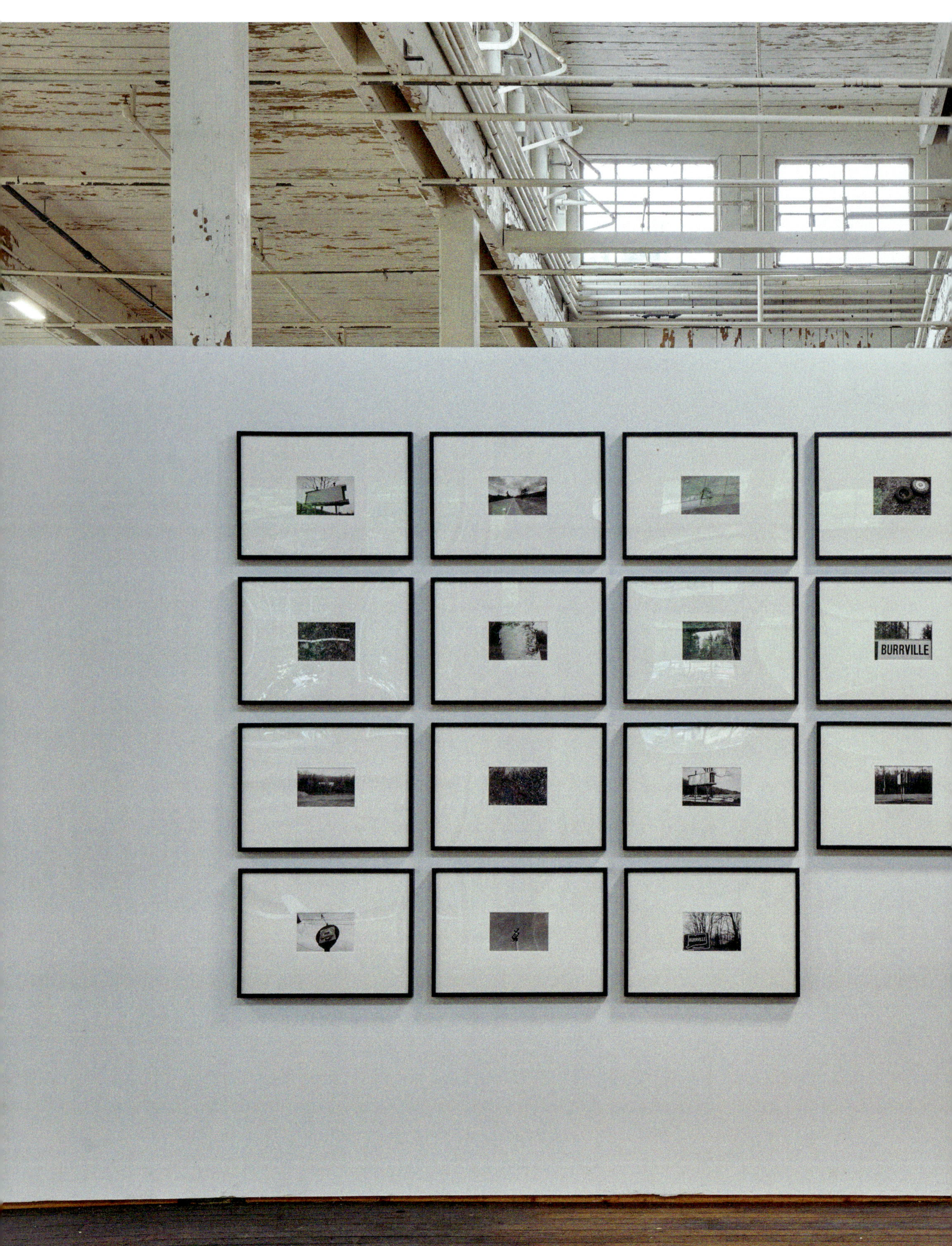

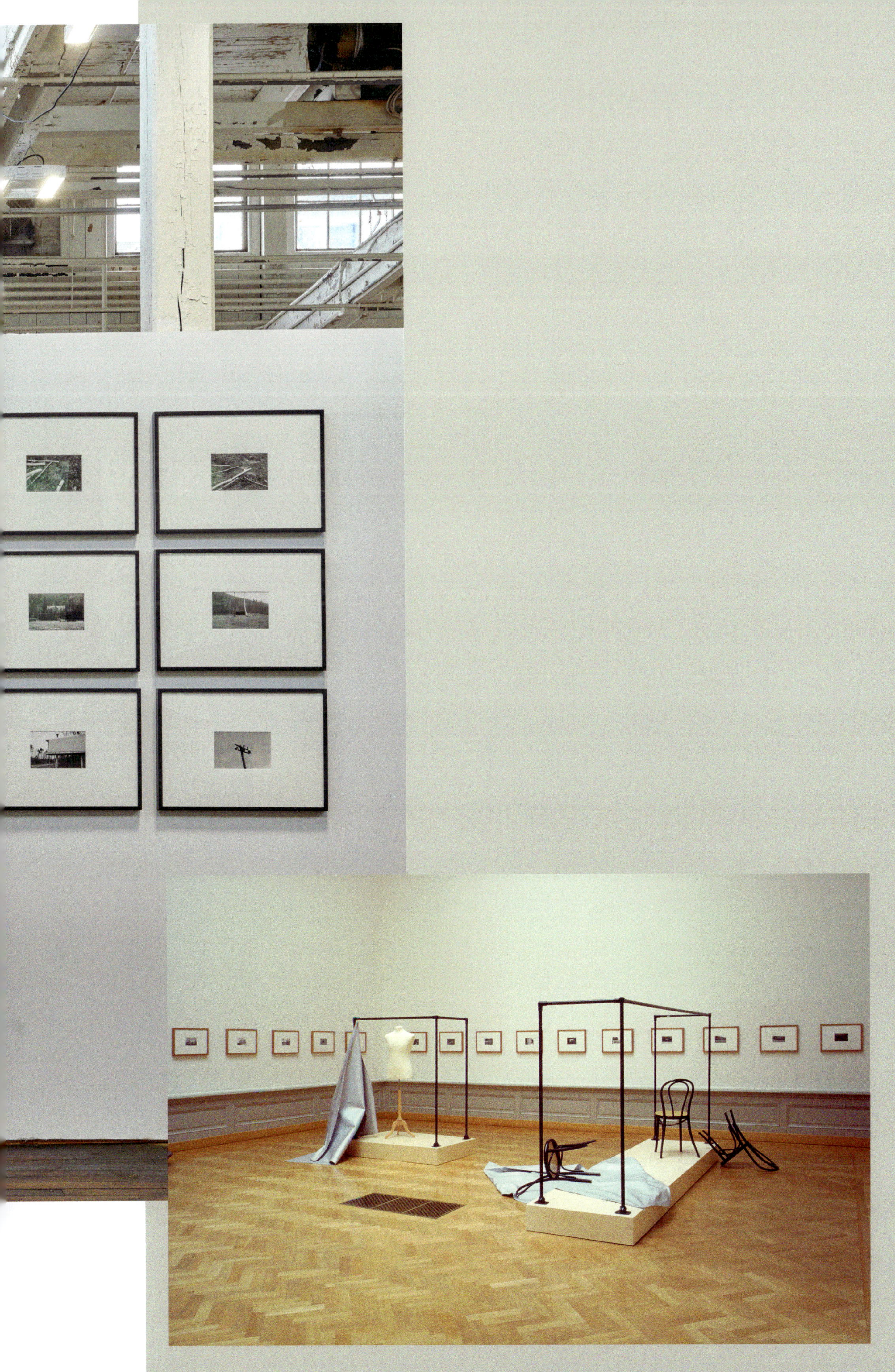

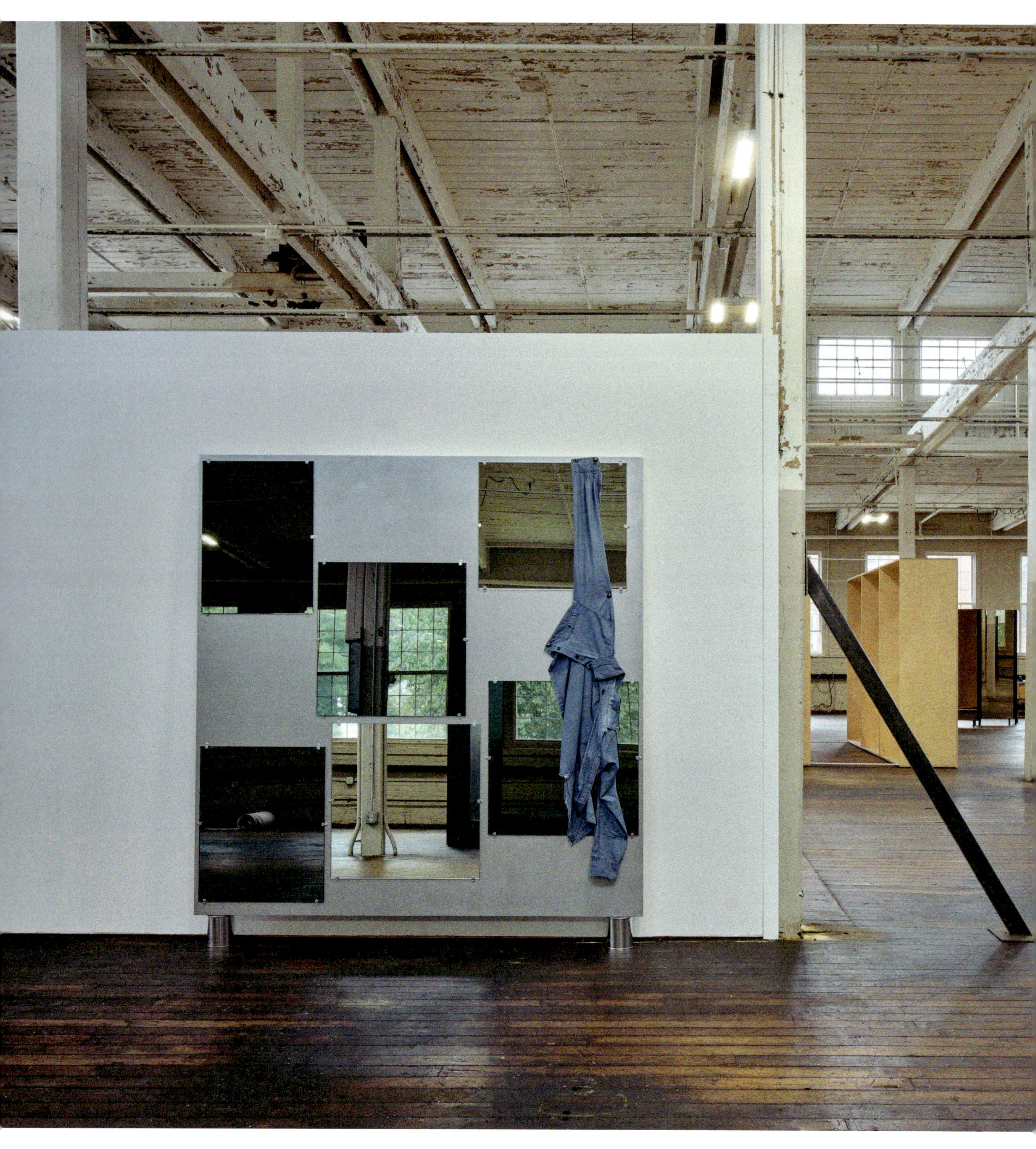

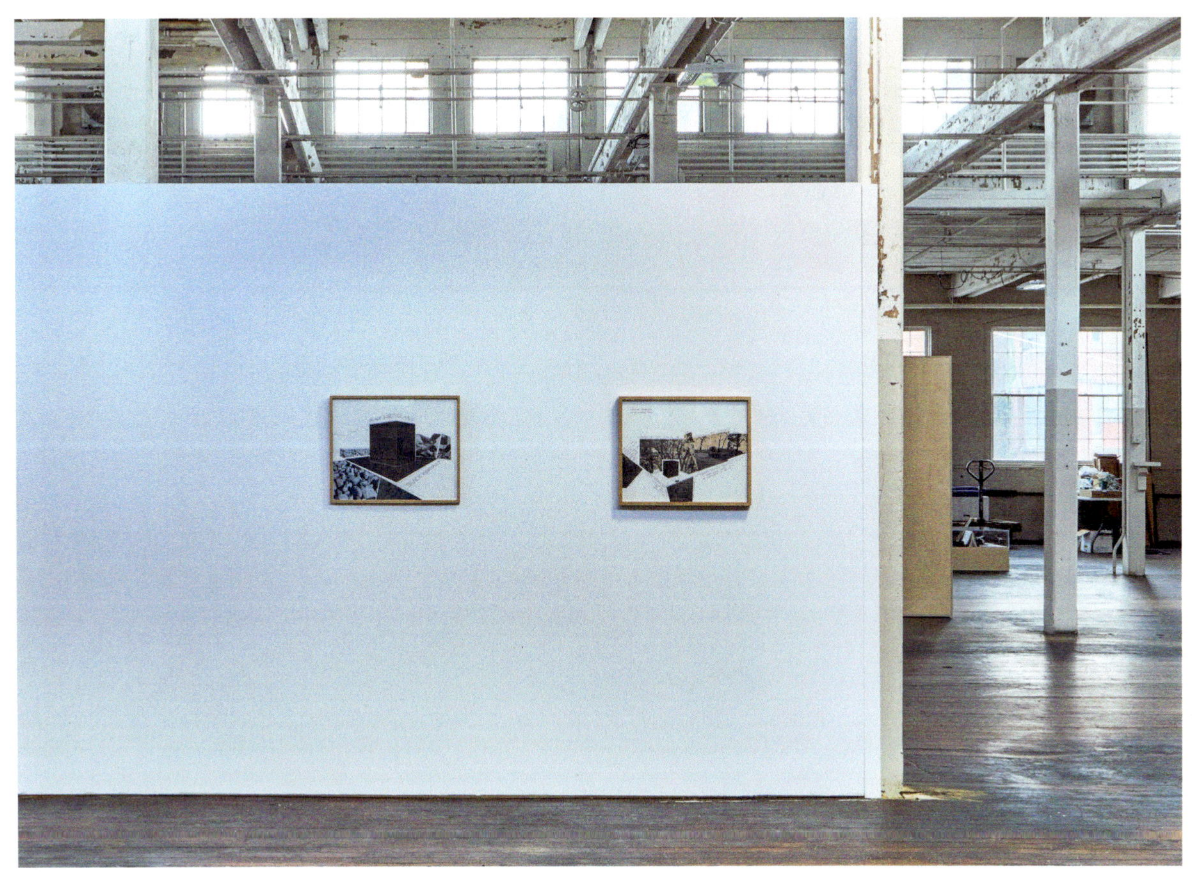

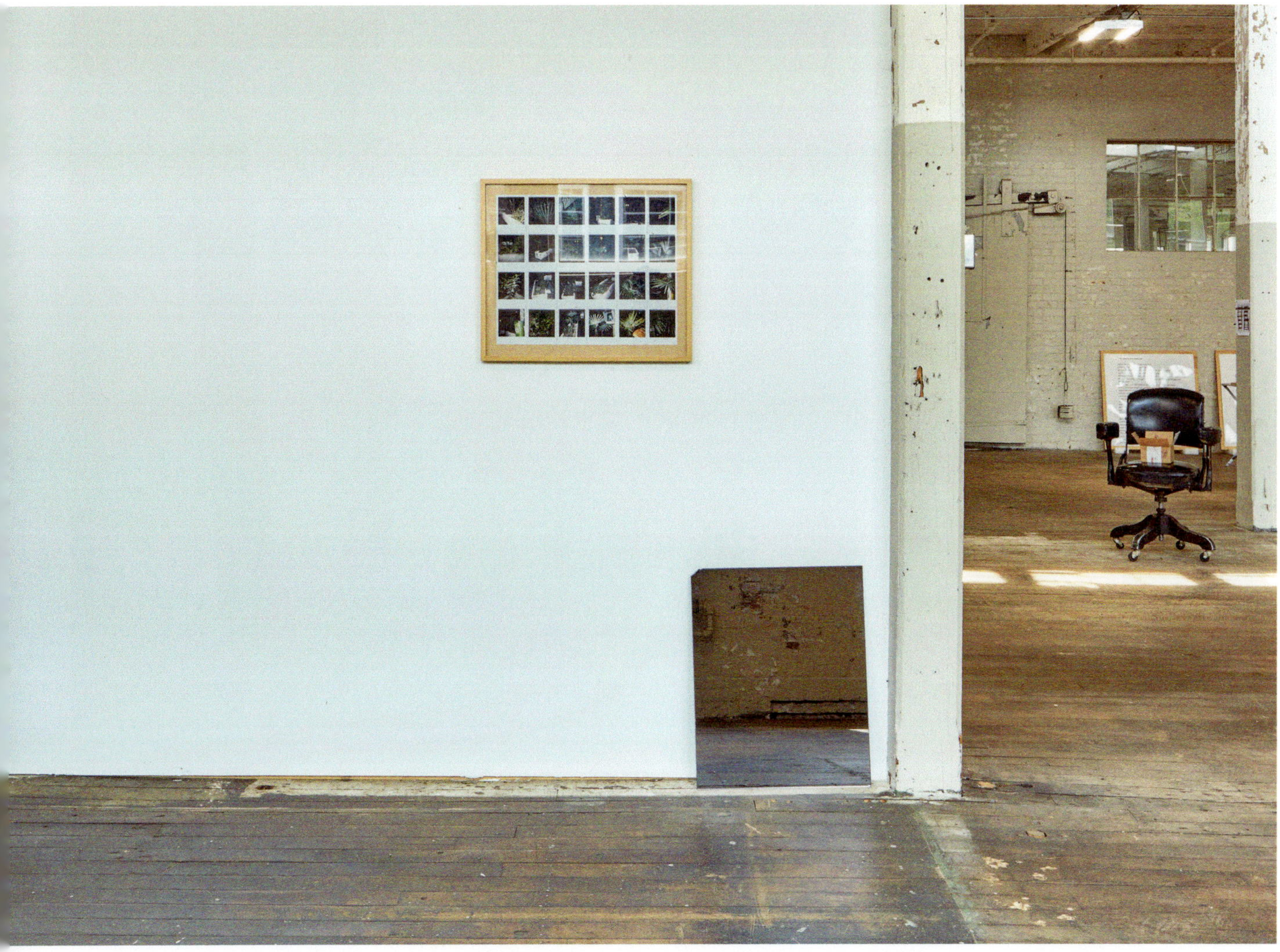

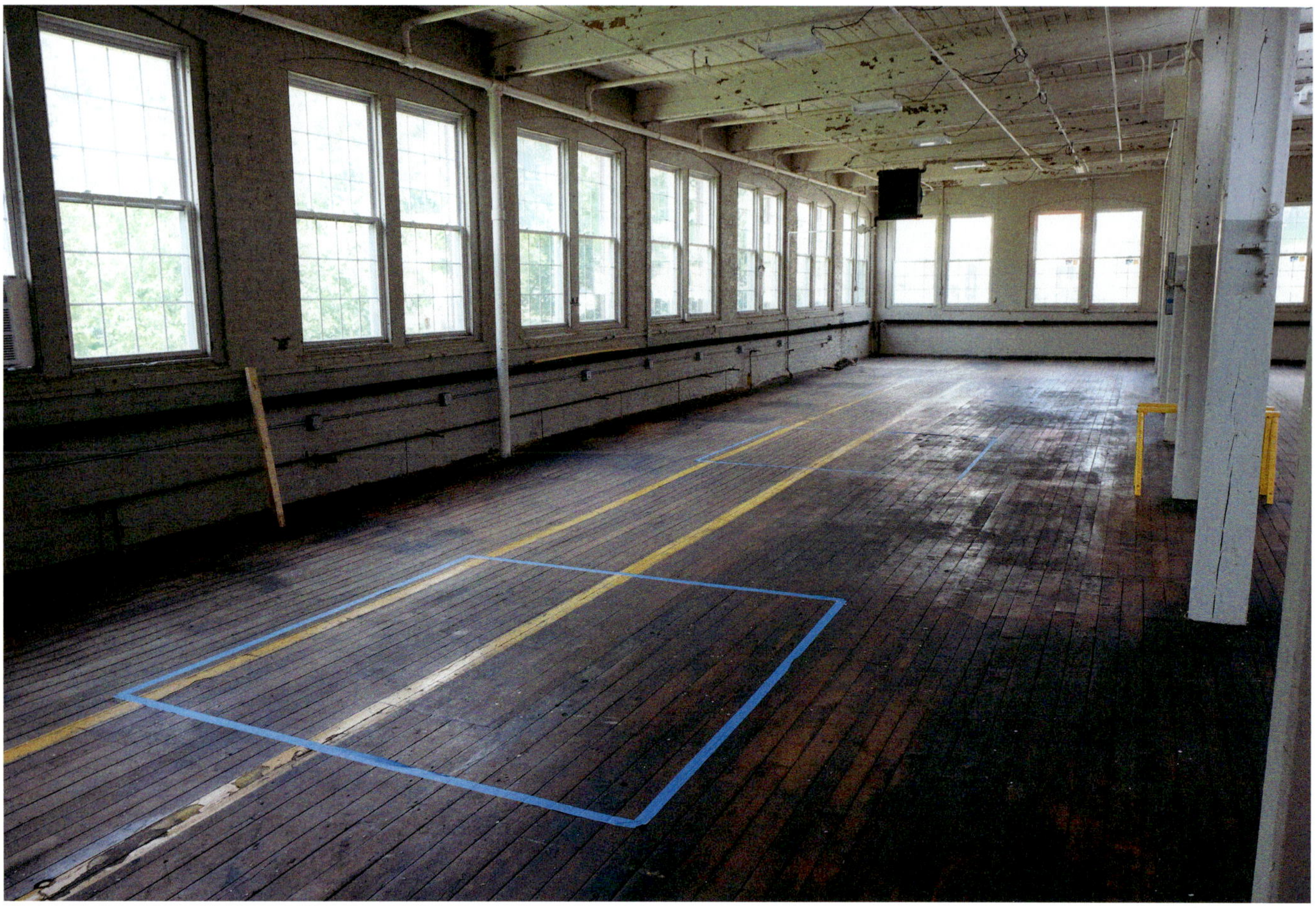

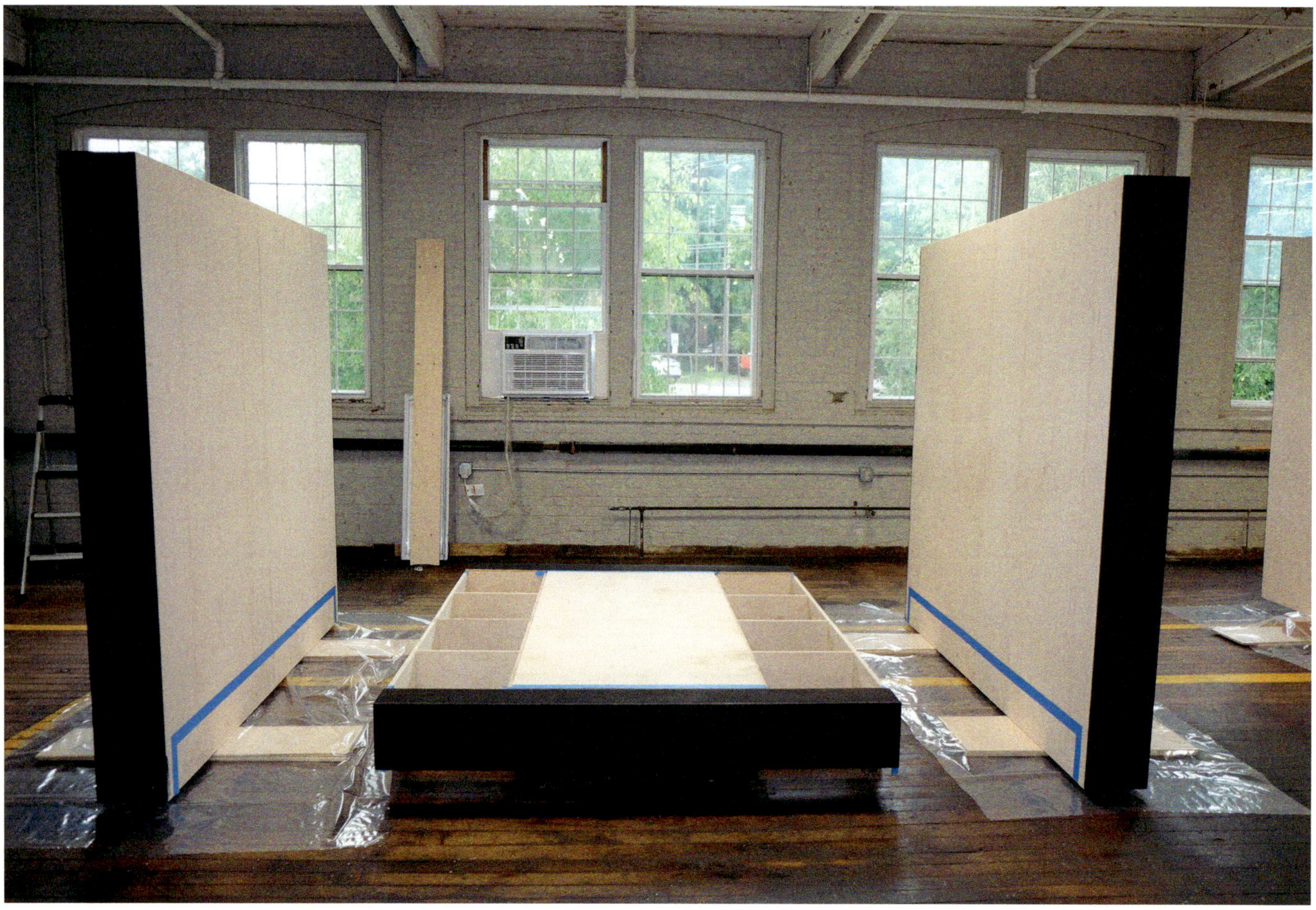

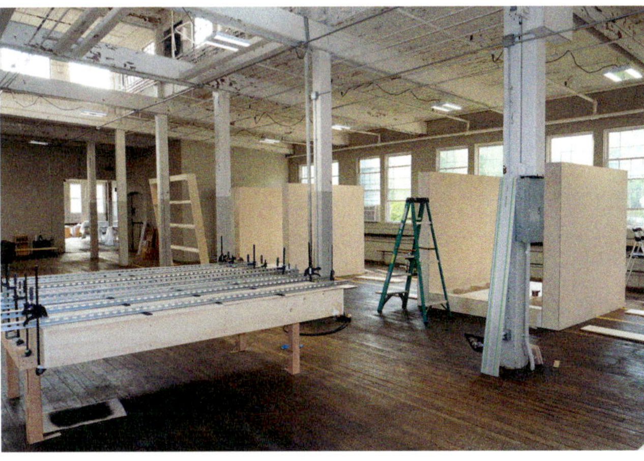

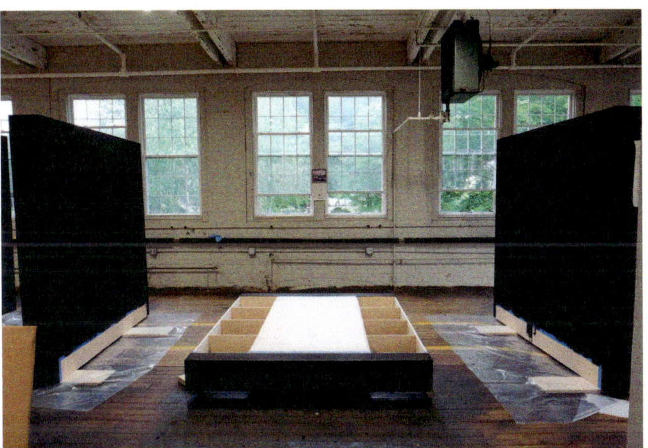

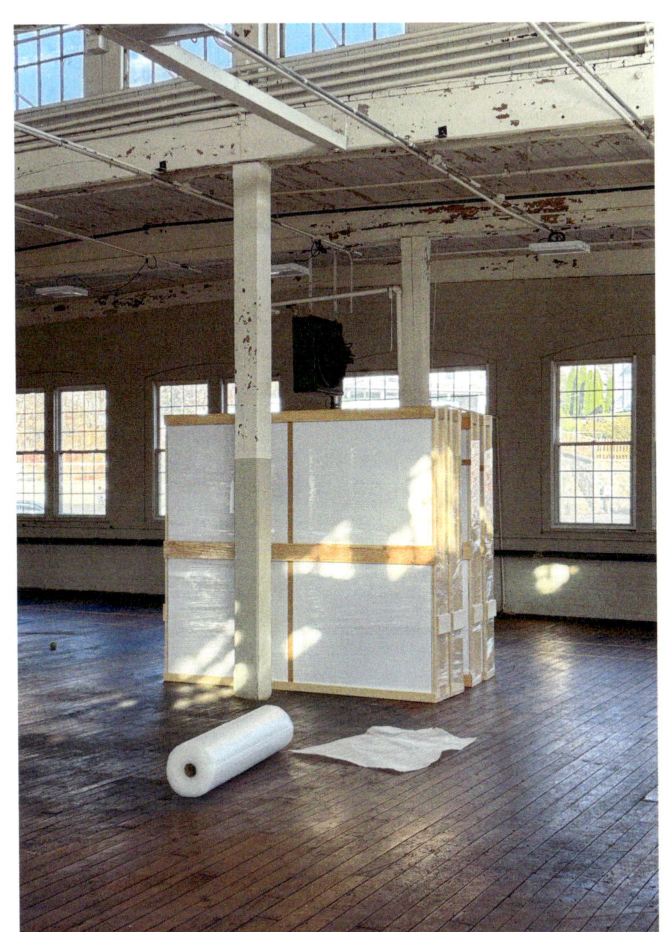

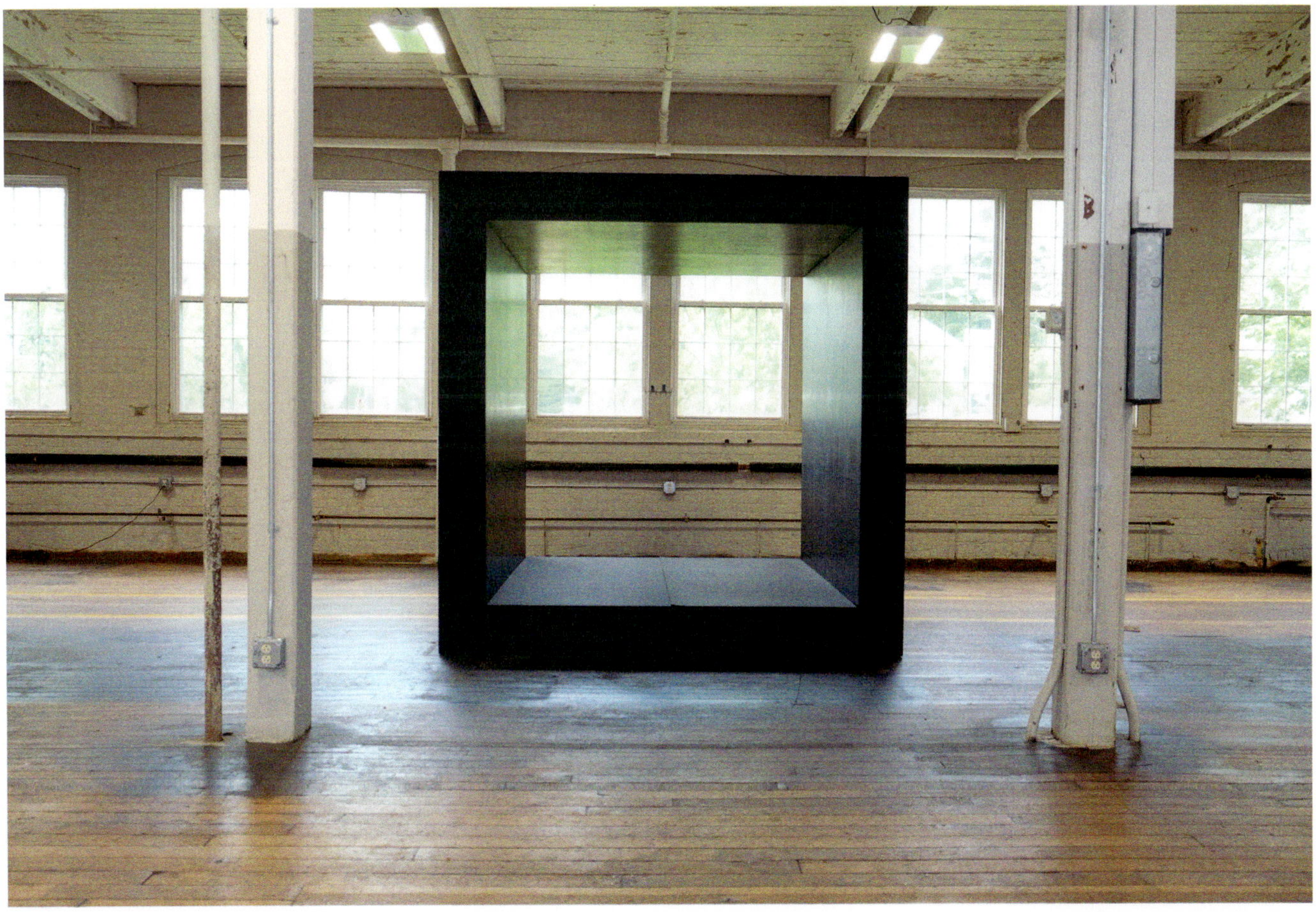

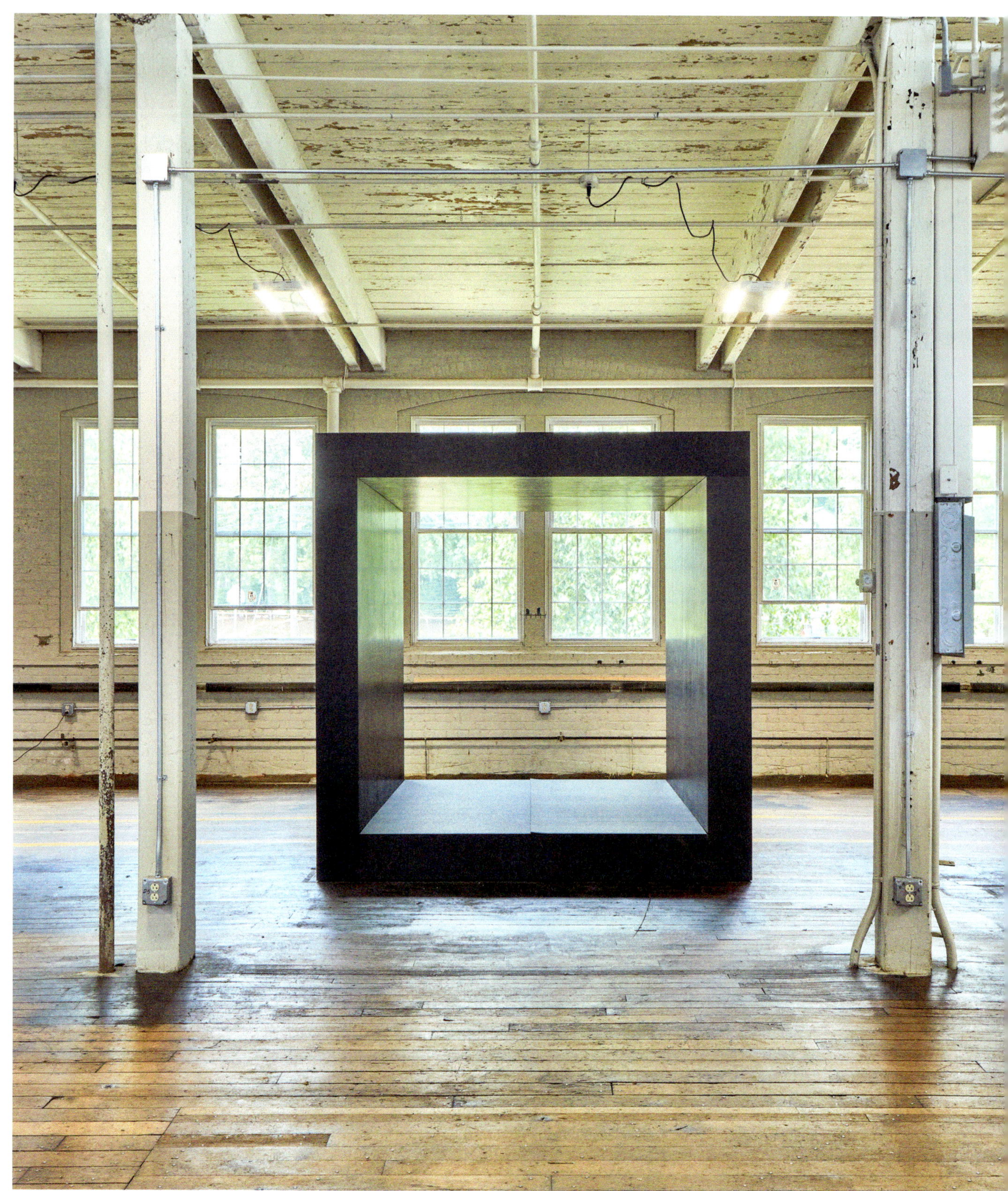

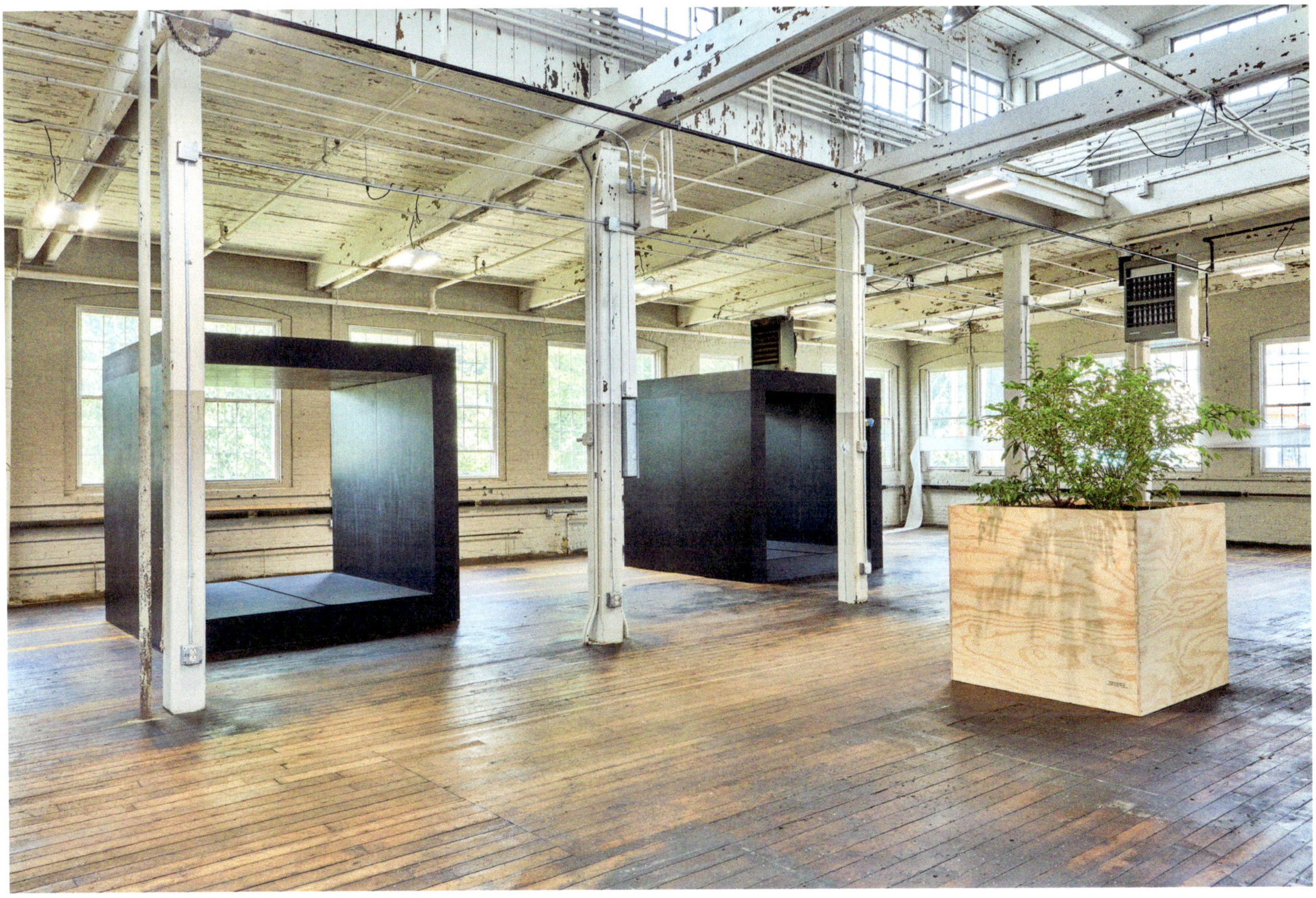

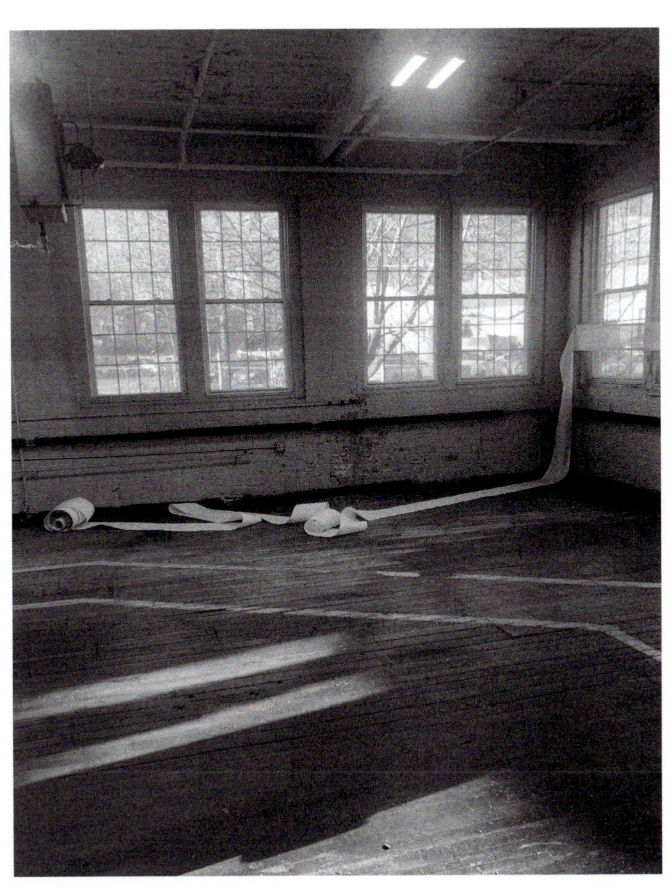

To encounter the hulking black frames that constitute Tom Burr's *Container (1–3)* (2001)—looming large compared to all their sculptural companions, like glowering lookouts in the densely populated space of the *Torrington Project*—is to encounter a work structured *as sculpture* by the work of memory. But everything I can say about these works starts from memory, from experiences: Of being *on top* of a work by Burr, delivering a talk while sitting on the sculpture *Anxiety* (2006) in Vienna during an event on sculpture and performance. Or locked up *inside* the cages of *Put Out* (2003), a carceral work I first saw in London in 2008. Or hiding *behind* the work, again inside the space the work creates, facilitating an unforgettable encounter with Colin de Land during the first gallery exhibition of *The Oblong Box* (2001)—where Colin put to immediate use the plastic ashtrays perched on shelves on the sculpture's hidden other side.

"All that your *Brillo Boxes* need," Paul Thek once supposedly said to Andy Warhol, "is a piece of flesh inside."[1] And so Thek upturned a *Brillo Box* and exposed its open bottom, turning it into a container for an inserted "meat piece," an erotic or desiring gesture that would subvert the Pop artist's insistence on the poetics of surface and superficiality with an immediate experience of depth, burrowing like a mole underneath and inside a prior work of art. Similarly, Burr's *Container (1–3)* "borrows" the formats of Minimalism, in this case a series of monumental concrete sculptures created by Donald Judd toward the end of his life at the Chinati Foundation in Marfa, Texas. Minimalism too was thought to be characterized by an evacuation of internal formal incident, with its push of all attention to the surface and to the outside, refocusing attention on the space surrounding the work itself. The Marfa sculptures' existence as outdoor works underlines this critical externality, one of the destinies of Minimalism at large.

1 See Margrit Brehm, Axel Heil, and Roberto Ohrt, *Paul Thek: Tales the Tortoise Taught Us* (Walther König, 2008), 32. Mike Kelley calls Thek's *Meat Piece with Warhol Brillo Box* a "collaboration" between Thek and Warhol, and offers the most compelling reading of the piece in his essay "Death and Transfiguration: A Letter from America," in *Paul Thek*, ed. Daniel Buchholz (Castello di Rivara, 1992). The critic Gregory Battcock—subject of Warhol films like *Eating Too Fast*, 1966 (the second version of *Blow Job*), like Thek who had been included in the Pop artist's *Thirteen Most Beautiful Boys*, 1964—shows up in the archival bulletin board pieces scattered throughout Burr's *Torrington Project*, and was the critic who linked Thek and Warhol most emphatically. See Battcock, "Humanism and Reality—Thek and Warhol," in *The New Art: A Critical Anthology*, ed. Gregory Battcock (Dutton, 1973), 13–20. Previously published in part as "Notes on 'Blow Job': A Film by Andy Warhol," *Film Culture* no. 37 (Summer 1965), pp. 20–21.

George Baker

2 Michael Fried decried the implicitly anthropomorphic "hollowness" of Minimalist sculpture in "Art and Objecthood," *Artforum*, Summer 1967, 12–23. Rosalind Krauss describes the external conditions claimed by Minimalist objects as "public" in "Sense and Sensibility: Reflection on Post '60s Sculpture," *Artforum*, November 1973, 43–53.

3 The original exhibition of Burr's *Container (1–3)* is documented in *Partnerschaften: Unterbrochene Karrieren* (Neue Gesellschaft für Bildende Kunst, 2002). My earlier account of this work and its many lessons can be found in "The Other Side of the Wall," *October*, no. 120 (Spring 2007): 106–37.

While some critics feared that this evacuation of the "internal" dimension of art would leave the Minimalist object "hollow," like a literal body, others claimed this exile as the highest critical value of the new forms of sculpture, a turn of art toward a condition of meaning-making that could only be called "public."[2] Burr's *Container (1–3)* intervenes within and transgresses these older critical agendas. When first shown in a group exhibition of artists who had been partners or couples at nGbK in Berlin, the dark black sculptures pressed close to the diminutive, decorative, and colorful paintings of Ull Hohn, Burr's former companion, who died of HIV/AIDS-related illnesses in 1995, when he was only thirty-five years old. The blank and dark forms seemed to lean toward Hohn's paintings, an installation strategy that embodied not only a kind of literal or spatial proximity but an *affective nearness*; through their overblown and borrowed Minimalist size, they also and just as often worked to block the paintings from view—so many momentary obliterations. In the most piercing moments of the nGbK installation, however, the open-form "containers" came to frame and encase views of Hohn's work, as if they were internalizing the paintings within their dark confines—a tragic and impossible attempt to hold on tight to that which is lost, to bring the outside back in.[3]

From the start, then, the sculptures that constitute Burr's *Container (1–3)*—like Thek's *Meat Piece with Warhol Brillo Box* (1965)—were fully relational objects. They embody a sculpture of relationality. To call Burr's sculpture "relational" would be to register this mode as Burr's specific manner of engaging artistic appropriation, his use of formats from prior artists like Judd, Serra, Smithson, Graham, or Warhol too—a kind of making, as with Thek, that is always between-two. But the elements of *Container (1–3)* then function to create further relations to the works and figures around them, to all that pass close to or visually enter their framing

        Containers

shape, their visual enclosure—what I also want to call their sculptural "embrace."

In the *Torrington Project*, the return of Burr's *Container (1–3)* seems doubly fraught, a relationality exacerbated—as the current installation underlines the retrospective aspect of Judd's original work at Marfa, an institution of the artist's making, just as Burr himself now takes a retrospective stance. But the existence of *Container (1–3)* in the *Torrington Project* also exacerbates the work's literal form, its "containing" sculptural function. Indeed, Burr's sculptures throw out all manner of visual echoes to the architectural frame that now surrounds them. And the *Torrington Project* is also a container, now containing the tripartite *Container* within its more general confines. We think of the "repackaging" of other retrospective projects, introjecting and transforming an artist's prior work, like Marcel Duchamp and his *Box in a Valise (From or by Marcel Duchamp or Rrose Sélavy)* (1935–41). The *Torrington Project* builds on the operation of the works in *Container (1–3)* as sculpture, their dedication to being relational objects, which is the shared labor of the greatest variety of the works by Burr that the *Project* regathers, re-creates, reinstalls, and displays. Many works in the *Torrington Project*, no matter how varied their forms and formats, echo individual aspects of the relational dynamics that *Container (1–3)* evidently clarified for Burr. With the wall-bound *Journal* series (2024), for example, abstract monochrome planes or panels come to be shaped in relation to work by Ellsworth Kelly, and function variously to block and reframe older objects and working remnants—like *Container (1–3)* and its blank, black "walls" obfuscating and revealing Hohn's paintings. The *Torrington Project* is filled with the scattered pieces of an expanded artistic project—often beyond the object-forms of sculpture—that takes the relational object as its "law" or deeper structure. Especially crucial in this regard

     George Baker

is the chain of "notational" works that the *Torrington Project* displays—always present in Burr's projects, but here prioritized—the bulletin boards, diagrammatic notes, and photo-displays that constitute so many breeding grounds of connection, locations where linkage can be both pondered and enacted. This becomes, in a sense, the *Torrington Project*'s overarching logic, as we witness a potentially narcissistic auto-retrospective, a rethinking of the vaunted privacy of the artist's studio space, suddenly transform and assume the guise of a fully relational practice, an endless chain, a promiscuous machine of new associations and reframings.

This is a lesson *Container (1–3)* taught, in a heartrending mode, a generation ago. This is a lesson now expanded. It is, we could say, the urgency of the *Torrington Project*. ◊

Containers

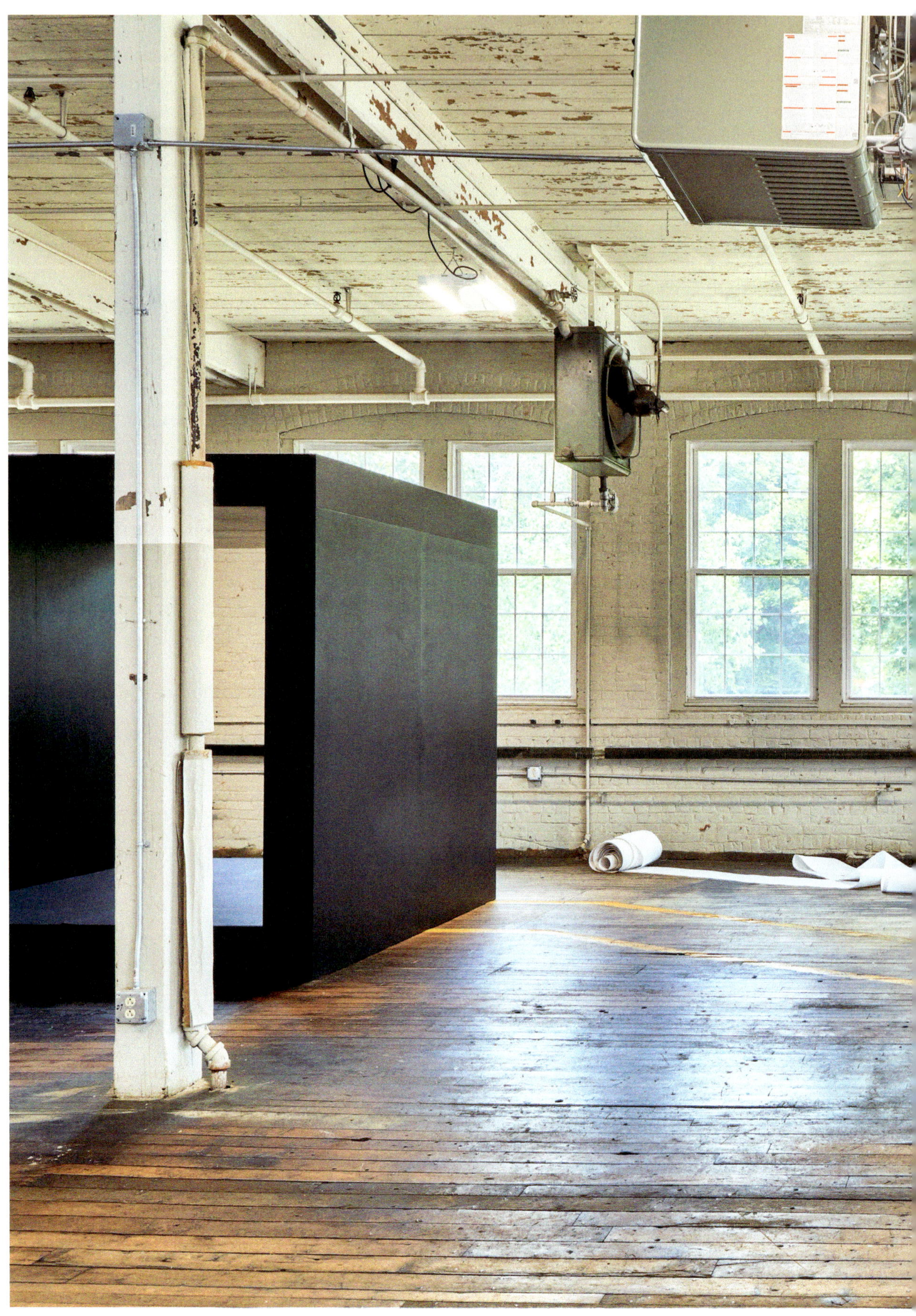

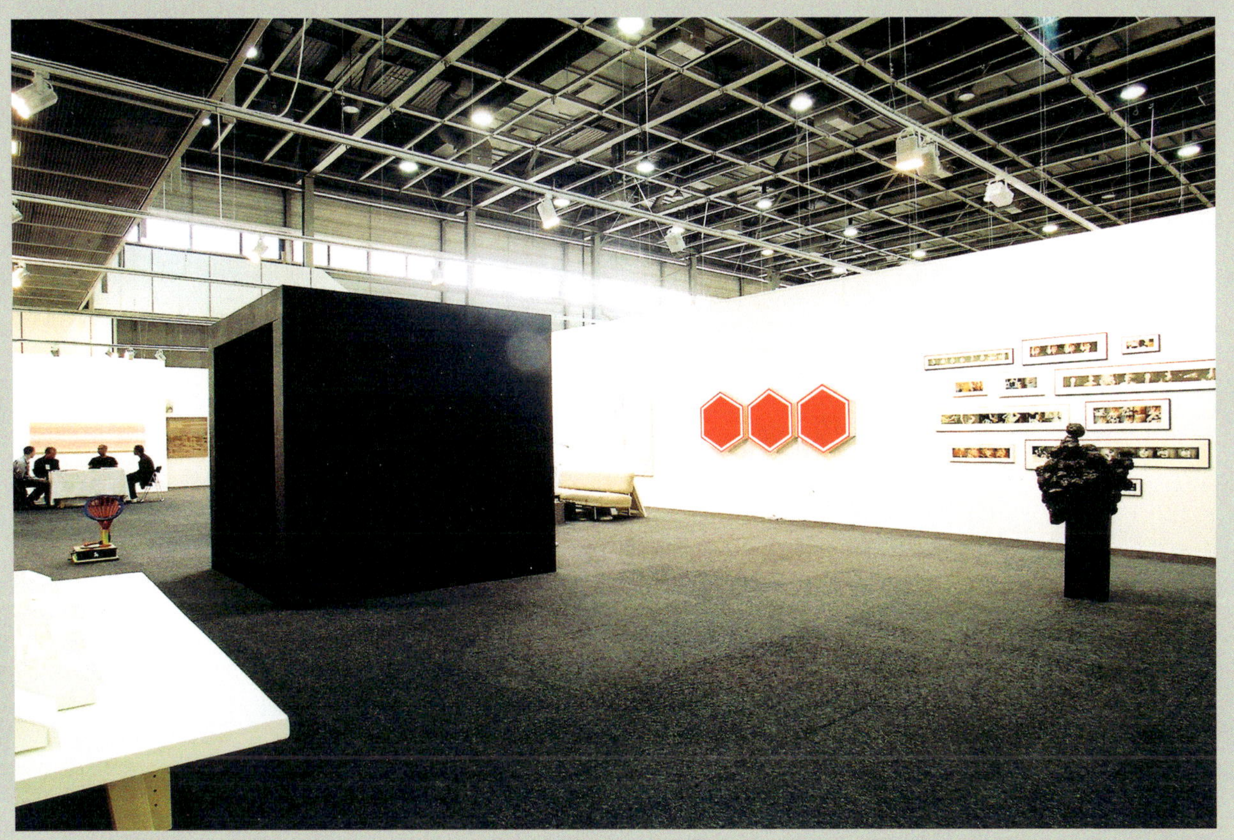

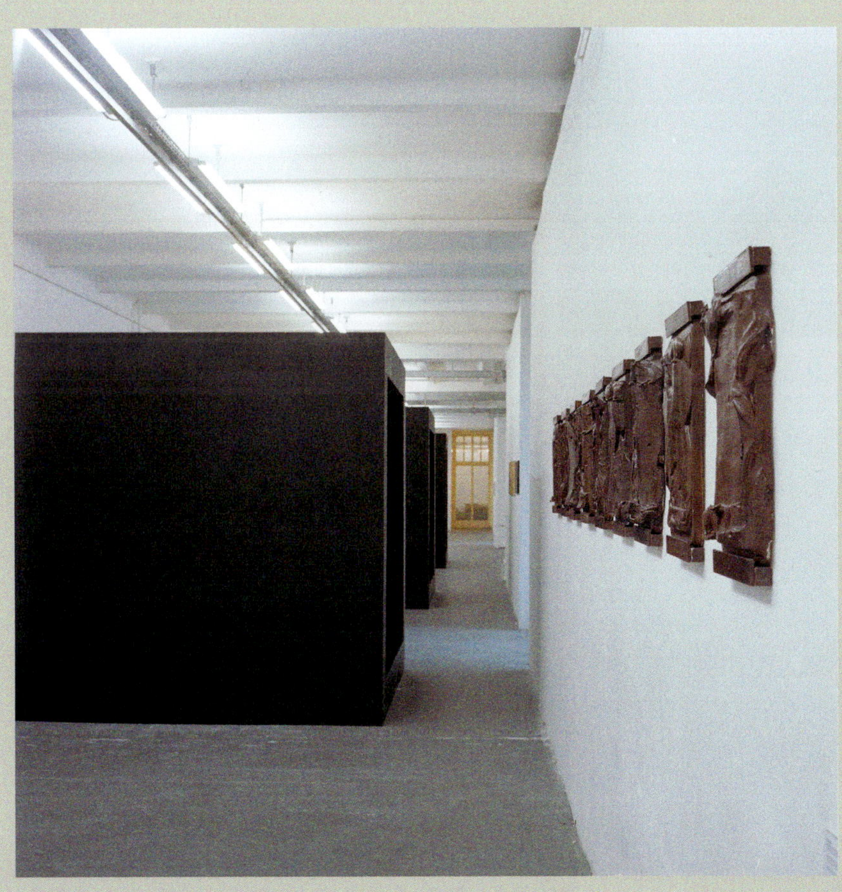

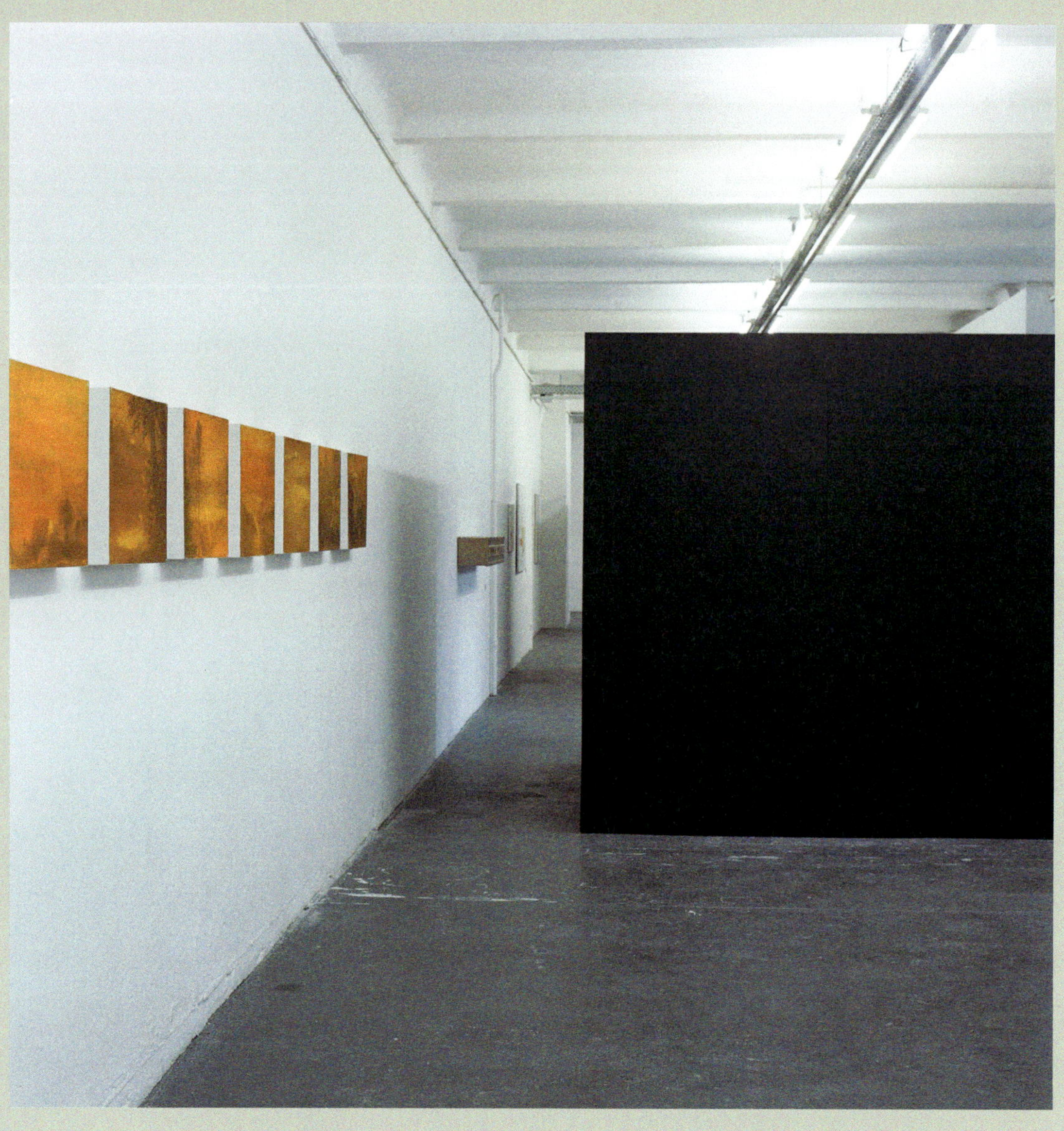

I created *An American Garden* in 1993, for Sonsbeek 93, an outdoor sculpture exhibition that had taken place in Arnhem, the Netherlands, every ten years or so since just after World War II. *An American Garden* was a part of a continuum of things I'd done, beginning in the late 1980s, which had emanated out of a piece of writing by Robert Smithson titled "Frederick Law Olmsted and the Dialectical Landscape." His final text, the piece took Central Park, and specifically the Ramble, as its site and subject. My series evolved through a group of topographical models, photographs, sculptures, and large-scale earthworks formed from plant and soil that resided both indoors, and in the case of *An American Garden*, directly outdoors in the existing landscape. These works collectively wove aspects of existing public park-scapes together with traces of their use, specifically aspects of queer cruising as it existed alongside and within other intersecting publics.

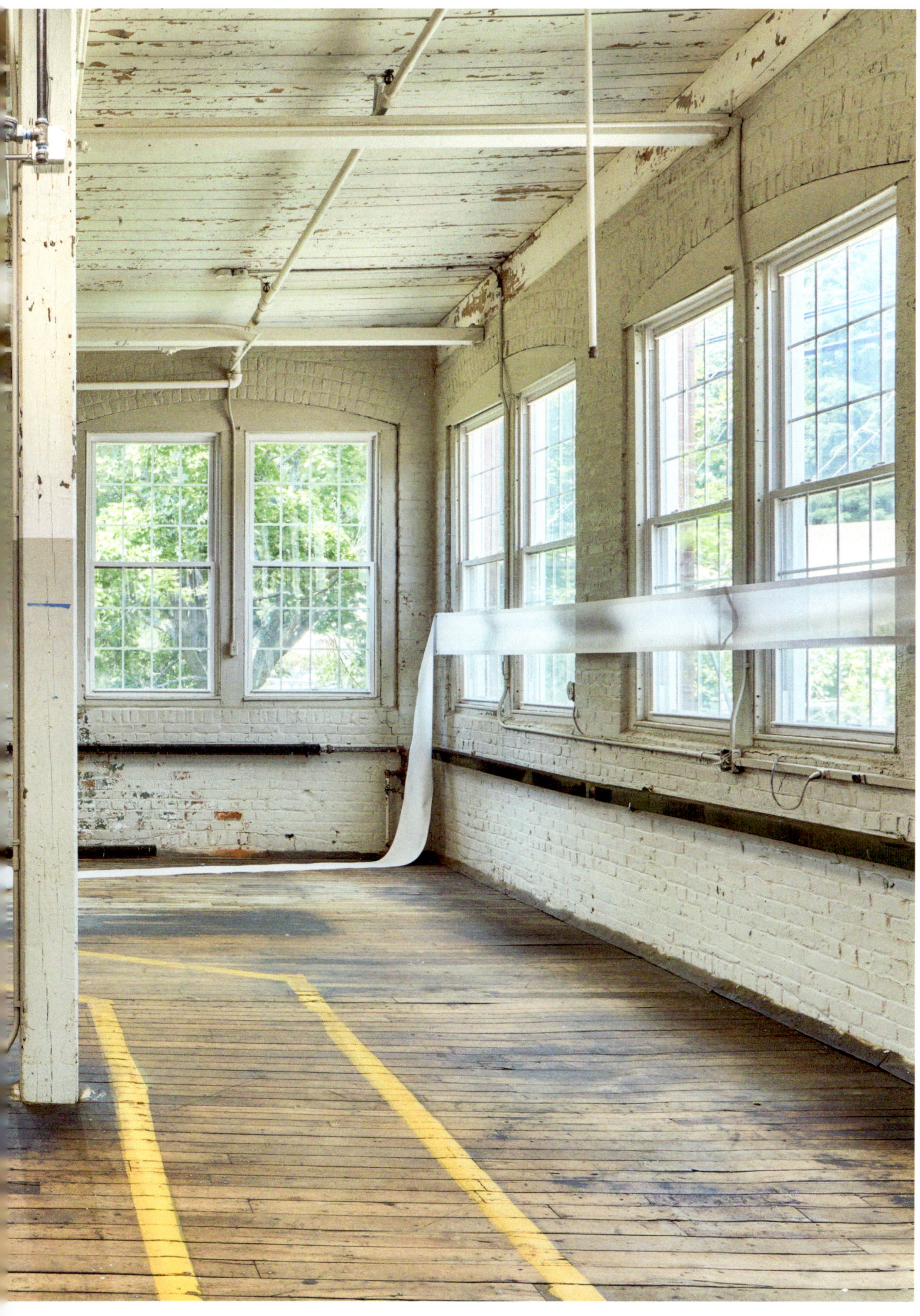

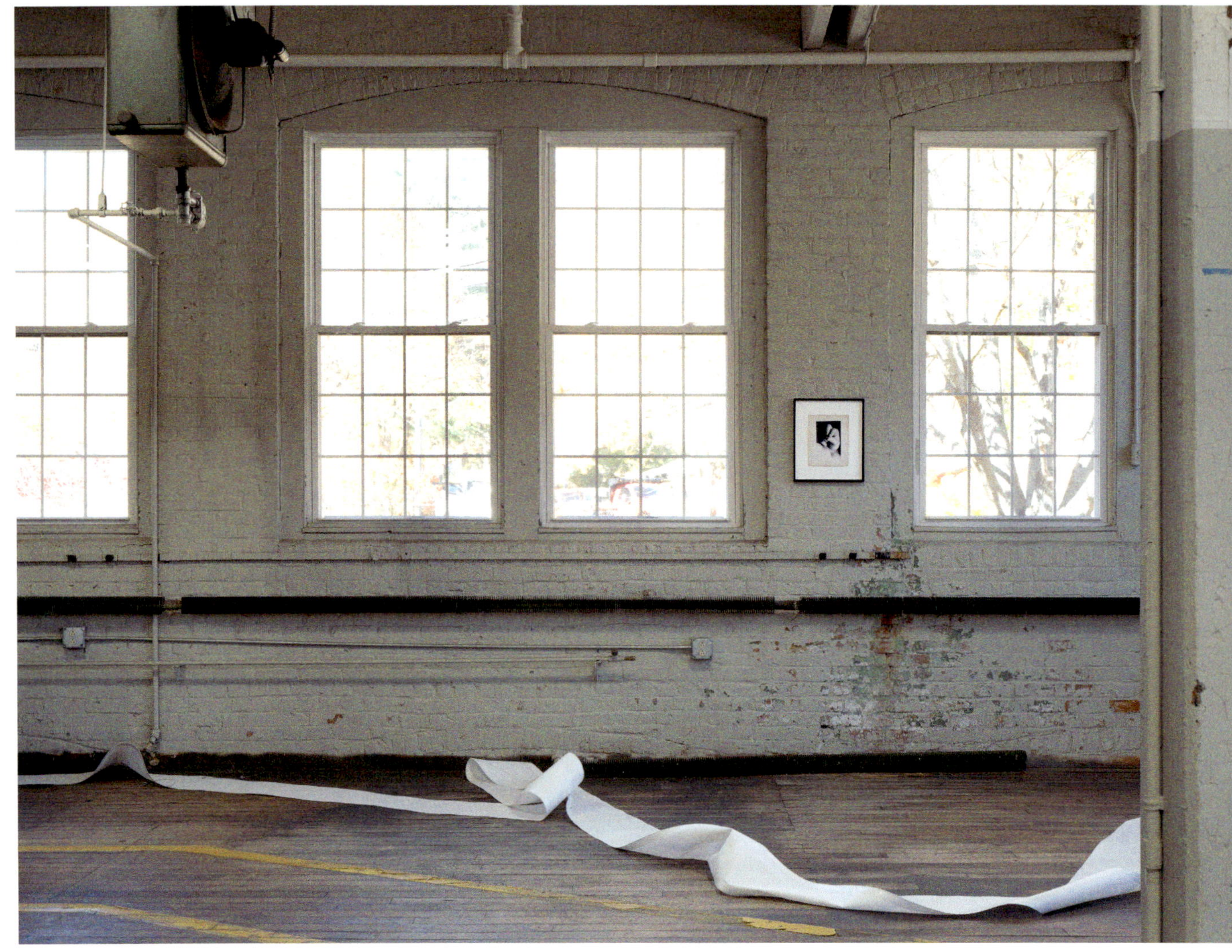

I operated a bit as if I were Smithson himself during that time, both enamored of his persona, and critically distanced from it, both inside and outside of him (and his writing and his work). I followed his own description of his steps through the park, steps which it seemed to me were as much a form of language as the written words that translated them, and I wanted, with these physical works of mine, to take particular *next* steps, to read between the lines of his prose and elaborate on them. I wandered through the Ramble a lot in those days. I loved it there; I felt safe and protected by the remove of it all, tucked away from the daily business of the nearby streets that housed all my obligations and routines. I loved the intricate pathways and rocky outcrops, the myriad rooms made within the foliage. I learned the names of many if not most of the plants that existed there. I felt the electricity of the place too, of other men walking through, pausing, connecting—with me, with others. There were the main arteries of traffic that led off into a web of secondary paths and into many pockets of solitude that felt far away from the passing of time. Often I would leave the gallery at 77th Street and Madison Avenue where I was working at the time, and traverse the park via the Ramble, following Smithson's charted choreography, out into the open spaces to the south, and then into the streets of Midtown until I got to Times Square, where I would slip into the Gaiety Theater, and slump down in one of the seats, and stay, sometimes for hours, watching the dancers—sometimes playing, mostly dreaming. I made work from these spaces and from these many walks through New York; they were the subject of my work, and they were my studios as well.

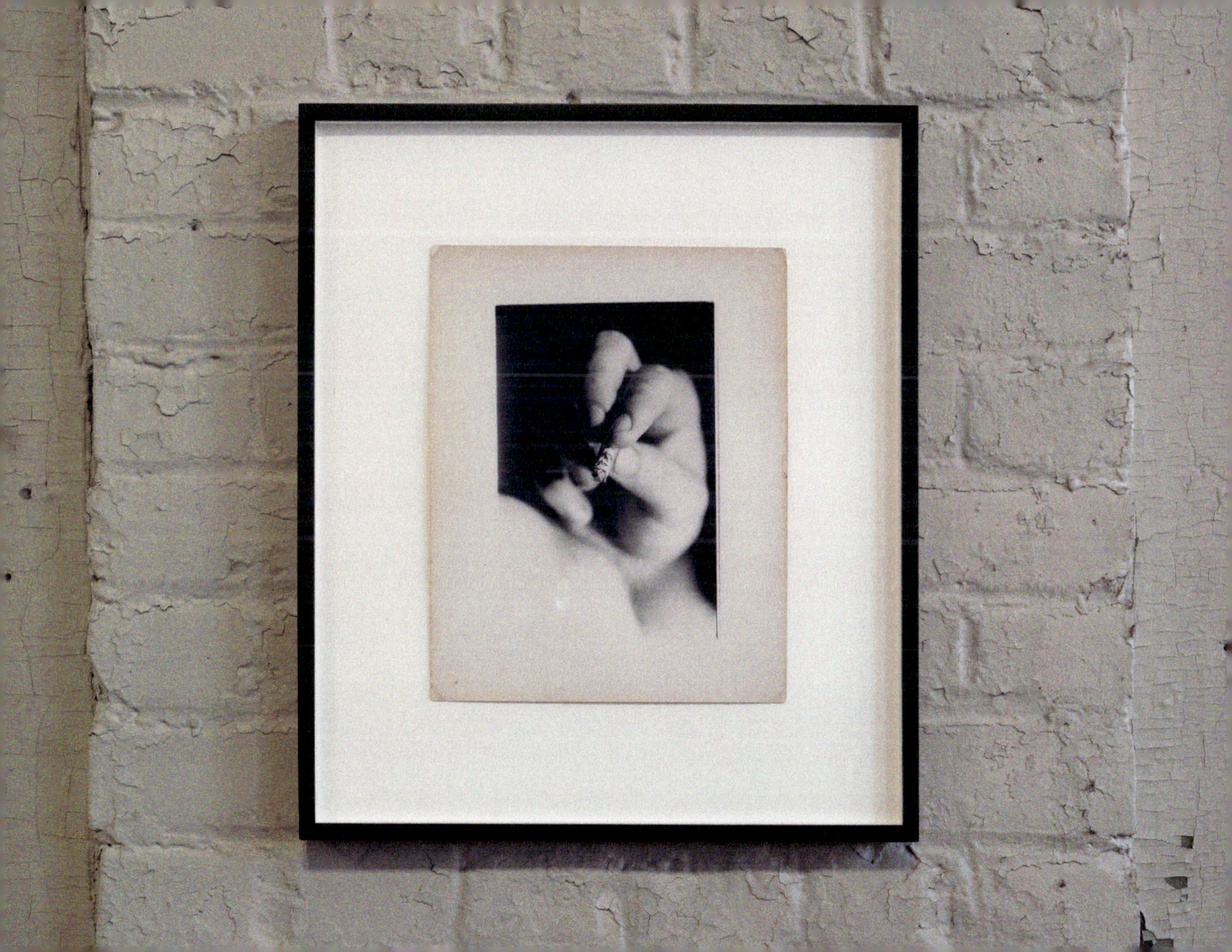

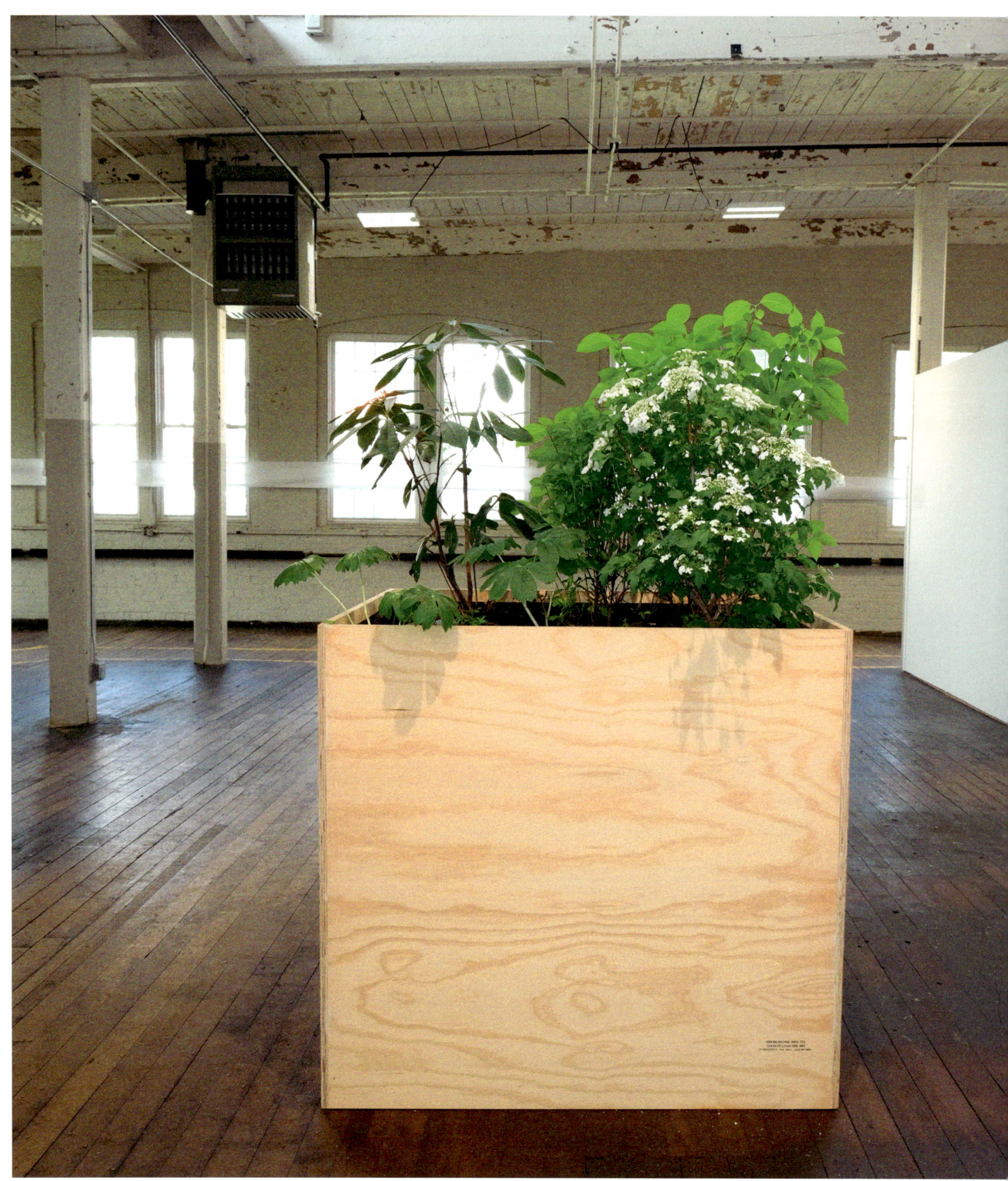

An American Garden was only exhibited one
time, in 1993. It was made of plants sourced from
Olmsted's list of the "native" foliage he selected
for the Ramble. The rocky topography of this
section of the park, which had been carefully
designed by Olmsted, was approximated in
my work through boulders we gathered in the
southern part of the Netherlands. All these
elements—the plans, and my drawings and
descriptions, and the photographs that outline
the specifications of the project—are what constitute the work in its downtime, while it is resting
in storage, before it is reinstalled again at another
time and place. In January 2020, I was plotting
how to make *Torrington Project* happen financially—well before I had begun the search for a
location—and I thought back to my conversation
with Patrick and decided to approach him, very
generally, about the possibility of his acquiring
An American Garden in its current resting state—
acquiring the plans of a past project in order to
realize the production of a new one.

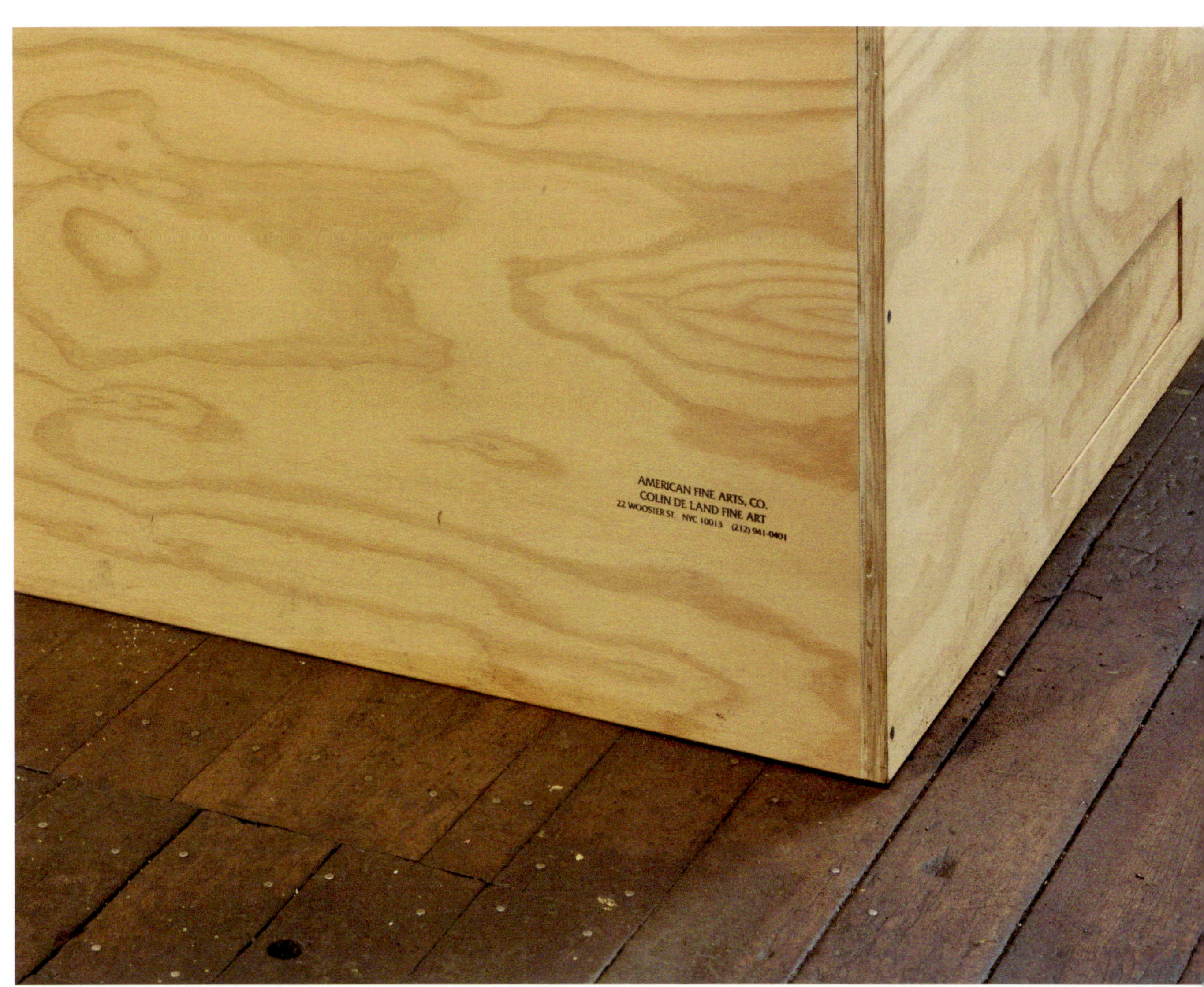

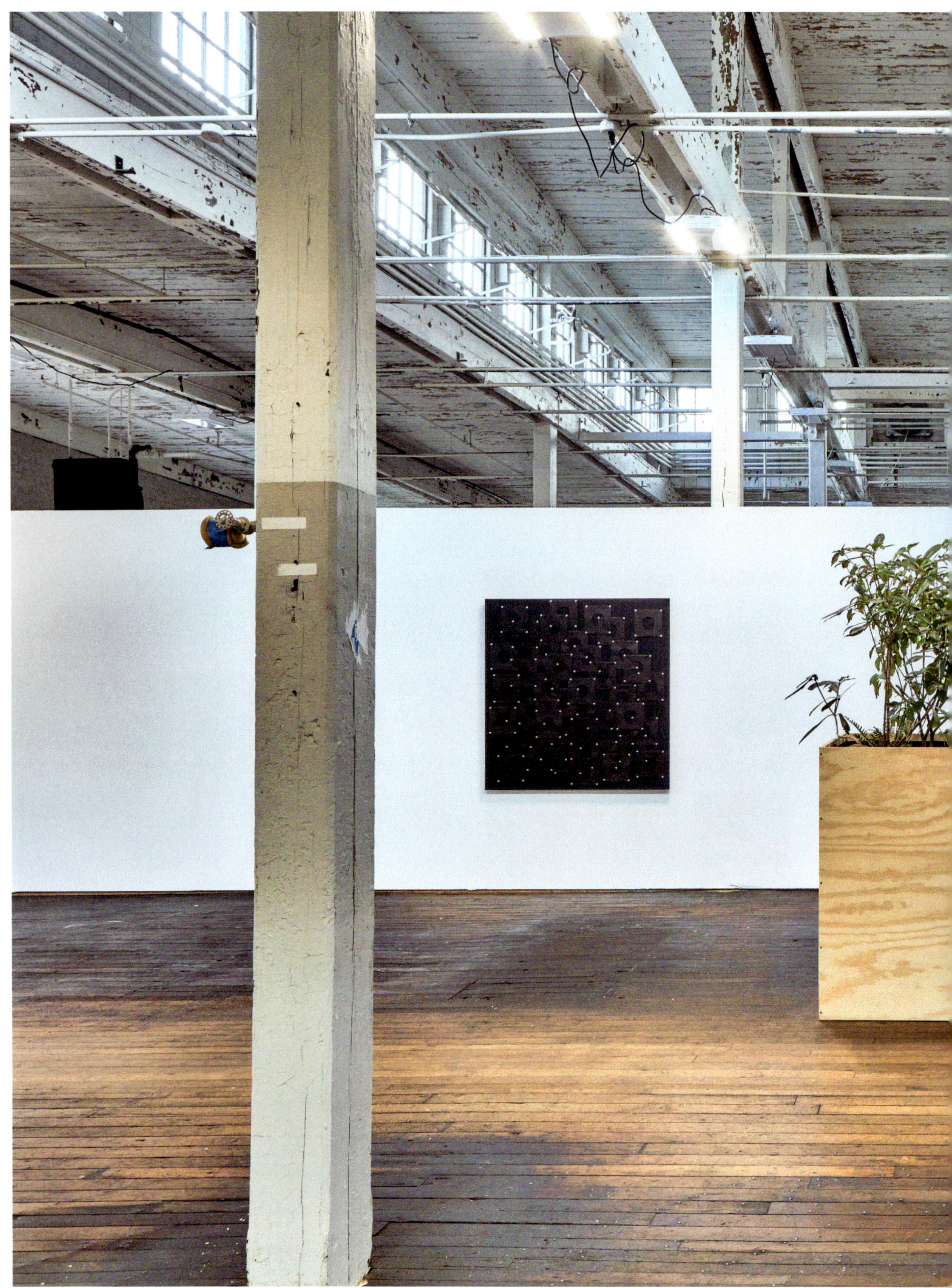

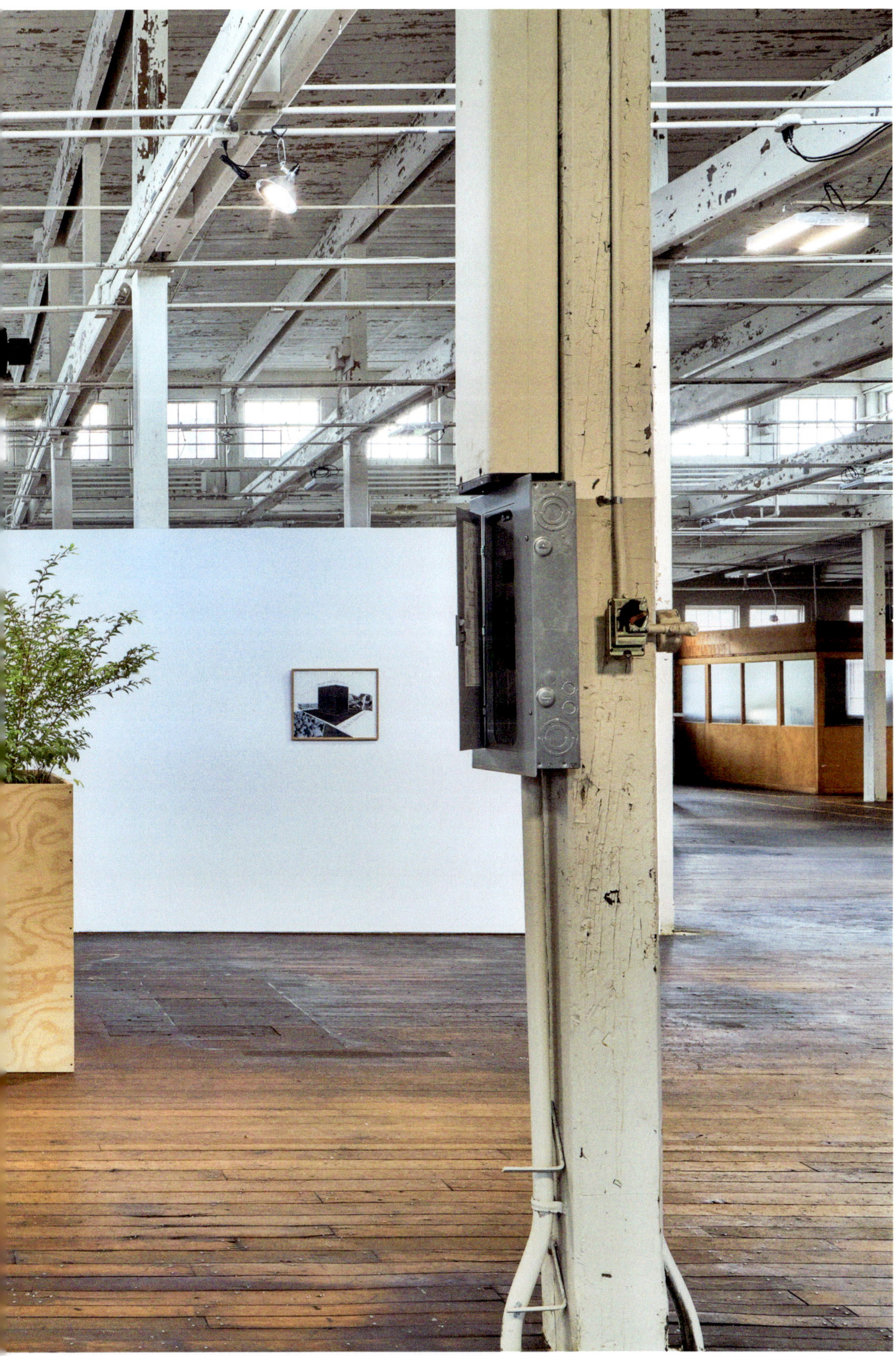

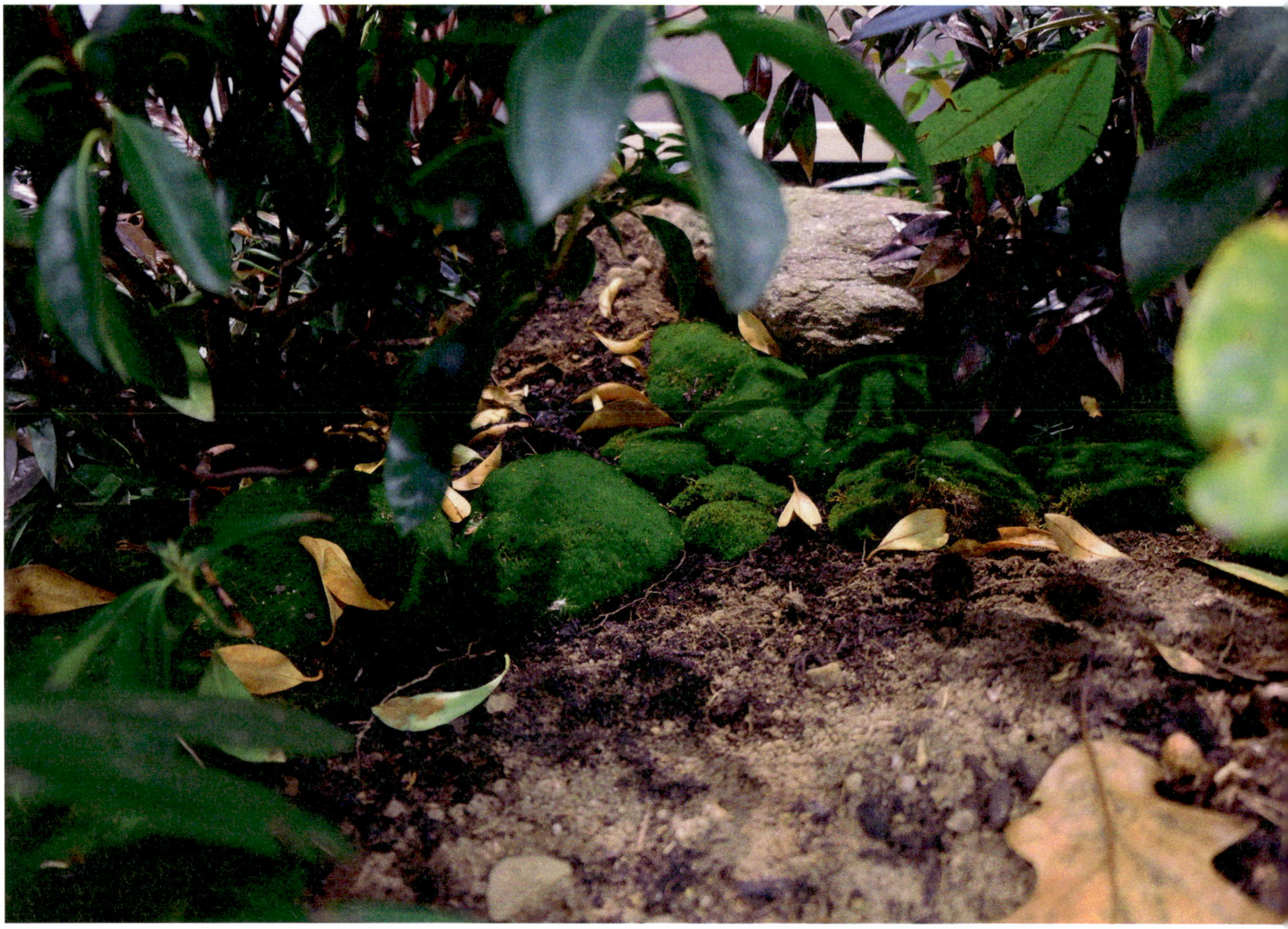

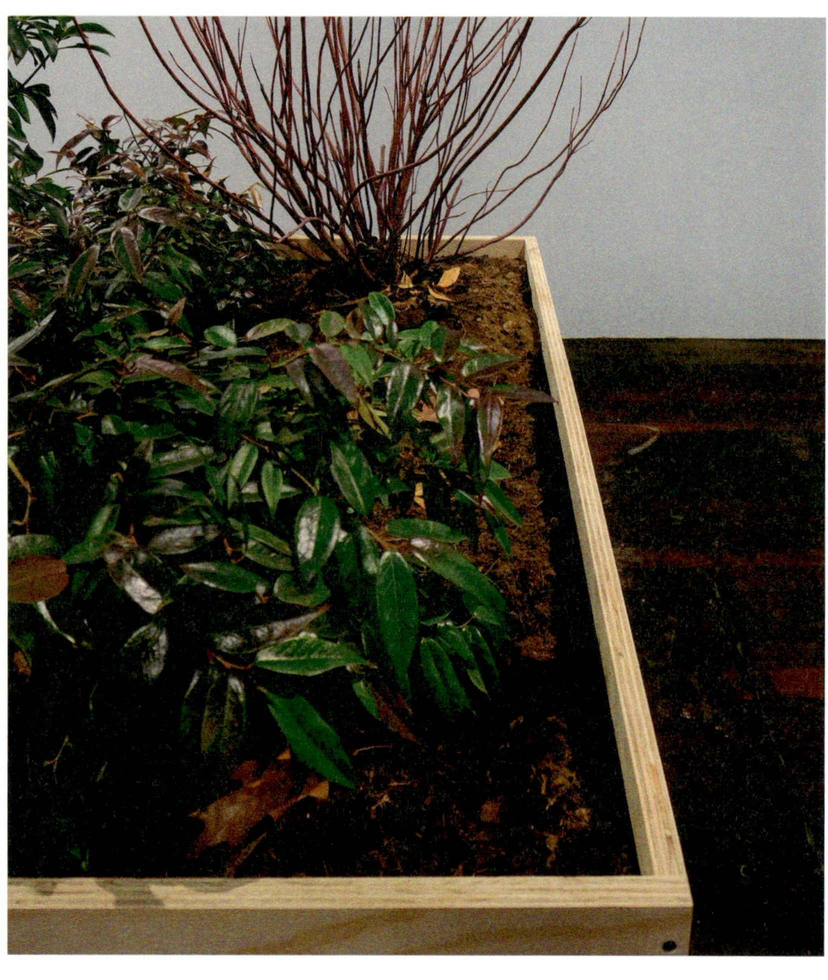

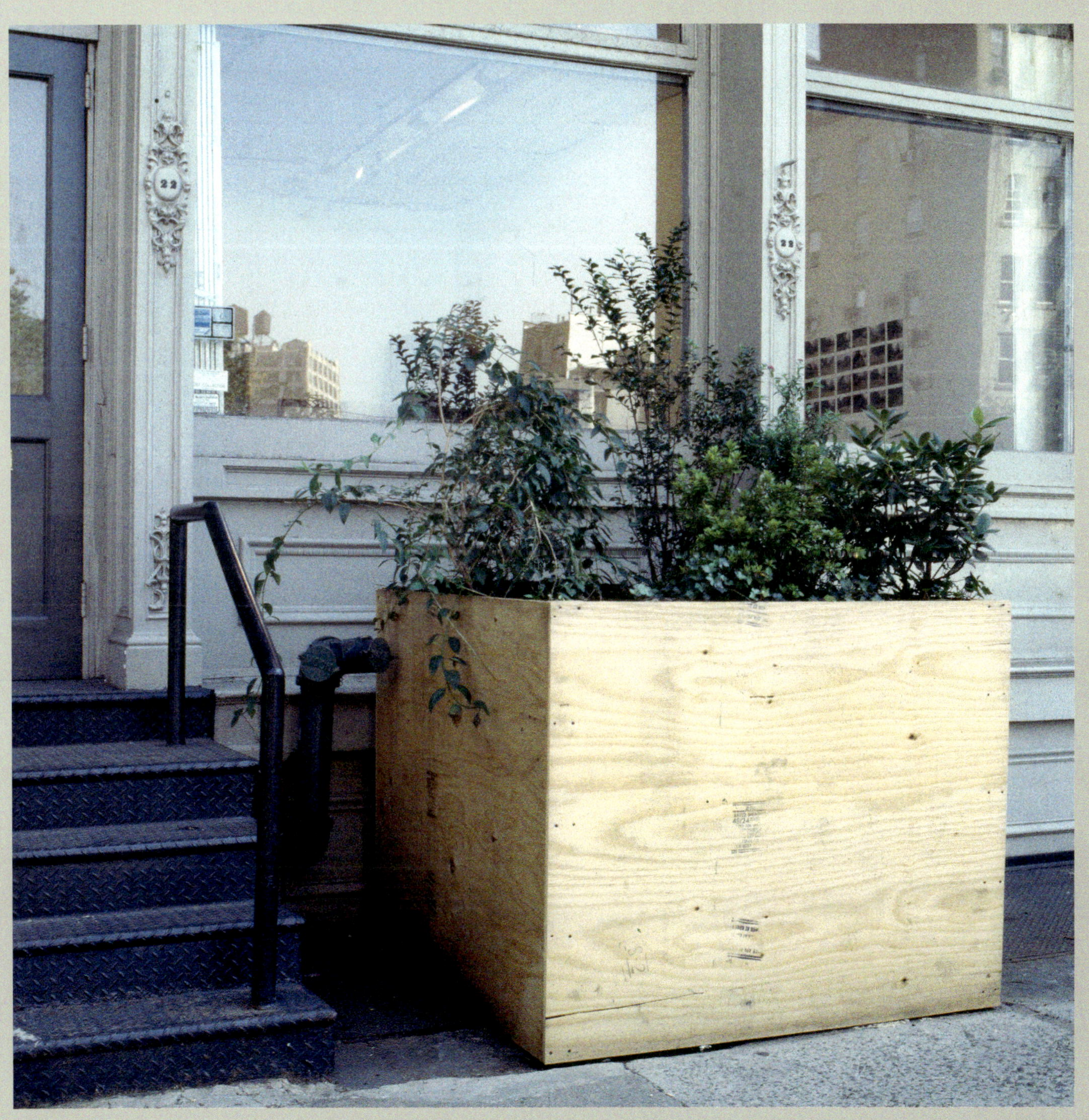

TOM BURR

PROPOSAL SONSBEEK 93

The proposal is to recreate, on a platform, within Sonsbeek Park itself, a section of Central Park, New York. The section will be landscaped with living plants, soil, etc., following the designs and groundplans set forth by Frederick Law Olmstead for the section of Central Park known as The Ramble. The platform will be built of wood, similar to a theater platform, or deck, and will float above the existing ground of the park. Approximate dimensions, still to be determined, will be somewhere in the area of 15 x 30feet. The platform will have legs, and will be lit by outdoor floodlights during the night.

The actual landscaping will follow the original plans for the Ramble. Olmstead was attempting to create what was being referred to at that time in Europe as an 'American Garden', a naturalistic landscape of woodsy, intricate detail, which was distinct from both the European formal garden traditions and the English landscape plans. The final landscaping will attempt to recreate a section as it was conceived, rather than as it has developed. The plants, in other words, would be young. There will be a path, or a few paths, which traverse the platform, with steps leading up to the platform, allowing viewers to walk through this 'model' of the Ramble.

The second level of the project has to do with its placement within Sonsbeek Park. It will be located on the slope of the hill between the Villa and the edge of trees which forms the border of the park. This places it between one of the central points of the park, the Villa, and the gay cruising area in the park, the area of trees bordering the park on that side, just next to the drive entrance. (It is interesting to note that this area has certain physical features which are similar to that of the Ramble, with small dirt paths winding through it, and areas of 'clearing' within the shrubs, etc., as well as the general fact that it is planted in a 'woodsy', naturalistic fashion.) This location also places the platform/model within a wide panoramic viewing, connecting it to the residential

I have quickly sketched what I have in mind:

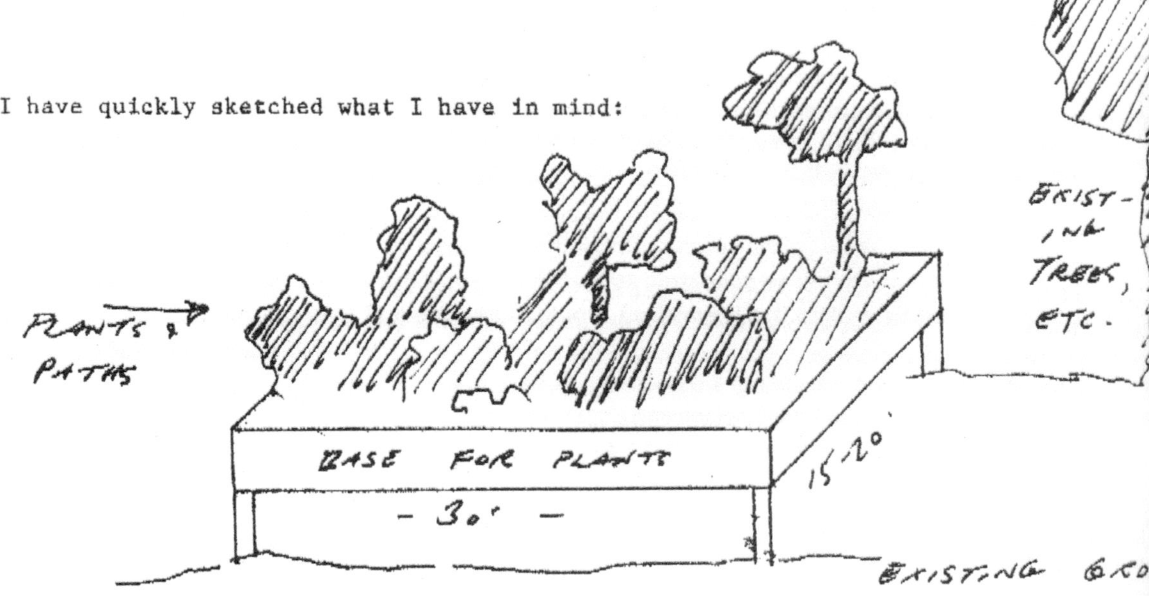

areas surrounding the park's perimeters. (This allows, for instance for an extreme 'long shot' of the platform, one which sees it in relation to the English landscape design of the front field, as well as the town surrounding the park. For instance, this location is immediately visible as one walks down the street from ‹Entre Nous›... as I found out).

The other level of the project will be textual, and will be located within the model landscape itself. Small, free-standing signs, of the kind commonly used in parks both in the United States and in Europe, will be dispersed throughout the Ramble landscape. The texts will address the nature of the present-day Ramble as a gay cruising/gathering place, and its relationship to perceptions of crime and safety, privacy, and public sexuality. These texts may come from a number of sources, I have much information to choose from. Probably they will be quotes/interviews from both 'with-in' and from 'out-side' the park, possibly producing a narrative quality. But all the texts will refer to the Ramble, in Central Park, not to Sonsbeek Park. The signs will be of the kind which would normally address the kind of trees, or plants, or possibly the history of the area.

There are two other components which may come into place. The first would be something which would engage, on some level, the area of Sonsbeek which I am pointing to with this 'model', the cruising area. This could possibly take place within the Villa itself (if you people are still able to occupy that space for the duration of the exhibition as you thought). From here, in the Villa, one could see both my 'model' and the Sonsbeek cruising area just beyond it, and there may be a way to employ this perspective. I am sure that I don't want to exploit, or 'endanger' the existing gay cruising area, so I must think this part through. I want the project to be a displacement which, through its placement and proximity, raises certain lines of thought. As well as the relationship of the 'American style', the reference to earth-art (other Sonsbeek exhibition, Smithson, etc.), and the notions of naturalism, design, function and perceived 'dis-function' of public spaces.

The other component of the project, which you mentioned, is the catalogue. For this project it would be best for me to write something, rather than engage in an interview, which will outline the ideas concerning Central Park, Sonsbeek Park, Olmstead and America, European perceptions, and then the role of these particular sites with regard to the gay constituency, its existence, role and relation to the existing context. I think that there is a way to write this, which rather than fostering an academic approach (which is the way it may sound now as I briefly outline the thematics), would illuminate and map out the project.

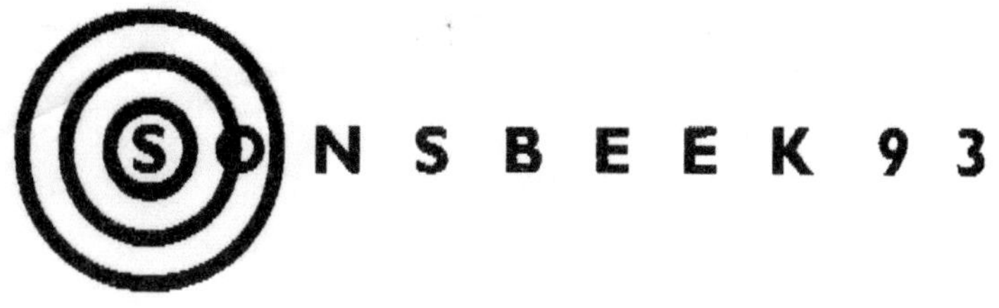

TO: Tom Burr
    c/o Adelson Galleries
    Fax: 212.439.68.70

FROM: Valerie Smith
      Sonsbeek 93
      Fax: 31.85.45.25.13

27 September, 1993

Dear Tom,

The last day of the exhibition went out with a bang. There were
lots of people here who were getting in the exhibition at the last
possible second and the negative local criticism was combated with
a brilliant defense by Jan Debbaut and Rudi Fuchs.

Your garden of eden is now turning red, but looks a little lonely
without the mingling of Sonsbeek visitors.

There is no chance that the city will give you a fee to keep the
garden in the Sonsbeek Park. The choices are that 1. the work be
destroyed or 2. you and the Stichting Sonsbeek donate it to the
city.* If we were to donate it to the city it would be without the
texts, because they are rather worn and weathered. Perhaps a more
permanent solution for the text could be devised, but as you can
imagine there is no money to make bronze plaques, so we might go
for something a little more modest.

Please let me know how you feel about all of this as soon as
possible, because I need and want to resolve this for both of us.
I am waiting for your decision.

Best,

Valerie

P.S. *I do not know if the city wants the work, but I wanted
to check with you first, to see if you are willing to give it to
them.

TELEFOONSTRAAT 3   TEL 31-(0)85 429060   ARN.AMRO 47 25 75 840   STICHTING SONSBEEK 93
6811 A3 ARNHEM NL   FAX 31+(0)85 432513   GIRO 1900 Y.P. BANK 818788   KVK ARNHEM NR S 51544

TOTAL P.01

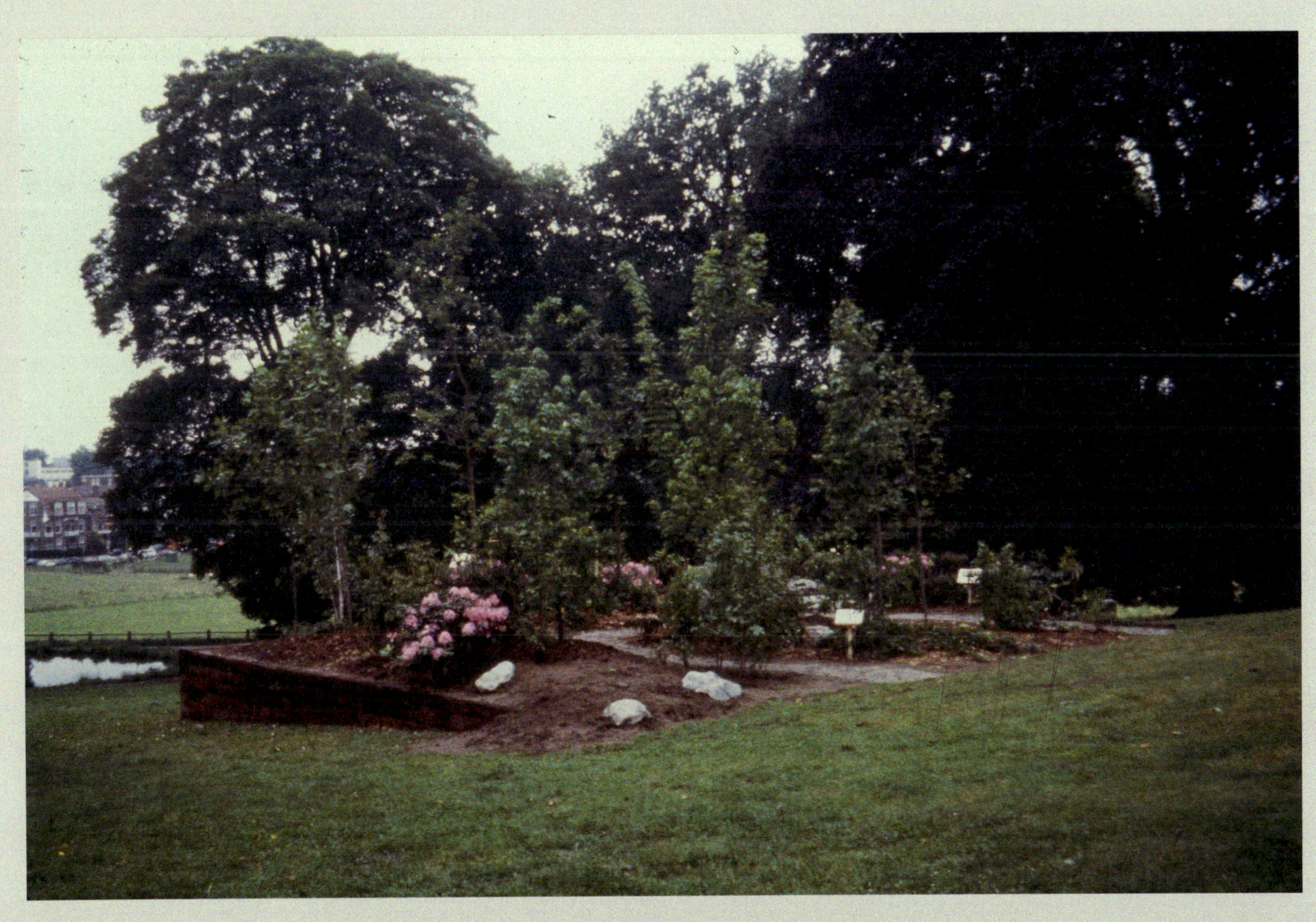

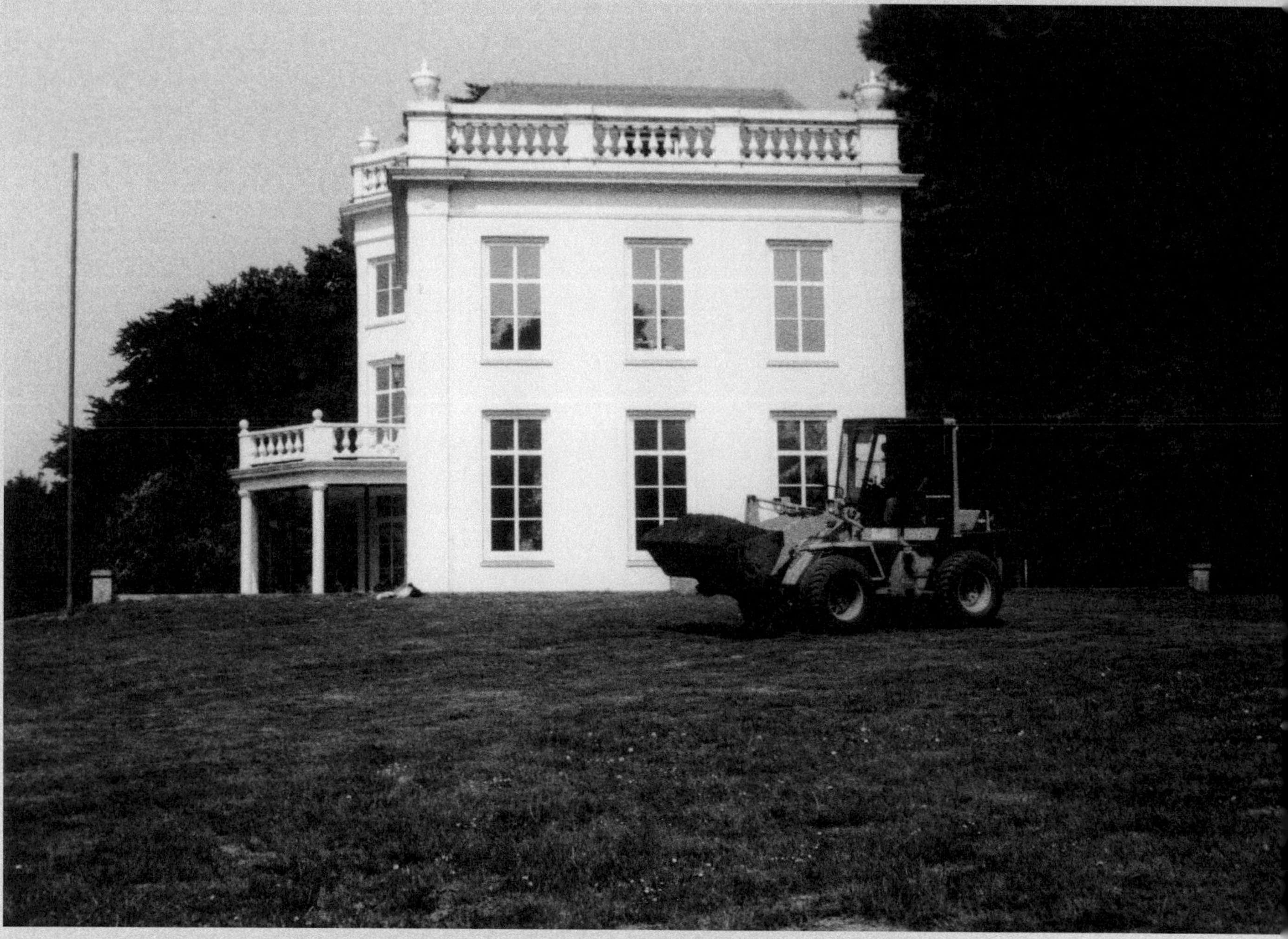

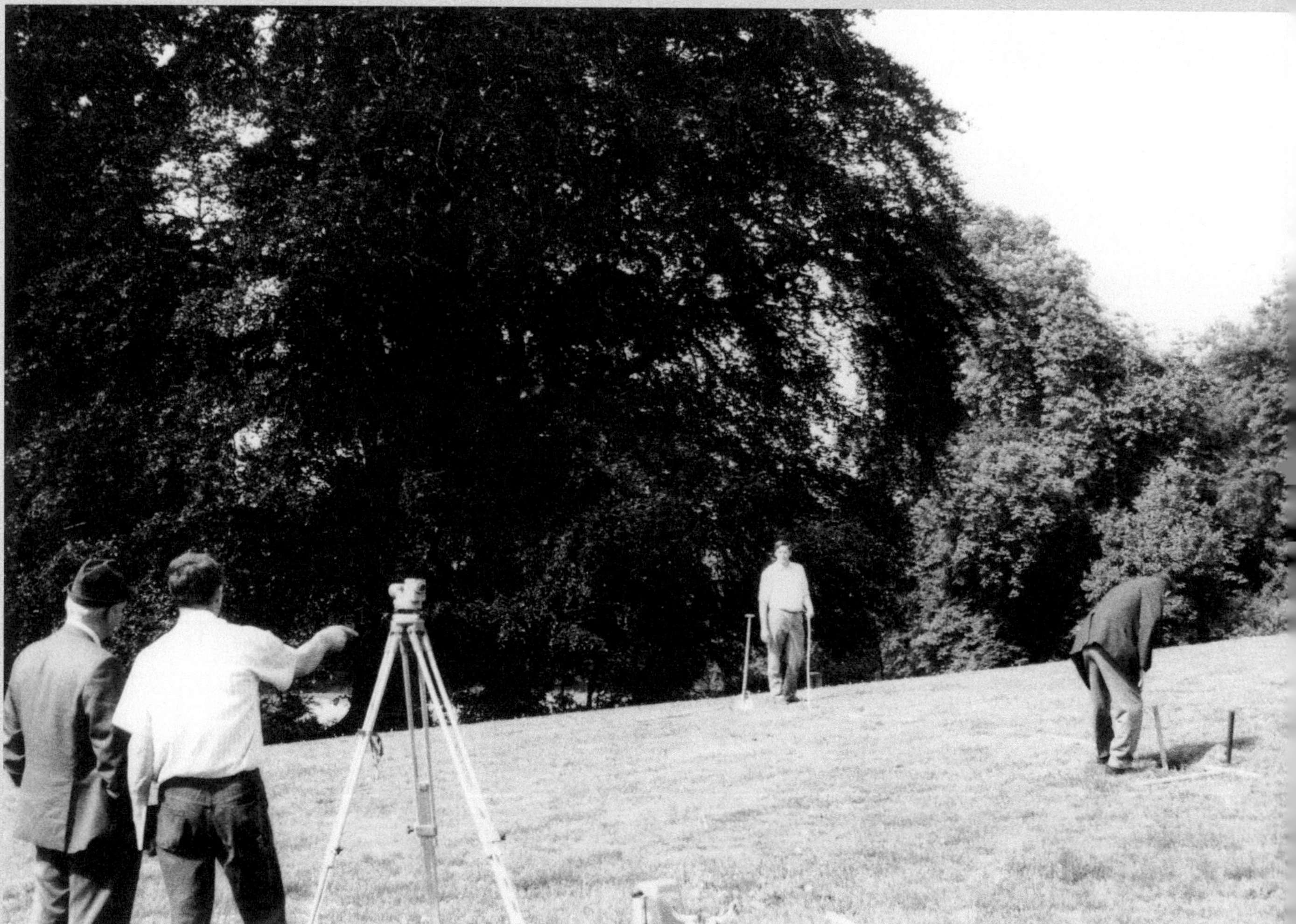

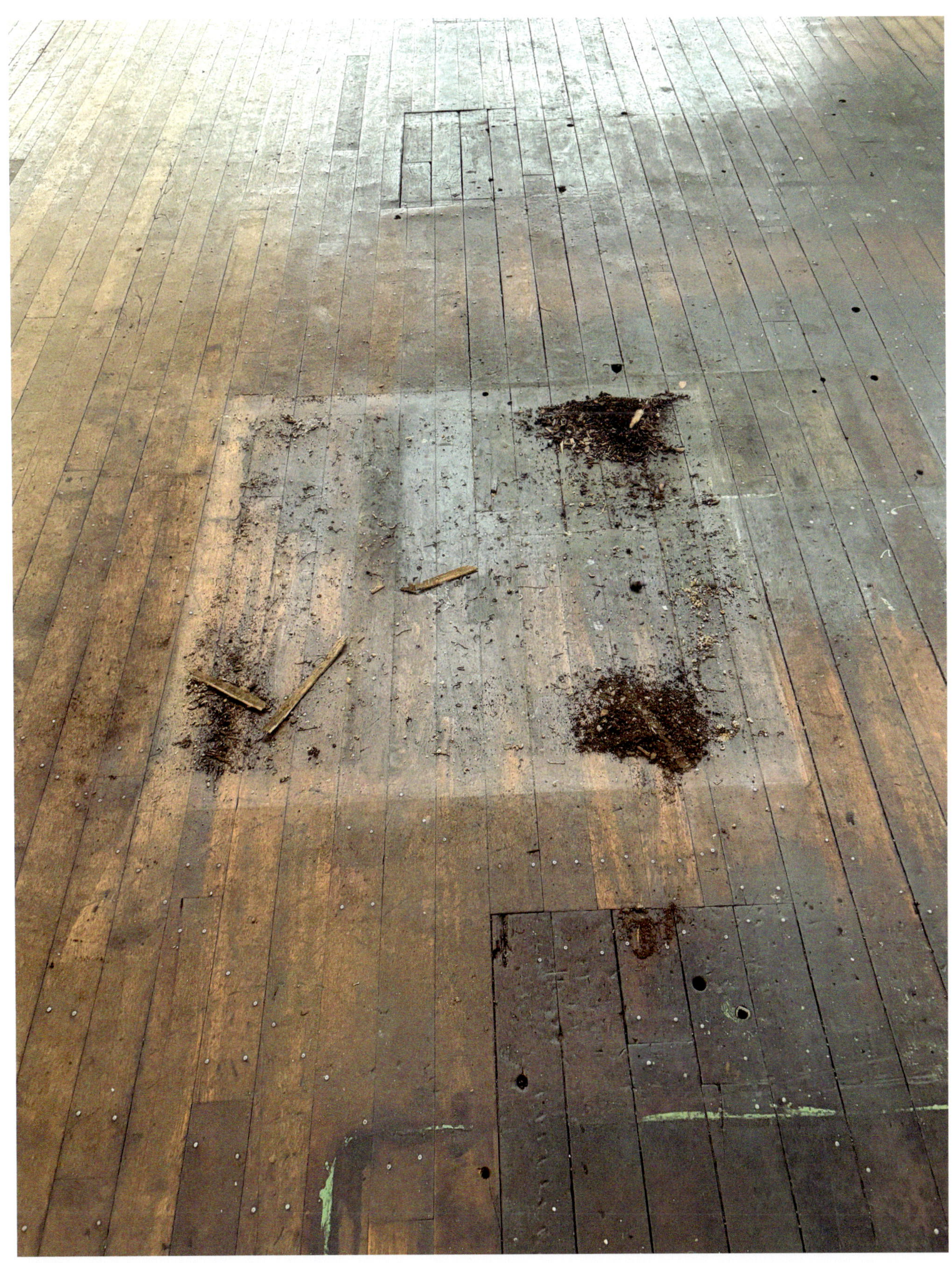

In Tom Burr's work, sites cruise—they generate meaning at the intersection of specificity and encounter, continuously redeveloped and rerouted. Just as the unplanned pedestrian paths made by gay men searching for sex in public parks chart deviant queer parcours—or desire lines—so do Tom's site-specific works link their point of origin with new coordinates of encounter in a sensitive, promiscuous interpenetration with context over time. Mobilizing what could anachronistically be considered a queer politics of site-specificity, Tom's iterative—at times fugitive—objects appropriate and displace charged elements of the built environment or the domestic interior, with a focus on forms and structures that permeate private and public, and artistic and historical personae. These stage-like works implicate viewers in site as an unfixed and unfolding drama. Initially spurred by the histories, behaviors, or architectural nuances of a particular location, they go on to develop distinct yet interconnected social lives, carrying these traces as new layers of meaning. Indeed, Tom's works are at once rooted and rhizomatic, informed by specific contexts while remaining fluid, open, and fundamentally irreducible.

This accretive and distributed approach to site was demonstrated early on in Tom's career with *Construction of an American Garden* (1993), a work that integrates site and cruising into its conceptual and compositional makeup. Initially conceived as a temporary and portable nonsite for the now-legendary exhibition *What Happened to the Institutional Critique?* (1993), curated by James Meyer at American Fine Arts, Co., the work replicates *An American Garden* (1993), which Tom originally created for the exhibition Sonsbeek 93 in Arnhem, the Netherlands. For the New York variation, however, Tom shrank the life-size garden so it fit snugly into a plywood crate, which he placed on the sidewalk in front of the SoHo gallery. Presenting as an everyday city planter, it was seeded with a selection of native plants from among

    Jordan Carter

those designated by Frederick Law Olmsted for his nineteenth-century "wild garden," a section of Central Park known as "The Ramble" that has historically been used by gay men for cruising.

Tom's micro cruising site subtly infiltrates urban space, merging the vocabulary of the Minimalist cube with coded emblems of queer desire. It establishes a dialectical relationship with the Ramble—existing between past and present, model and landscape, official use and subversive reinterpretation. While *An American Garden* layers one landscape atop another, *Construction of an American Garden* takes this compression a step further, revealing itself as an artwork only when a visitor steps into the gallery and consults the checklist. In this way, the work mirrors the logic of cruising, where coded cues disclose desire in public space. Its evolving form constellates Central Park, Arnhem, and SoHo into a matrix of desire lines. As a work whose subject is a cruising ground, it embarks on a cruise of its own, eventually resurfacing in Tom's *Torrington Project* after a thirty-year retreat from public view.

Also emblematic of Tom's queer compression and redistribution of site is *Deep Purple* (2000), his iconoclastic and critically diminutive citation of Richard Serra's *Tilted Arc* (1981). A modular, portable, and playfully purple adaptation of Serra's notoriously obstinate work, *Deep Purple* refuses the fixed monumentality and chromophobia of its predecessor, adapting fluidly, flamboyantly, yet fugitively to variable conditions of display. Whereas Serra declared that his 120-foot-long, 12-foot-high monolithic Cor-Ten steel sculpture set in Manhattan's Federal Plaza was essentially destroyed when it was removed in 1989, Tom's 82-foot-high, 8-foot-wide wood construction is intended to come apart and be packaged, shipped, and put back together again, adjusting to fit the designated exhibition venue and, in the process, radically shifting its predecessor's unbudgeable articulation of site-specificity. In its

Distributing Desire Lines

nomadic promiscuity, *Deep Purple* proposes a queer relation to site as one wherein adaptability and transport become constitutive elements of the work itself. Site does not so much suggest a final destination, but rather a point of departure and connection. The work's iterations and exhibition histories become meandering pathways mapping collisions of artistic, personal, institutional, and public desires, from the garden of Kunstverein Braunschweig, where *Deep Purple* made its debut in 2000, to the Brutalist foundation of the Whitney's Breuer Building in 2002, to the interior galleries of the Musée Cantonal des Beaux-Arts de Lausanne for Tom's 2006 survey, to the courtyard of FRAC Champagne-Ardenne in 2008, and, most recently, to the Des Moines Art Center in 2019, where it stood next to the cascades of blue beaded curtains in Felix Gonzalez-Torres's *"Untitled" (Water)* (1995) on the occasion of the group exhibition *Queer Abstraction*.

Following these nonlinear desire lines leads us to a few sites and contingent works that have linked Tom and me over the past decade. Tom and I first met in Minneapolis in 2015 during my time as a curatorial fellow at the Walker Art Center. During his visit, we decided to take the elevator to the top of the tallest building in the city: the IDS Center, designed by mid-century architect Philip Johnson. Tom was drawn to this iconic edifice for various reasons—not least of which was its inclusion in the opening sequence of *The Mary Tyler Moore Show*—as we were planning his commission for the 2016–17 group exhibition *Question the Wall Itself*, a show that explored the politics of the constructed interior scene.

Compression reemerged as an operative strategy as Tom homed in on the zigzagging corners of the IDS Center, which functioned as quasi-ornamental accents on the towering postmodern construction. Inside the building, this series of setbacks, or "zogs," as Johnson referred to them, increased the number of corner

     Jordan Carter

1   Tom Burr, "Tom Burr by Alan Ruiz," interview by Alan Ruiz, *BOMB*, Winter 2016, https://bombmagazine.org/articles/2015/12/15/tom-burr/.

offices per floor, connecting interior architecture with business psychology. In his now-signature methodological variation on Robert Smithson's site/nonsite dialectic, for the show at the Walker, Tom shifted the terms of engagement from the natural landscape to the built environment, with an emphasis on queer figures, structures, and behaviors that register moments "when certain hard forms or movements or gestures or attitudes become 'soft.'"[1] Excerpting the "zog" design and restaging it in the Walker's galleries, Tom's scaled-down plywood appropriation, *Zog (a series of setbacks)* (2016), also bears photographic panels on its backside that feature the artist taking selfies in the reflection of Johnson's Glass House in New Canaan, Connecticut, not far from his hometown of New Haven. Johnson hid his sexuality during his lifetime, but with this nested nod to the closeted homosexual who lived in a glass house, Tom collapses corporate and domestic architectures and integrates his own body and biography into this complex network of citation and critique.

Indeed, Tom often shows up by way of others—positioning figures both past and present as proxies or stand-ins. In this way, his works become surrogates for architectural sites and art historical or queer personae, and, by extension, for himself, as he performs in drag as Richard Serra, Philip Johnson, or, in the case of our wayward itinerary, French novelist and playwright Jean Genet vis-à-vis *The Railings (May, 1970)* (2017). I joined the Art Institute of Chicago in 2017, the same year that Tom embarked on a deeply personal and historically informed exhibition sited in the Marcel Breuer-designed Pirelli Tire Building in New Haven. In response to the building's safety regulations, Tom fabricated a 103-foot-long railing to guard visitors from potentially falling into a sunken area in the floor, referred to by the architect as "the depression." This code-compliant railing doubled as an act of resistance, inscribed as it was with a 1970 May Day speech written by Genet in support of the Black Panther Party

Distributing Desire Lines

and delivered on the nearby New Haven Green by a Panther representative advocating for the release of founder Bobby Seale, who was standing trial in the city for murder.

In a willed and spirited instance of site-serendipity, Tom and I collaborated on the acquisition of this piece by the Art Institute of Chicago, where, in 2018, it fit perfectly along the garden pathway traversing the museum's Stanley McCormick Memorial Court. Here, it took on new meaning and function: No longer a protective barrier, it functioned as a handrail guiding visitors along the placid alley. This seemingly innocuous extension of the landscape architecture critically resonated with Chicago's specific history involving Genet and the Black Panthers. It was in Chicago that the solidarity between Genet and the Panthers was first established, spurred by their collective witnessing of the brutal police response to protesters during the 1968 Democratic National Convention.

"When I was grappling with the New Haven project," Tom reflects, "I wanted to weave in and out of a personal voice. In the writings around the project, as well as within the work itself, there was going to be a prevalence of 'I'—of my own narrative, New Haven being where I was born[—]and that fact was meant to frame the work. But I also wanted to have distance, and to have a surrogate figure that allowed fluidity into a wider trans historical [sic] space and voice."[2]

Accordingly, *The Railings* links Tom, Genet, and the Panthers within a continuum of social and political address that transgresses the boundaries of race, gender, and sexuality. The fence-like sculpture imposes order and regulation, modulating the body's movements while simultaneously communicating a provocative message of defiant solidarity. The work also became a material metaphor for the intertwined history that Tom and I share, weaving together a relay of citations

2   Tom Burr, preparatory notes for *Abridged* at Galerie Neu, Berlin, 2017.

   Jordan Carter

emblematic of his practice and its ricochet of sites and contexts. Folding the micro and macro, these references and relations across time, space, and context speak to the protean nature of Tom's roving reconfigurations of site and self—which, as they did in *Torrington Project*, chart new paths and possibilities in ways that embrace the transformative possibility of encounter—fraternizing, propagating, and cruising within the context of the artist's own corpus. ◇

Distributing Desire Lines

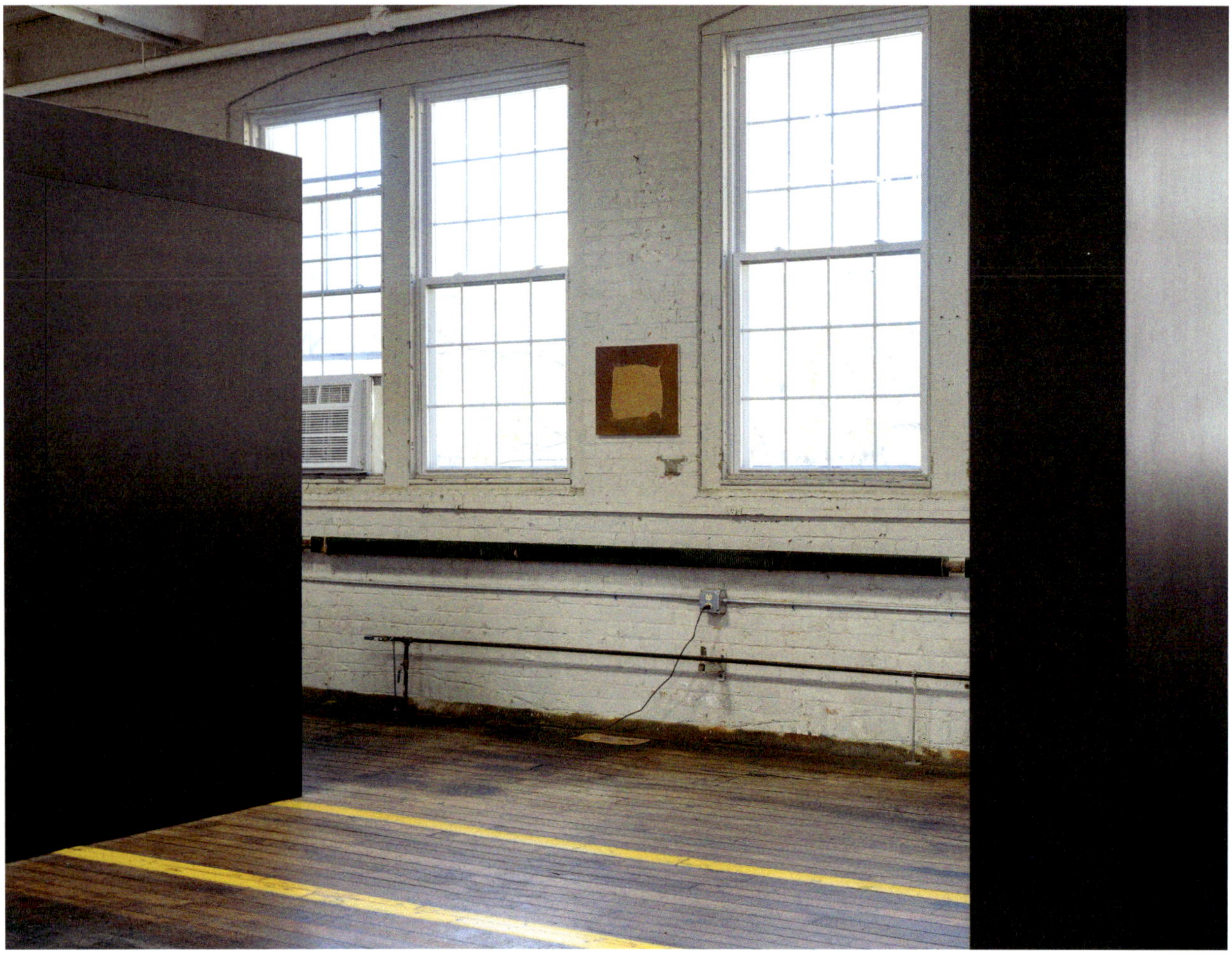

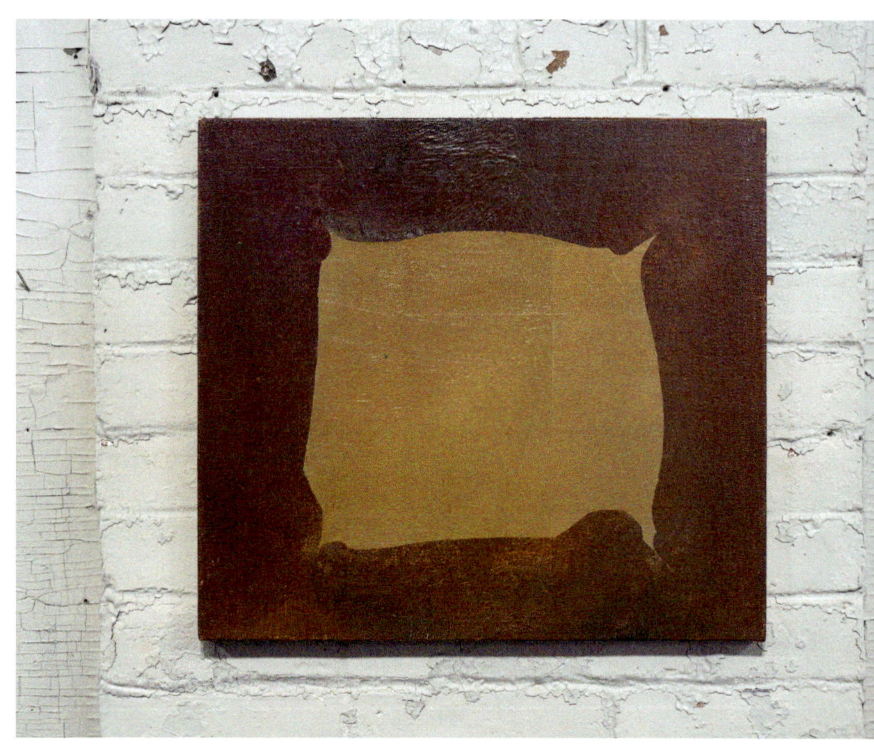

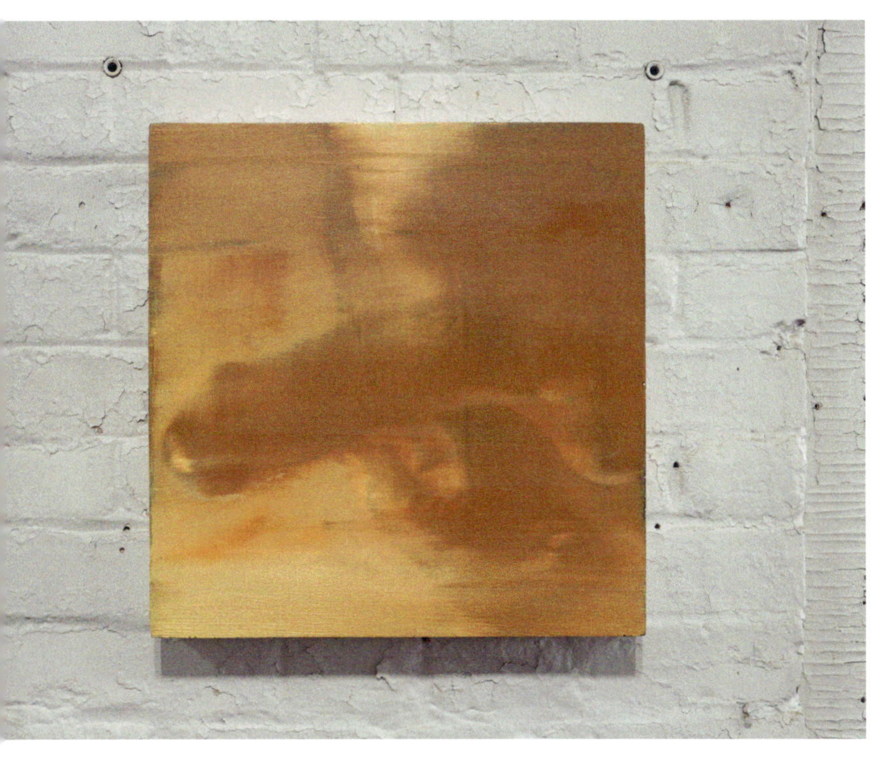

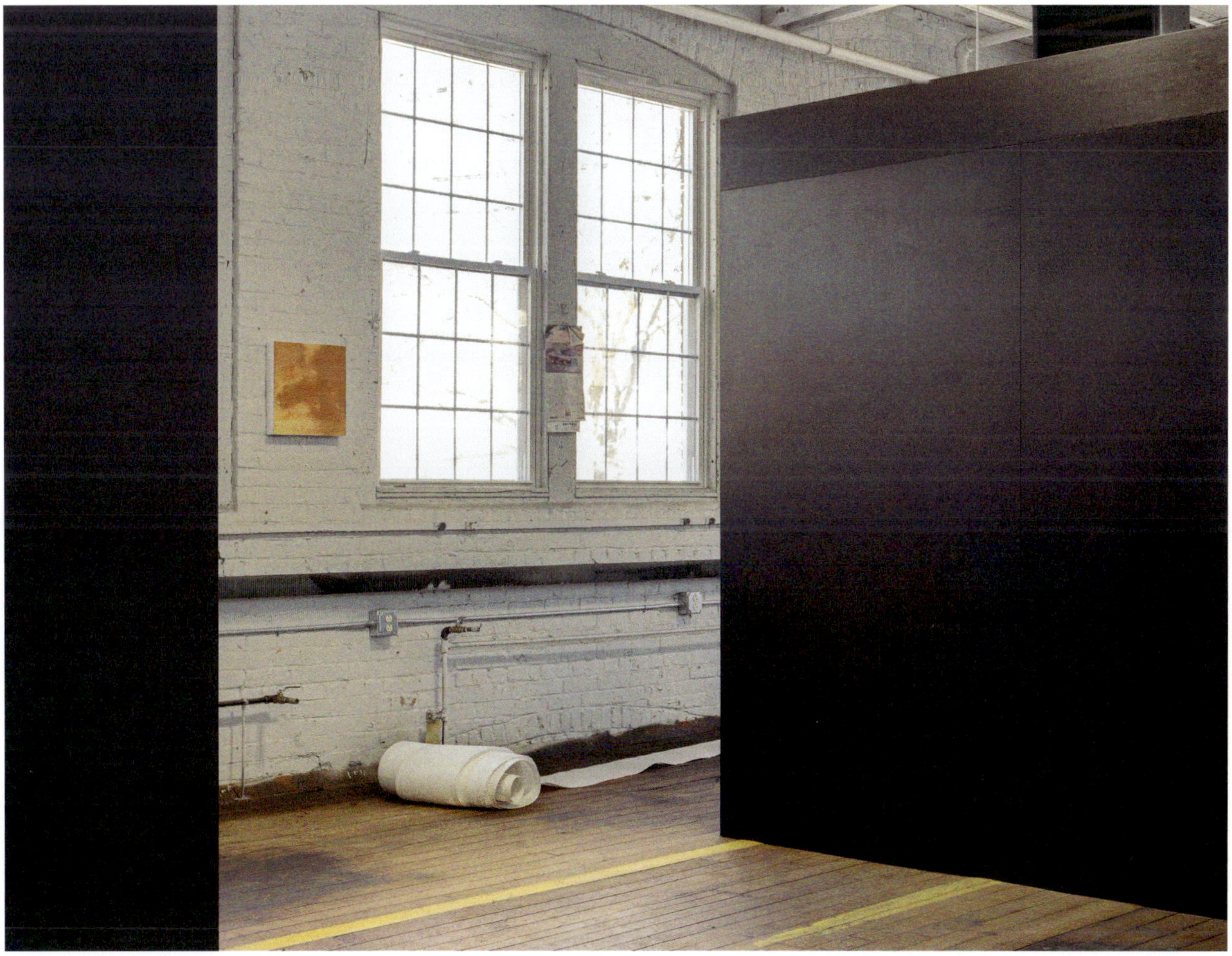

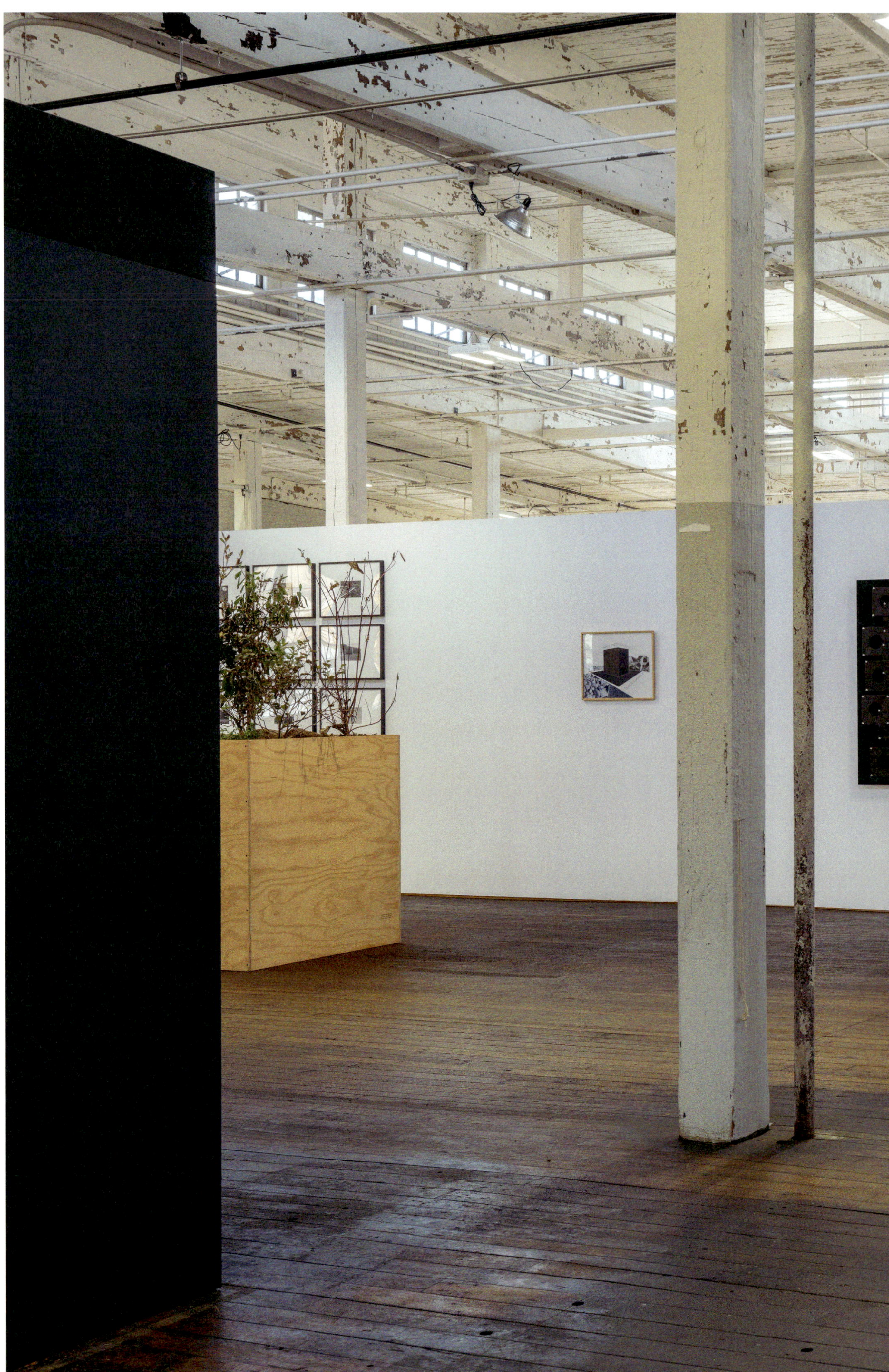

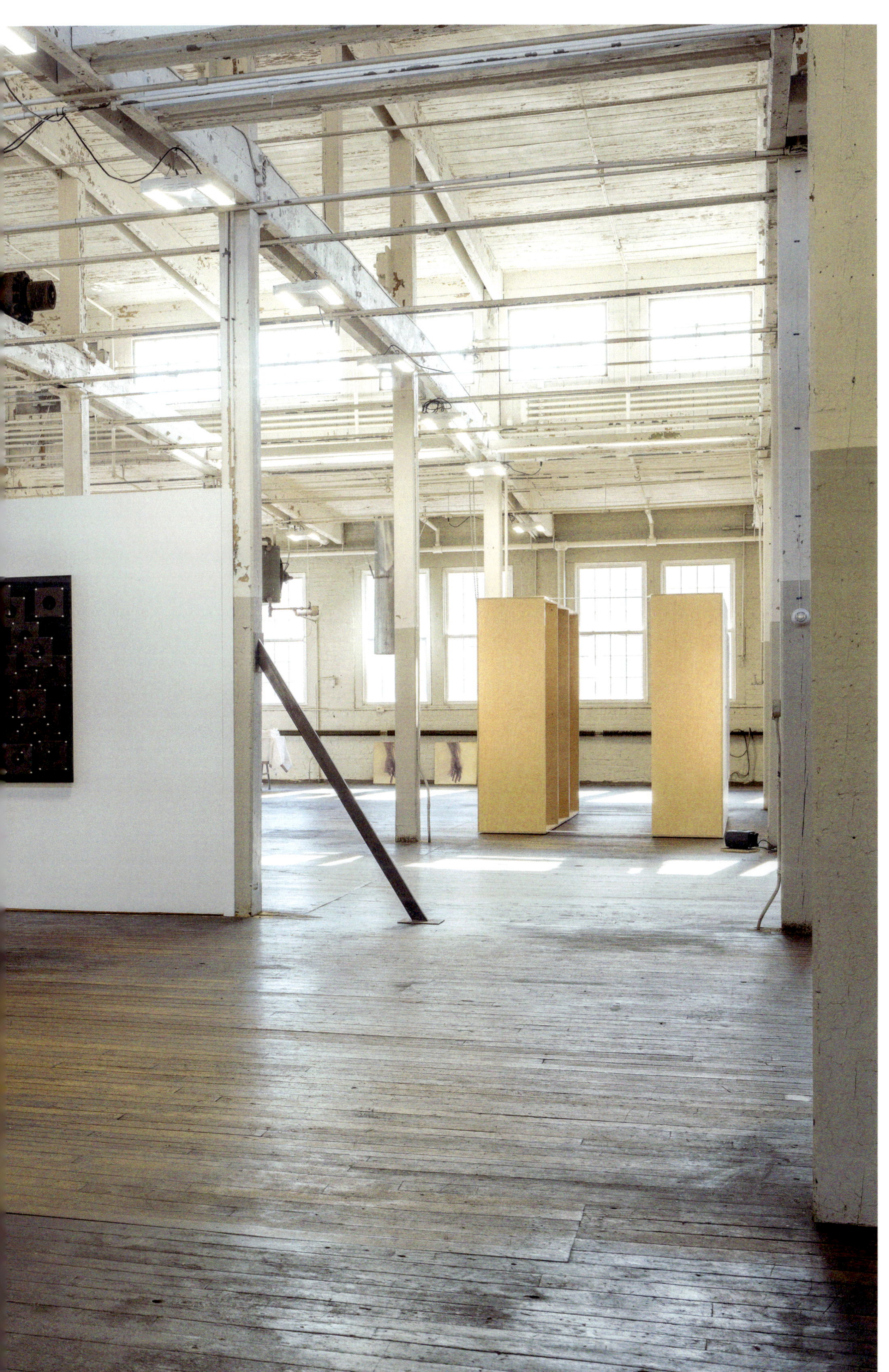

5

I spoke with Stefania and with Christine, and with Spencer Young, who was working with Patrick at the time, about the logistics of it all, and we set out to craft a proposal. Christine was on board at this point as a collaborator in the research and development of it all, and was central to thinking through the ways in which the project could happen, and face the world, and interact with the public, as well as leading the deep dive we took into archival materials. Patrick was immediately receptive, and I felt an enormous wave of relief, and a thrill, that this was going to be realized. I found the building on Migeon Avenue and began the process of reconceptualizing how the space would work, how it would flow, where I would alter it with additional walls, what architectural elements would stay and what might be removed. I slowly started to design a series of zones: some quite

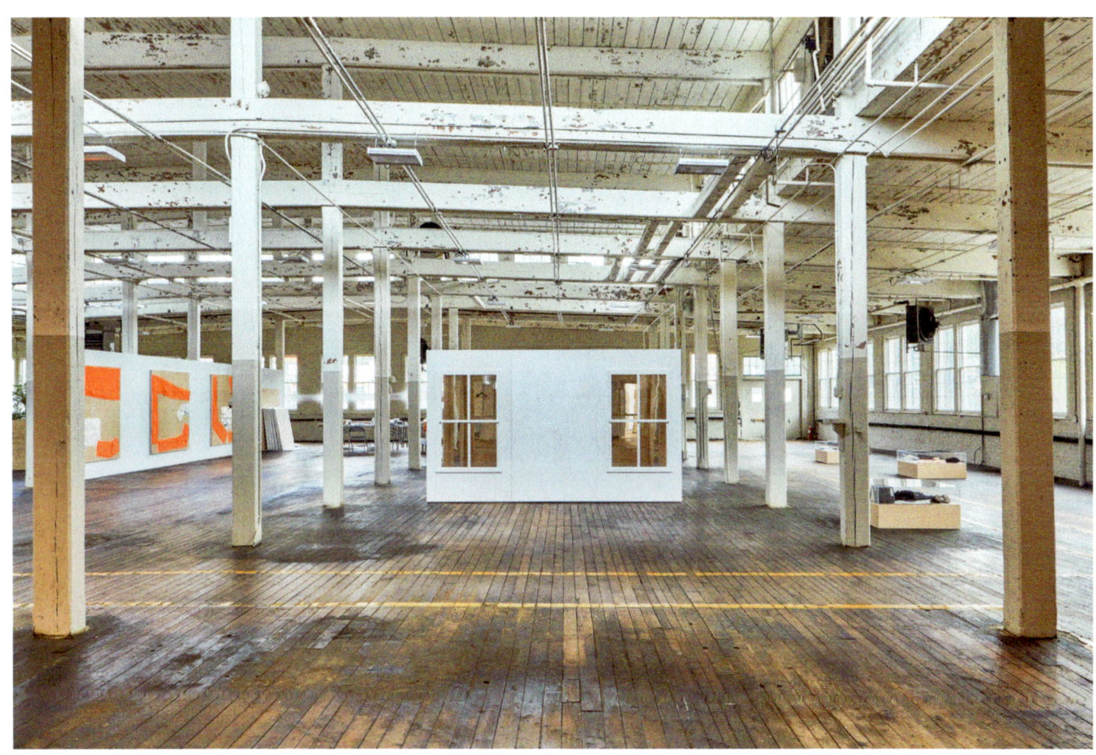

architecturally distinct with new walls defining their limits; others more openly spatial, existing as floating areas within the vast spaces of the two large rooms, which were punctuated by a grid of wooden columns, spaced every twenty feet along the north/south axis, and every ten feet along the east/west. This plan proposed the interplay I was interested in, of partly open and partly closed spaces unfolding across the floor, defined in the middle by an existing brick wall that divided the two rooms, with a series of three large doors, an interior glass window, and a small lower opening we dubbed "The Fireplace," punching holes through it and allowing even this heavy structural wall to oscillate between open and closed. It was a lengthy process, of deciding this scenography, and imagining sight lines between works, and also envisioning how it would unfold as bodies passed through it.

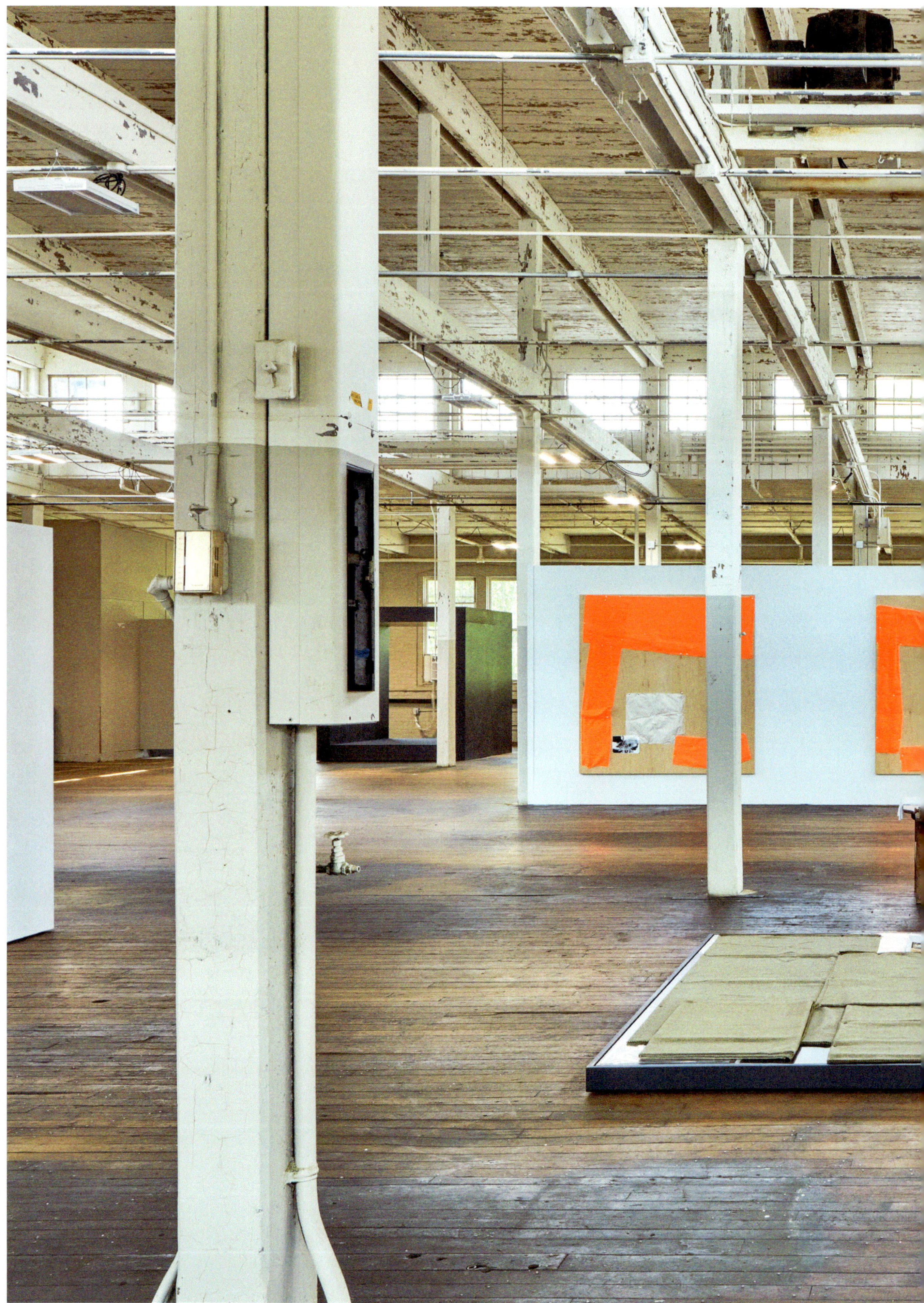

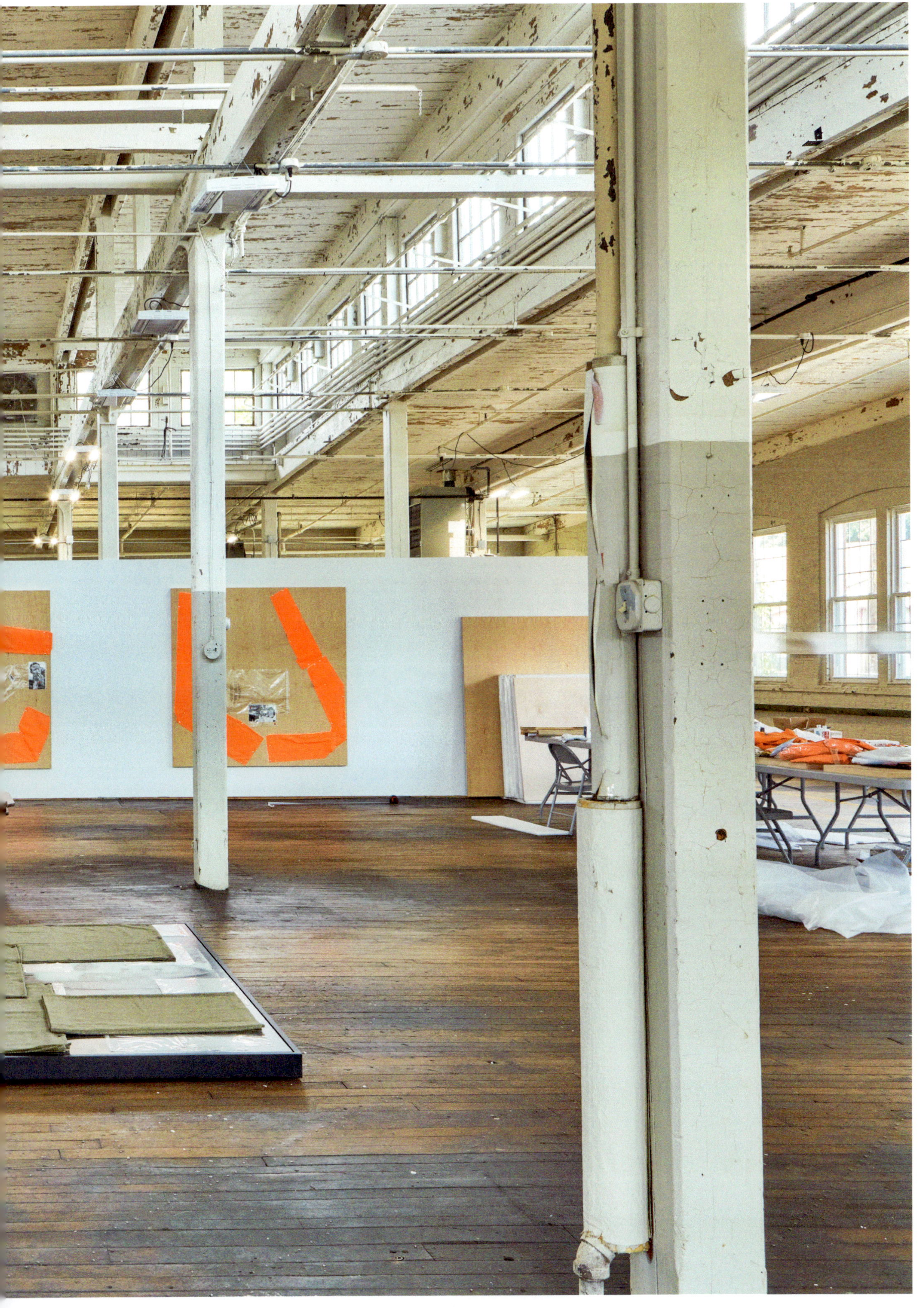

Charles Atlas

Photo- LEVISON
12/20/85

Sun. Ent.

pany. When Cunningham became intrigued by the new concept of dance
video — a medium in which he had
no experience — trained filmmaker
Atlas jumped in.

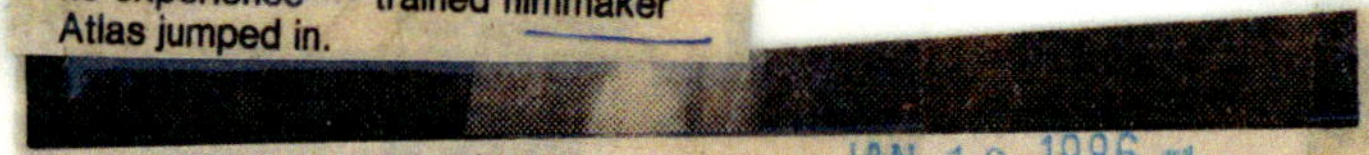

Staff Photo by Marlin Levison   JAN 12 1986

Charles Atlas, the world's leading experimenter in dance video.

"I certainly never intended to make
dance videos when I joined Merce,"
said Atlas, 40, on a recent visit to
the Twin Cities. Yet Cunningham's
trust and his willingness to experiment led to an enormously creative
13-year partnership, with Atlas carrying the title of filmmaker-in-resi-
dence through 1983.

13

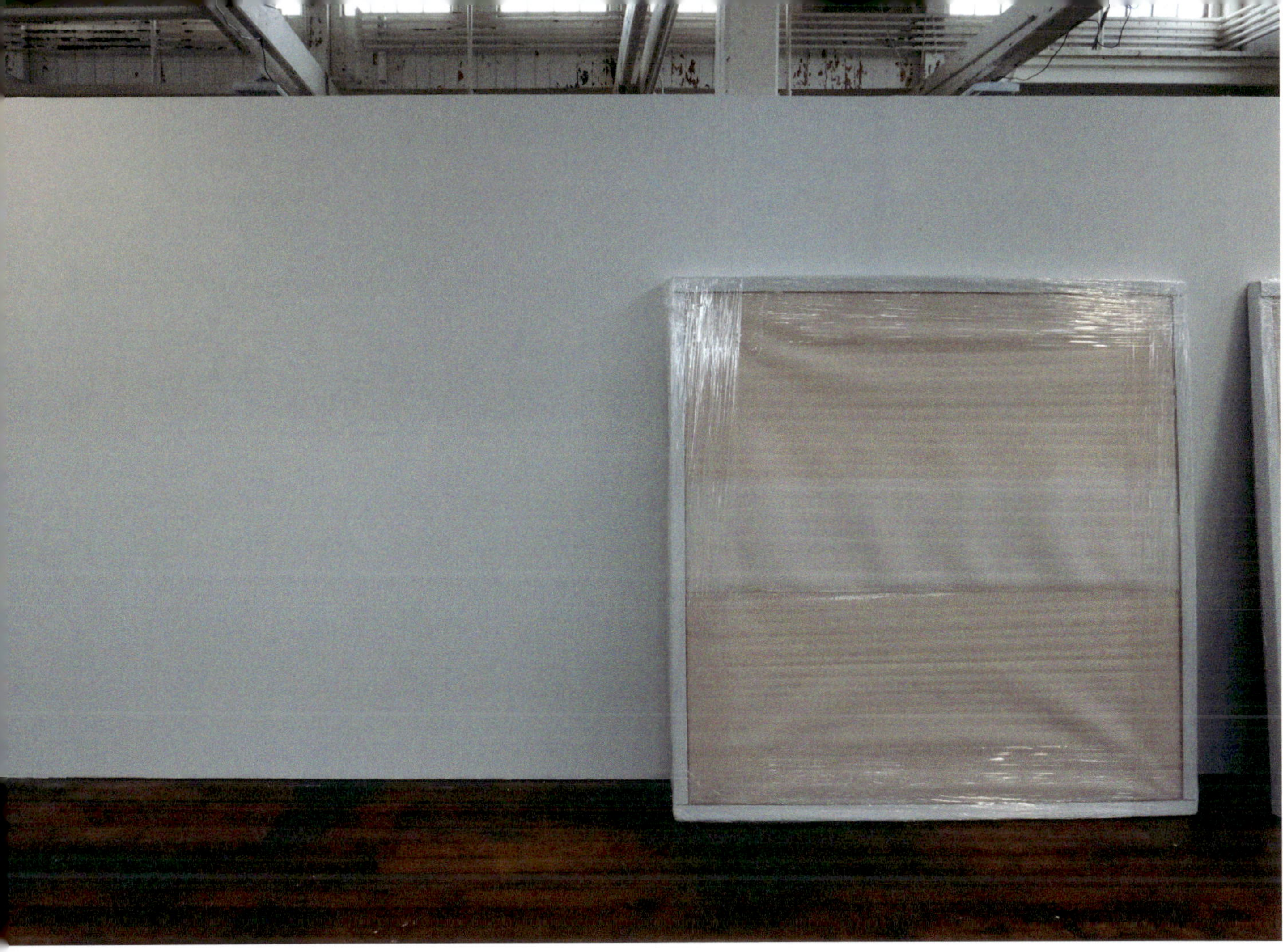

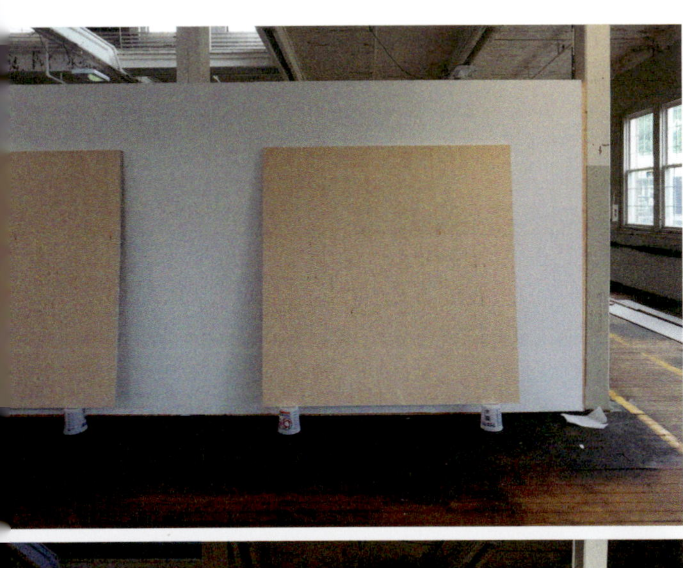

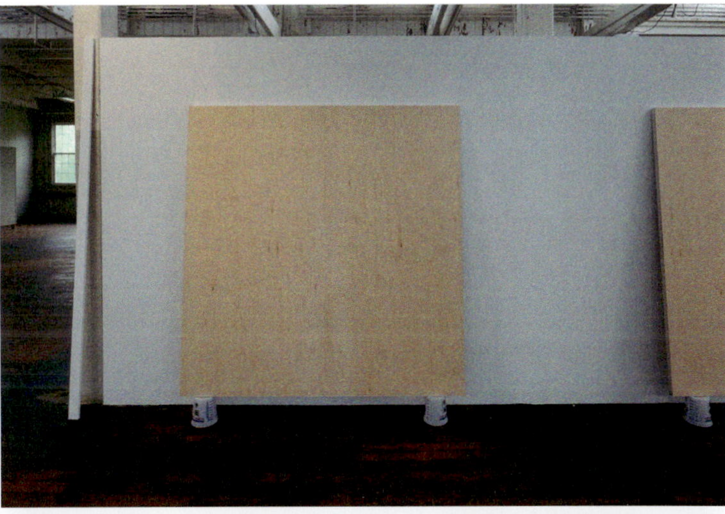

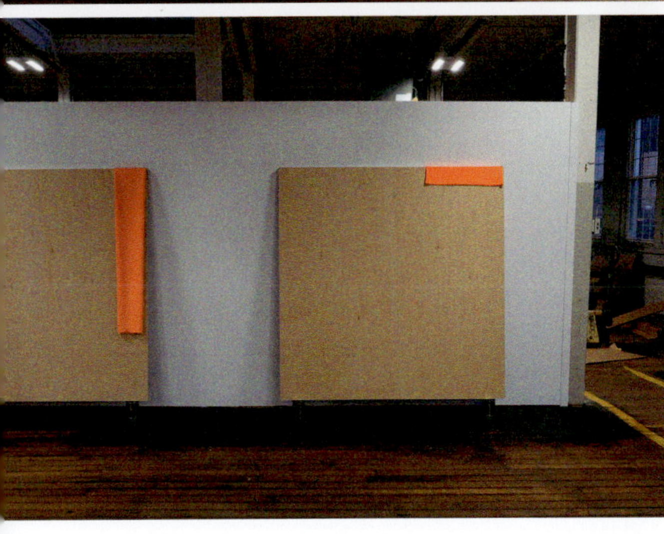

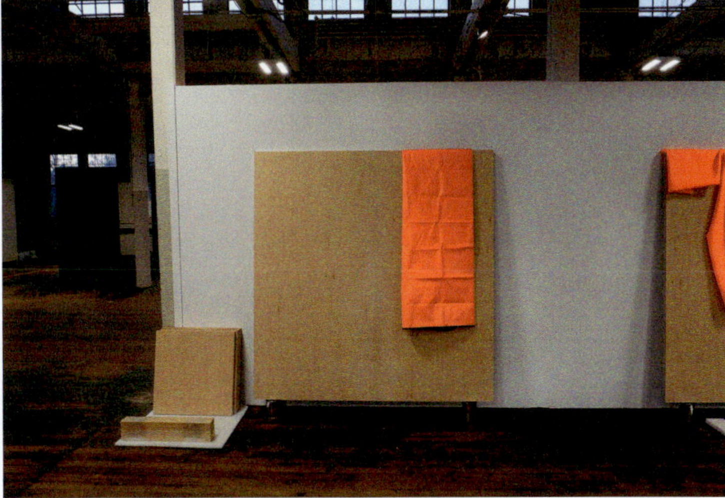

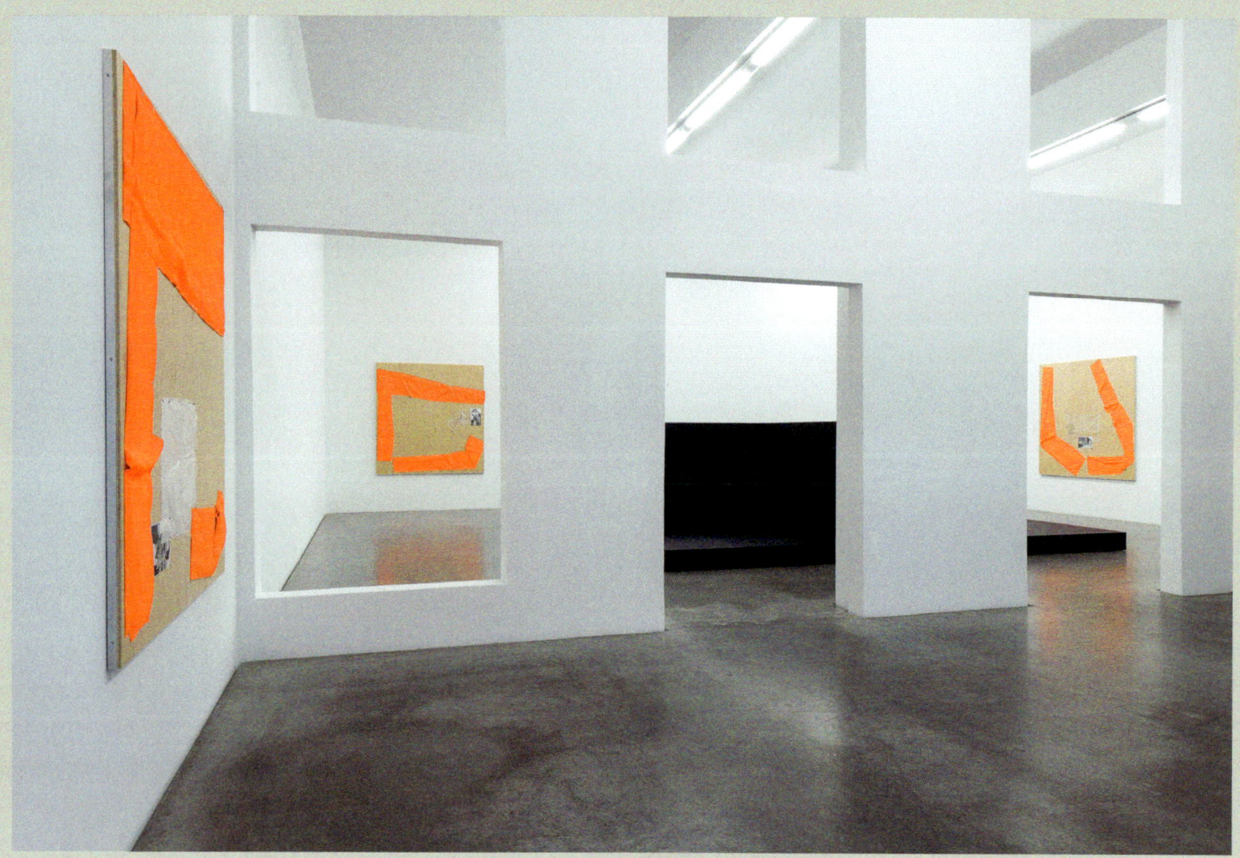

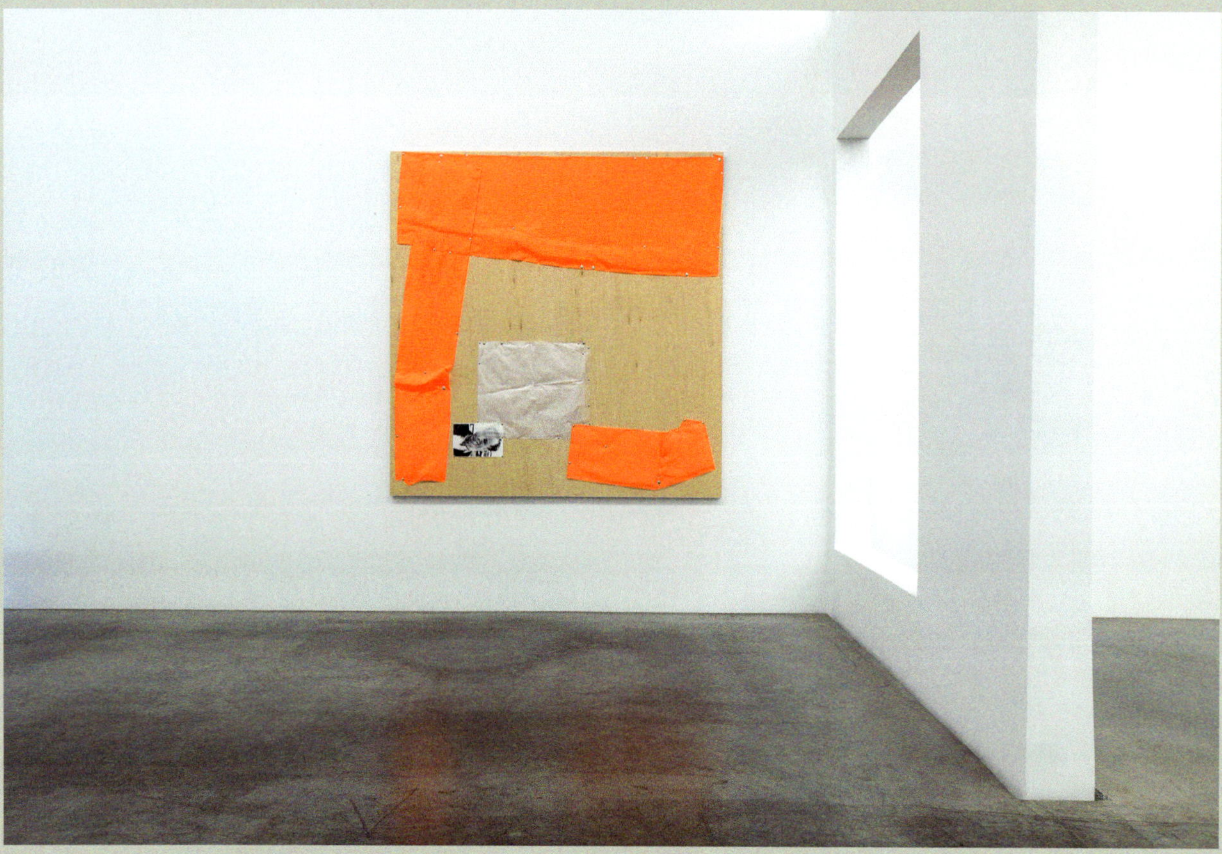

We had already chosen a few works that would be involved in the project, but they needed to be remade, like *Container (1–3)*, or, in other instances, simply repaired. None of this was easy, and Nick Hochstetler and the team he assembled struggled to get the materials we needed when supply was an issue—particularly when it came to plywood. I was drawn to plywood early on in my life. I like its democratic nature. I like the way it is constructed, its layers, and the many different woods it can be made up of, as well as the multiple grades available. It can be fancy or drab, and with each wood type or grade another patterning, surface grain, and texture is visible, from smooth to rough, bland to something almost psychedelic. When the swirls and blobs of a highly visible grain are present, a kind of persistent ornamentation takes over the otherwise ubiquitous and pedestrian material, as if it just can't help itself. Like laughing, or blushing. A sort of eruption of emotive décor, which is tempered by the utilitarian nature of the thing.

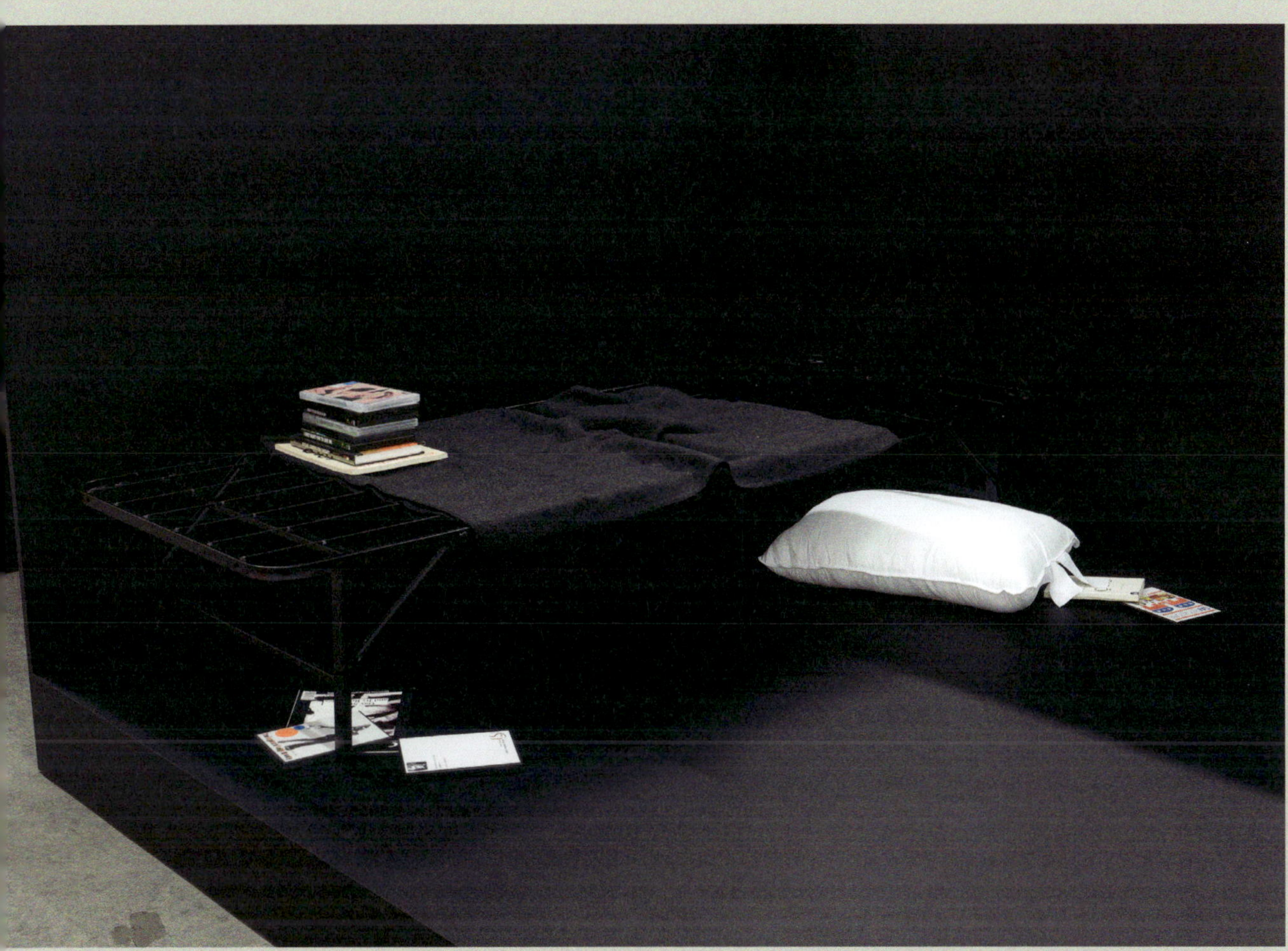

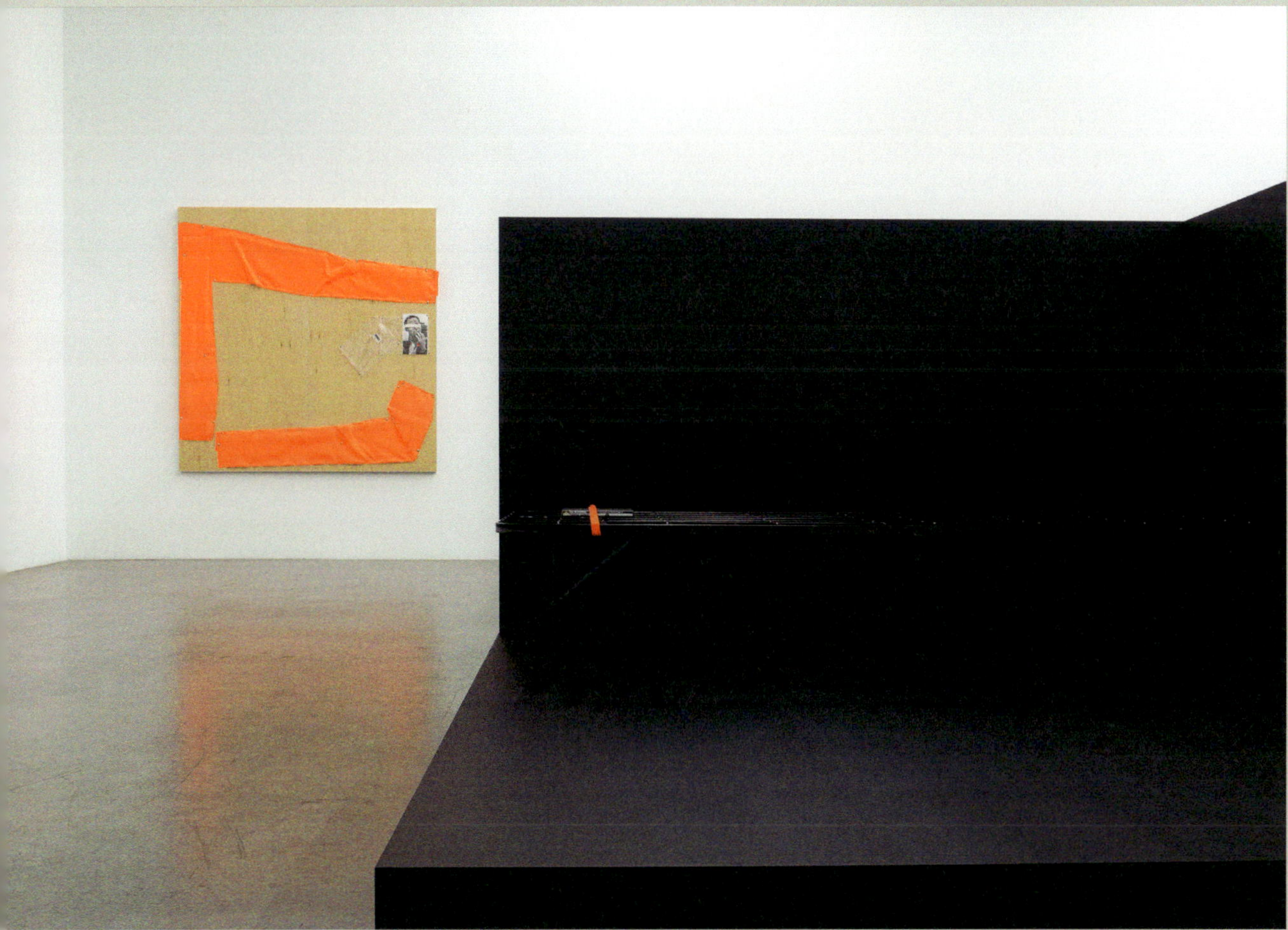

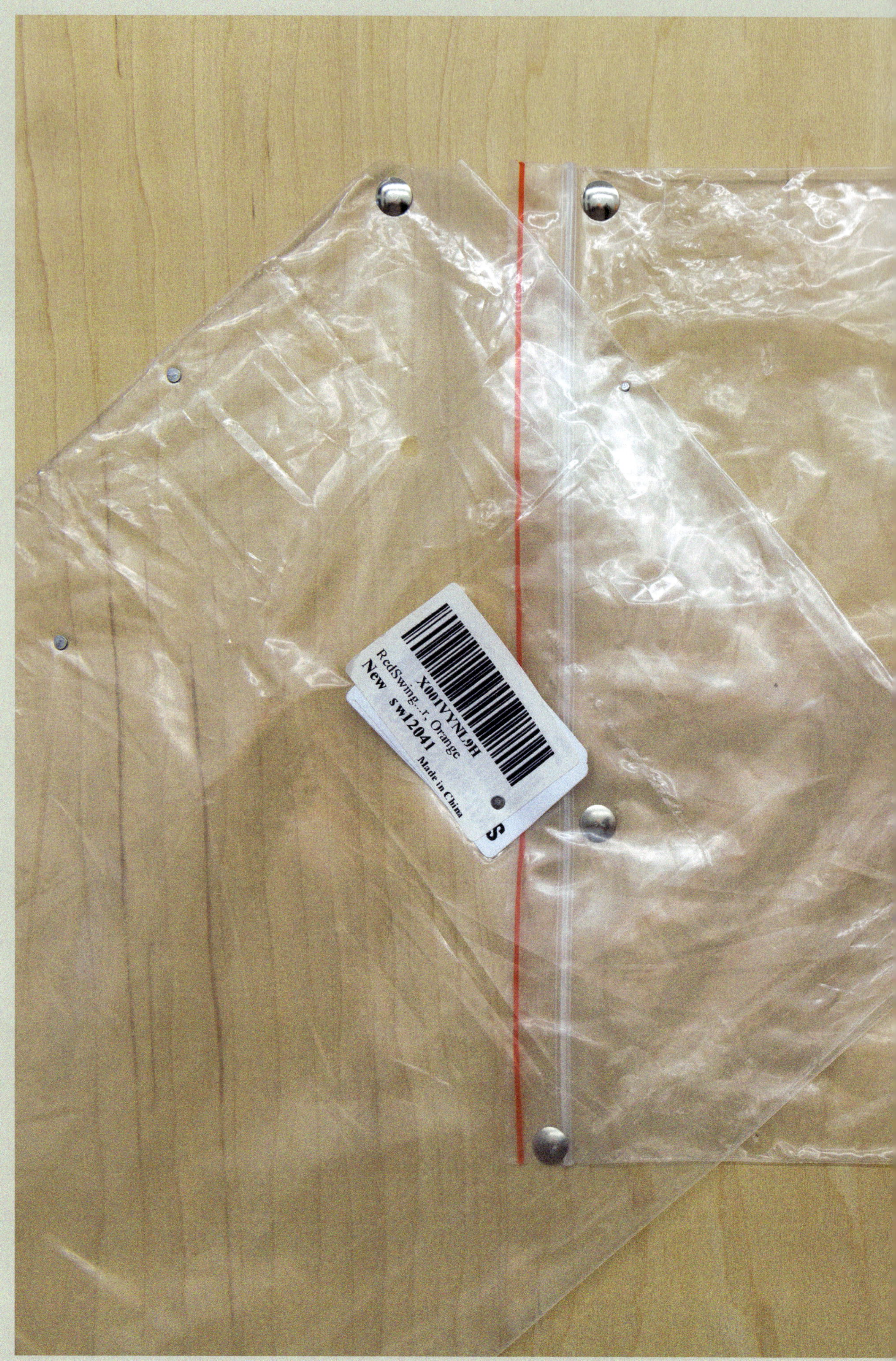

X001VYNL9H
RedSwing...r, Orange
New SW12041
Made in China
S

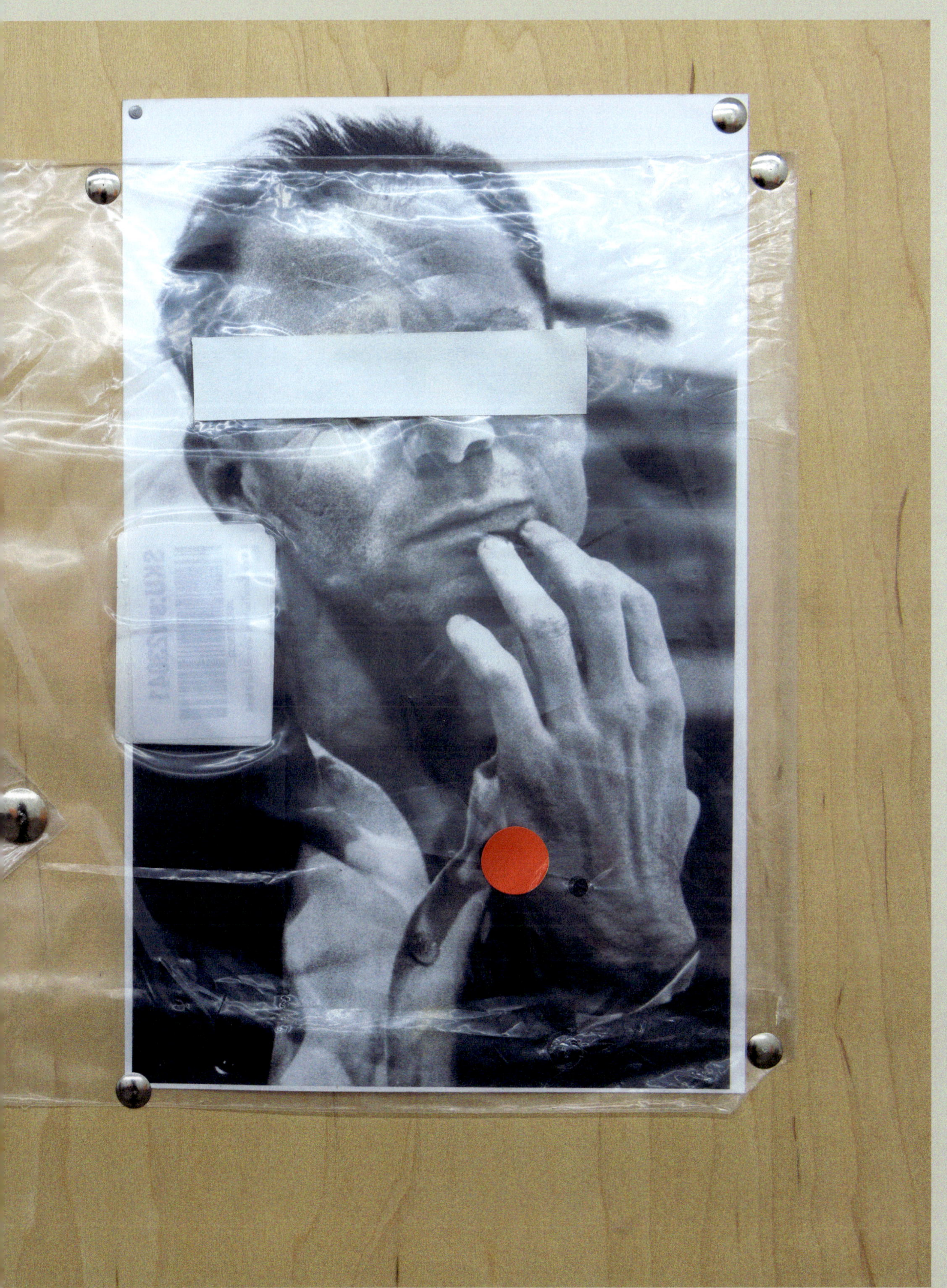

Plywood is meant to be underneath other
surfaces and materials most of the time,
covered up by them, so when it's not, when it's
the unadorned material itself, it feels exposed.
I've used a wide range of different plywoods
over the years, changing the type or the grade
according to the project and what I felt it needed,
and whether the surface was to be stained or not,
and if so, deciding which grains would remain
visible through the stain so you could still feel
the material coming through. I also started to
consider that these different works might come
together in the future in various configurations,
in survey exhibitions where you might see one
application of this material in relation to another,
or in books or magazine spreads, where you can
see the juxtapositions clearly. I wanted plywood's
different moods and applications to take on a
role over time, over many different works, and not
be a neutralized material; sometimes it should
be blank and somber, or feigning neutrality, and
other times it sings more loudly.

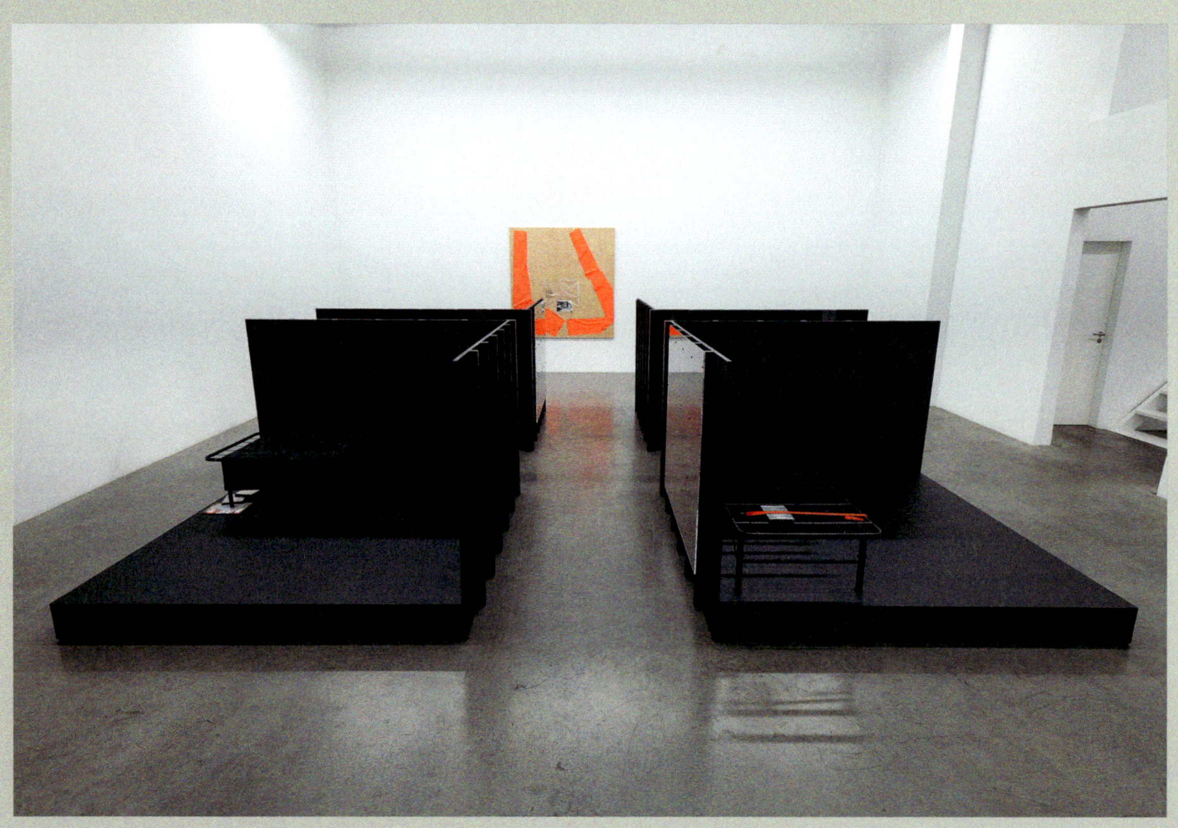

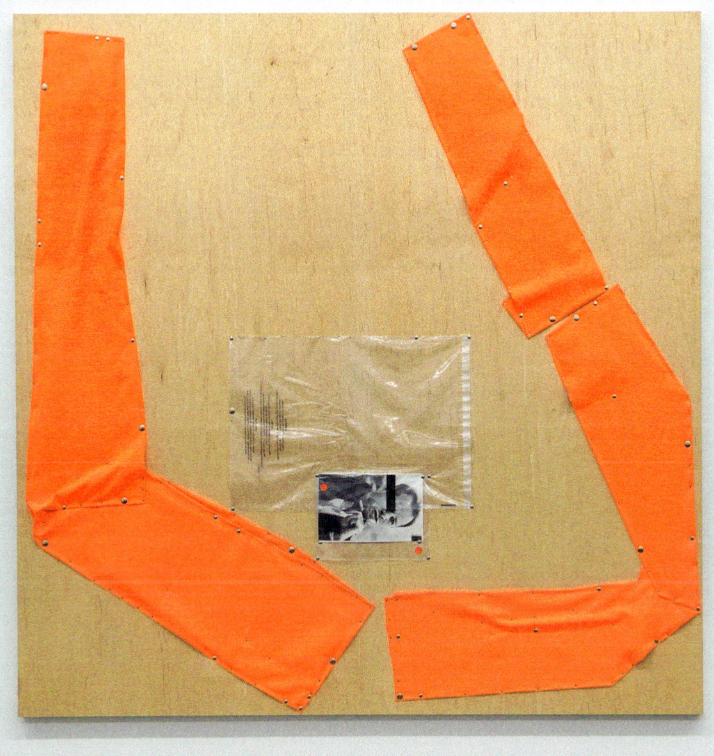

Plywood was difficult to acquire during the early months of *Torrington Project*. And when you could find it, it had soared in price. Suddenly, it was precious. After looking all over New York and southern New England, Nick was able to find a lumberyard not far from where we were in Torrington that not only had a large volume of plywood, but would allow us to come and hand-select our own sheets. This was particularly important to the re-fabrication of *Construction of an American Garden*, the smaller satellite version of the earlier, larger *An American Garden*, which, like the full-scale version, had only been exhibited once before, also in 1993. *Construction of an American Garden* was installed on Wooster Street outside of American Fine Arts, Co. It was something of a postcard or souvenir sent back from the Netherlands, where the larger work had been installed, and took the form of a four-by-four-foot plywood crate-as-planter, delivered to the front door of the gallery and landscaped with plants from Olmsted's list.

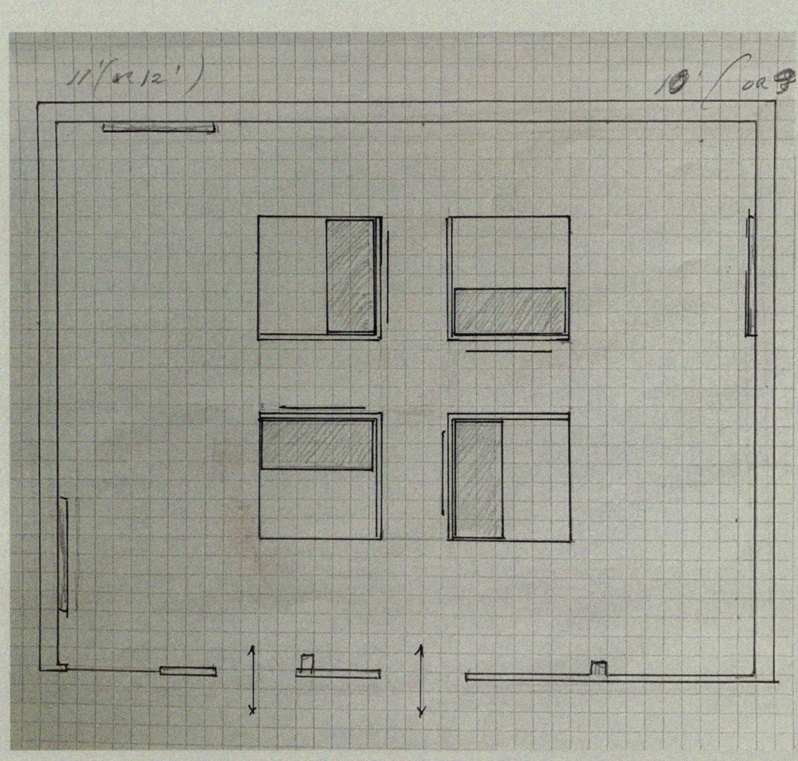

Dear Tom,

Between November and now, winter solstice, I've been wanting to respond to your stimulating message, as a follow-up to our summer conversation.

At last, the end of this year is here. It's been a miraculous year—full of joy, sadness, and many nuances in between, so I'm glad to at last be able to take time to pause and reflect.

I feel we are linked and share relations in compelling ways that are still unfolding. I keep learning of more ways. It is a gift to be able to realize that we are still alive and have lived through so many years, perceiving many things, no matter how these may have momentarily seemed or felt at various times, to now be able to acknowledge having survived, with a possibility to reflect as well as to relay some of the relations we've perceived—not yet articulated, impressions still gradually emerging. Thank you for your patience and for your invitation to be in dialogue now.

I still value remembering, as I have in various ways through time. Of course, taking Borges's reflections on memory mania into consideration as well, yet finding there is still quite a lot to consider regarding what any of us arrived into, and how it has gone on; what is remembered, or promoted, or retained, or obliterated, or partially buried. Today I'm rereading Bergson's *Matter and Memory*, for instance. I'm just beginning to reread it, which led me to thinking about you.

After having lived through the years, I imagine it is inevitable to reflect. And for artists, in particular, it

     Renée Green

seems impossible not to do this, especially if you've managed to make it to the age of thirty, let alone twice that age. It seems remarkable, to have lived this long. I remember feeling very old at the age of twenty-six, but as you mentioned, those were other times, the 1980s. I think that realizing you are not alone, in terms of having shared with another what through survivance become historical moments is significant, not to be denigrated; actually, a form of sustenance.

I like what you wrote in our email exchange about returning to notions of "a group of artists linked through time and place and general tendencies of concerns, sometimes self-determined as such, other times grouped or framed from the outside, by exhibitions, by writers, by curators, by circumstance, by chance. The notion of belonging—or not belonging—is a fraught one. And what about once belonging." I'd like to take a moment now to write briefly—and in the future, to talk more with you—about these things, as I too think and wonder about these configurations, imaginary and actual, identifiable, even if fleeting. I guess that's how I recurrently think of these combinations between artists and the entire cultural and economic infrastructure we are engaged with: as constantly shifting, with specific tendencies depending on what compels the participants, amid varying conditions, certain repetitions, and, of course, also differences. I'm not blasé about it, but it feels familiar. I used to very much like the idea of working in an ensemble, and I guess Free Agent Media (FAM) has been one way for me to enact this wish. I created FAM in Berlin, in 1994. We were both there, at different and crossing times. I'm curious to learn more about your recollections through time shifts, to present perceptions and feelings.

Matter and Memory

In wintery New England again. After reading and rereading and recollecting: books, words, images, photos.

Dear Tom,

Again, I'm thrilled to be asked to contribute to this book reflecting on the *Torrington Project*. I appreciate your and the editors' patience regarding my slow reply. You may have discerned that despite my enthusiasm, I've been challenged for various reasons to respond with the lightness I had imagined, based on remembering how good it felt to be in the midst of the *Torrington Project* gathering back in May 2022. To be honest, I found this invitation to be something I very much wanted to do, despite back-to-back deadlines, as I imagined it would give me a chance to participate in thinking with you and with others about questions that have arisen in recent years regarding the contexts we've had as artists: our trajectories, our productions, and the span between two centuries, from C20 to C21. We've been asked questions by different generations from those interested in the realm of contemporary art.

What I found as I began to write were blockages—scary, shadowy feelings of a heavy and strange past, partially submerged—and it felt exhausting to confront them while in the midst of many activities, yet necessary in order to engage via matter and memory. What helped me move through this impasse was to read our words, in your books and in mine. We both have catalogues from our survey exhibitions that took place at the Musée cantonal des Beaux-Arts, in Lausanne: yours in 2006, mine in 2009. We both also have books of our writings that cover spans of time: mine are selections of writings between from 1981 to 2010; yours

     Renée Green

span 1991 to 2015. I needed specific matter to come into contact with our voices and with other times. I also read "Institutional Critique," the roundtable conversation I was unable to attend that was published online in *November*; I felt as if I were a listening participant. I learned things and found further resonances, shared intersections in our pasts, our interests, our schools—I attended SVA between 1979 and 1980—and our friends: Ull, Pat, Colin; the many unstated complexities. Coming into contact with each of these sources opened a possibility to further think and remember my encounter with the *Torrington Project*, which I still ponder; this process also allowed me to touch on a variety of impressions and feelings that passed through me when I visited the location, of past meetings and disparate times and places, yet in the present. These were also layered. Having known you personally during the 1990s in relation to the milieux we both circulated through was another factor of stimulation.

One significant layer to mention is location, that being the state of Connecticut. I hadn't in the past, when we'd met in New York or in Europe, stressed a relation to having spent time there, but I did live there for a duration of time to attend university: Wesleyan. The brutalist architecture of its Center for the Arts was an attraction, and I was also familiar with Yale and New Haven, Hartford—as a student I'd worked on cataloguing and writing about the Sol LeWitt Collection when it was housed in the Wadsworth Atheneum. A variety of perceptions regarding New England throughout my life were resonant, from childhood and adolescence through adulthood. These were also links to Pat Hearn, who'd grown up in Providence and later lived in Boston before moving to New York. The New England Atlantic coastal region vibe created bonds.

I'd not been to Torrington specifically before going to visit the *Project*, yet there was a regional familiarity.

Matter and Memory

Many times during the past years, while on the train between New York and New Haven, on the way to Massachusetts, I'd look at the abandoned warehouses and wonder what it could be like to use this kind of space. I liked very much that you'd done the project in such a space, the kind I often peer into while walking by. It seemed as if you were taking matters into your own hands, in terms of a kind of agency with the arrangements made for leasing, in the present, based on what I'd learned via conversations at Bortolami. Of course I thought of Donald Judd, yet I was intrigued by the limited time period of the lease, as I'd understood it. Different than buying a town in Texas. I imagined you living nearby. For many years, while passing near Norfolk or Milford, I'd imagined you living in a house there, and I'd think in a vague way of James Laughlin and New Directions Press, both of which I note you mention in your writings.

At *Torrington*, I walked slowly around the entire space, looking at the structure of the building and the light from the windows, finding surprise areas throughout the spaces that were variegated in scale. I loved the expanse of it, the wooden floors, the vertical and horizontal structural beams, the wooden ceiling, the many surrounding windows, the ability to spread throughout the entire space in any way you decided, with generous amounts of space between everything. A certain bare luxuriousness, meaning the luxury of so much space. Not precious; specific, yet not conclusive; somehow open-ended. I enjoyed that it was not an "exhibition space," but rather, an ongoing space, with indications of work taking place with visible storage containers. I also enjoyed that you could decide how you wanted to use the space—you could continue to experiment with and work with, play with, whatever you chose in whatever way you chose. I noticed that you could return to things at your own pace.

     Renée Green

Through the windows you could see trees and other brick buildings. I imagined you roaming there at different times of the day or night. I noticed in particular the tables and what was on them, what these indicated; for example, the same paperback of *The Bell Jar* that I remembered from my youth. As I moved through the spaces I found different details that I felt links to, including colors, like a particular orange you associated with Charles Atlas, whom I told you I liked very much to spend time with. It seemed like a place to be in solitude, as well as with others if you chose. Residue of previous party zones, remembered and actual, seemed possible. Movement and stillness. It definitely didn't feel like a production factory; rather, it resonated as a conscious project about another possible existence as an artist. And this I liked very much.

I'll stop now, but I look forward to our unfinished conversations.

Love,

Renée ◇

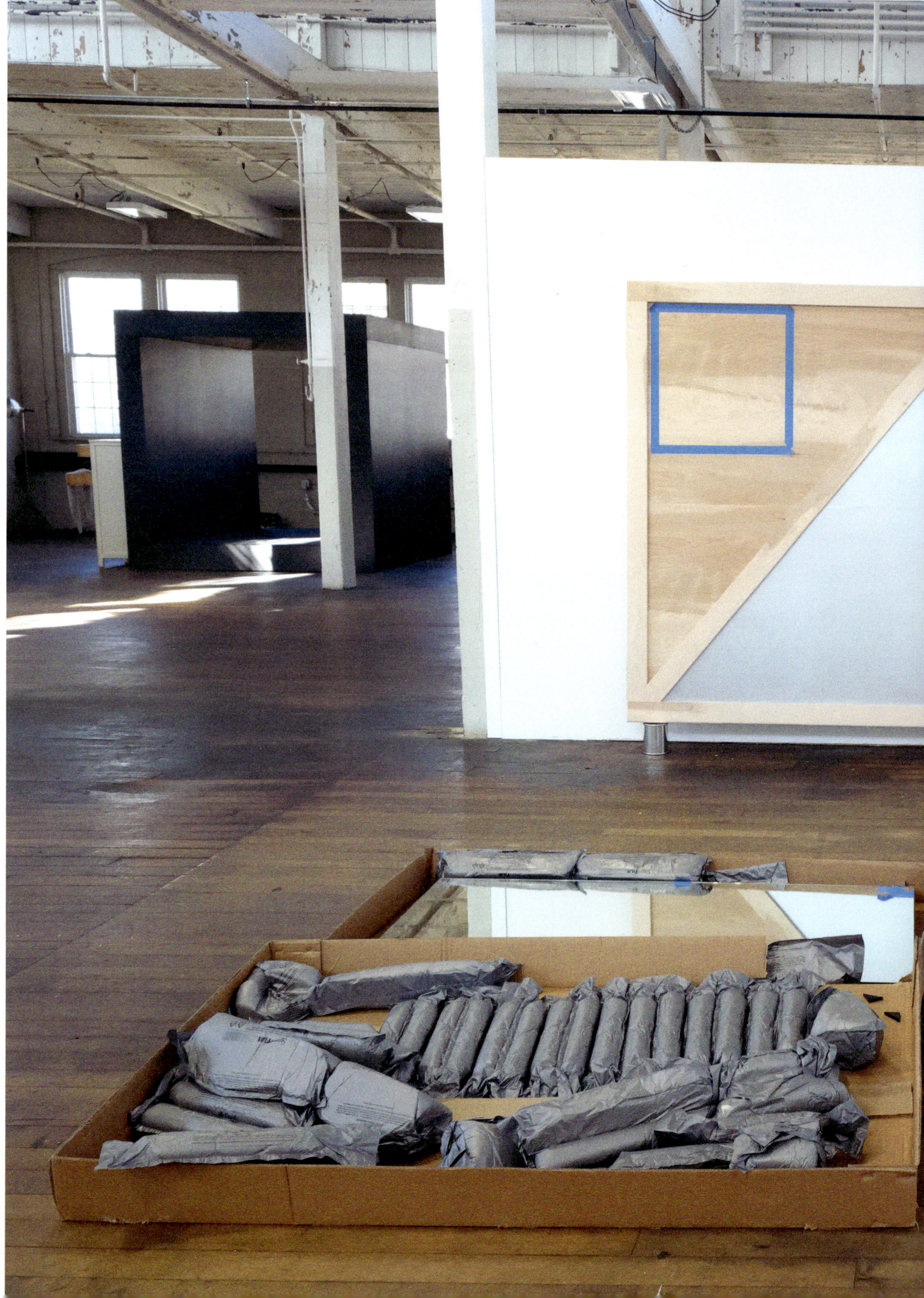

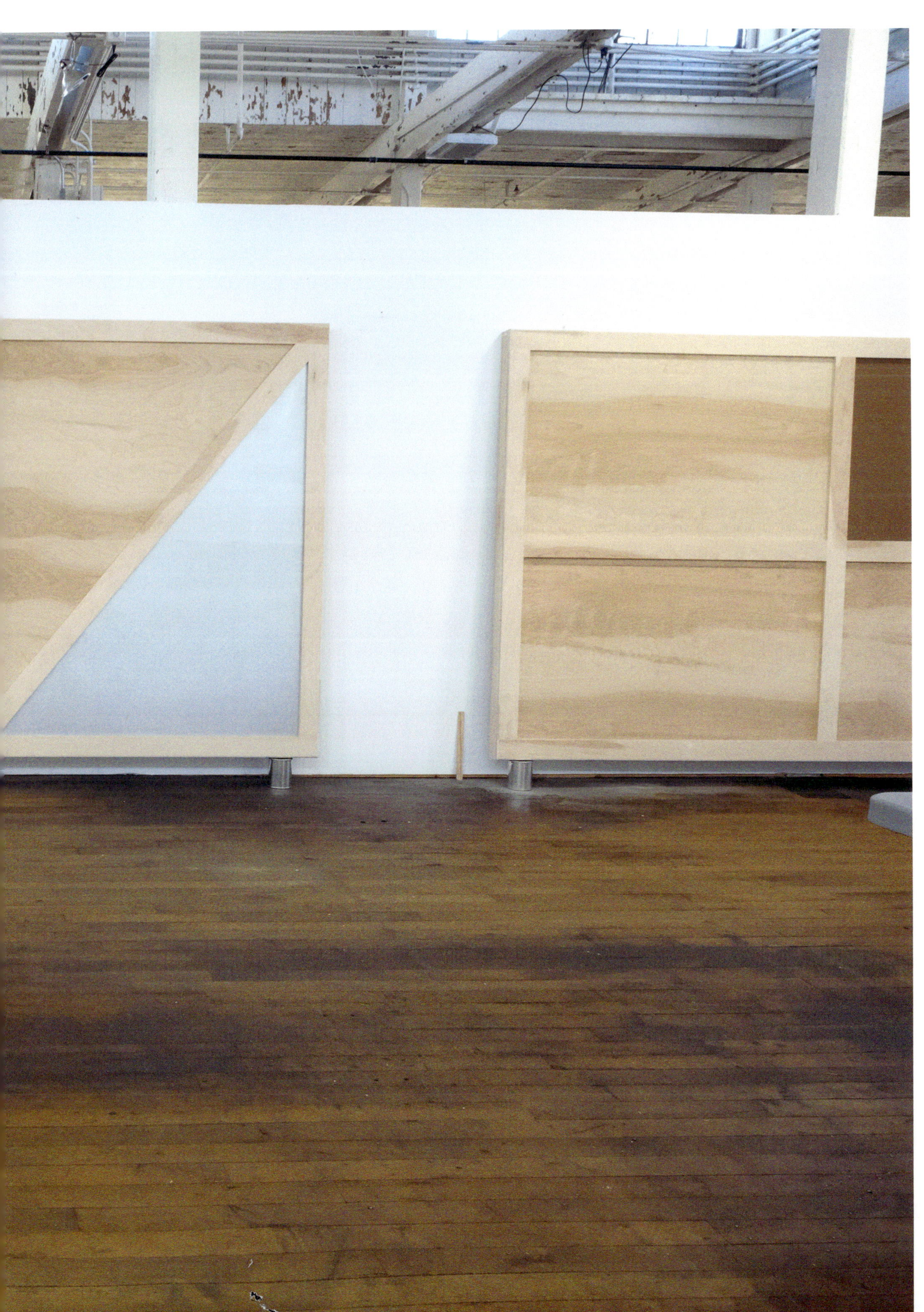

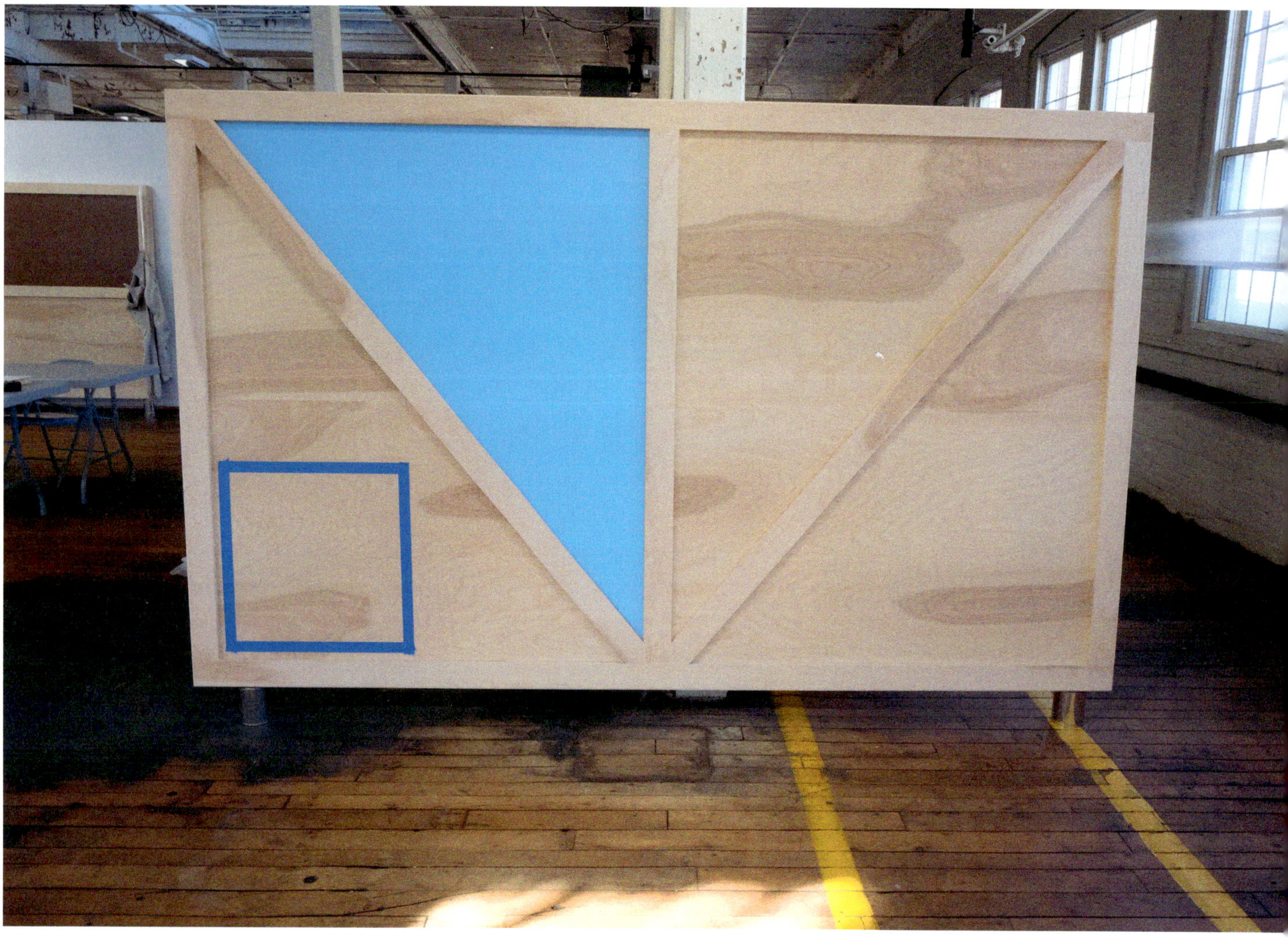

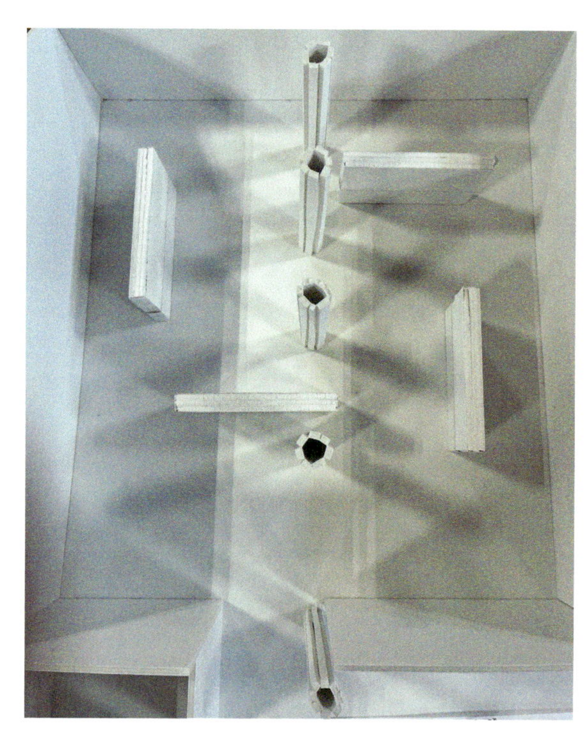

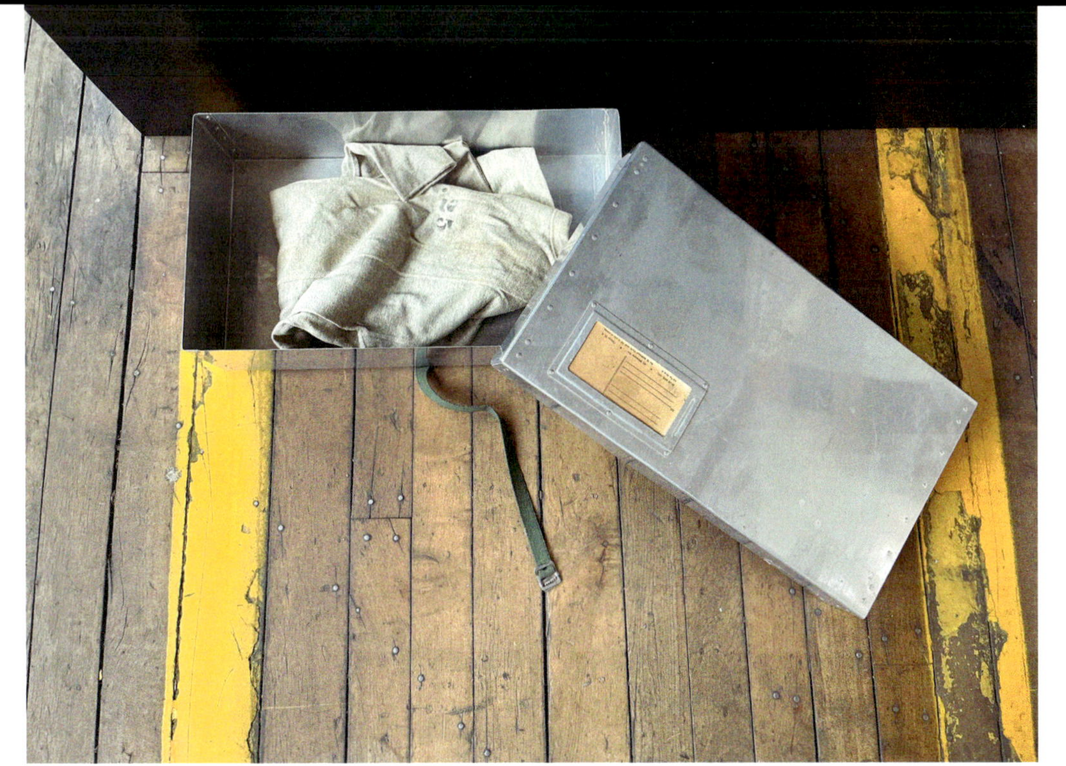

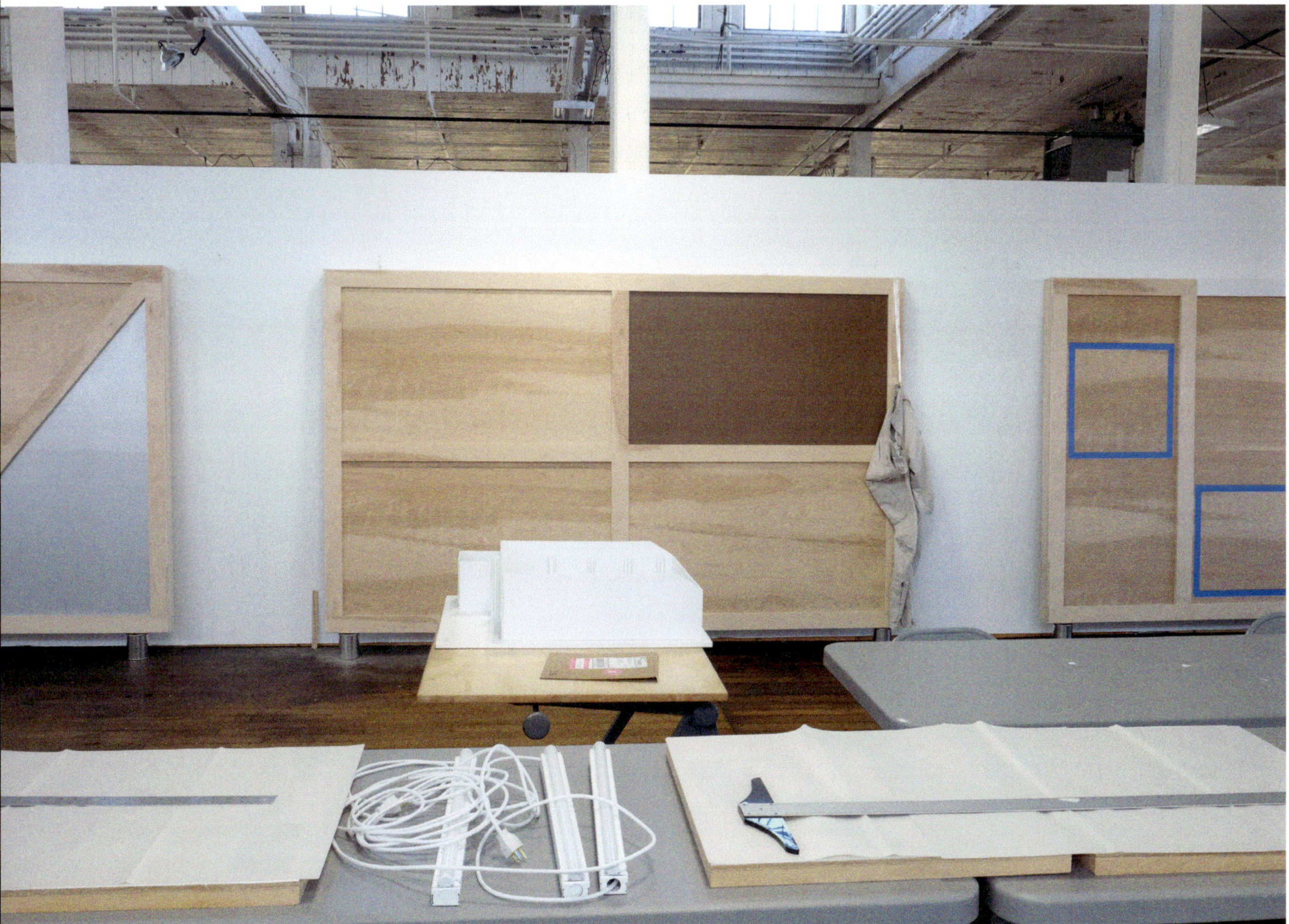

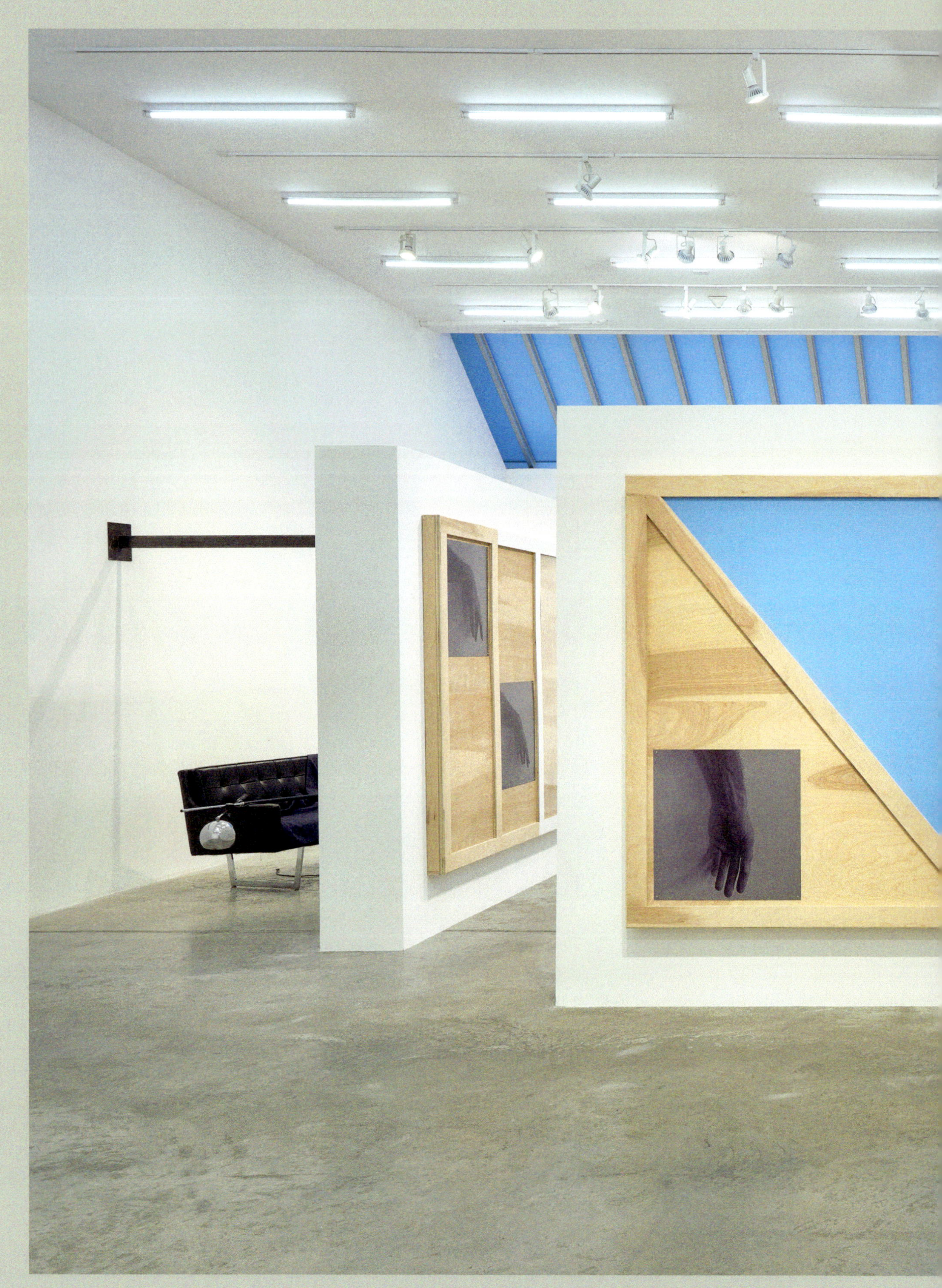

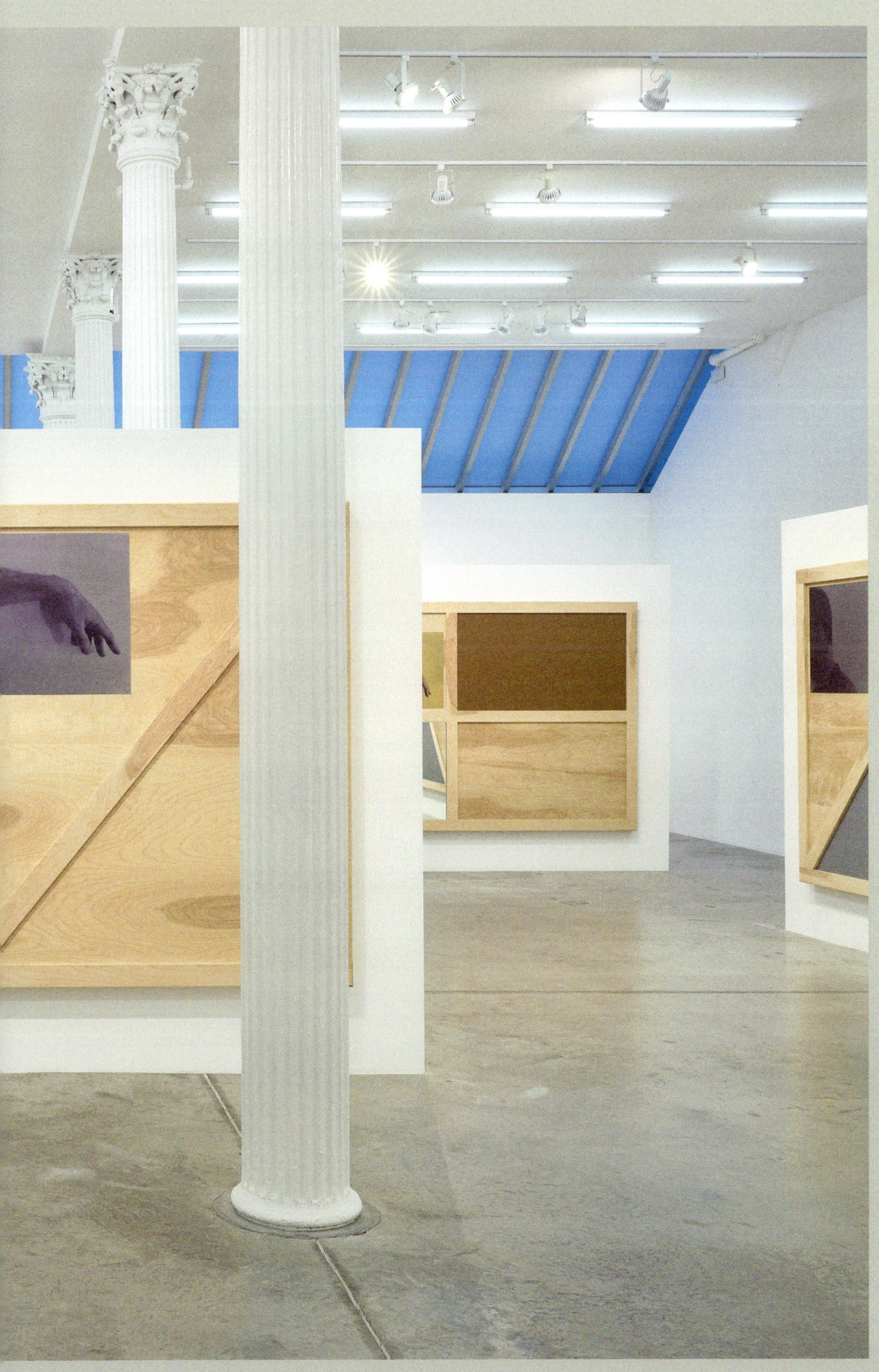

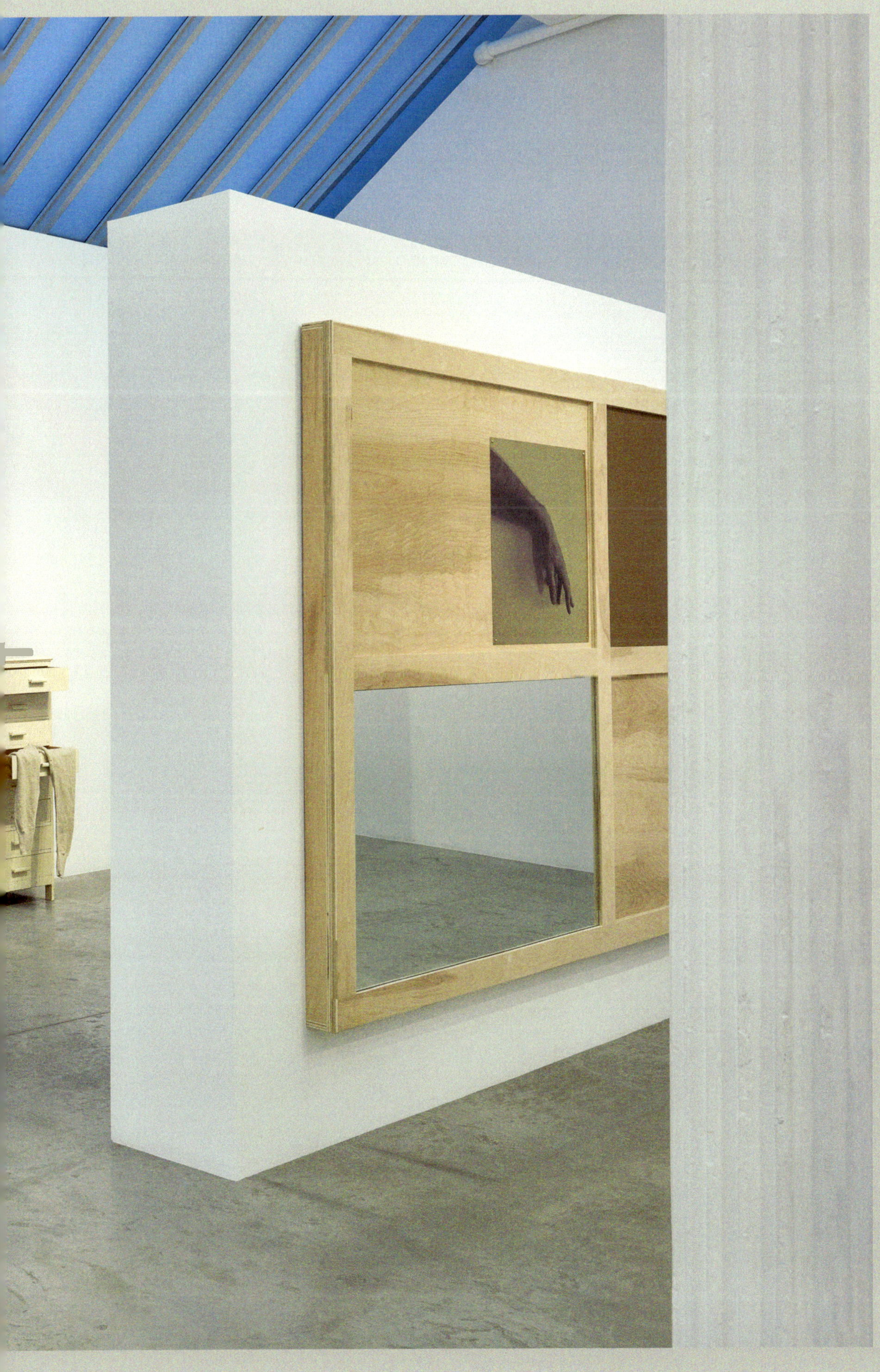

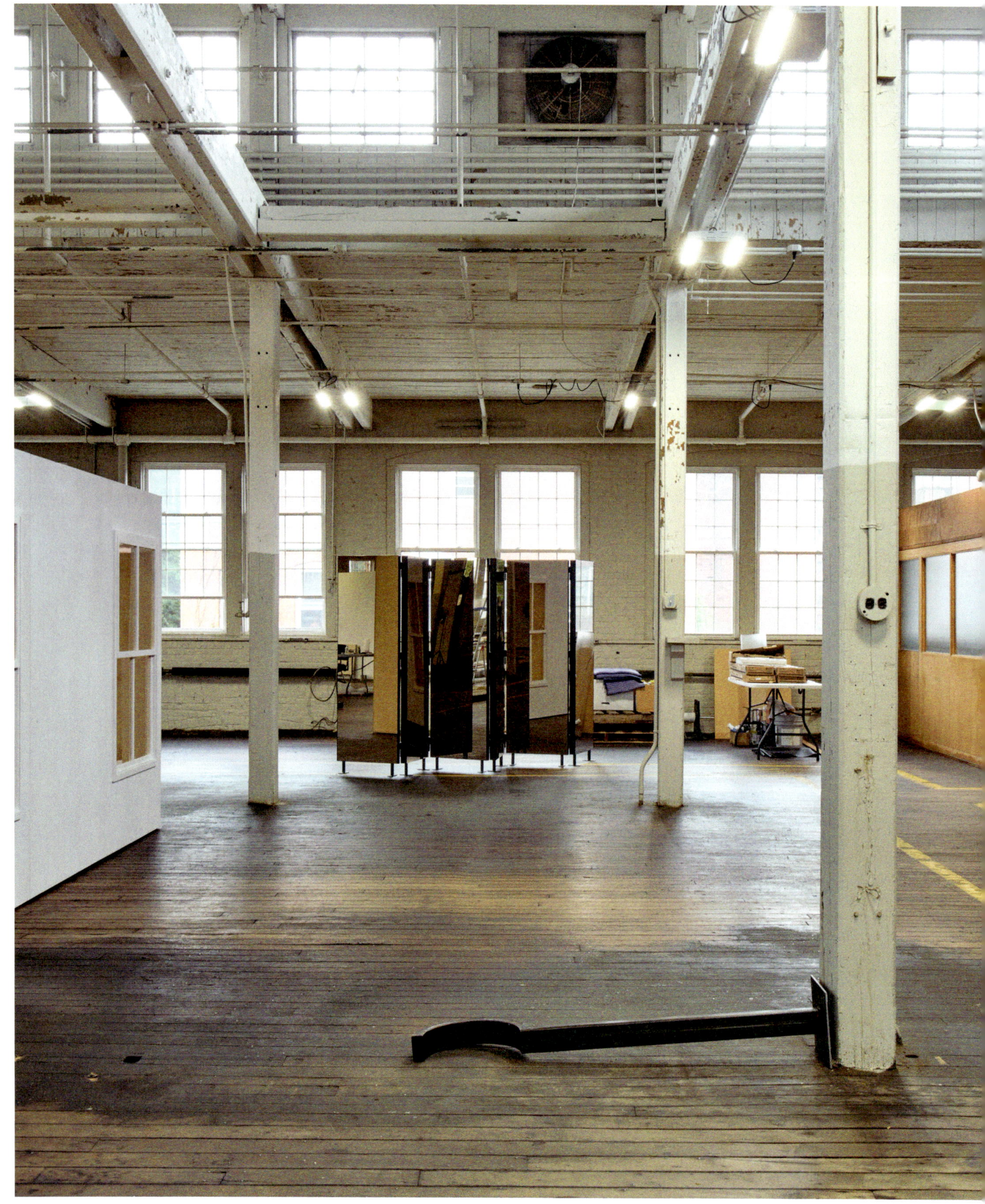

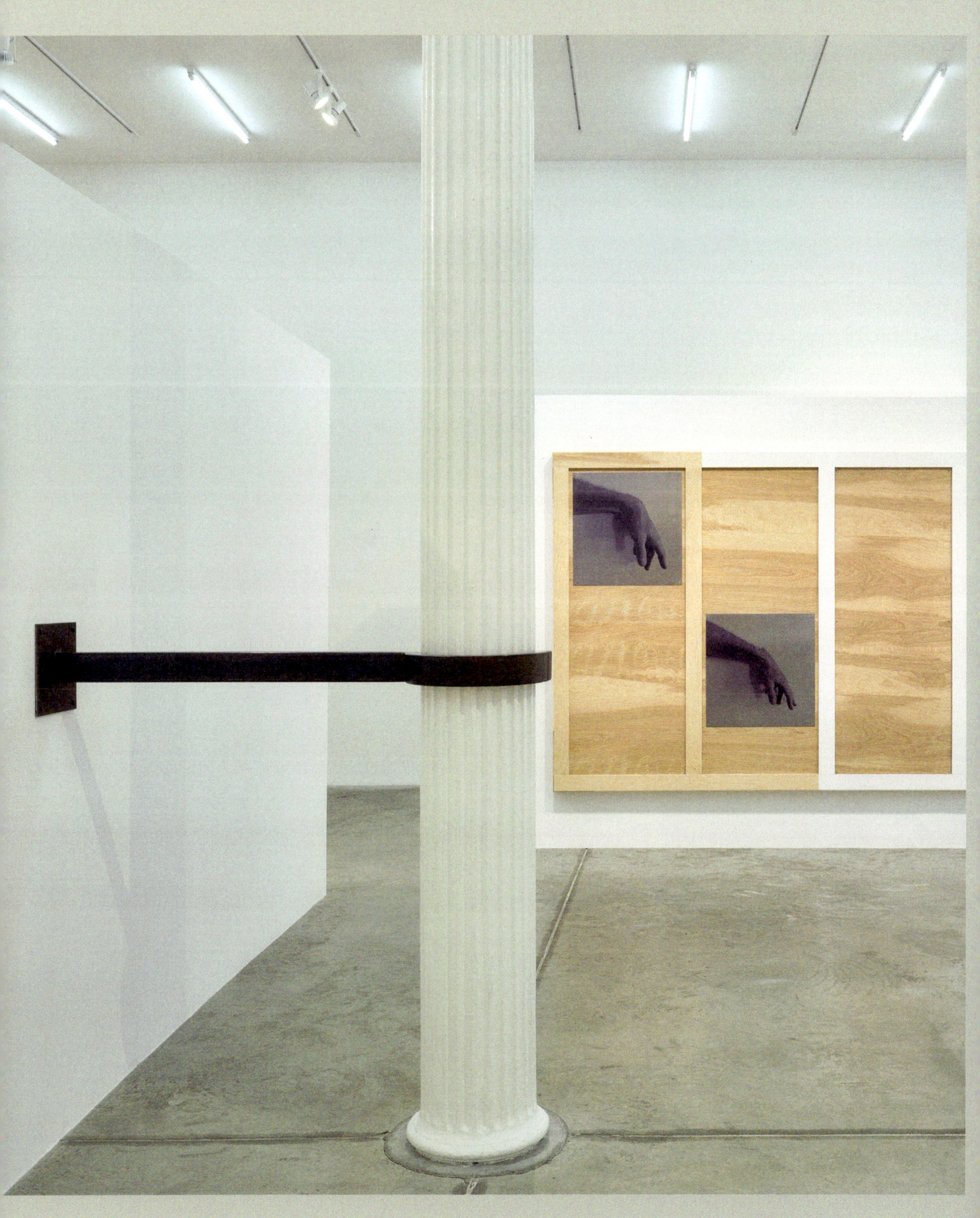

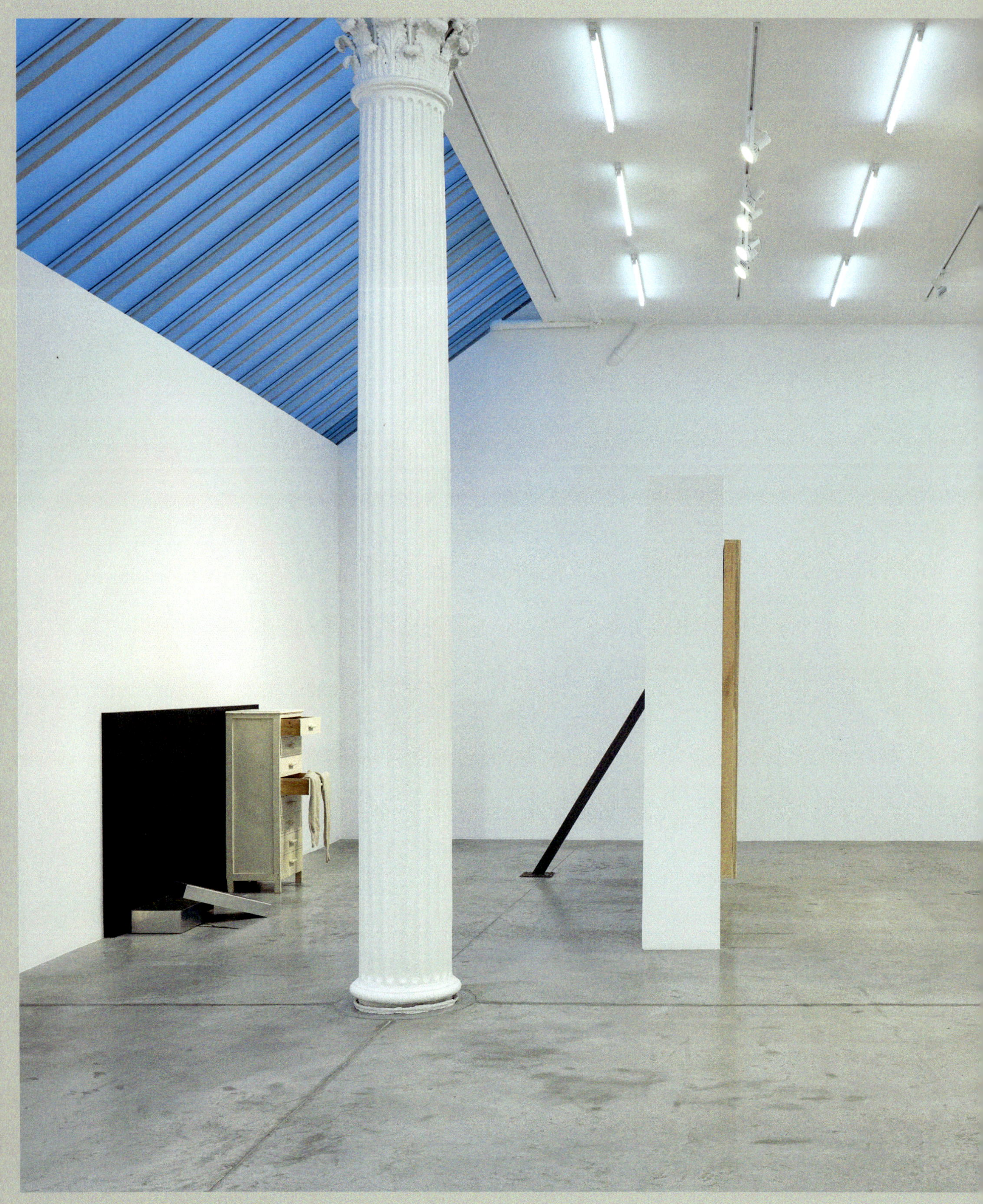

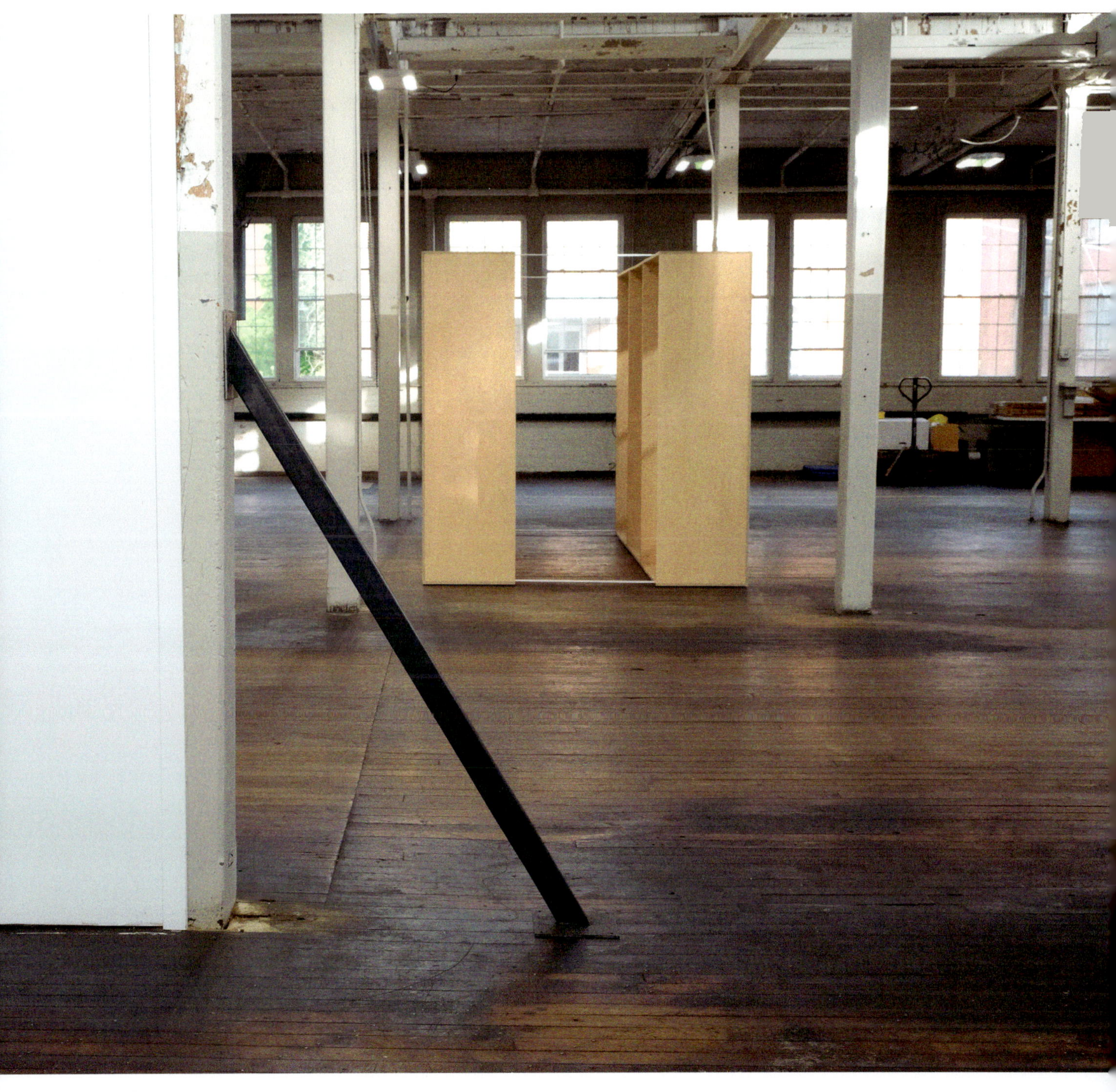

Artworks change their look over time and plywood can make change visible in multiple ways: The color will darken if it's not sealed, and many times even if it is. The layers can shift, the knots become more pronounced, or the surface begins to ripple from underneath, or the whole sheet can warp. *Construction of an American Garden* was built better in Torrington than it had been originally. Back in 1993 the piece was put together quickly—we were always up against the clock, it seemed—and because it was installed outside where it would be exposed to the elements, to the street, and only had to last for a month, it was fairly rudimentary in its construction. For *Torrington Project*, Nick devised an entire drainage system within the plywood planter, complete with a small drawer to periodically empty the runoff, making it easier to preserve the foliage. It was built of a tougher grade of plywood, though not so high as to eliminate the visible grain and the swirls and patterning of the wood, which kept its crate-like language in place. These changes allowed it to last for the duration of the project with water flowing through it and the weight of multiple bags of soil suspended within its volume. They also gave the work, as I had hoped, a slightly more mature presence, emphasizing its versions, iterations, or the difference between that moment and this one. To update the work from the original, I created a rubber stamp with the name and address of the gallery, AFA, in the font Colin used, and stamped the container on the lower right corner of one of the plywood panels, like a tattoo or livestock brand.

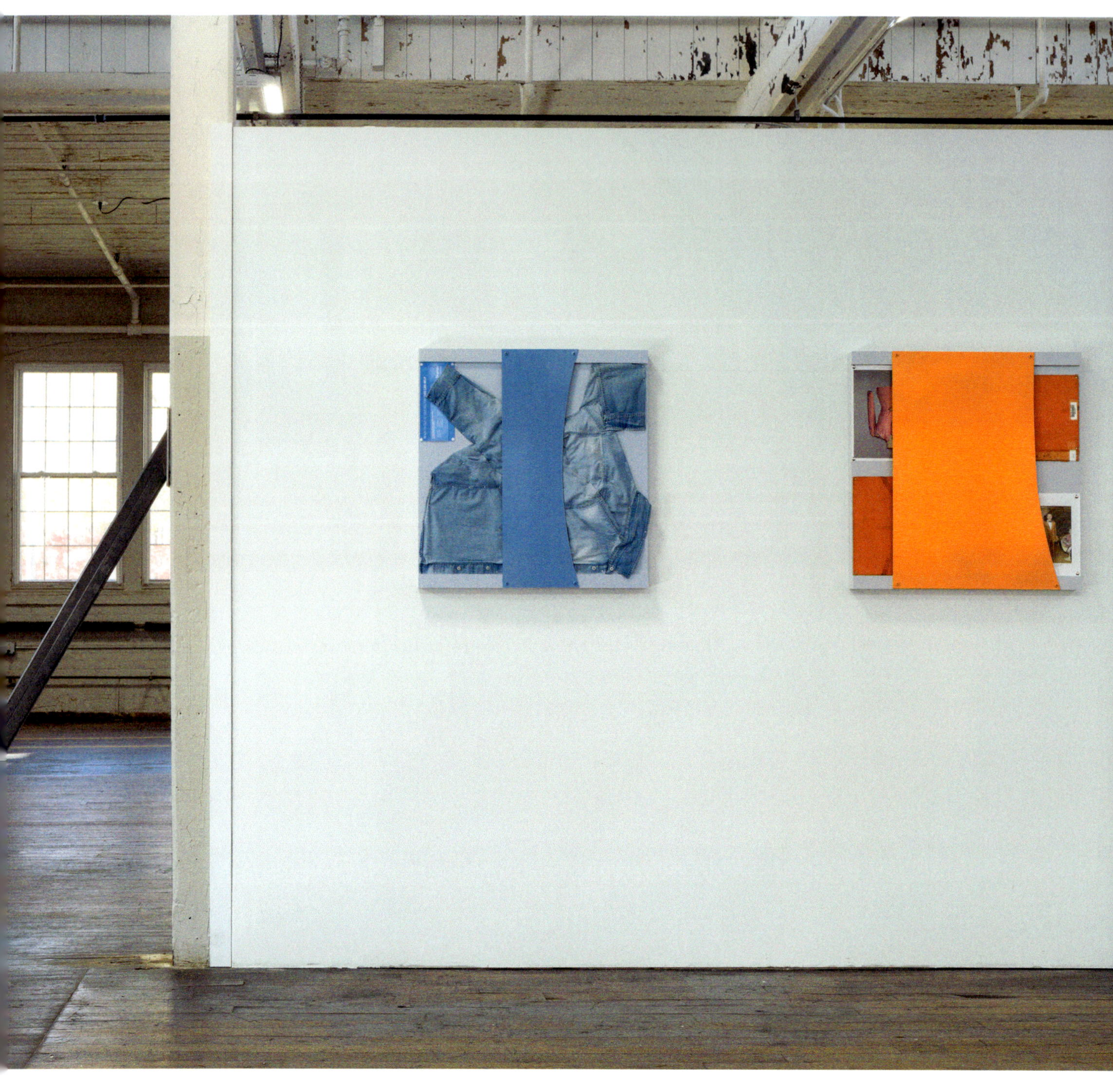

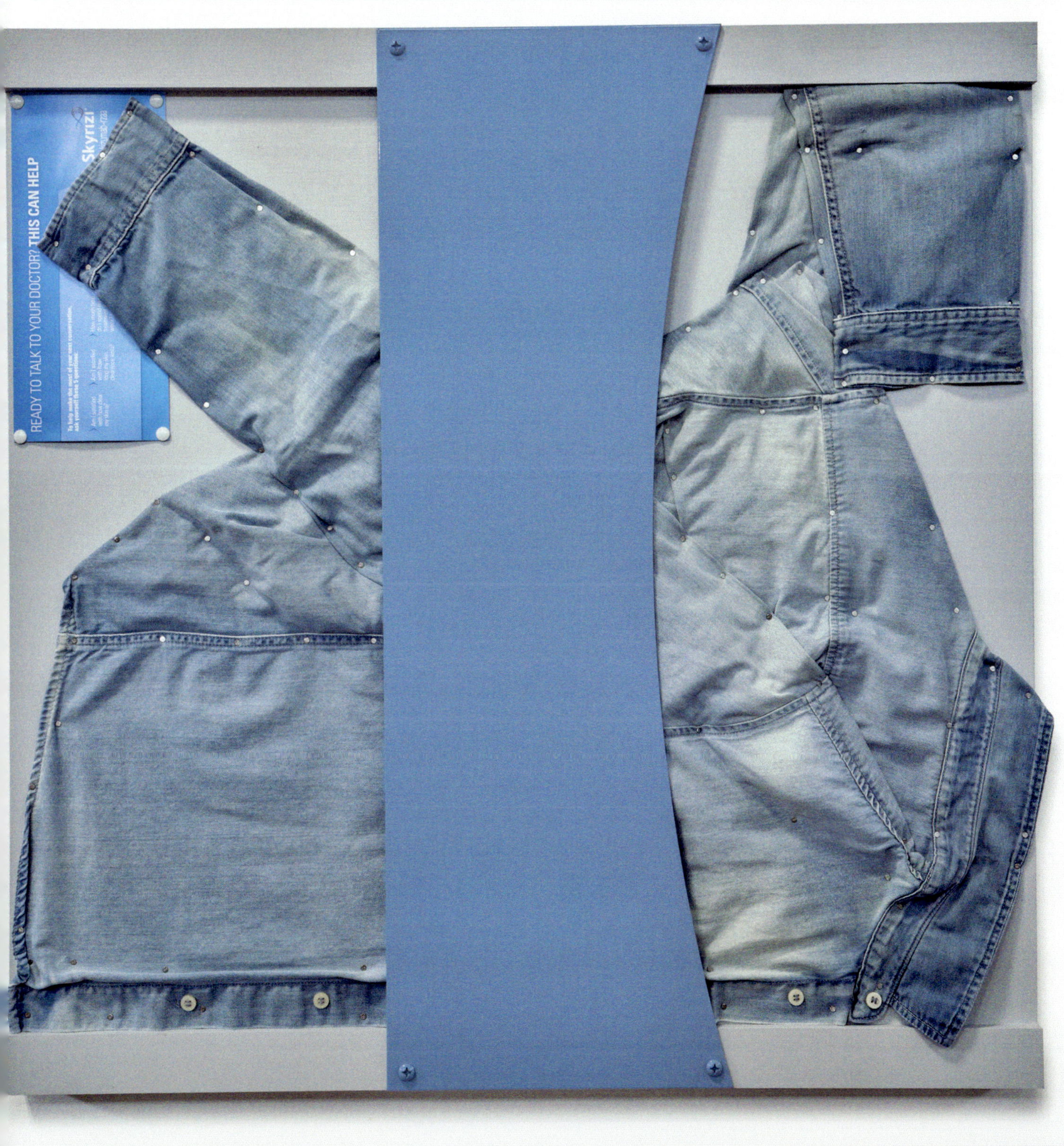

Skyrizi
READY TO TALK TO YOUR DOCTOR? THIS CAN HELP

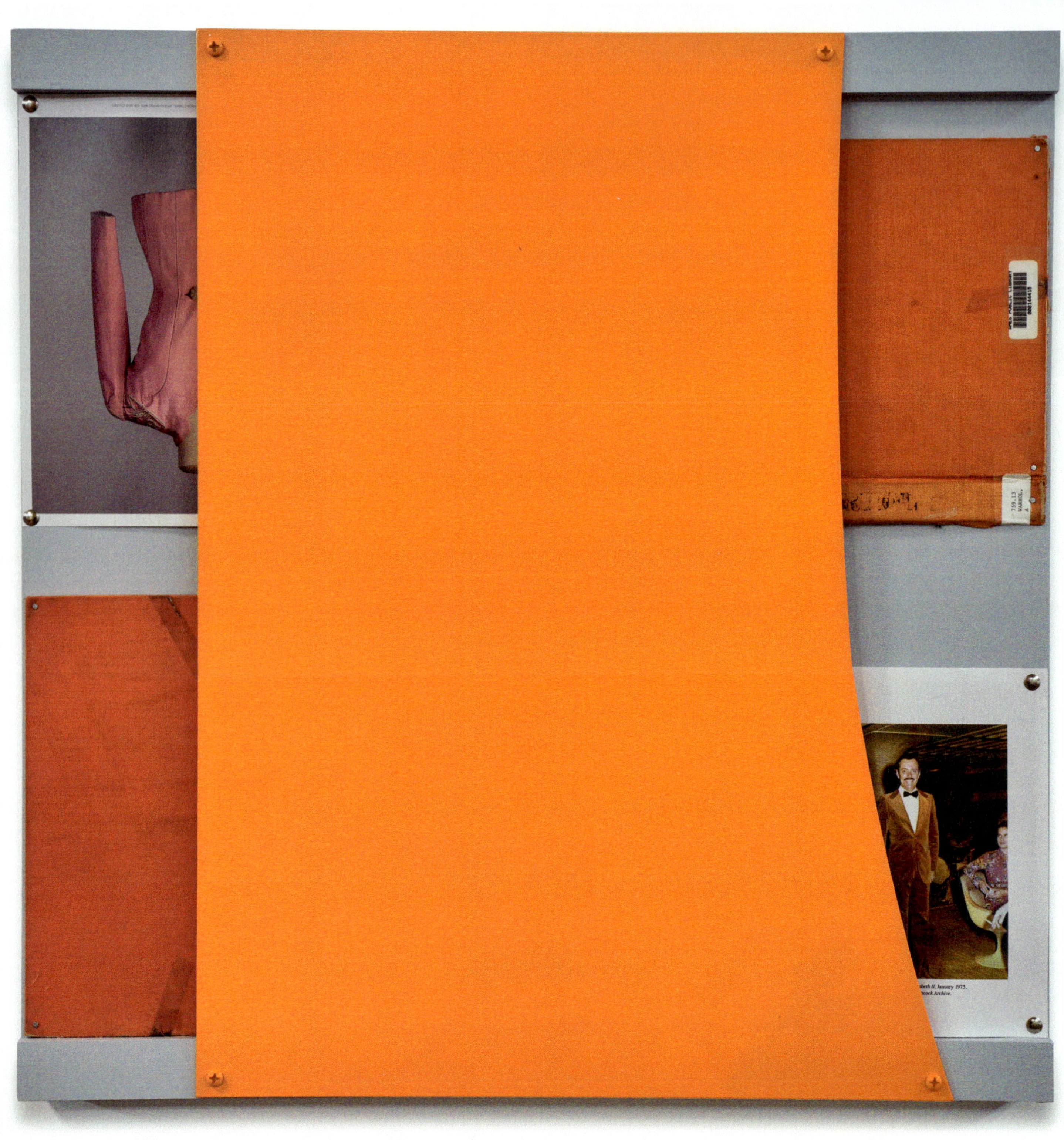

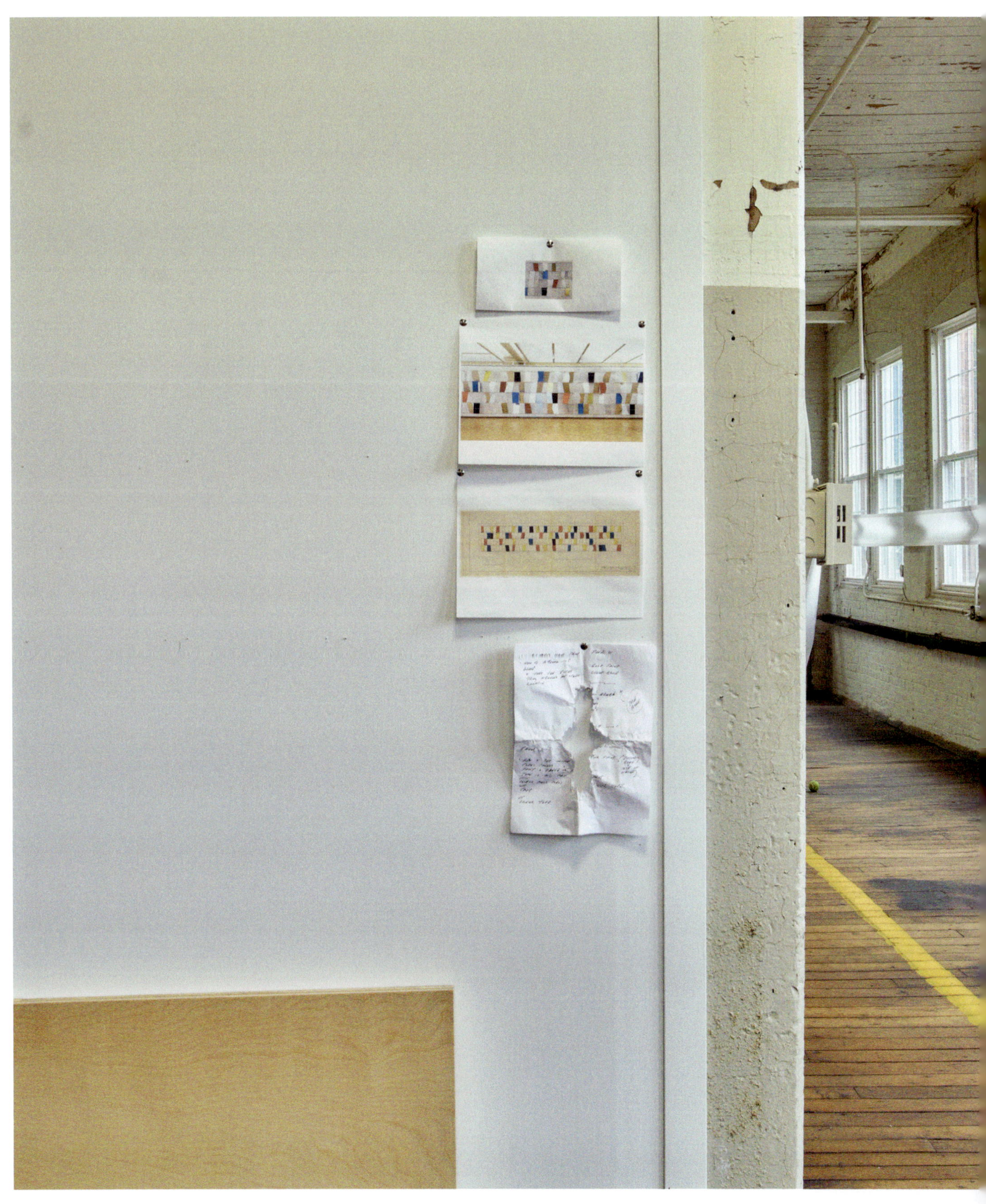

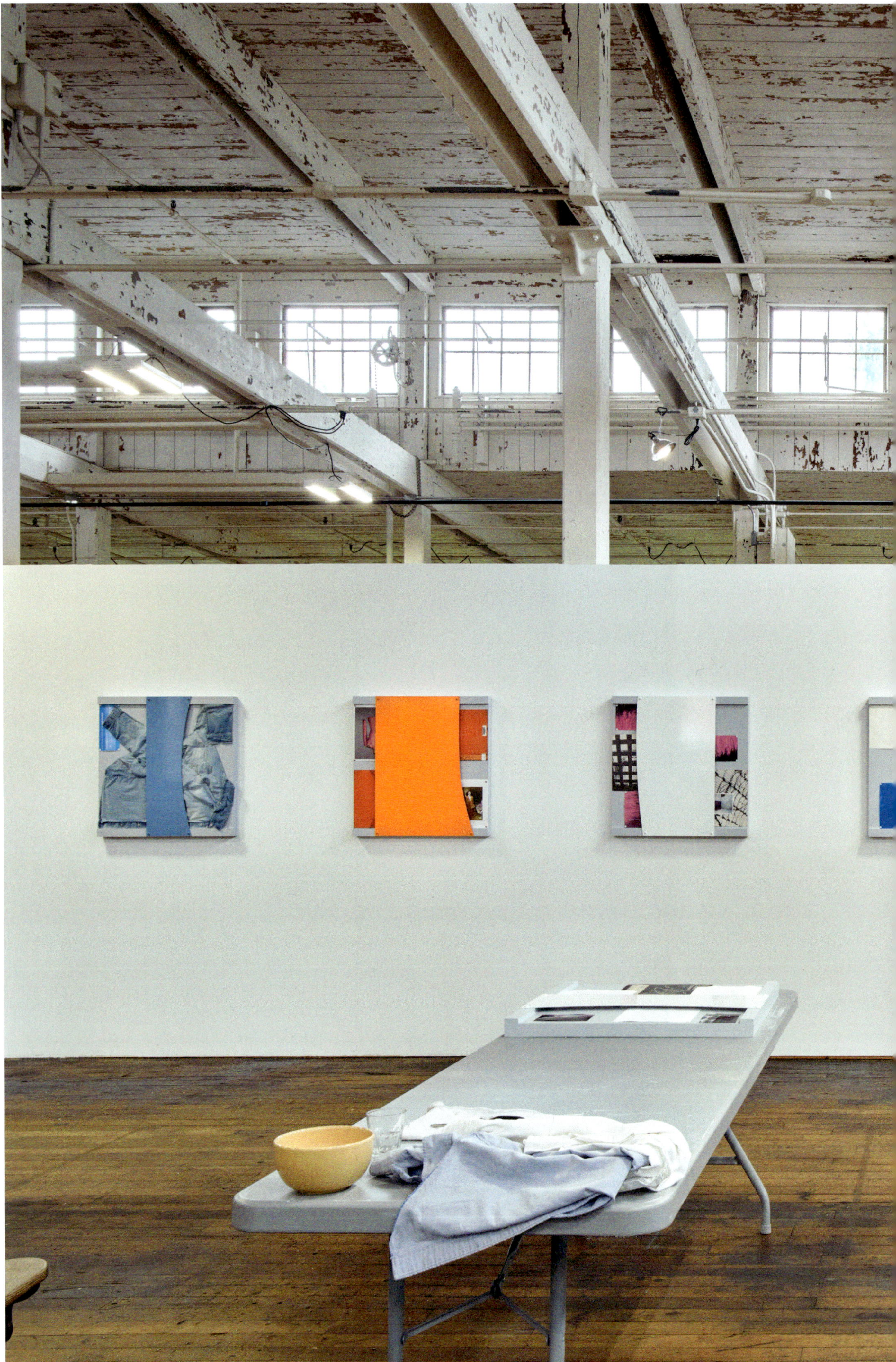

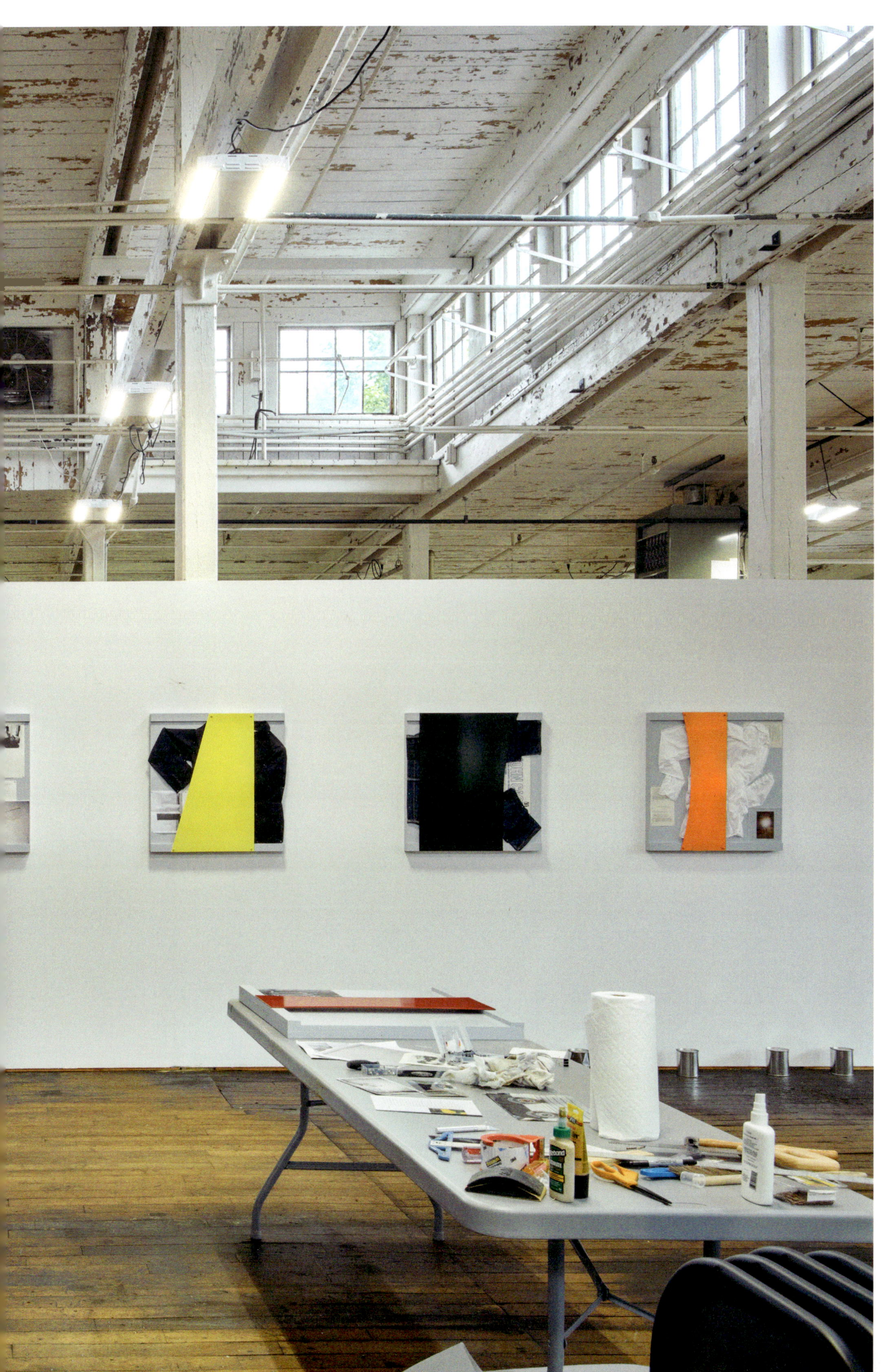

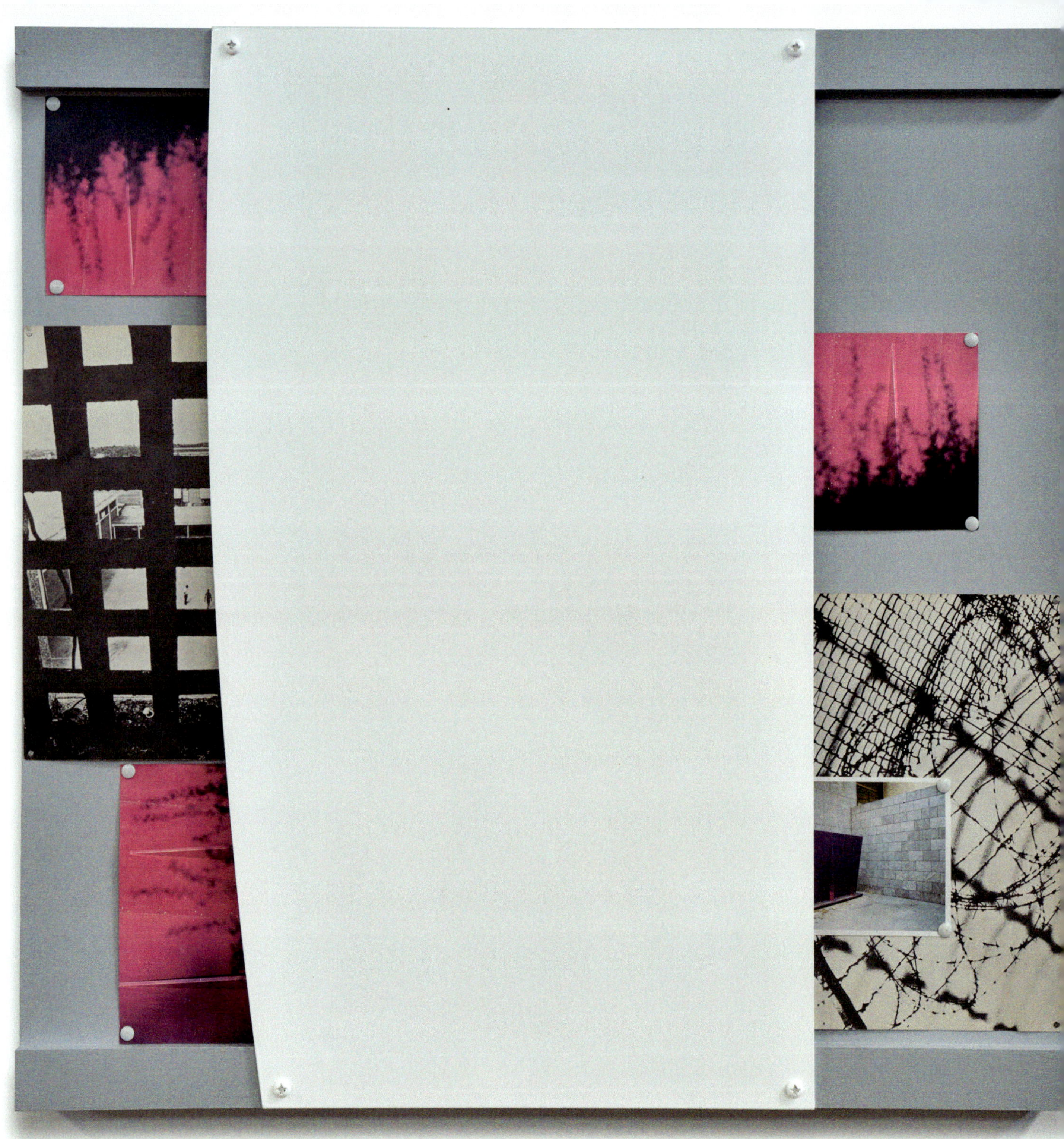

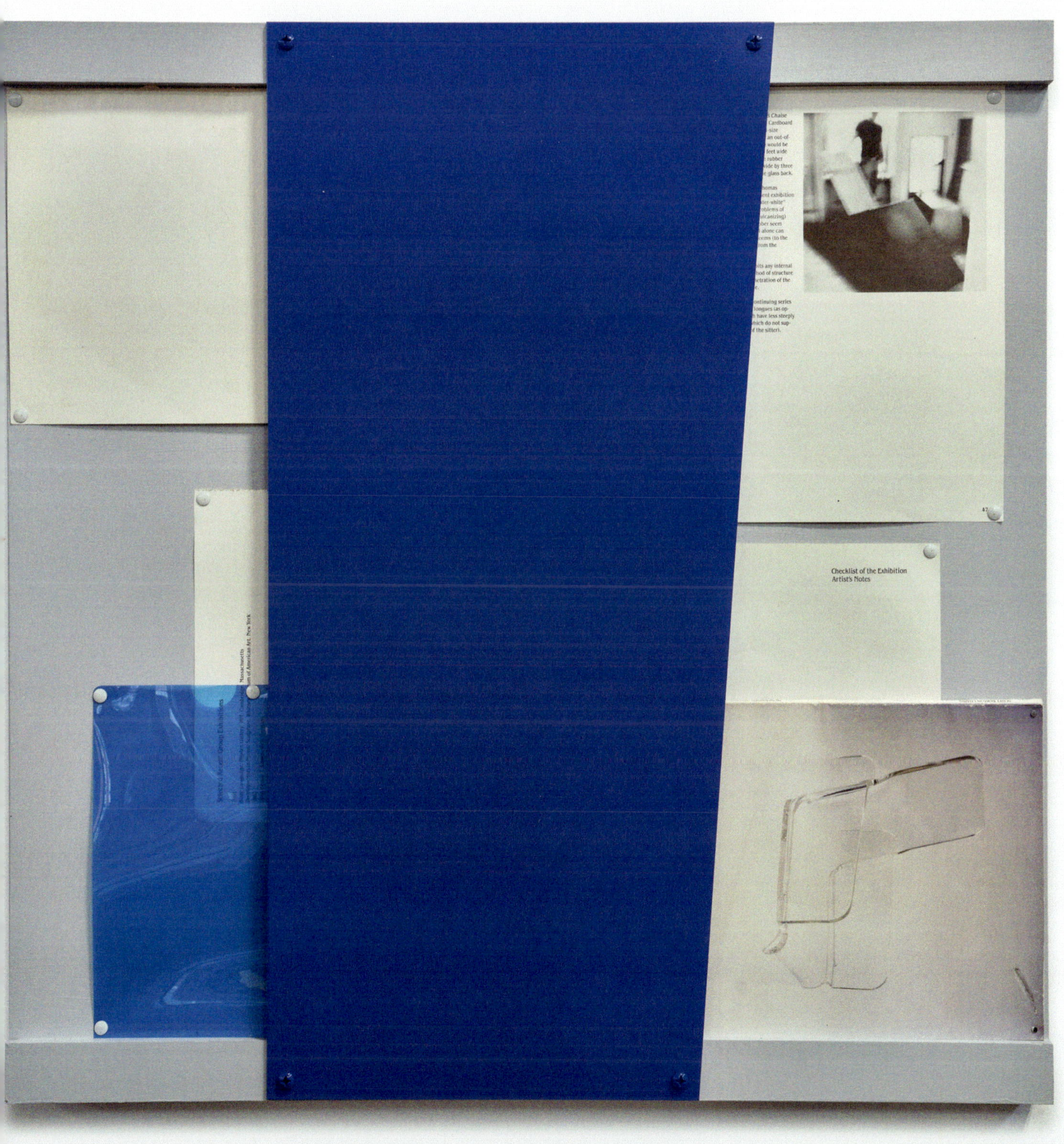

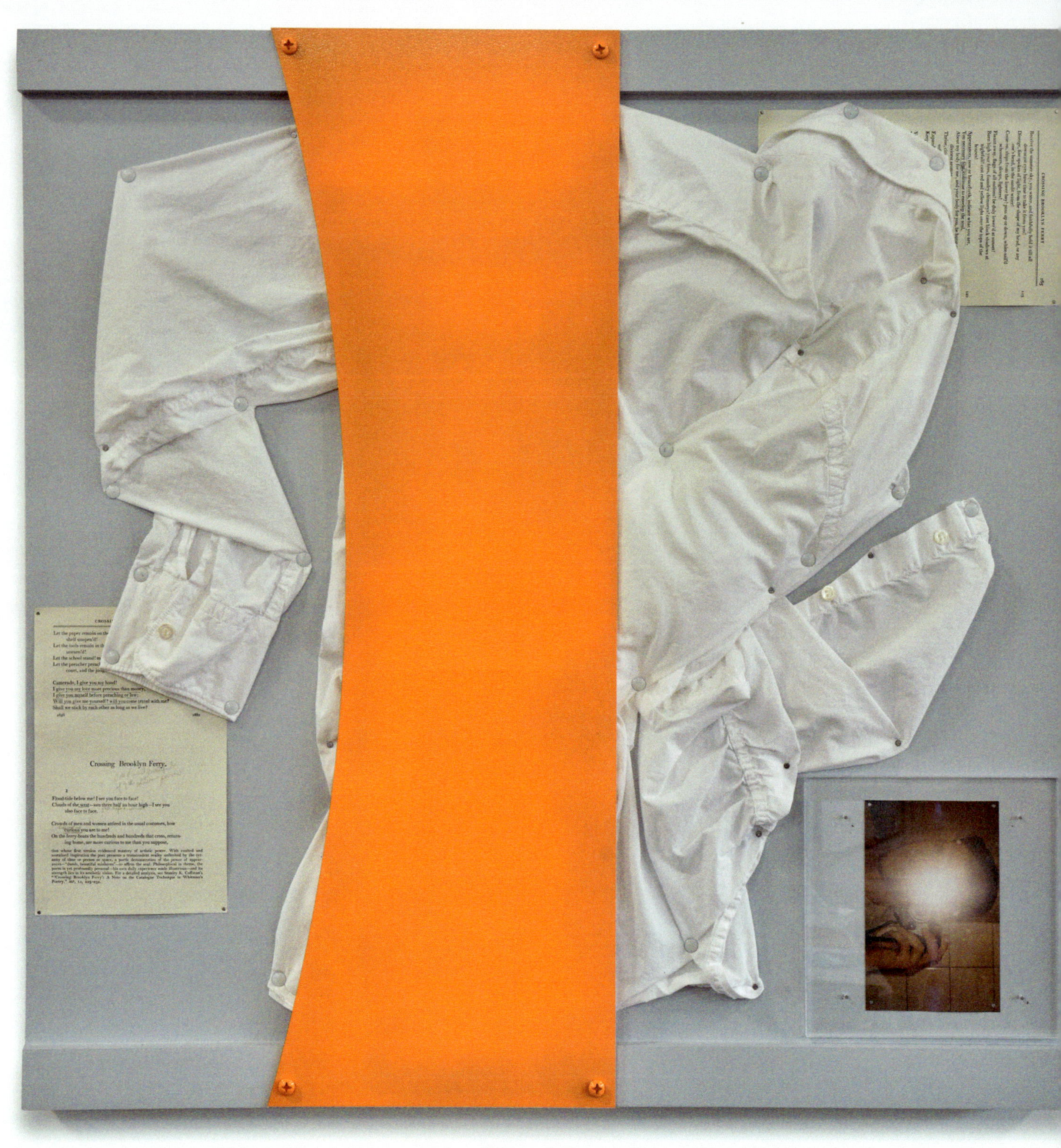

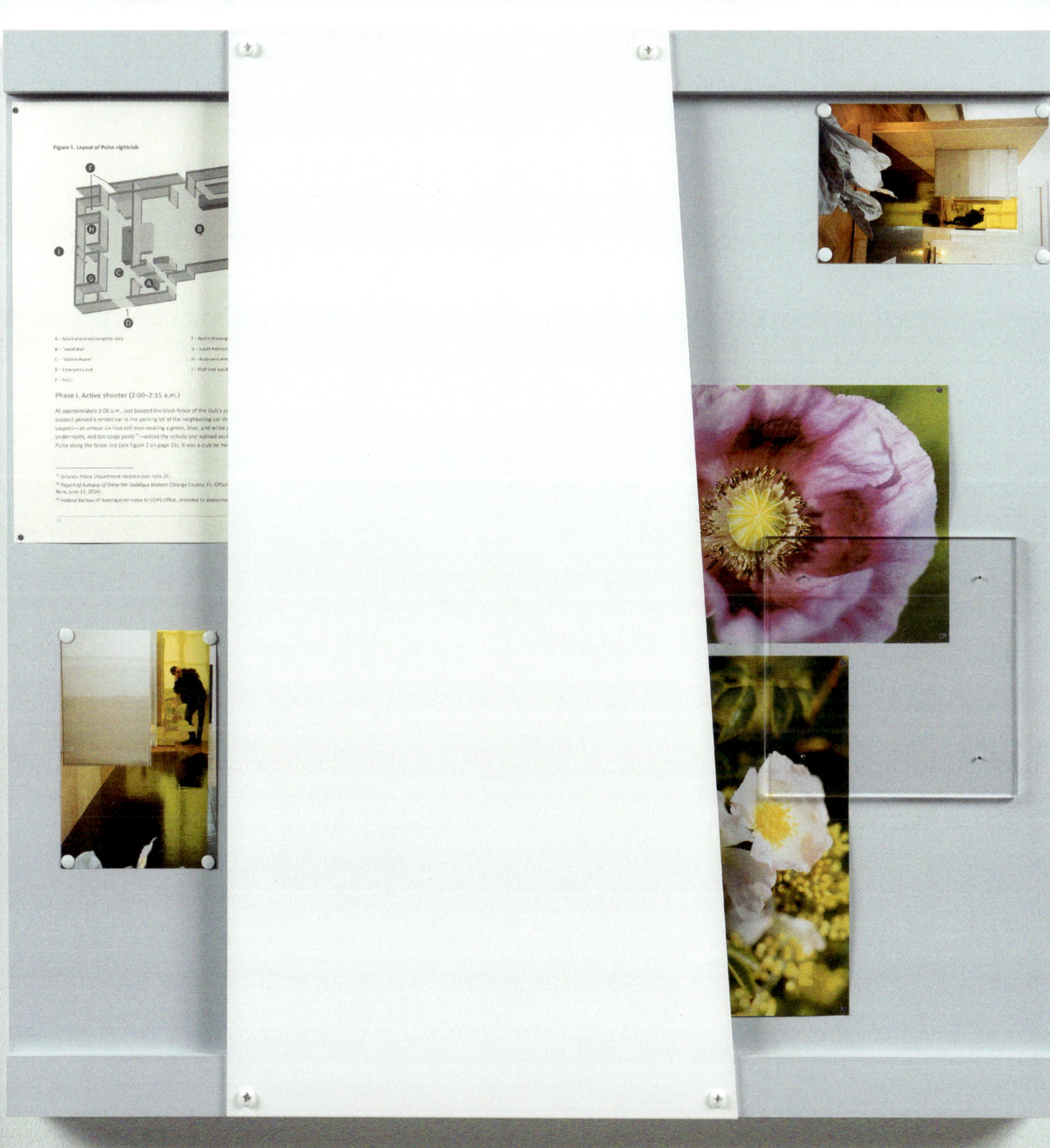

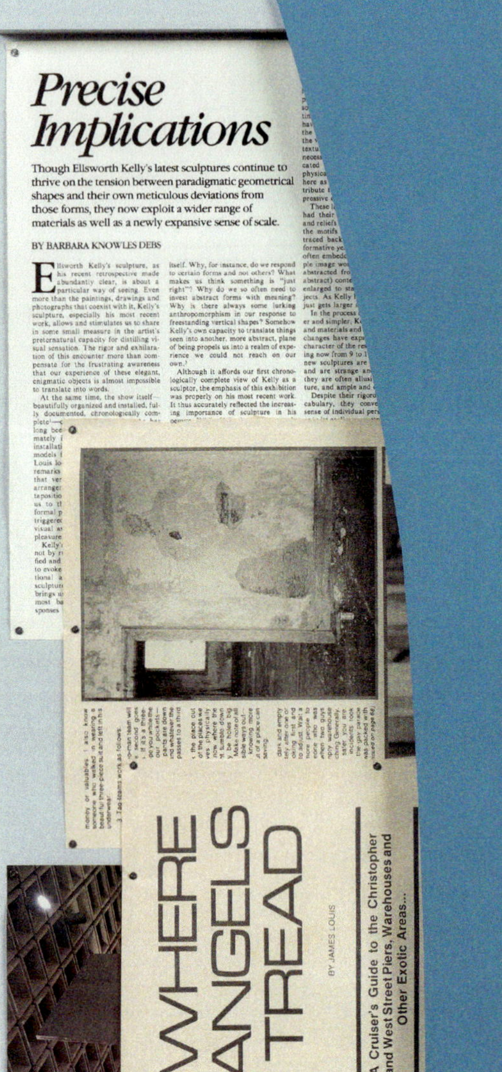

Precise
Implications
Though Ellsworth Kelly's latest sculptures continue to thrive on the tension between paradigmatic geometrical shapes and their own meticulous deviations from those forms, they now exploit a wider range of materials as well as a newly expansive sense of scale.
BY BARBARA KNOWLES DEBS
WHERE ANGELS TREAD
BY JAMES LOUIS
A Cruiser's Guide to the Christopher and West Street Piers, Warehouses and Other Exotic Areas...
ANGELS
Keep your money and valuables at home because the slimmer the pickings, the safer for all of us.

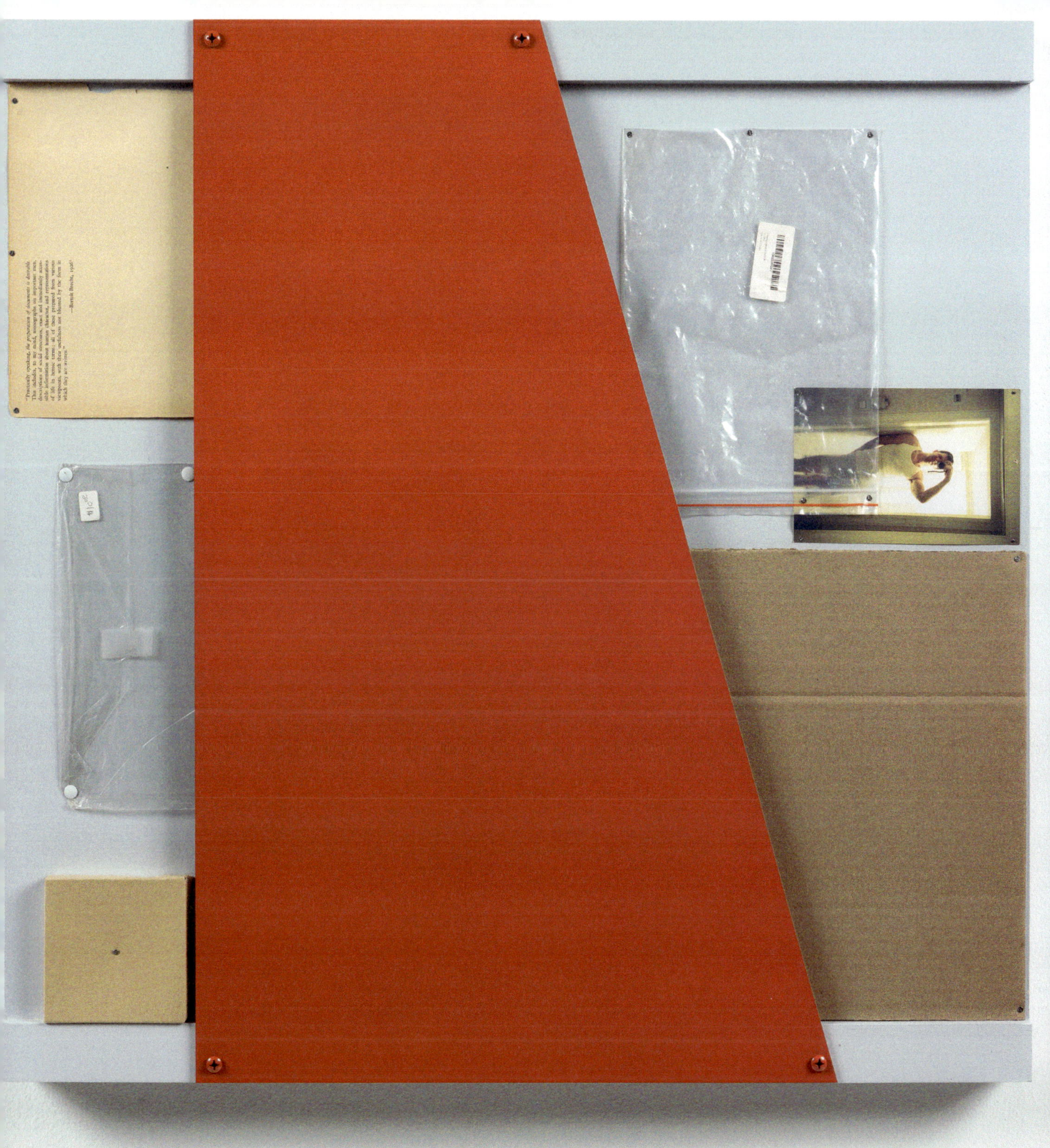

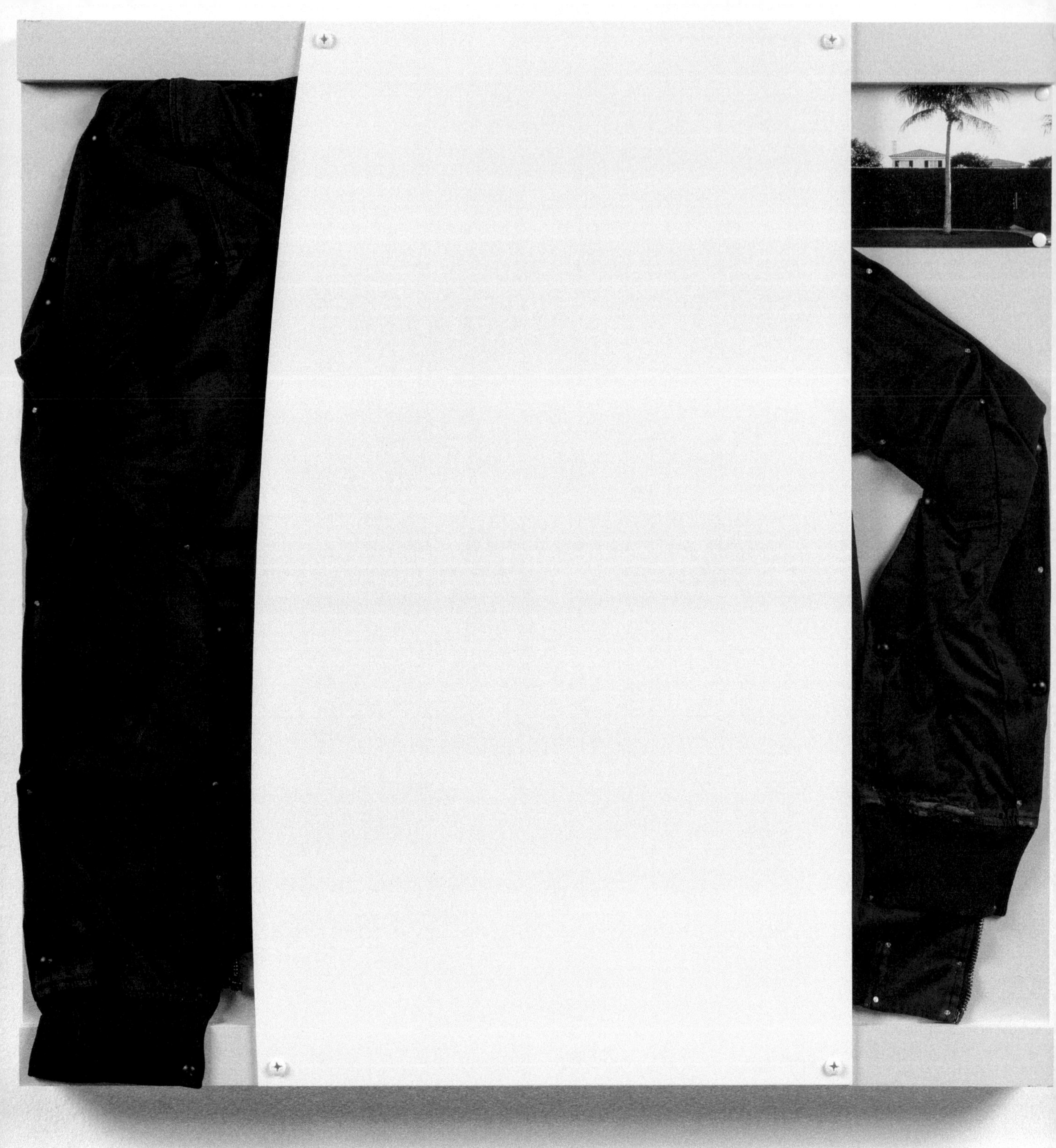

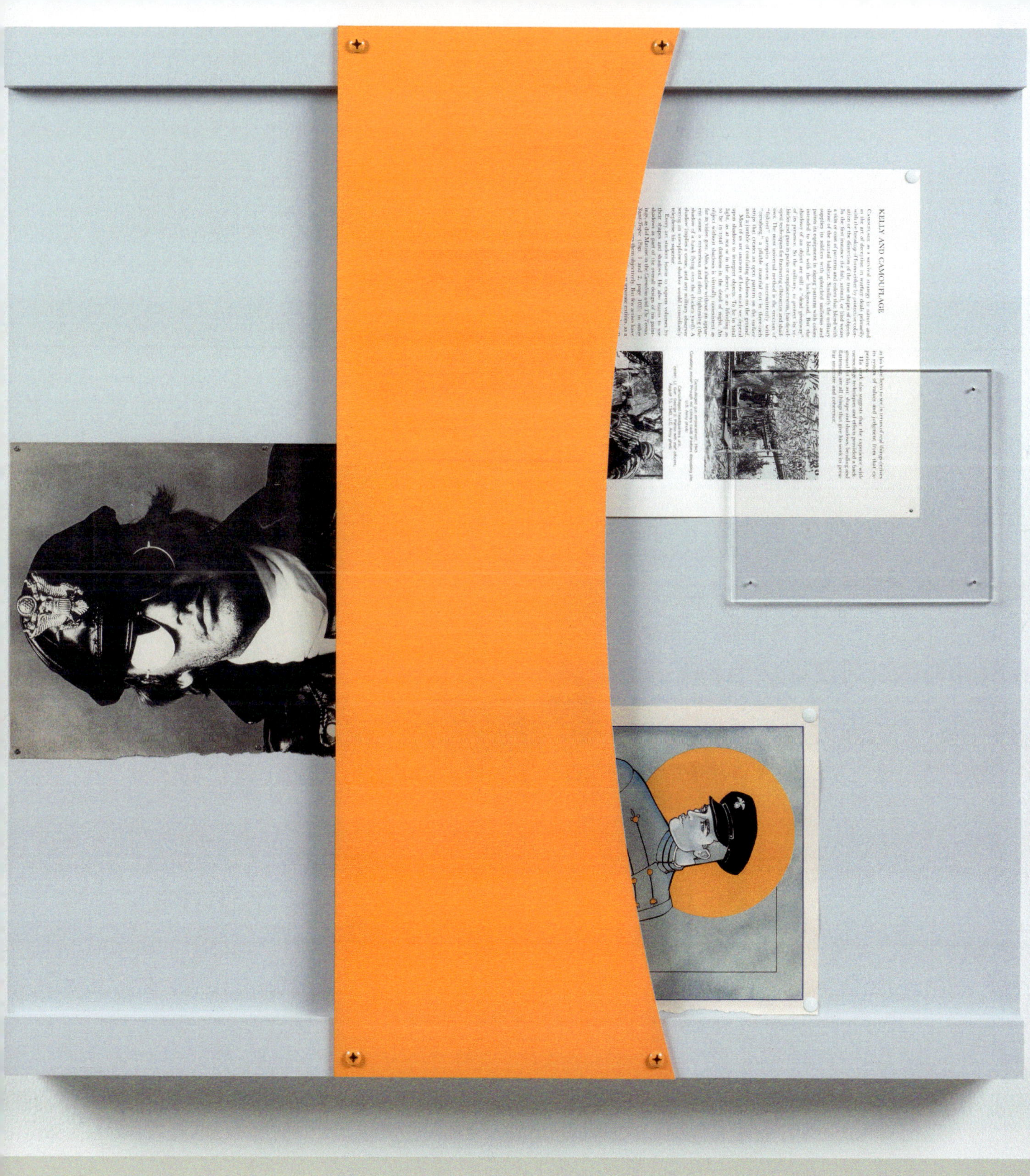

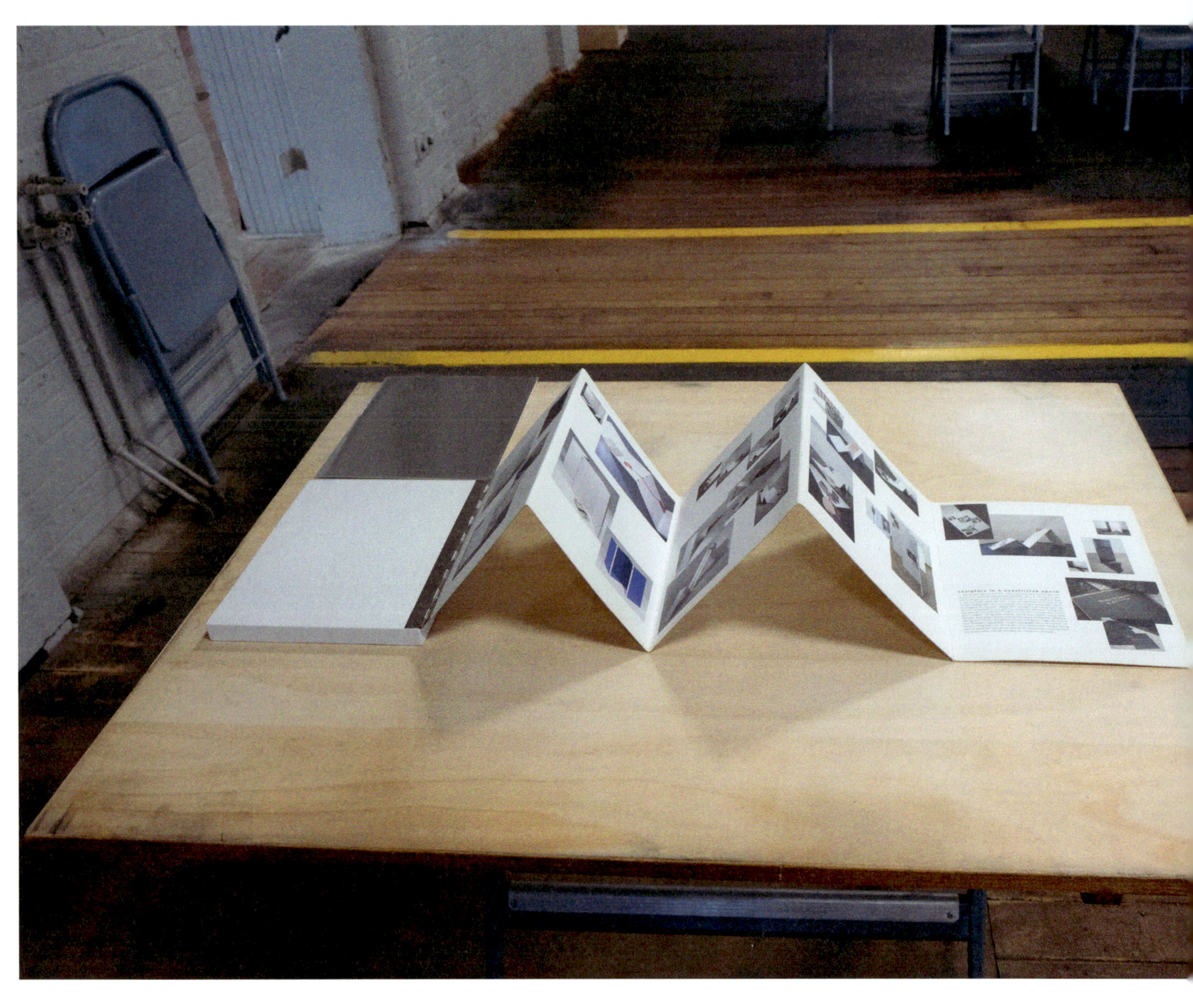

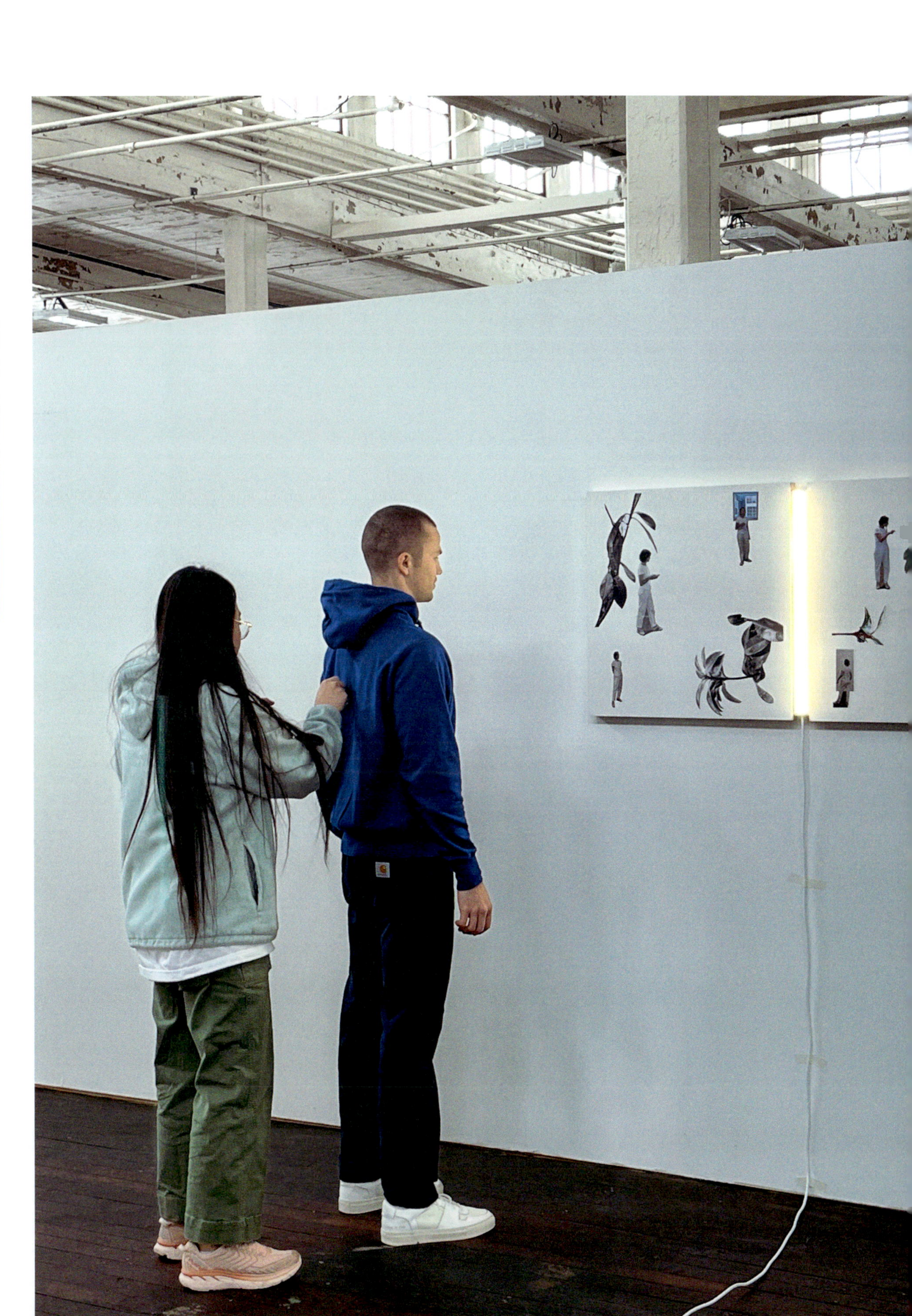

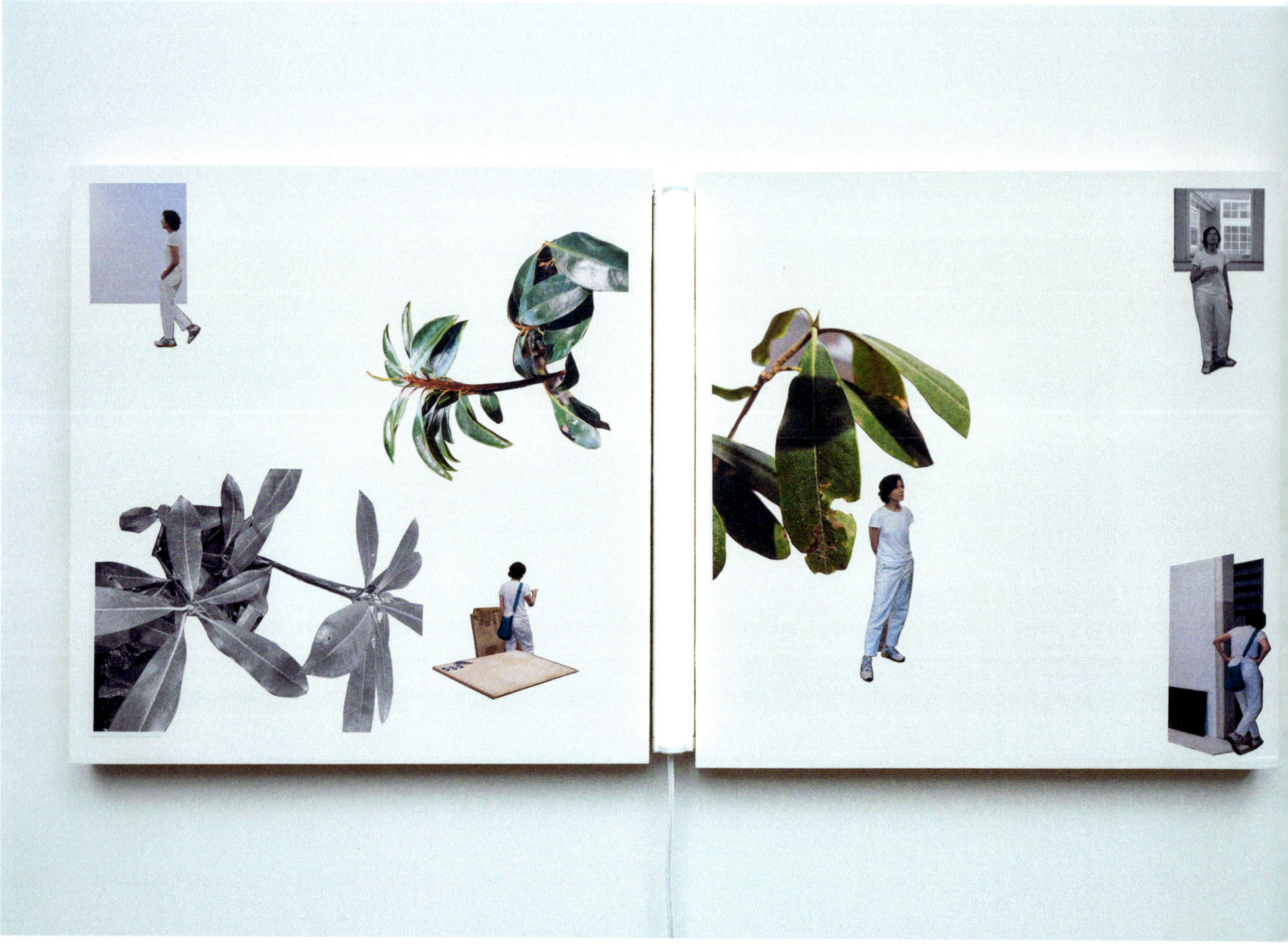

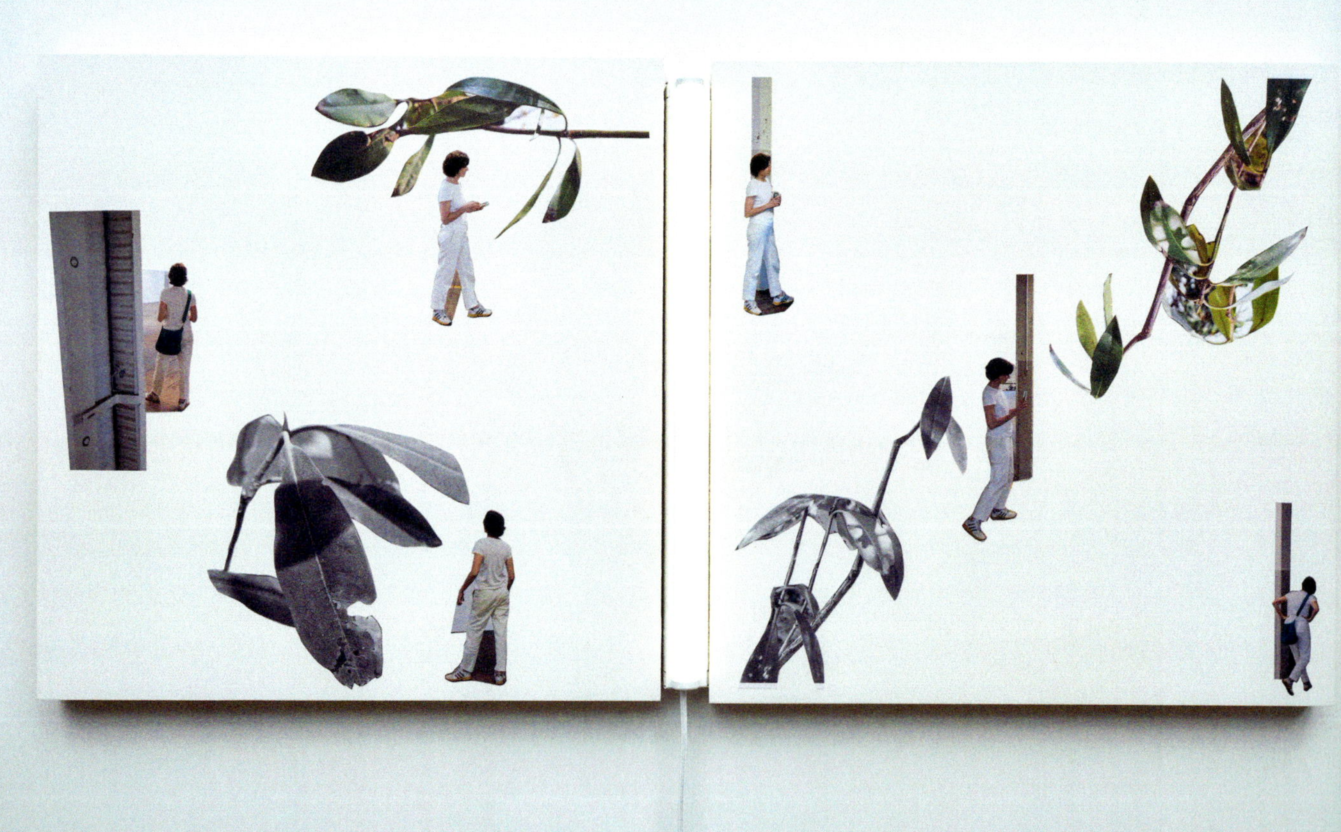

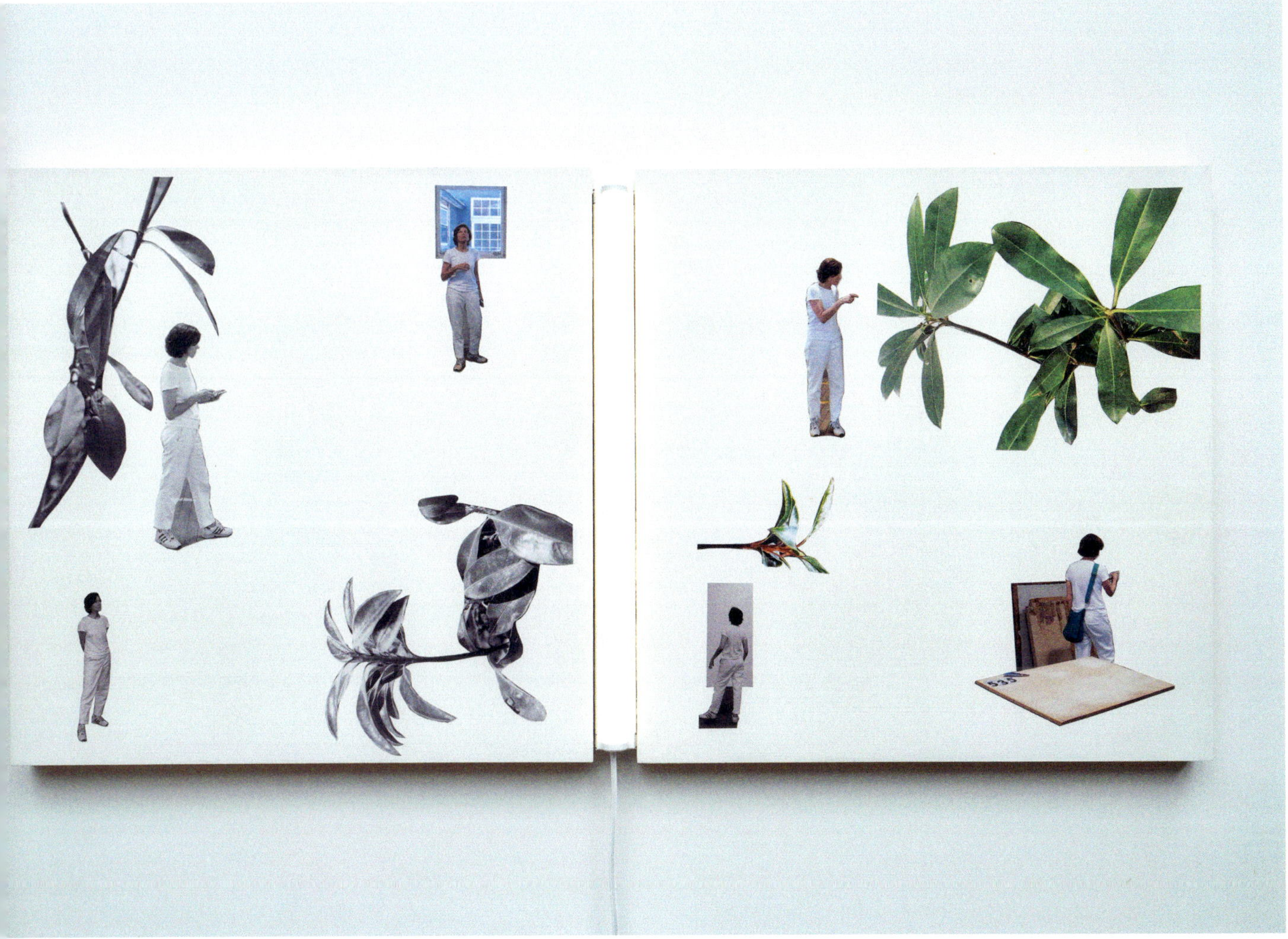

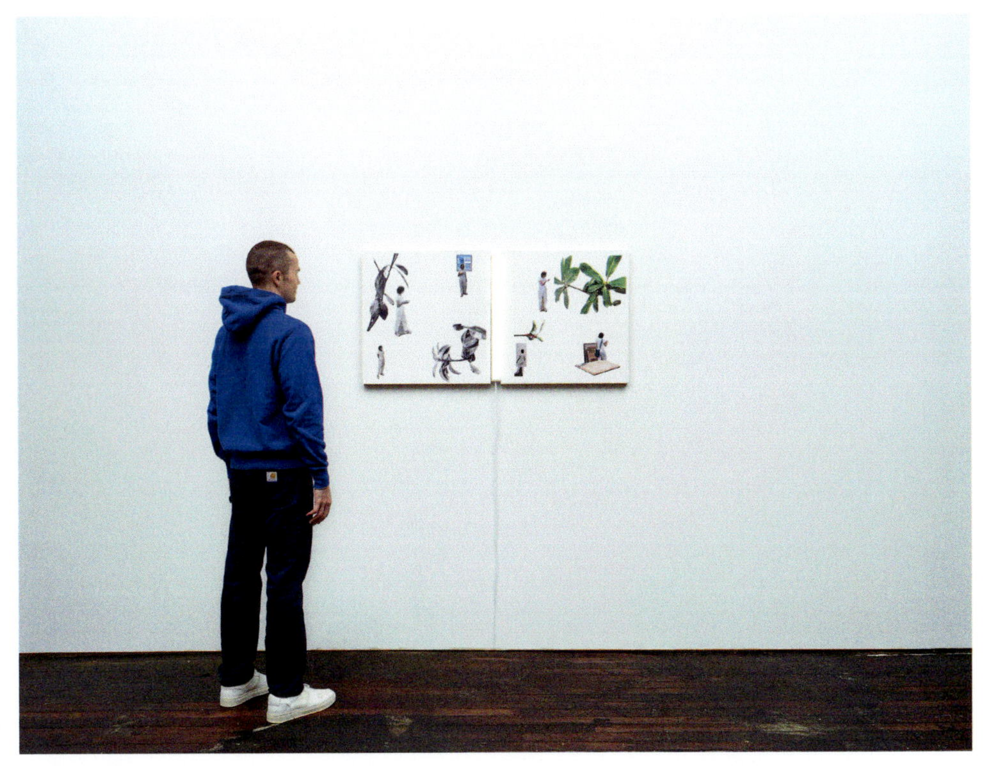

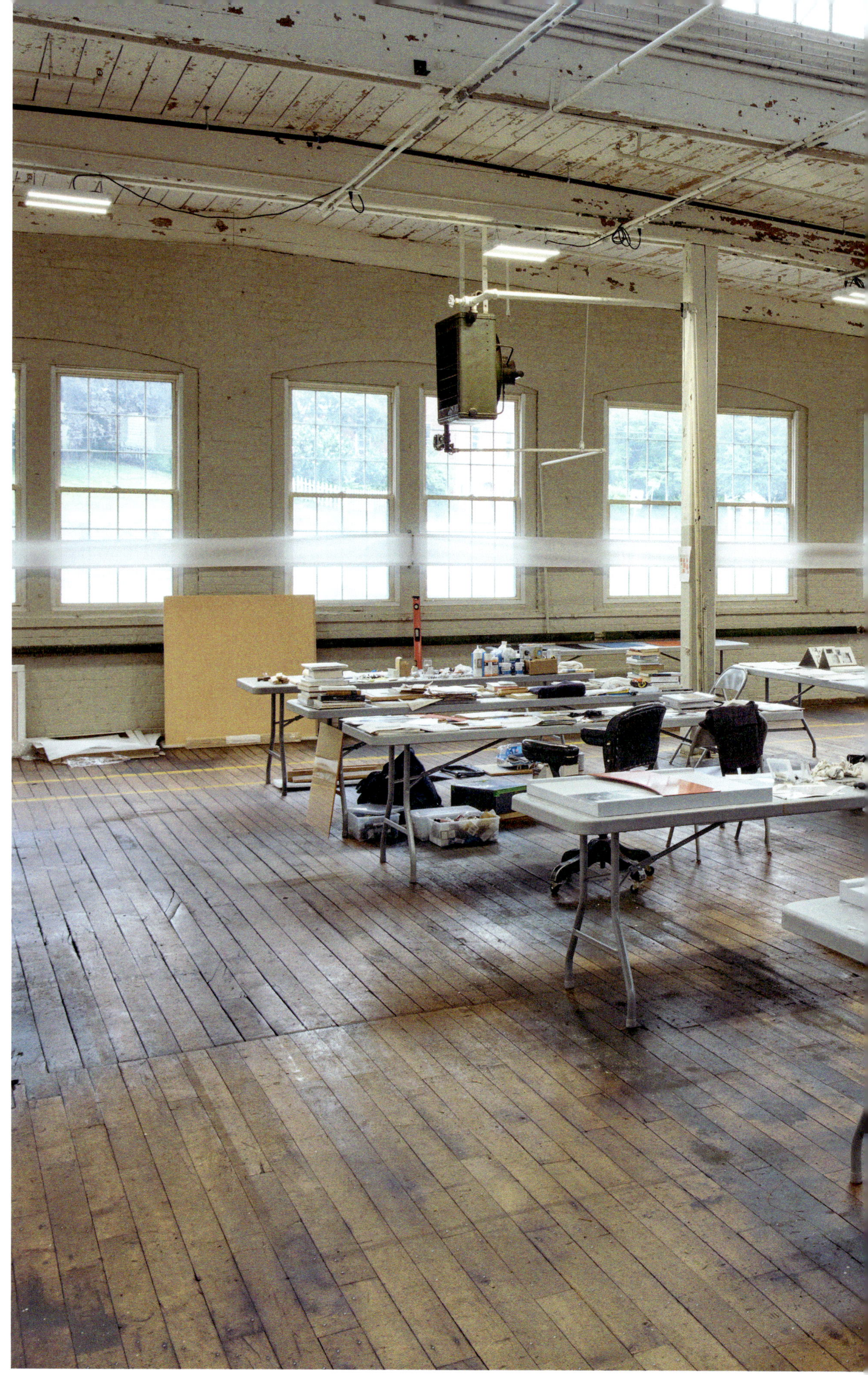

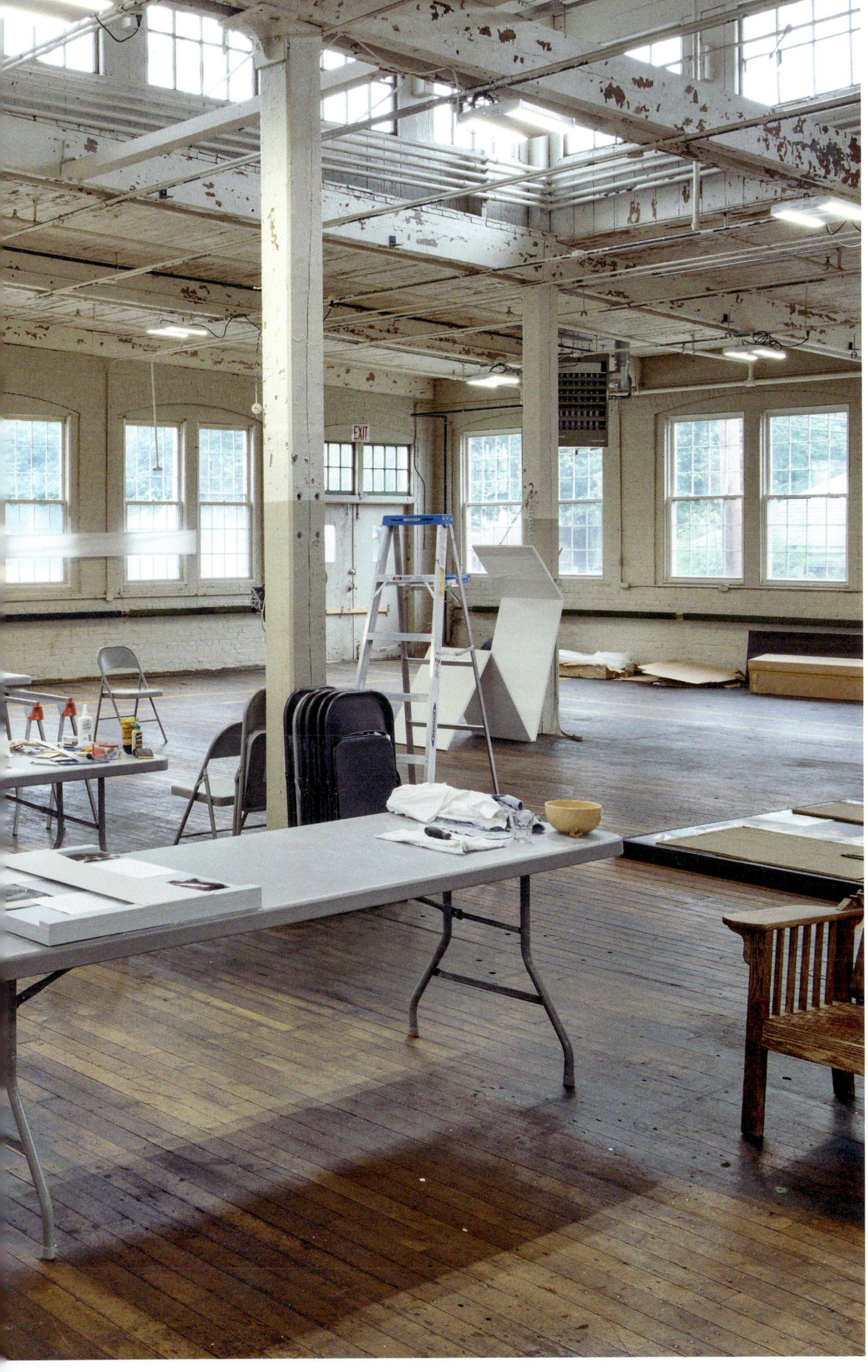

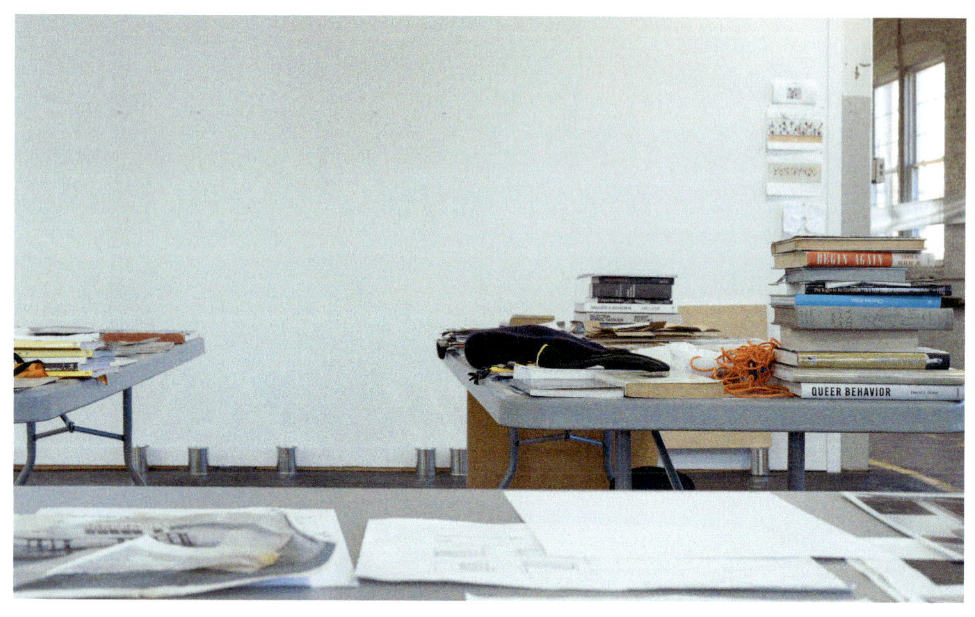

170

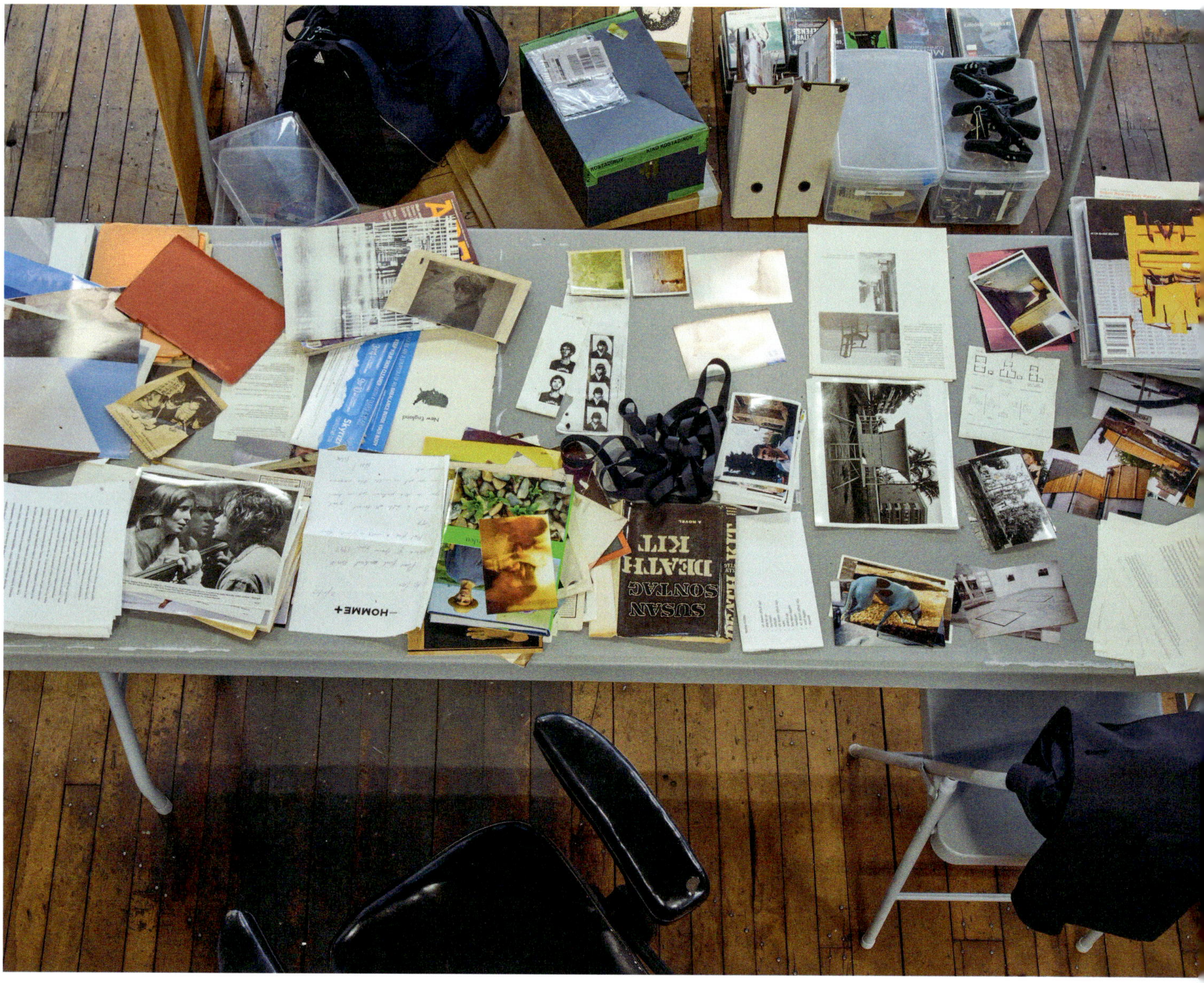

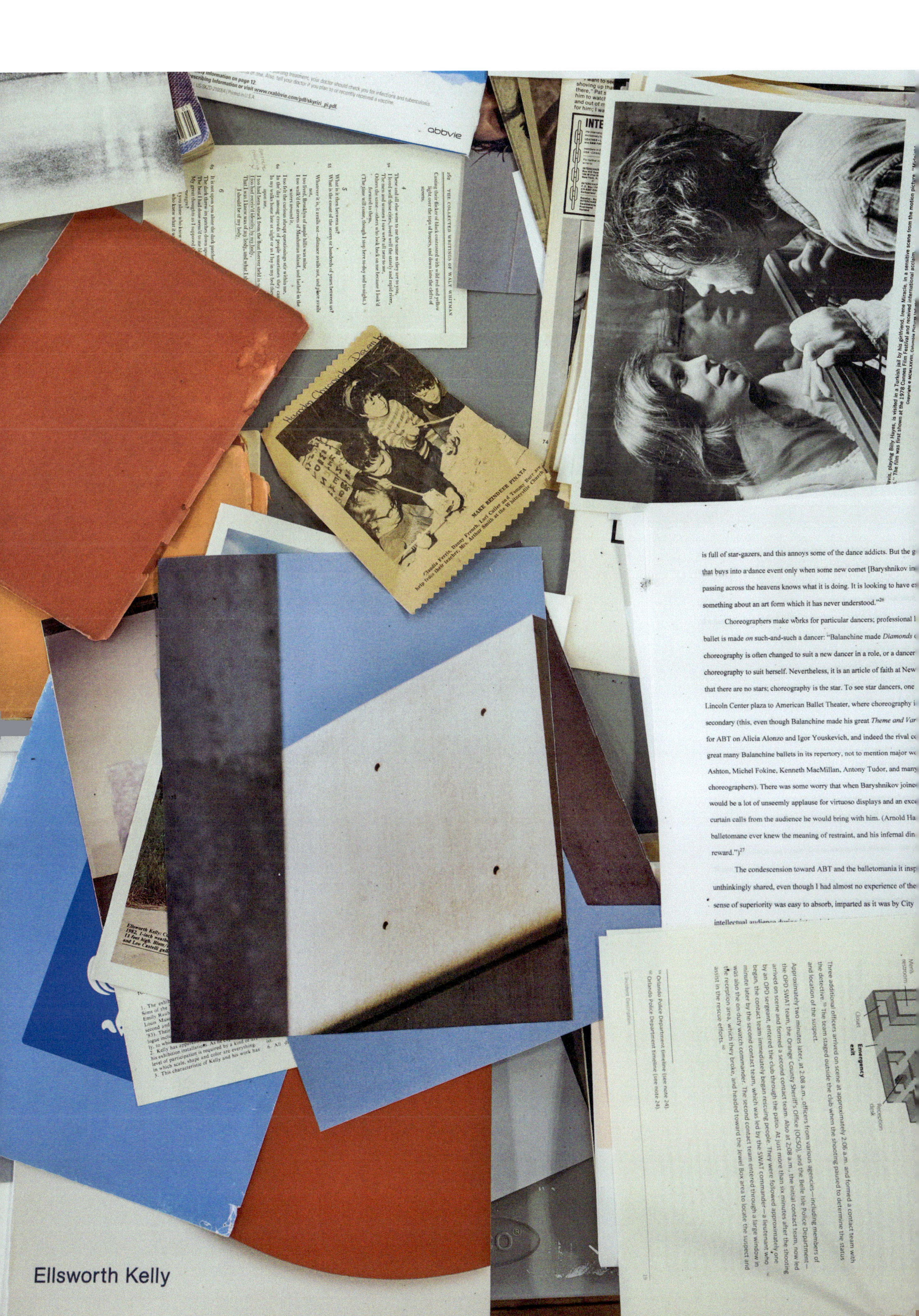

Ellsworth Kelly

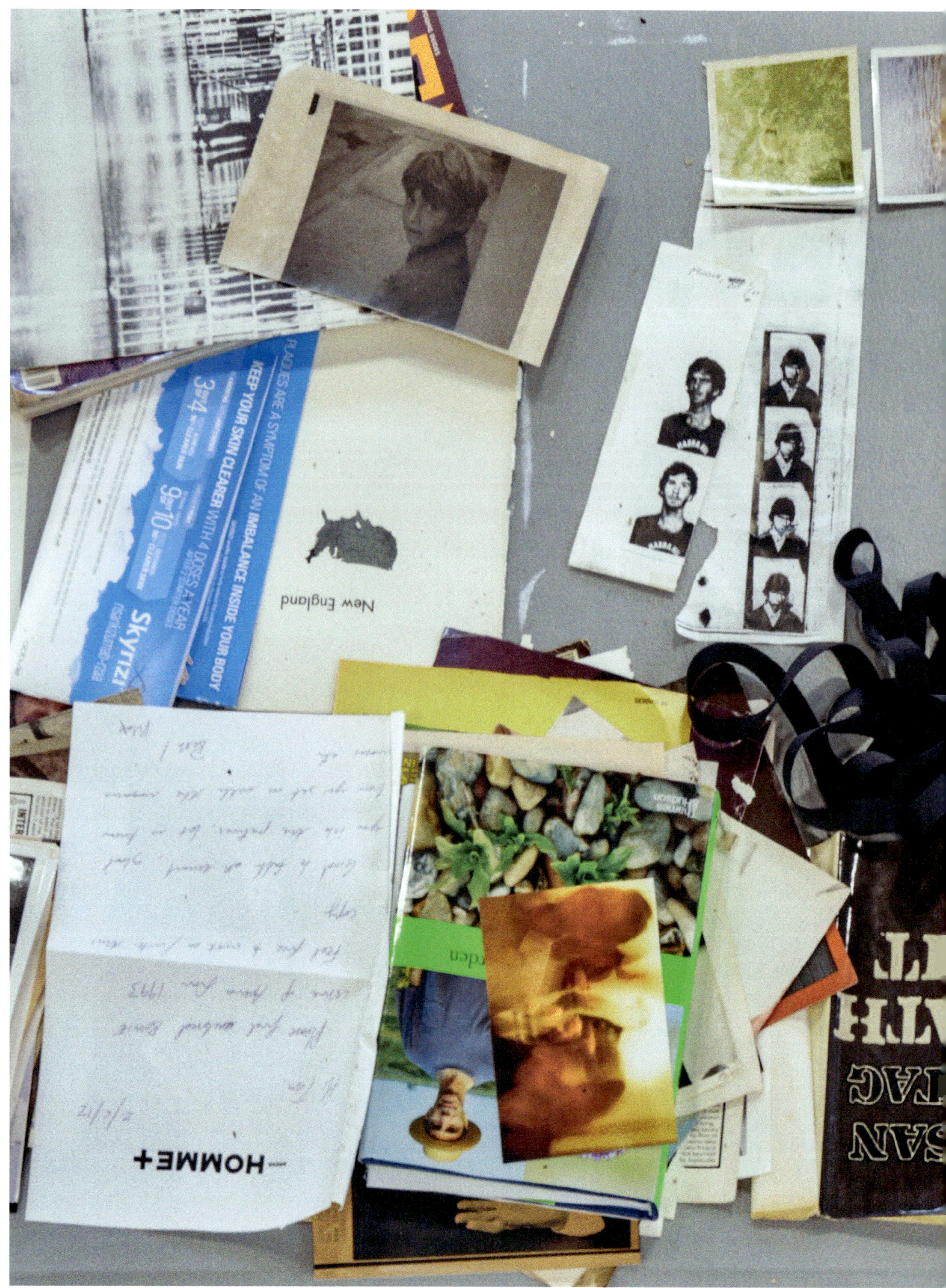

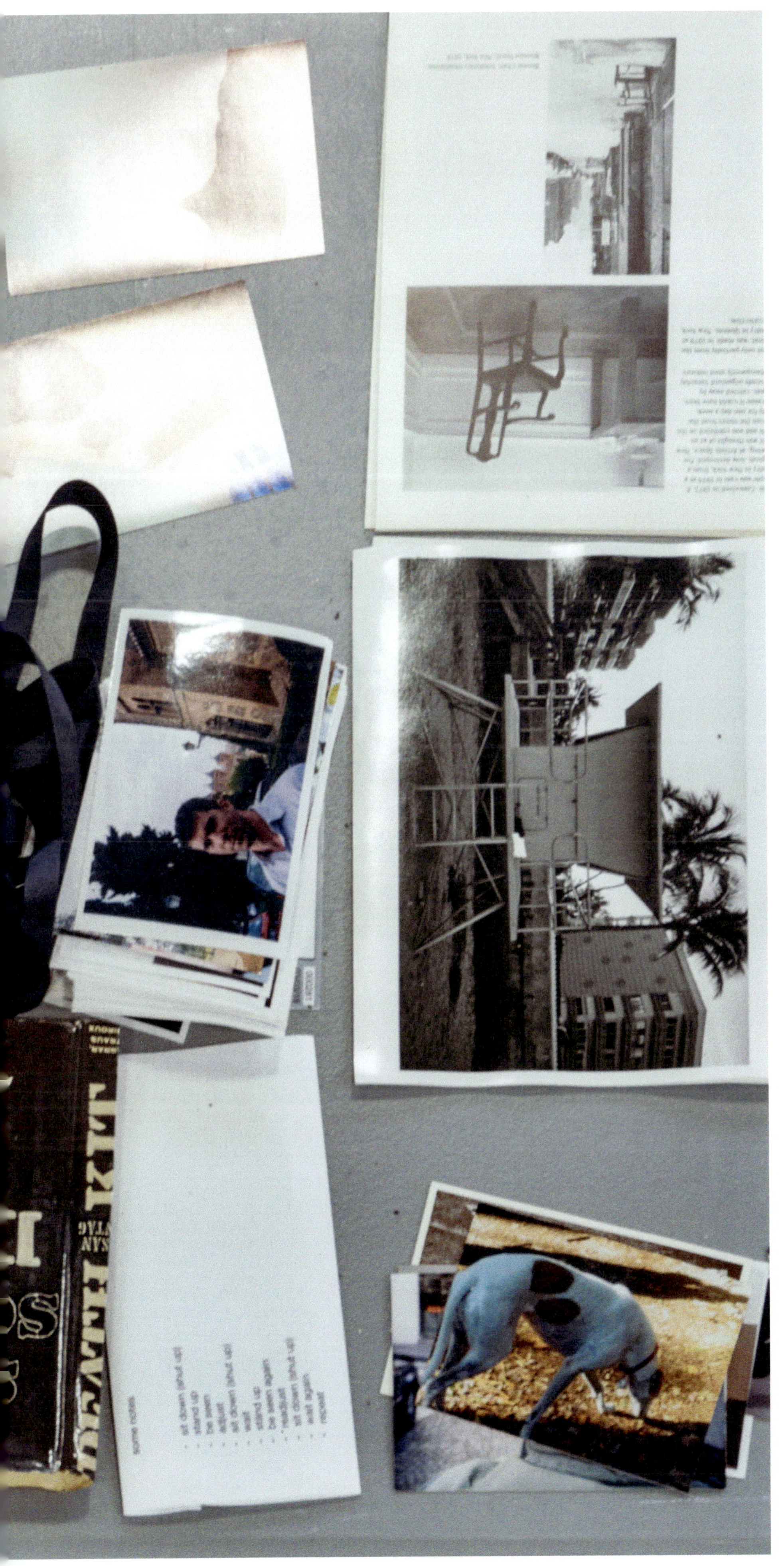

Other works needed restoration. I dedicated
a zone in the northwest corner of the smaller
room to this activity; the area was affectionately
coined "The Clinic," and several works from the
late 1980s and early 1990s were located there,
some on tables and sawhorses, covered with
plastic sheets. The works that were in good condition or only needed minimal touch-ups were
eventually hung on the adjacent walls. Others,
like the Ramble models from my exhibition at
White Columns in 1992, needed some careful
restoration, which I did myself, sealing them this
time under protective plexiglass bonnets that
could be moved easily on and off, something I
had planned to do for twenty years or more but
had never gotten to. A few other works remained
under plastic tarps throughout the process, the
project's three and a half years not long enough
to get to everything.

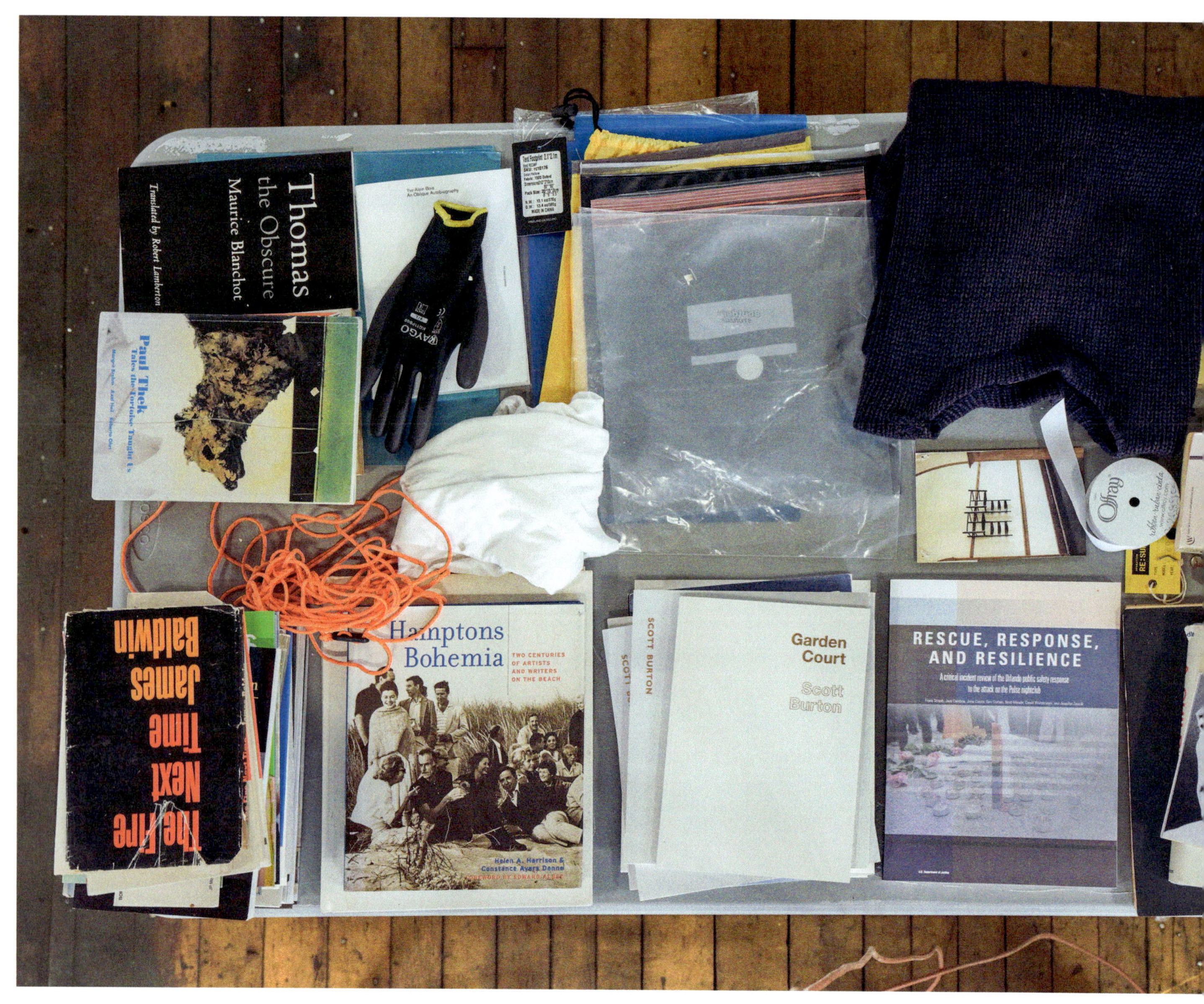

174

I hung drawings in this area, a vertically pinned suite I made for the design of the tan-painted "Ull" boxes installed on either side. The drawings were partially damaged by water at some point in a Manhattan Mini Storage unit, and the blue and black ink and sharp pencil lines are slightly blurred in certain places, which is oddly attractive and doesn't seem to degrade their appearance. I was surprised when I saw them again. It felt as if I had opened the pages of an old journal. The drawings seemed familiar and very close, but at the same time vaguely embarrassing because of that. Drawings can exhibit extreme intimacy—at least mine do, at least for me—in part because they weren't meant to be seen like this, displayed in this way. Seeing my handwriting from the past can conjure up the same sensation. But this suite of drawings felt compelling, particularly in the space that I was creating, where the larger, more architectural works might sit alongside these preparatory, awkwardly personal, gestures. I decided to look further into the many files of drawings and notes I have from a range of periods, assembling several of them on two sections of wall just around the corner from the first ones.

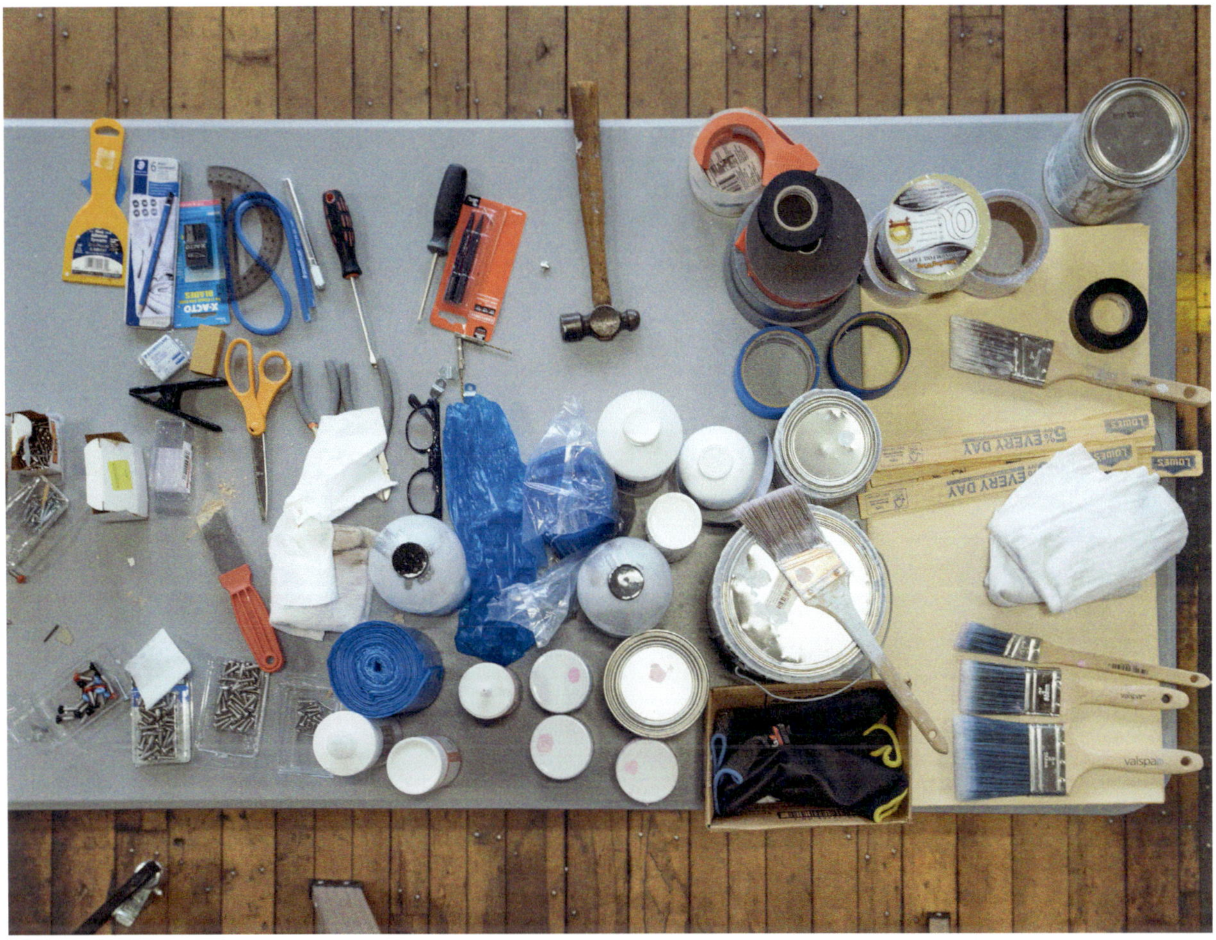

Lowe's
5x EVERY DAY
Valspar

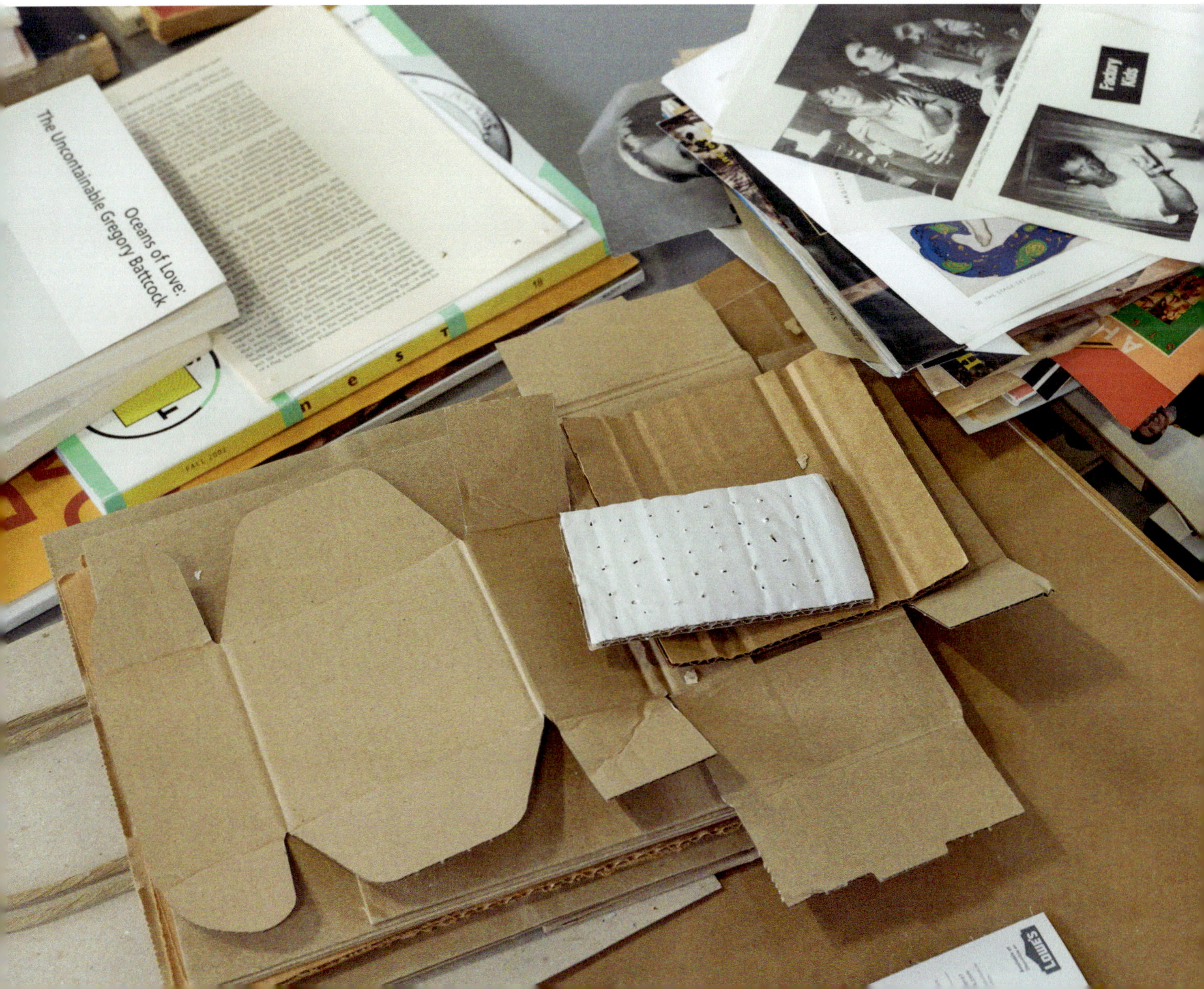

Oceans of Love:
The Uncontainable Gregory Battcock
nest
FALL 2002
Factory Kids
Lowe's

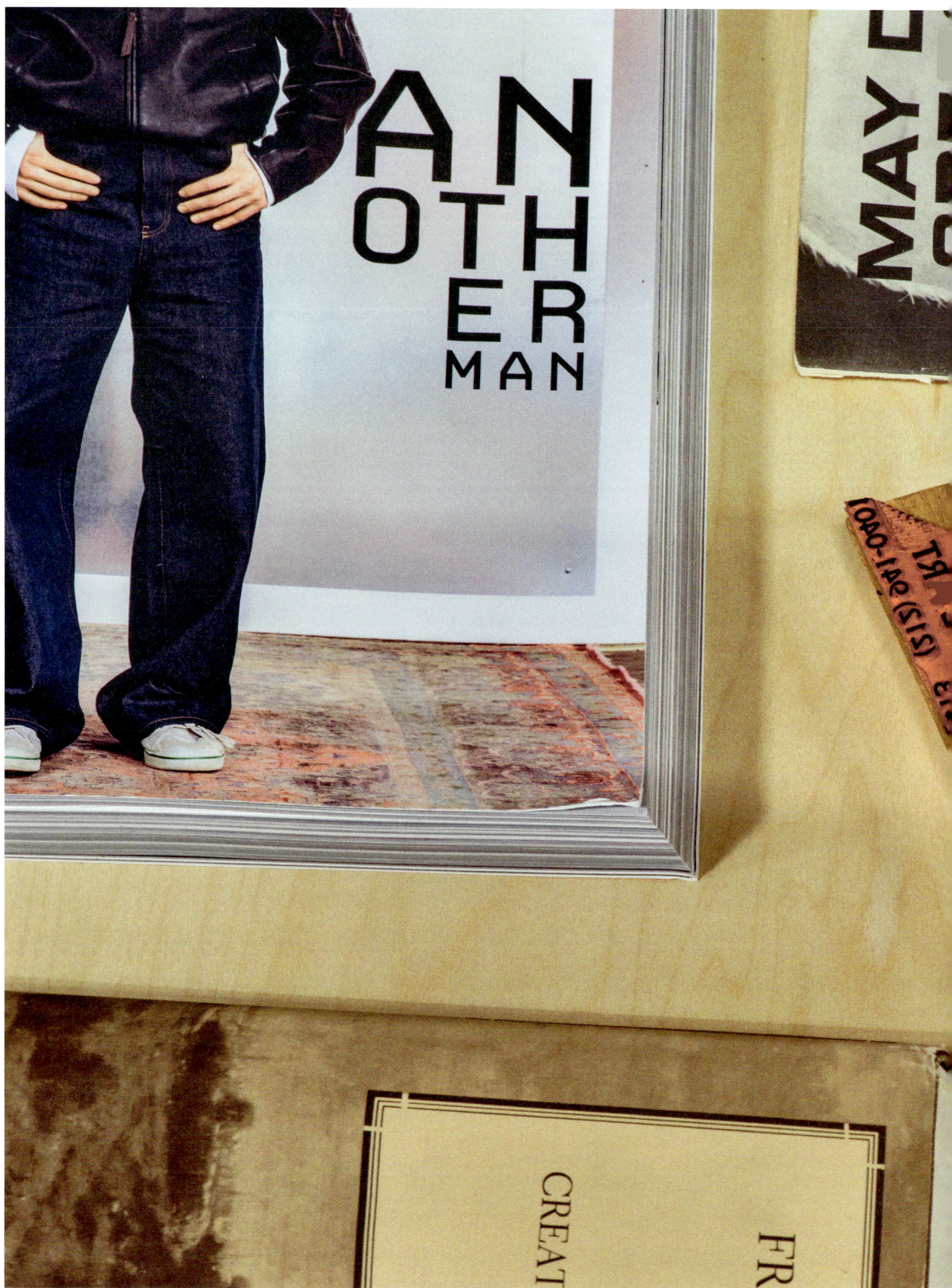
AN
OTH
ER
MAN
MAY
(515) 941-0400 Rl
CREAT
FR

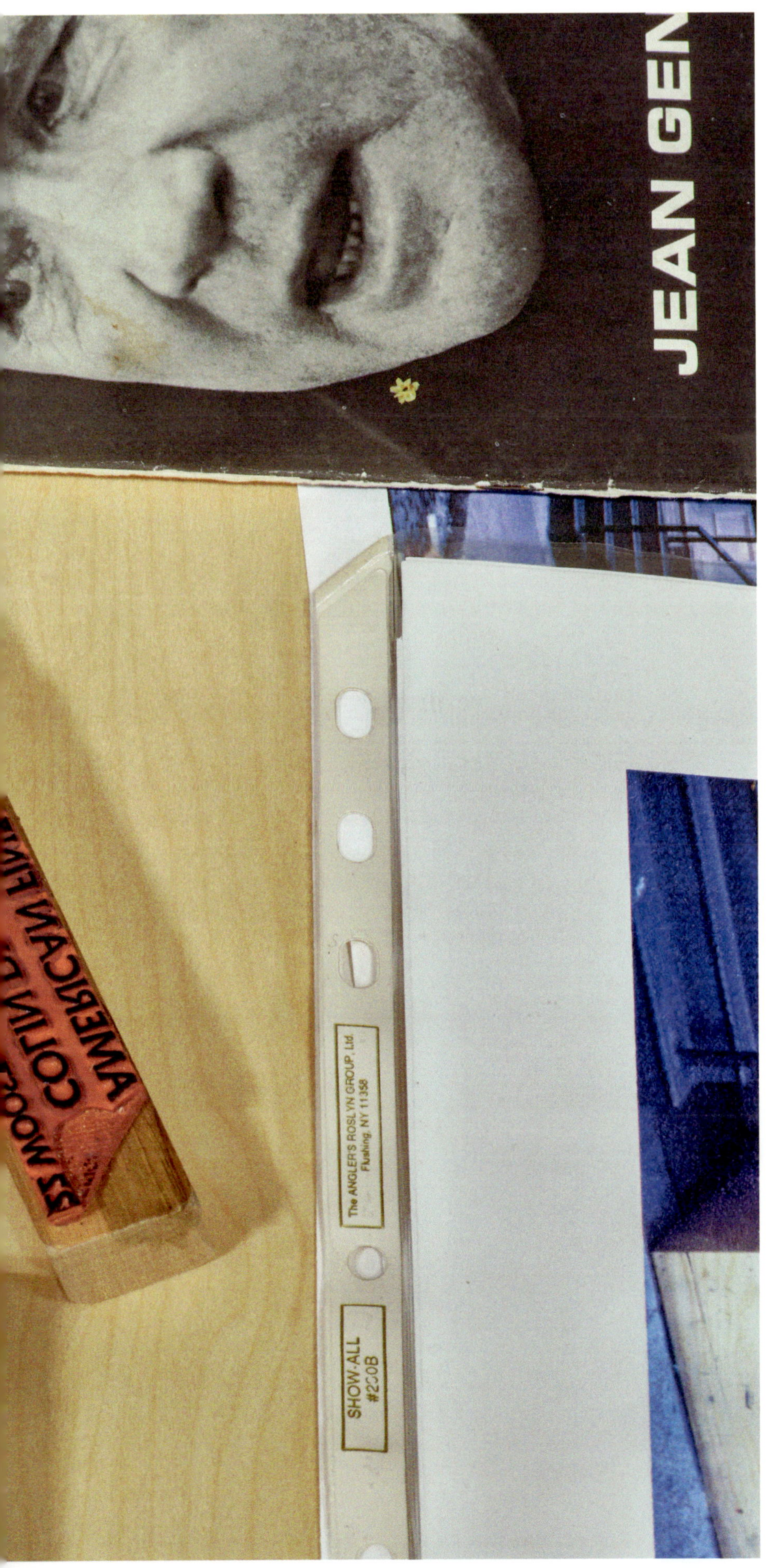

The first of these sections was precisely focused on a group of drawings from the mid-1980s, when I was attending art school in New York. Many of them were on architectural tracing paper, the amber-yellowish kind, and elements of collage were glued onto them, with my pen sketches and notes scattered around in black and red. All manner of patina had occurred on their surface since their creation—glues had dried up, tape had yellowed, edges had curled—but they were intact and legible, and, hung together like this, produced a sensuous chromatic tonality of semitransparent yellows, oranges, and greens. They also described a time and my thinking at that time, which strangely didn't seem that far away, or changed, with thematics and forms that still made sense to me—along with ideas that I still wanted to make material. Some of the works outlined in the drawings I have realized either at the time or shortly after, others not at all. One showed silver mirrored boxes that were produced and hung in the AFA bathroom for a few years before Barbara and Howard acquired them, while the orange boxes depicted in at least one of the sketches were produced but never exhibited outside my home studio until 2021, when they were included in a group exhibition at Galerie Neu in Berlin called *Divine*. The grid of eight orange boxes was hung in proximity to a beige-ish abstract monochrome by Ull, the works at right angles to one another.

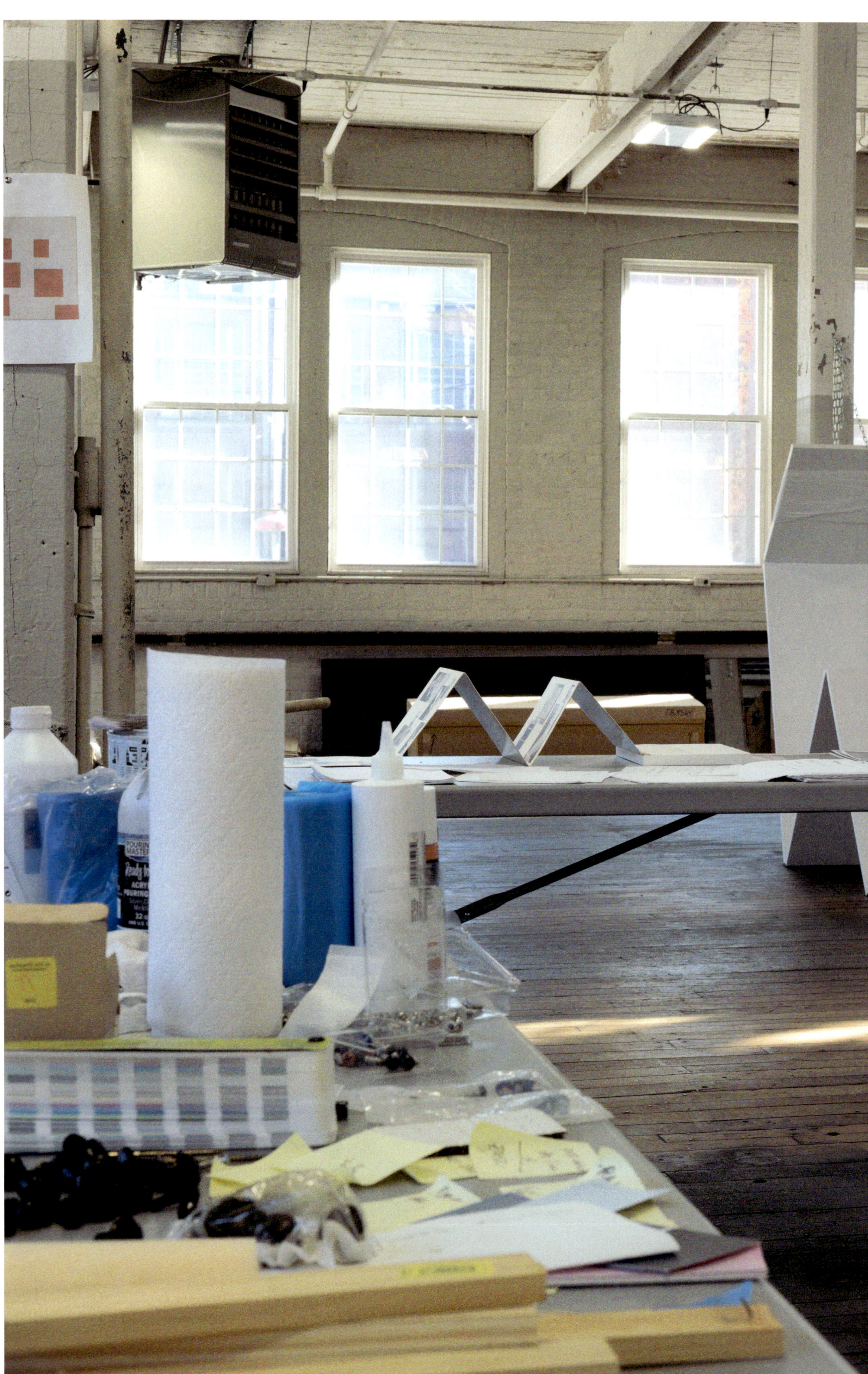

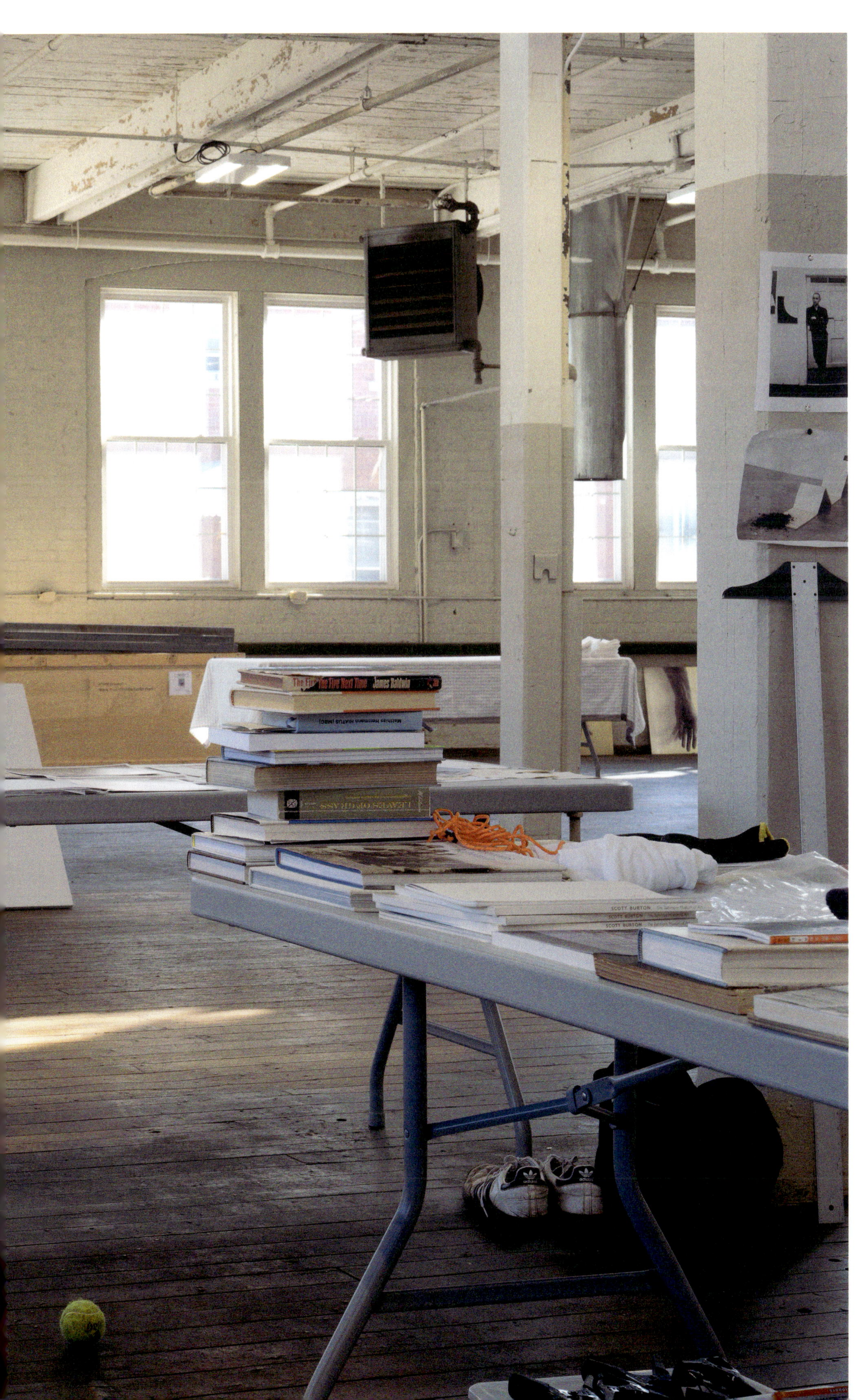

6

The drawings wall also did something else, I think. For many years, I chose to remove myself from my work, conspicuously removing any references to me or my biography. There was a de facto identification that happened anyways, because I was dealing in part with differentiated subjectivity, and queerness, in the work. I knew that I would be read into the work already, and that I couldn't escape it, and this proved true. I consciously reduced my presence and personal footprint in the work at a moment when there were steep demands and desires in the art orbit to locate and secure identity, and to traffic in it.

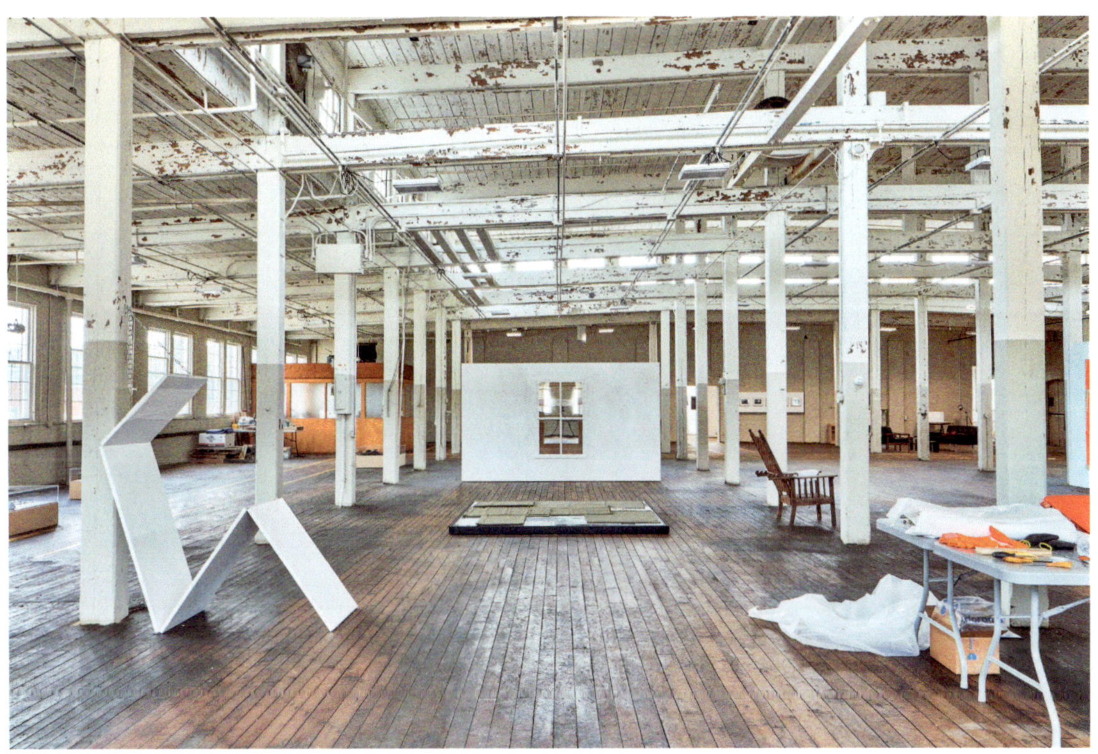

Later I shifted somewhat, so as to consciously devise ways to expose myself, or some suggestion of myself, as a reaction to what I saw as being categorized within the same mythically anonymized zone of Conceptual art that I had wanted to break from. The drawings wall was an extension of this thinking, a sort of highly personal punctuation within the overall tableau of *Torrington*, but one that, given the nature of many of the drawings as "working drawings" that were sent to galleries, fabricators, and institutions, still situated me within a network of complex external forces.

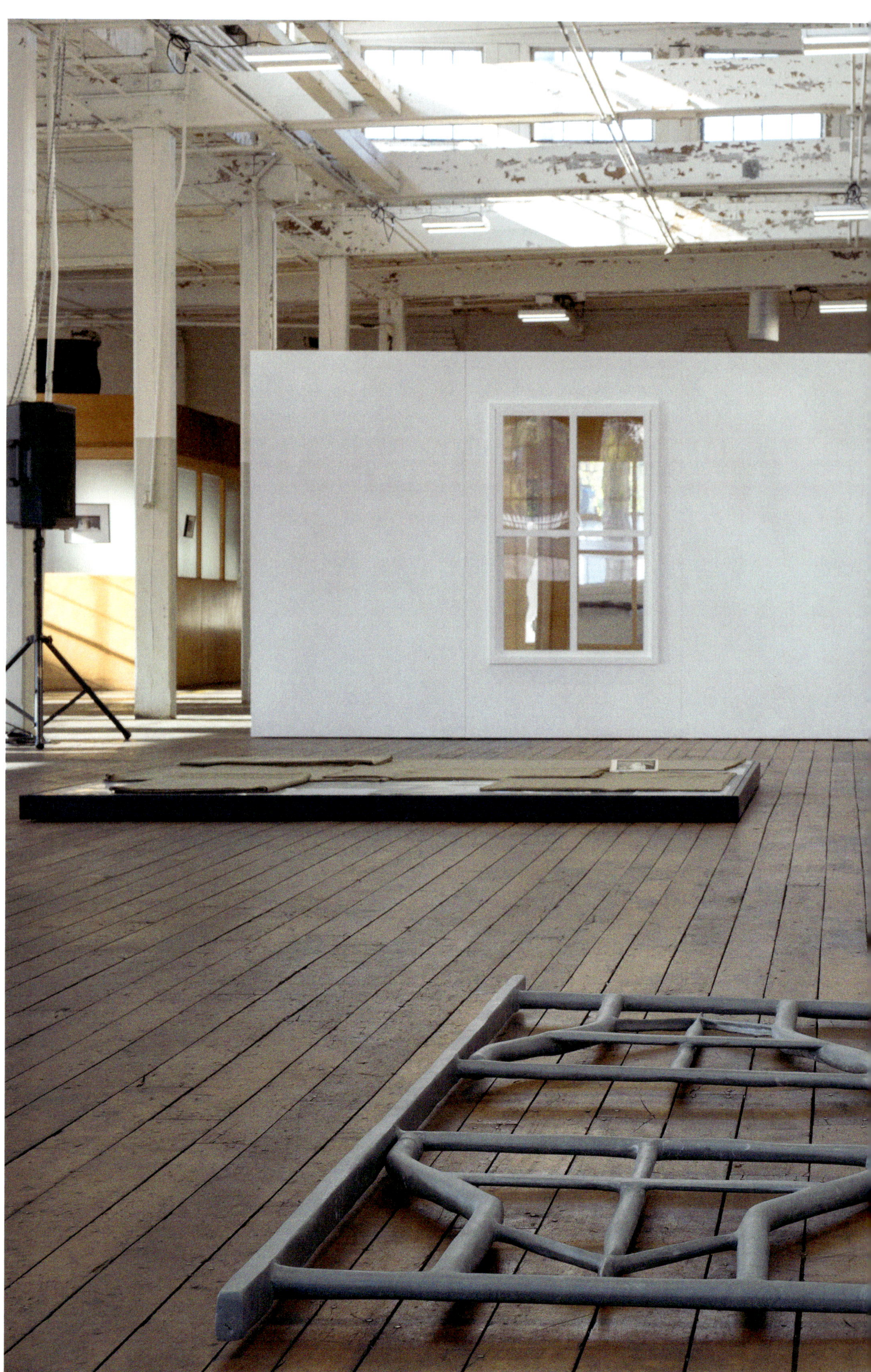

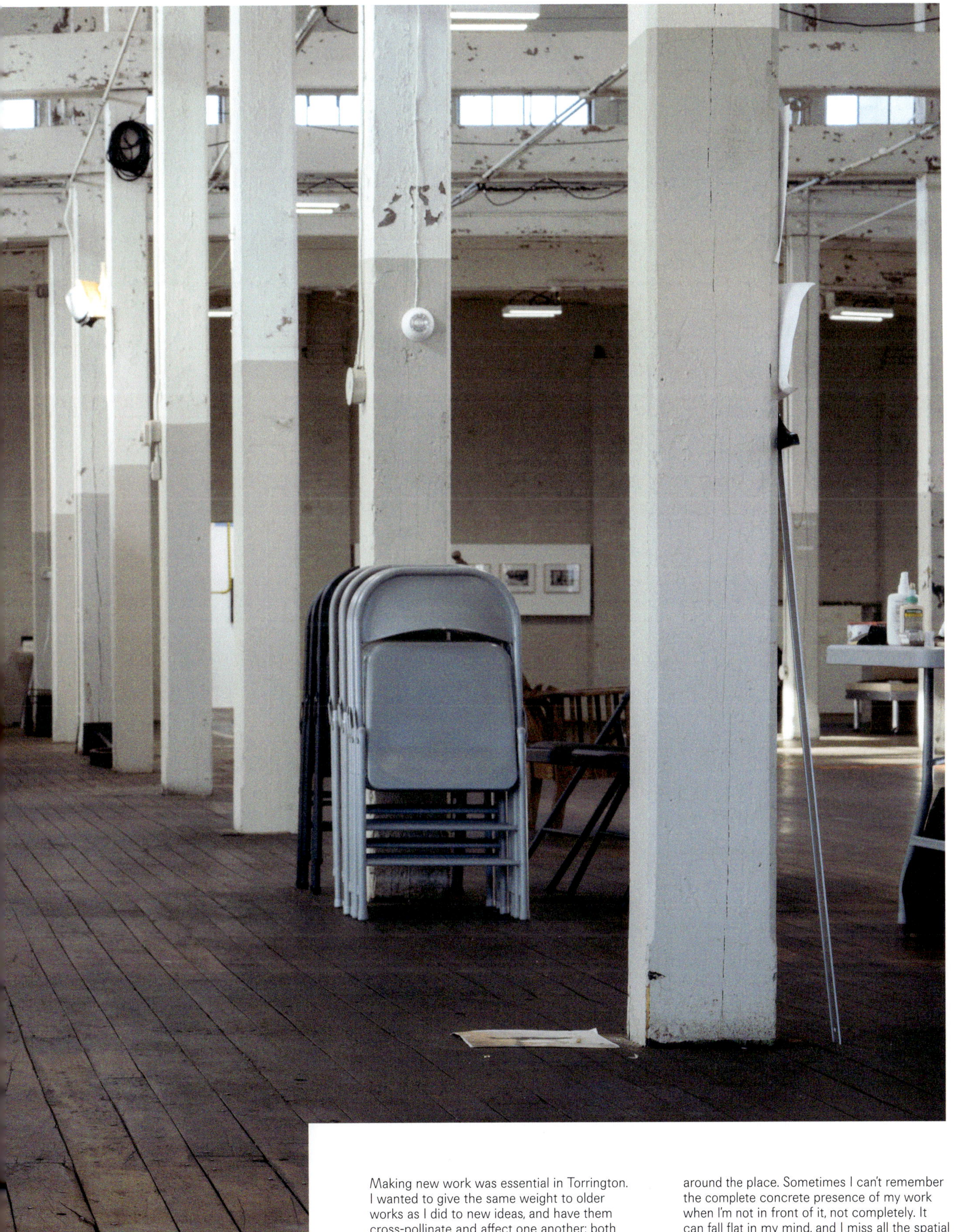

Making new work was essential in Torrington. I wanted to give the same weight to older works as I did to new ideas, and have them cross-pollinate and affect one another; both sorts of work and both sorts of contemplation mattered. I had exhibitions I was committed to outside of this project, the work for which would leave Torrington and not return, but I also wanted to create new projects specifically for the space, ones that would remain in dialogue with the growing constellation of early works I was assembling. I imagined there could be a motivational charge, and playfulness, in working within an archive, where I could be continuously prompted by the ideas floating around the place. Sometimes I can't remember the complete concrete presence of my work when I'm not in front of it, not completely. It can fall flat in my mind, and I miss all the spatial elements. A big part of what I longed for was the idea of lingering in an exhibition setting after hours, of being able to dance through the space mentally—physically, too—unencumbered by the trappings of installation, openings, tours, talks, etc. To be outside of that sort of time restriction and be able to experience the works and the spaces between and around the works over an extended period of time, luxuriating in that suspension. I wanted to create the possibility for these encounters.

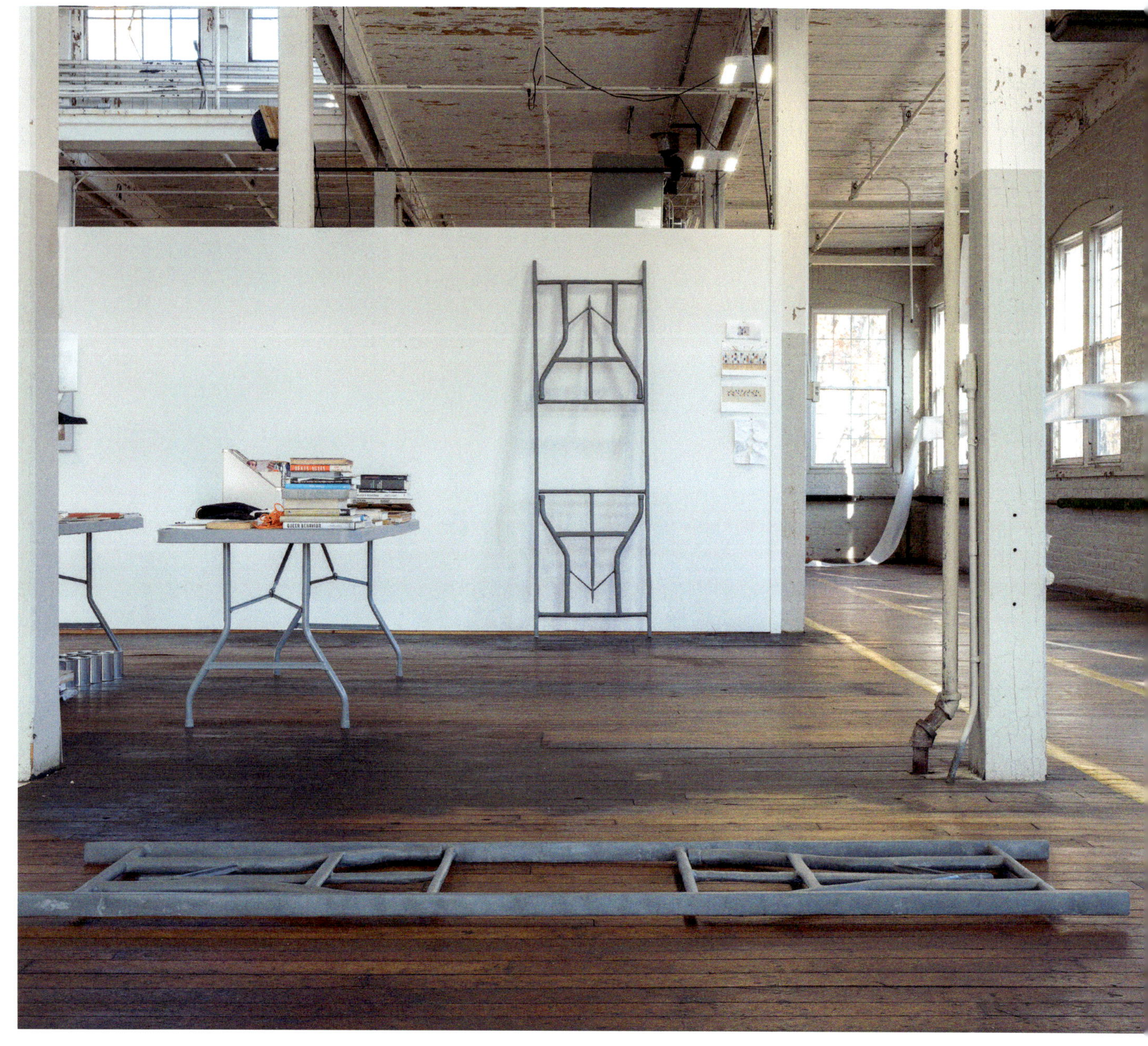

I built a room in the center of the smaller room—a room within a room—with Sheetrock walls on three sides and open at one end, creating a tightly contained, box-like space, which in turn created corridor-like spaces around it that elongated, spatially and temporally, the experience of walking through the whole of the project. The walls here were eight feet high, significantly lower than the existing walls of the building. The effect was that of being in a model, or on an isolated stage set in the middle of a theater: heterotopia within heterotopia. Because of the size and shape of the room, the lighting felt more intense than anywhere else in the building, which made it feel overexposed and somewhat antiseptic; a sort of observation capsule that we would usually just call "The Gallery."

Originally the intention was to make a long, continuous bulletin-board work in this room, a format I have engaged from time to time. I laid out all the black-stained panels along the floor, end to end, and would come in to take a break from the projects taking shape in the other rooms, sitting in one of the many black or gray folding chairs scattered around, and thinking. Some months went by. I ordered a series of glass mirrors, mostly gray "smoked" ones and a few clear, of various dimensions. I leaned these sporadically against the panels. I shifted some of the panels, and each time I subtracted one of them, creating space between panels, I felt it was closer to what I wanted. The process was about acting and then pausing, moving elements around and then sitting, standing up again, leaving, returning, sitting, getting up to play with the panels again, pulling back, and so on.

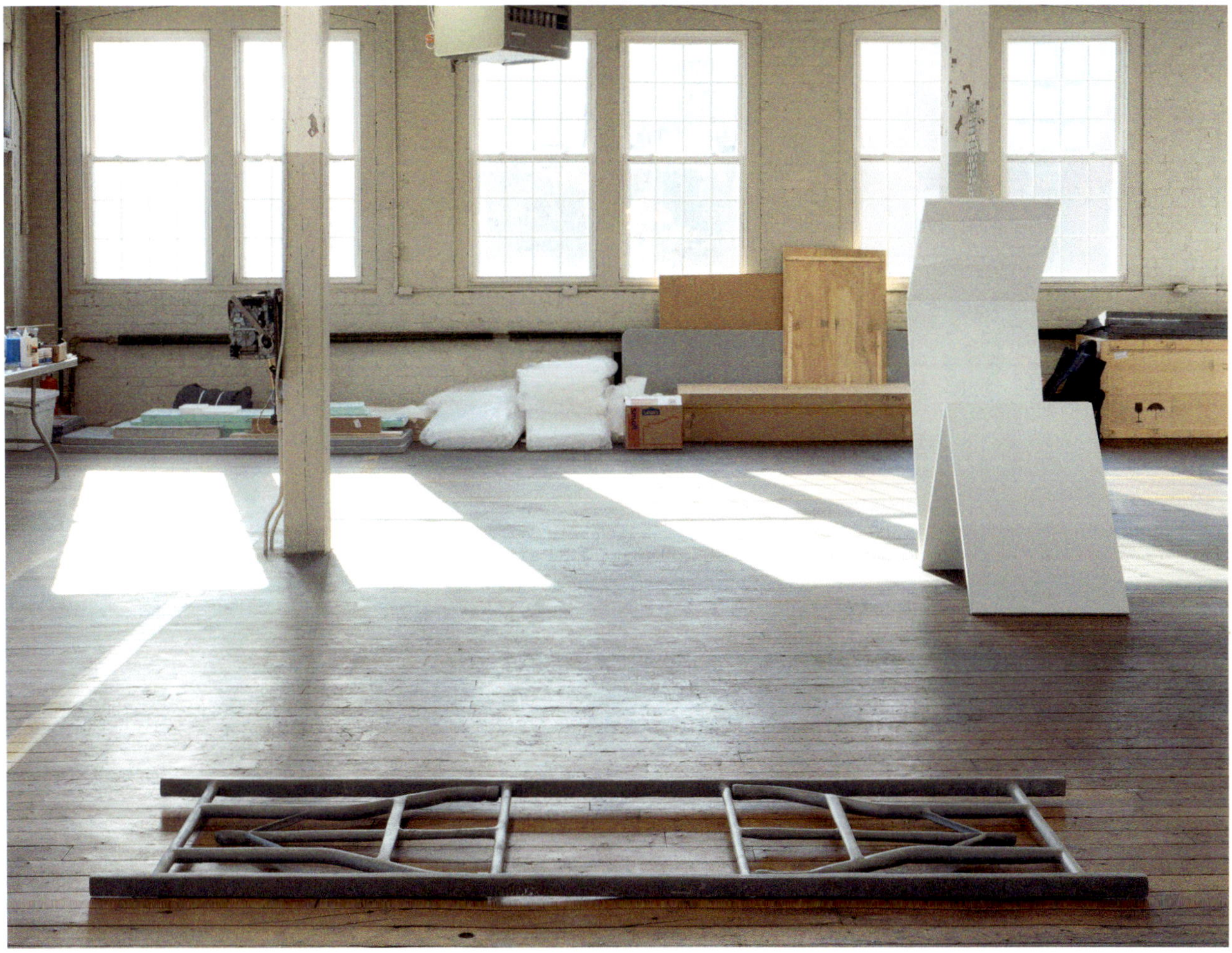

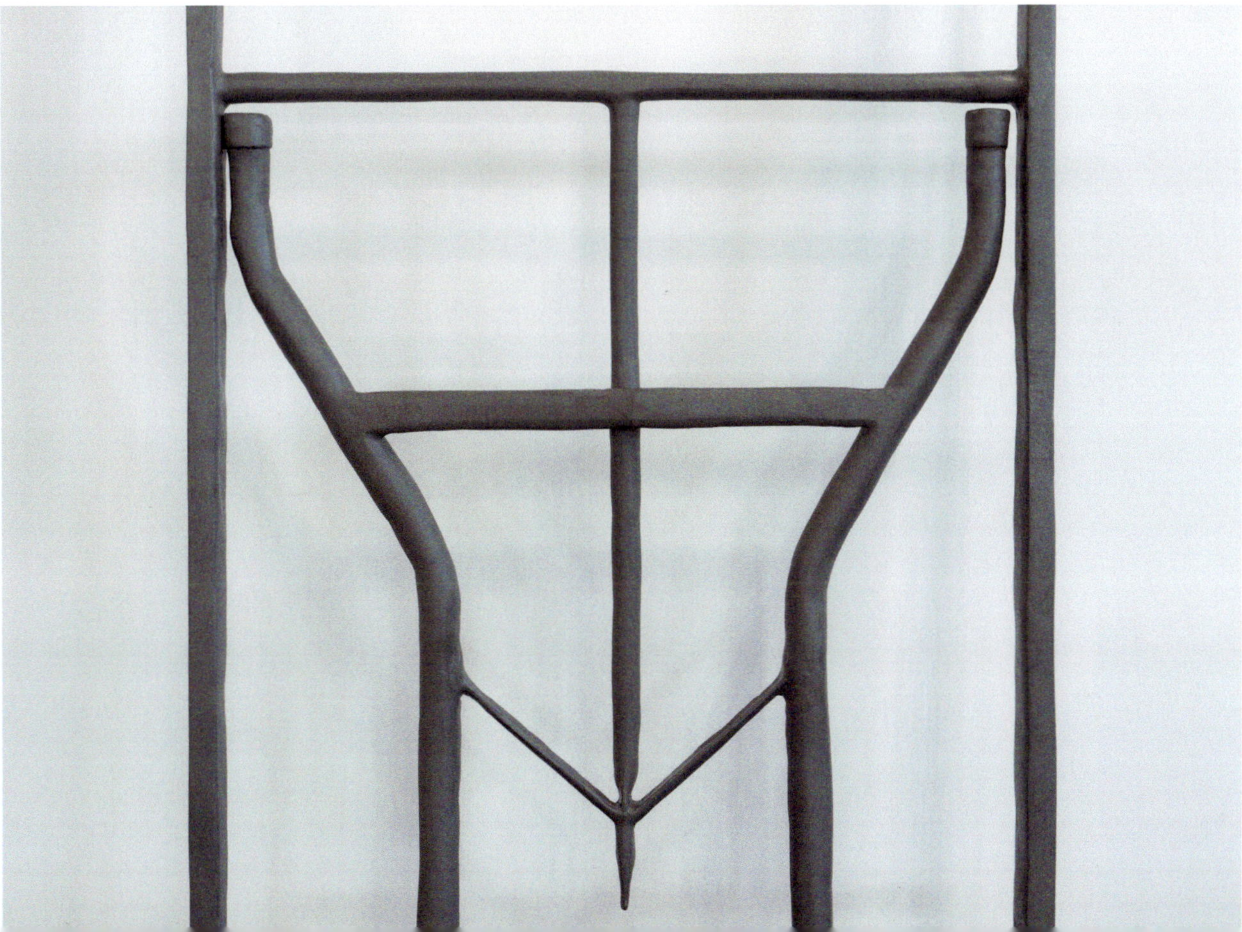

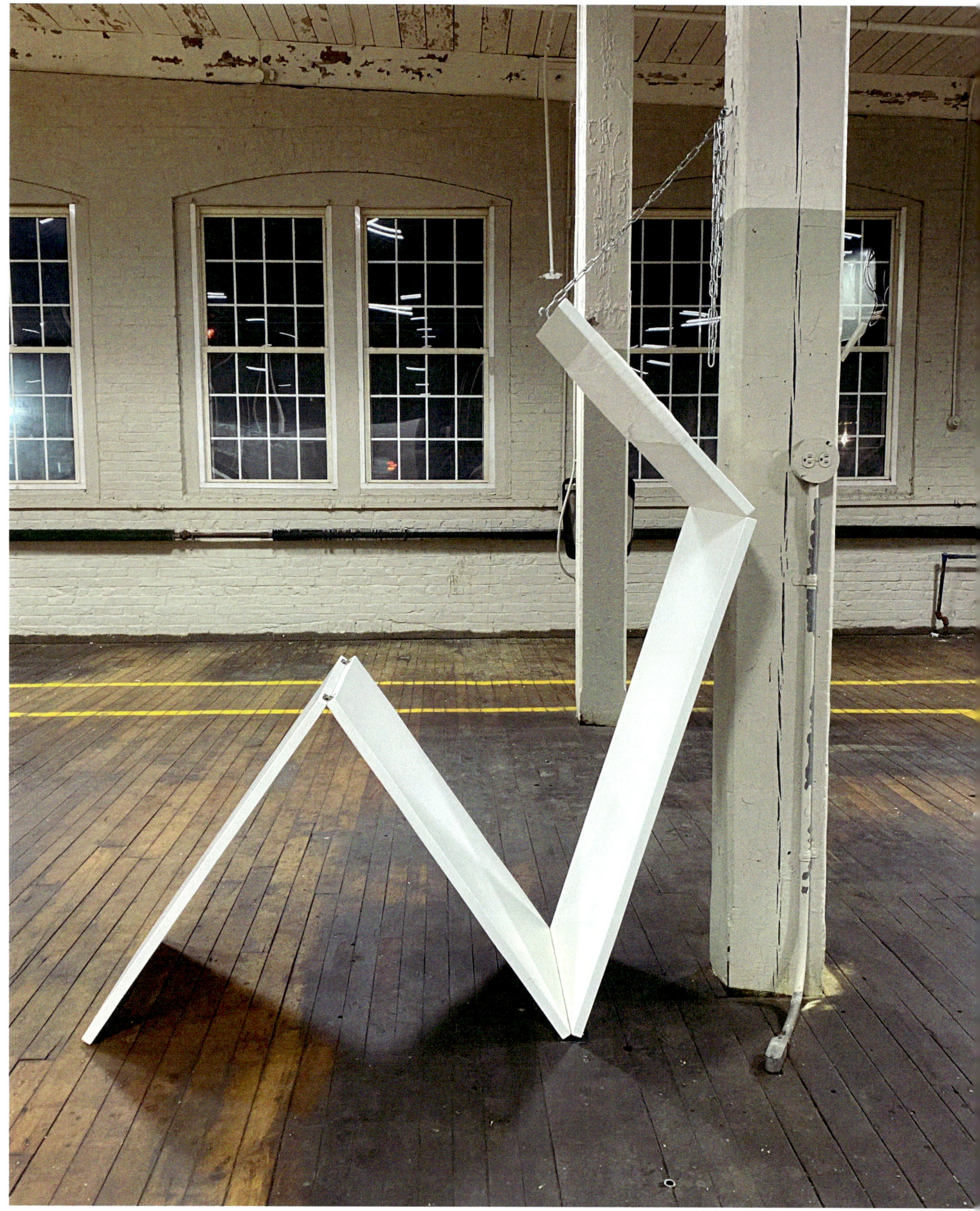

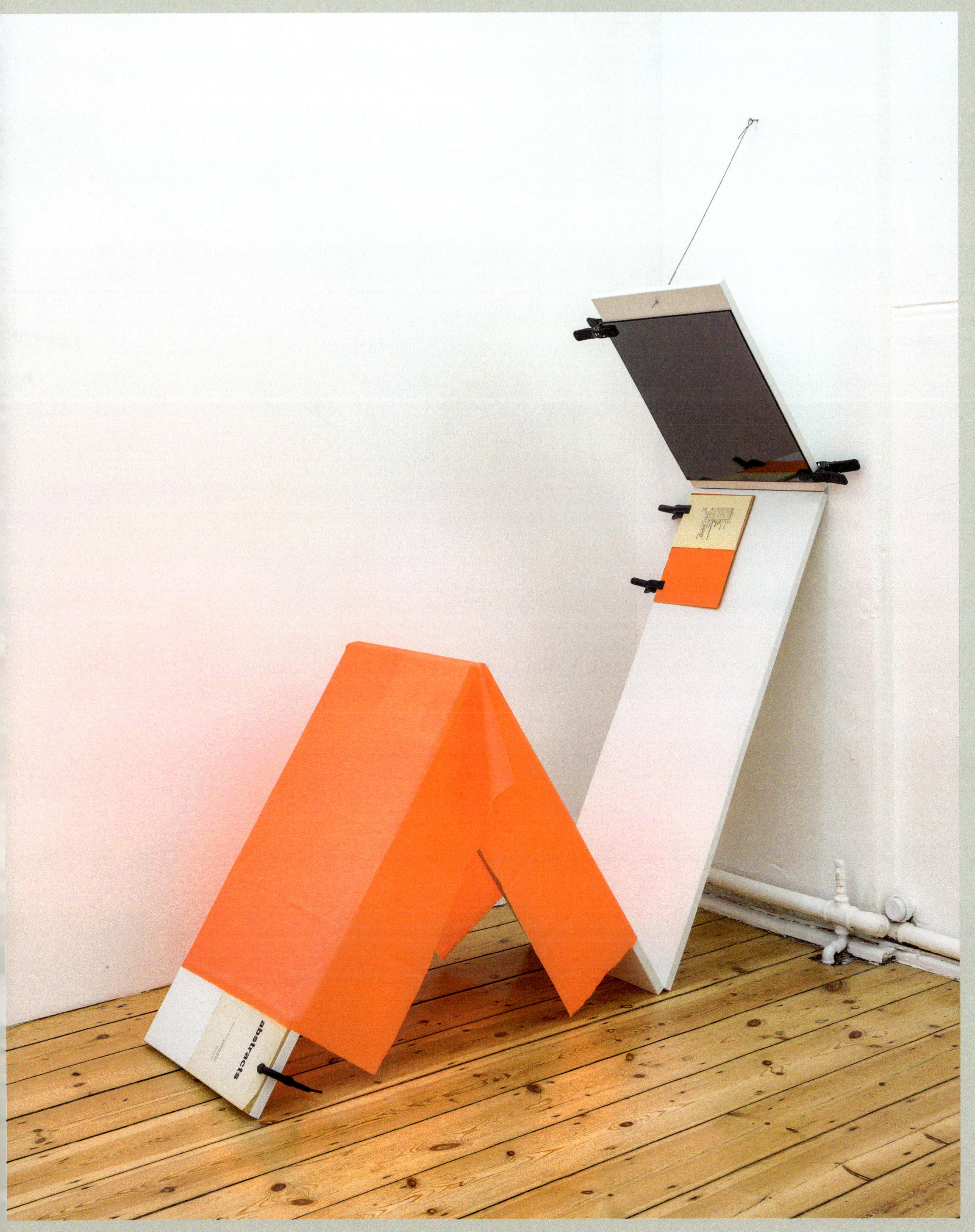
abstracts

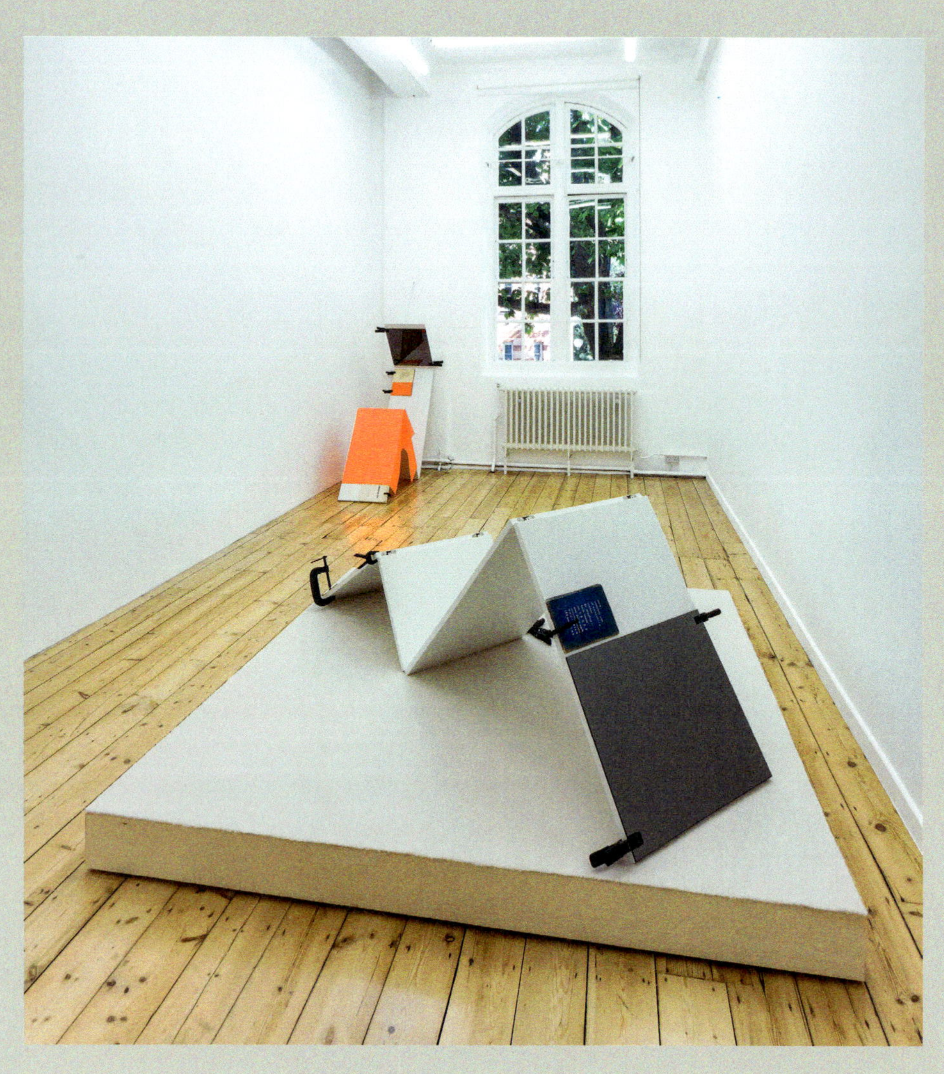

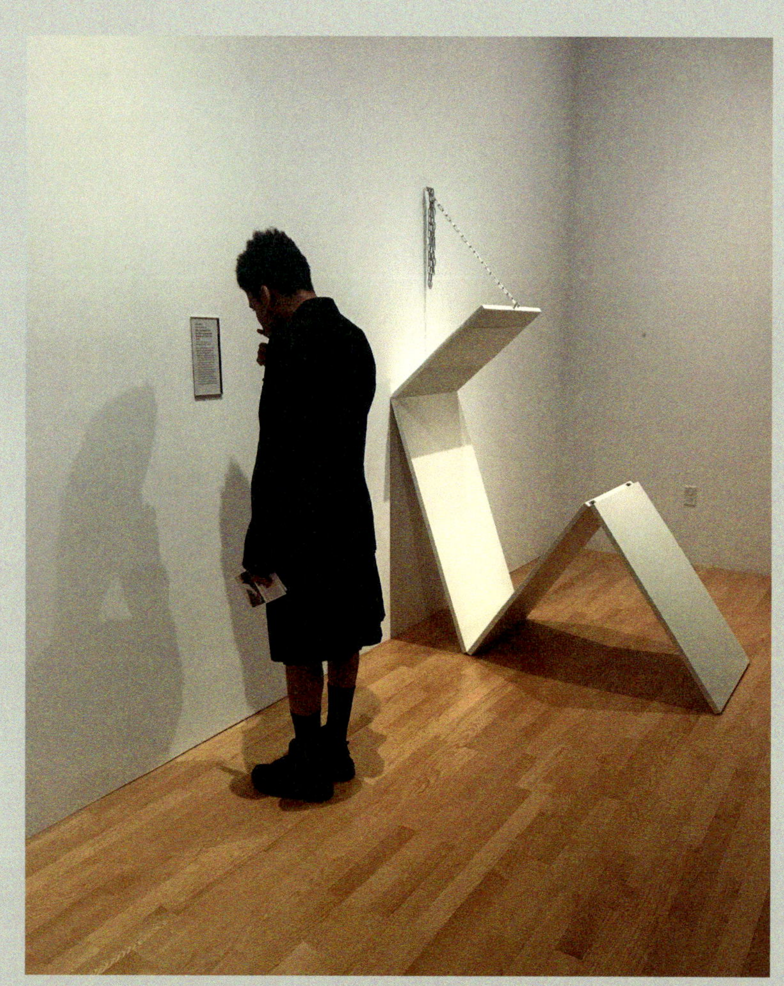

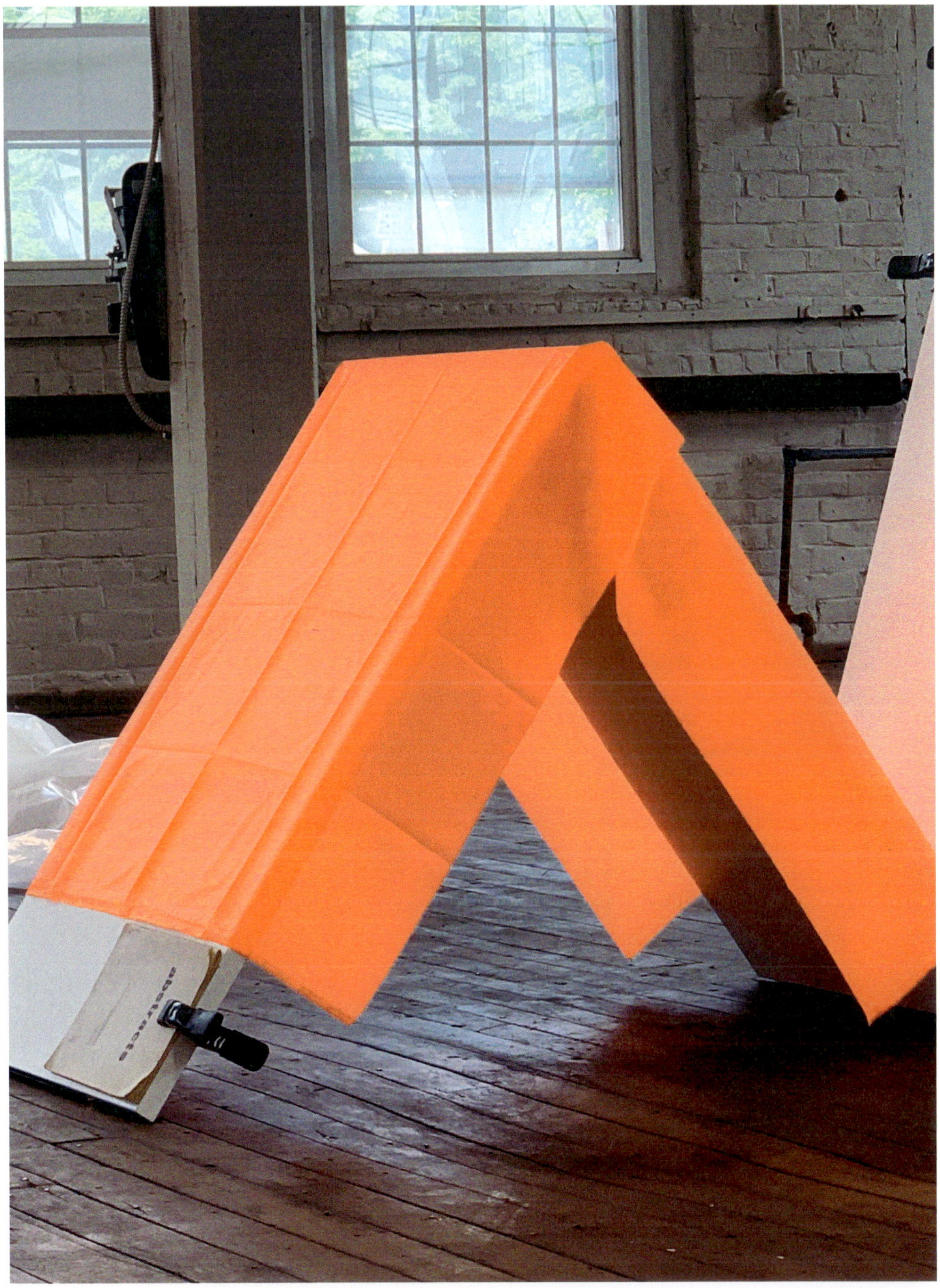

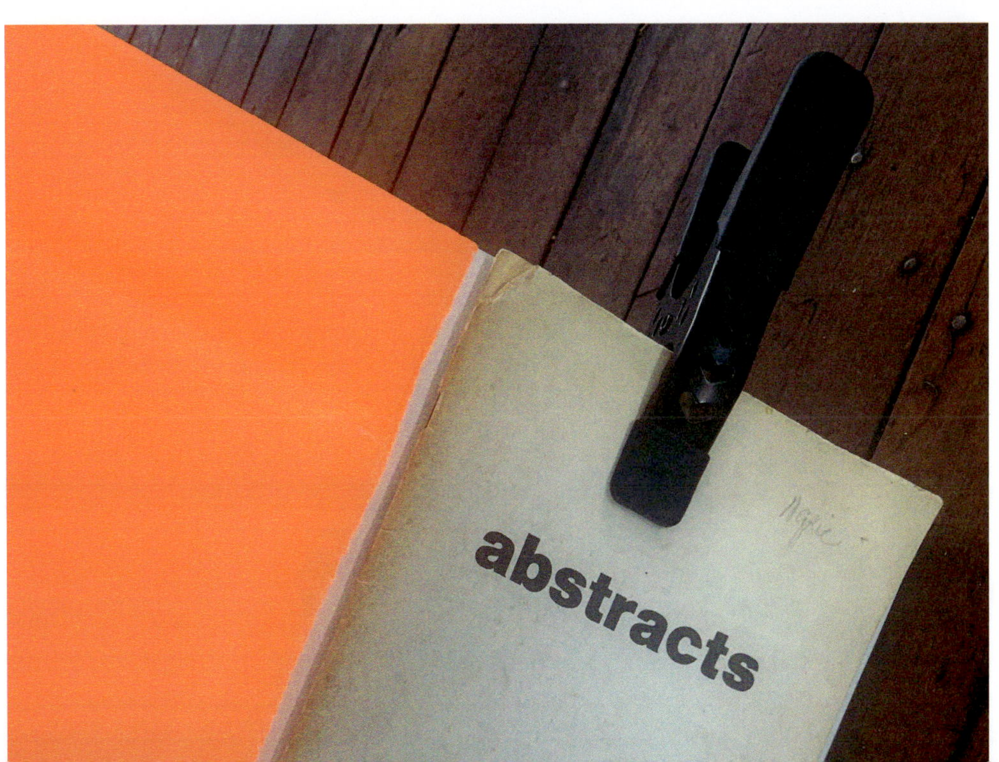

abstracts

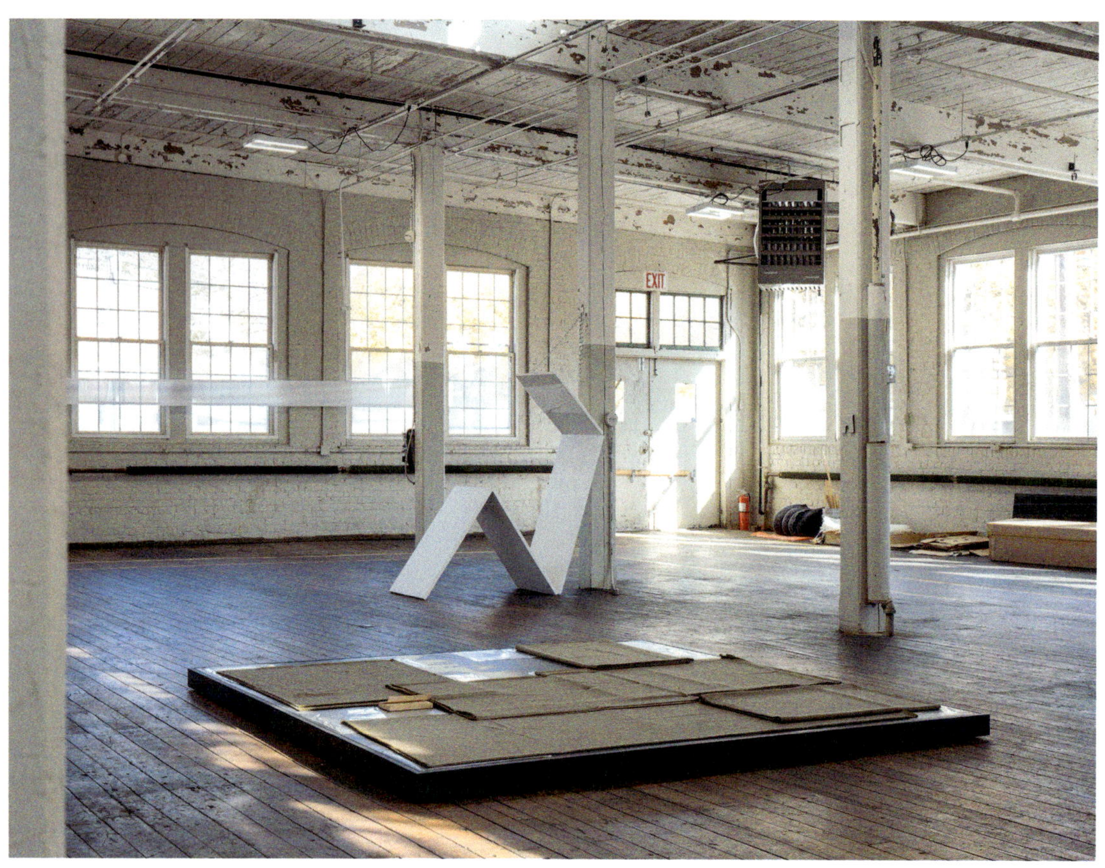

Studios and how to conceive of them were on my mind. I was always struck by how imagination often seemed to come to a halt when it came to the space of the studio, that all the brainpower and creative energy was focused solely on "the work," while the surroundings were dulled down and made to be simply in the service of that object or art-thing. I was searching for some alternative path to lead me out of my disbelief in this model, at least for the duration of the project—to turn it sideways and make it strange, less known. I thought about Warhol, of course, and of Adrian Piper's bureaucracies and administration-as-studio as a form of agency; I thought about the many so-called post-studio practices, often coming out of feminist thought, that had been so important to me during the time I was a student, where the studio in a traditional manner was no longer the only solution to an art practice. I thought about site-specific approaches, including my own at many times, that descend upon locations, perhaps as a mobile studio in some sense. And I also thought about Bruce Nauman in a way that I hadn't before, looking at him afresh as someone who had focused his gaze on the studio, and had used that space and the ideas that circulate around it as some of the very substance of his work, performing his way through his studio, registering its sounds and its nocturnal movements, considering it as a nuanced context and not a seemingly neutral export department. I watched his body at various stages of his life, walking tightly, awkwardly, but elegantly too, in his contrapposto works. It's like walking a tightrope, or following a very strict set of choreographed movements for some unknown audience at some future point in time. I felt this way about studios, and about being in the current Torrington situation, being present there and expecting and hosting viewers, and contemplating what my body might do, what my walking might be like as it wove through the space, and my talking as well, and how to expand from that, and how to exist within the constrictions of it all, and allow my works—and myself—to breathe, if I can say that. I wanted things to breathe.

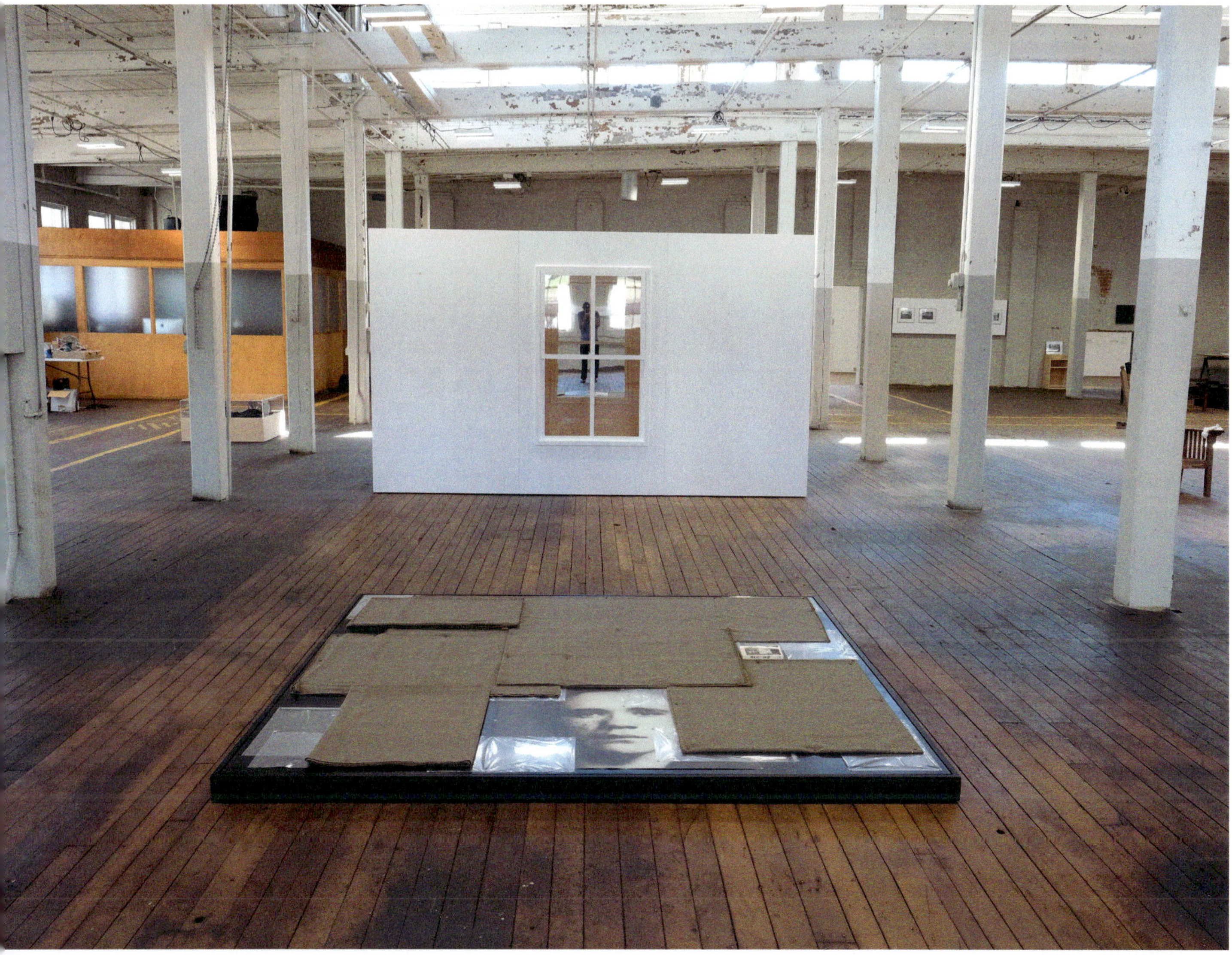

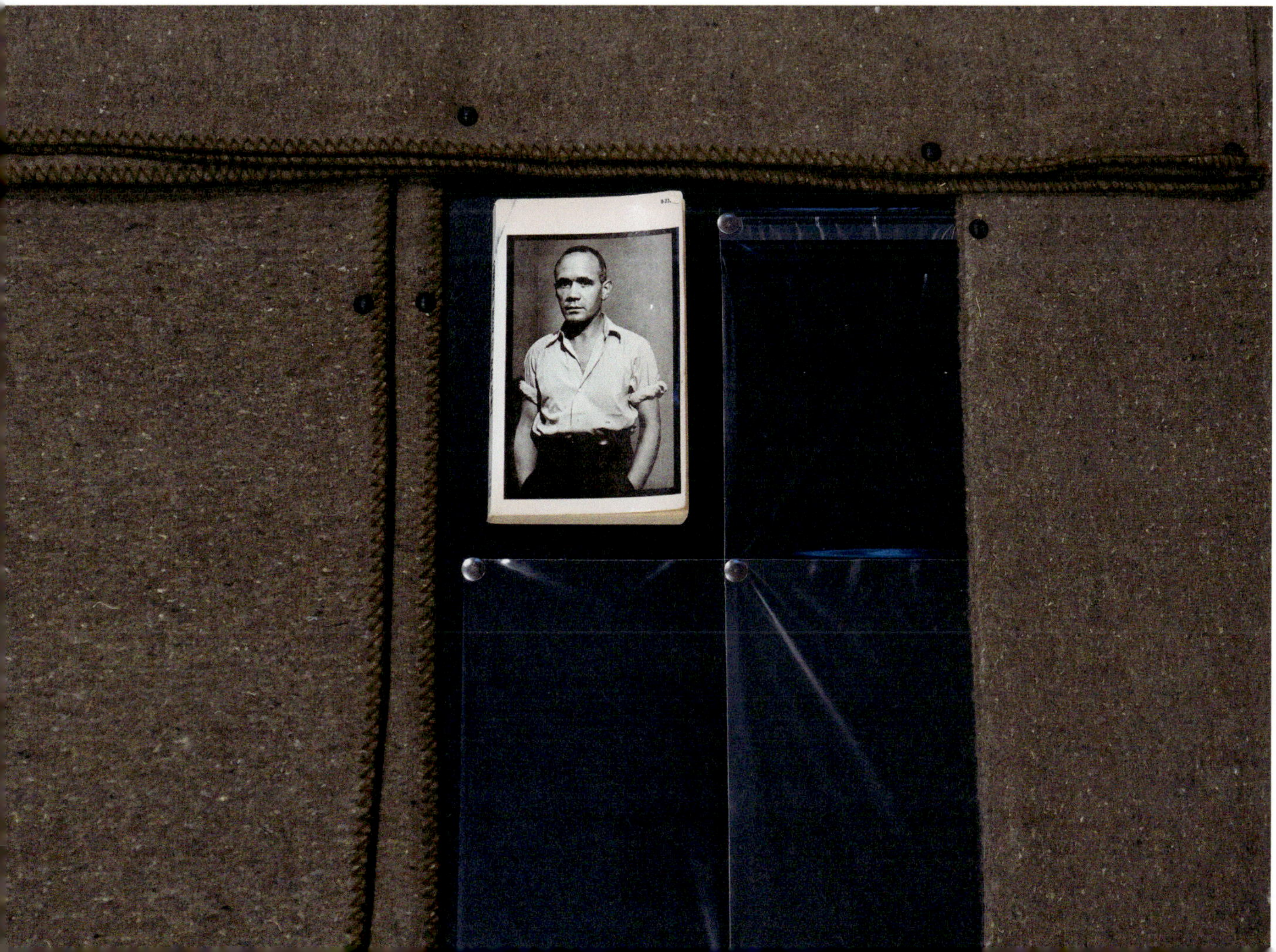

Stasis 1: *Immobility*

but there is life in immobility

    you know?

Deep
deep
deep
purple

bent, not straight
in between standing and falling
slowly moving towards both sides

infiltrating a system
pressure
to make it raw
bleed

infiltrating history, and the white boys
in their sleep
they will never sleep again

in between
the oscillation
concealing and revealing
just enough

to see

the arc of history bending towards what?
Monuments?
No, ruins

OK if I start with the idea that we're born into a completely pre-invented existence where everything is regulated [?][1]

… if you're the spy—always "straight acting," always within the system—you are the person that they fear the most because you're one of them and you become impossible to define …[2]

Any sensibility which can be crammed into the mold of a system […] is no longer a sensibility at all.[3]

1   David Wojnarowicz, *Weight of the Earth: The Tape Journals of David Wojnarowicz*, ed. Lisa Darms and David O'Neill (Semiotext(e), 2018), 117.

2   Felix Gonzalez-Torres, "Interview by Tim Rollins," in *Felix Gonzalez-Torres*, ed. Bill Bartman (A.R.T. Press, 1993), 5–31. Republished on the website of the Felix Gonzalez-Torres Foundation: [https://www.felix gonzalez-torresfoundation.org/attachment /en/5b844b306aa72cea5f8b4567/Down-loadableItem/639385f3fa829db6a90469fb]. Accessed April 14, 2025.

3   Susan Sontag, *Notes on "Camp"* (Penguin Random House, 2018), 1.

     Humberto Moro

Stasis 2: *Sedimental*

A forensic exploration,
of objects outside of time
unearthing the overburden,
the burdens
excavating what is left in form
to reveal what is possible in meaning
by approximating what cannot be grasped

making sense of the mise-en-scène
a screen that holds no image
which reflects no light
but only stands
for what once was

an operational dexterity
result of sentimental procedures placed
almost too long ago
repeated one after the other
on top of each other
accumulating, blending, bending
from the dematerialization of art
to the materialization of thought
via the reconfiguration of space
sculpture?

No, but the feeling of it
an oscillation between the end of language
and the beginning of an object

what was, stayed, sediment of memory[4]

the erosion of public space, the erosion of different publics' use of urban spaces[5]

works would release certain elements, certain layers of their sedimental makeup[6]

what is the role of the artist now, vis-à-vis the urban landscape of privatization and hyper-development[7]

4 Hélio Oiticica, *Secret Poetics*, trans. Rebecca Kosick (Soberscove Press, 2023), 47.

5 Tom Burr, "Tom Burr revisits, reflects, and thinks anew," interview by Robert Sandler, *Art21*, July 2023: [https://art21.org/read/in-the-studio-tom-burr/.]

6 Ibid.

7 Tom Burr and Humberto Moro, *Sedimental* (SCAD Museum of Art, 2018), 20.

8 Burr and Moro, *Sedimental*, 30.

Forms of Stasis[8]

Stasis 3: *A Methodological Muscle*

You said you were flexing
in order to achieve some equilibrium

a moment of centrifugal and centripetal
forces in equal measure
finally giving control away
so something external can gain it again

a stasis

anyhow,
the training you need
to bend words into objects

to bend chairs
the political potential of a chair
sit down
stand up
walk like a boy
thoughts into buildings

bodies into walls
the body as a building
with decorated rail guards
incomplete open cubes
from the sexual minorities
flexing again and again
trying to escape into the wilderness of
concrete utopia
the confines of a closet's insides
the shapes of twentieth-century delirium

finding a kind of solace there
as a method

so brutal

Volume, gravity, propping and support, display
and maintenance[9]

[a] poet from the waist up[10]

Here's to the asses that sit on the chairs,
The muscles and fat warmly upholstered in
hair…[11]

…between architectural language, social
space and the expanded field of sculpture/the
body…[12]

9   Ibid., 17.

10 After Tom Burr's *The Poet from the Waist Up*,
    2005, plywood, mirror, drawing pins, hinges,
    and a copy of *The Blood of a Poet* by Jean
    Cocteau, 42.9 × 23.6 × 116.5 in. (109 × 60 ×
    296 cm). Guilbaud Collection, Martinique.

11 Tom Burr, "Anxiety, or An Ode to the Chair,
    or Lullaby to a Stranger, or These Many
    Mirrored Moods of Mine" in *Anthology:
    Writings 1991-2015*, ed. Florence Derieux
    (Sternberg Press, 2015), 79. This text also
    constituted a 2006 performance at Mumok-
    Museum moderner Kunst Stiftung Ludwig in
    Vienna as part of the exhibition *Wieder und
    Wider: Performance Appropriated*, co-curated
    by Barbara Clausen and Achim Hochdörfer.

12 Florence Derieux, "Forward" in *Anthology*, 5.

Stasis 4: *Cease to Exist*

Some things can't be rushed
a sunrise, a kiss
the weight of the earth
an idea, a stone

In Torrington, like in all corners of the
cardinal points
the clock is ticking
is time the enemy?
No, it's space

Right after post-industrial,
but not quite at the end of an already
underway apocalypse

reunited to be together
in Burrville

to think about the urgencies of oblivion
the infamies of re-embodiments
and the dangers of archiving

to be there and think

before things slip

I don't want to be the enemy anymore.
The enemy is too easy to dismiss and to
attack.[13]

What was I then if not my name?[14]

Whenever we discover what we are, we cease
becoming that [...] Once you have that cogni-
zance of what you are, your totality, then you
cease to exist.[15]

13 Felix Gonzalez-Torres, "Felix Gonzalez-Torres,
Être un Espion," interview by Robert Storr,
ArtPress, January 1995, 24–32. Republished
on the website of Creative Time: [https://cre-
ativetime.org/programs/archive/2000/Torres/
torres/storr.html]. Accessed April 14, 2025.

14 Hieu Minh Nguyen, *Not Here* (Coffee House
Press, 2018), 13.

15 Wojnarowicz, *Weight of the Earth*, 85.

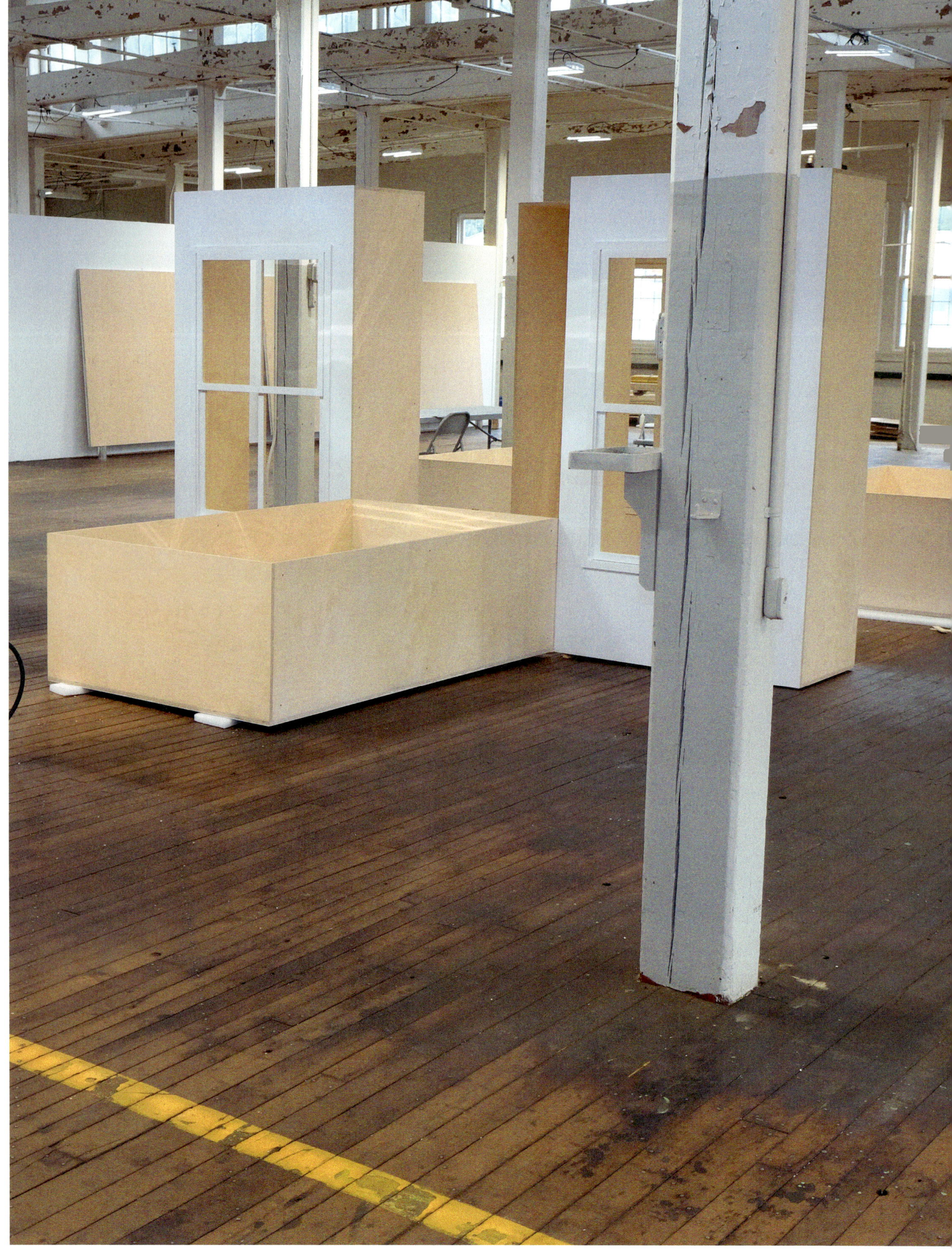

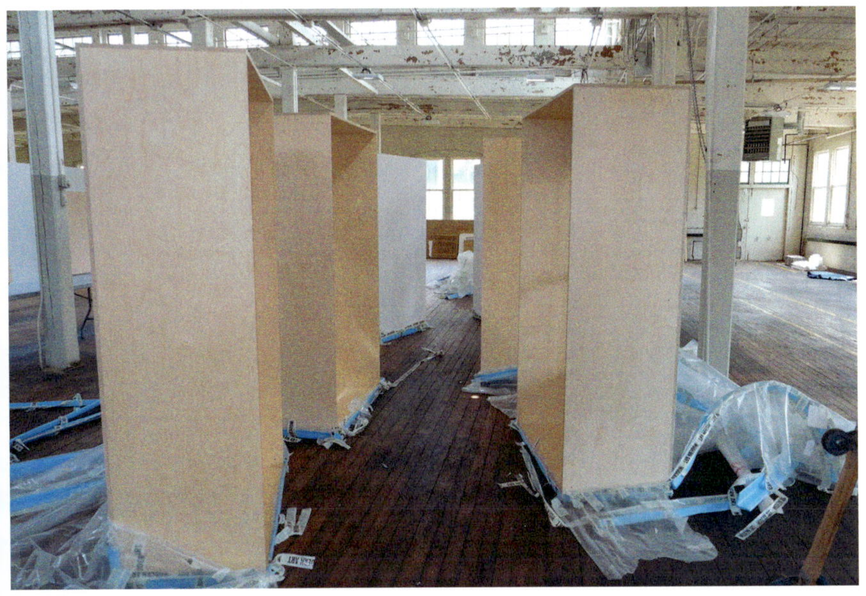

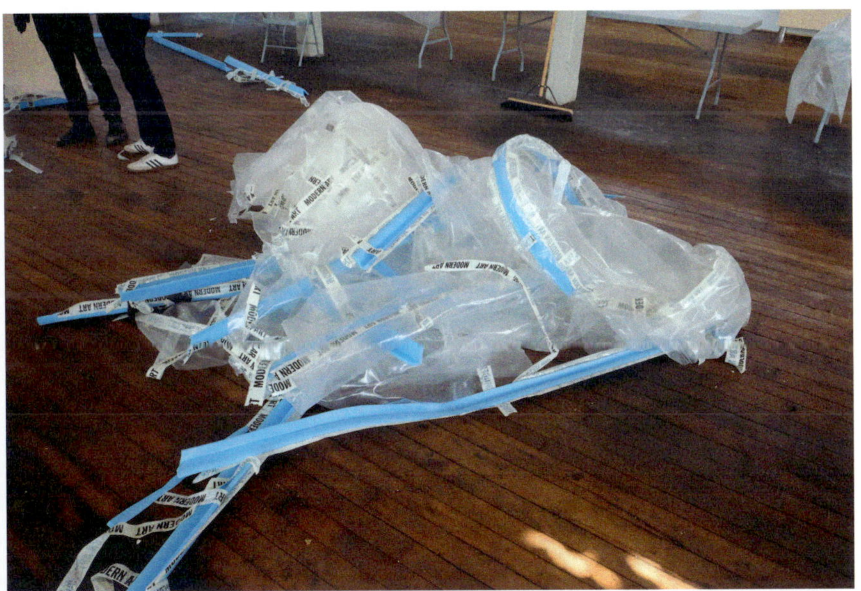

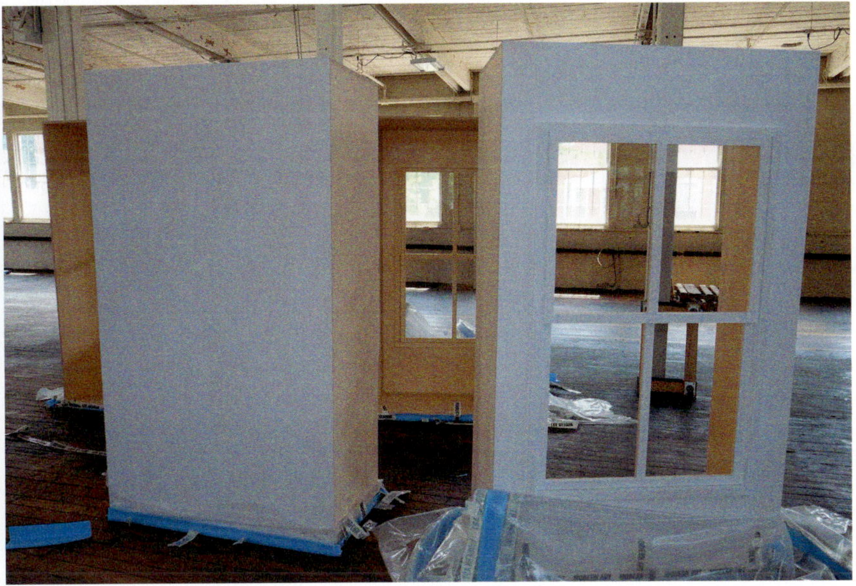

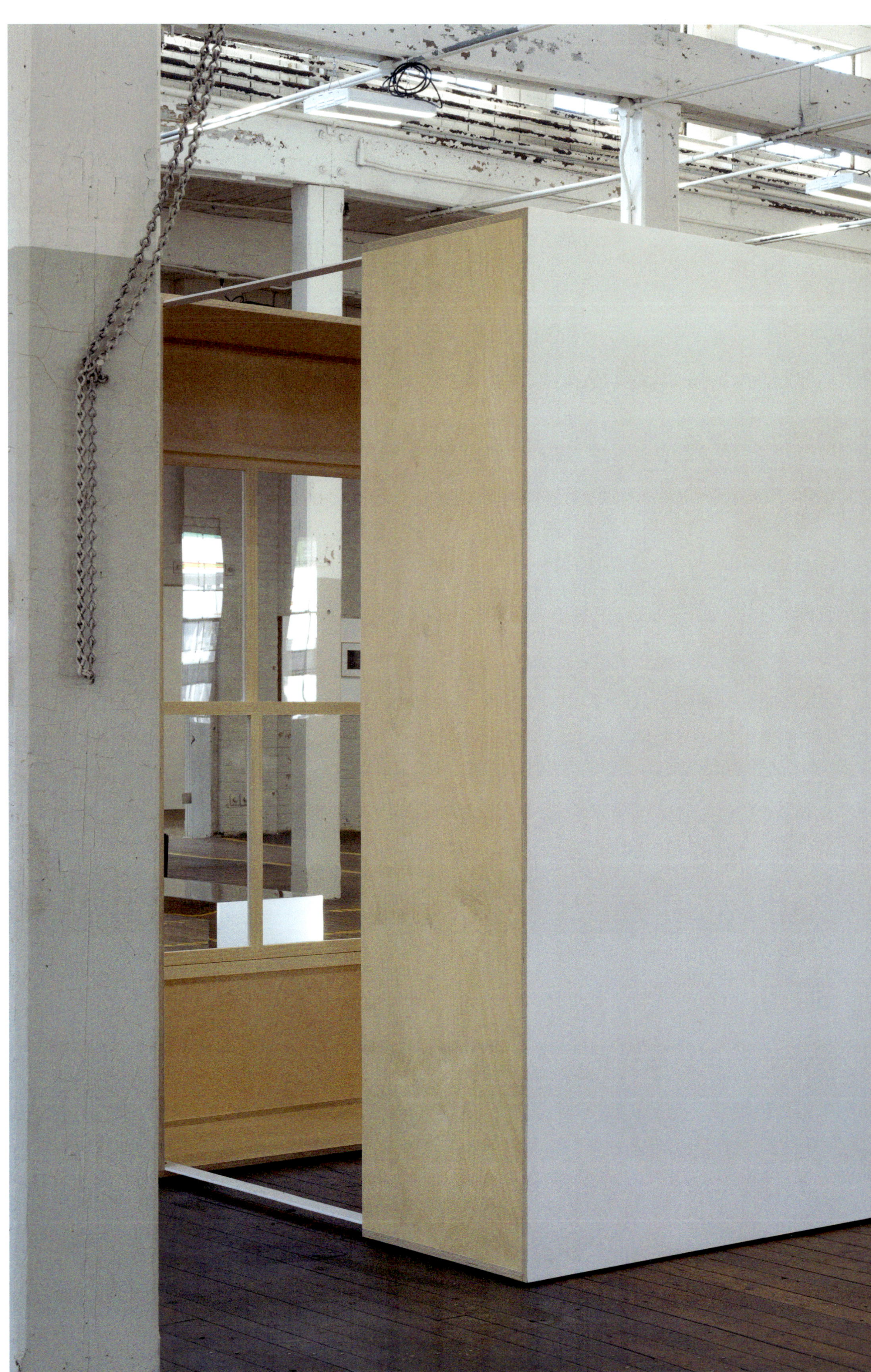

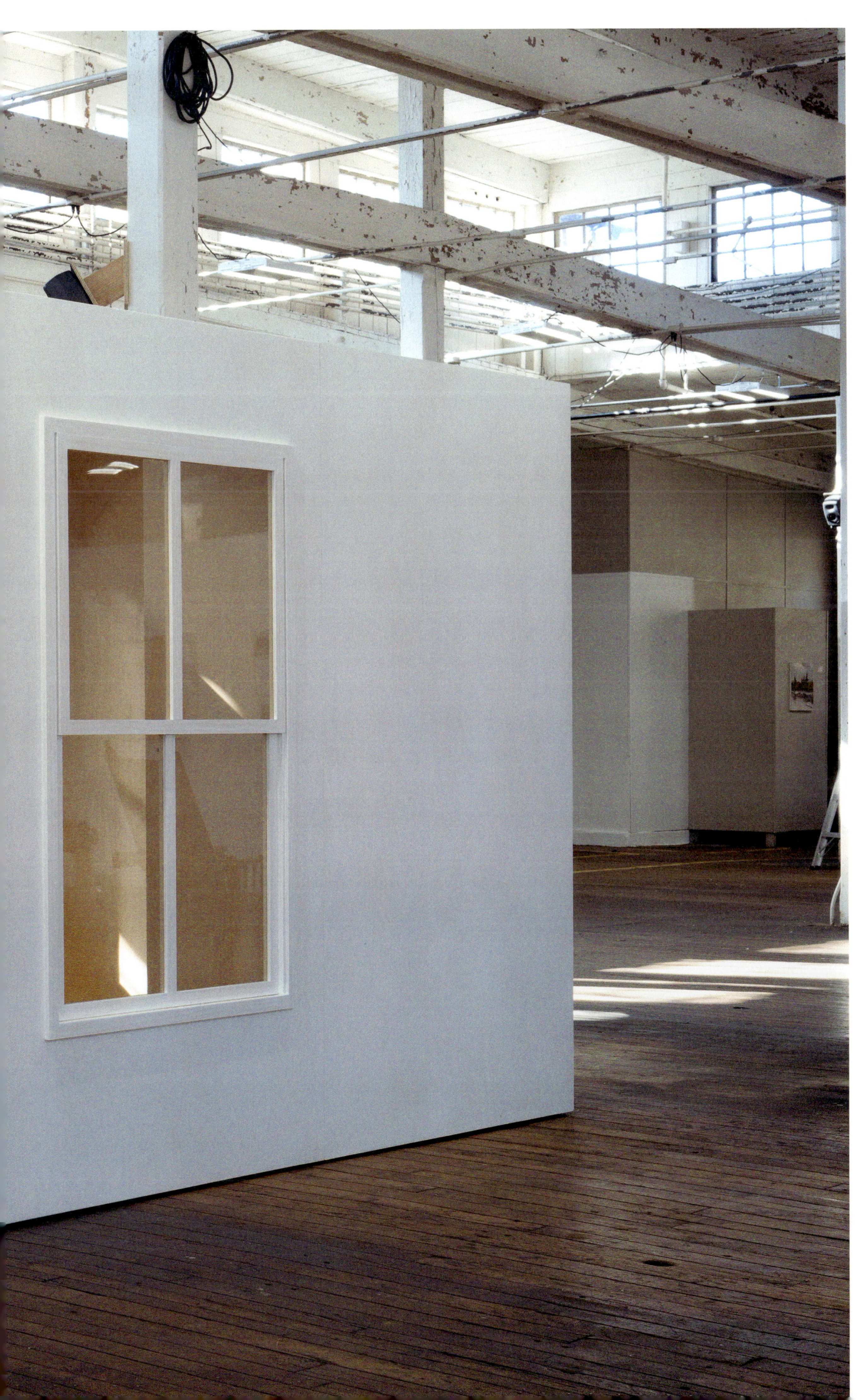

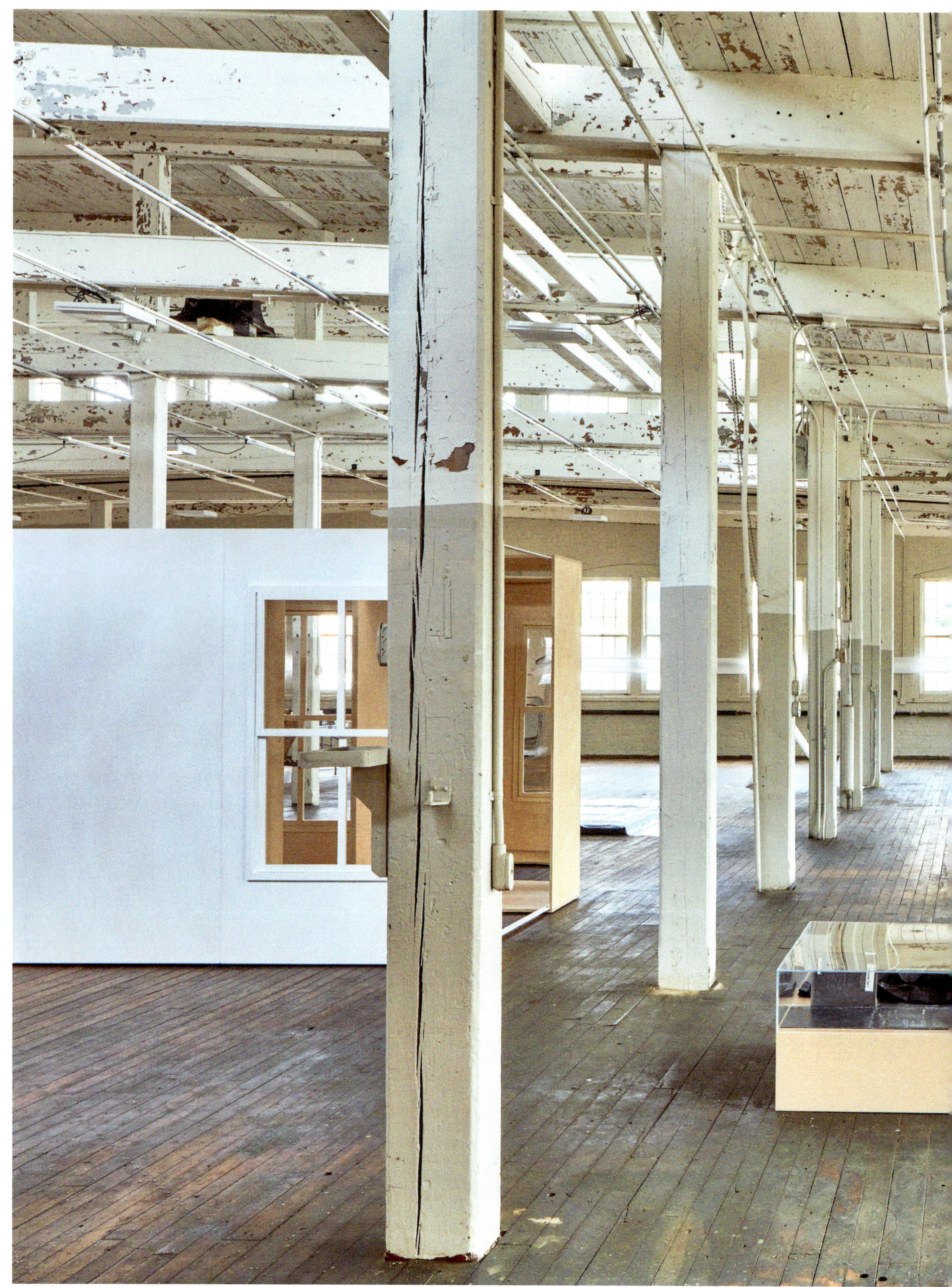

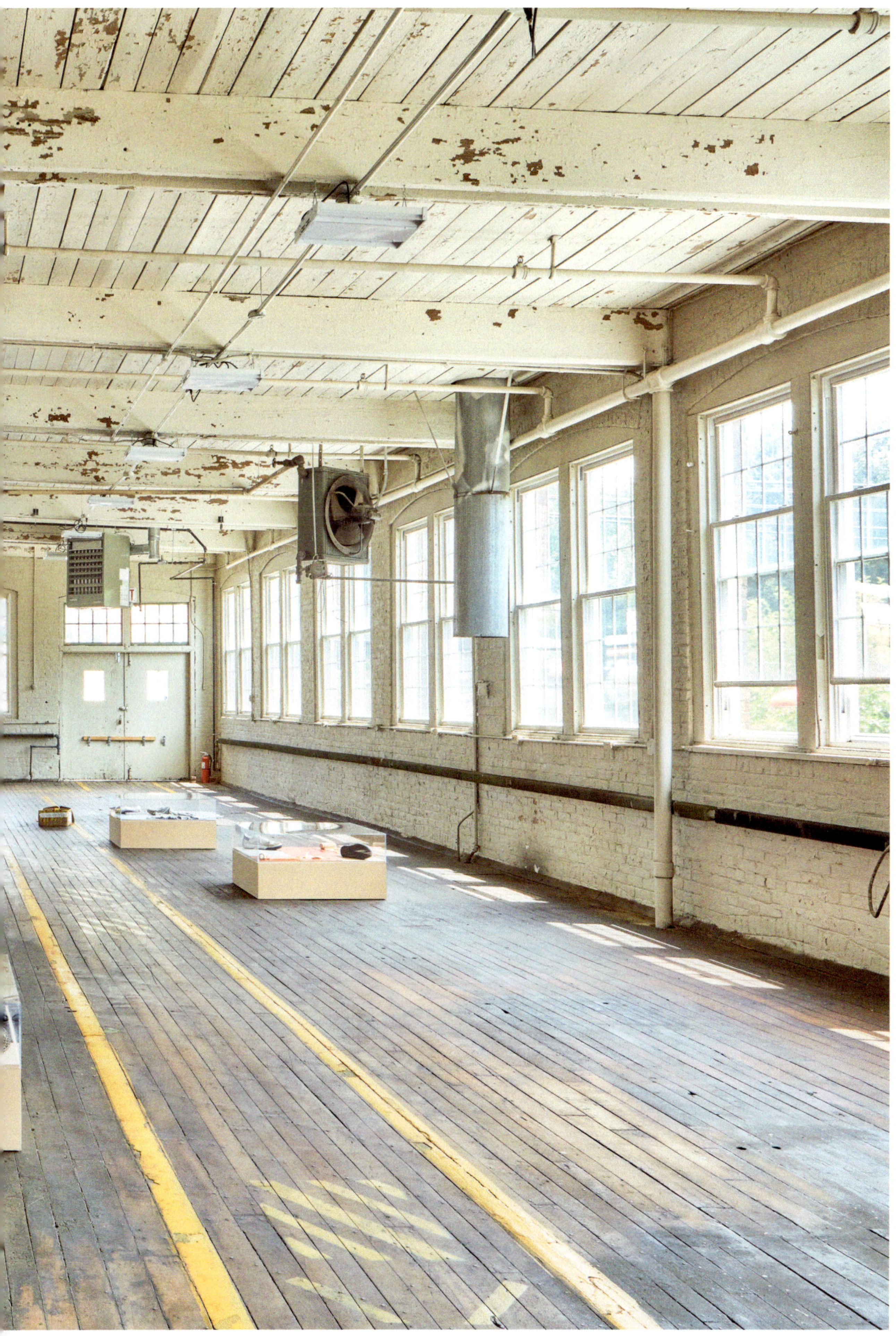

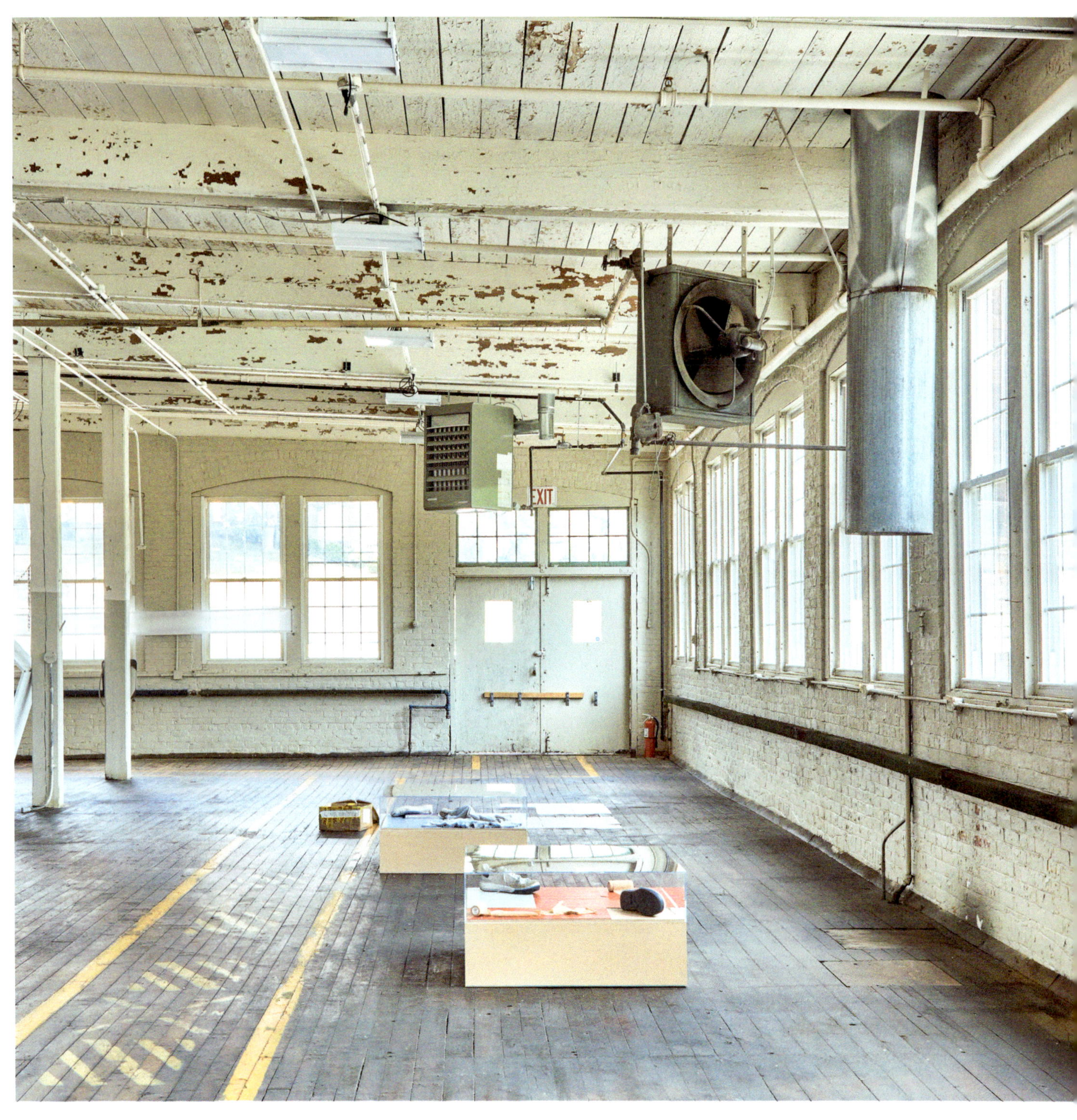

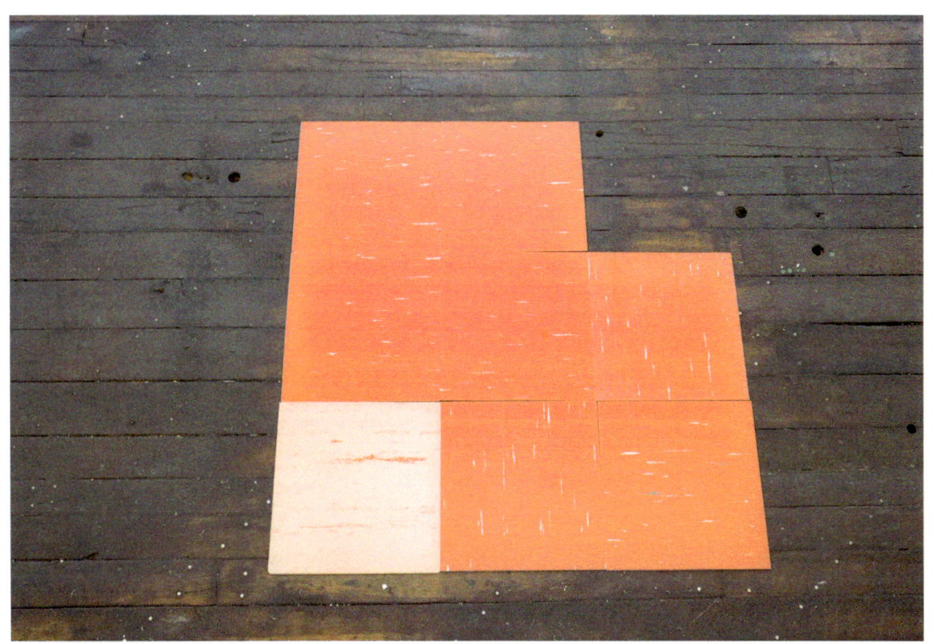

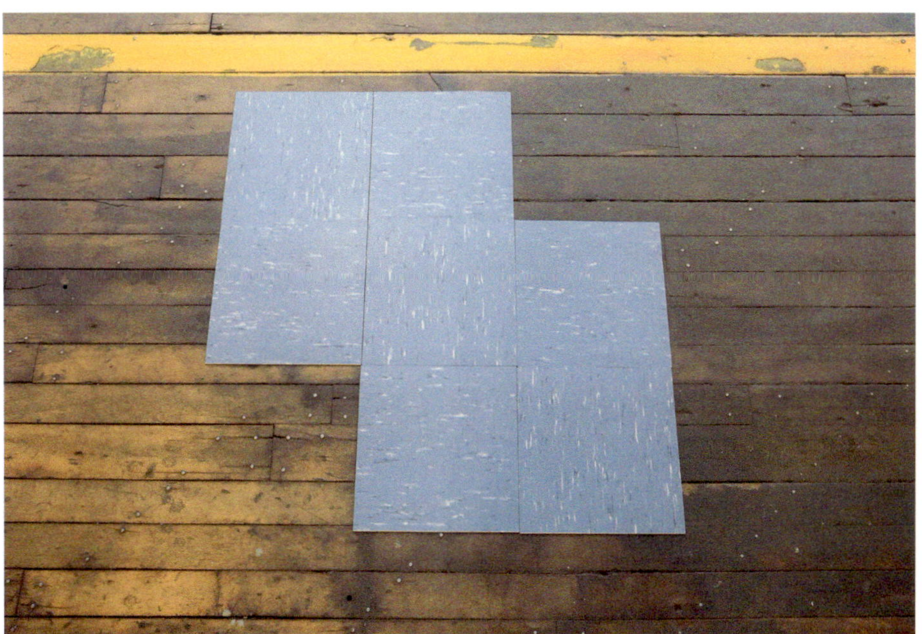

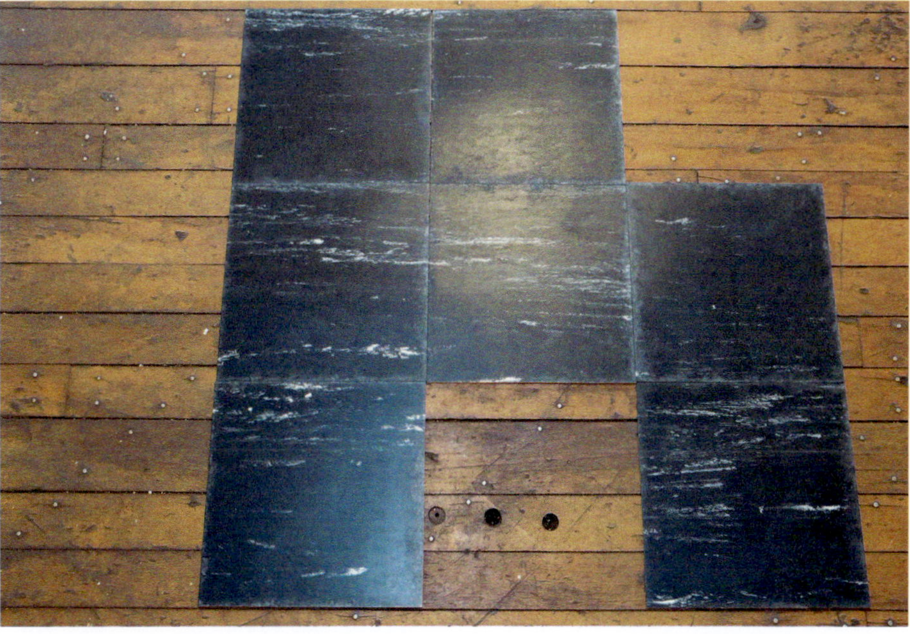

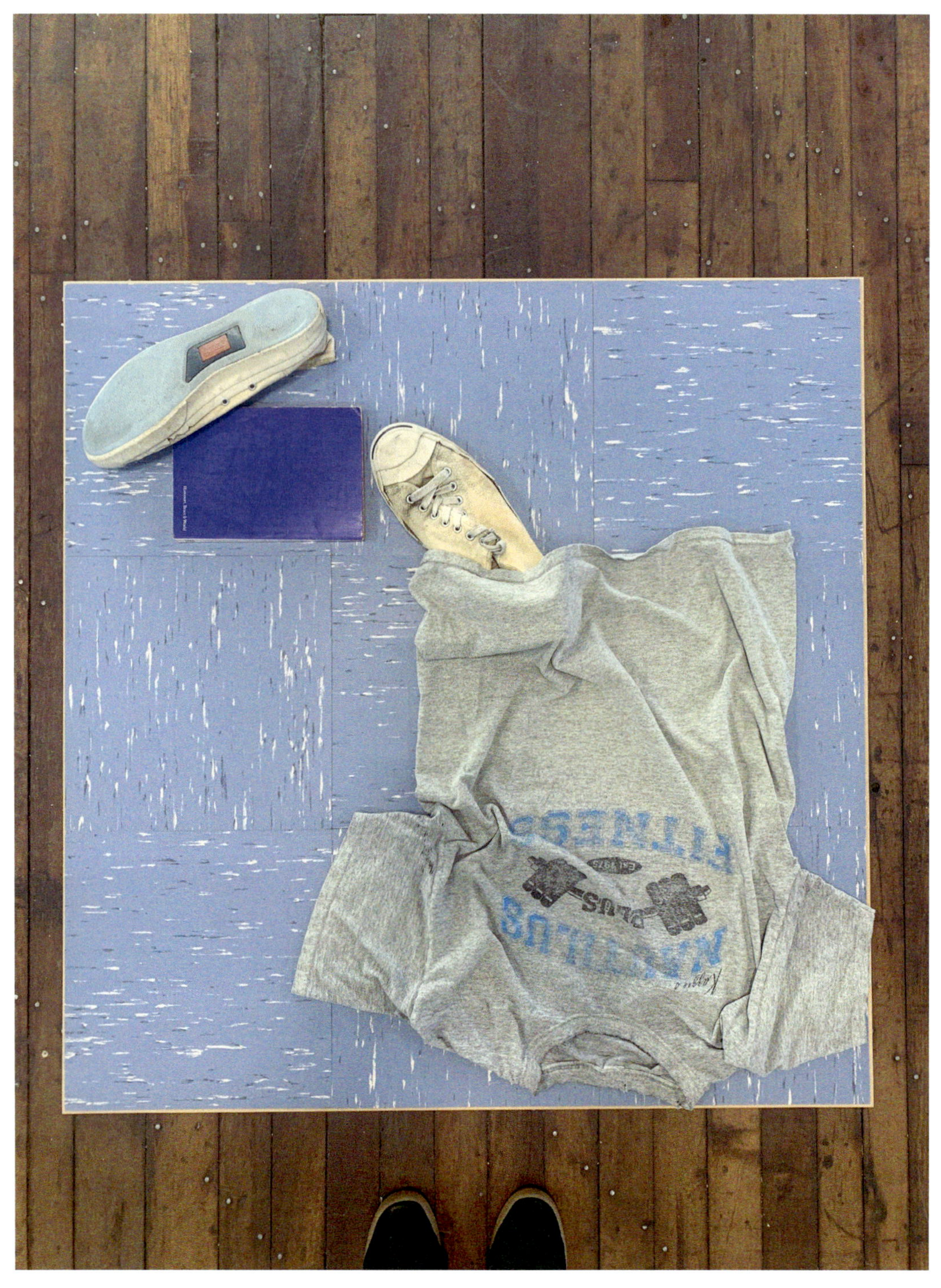

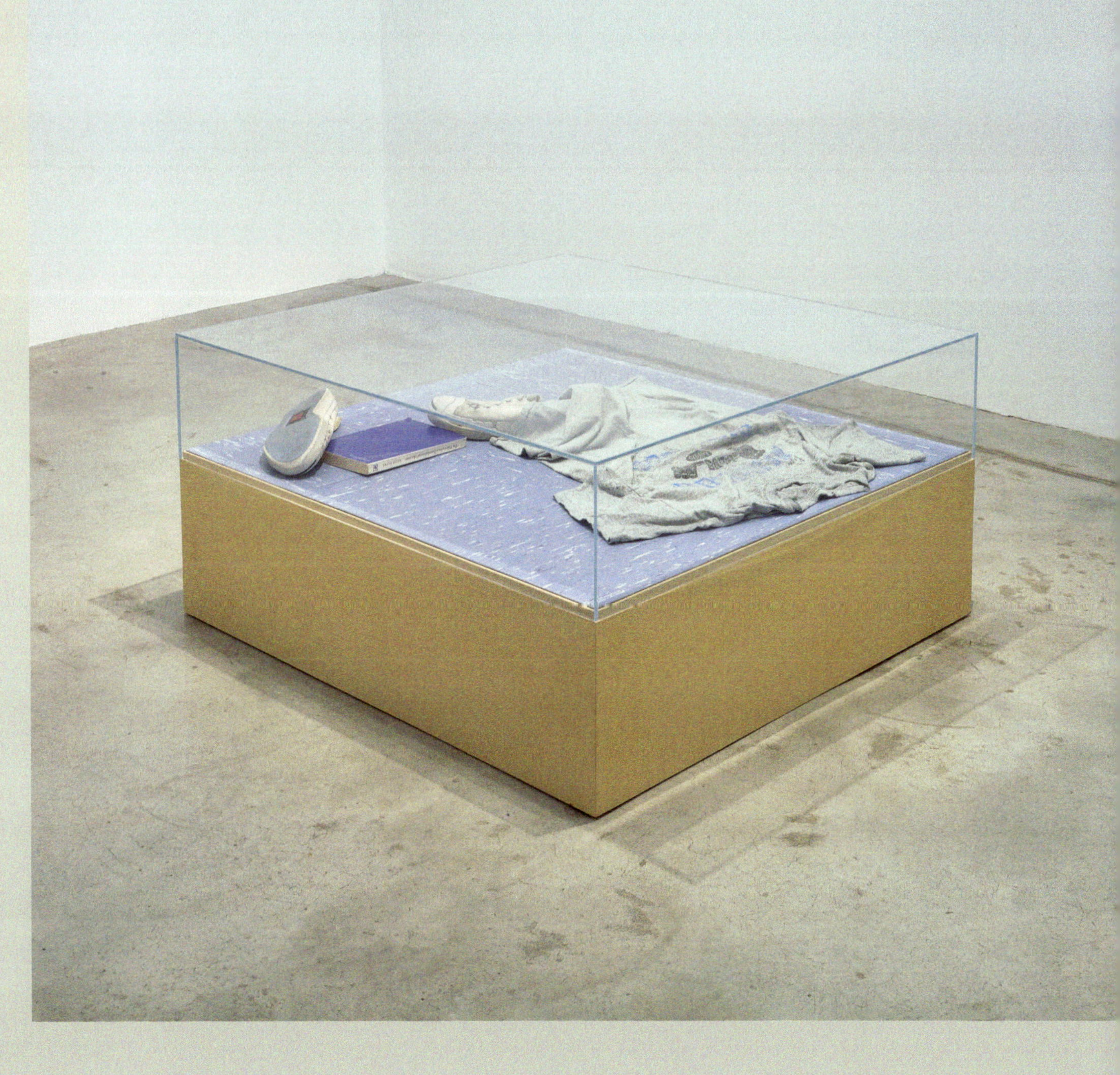

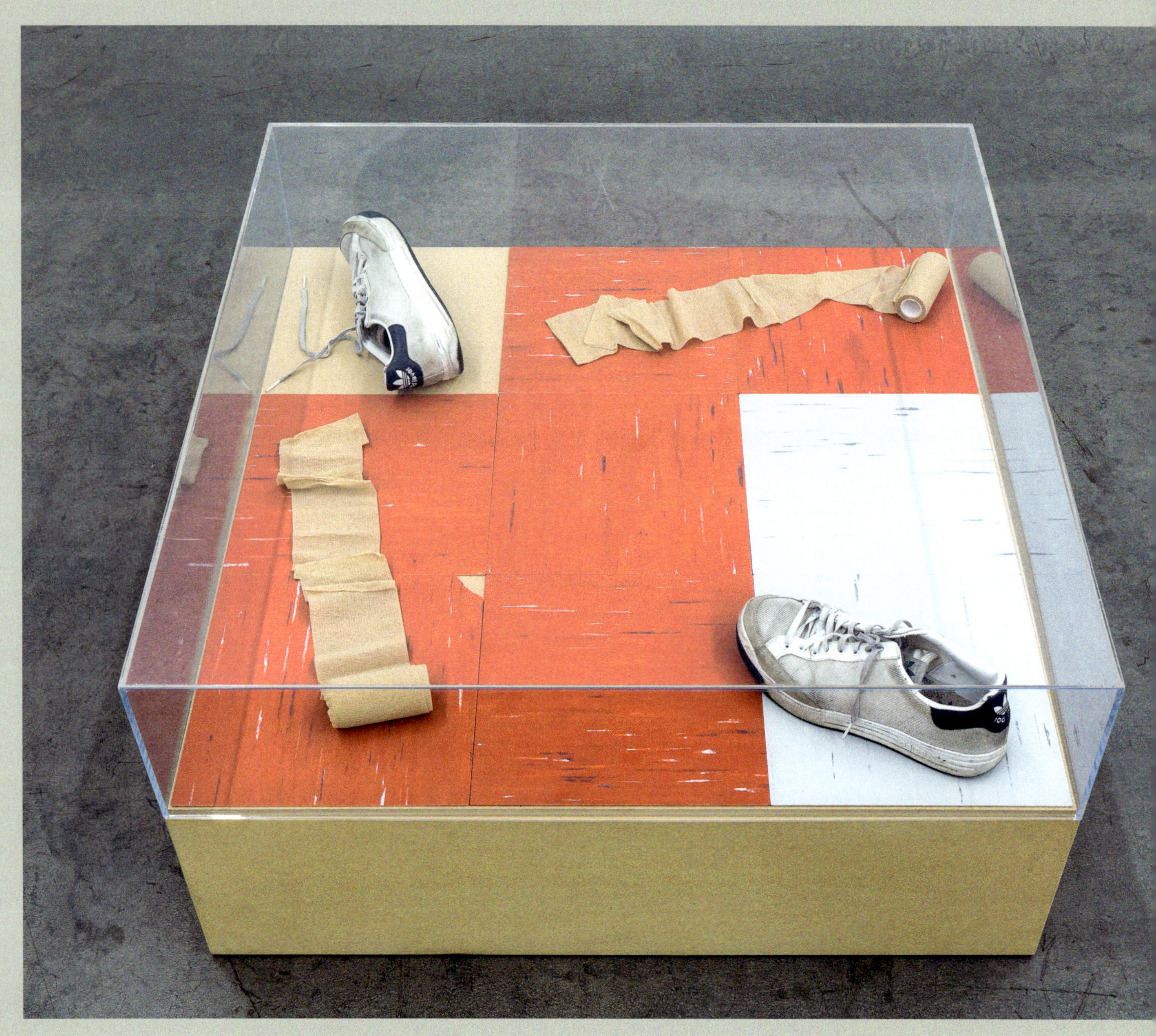

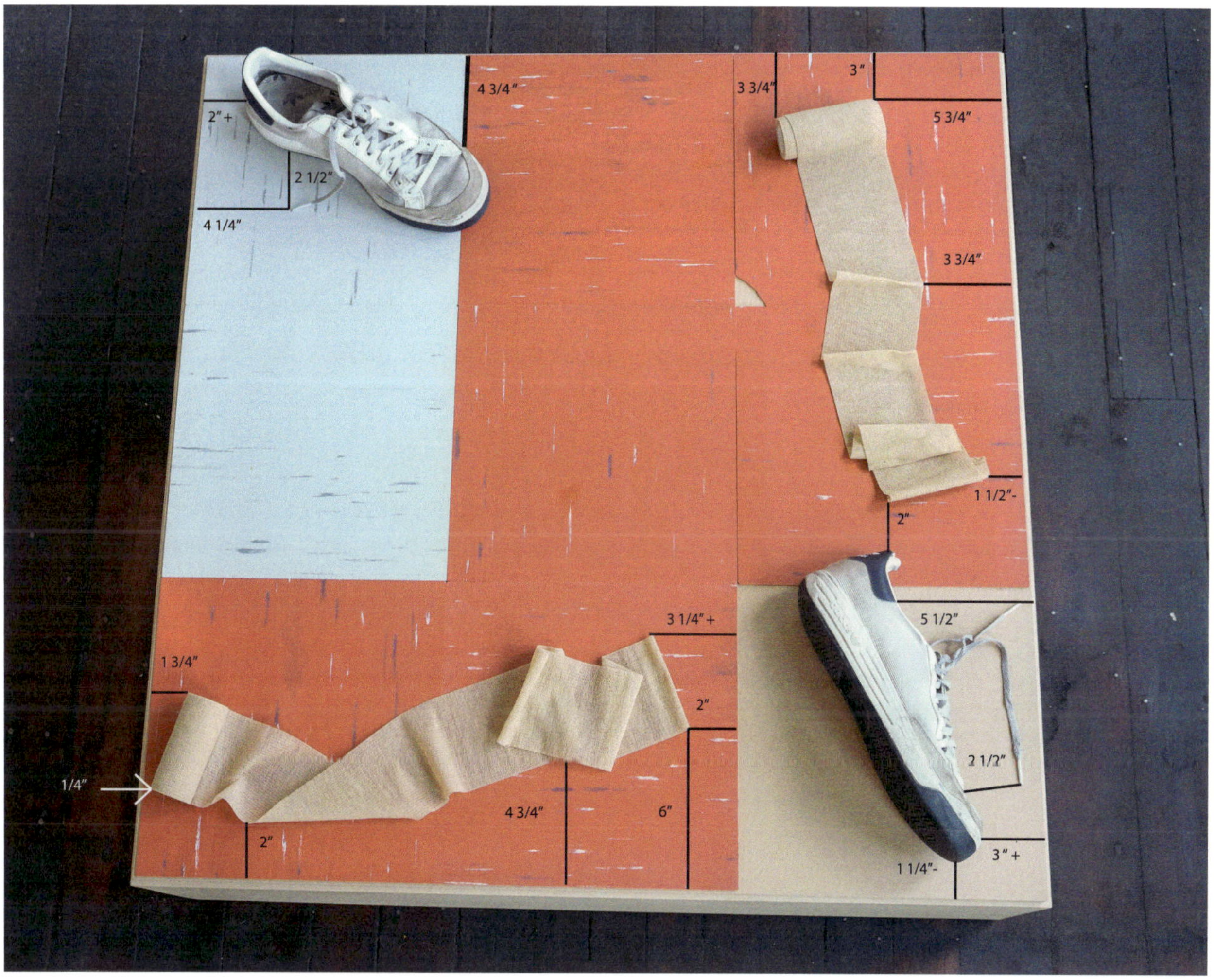

2" +
2 1/2"
4 1/4"
4 3/4"
3 3/4"
3"
5 3/4"
3 3/4"
1 1/2"-
2"
1 3/4"
3 1/4"+
2"
5 1/2"
2 1/2"
1/4"
2"
4 3/4"
6"
1 1/4"-
3" +

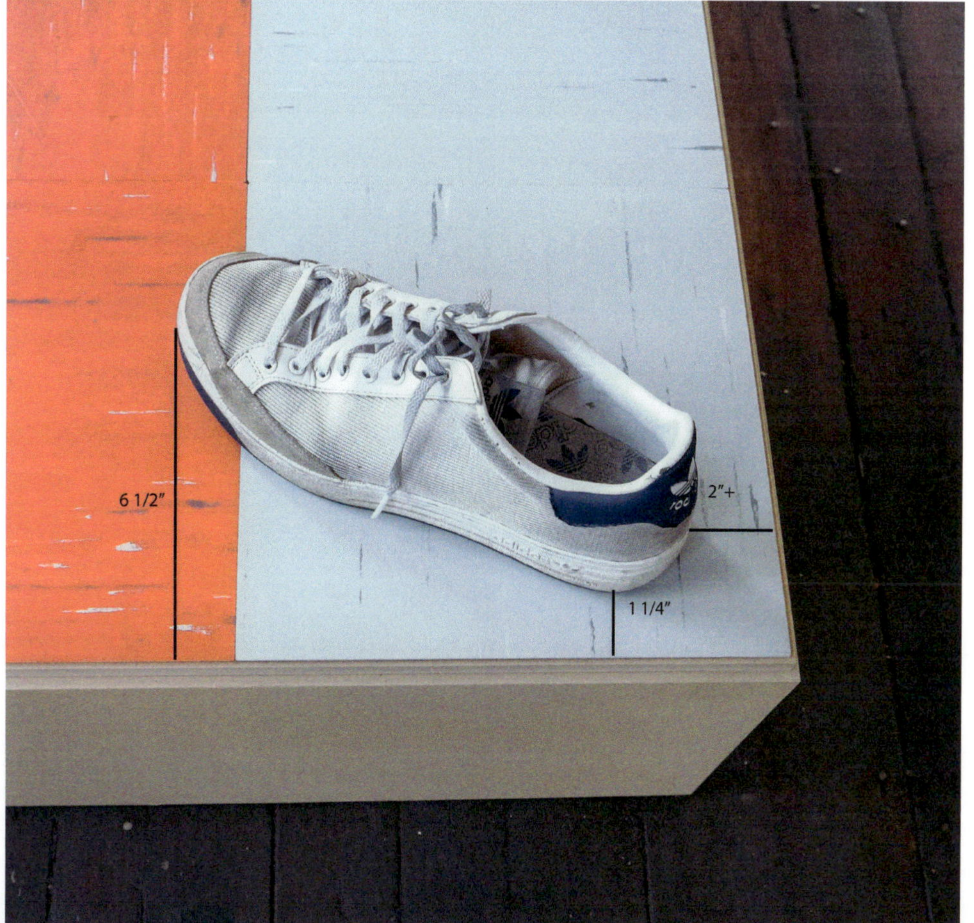

6 1/2"
2"+
1 1/4"

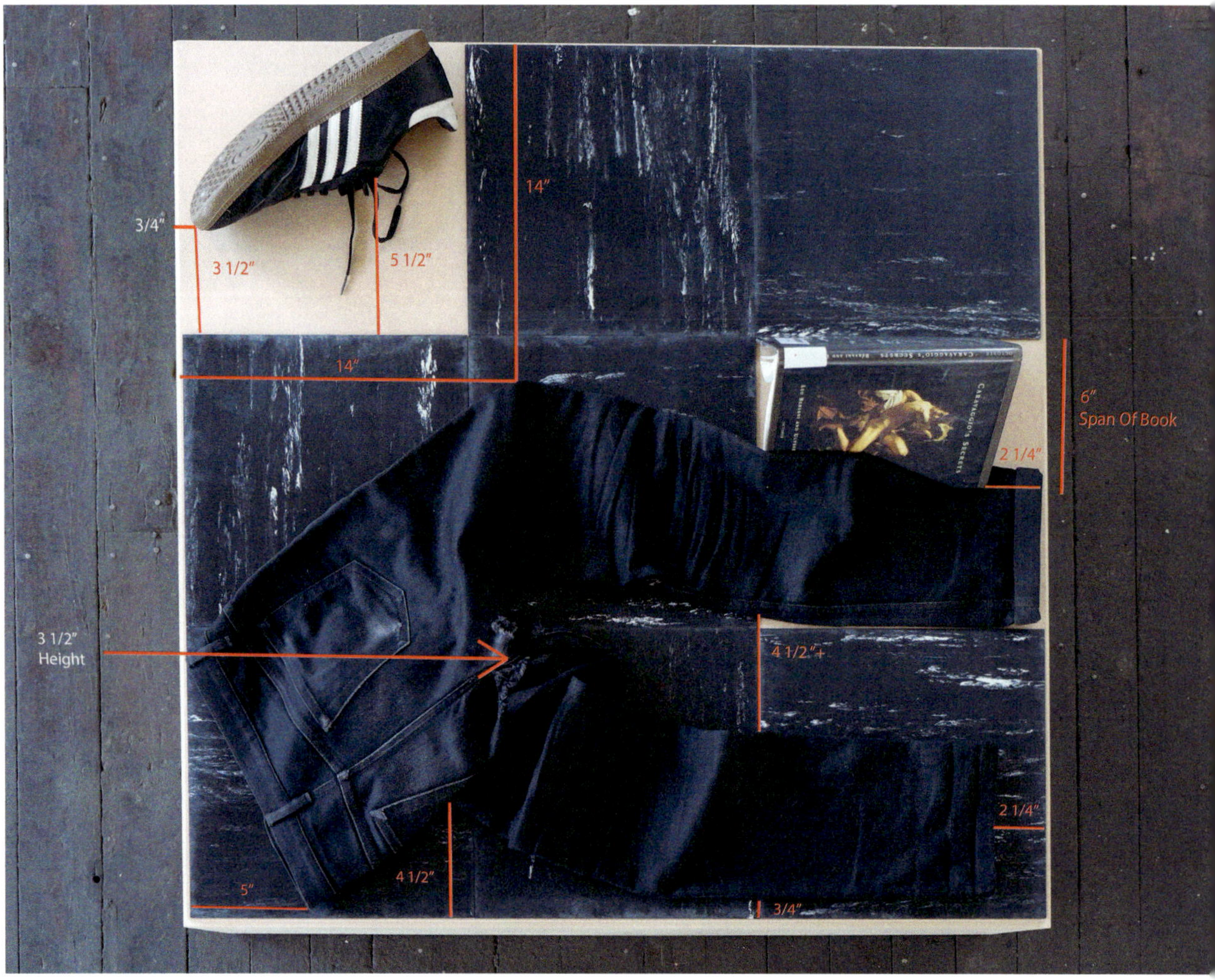

3/4"
3 1/2"
5 1/2"
14"
14"
6"
Span Of Book
2 1/4"
3 1/2"
Height
4 1/2"+
2 1/4"
5"
4 1/2"
3/4"

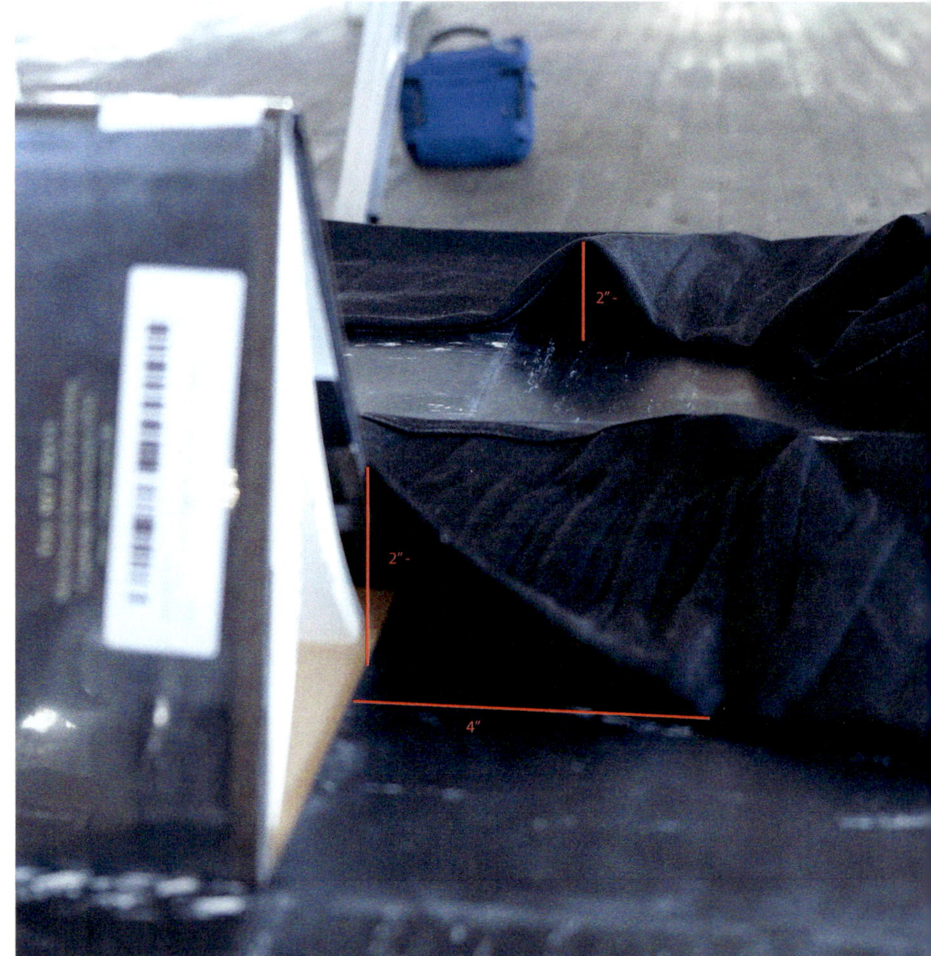
2" -
2" -
4"

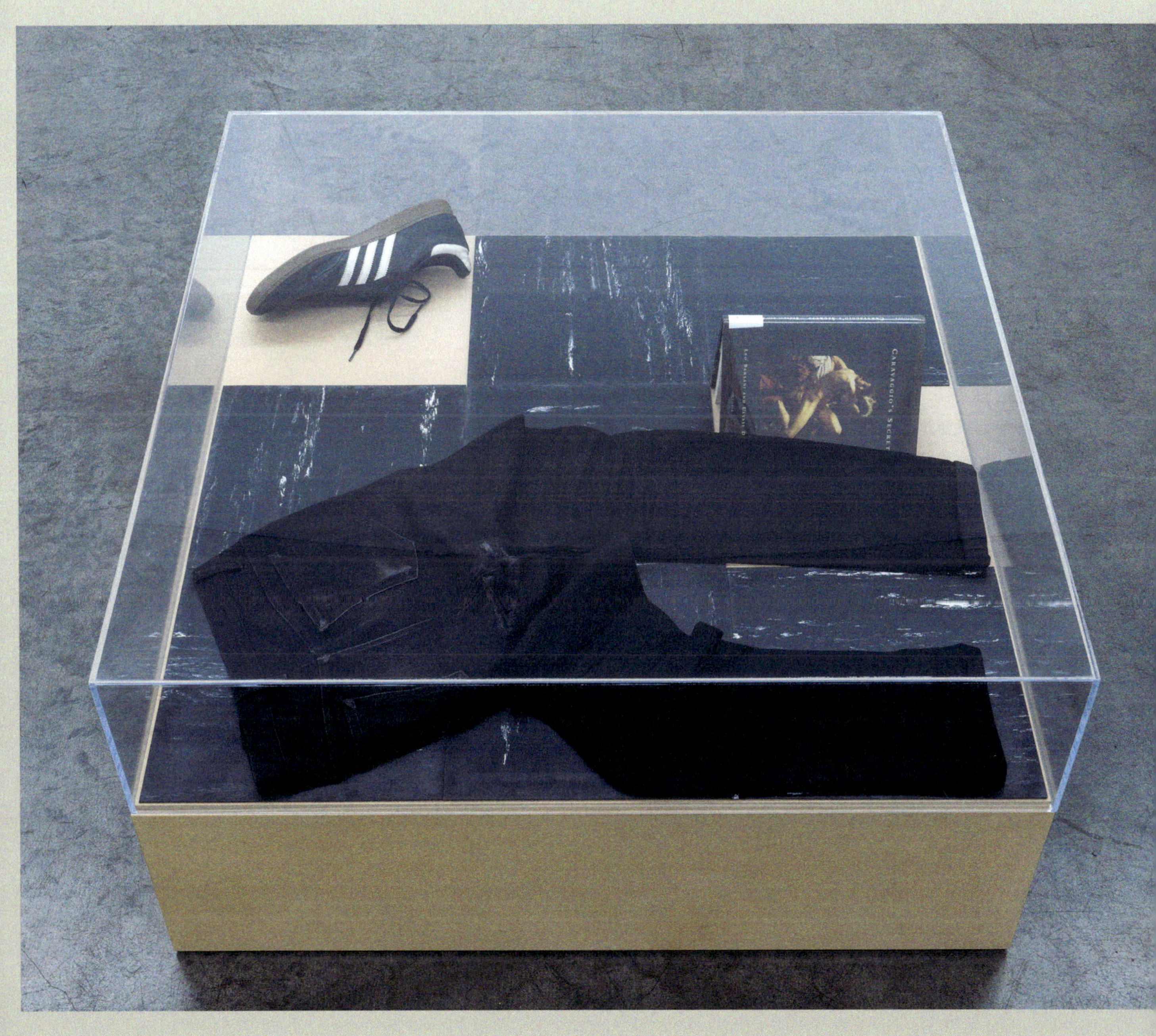

CARAVAGGIO'S SECRETS

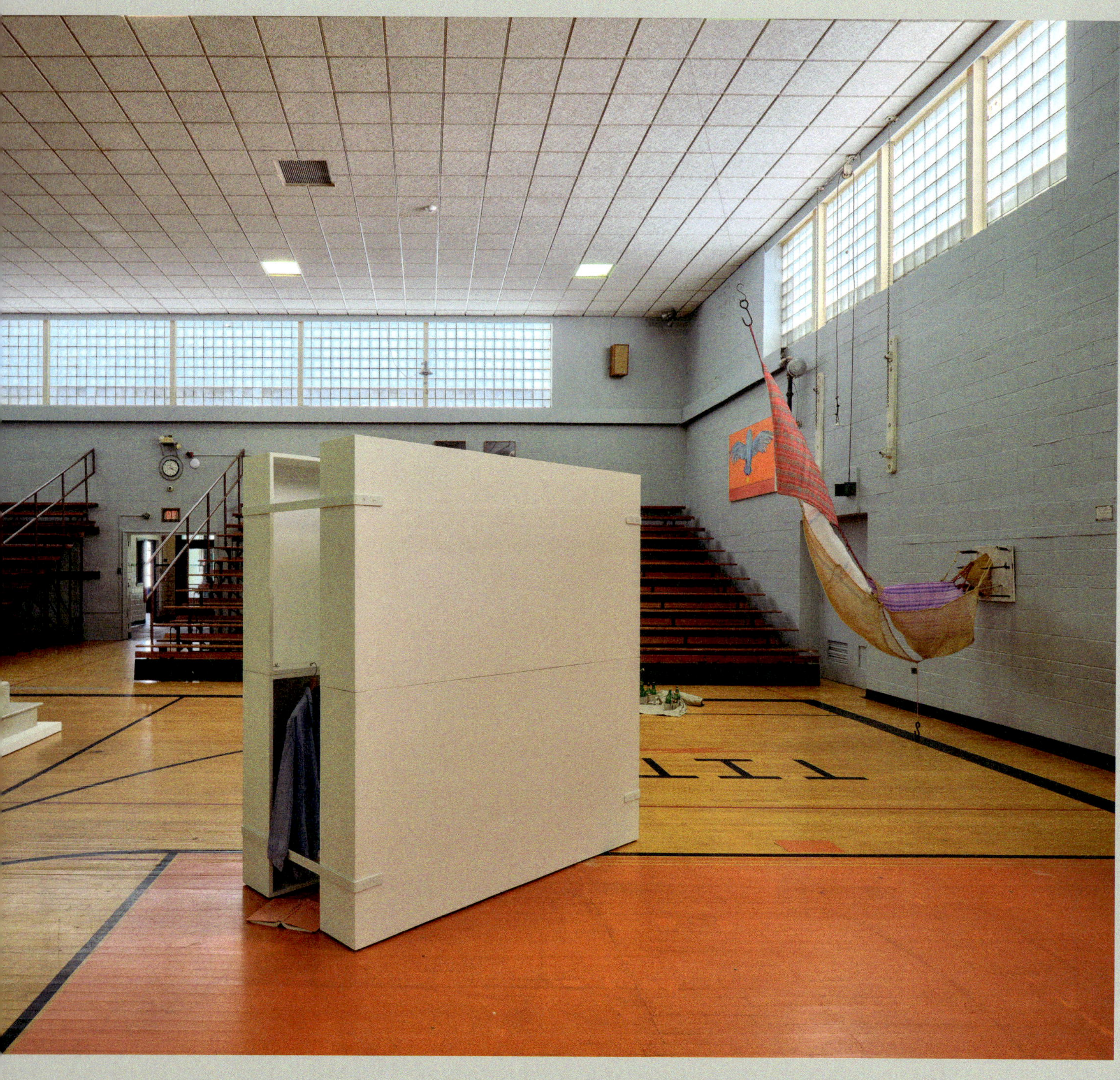

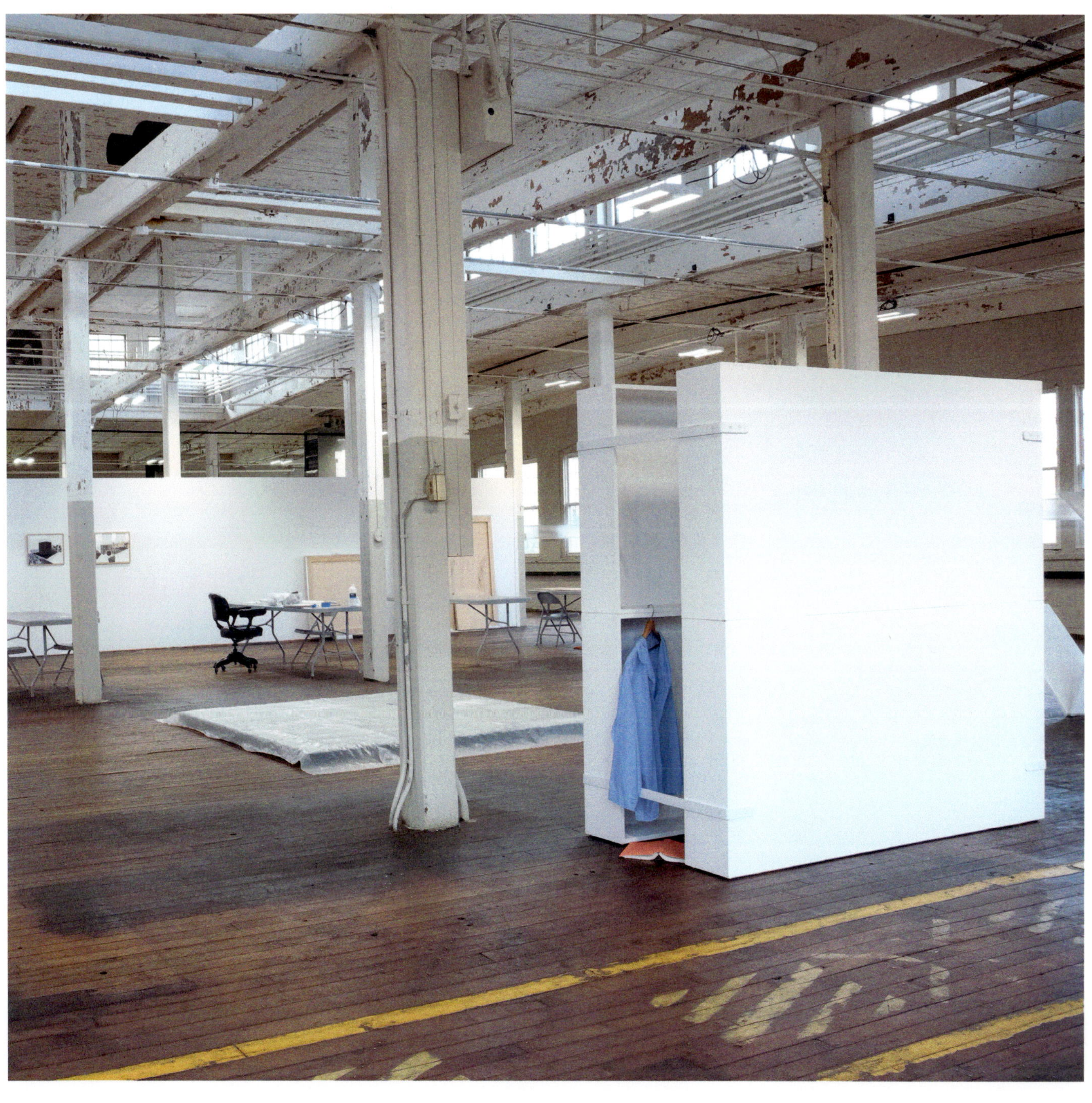

211

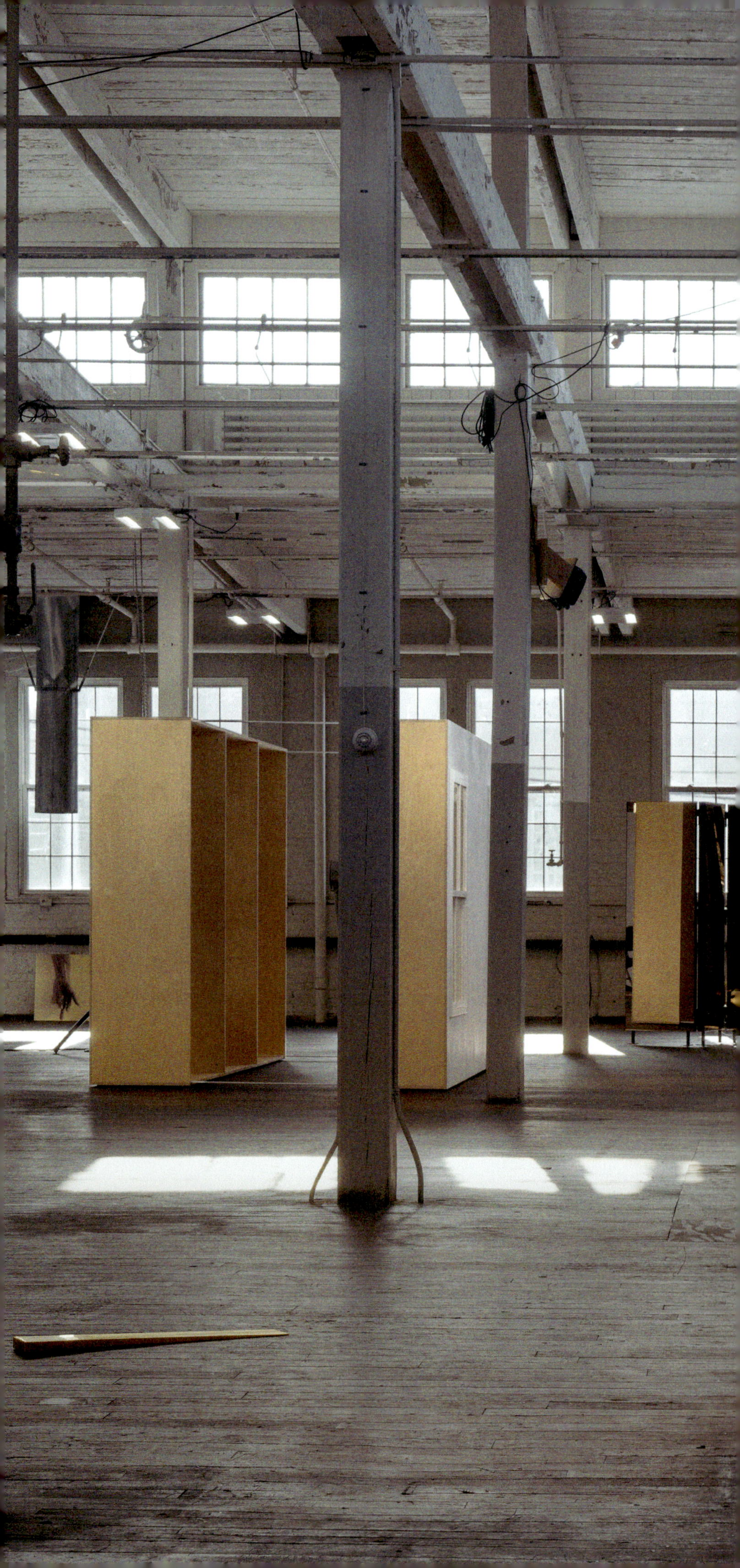

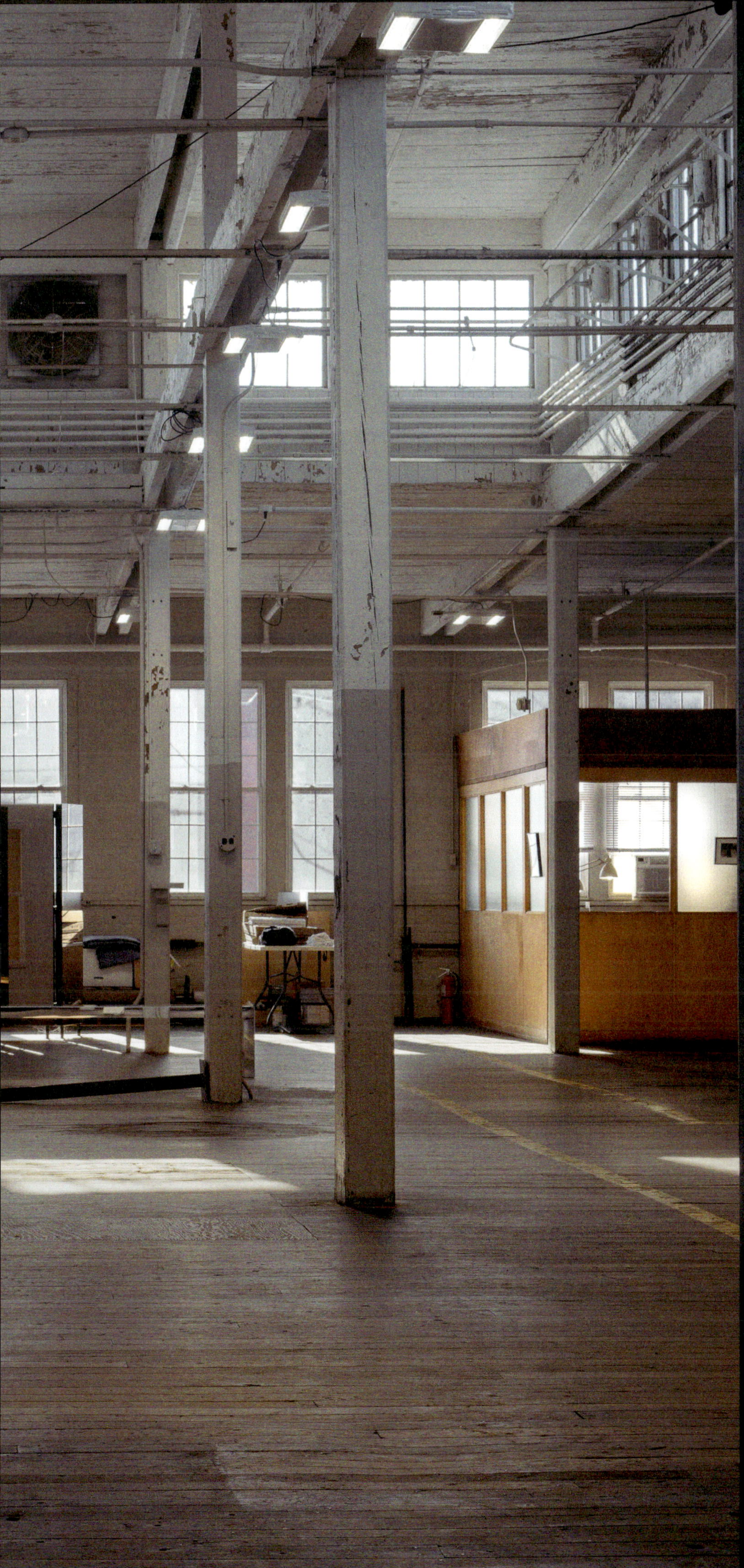

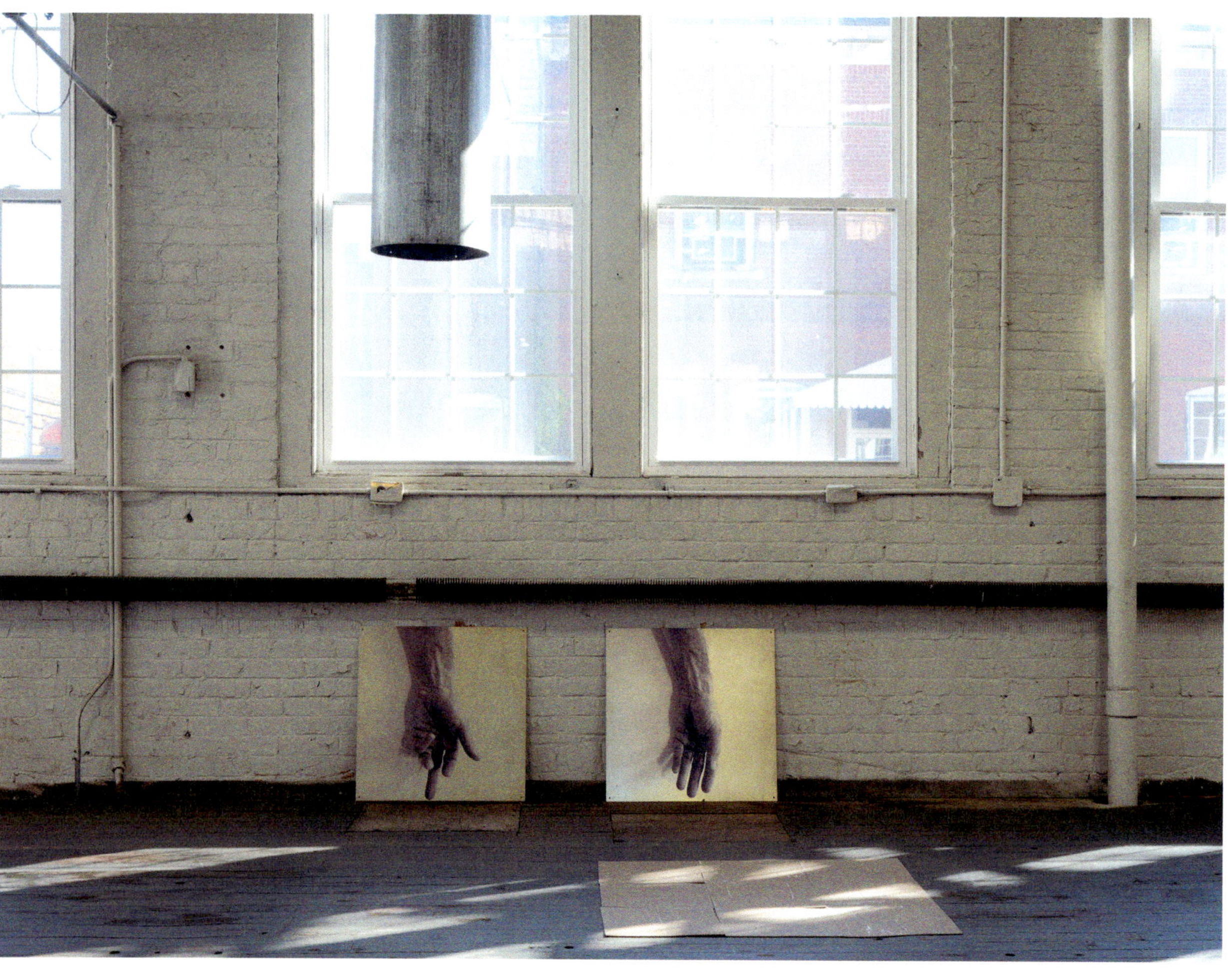

Editing several of the panels out of the room
accomplished what I was after and whittled
the work down from one continuous span to
something closer to the rhythm of intervals, with
the lengths of blank wall between what turned
out to be four distinct panels also playing a role.
Studio Contortion Sequence I–IV remained in place
throughout the project. I made two additional
iterations that were included in the works I sent
to Berlin for my exhibition at Neu, but the original
four never budged from their location in the room
within a room. Each time I consideedr a new
possible plan for the space, I would hesitate and
couldn't commit to taking *Sequence* down; it was
too well calibrated there, and worked in tandem
with the active studio area on the far side of the
next room. The mirrors interplayed with the steel
braces in a way I hadn't quite expected, with the
braces acting as an arm that links the panel on
the wall to the floor in a gesture of codepen-
dency, while simultaneously blocking anyone who
approached to catch their reflection. The folding
chairs that I would sit in for hours, contemplating
this box of a room, at some point made their way
into the equation and completed the series. It's
the chairs and their slight shift and turn in each
of the four instances, producing variations, that
emerged out of the contrapposto video works, I
think, and became the very limited dance steps of
the composition.

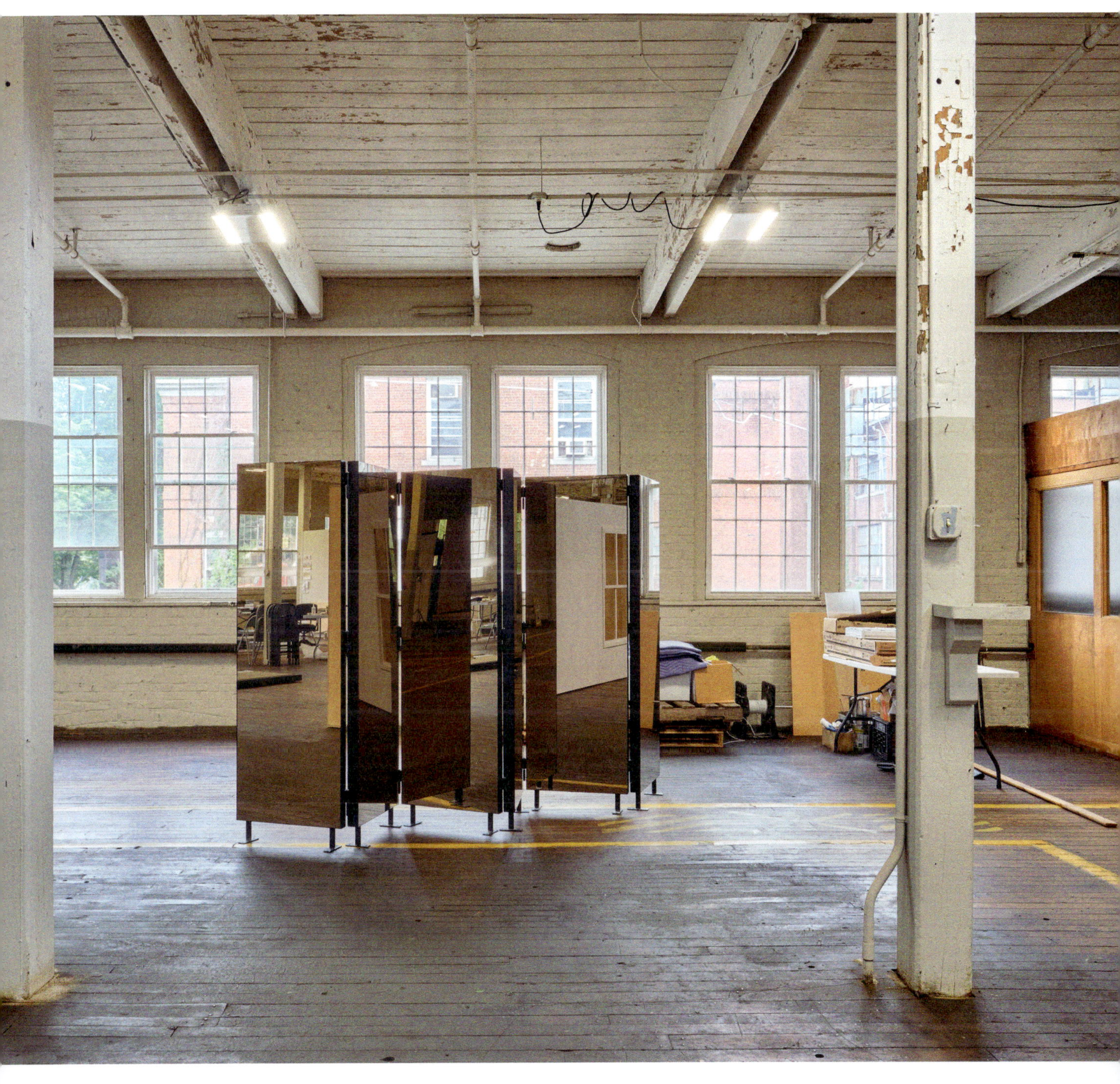

Claire Bergeal recently shared with me a thought she had, which somehow I hadn't thought about so clearly, which connects to all this, and to the shift I made in designing this project in Torrington. She referred to the idea of hosting, and that for so long, throughout my working life in fact, I had been hosted by institutions or art spaces, galleries, etc., invited to a particular location, and that invitation had been the structural backbone of my work, prompting my response. This project reversed those terms, and I became the host. I became more anchored in place. The pandemic—and other reasons, too—determined this to some degree. But I also wanted to feel grounded in this space, and have others, periodically, come to me, in a form of role reversal. I wanted the structural shift of it to occur, to experience that reversal-as-refusal.

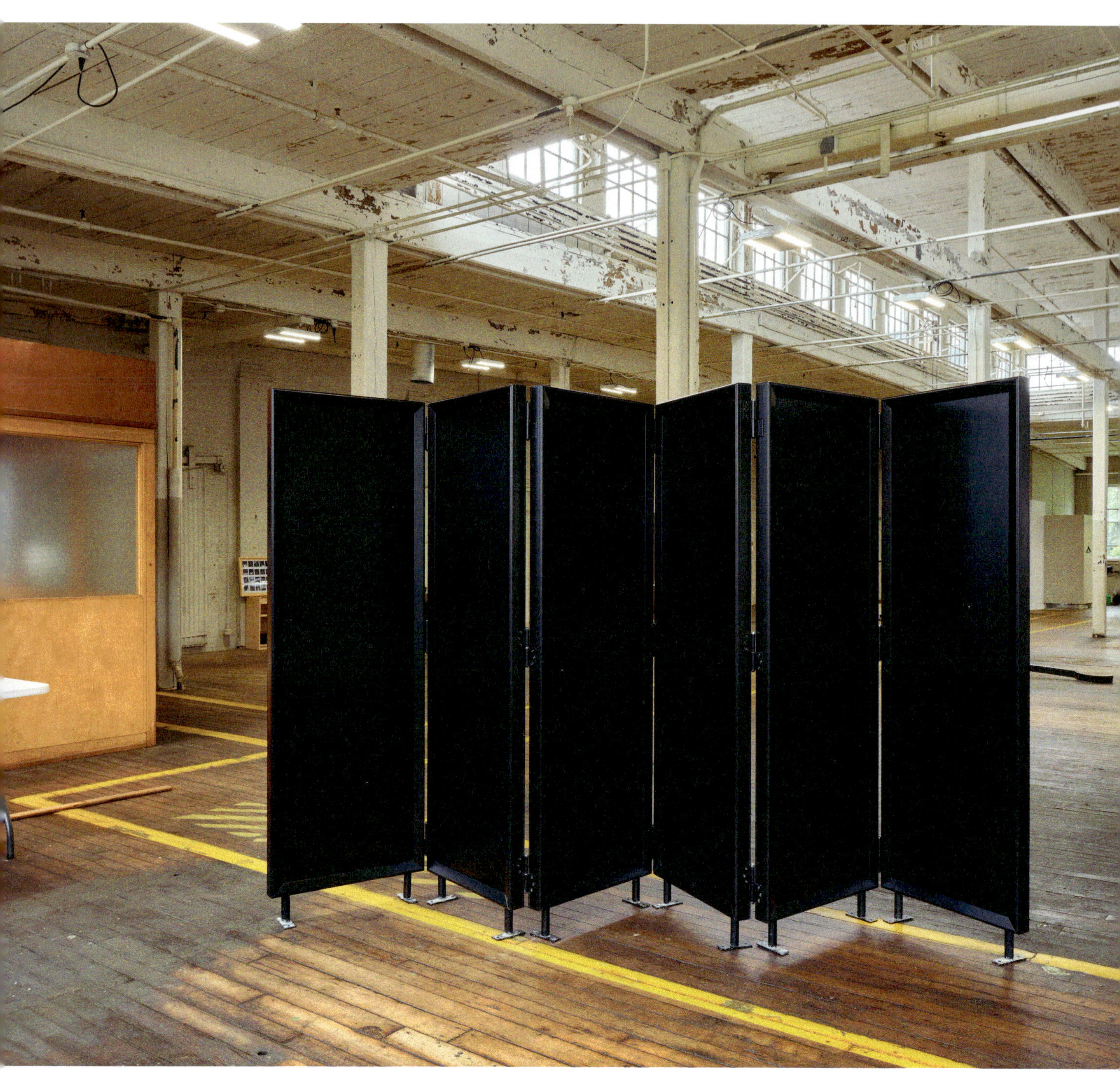

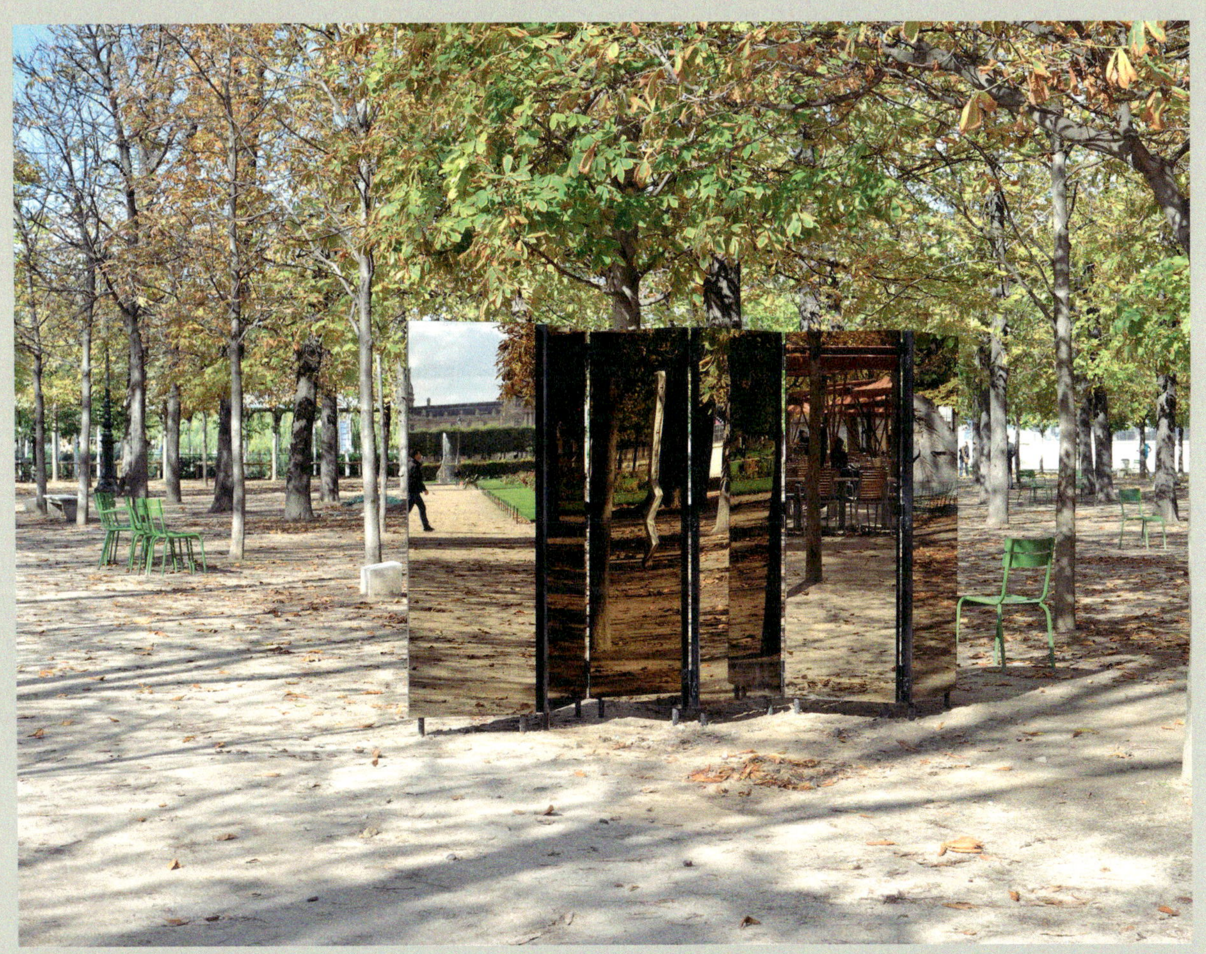

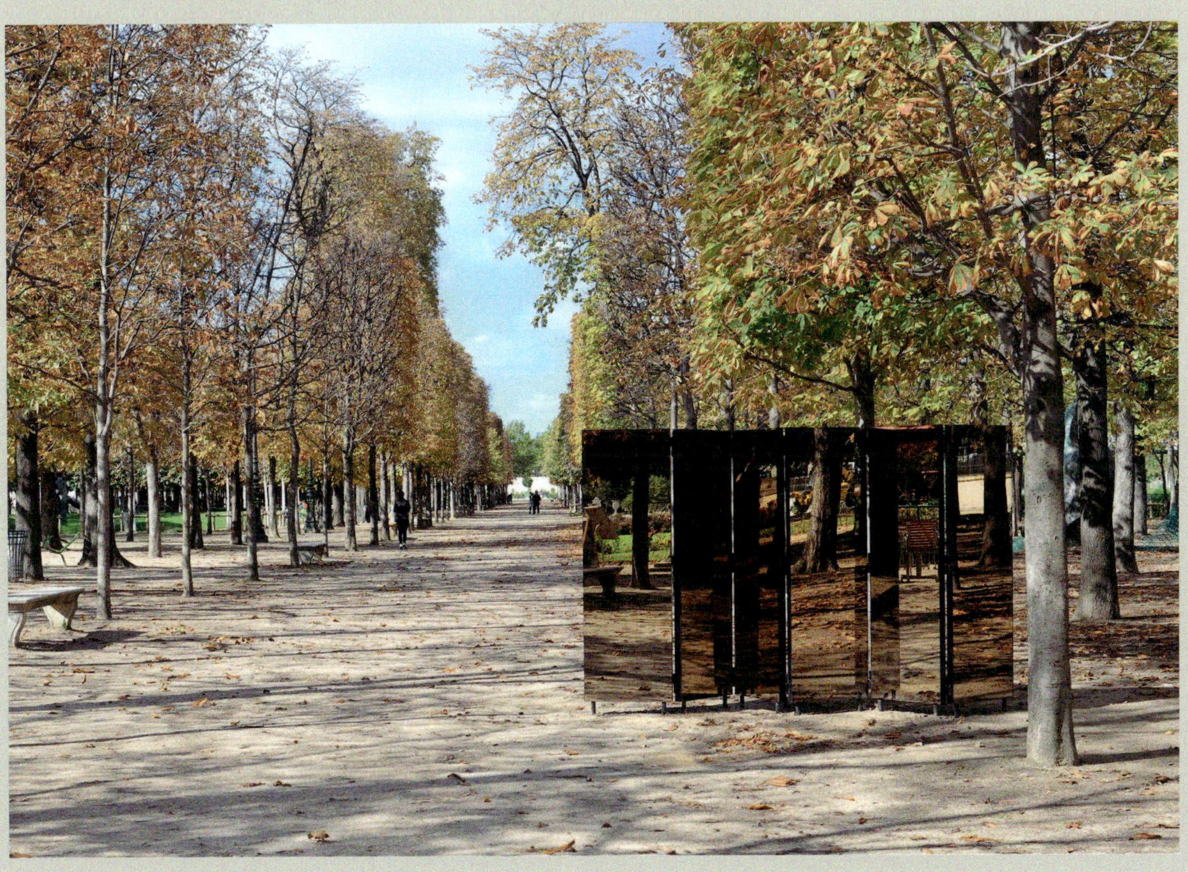

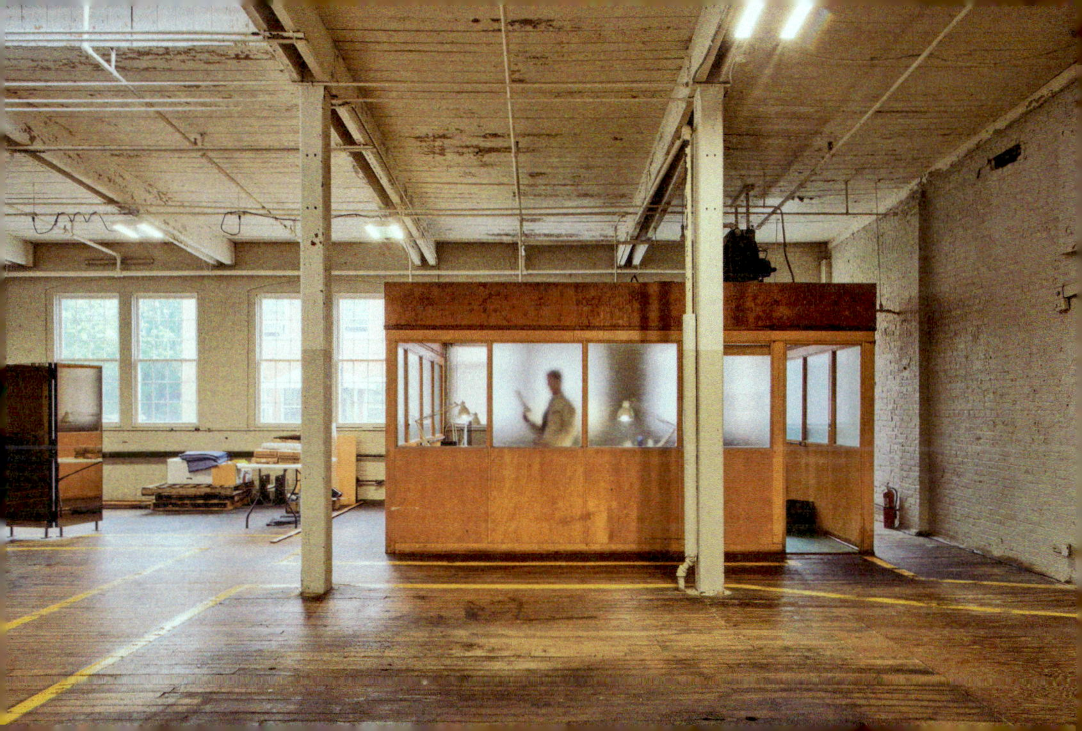

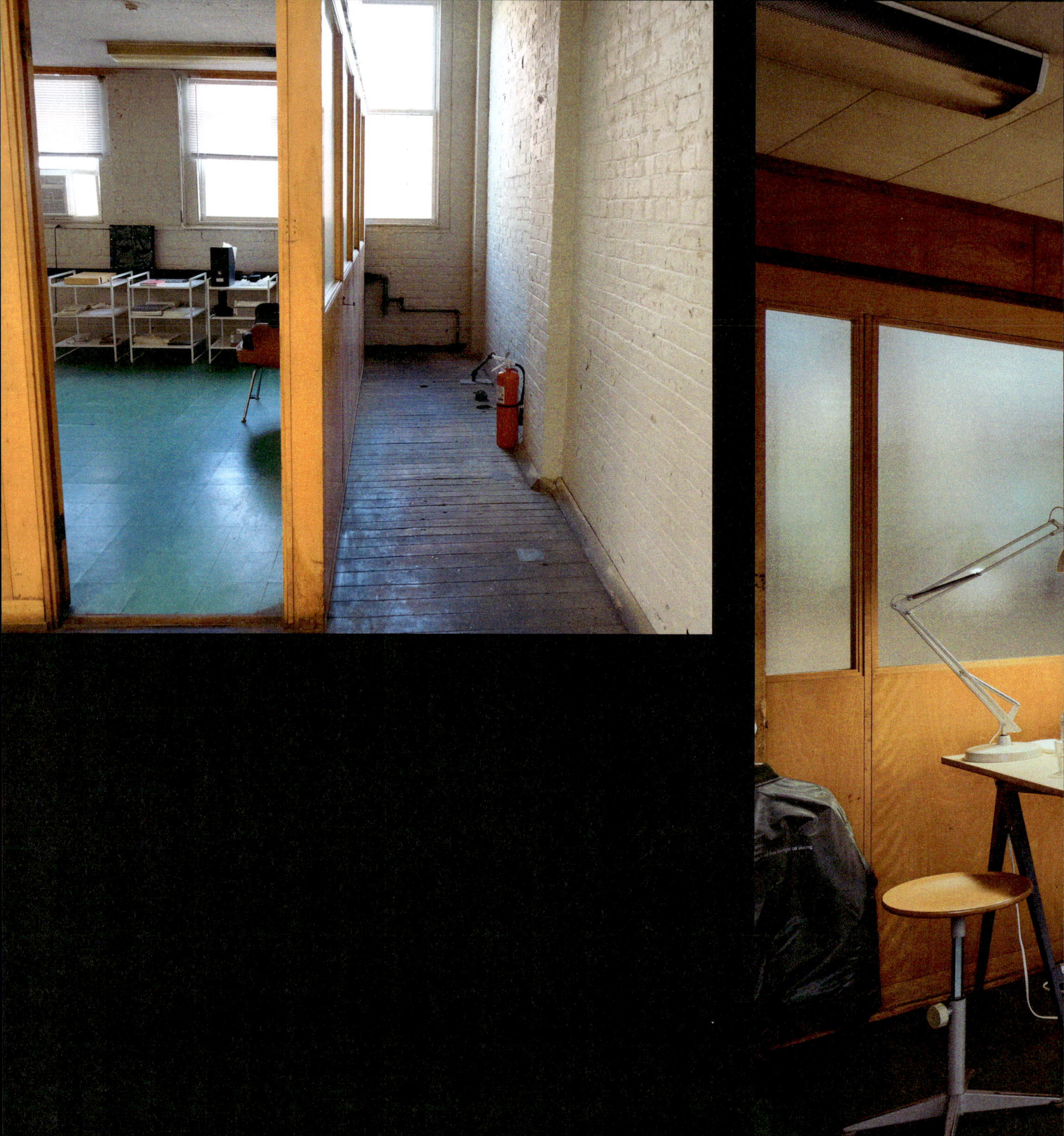

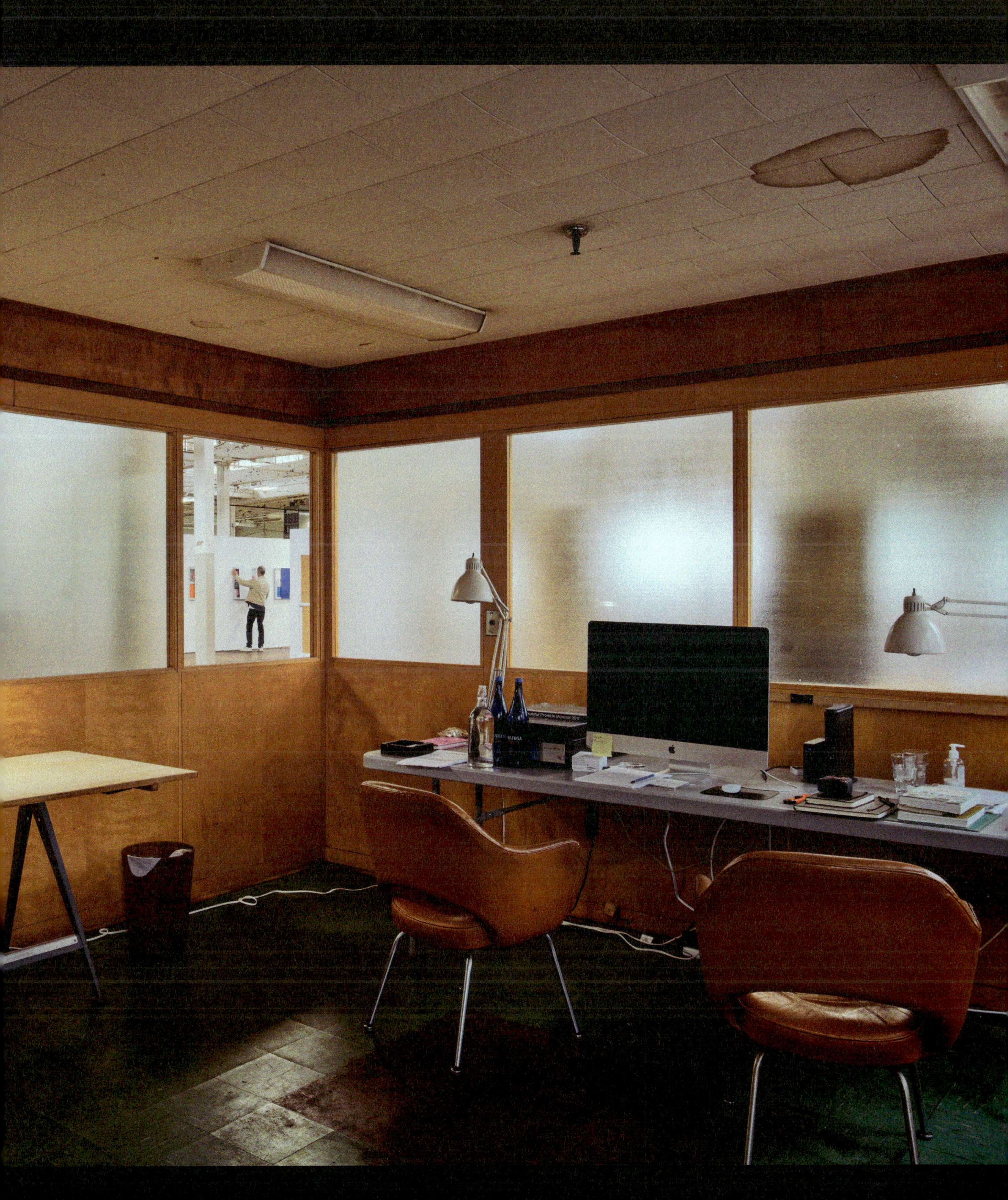

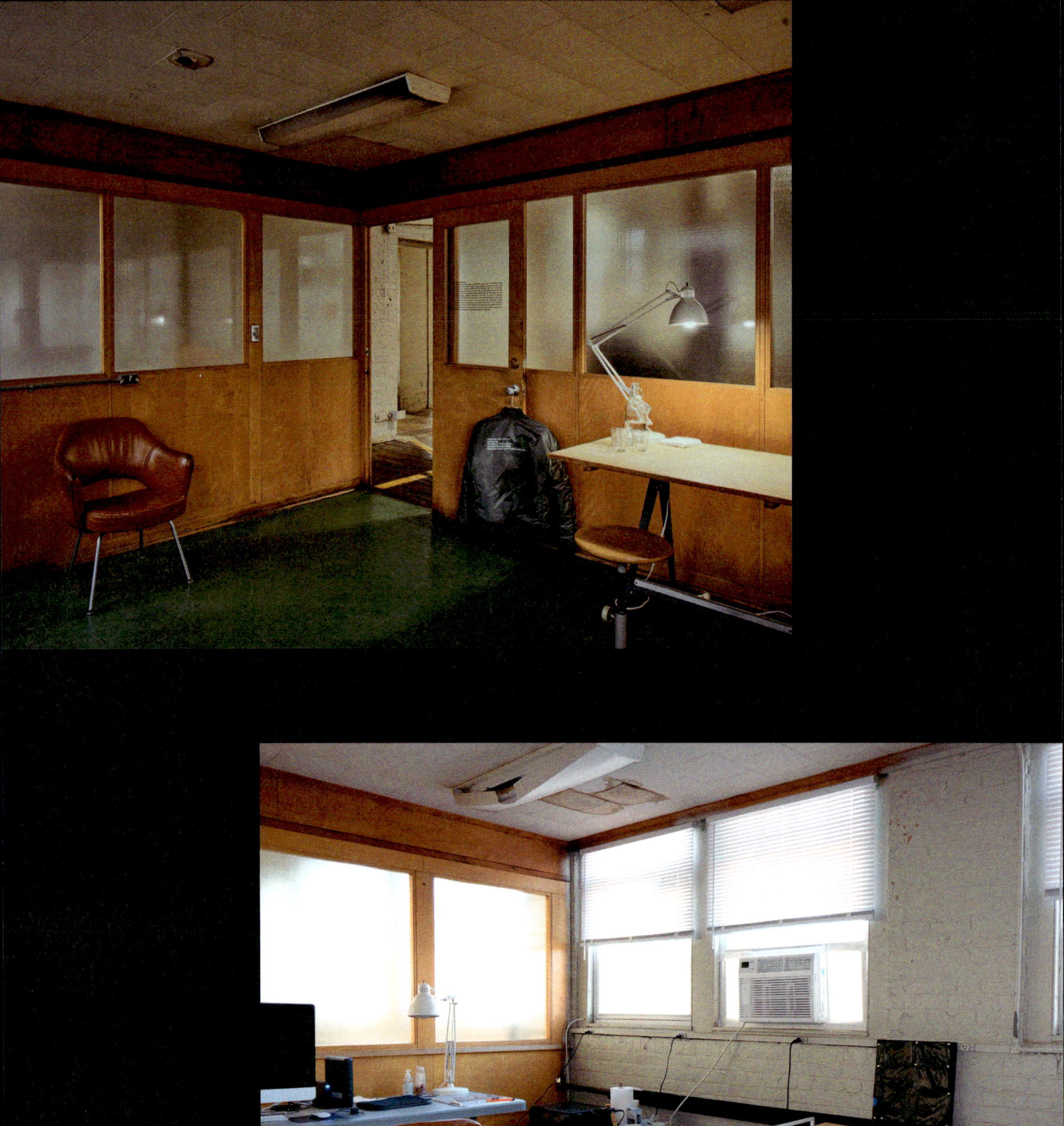

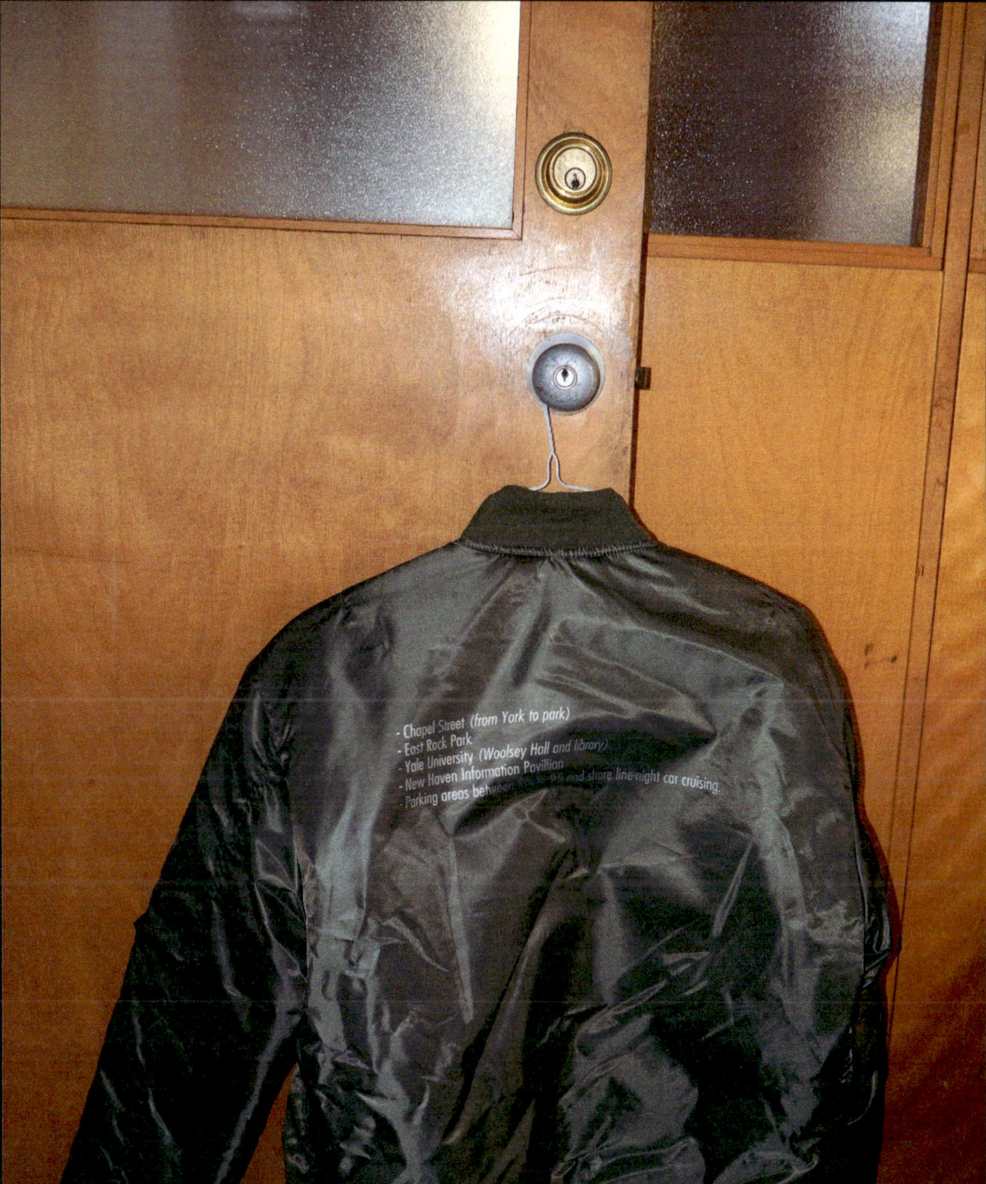
- Chapel Street (from York to park)
- East Rock Park
- Yale University (Woolsey Hall and library)
- New Haven Information Pavillion
- Parking areas between 8pm - 6am and share line-night car cruising.

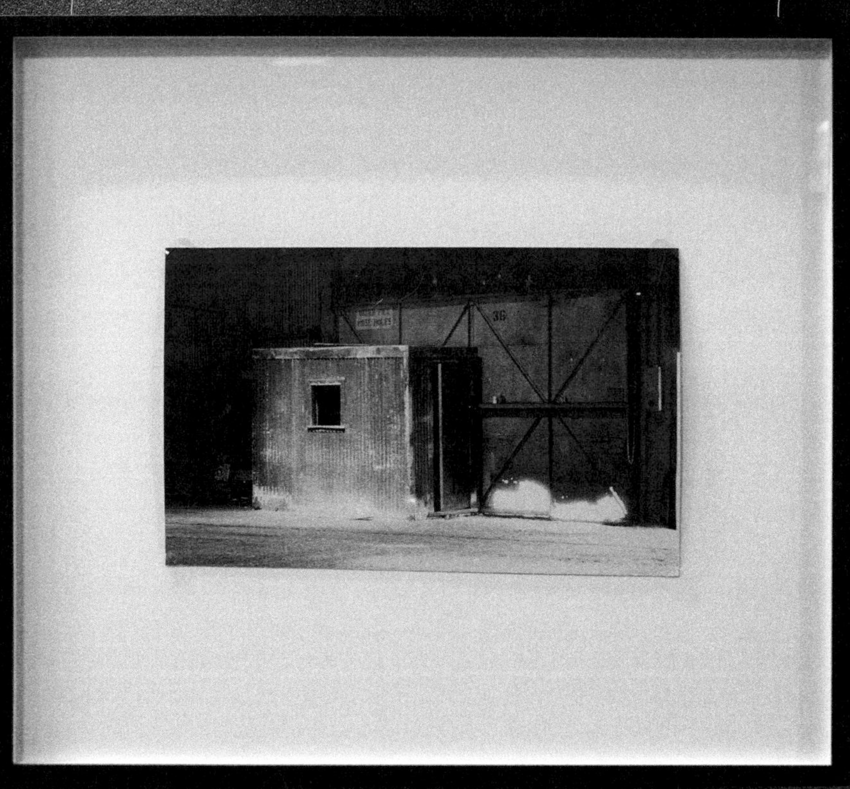
36

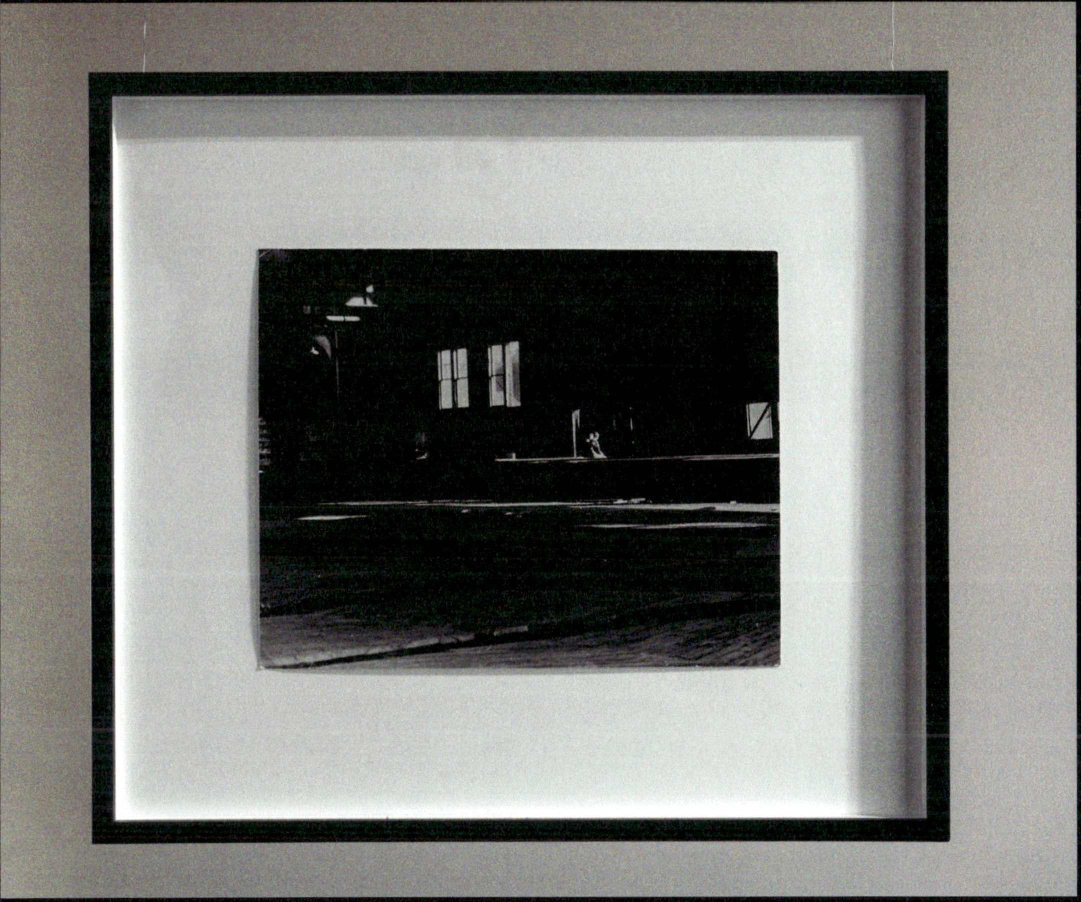

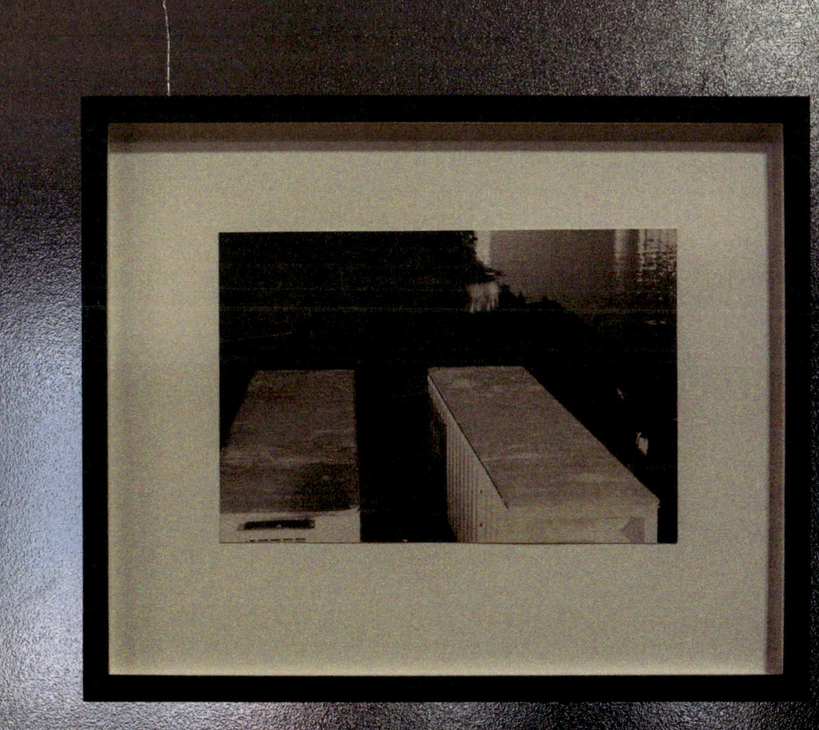

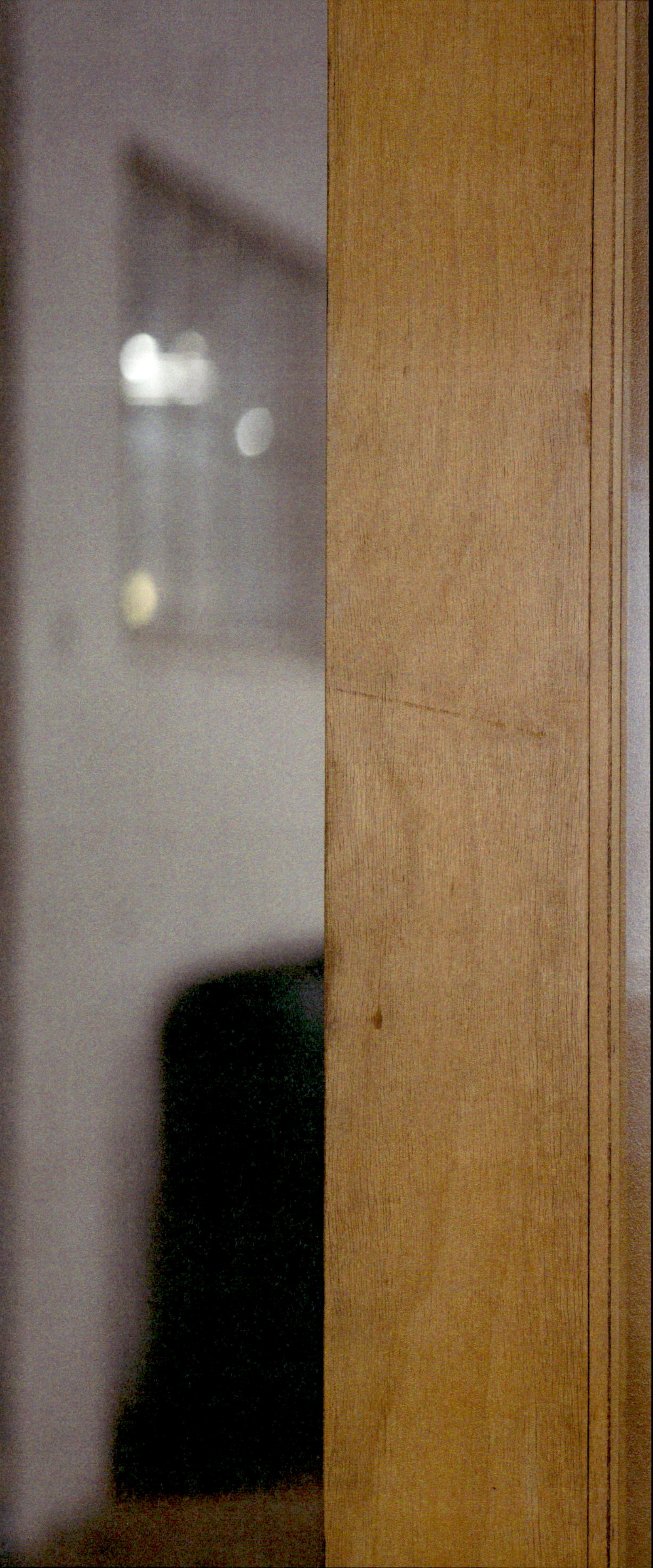

The third renovation:
The Wonder Bar is a small neighborhood gay bar on 6th Street just off Avenue A, in the East Village. It has recently changed owners, and changed decor. The film screen and the Monday night film screenings have been removed and a DJ booth with a large elliptical opening has been added. The original Wonder Bar opened around 1990 when the last of the East Village galleries (American Fine Arts, Co. and 303 Gallery) moved off of this block and into SoHo. The new incarnation of Wonder Bar is hipper and more popular than its predecessor, attracting a large mixed gay and lesbian crowd on most nights of the week. The renovation will take place on the inside of the bar, running along the west wall of the space, across from the long bar and up to the large elliptical opening of the DJ booth, creating a long green sheath of wallpaper.

8

Just to the side of *Studio Contortion Sequence I–IV*, partially blocking the passage that leads to the older park models and wall boards and UII boxes and their related drawings, I installed *Hélio-Screen* to act as a barrier or filter between the two groups of works. *Hélio-Screen* was made in 2019, not that long ago, but it felt linked to some earlier bodies of work that I was considering again, like *Oblong Box*, which was placed nearby, or maybe it was just another moment of *détournement*, which was the whole of *Torrington* at this point, with its broad spectrum of borrowing and repurposing staged across the architectural expanse. It's also the case that specific works speak this language more emphatically than others, and *Hélio-Screen* is one of these.

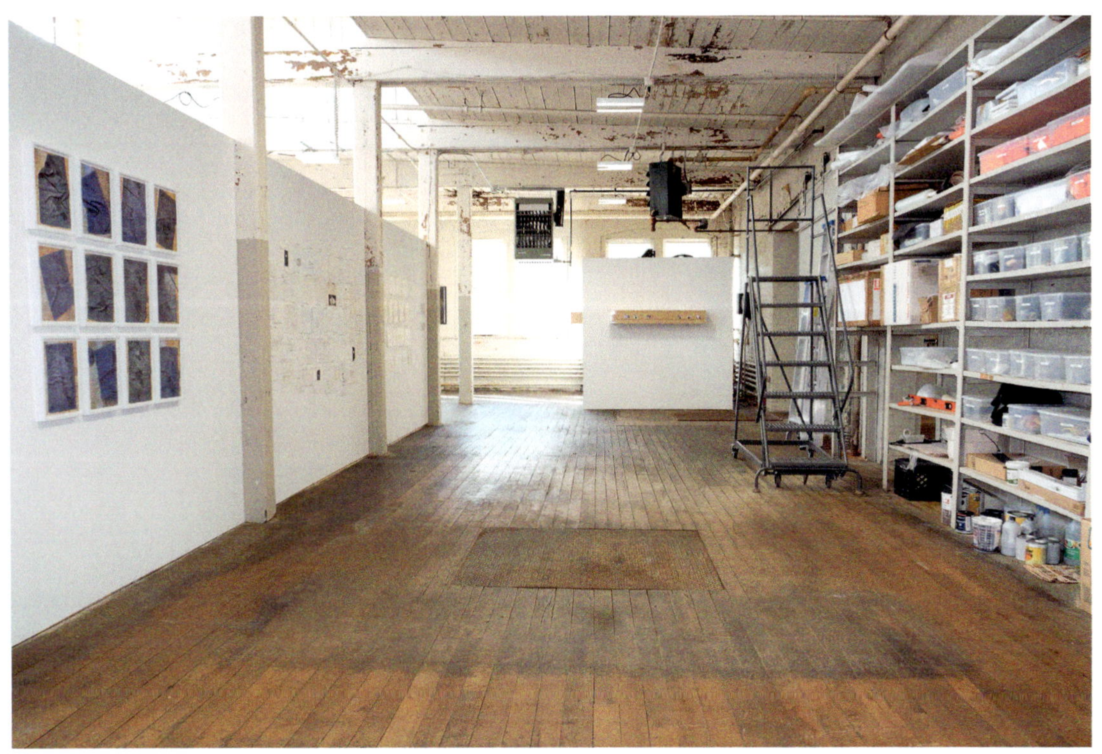

The screen was a central component of *Hélio-Centricities* which I installed in March 2019 at *auroras*, an art space in São Paulo housed in a modernist villa. I spent a month there thinking and plotting, sleeping in a bedroom just above the exhibition rooms. This was an intimate way to process an exhibition space I would soon make work within: to sleep, wake up, wander through the house alone at any hour, through the furnished rooms, the library, the kitchen, and out into the spaces that were once used as the living and dining rooms and were now empty, waiting for what I would do. I didn't know what I would do there exactly before I arrived; I had left it somewhat open. I wanted to act like the very young artist I once was, and to make the work there on location without enormous preparation, bringing only a few basic materials, mostly pushpins and some books and an inventory of possibilities in my notebooks.

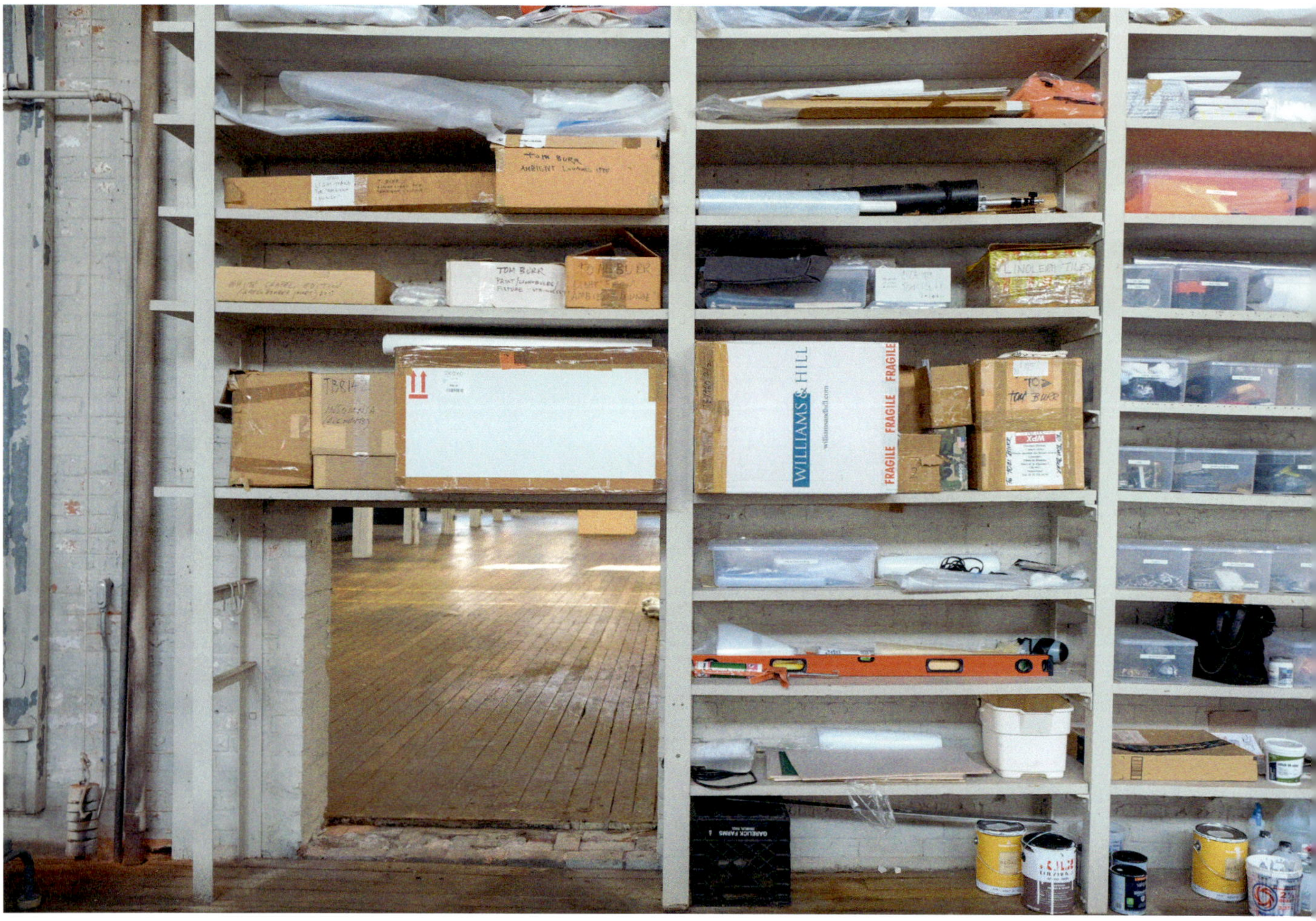

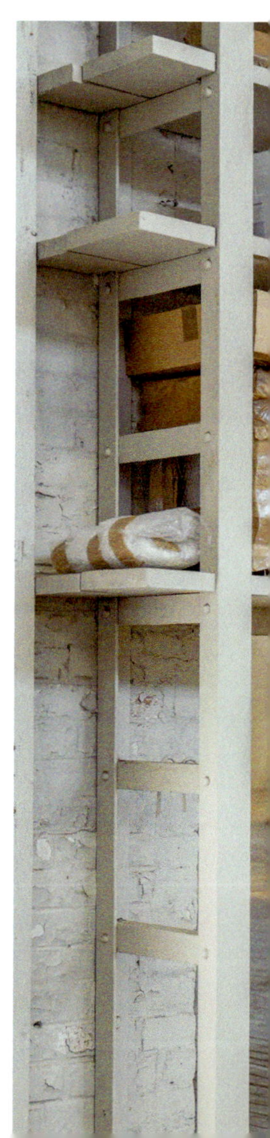

But in reality I had never been that particular
artist. I had always been prepared, or mostly
prepared, most of the time, for what I would
do at a site, which isn't to say I didn't fall on my
face, or fail, but making work on-site, or develop-
ing it out of the site to some degree, required
this advance preparation. The fantasy I was
projecting on the *auroras* experience was less
about who I was or had been, and more about
who or what I wanted to be at this precise
moment. I didn't want to fail, but I also decided
not to concern myself with that problem as
much anymore. And so I imagined some sort
of freedom for myself, brought on by the open
nature of the invitation, by the prospect of
traveling to a place I'd never been and brought
on by my latching on to Hélio Oiticica as a
figure to somehow accompany me through all
of this, inspired in part by his own trajectory
between Brazil and the East Village, thinking of
it as a road map of my own bodily and artistic
movements as well.

The psychology of the house struck me: its anx-
iously rigorous sense of privacy, of protection,
blocked from the street by opaque walls and
gates, and open to the back garden with wide
expanses of sliding glass panels. The house was
built in 1957, the same year that Oiticica was
creating his *Metaesquema* works. They were
on my mind already. I had been immersed in
Oiticica's work for a long time, decades, first
hearing his name, I think, in the early 1980s. I
was attracted to the yellow dangling forms and
the unique oddball direction he took out of the
Neo-Concrete movement almost as an escape,
forging a queer trajectory, I think, one that I
sensed early on.

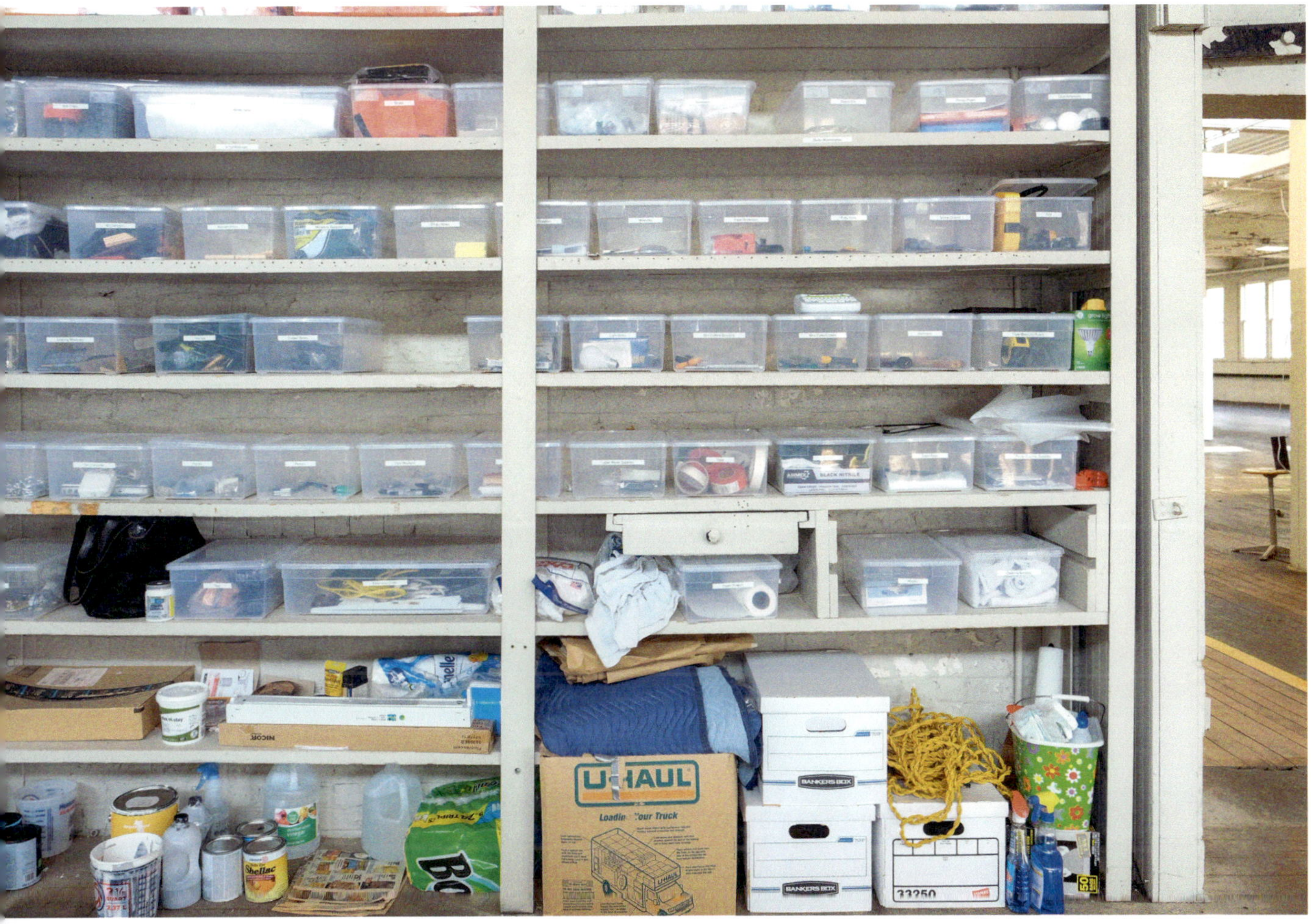
U-HAUL
BANKERS BOX
33250

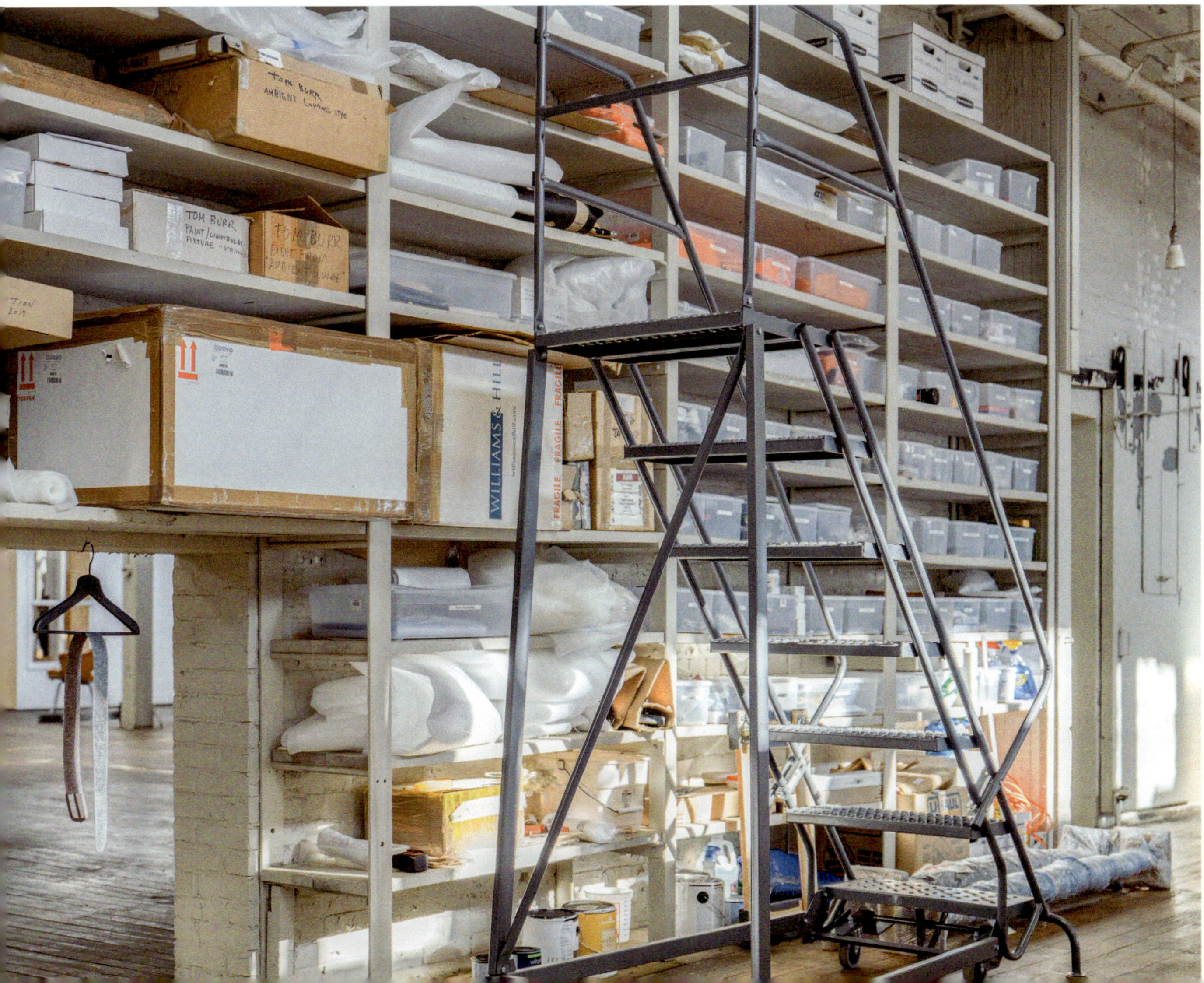
TOM BURR
WILLIAMS & HILL
FRAGILE

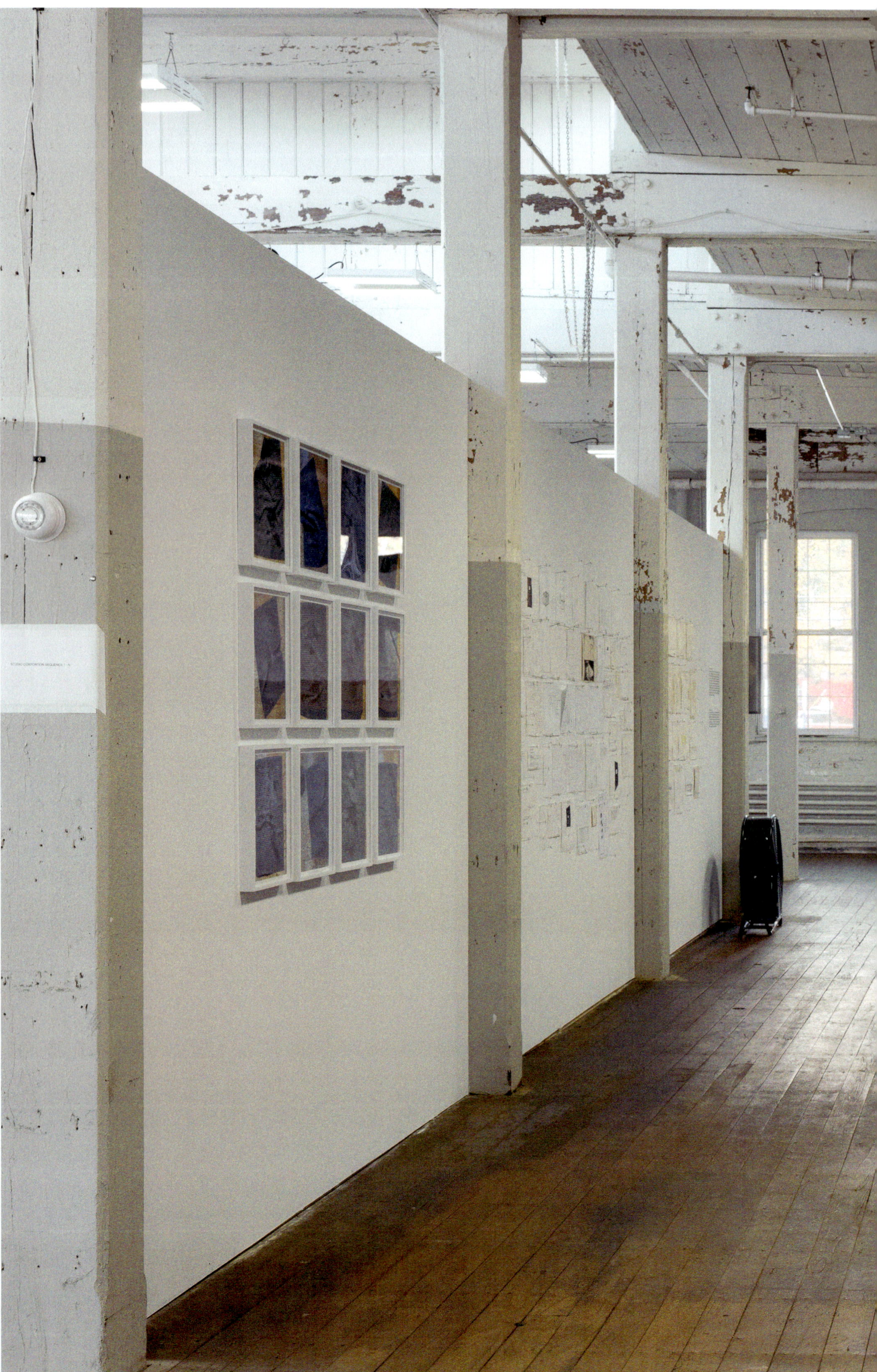

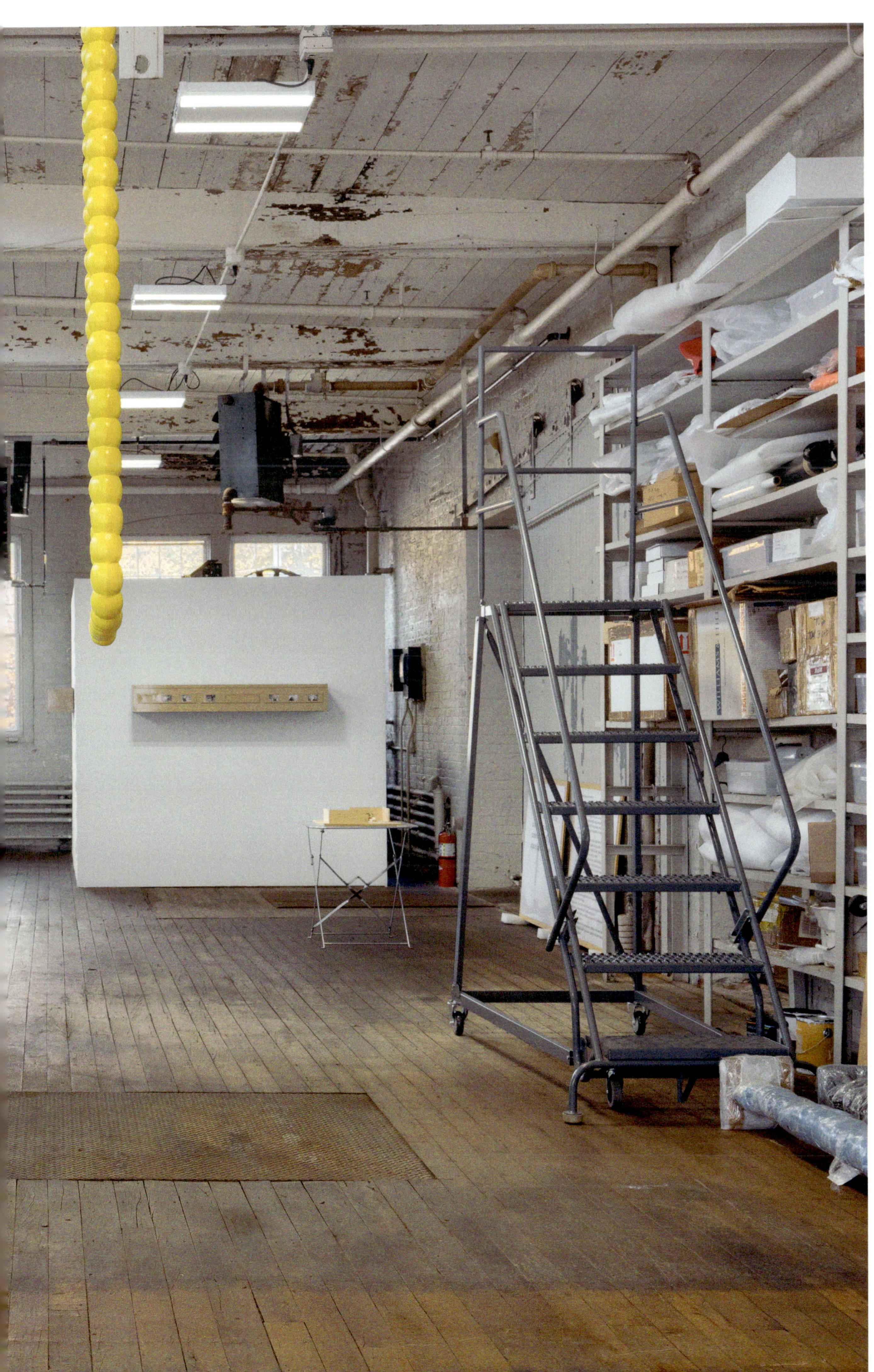

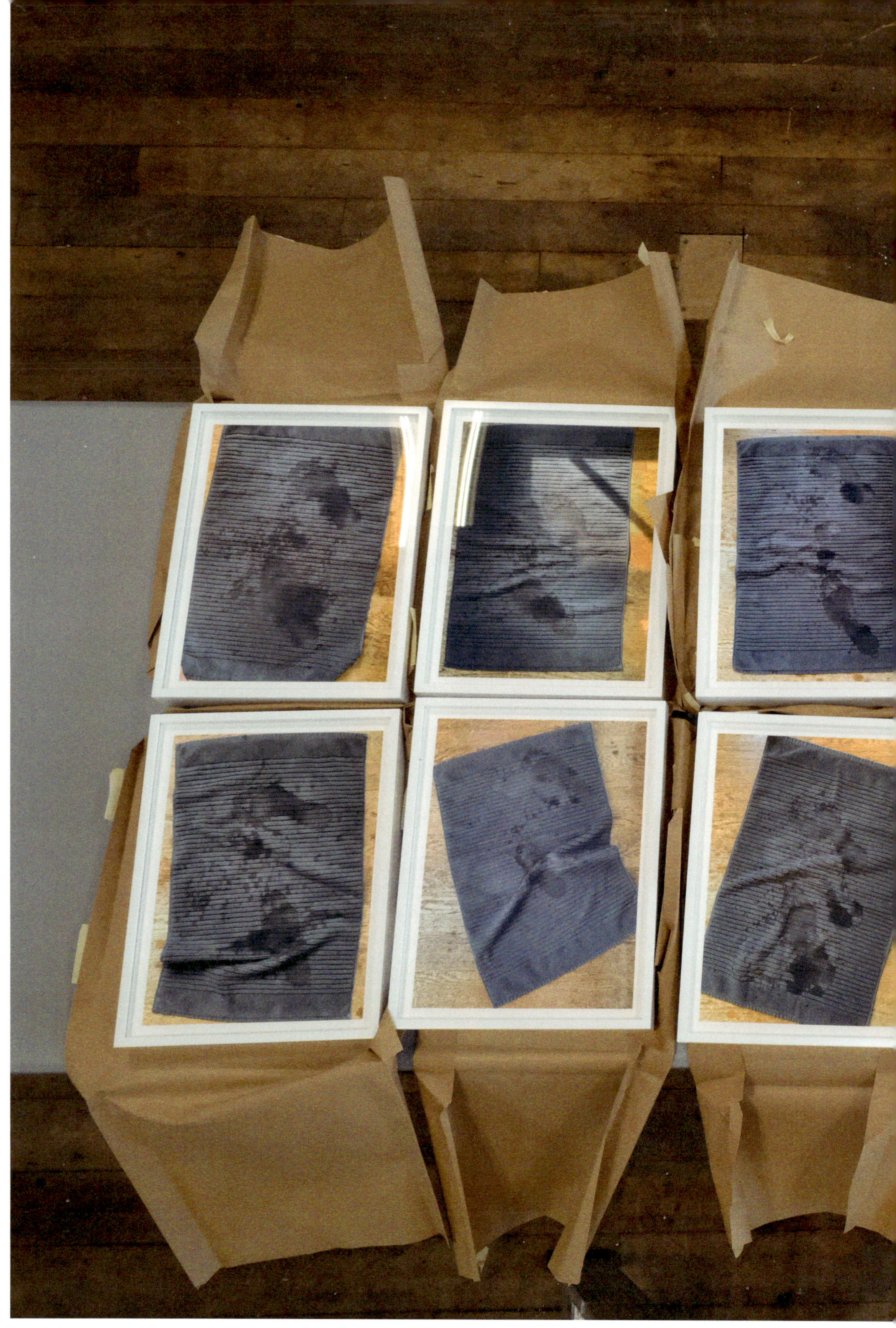

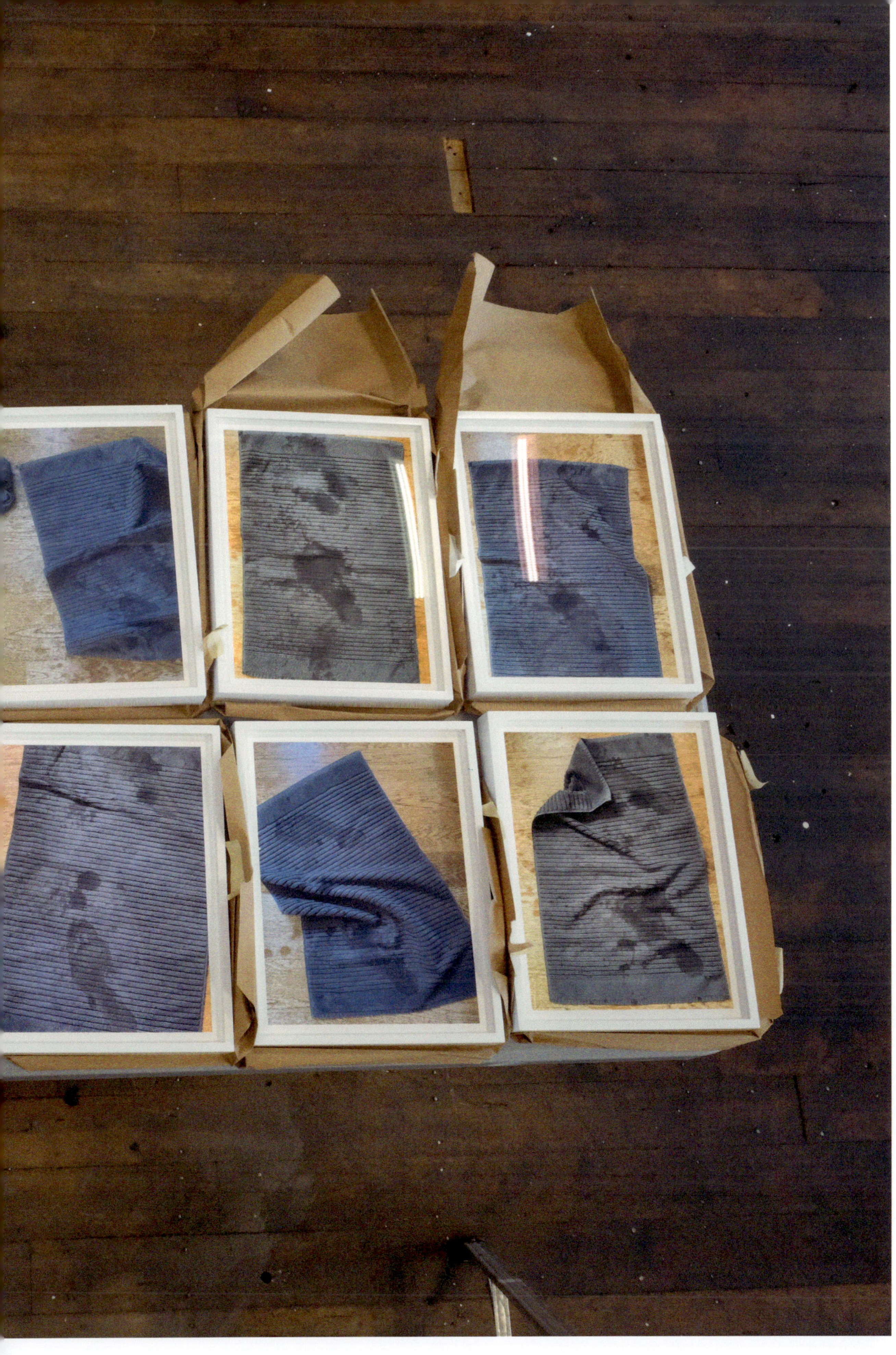

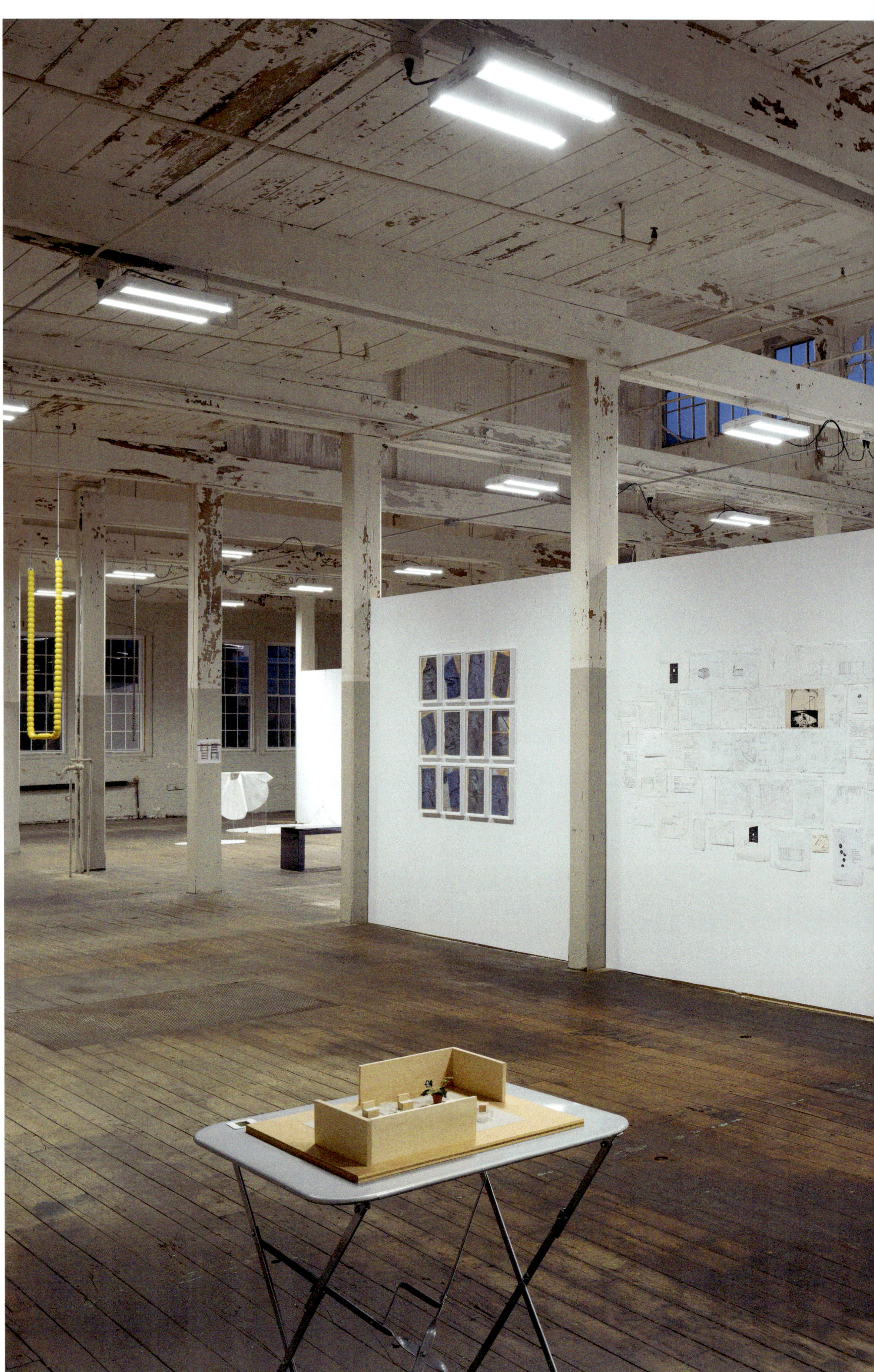

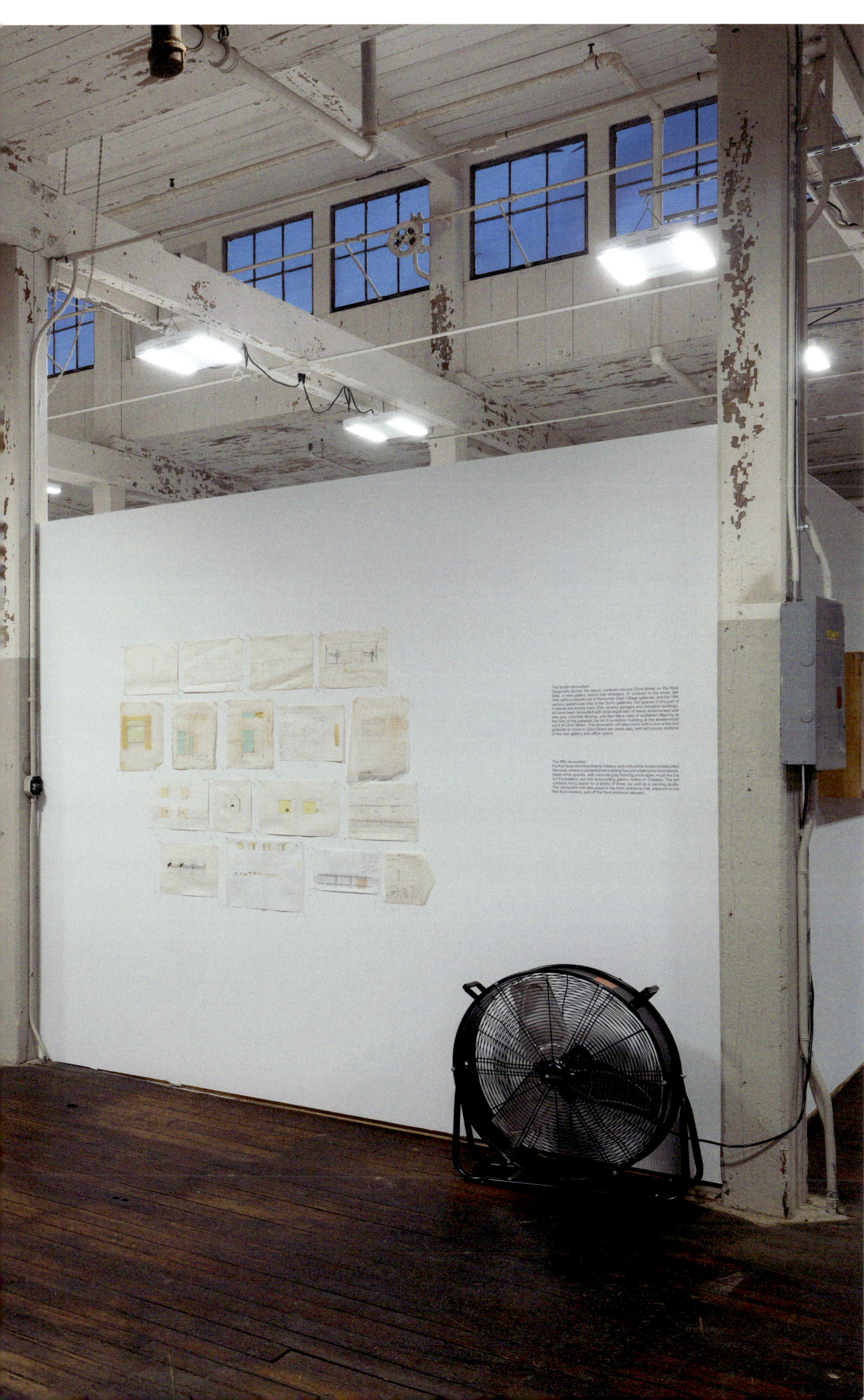
The fourth renovation:
Diagonally across the island, centered around 22nd Street on the West Side, a new gallery district has emerged. In contrast to the small, late 19th century storefronts of the former East Village galleries, and the 19th century warehouse lofts of the SoHo galleries, the spaces in this part of Chelsea are mostly early 20th century garages and industrial buildings. All have been renovated with large expanses of newly sheet-rocked wall and gray concrete flooring, and feel like a nest of scattered offspring at the feet of the parental Dia Art Foundation building at the westernmost point of 22nd Street. The renovation will take place within one of the first galleries to move to 22nd Street two years ago, and will occupy sections of the rear gallery and office space.

The fifth renovation:
Further down the West Side to Tribeca, and onto a little-known street called Renwick, where a residential loft building has just undergone renovations. Sleek white spaces, with concrete gray flooring once again recall the Dia Art Foundation and the surrounding gallery milieu in Chelsea. The loft contains living space for a family of three, as well as a painting studio. The renovation will take place in the front entrance hall, adjacent to the first floor lavatory, just off the front entrance elevator.

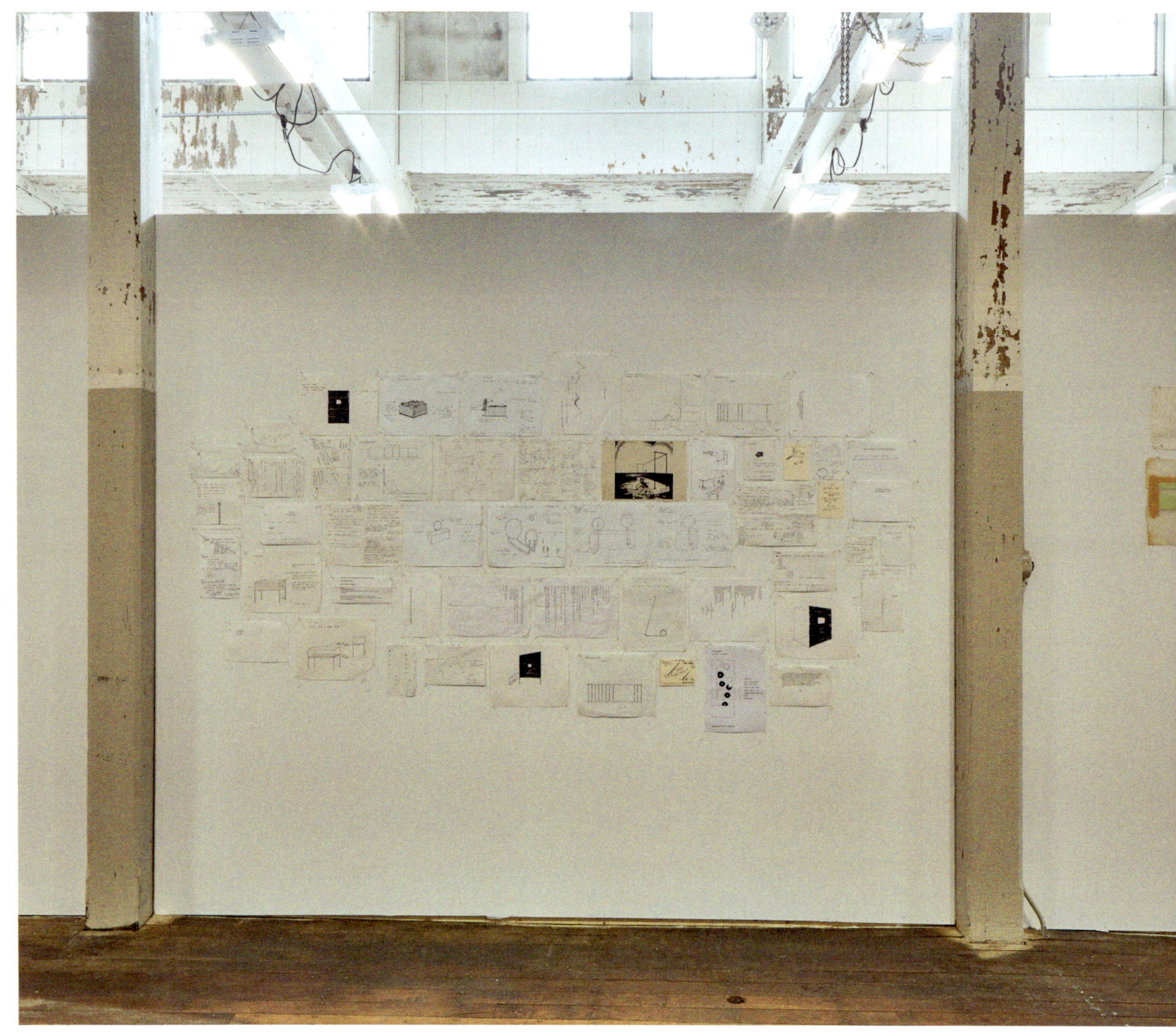

I woke the first morning in São Paulo to see the bedroom's heavy black wooden window shutters letting a graphic play of light through their irregular horizontal cracks, shifting slowly around the walls and across the ceiling of the room. The patterns felt like Hélio dancing, slowly, almost imperceptibly, and they also looked like the sharp bands of constraint emanating from the skin of the building and into the room. Forms of delirium and sedation, combined. I imitated that effect, and the effect of the *Metaesquema* works themselves, which the window shutters resembled, in the design of a wall, or screen, that would behave similarly, allowing light in while conspicuously blocking the view. I jotted down in my notebook, "I want to think about where Oiticica ends and I begin, or where I end and he begins." Along with the pile of Oiticica books I had flown down with, I brought my dog-eared copy of Roland Barthes's *A Lover's Discourse*, which sat on the bedside table, under the extraordinary lamp with a mirrored base.

Hélio-Screen was the result, as well as two large wall panels and a series of smaller collage works I called *Spatial Constraints*, which I made in the room next to my bedroom in the weeks leading up to the opening, incorporating into the panels various T-shirts I had brought with me to wear. I hadn't intended to use them, but they were there and started to make some kind of sense coupled with the other materials I had sourced in São Paulo. There was a persistent use of that bright yellow in these collages, which I had always thought of as Oiticica's color, and now thought of it as mine in this strange quasi-amorous exchange.

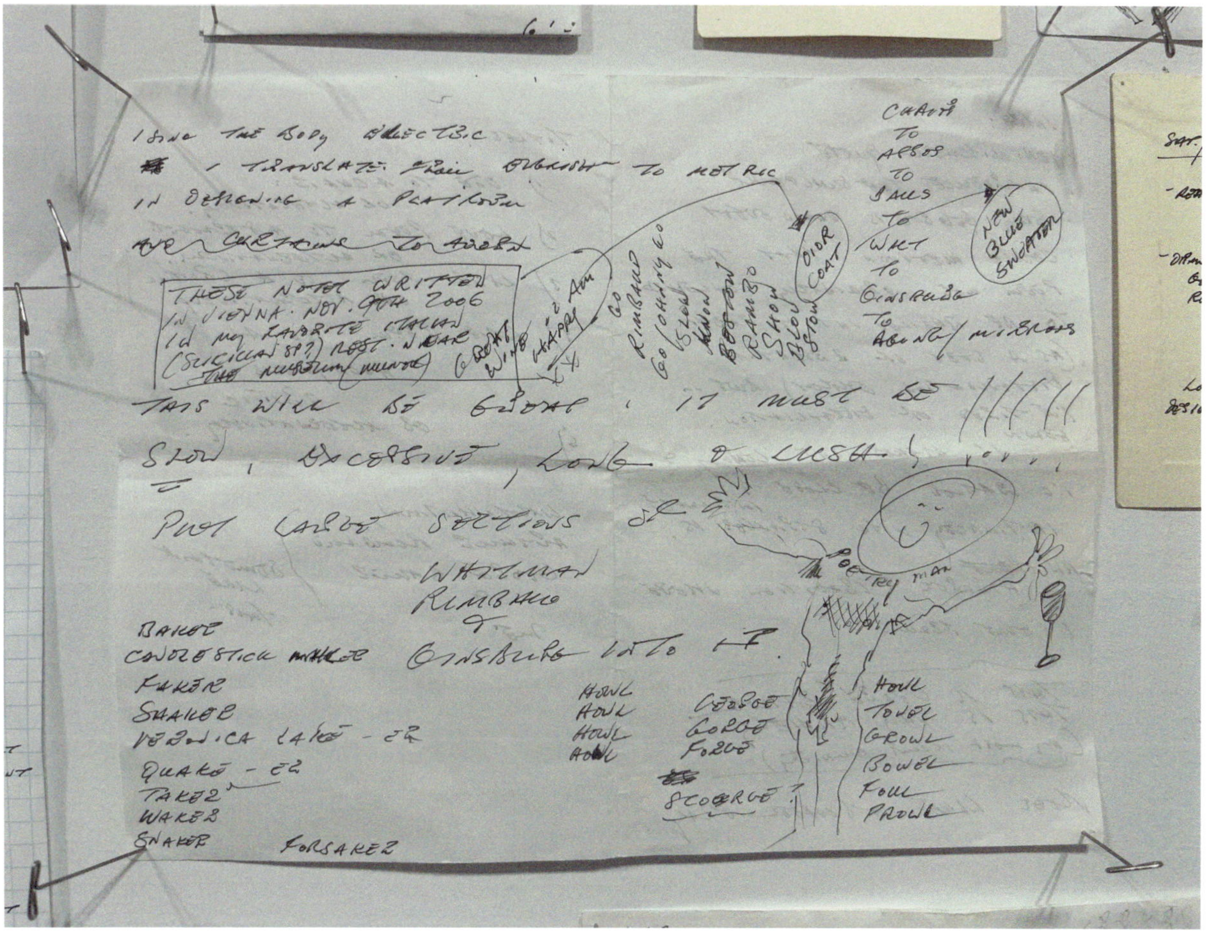

I SING THE BODY ELECTRIC

I TRANSLATE THEIR ENGLISH TO METRIC

IN DESIGNING A PLATFORM

WE CATERING TO AVERT

THESE NOTES WRITTEN
IN VIENNA · NOV. 9TH 2006
(D MY FAVORITE ITALIAN
(SICILIAN S?) REST. NEAR
THE MUSEUM / MUMOK)   GREAT
WINE   HAPPY

CHAOS
TO
ARBUS
TO
SAILS
TO
WHT
TO
GINSBERG
TO
ABONY / MIRRORS

NEW
BLUE
SWEATER

DIOR
COAT

THIS WILL BE GREAT. IT MUST BE

SLOW, EXCESSIVE, LONG & LUSH,

PLUS CAPET SECTIONS

WHITMAN
RIMBAUD
&
BAKE
CANDLESTICK MAKER   GINSBERG INTO IT.
FAKER
SHAKER
VERONICA LAKE — CZ
QUAKE — CZ
TAKE
WAKE
SNAKE   FORSAKE

HOWL   GEORGE   HOWL
HOWL   GORGE   TOWEL
HOWL   FORGE   GROWL
HOWL   BOWEL
           SCOURGE   FOUL
                        PROWL

POETRY MAN

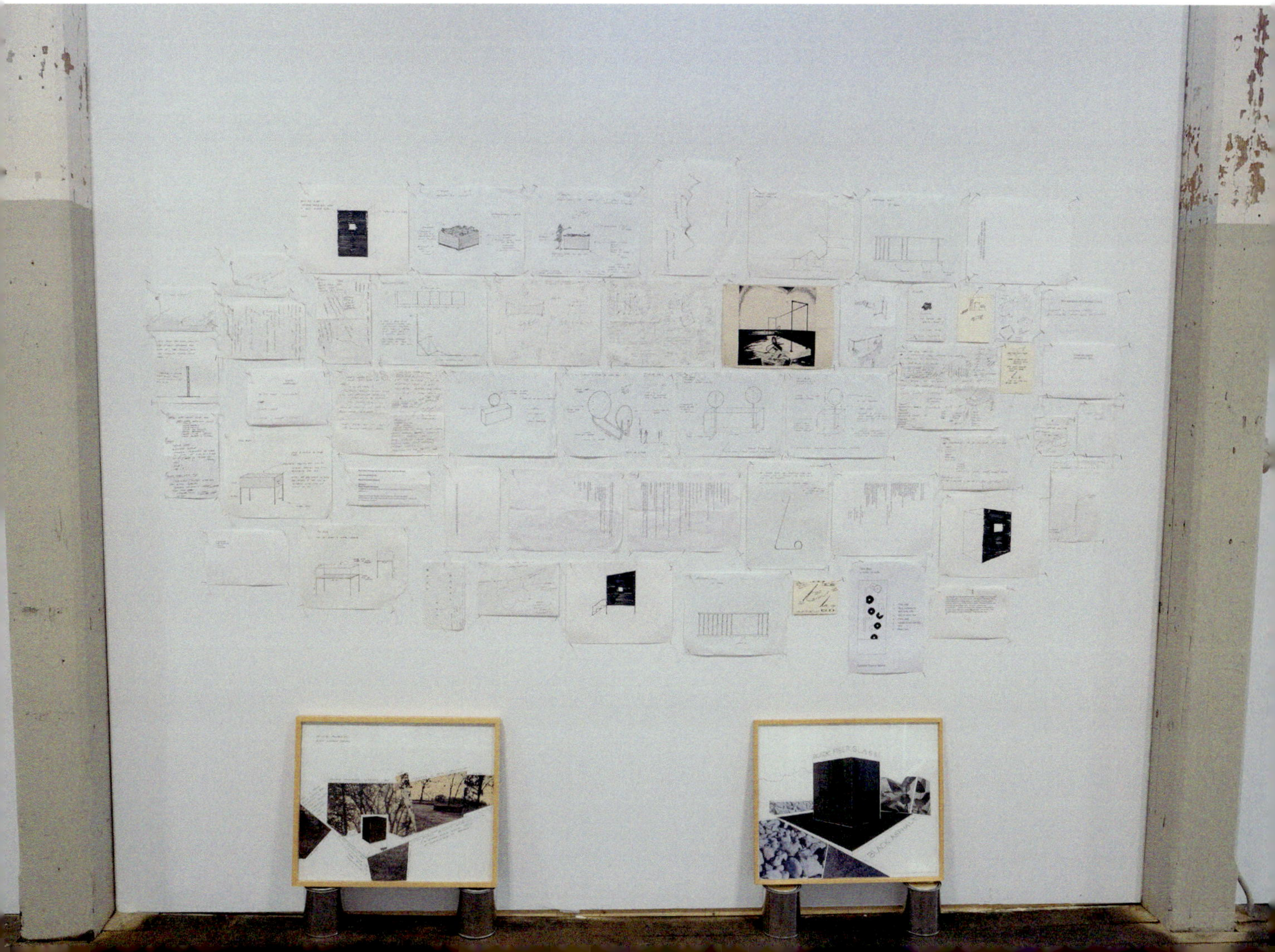

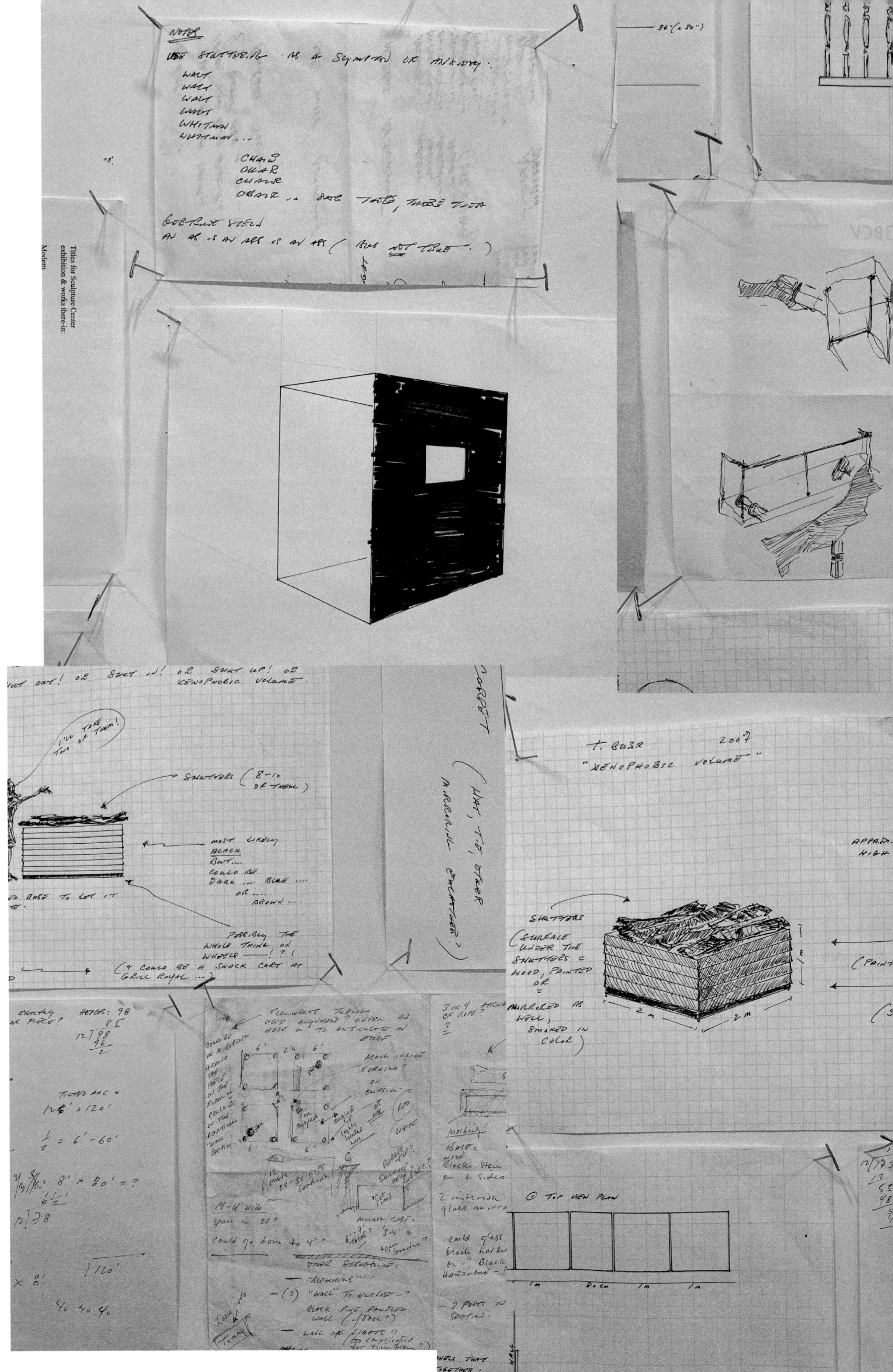

NOTES
t. BURR   2007
"XENOPHOBIC VOLUME"
Titles for Sculpture Center
exhibition & works therein:
Modern
SHUTTERS
@ TOP VIEW PLAN

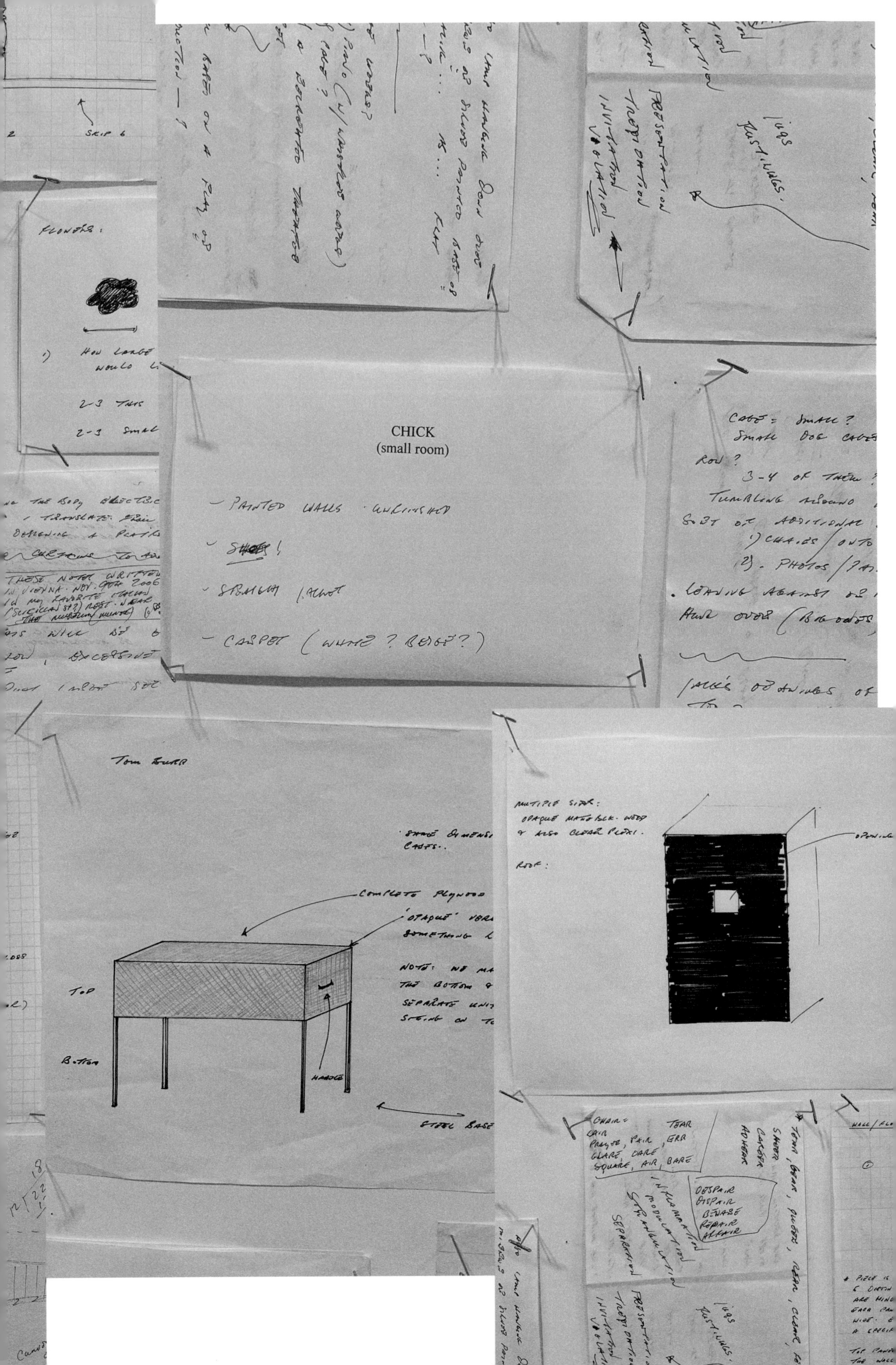

CHICK
(small room)

PAINTED WALLS · UNFINISHED
SHEET !
STRAIGHT / RAW
CARPET (WHITE ? BEIGE ?)

FLOWERS:
HOW LARGE
2-3 THIS
2-3 SMALL

SKIP 6

TOP
BOTTOM
HANDLE
STEEL BASE

OPENING
ROOF:
MULTIPLE SIZE:
OPAQUE MATT BLK. WOOD
& ALSO CLEAR PLEXI.

DESPAIR
DISPAIR
DEVASE
REPAIR
AFFAIR

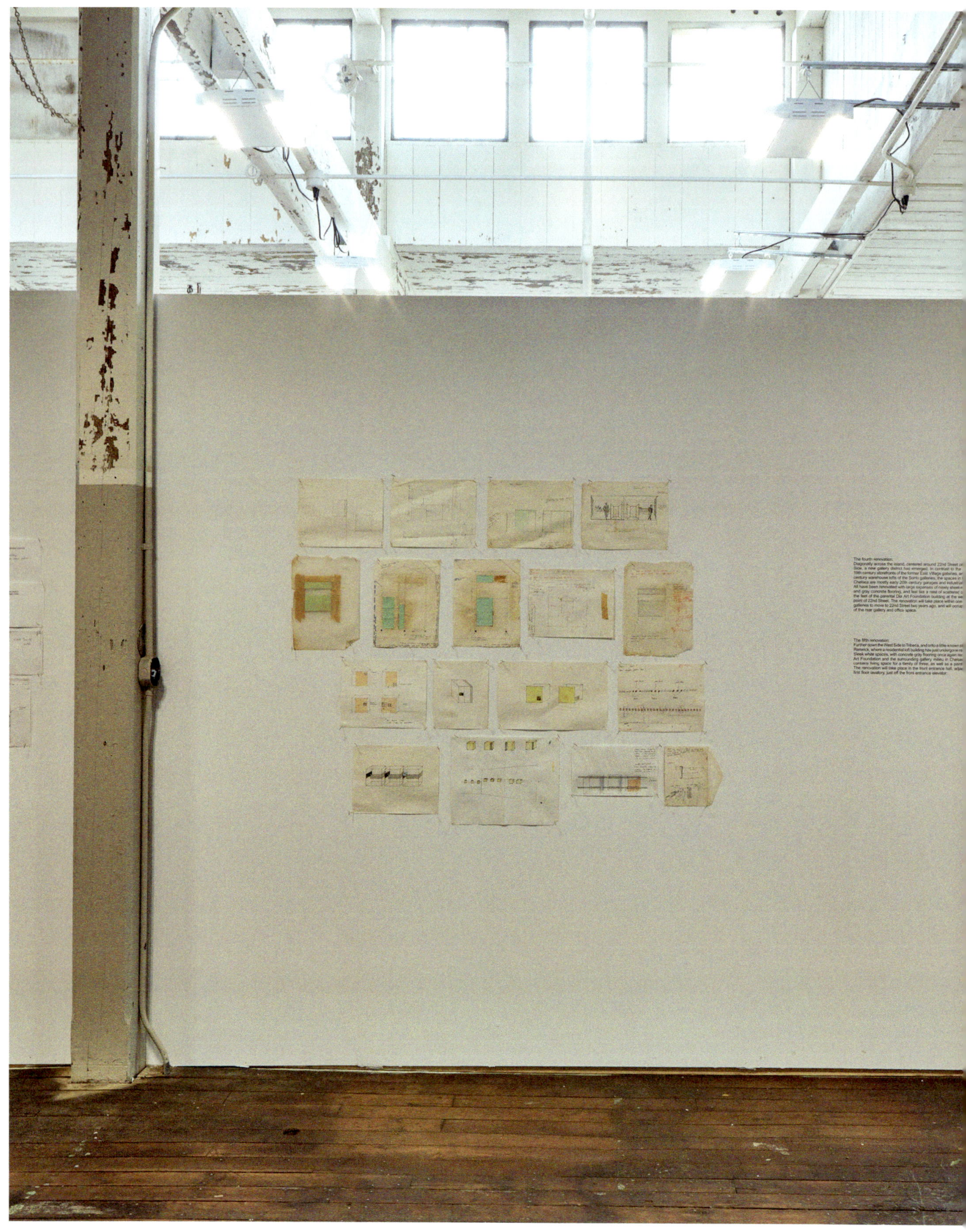

242

The fourth renovation:
Diagonally across the island, centered around 22nd Street on the West
Side, a new gallery district has emerged. In contrast to the small, late
19th century storefronts of the former East Village galleries, and the 19th
century warehouse lofts of the SoHo galleries, the spaces in this part of
Chelsea are mostly early 20th century garages and industrial buildings.
All have been renovated with large expanses of newly sheet-rocked wall
and gray concrete flooring, and feel like a nest of scattered offspring at
the feet of the parental Dia Art Foundation building at the westernmost
point of 22nd Street. The renovation will take place within one of the first
galleries to move to 22nd Street two years ago, and will occupy sections
of the rear gallery and office space.

The fifth renovation:
Further down the West Side to Tribeca, and onto a little-known street called
Renwick, where a residential loft building has just undergone renovations.
Sleek white spaces, with concrete gray flooring once again recall the Dia
Art Foundation and the surrounding gallery milieu in Chelsea. The loft
contains living space for a family of three, as well as a painting studio.
The renovation will take place in the front entrance hall, adjacent to the
first floor lavatory, just off the front entrance elevator.

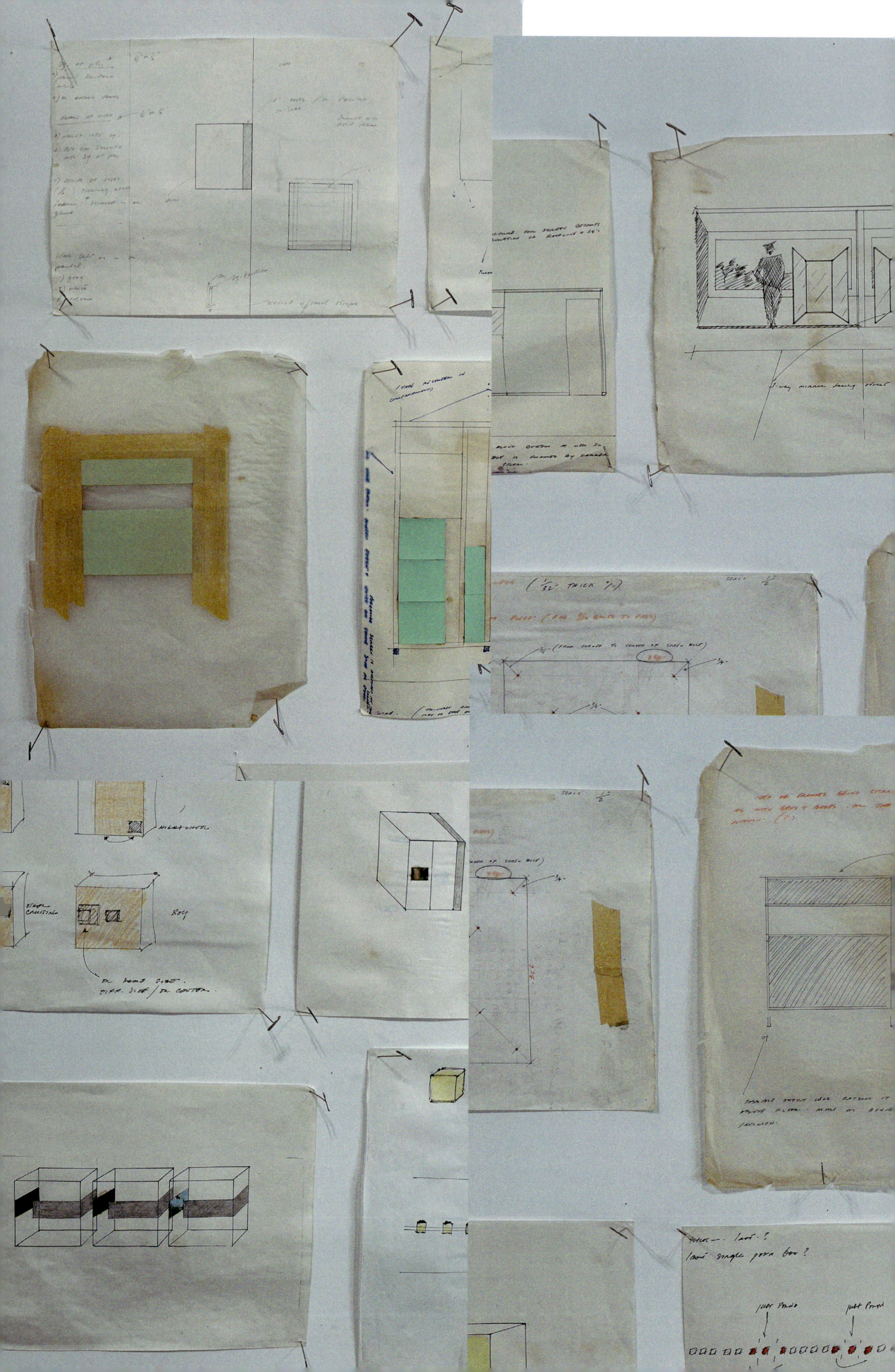

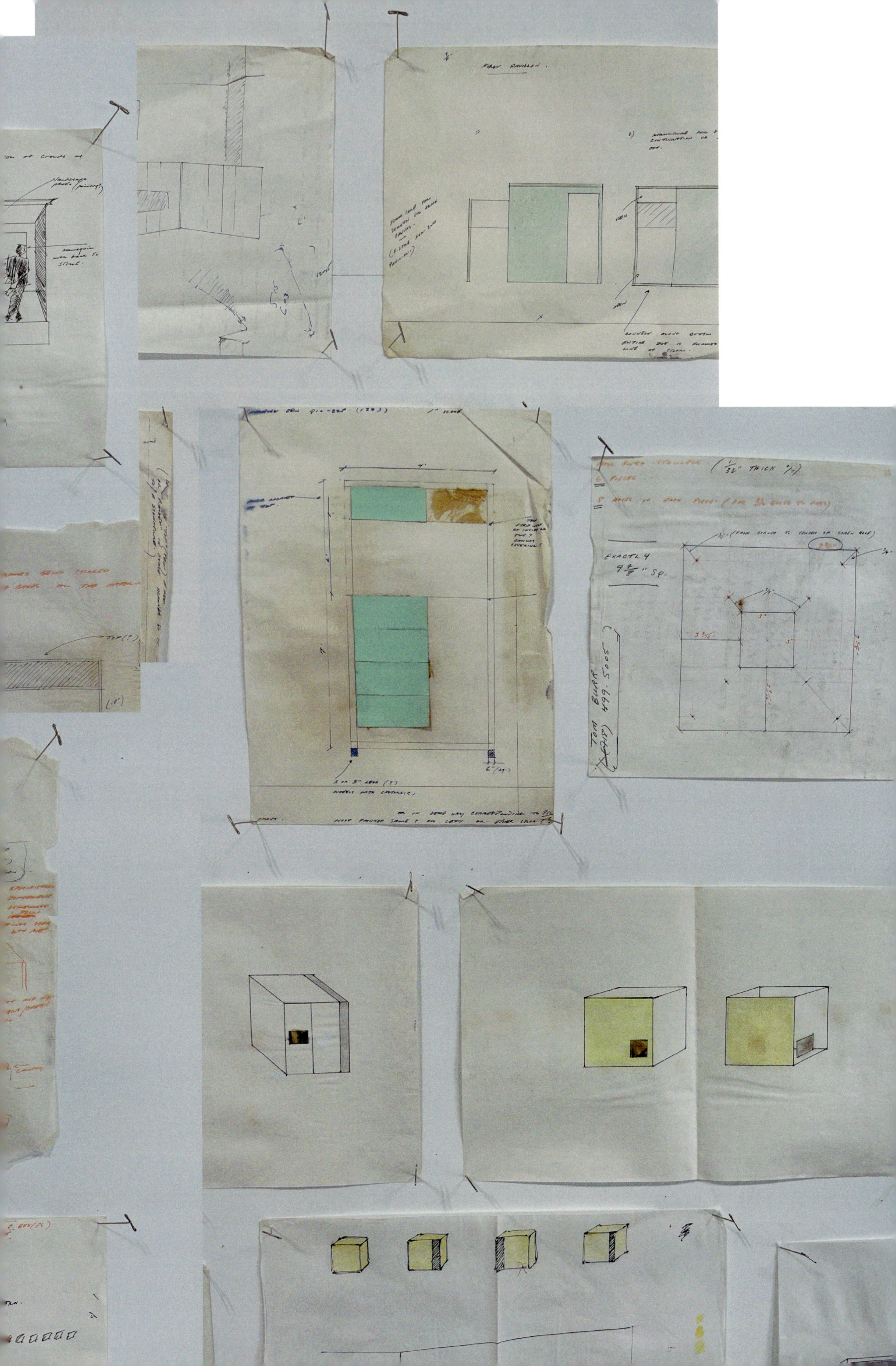

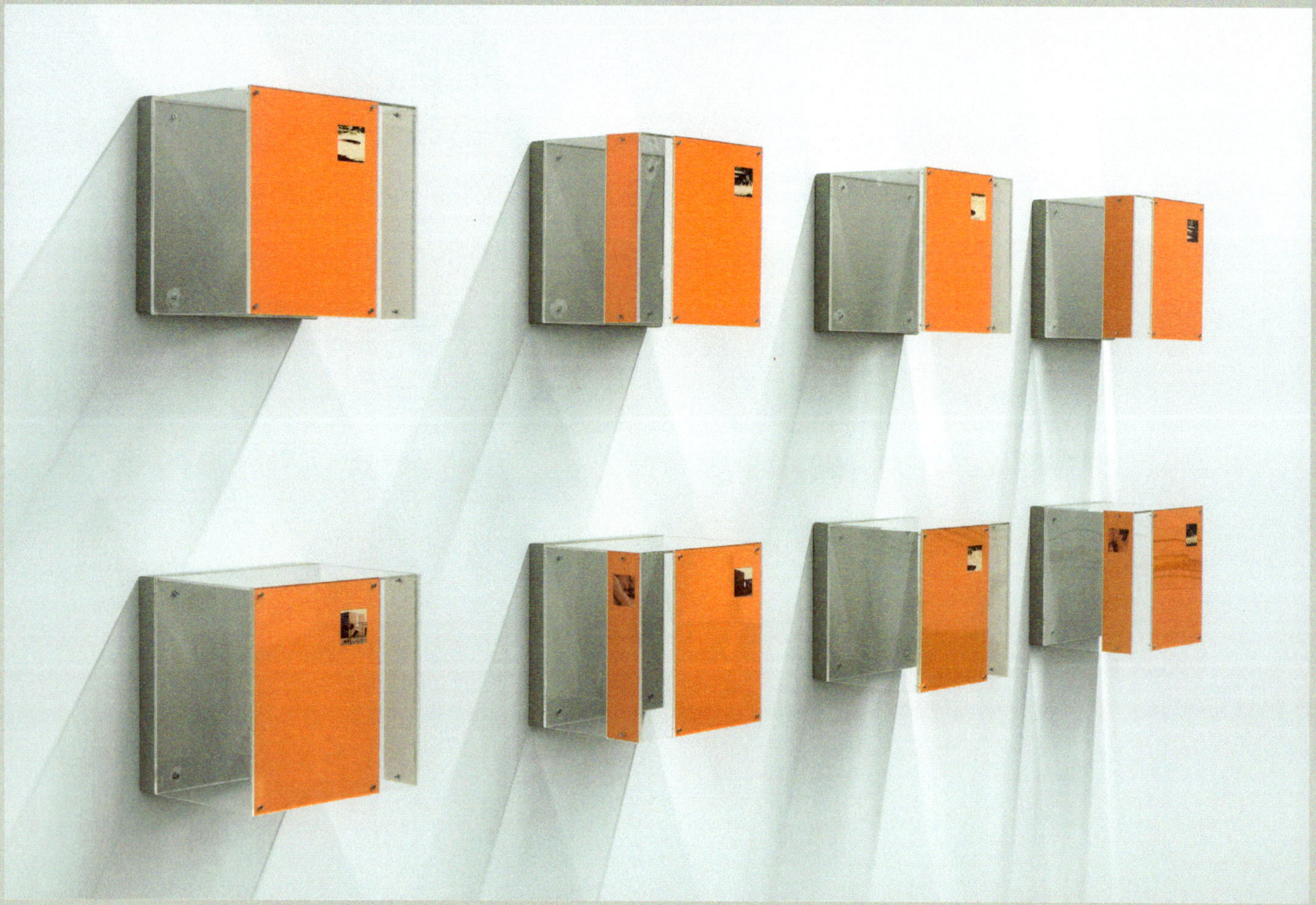

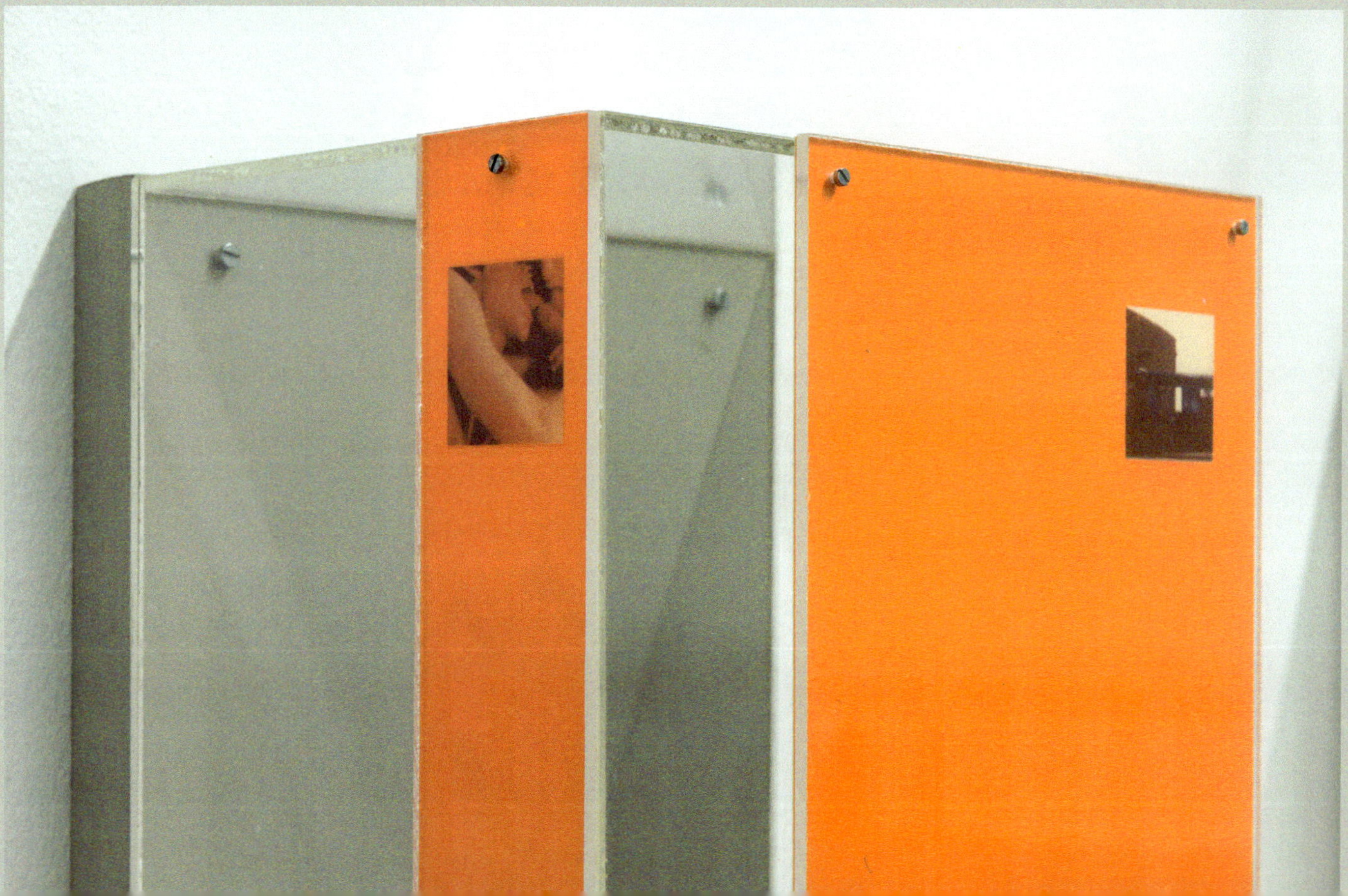

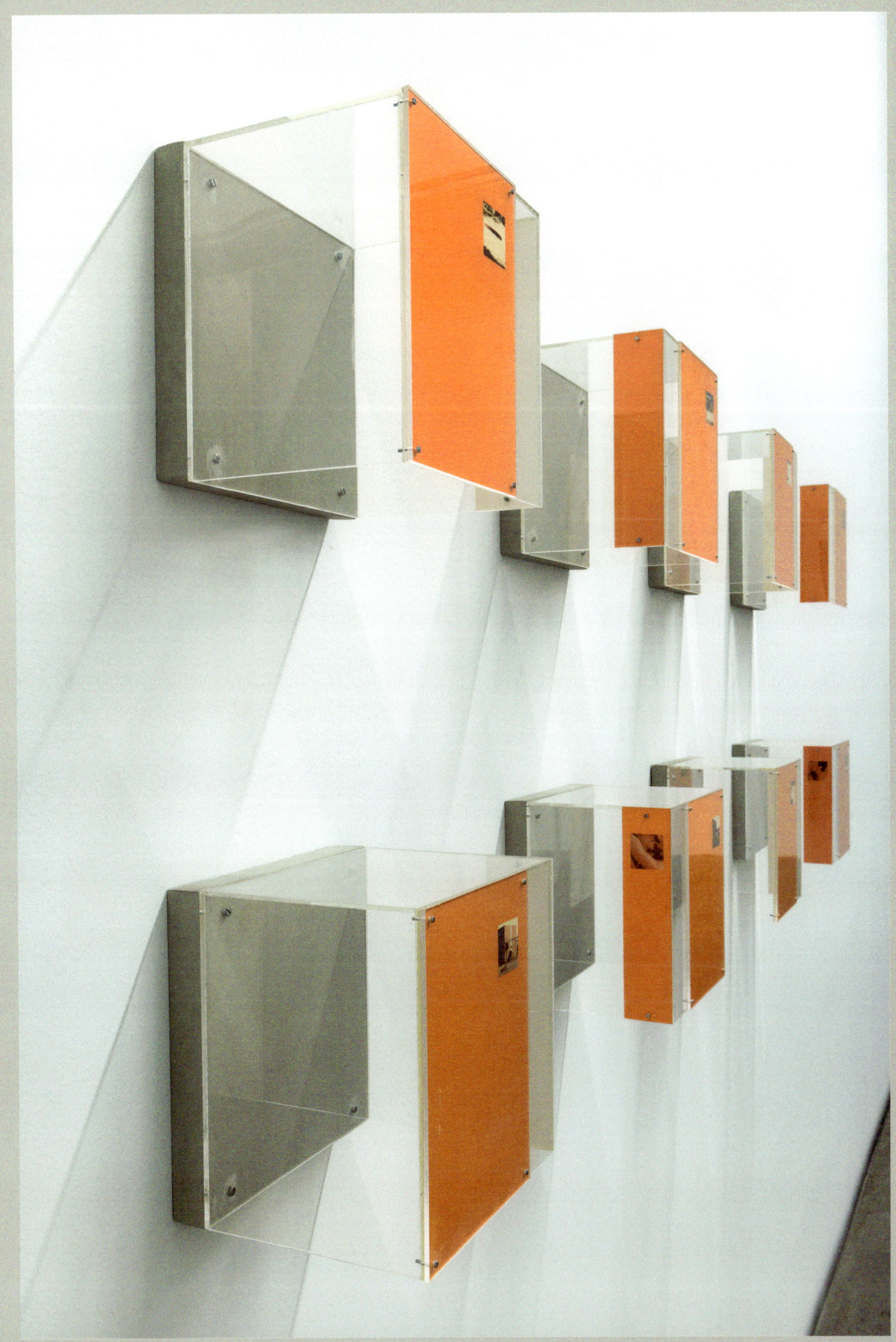

247

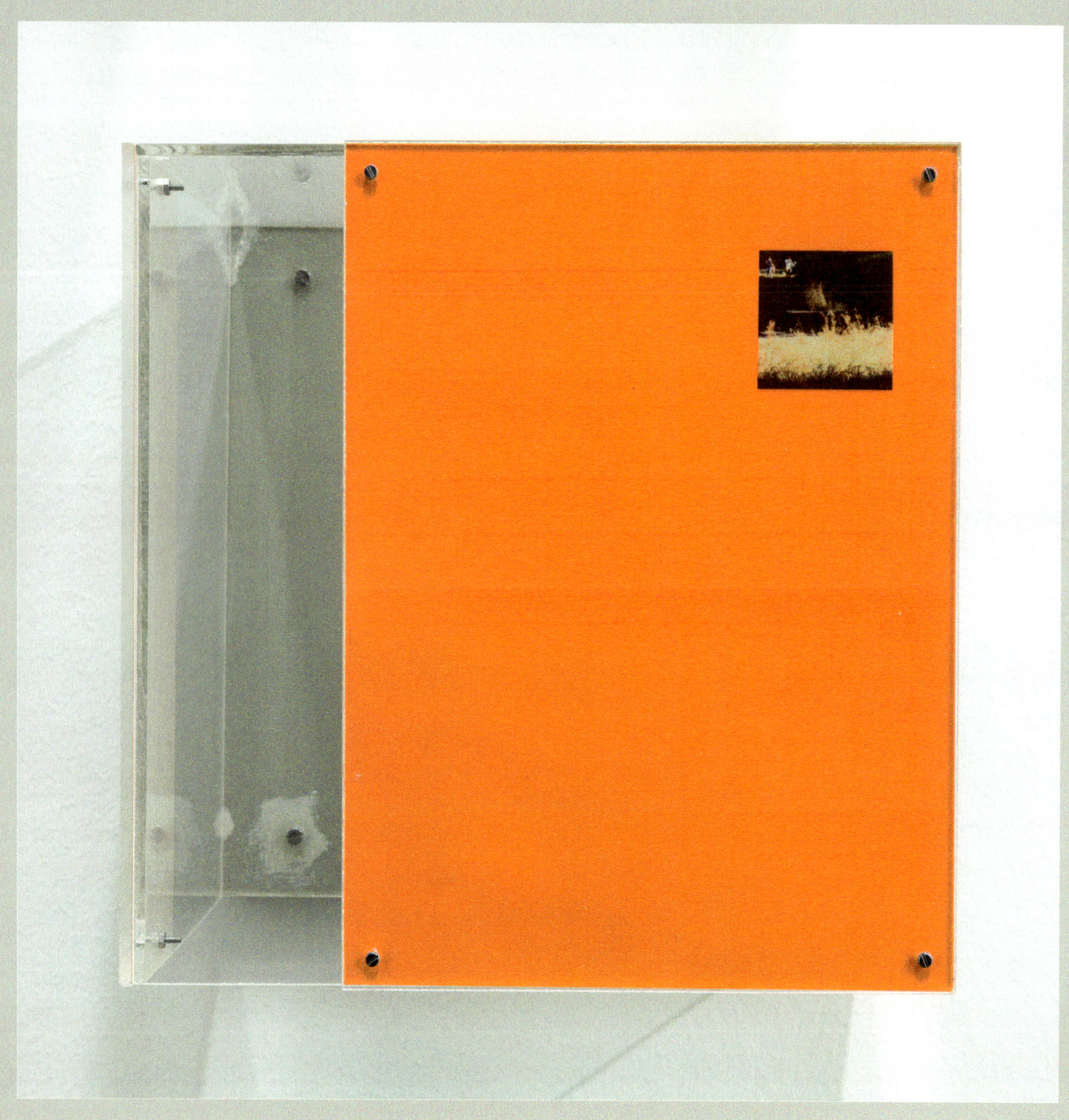

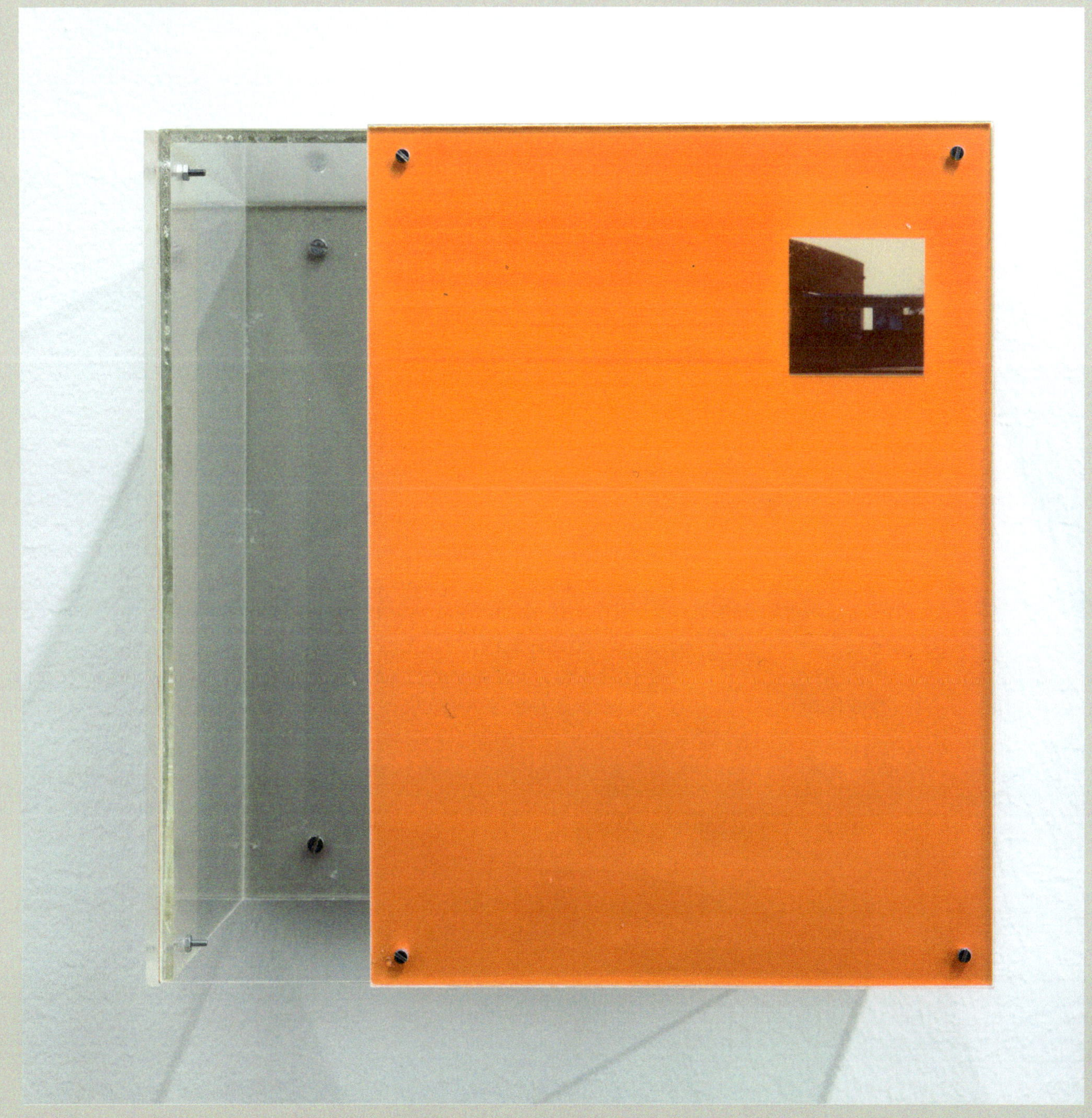

When we go to Torrington one sunny August afternoon, there's a problem hanging over my head. A
sculpture I made is falling apart somewhere in Sweden,
or somewhere between here and Sweden. Its skin is
falling off its bones. I haven't seen it happening, but I
was told, and I am told it is a problem. The sculpture
was already remade once, and somehow it's decom-
posing again. I am emailed a picture. Its once-glossy
black skin looks gray, dusty, and mottled. Maybe it
doesn't want to exist.

What is the thing? What is the artwork? These questions are still subjected to the many unnecessary
bifurcations that undergird our understanding of art
(and, necessarily, of value): The relationship between
concept and material, form and content, process
and object, artist and curator, studio and exhibition.
Bifurcations that, in our schooling, we were assured
had fallen away, thanks to artists twenty to thirty years
our senior.

Art history looks mucky with your nose pressed this
hard against its frosted glass. There are many questions that, indeed, have fallen away in its course
(e.g., Is it a painting or is it a sculpture? It's painfully obvious that no one—except maybe a certain
kind of buyer—cares), but there are others (some
of those mentioned above, for instance) that have
reared their heads and reified themselves. They produce a haze that bucks real inquiry. We now know
that it is not so interesting to spend one's time arguing
about whether something is a film or a performance,
whether it is architecture or not architecture, and so
forth, because being post-medium is definitely okay.
Now, a more distressing and urgent set of questions
has come to the fore—risen out of the muck—and
these questions are maddeningly straightforward: At
what point does a thing cease to be itself? How could
you ever know for certain, and would you want to?

     Aria Dean

Historically, to produce, or rather, to maintain art, as an *activity*, seems to have meant staving off objects, which appear to supply art with telos, and focusing on ends when the artist is concerned with means. The artist preoccupied with means is herded toward concepts and performativity. Perhaps, to maintain their focus, they must get rid of the world—pushing toward art for its own sake until the studio / the gallery / the catalogue become a hermetically sealed loop whose materials are its symbols, and whose symbols are really just its icons. Or perhaps one must cannibalize the world, metabolizing all that interests and troubles us about it, forcing it through the sieve of the artist's critical perspective and hardening it into pellets.

Is "getting rid of" the modernist way, and "cannibalizing" the postmodernist? Getting rid of the world is a difficult thing for artists who come to their practice with any enjoyment of material—the Conceptualist with a Minimalist heritage, the Minimalist with a Conceptual ground. Perhaps, instead of the world, this artist must get rid of or cannibalize themself. Getting rid of yourself is also difficult when the self still screams out to be grappled with. Cannibalizing the self and the world, embalming them in the belly of a sculpture, or worse, decorating the sculpture-tomb with them, leads to horrors as well.

In Tom Burr's studio, things are ever evolving, though not in the way an organism, ecosystem, or computational process might change over time. It's more like the problem of the ship of Theseus's story. A story that is a question: If a ship departs, and in the course of its journey all its parts are replaced—every part, down to the last plank—is it the same ship upon its return? It's that maddeningly simple question of what constitutes the object, and when it can or must no longer be considered *itself*, whatever *itself* was. Must the acrylic panel be the same acrylic panel that you saw before?

Could you know whether it is whatever it was, or if it isn't or wasn't it?

At *Torrington*, objects have lives and lifespans. These are more complicated—in terms of when they began, what stage they're in—than many works that venture to make their primary subject their own temporal or conceptual durability. Here, the passage of time is factual—the objects neither move with objective time (moments, days, months, years), nor do they protest it. Their disposition is neither eternal nor out of joint. There is one work that is not present but looms in the background as Tom shows us the decades' worth of works staged throughout the former factory—some left as they were in their original state of coming into being, some "reproduced," though I'm not convinced of this word. That is Burr's *Deep Purple* (2000). This send-up of Richard Serra's *Tilted Arc* (1981) is surely interesting to me for its hailing of Post-Minimalism, but it is more interesting for how Burr speaks of the relationship between the idea of the work and the work as a thing in itself: a huge yet flimsy wooden thing that has to be allowed to live out its days, weathering and decaying, but that just as well may be revitalized and reset. (And sure, the difference in materiality between *Deep Purple* and the Serra piece is charged and funny, calling attention to the way a simple shift in materials turns *Tilted Arc* into a set piece, and making you realize that Serra wielded his own form of camp. What is campier than bravura as such?)

I suppose it's all painfully simple: The experiment at *Torrington* is in letting something be itself, without necessarily categorizing it as such. Like us, objects are shifting constantly, and like Burr's *Construction of an American Garden* (1993), they need to be tended to in order to maintain their constitution. A true reproduction might have a provenance that ensures its value,

    Aria Dean

but the ongoing activity of the artist in relation to the fruits of his labor may, with great effort, ensure both artist and object life without reification. Perhaps use value hangs in the balance; despite being art, and therefore *useless*, the way these objects in Torrington live is more like objects that have and maintain their value through their use. Maybe they do have use value—being that being, or appearing, is indeed a form of labor after all. ◊

9

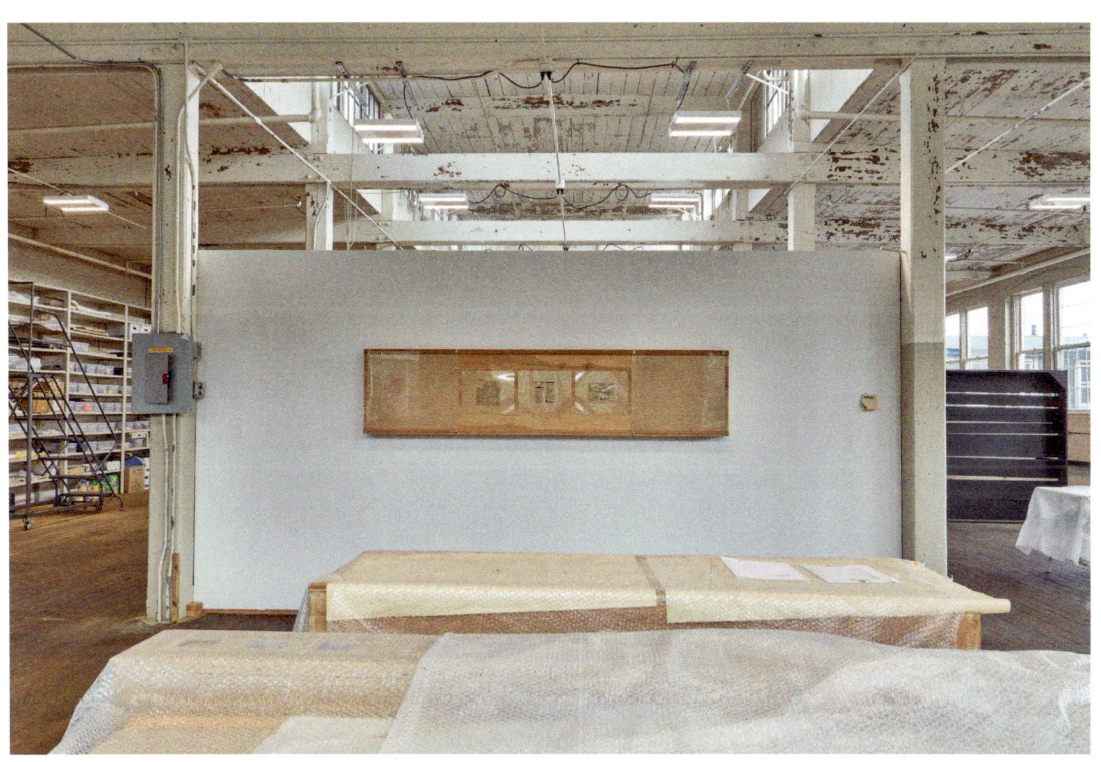

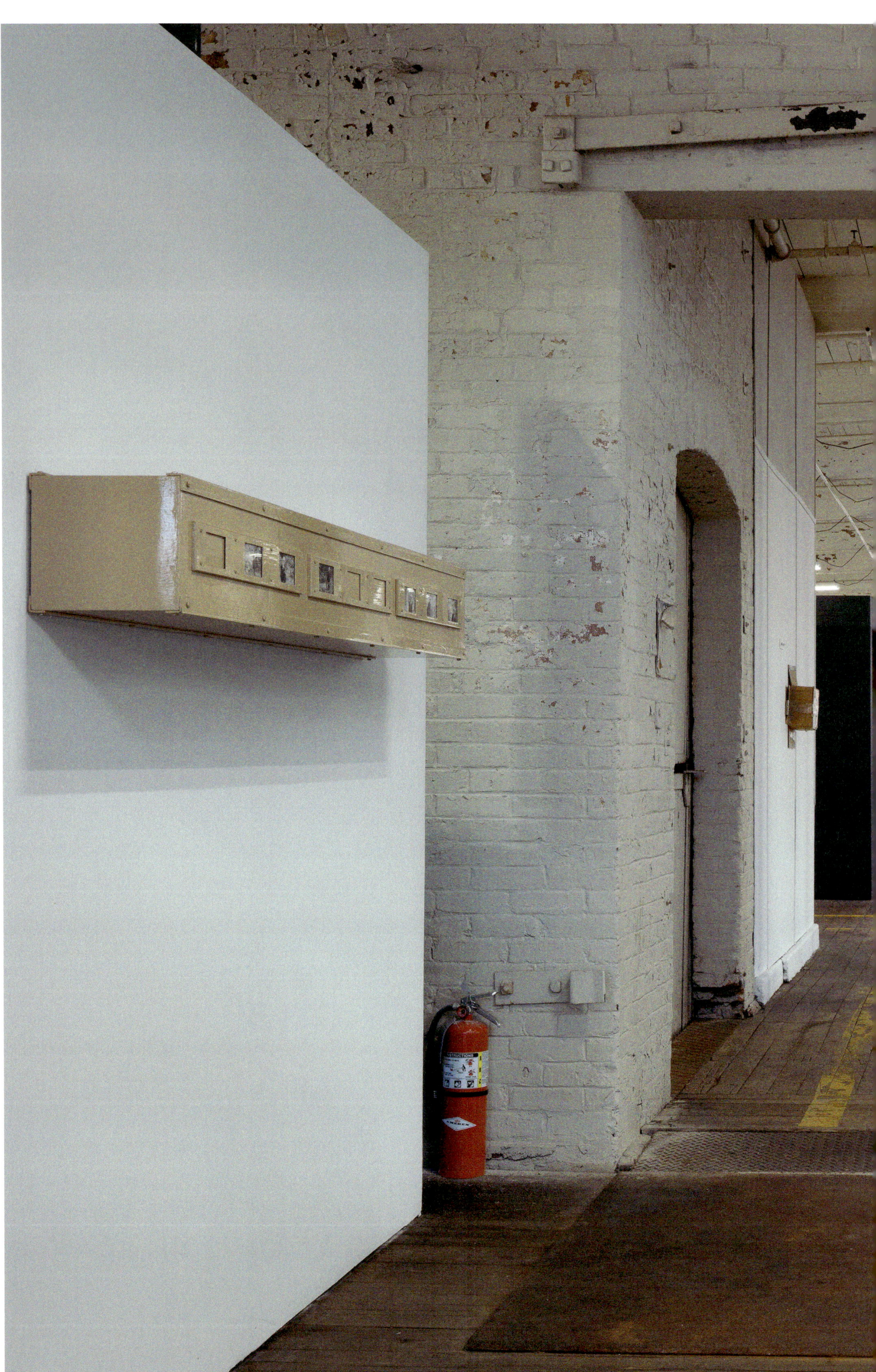

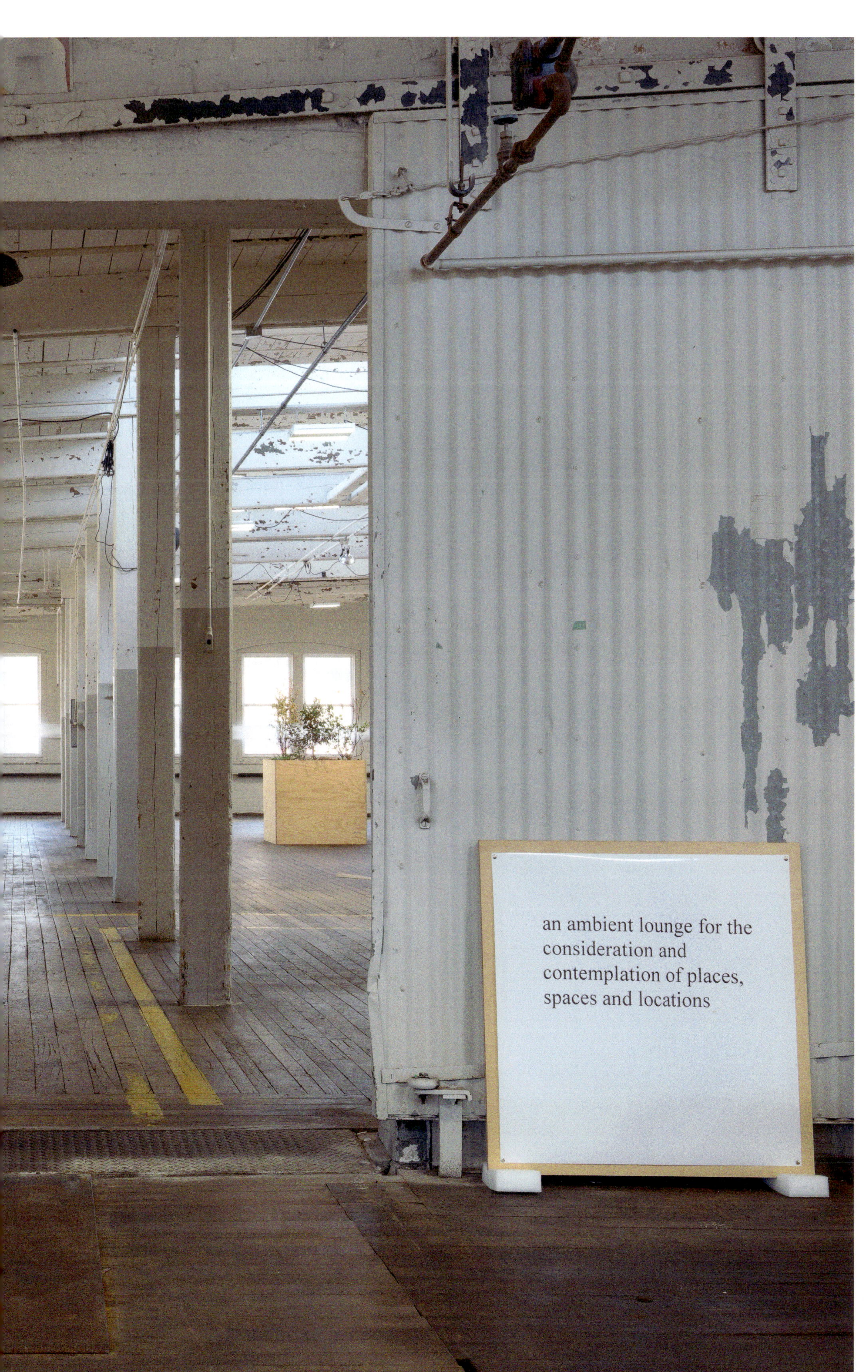
an ambient lounge for the
consideration and
contemplation of places,
spaces and locations

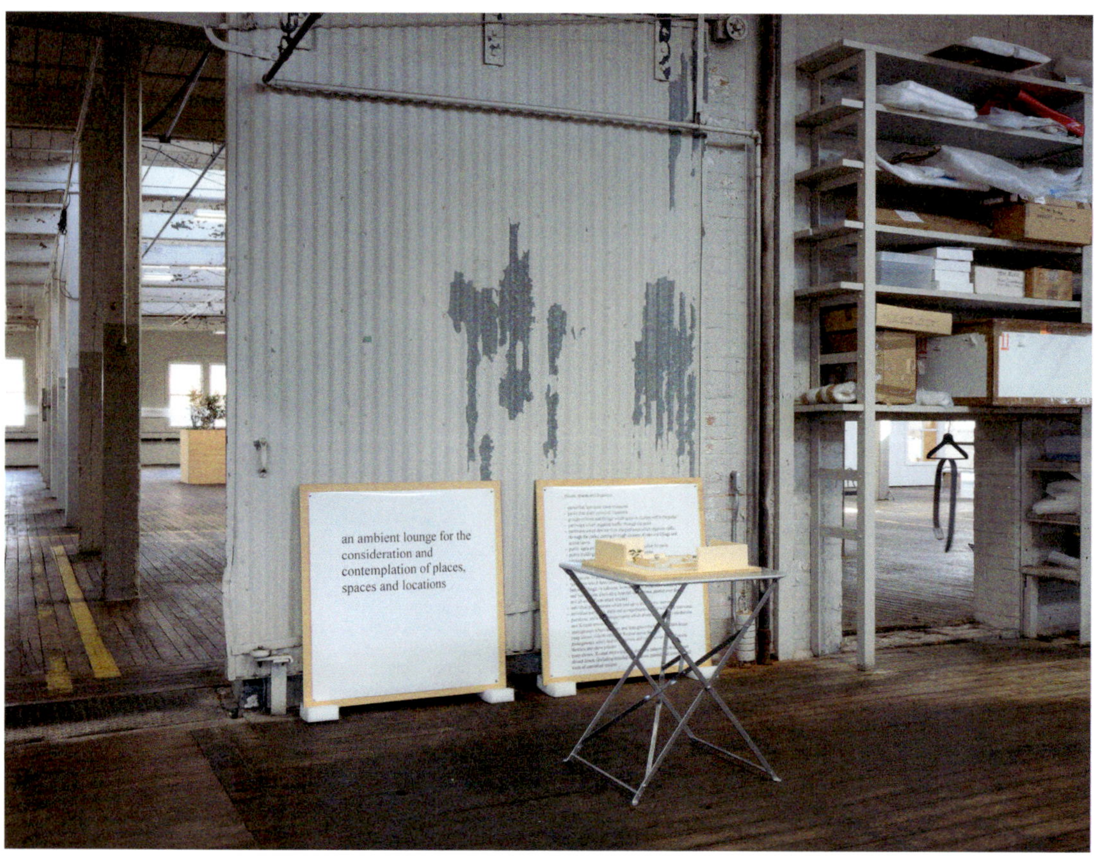
an ambient lounge for the
consideration and
contemplation of places,
spaces and locations

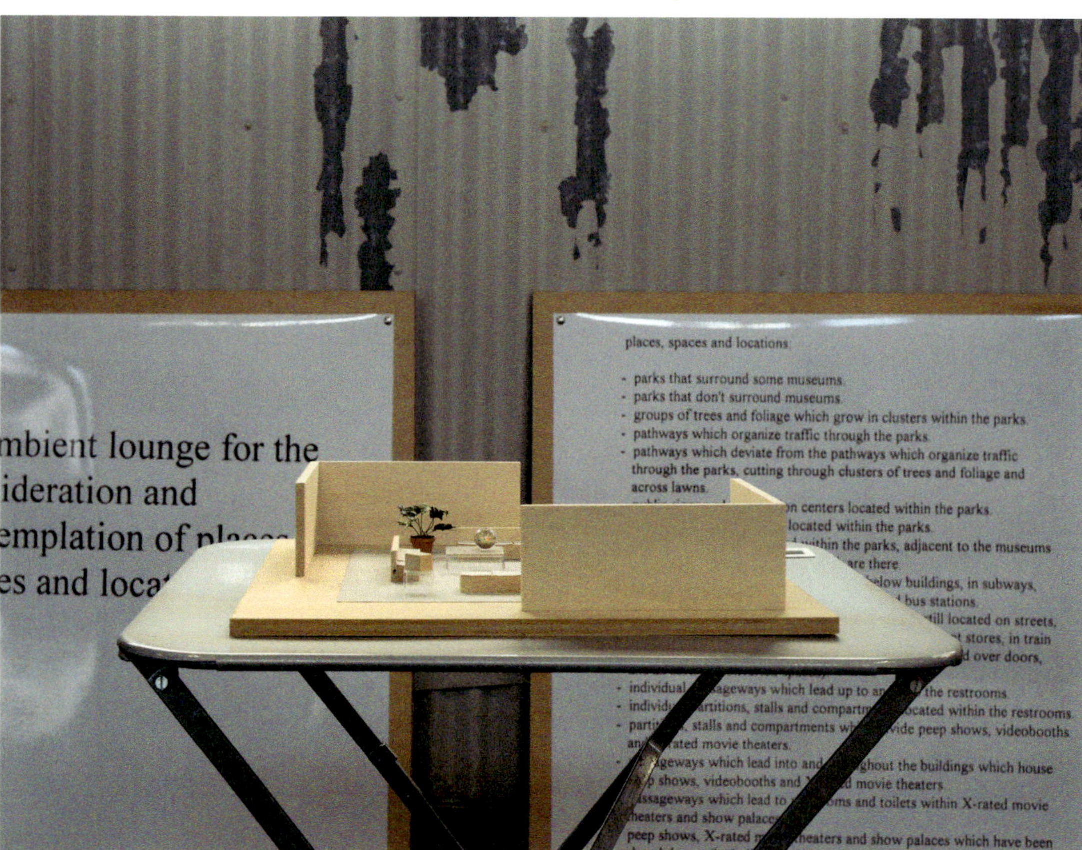
mbient lounge for the
iideration and
emplation of places
es and locat

places, spaces and locations:

- parks that surround some museums.
- parks that don't surround museums.
- groups of trees and foliage which grow in clusters within the parks.
- pathways which organize traffic through the parks.
- pathways which deviate from the pathways which organize traffic
  through the parks, cutting through clusters of trees and foliage and
  across lawns.

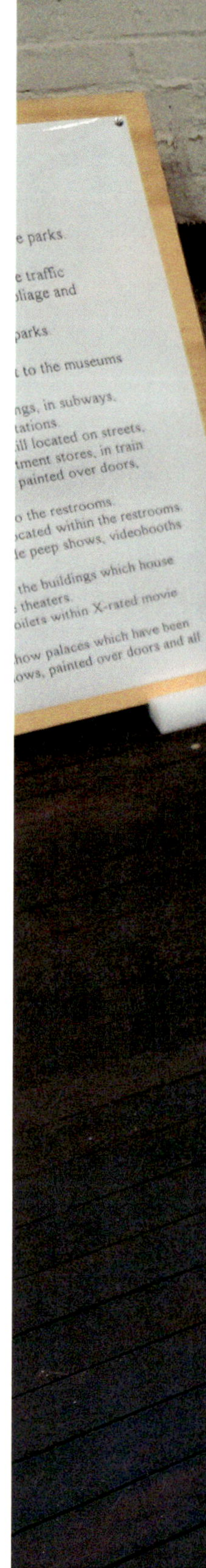
e parks.

e traffic
oliage and

parks.

to the museums

ngs, in subways,
tations
ill located on streets,
ment stores, in train
painted over doors,

o the restrooms.
ocated within the restrooms.
e peep shows, videobooths

the buildings which house
theaters.
oilets within X-rated movie

how palaces which have been
ows, painted over doors and all

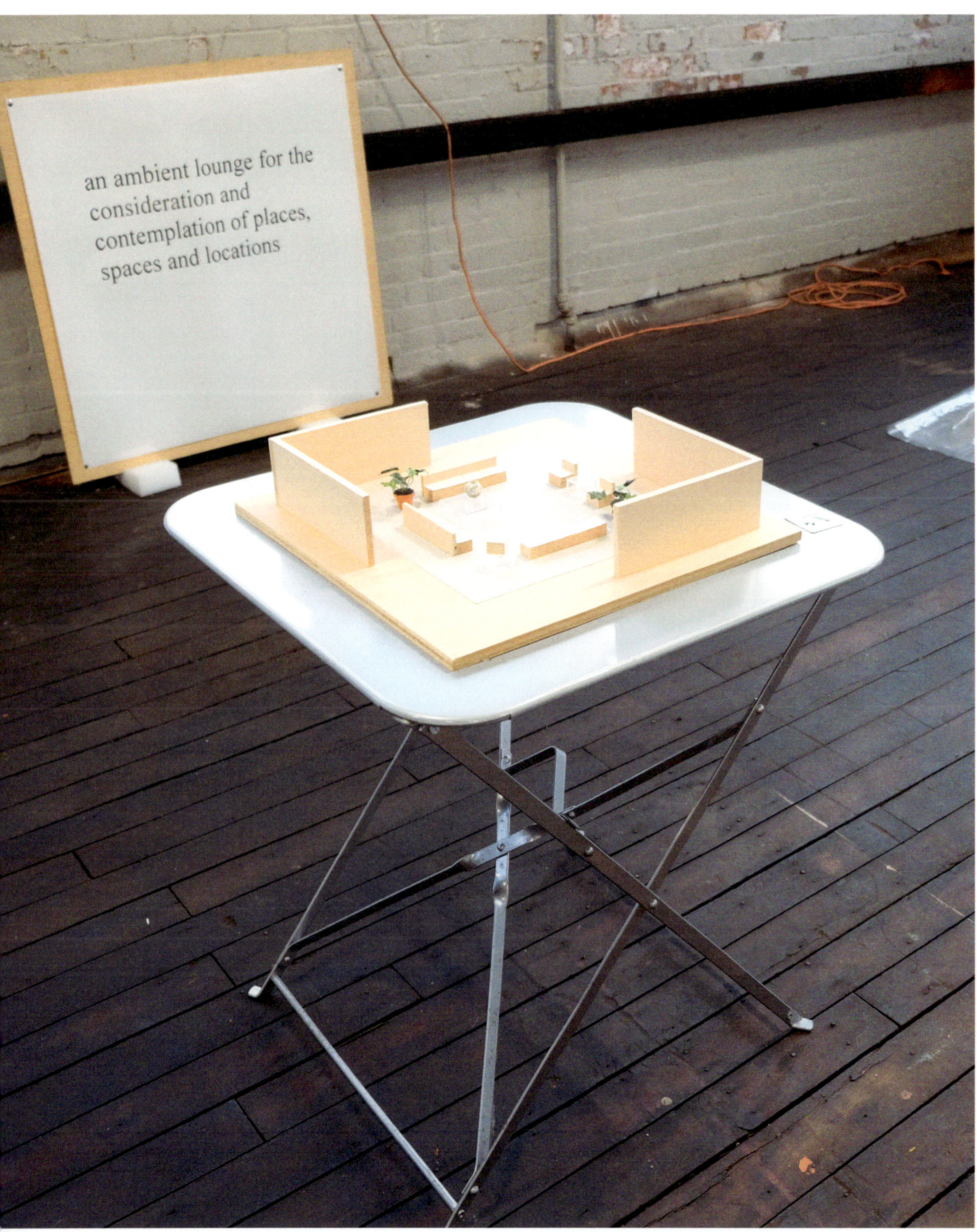

an ambient lounge for the
consideration and
contemplation of places,
spaces and locations

259

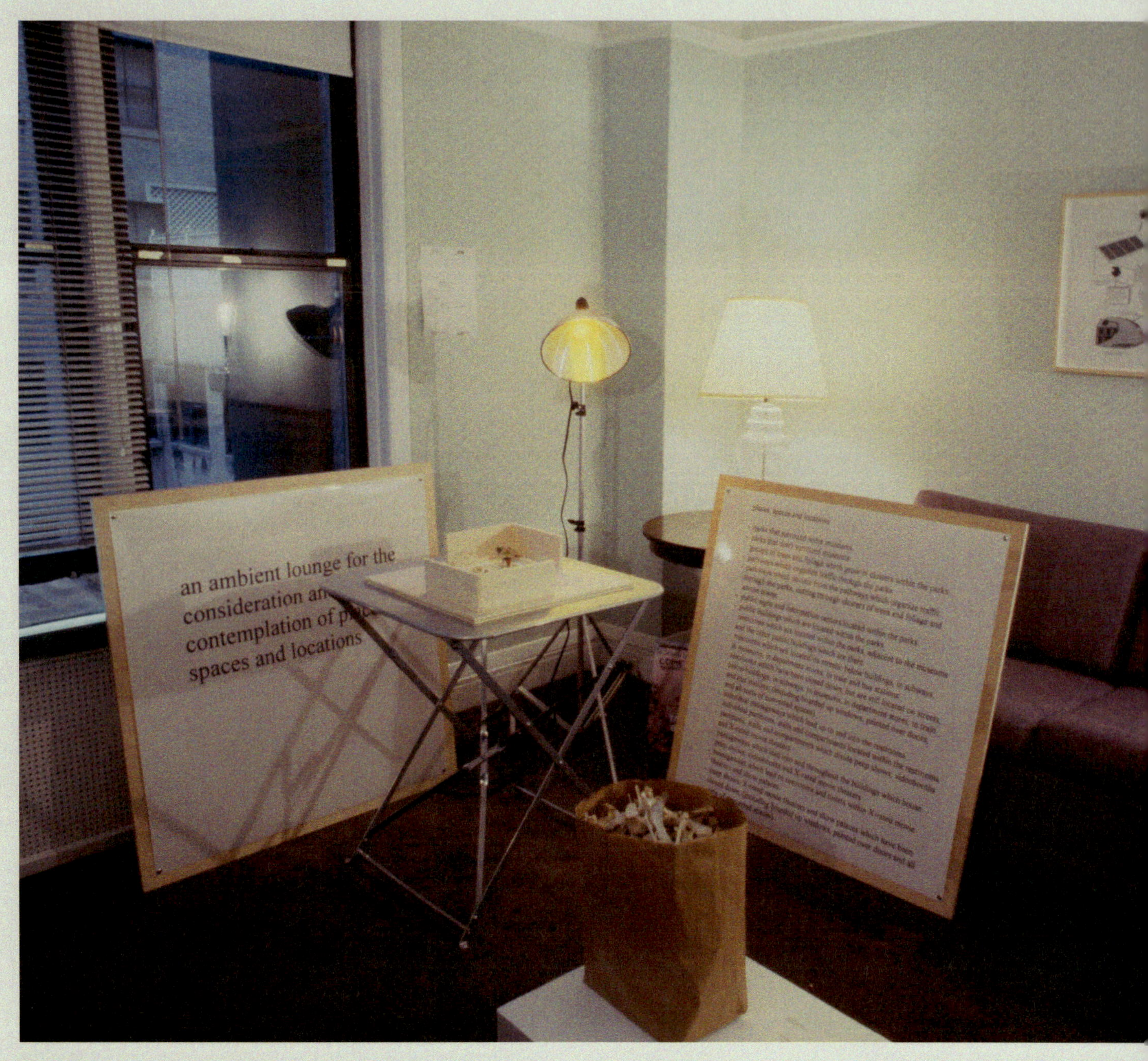
an ambient lounge for the
consideration and
contemplation of
spaces and locations

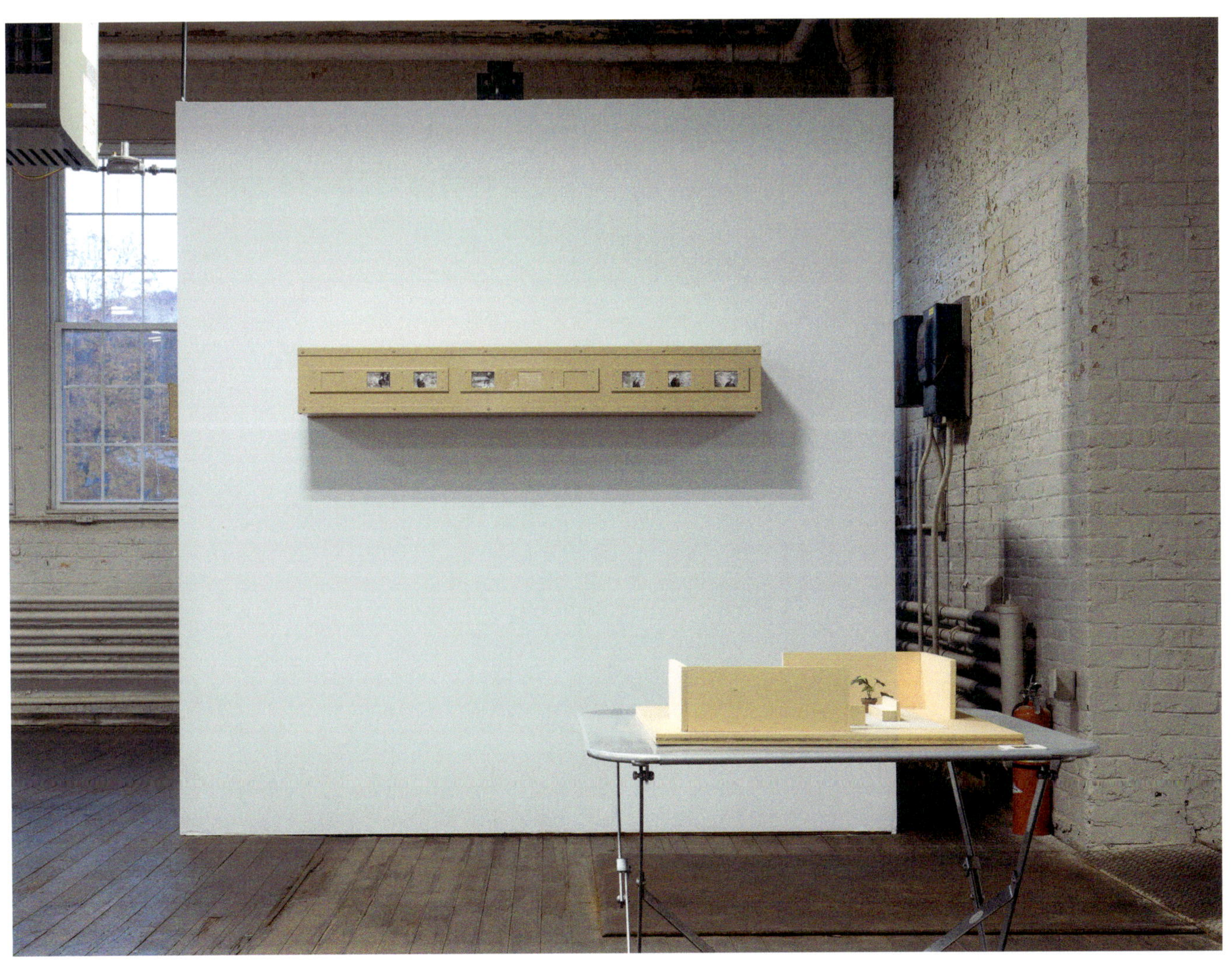

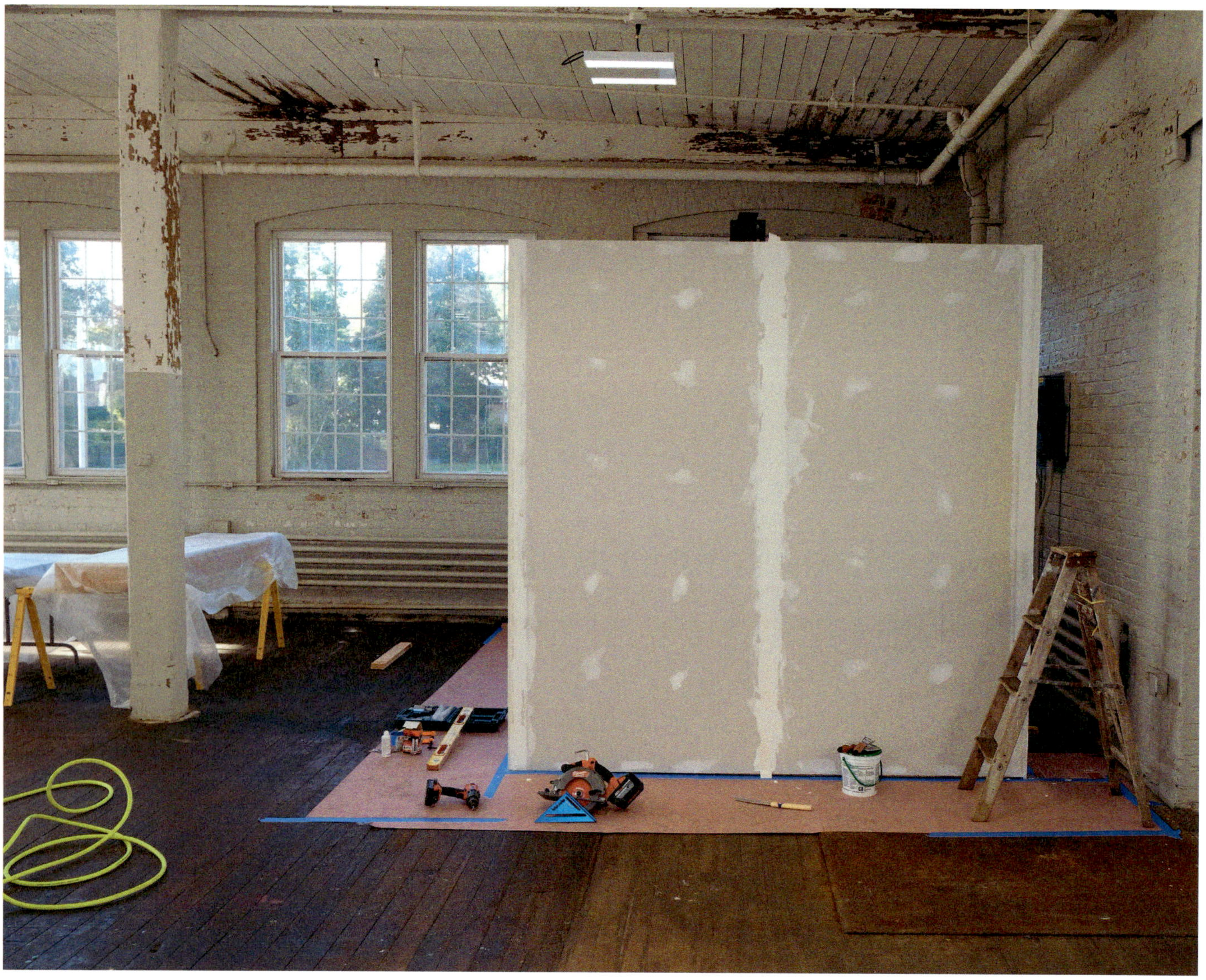

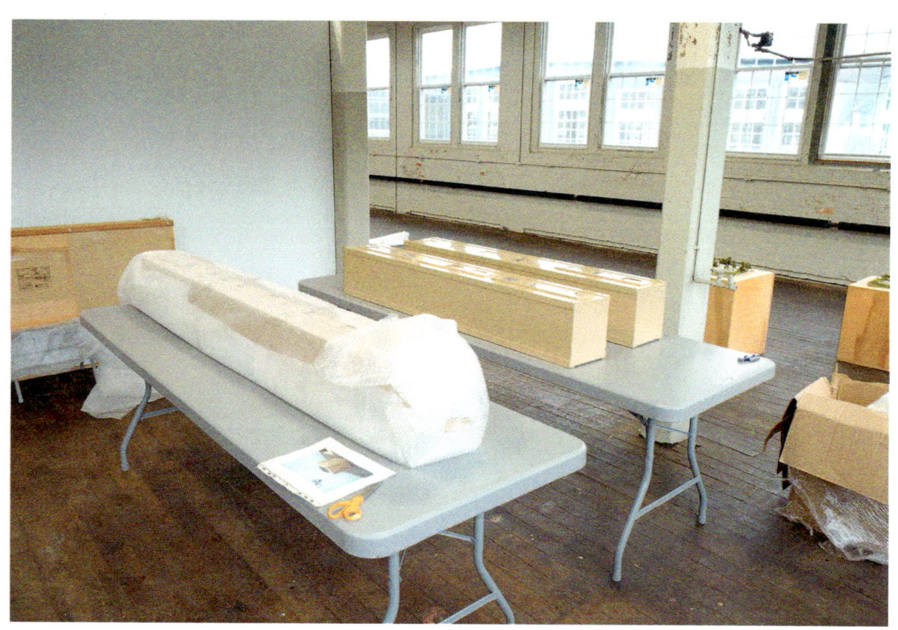

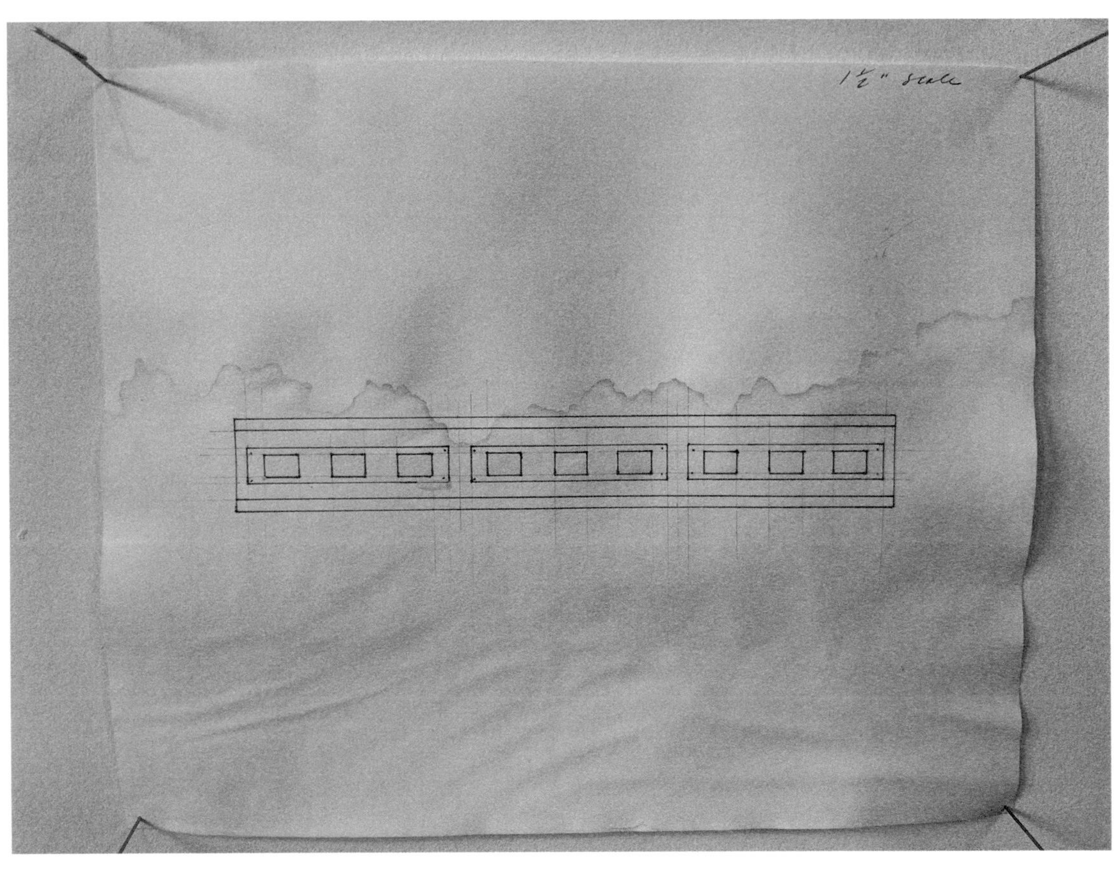

1½" scale

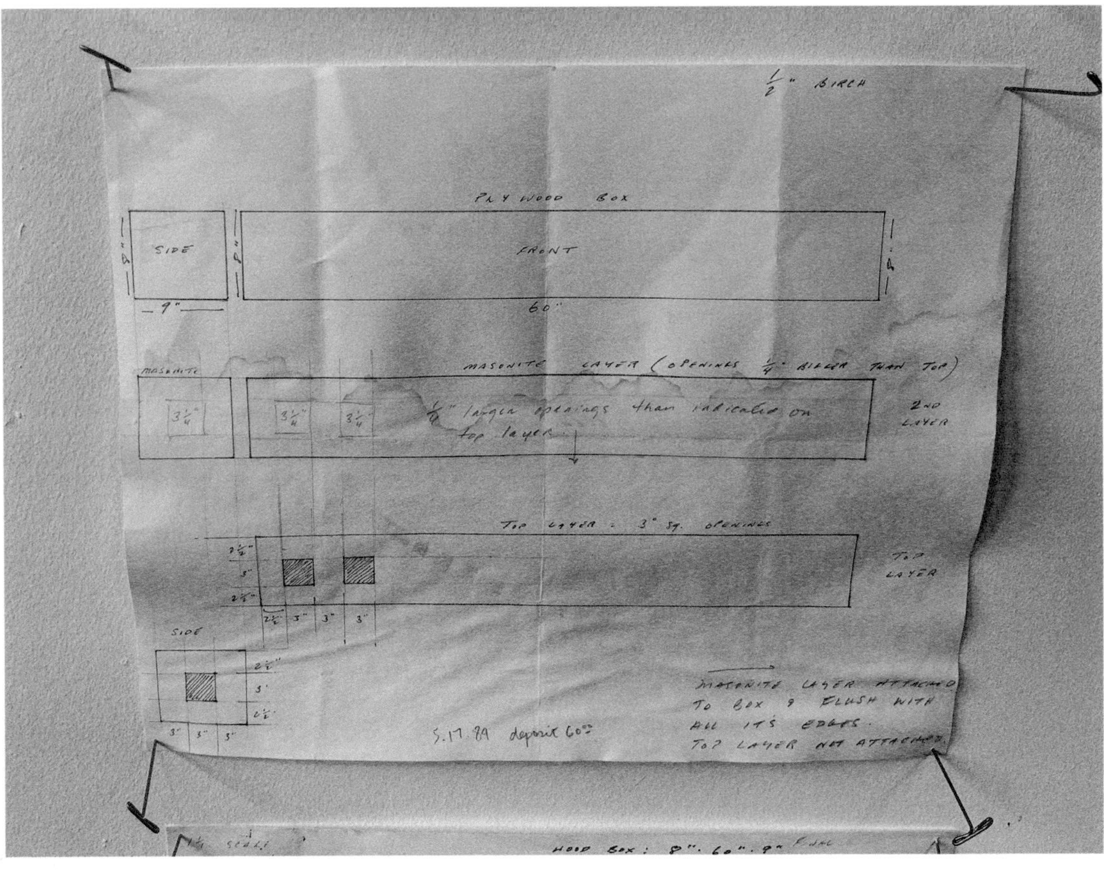

½" BIRCH
PLYWOOD BOX
SIDE
FRONT
9"
60"
MASONITE LAYER (OPENINGS ¼" BIGGER THAN TOP)
MASONITE
3¼"
3¼"
3¼"
¼" larger openings than indicated on
top layer
2ND
LAYER
TOP LAYER : 3" sq. OPENINGS
2½"
3"
2½"
2½"
3"
3"
3"
TOP
LAYER
SIDE
2½"
3"
2½"
3"
3"
3"
5.17.89 deposit 60⁰⁰
MASONITE LAYER ATTACHED
TO BOX & FLUSH WITH
ALL IT'S EDGES.
TOP LAYER NOT ATTACHED.
HOOD BOX : 8" . 60" . 9"

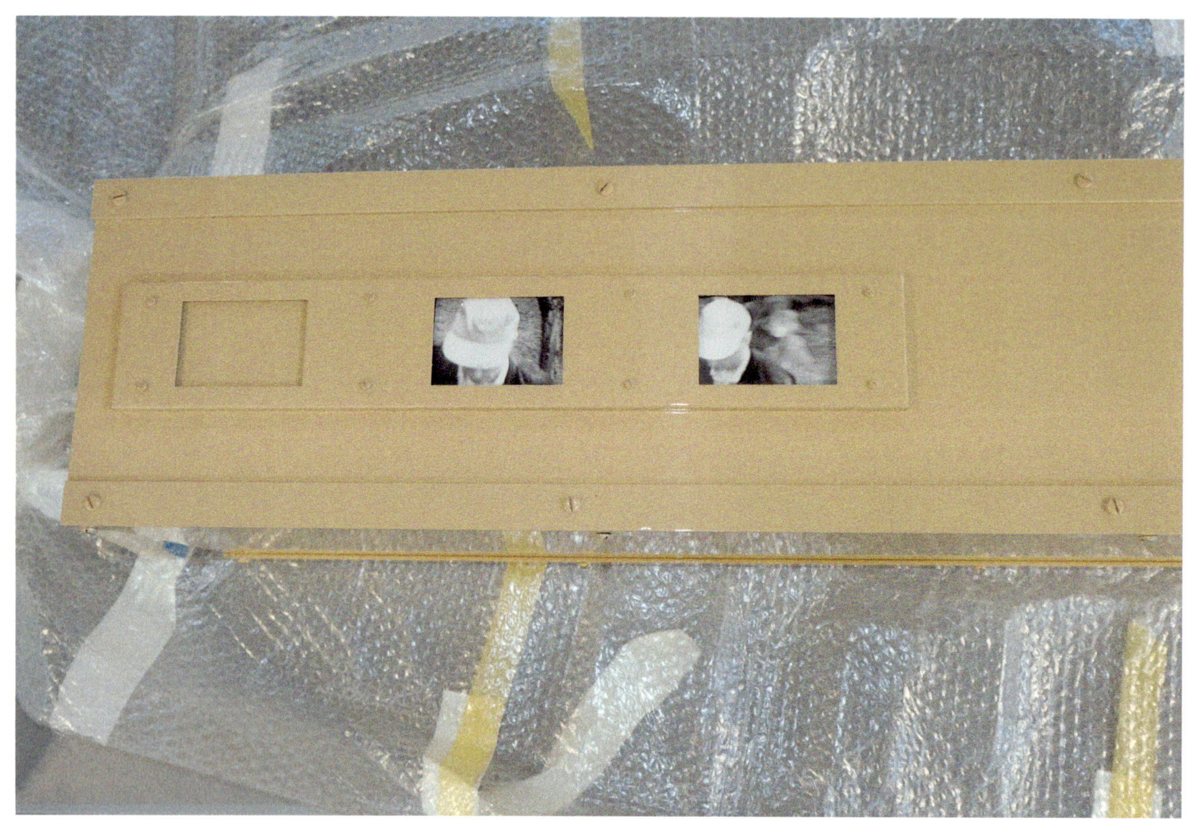

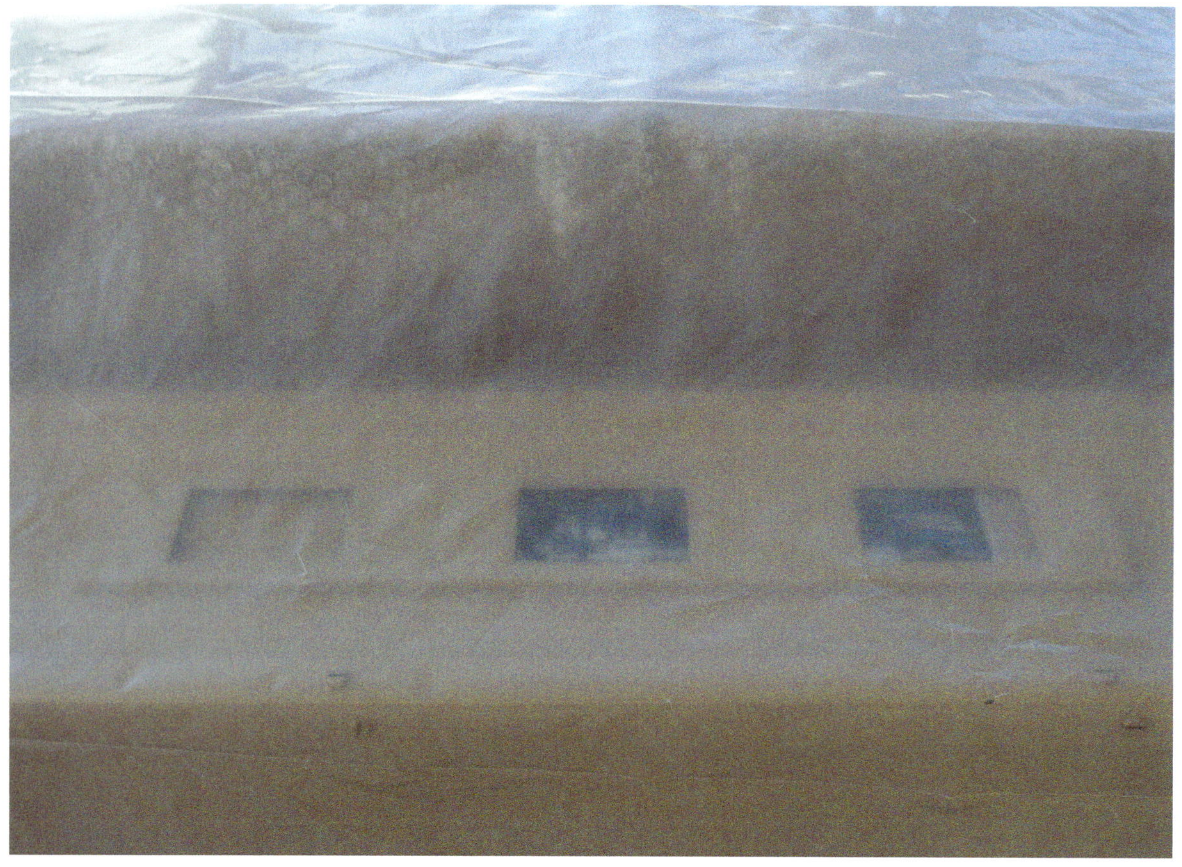

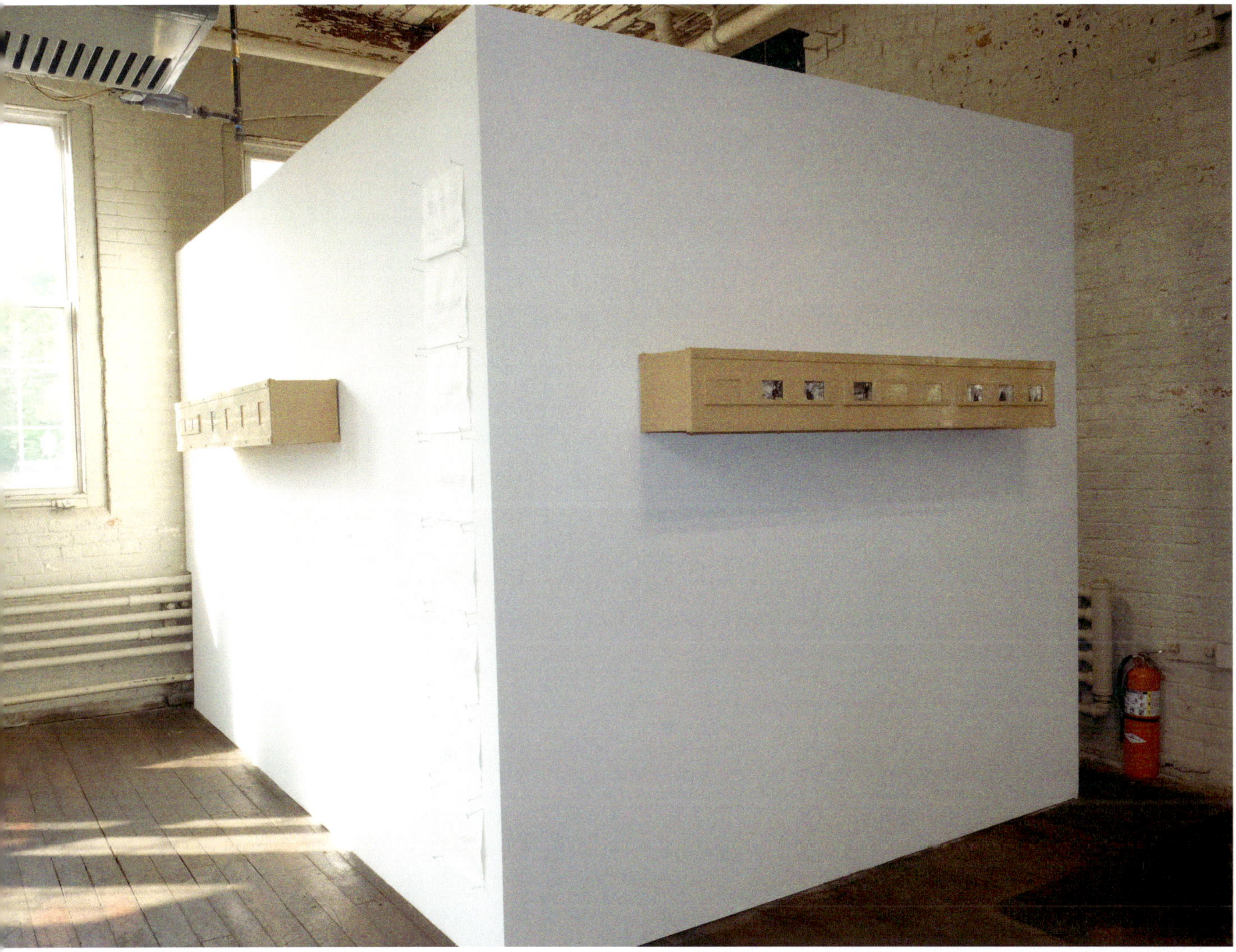

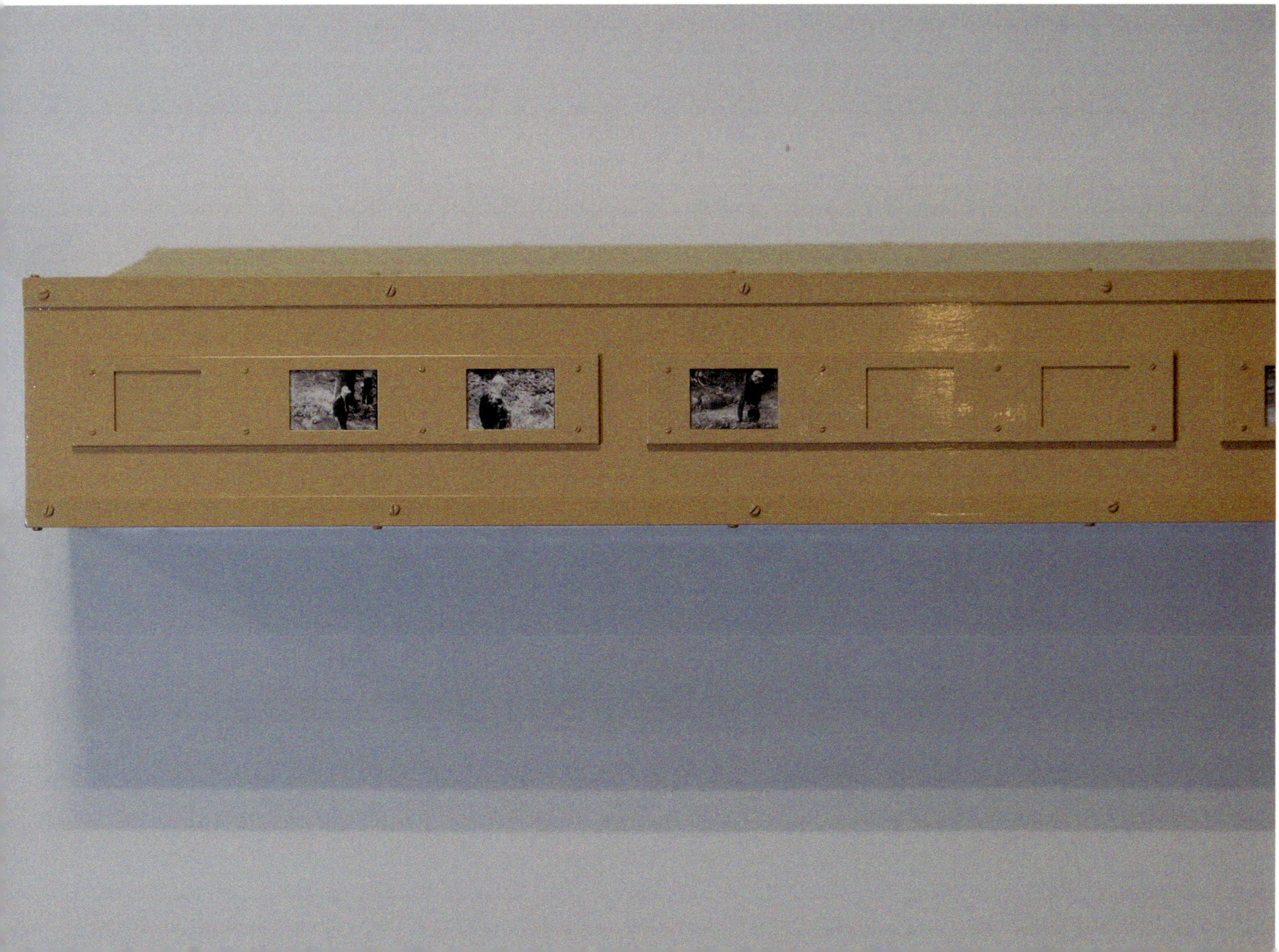

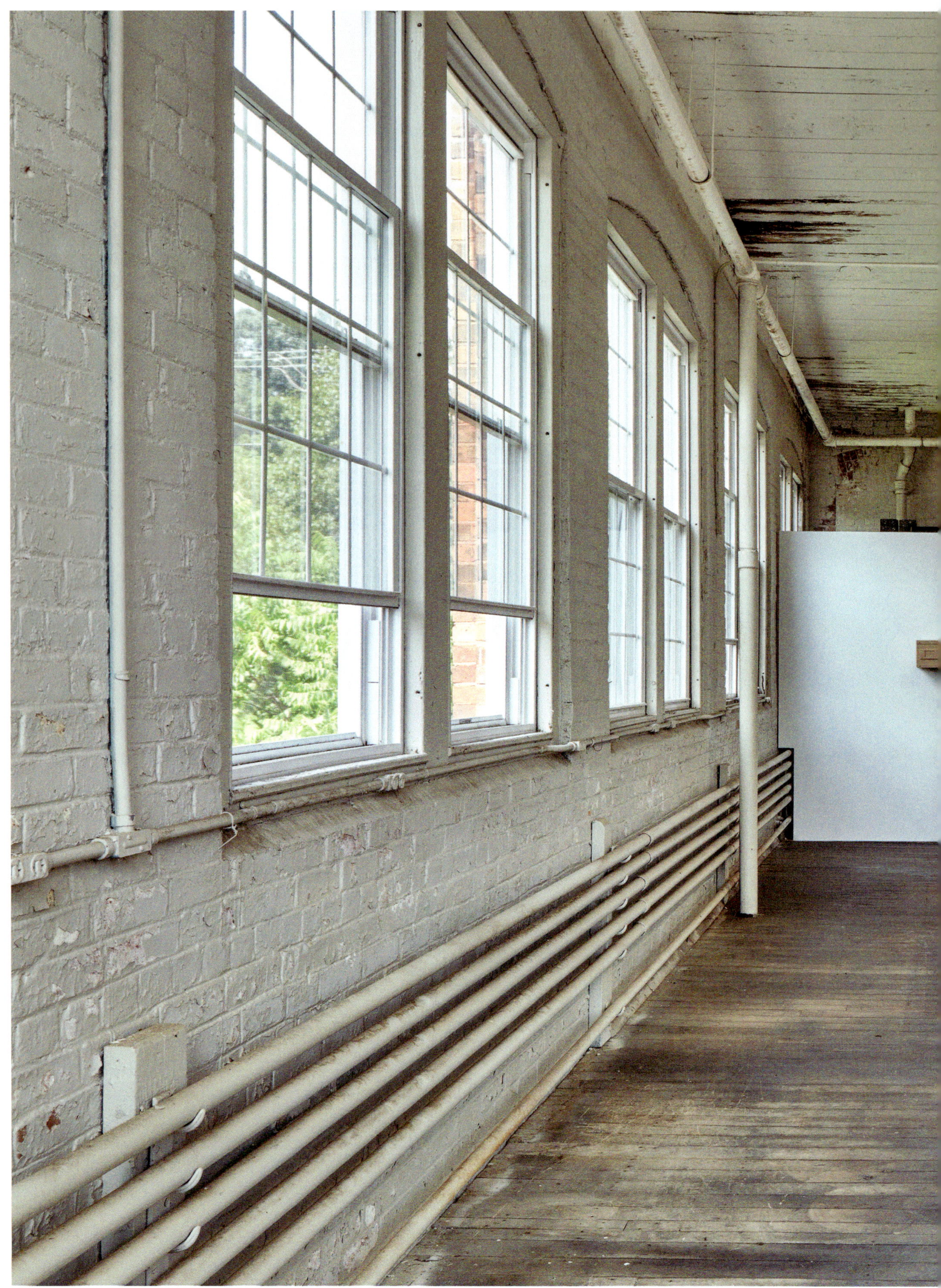

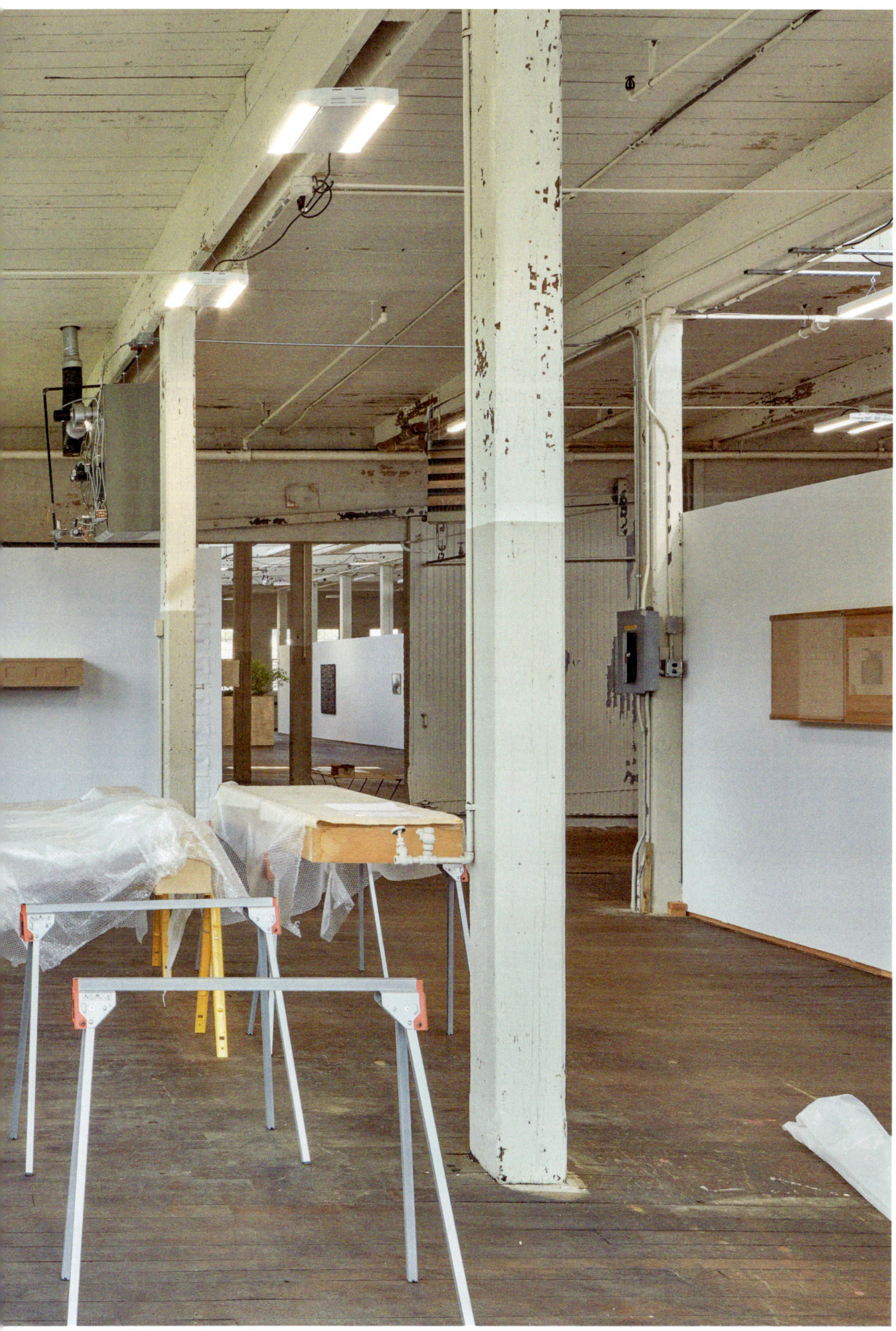

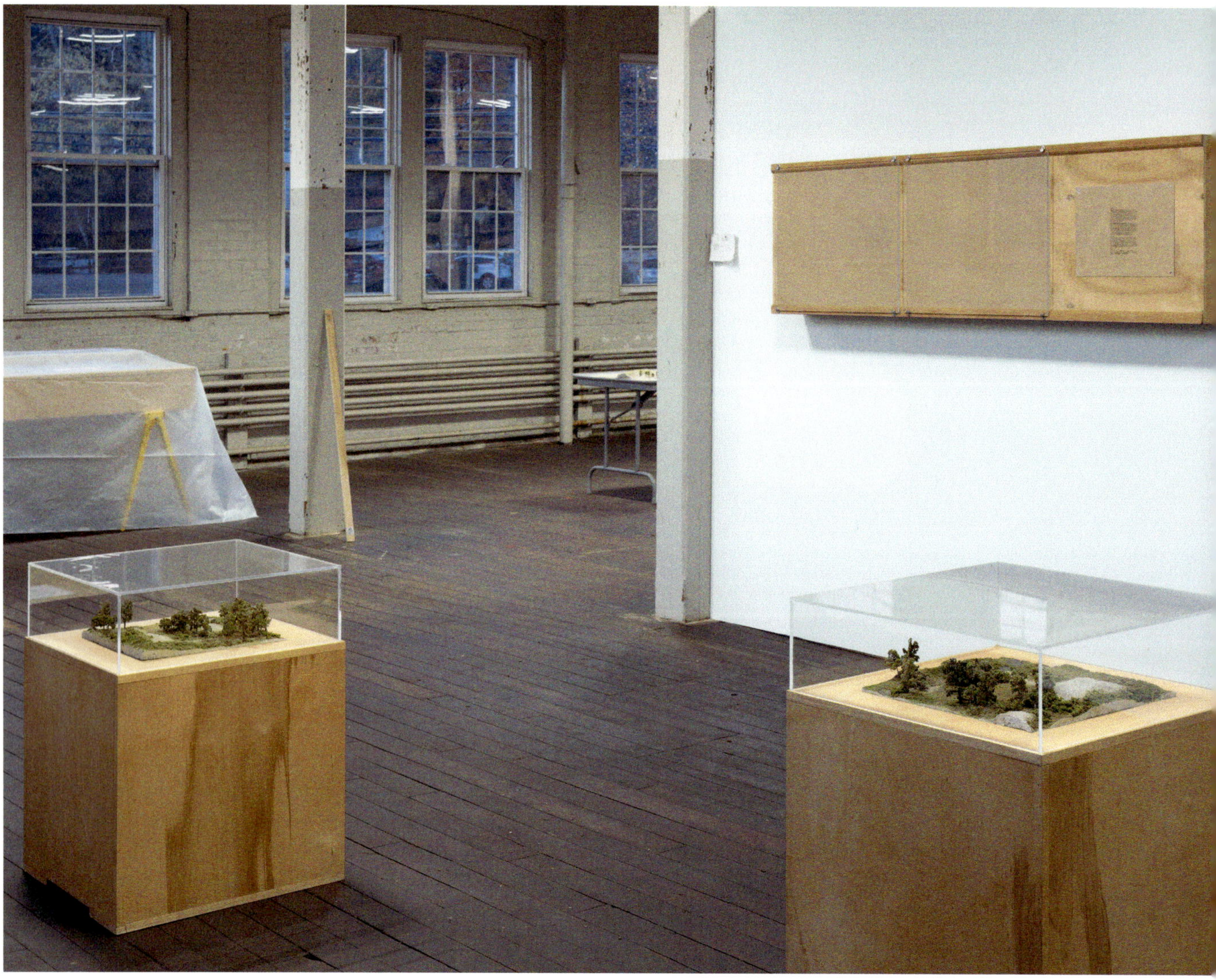

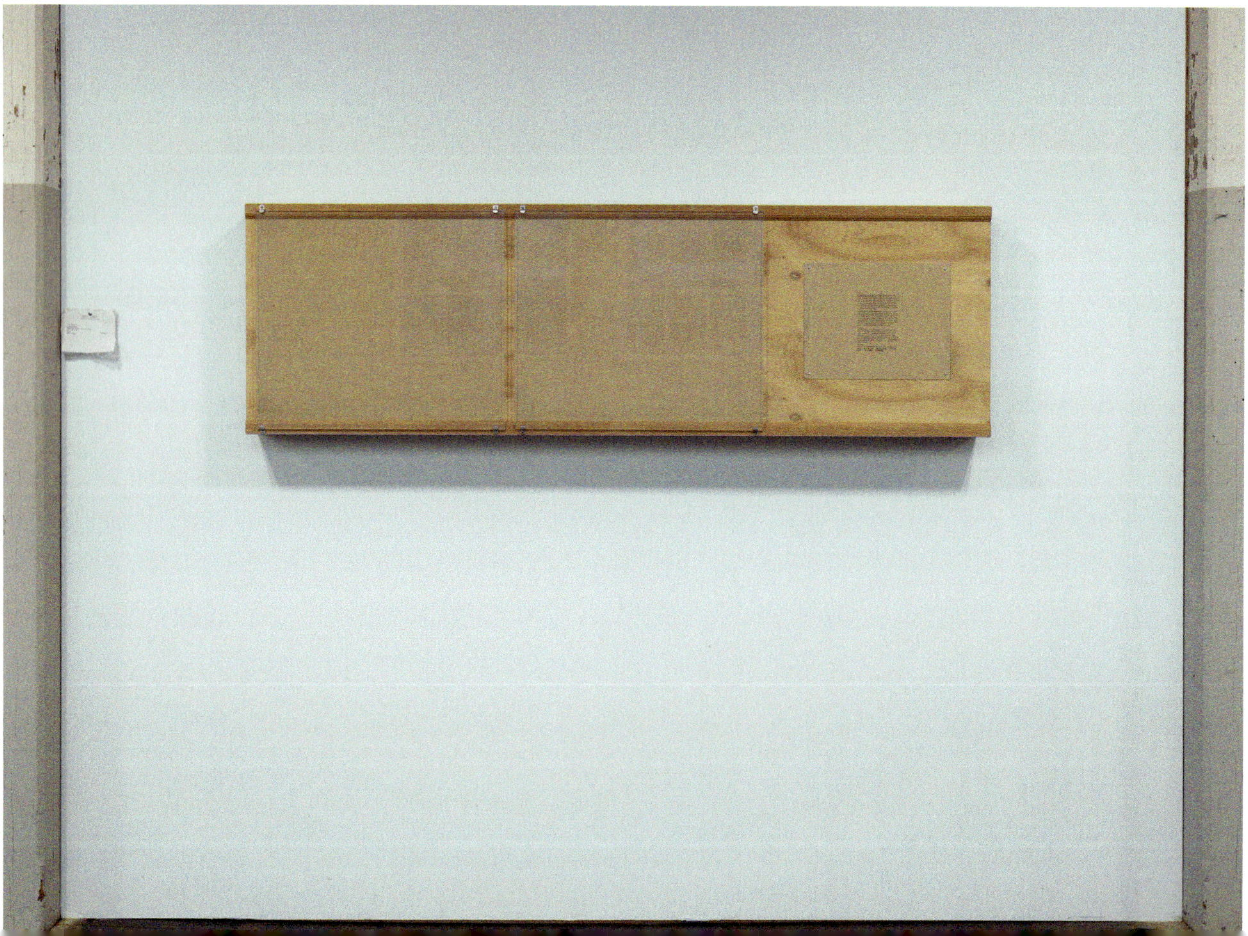

Q. What kind of place is this?

A. ...right here I feel like it's a chance to get back to something wild and
   natural. I like these parts of the park a lot where there're paths winding
   through and the trees are pouring over and it's sort of disorganized and
   real, you know...

B. That's it, it's a chance to get to something that's sort of real, after
   spending all week in the not very real enviroment.

Q. You mean the city?

B. In the city, yeah...

A. ...the trees and stuff just the way it is is fine. Just fine... I know things
   were planned, I know this park was very carefully planned, and probably more
   carefully planned than Versailles was planned, but now that it's been a period
   of time it doesn't look as if it was planned...

A. Okay, this looks designed, this looks completely designed.

B. Sure.

Q. This meadow?

A. yeah...

(two men strolling)

JANUARY 17 - FEBRUARY 9, 1992
NO TITLE, 1992, TEXT.

TOM BURR

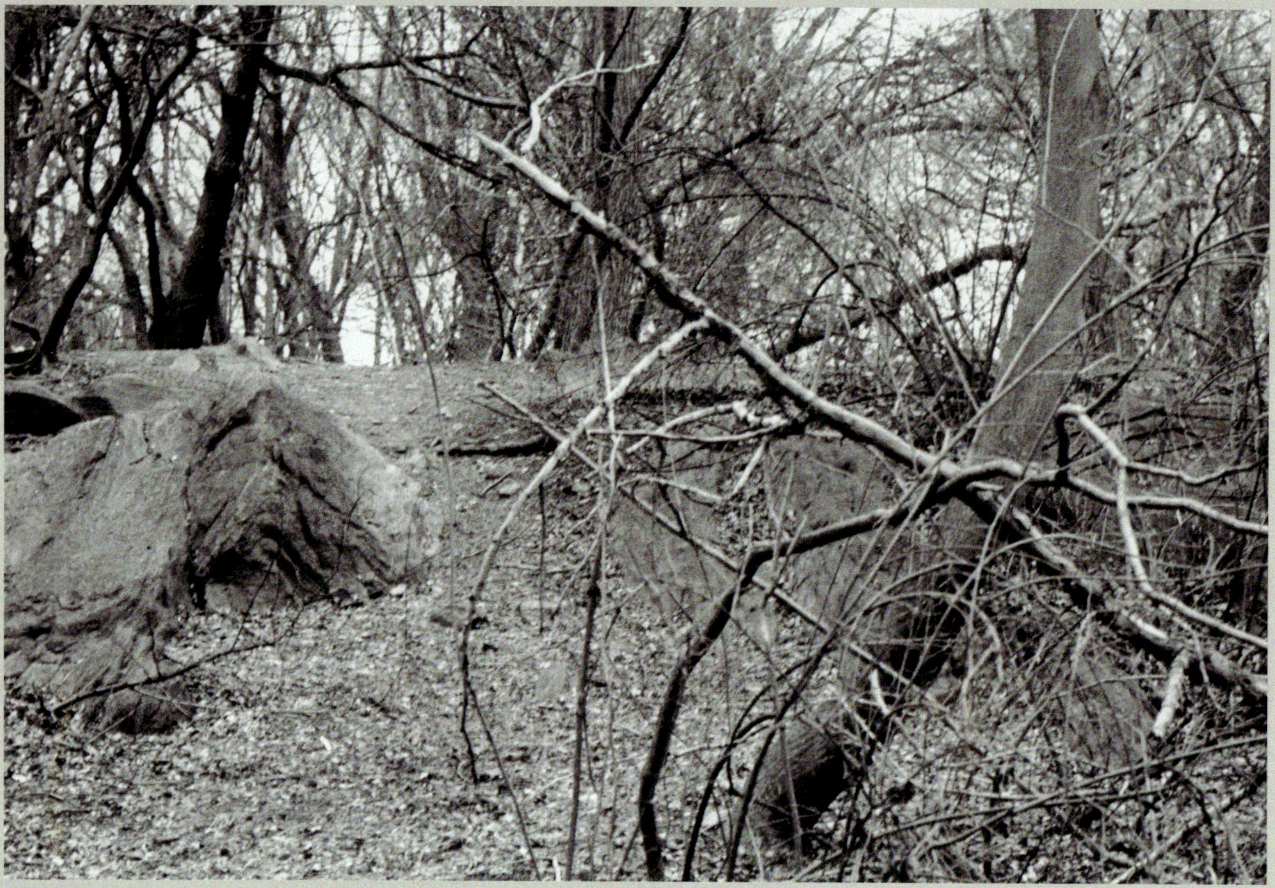

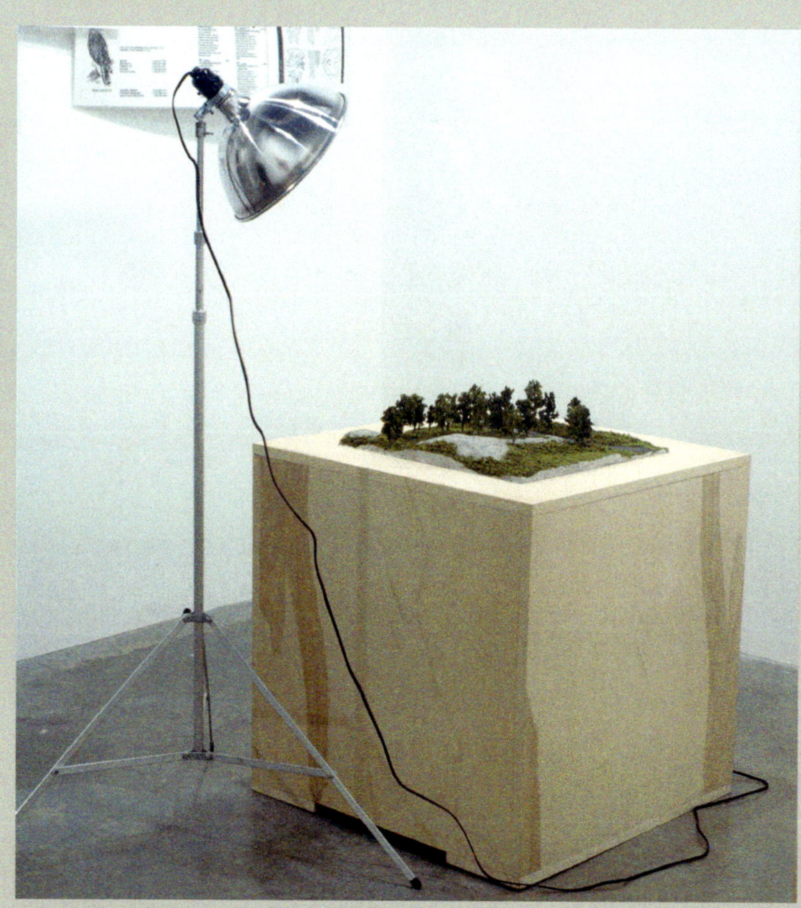

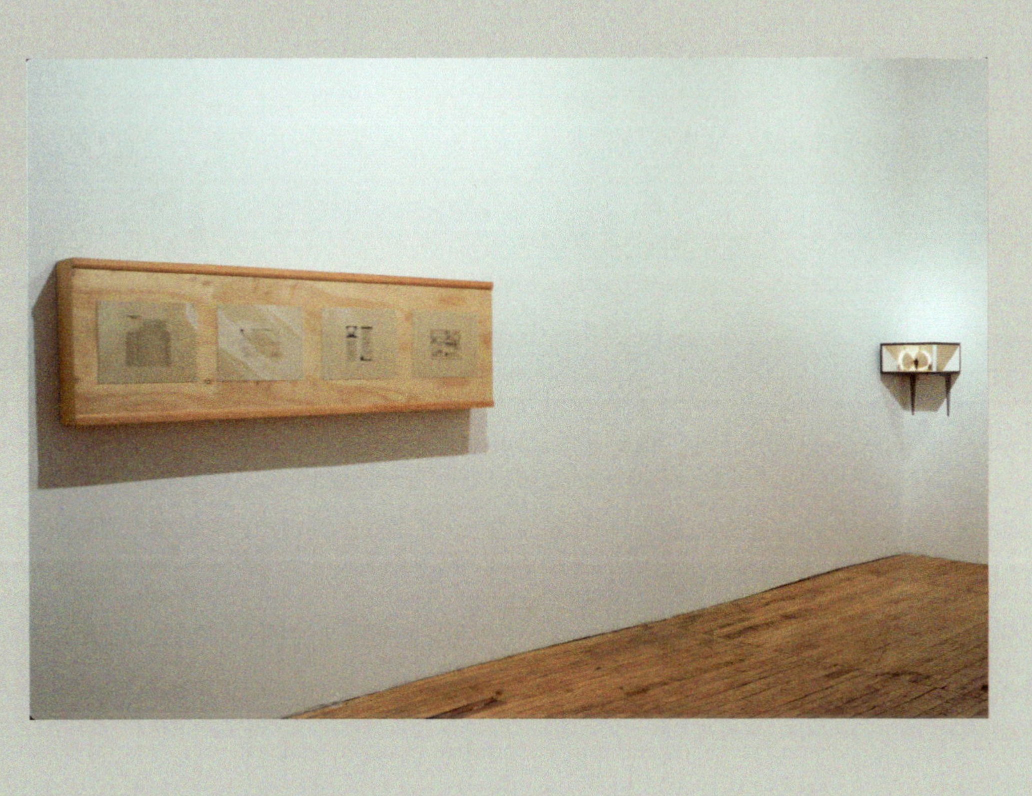

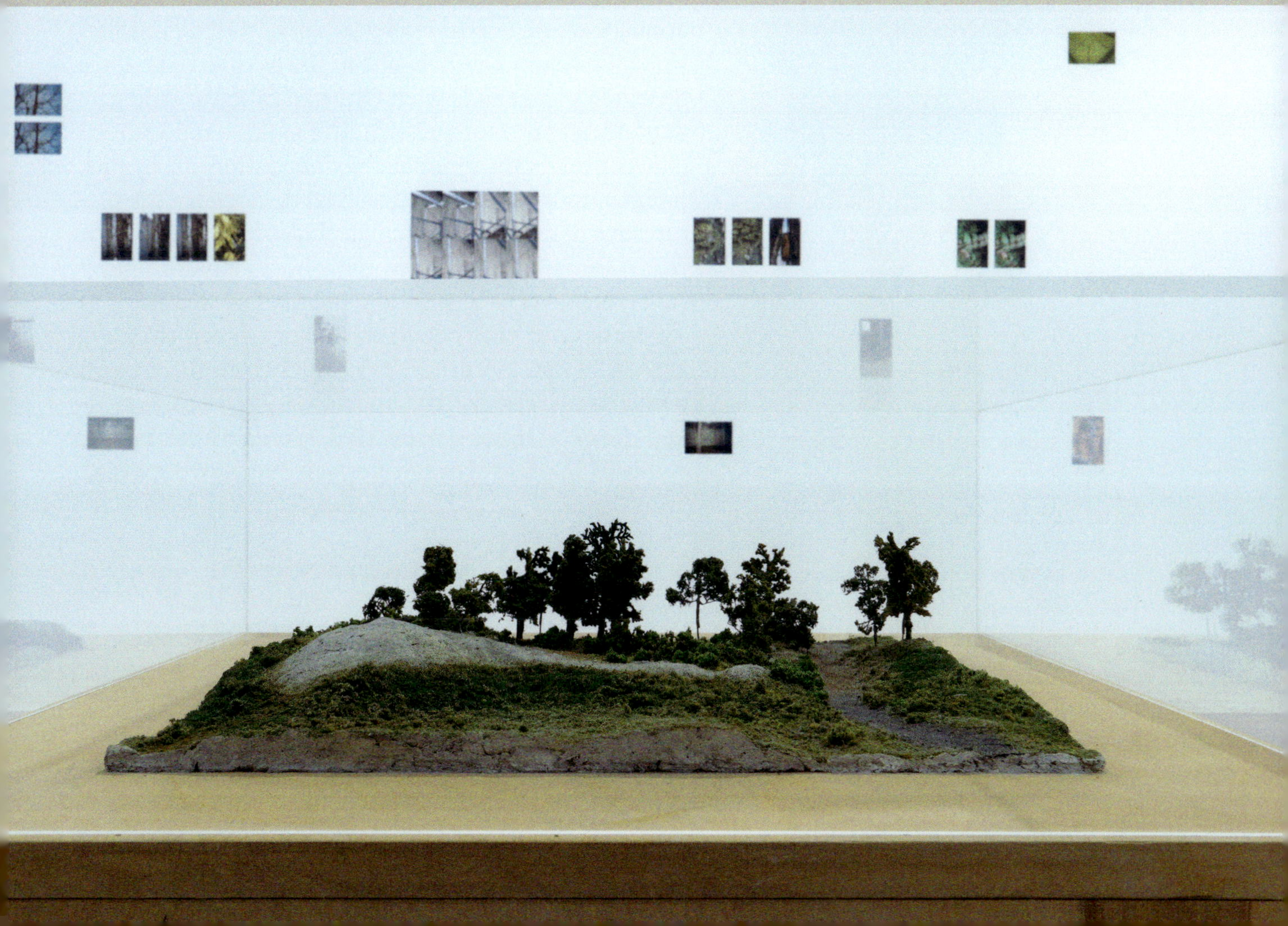

1   The exhibition, titled *Life Between Buildings*, was held at MoMA PS1, June 2, 2022–January 16, 2023, and included these two works by Burr.

I first saw Tom Burr's *A Ramble in Central Park (one)* and *A Ramble in Central Park (two)* (both 1992) in his Torrington studio; it was early 2022, and I was preparing for an exhibition looking at artists who have engaged liminal areas of New York City through an ecological lens.[1] Sunlight streamed into the space, lending the miniature landscapes a seraphic bent. Burr's works replicate the rocky hillocks and footpaths of the Ramble, an area in Central Park, with the material language and precision of a model train enthusiast, offering excerpted god's-eye views displayed on sleek wood plinths. One might be hard-pressed to say if they are records or projections, meant to immortalize a past landscape or sell a future one.

In 1858, Frederick Law Olmsted and Calvert Vaux presented before and after views of their proposed design for what would become the Ramble. The before: a photograph taken from around West 74th Street, capturing a deforested terrain dotted with cottages. The after, or "rendered effect," as Olmsted and Vaux captioned it: a painted vista of dense woodlands encircling a lake, seen slightly from above and suffused with the gauzy atmosphere of a Poussin. A year later, in 1859, this picturesque vision was brought to life as thirty-six acres groomed to resemble what Olmsted called a "wild garden" of native trees and winding paths—an idealized (and conveniently unpopulated) fabrication of a bygone indigenous landscape. As an aesthetic category, the picturesque designates that which eludes full cognition or control—dark forests, dissolving horizons, crumbling ruins, the ravages of time and caprices of weather—as "expressive of that peculiar kind of beauty, which is agreeable in a picture."[2] It emerges from the frisson between a desire for the unbridled—and *unseeable*—and the crystalline perspective offered by the image. A nexus, in other words, of opacity and scopophilia.

2   William Gilpin, *An Essay on Prints* (London, 1802), xii.

     Jody Graf

3   Robert Smithson, "Frederick Law Olmsted and the Dialectical Landscape," *Artforum*, February 1973, 67.

The Ramble remains more or less as Olmsted and Vaux designed it. Elsewhere, the park features grassy lawns, ornate fountains, and plumb boulevards with long vistas. But the Ramble swallows you into a glut of snaking paths. On a recent visit—an oppressively sunny and eerily warm fall day—tourists strolled while reflexively consulting their iPhone maps, self-soothingly monitoring their dot-shaped avatars as they wrestled with the ingrained impulse to *get somewhere*. The Ramble "out-labyrinthed labyrinths," as Robert Smithson put it in his 1973 article "Frederick Law Olmsted and the Dialectical Landscape." "For what really is a Ramble," he wrote, "but a place to walk aimlessly and idly—it is a maze that spreads in all directions."[3] The Ramble certainly encourages an aleatory meandering unsolicited by the rest of the grid-stamped city. But its spatial "aimlessness" has given rise to other quite specific aims and uses.

Since the early twentieth century, it has been a popular site for cruising, its shady thickets and alcoves well suited for trysts—a place for people to see each other, but also remain unseen. A photograph from the 1950s offers a rare illustration. Groups of men saunter down sun-dappled paths, their shoulders just touching and hands seeming to graze beneath suit cuffs. Over time, the Ramble became crisscrossed with "desire lines"— unplanned footpaths etched into the landscape by those seeking cloistered spots for a hookup, or the possibility of one. The same tangled sight lines and dense foliage that make the Ramble a prime spot for lovemaking also render it suitable for bird-watching—indeed, people come to the Ramble to pursue both activities. Bird-watching involves a different kind of unplanned encounter and close looking, one much more accepted by the park administration.

Shadow Play

4   Quoted in Manfred Hermes, "Cruising and Birdwatchers," *Texte Zur Kunst*, February 1992, 192–93.

5   For a discussion of anti-gay violence in the Ramble in the 1970s and the conflicted responses to the NYPD's neglect of the area, see Doug Ireland, "Rendezvous in the Ramble," *New York*, July 24, 1978, https://nymag.com/news/features/47179/.

Burr invoked these two unanticipated uses—cruising and bird-watching—in a 1992 show at White Columns entitled *Central Park Visitor Center. Focus: 'The Ramble,'* where he first showed his models of the Ramble. The sculptures were positioned in the middle of the gallery, while a bevy of texts pulled from the Central Park Visitor Center lined the walls. These extolled the Ramble as an area for bird-watching and omitted mention of its alternate use as a refuge for oppressed desire. Not that park administrators didn't know; an internal report from the time states: "The gay activity includes cruising or strolling through the area which is harmless enough. Also part of the activity is orgies or active sexual activity in the shrubbery. This has caused damage to the plants and more importantly, the trampling has resulted in erosion."[4] It may have been "harmless enough," but not so harmless that police didn't periodically sweep the area; at the same time, they declined to prevent or prosecute the anti-gay violence that often took place there.[5]

Looking at installation shots of Burr's 1992 presentation, I was intrigued to see a single metal lamp positioned next to one of the Ramble models, illuminating the scene with a cold, unnatural light reminiscent of a surgical theater or interrogation room. It struck me that my initial understanding of these works as critical re-romanticizations of the Ramble, replicas of what is, at core, a replica, was not the whole story. Rather, the works' bite emerges in their reenactment of the Ramble as *picture* rather than space of possibility. In 1992, a time when public space was being increasingly privatized and "sanitized" (see Burr's works about Times Square, namely those making up *42nd Street Structures* from 1995, for another example of the artist's incisive attention to this issue), this bracing light underscored how, in Giuliani-era New York, a term like "visibility" was often synonymous

     Jody Graf

6   Burr's installation also makes me think of the
blinding high-intensity mobile floodlights
installed by the NYPD on street corners, in
parks, and in public housing developments
across New York City beginning in 2014. This
was part of a strategy called "Omnipresence,"
which, according to Mayor Bill de Blasio, was
designed to "light up the areas that have previously been obscure and problematic." See
"Transcript: Mayor de Blasio Announces Plan
to Make New York City's Neighborhoods and
Housing Developments Safer," NYC Office
of the Mayor, July 8, 2014, https://www.
nyc.gov/office-of-the-mayor/news/338-14/
transcript-mayor-de-blasio-plan-make-new-
york-city-s-neighborhoods-housing#/0.

7   Frederick Law Olmsted, *The Spoils of the Park:
With a Few Leaves from the Deep-Laden Note-
Books of "A Wholly Unpractical Man"* (1882),
26.

8   Ibid., 50.

9   "Compromise for the Ramble Is Pressed on
Park Tour," *New York Times*, November 27,
1955, 86.

with the surveillance and discipline of marginalized groups, such as the queer community, under the guise of safety. Leaving the Platonic cave for the blinding light of day does not, for everyone, lead to freedom.[6]

Interestingly, the question of light plagued opinions about the Ramble from the beginning. In an 1882 treatise titled (incredibly) *The Spoils of the Park: With a Few Leaves from the Deep-Laden Note-Books of "A Wholly Unpractical Man,"* an aggrieved Olmsted derides municipal efforts to tame the Ramble, complaining, "Rocky passages of the Park, which had been furnished under my direction with a natural growth of characteristic rocky hillside perennials, have been more than once 'cleaned up,' and so thoroughly that the leaf-mould, with which the crevices of the ledge had been carefully filled for the sustenance of the plants, was swept out with house-brooms in the interest of that good taste which delights in a house painted white with green blinds."[7] And later: "How will it be when 'a free circulation of air and light' beneath every bush and brooding conifer has been secured; when the way of the lawn-mower has at all points been made plain, and the face of nature shall everywhere have become as natty as a new silk hat?"[8] The Ramble never quite became the "silk hat" of Olmsted's nightmares, but efforts were made in that proverbial direction. In the 1930s, the city closed access to "The Cave," a dark grotto used for covert rendezvous. In 1955, Robert Moses tried replacing the Ramble with a senior center, to the dismay of the public. As one Mr. Harrison of Midtown carped, "In a Moses park everybody must do something—row a boat, ride a horse, play shuffleboard.... The Ramble is a place just to sit quietly and look at the trees, but Moses doesn't understand that. The bird watchers are wrong, too. Except for a few weeks in spring and fall, there are no birds here except common sparrows and gulls."[9]

          Shadow Play

The tensions, simultaneities, and collisions that reside at the heart of the Ramble—between shadow and illumination, privacy and public space, planned disorientation and control, embodied perspectives and omniscient views—persist. As I write this, the technophilic and crime-obsessed Mayor Adams has big plans for tipping the scales toward omniscience, with a fleet of autonomous drones soon to be flying over the park. In August 2024, NYPD Deputy Commissioner for Public Information Tarik Sheppard stated, "We've got the autonomous drones coming by the end of the month.... It's going to allow us to cover a big territory very quickly and also allow us to get images and video in places [of the park] where we don't have cameras." "There are no secrets being kept here," said NYPD Chief of Patrol John Chell in a separate news conference.[10] So here we are, in the city without shadows that Burr's works presaged those thirty-two years ago, subjected to the watchful glare of a lamp we might not even know is on, living under the light of a sun getting ever hotter, wondering where on earth we will keep our secrets. ◊

10 Bill Hutchinson, "Largest US police force is using drones to curb a Central Park crime spree," ABC News, August 22, 2024, https://abcnews.go.com/US/largest-us-police-force-drones-curb-central-park/story?id=112995925.

  Jody Graf

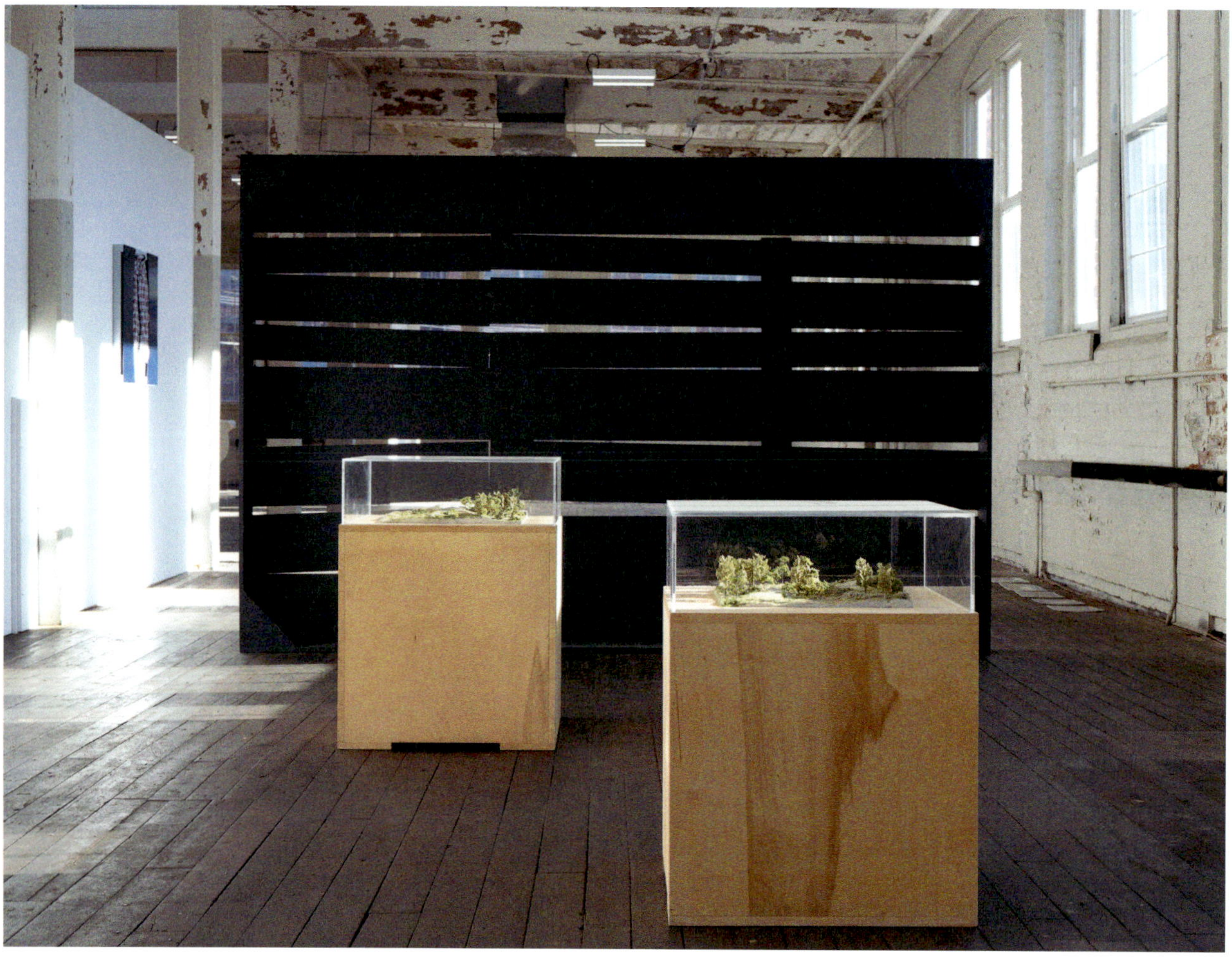

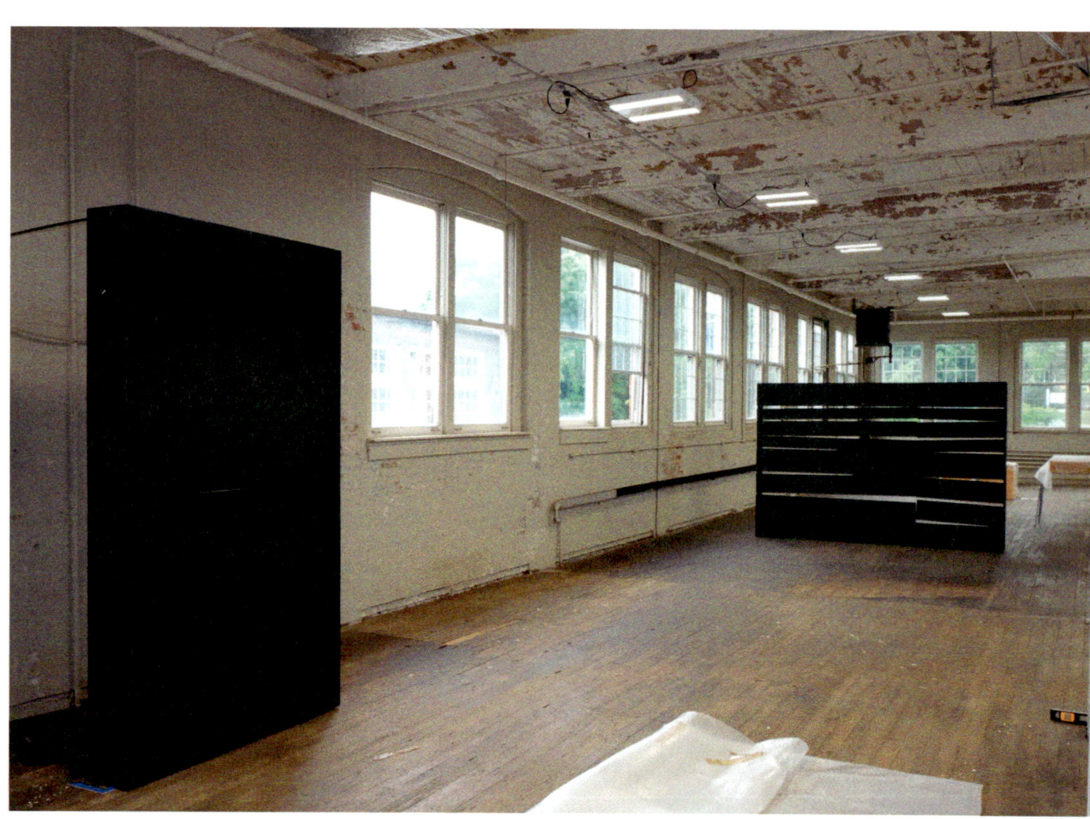

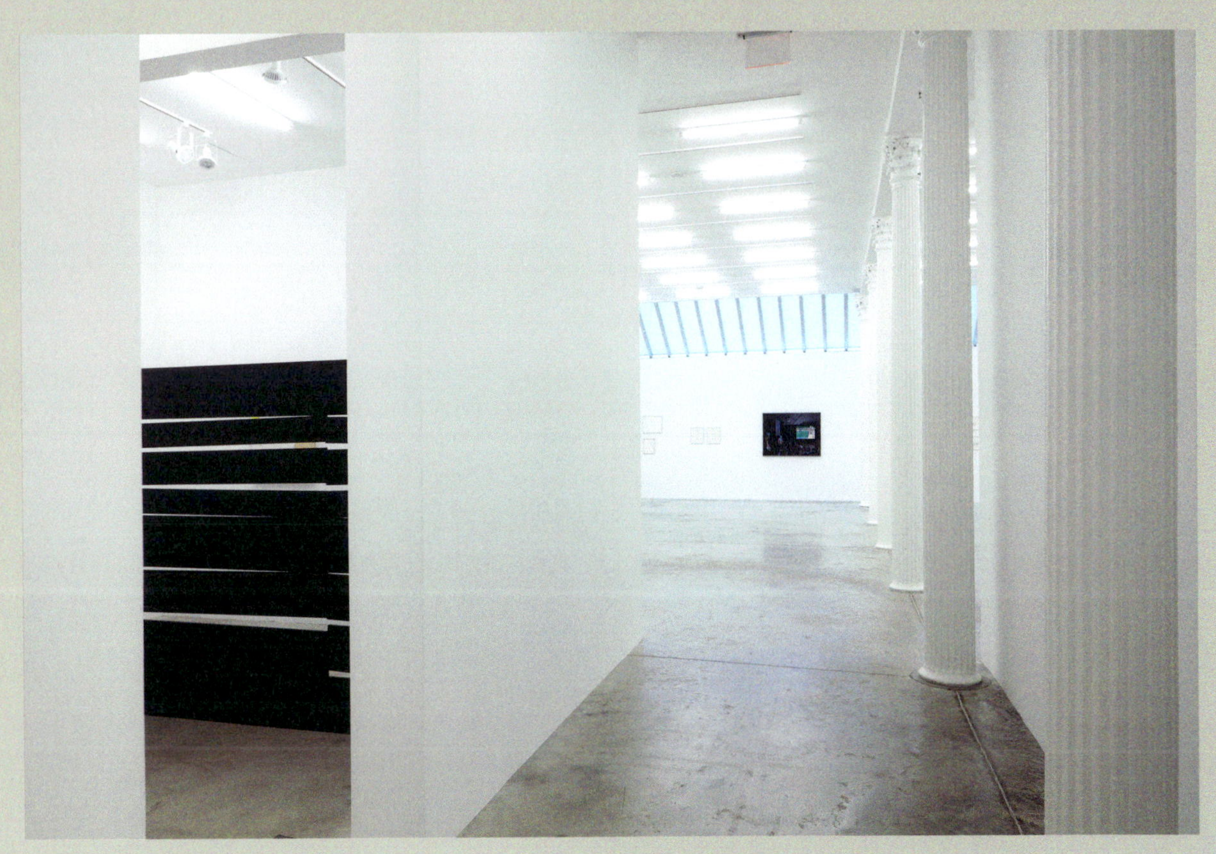

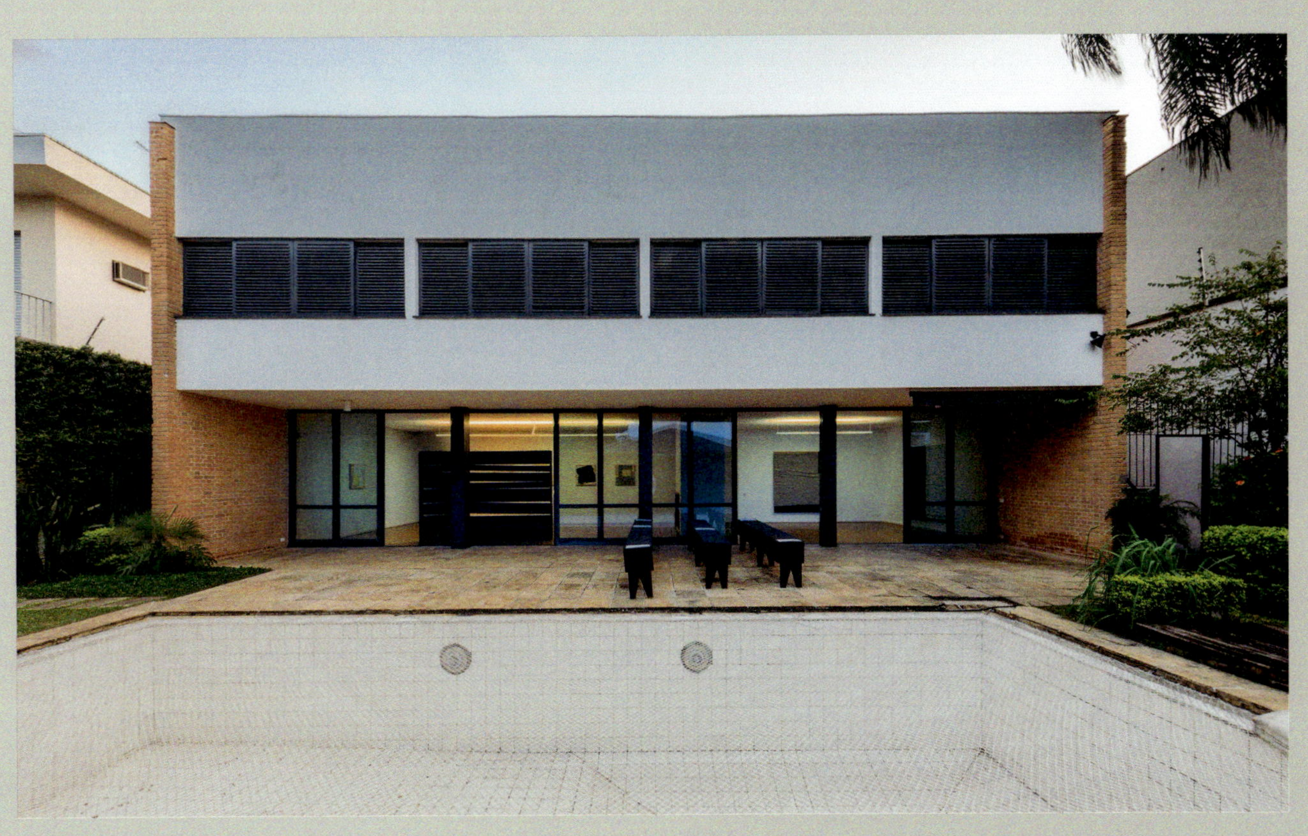

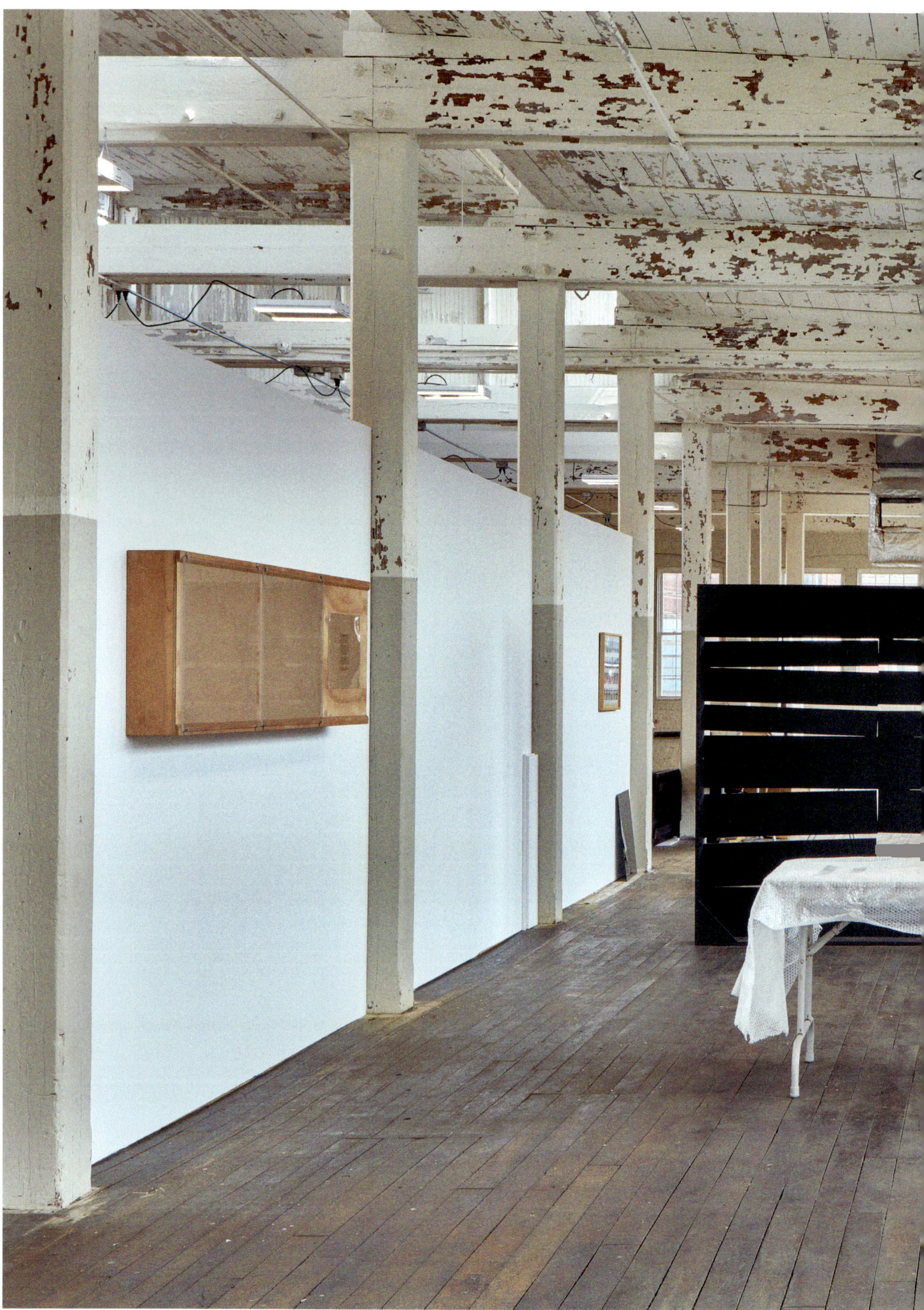

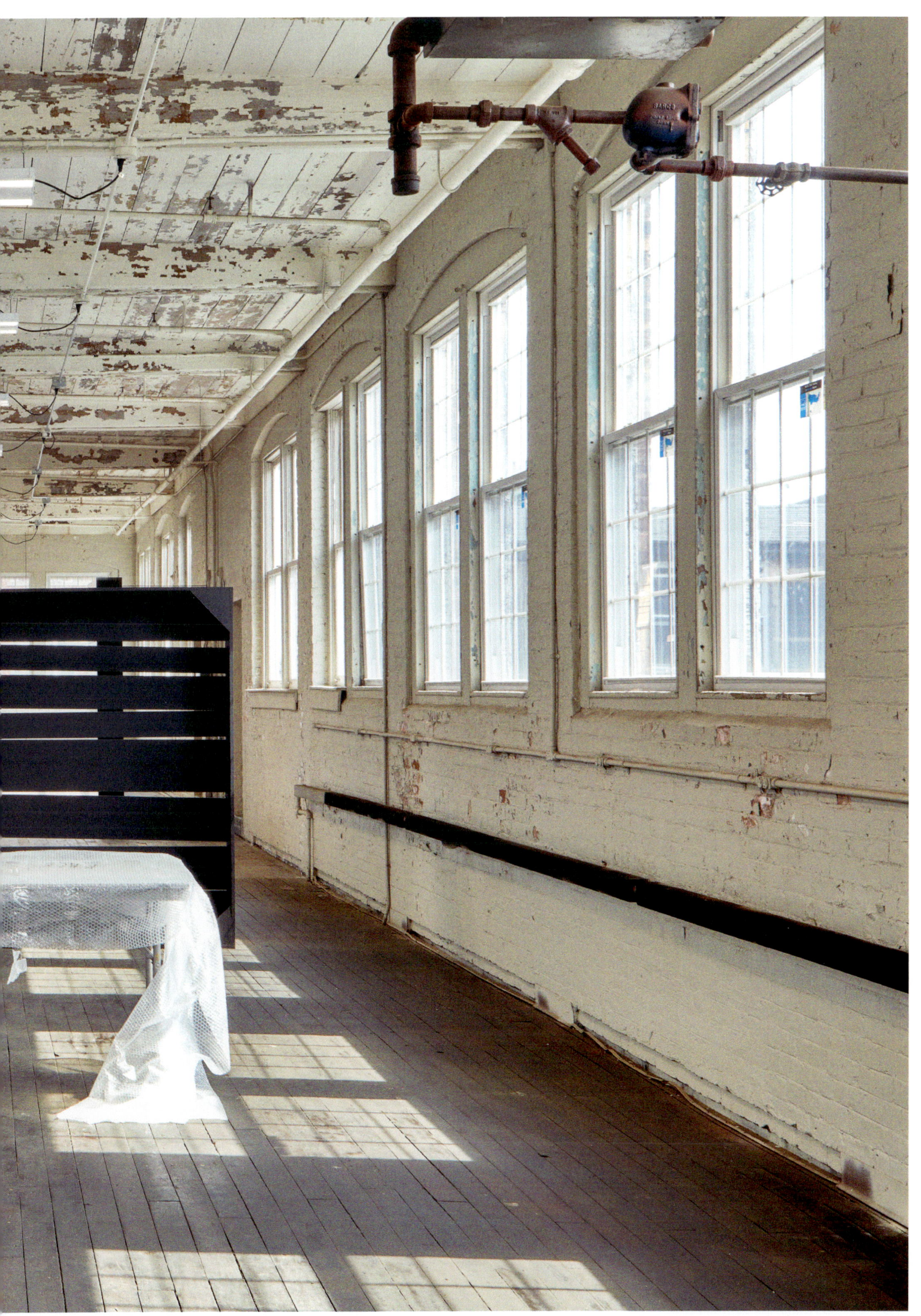

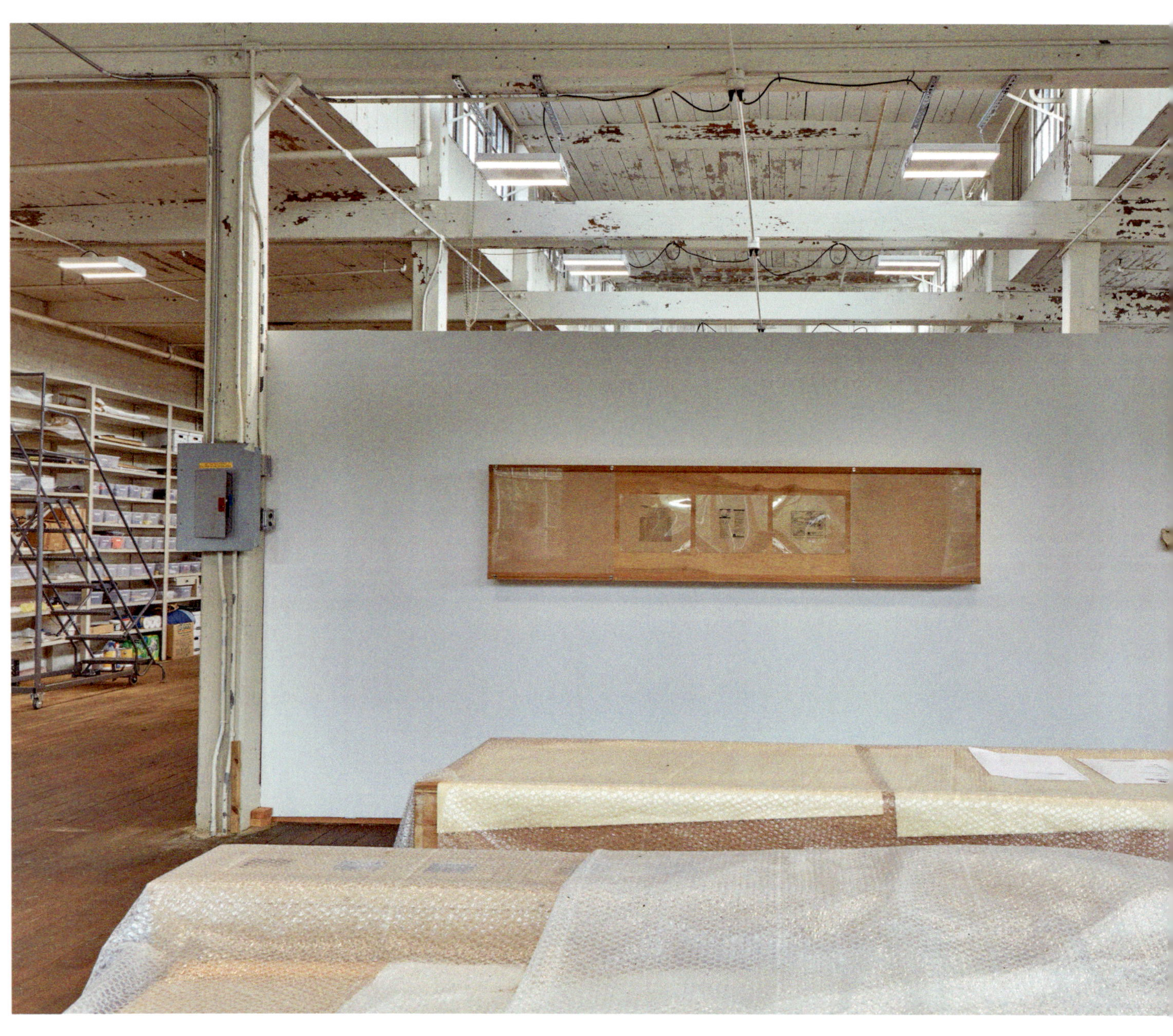

282

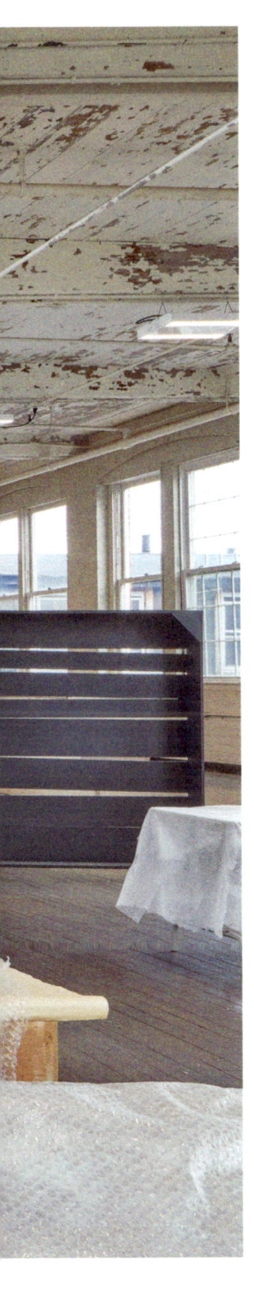

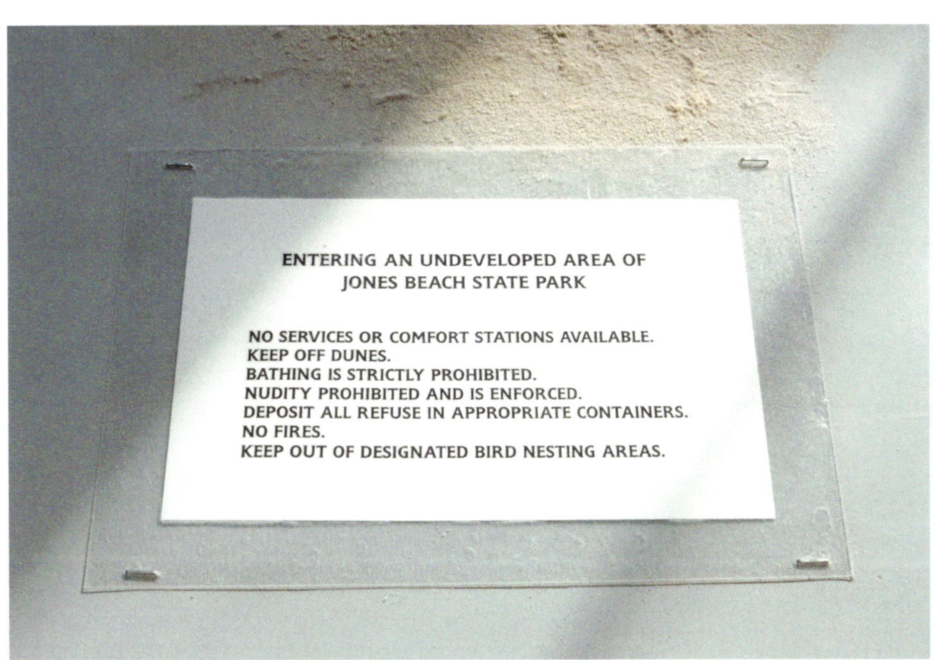
ENTERING AN UNDEVELOPED AREA OF
JONES BEACH STATE PARK

NO SERVICES OR COMFORT STATIONS AVAILABLE.
KEEP OFF DUNES.
BATHING IS STRICTLY PROHIBITED.
NUDITY PROHIBITED AND IS ENFORCED.
DEPOSIT ALL REFUSE IN APPROPRIATE CONTAINERS.
NO FIRES.
KEEP OUT OF DESIGNATED BIRD NESTING AREAS.

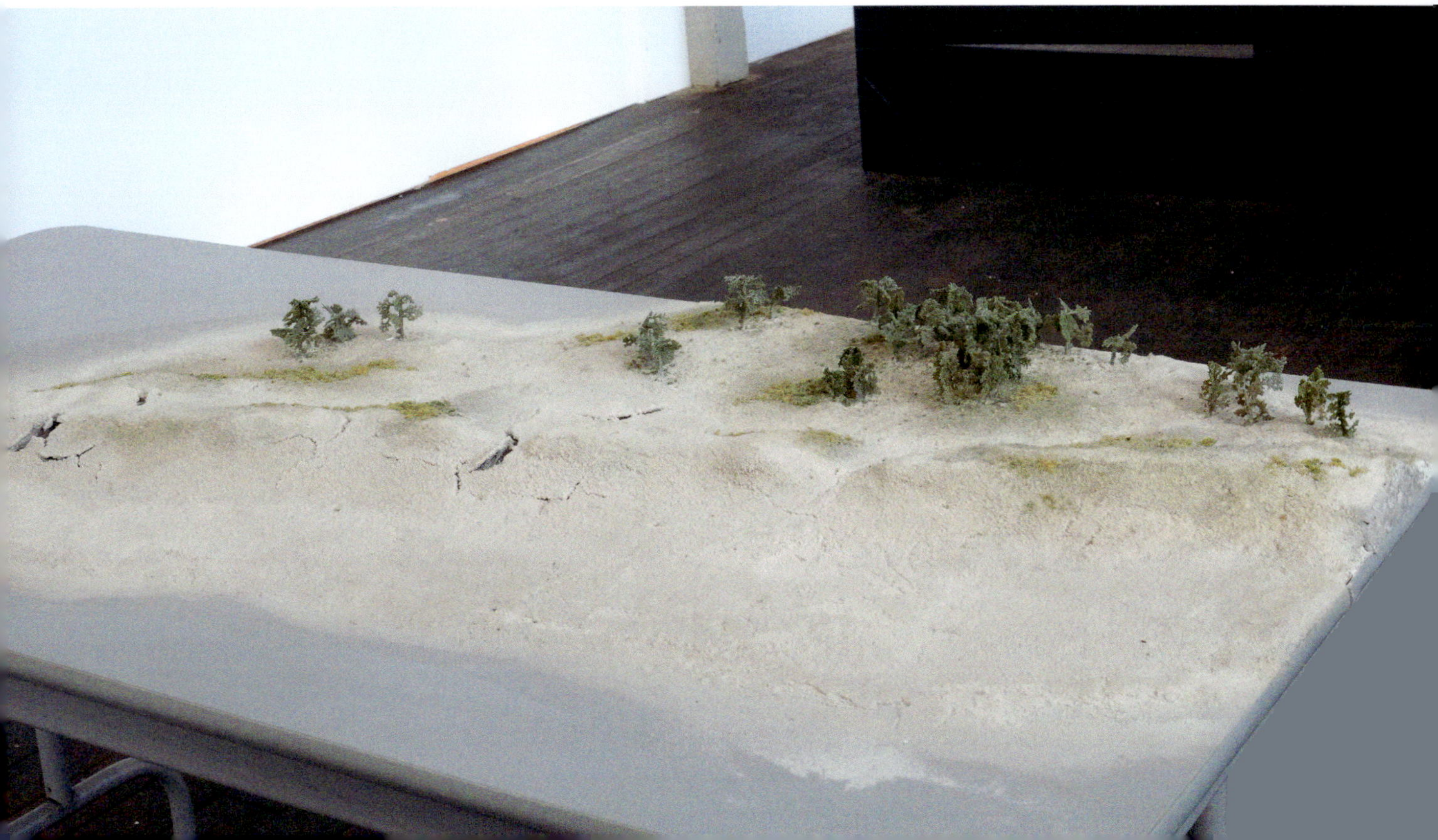

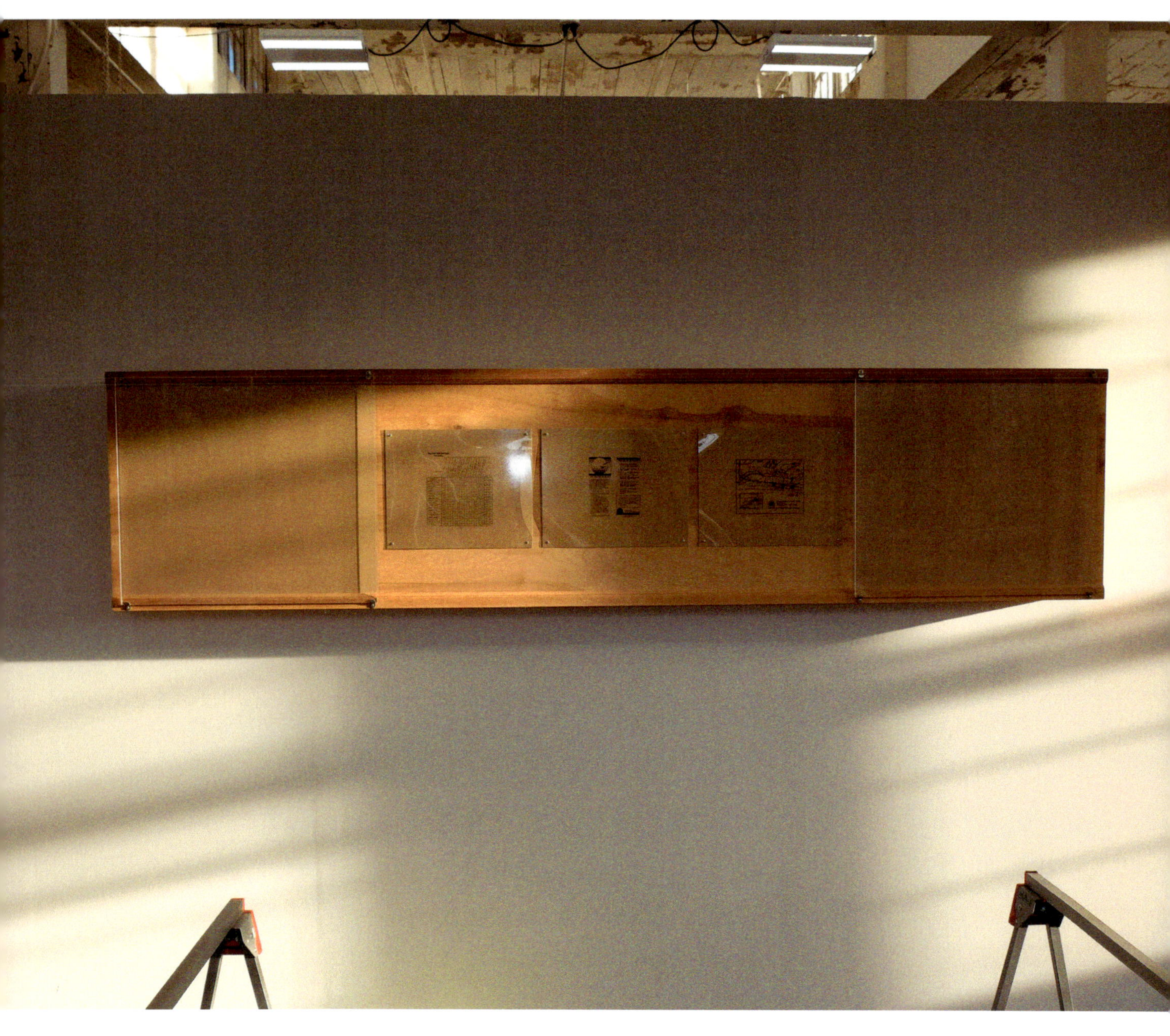

Torrington Project had in its makeup a form of beckoning and drawing in. I thought of it at times as a lure, as thinking through the structure of desire. It was about consolidation, too—of work, of ideas—in order to make sense of patterns and habits and passages of time while being able to expand in place, a very fixed place. Various artworks and people came to that site, which is where I wanted to be and where I wanted conversations to be had, meandering through this opened-up and animated archive. Sometimes I imagined the space as a warehouse of ideas, where you could quite physically bump into those ideas, and then ricochet off into another, or pass through the space between these propositions and sense the gravitational weight of the questions I had asked and was asking again. Blake referred to it as "a conceptual loading dock," which seems about right to me.

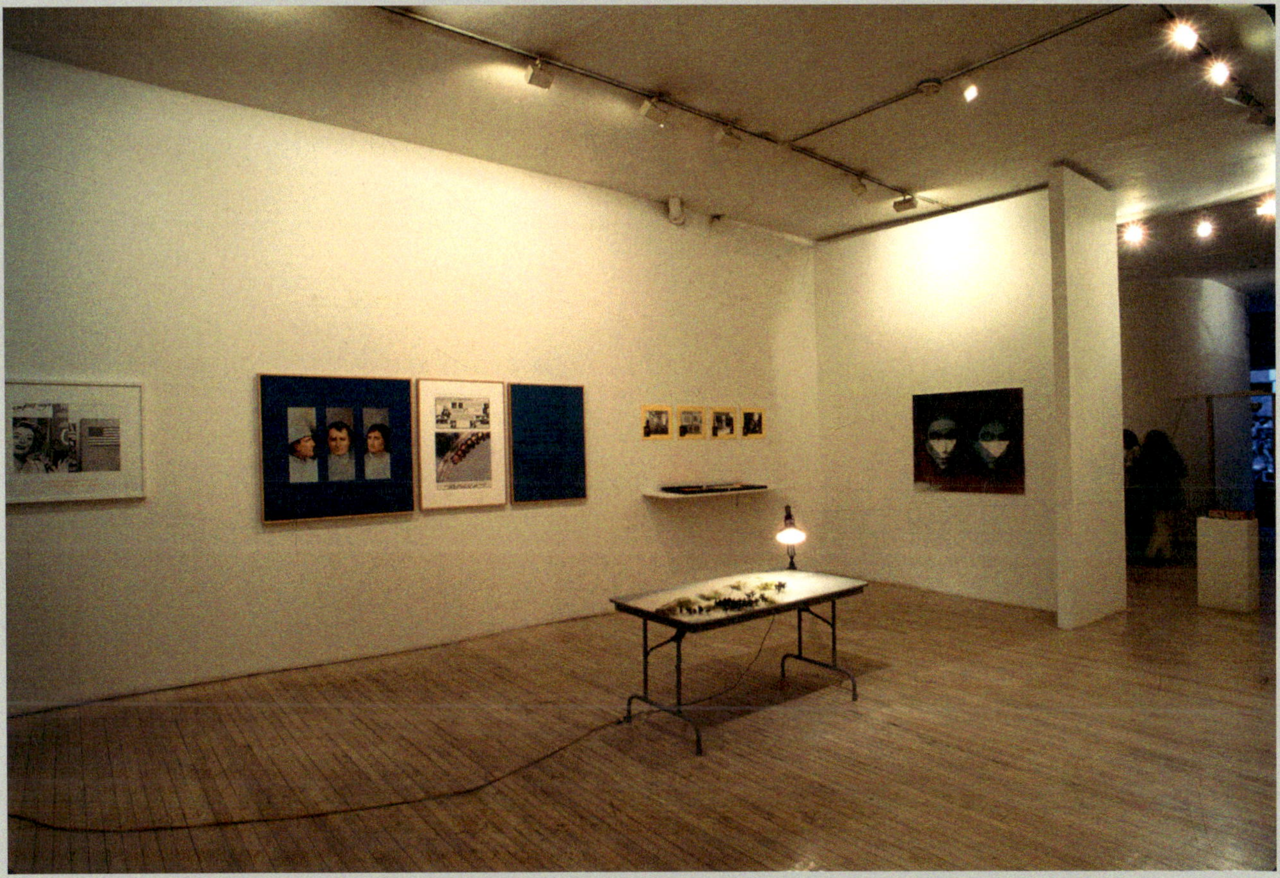

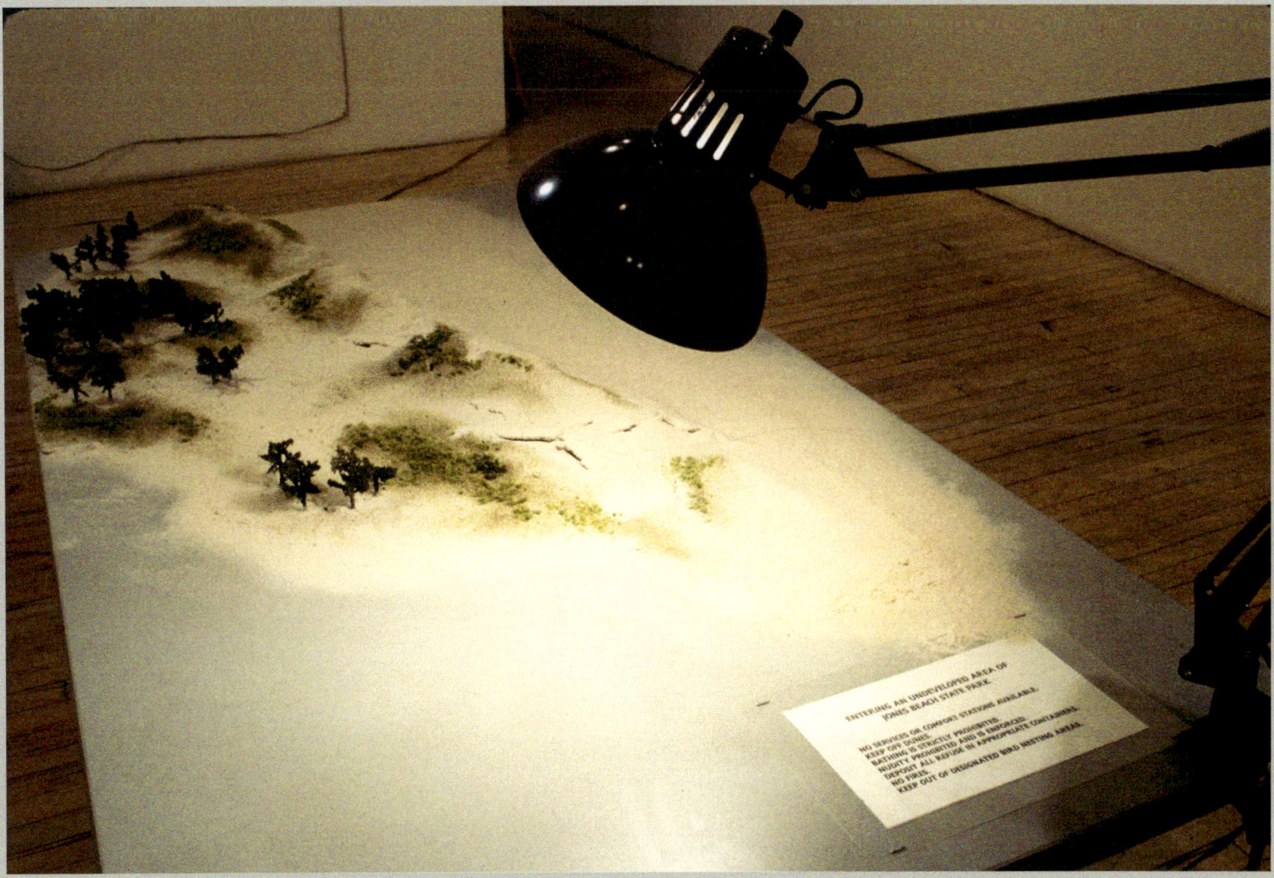

ENTERING AN UNDEVELOPED AREA OF
JONES BEACH STATE PARK

NO SERVICES OR COMFORT STATIONS AVAILABLE.
KEEP OFF DUNES.
BATHING IS STRICTLY PROHIBITED.
NUDITY PROHIBITED AND IS ENFORCED.
DEPOSIT ALL REFUSE IN APPROPRIATE CONTAINERS.
NO FIRES.
KEEP OUT OF DESIGNATED BIRD NESTING AREAS.

10

Ull's work had been there from the beginning.
I had brought three works of his to Torrington:
the shoe drawing and two of the "Bob Ross"
landscapes. Ull was also present in the tan boxes
of mine from 1989, where I had used a group of
stills from video footage I shot of him walking
through the woods of Prospect Park, wearing his
bomber jacket and baseball cap. But I wanted
to have additional examples of his work present
to approximate the dynamic created in 2001 at
nGbK in Berlin, where I built *Container (1–3)* to
stand alongside and partially frame a group of Ull's
paintings and wall reliefs.

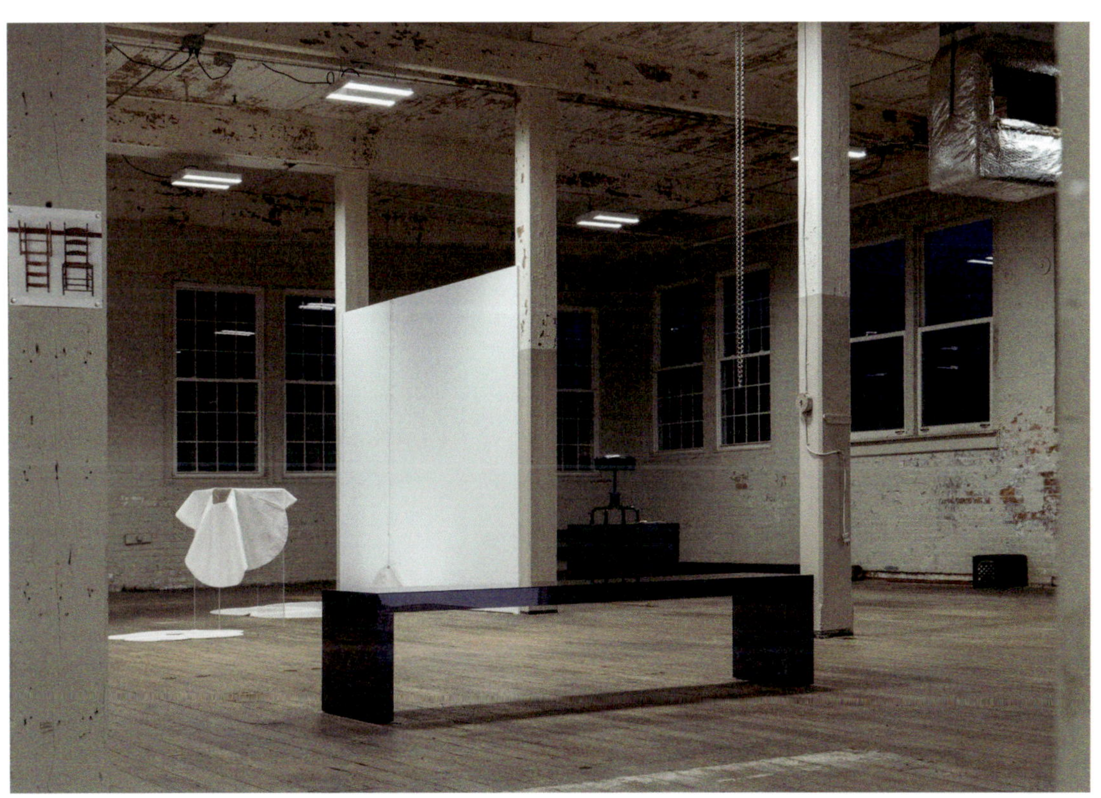

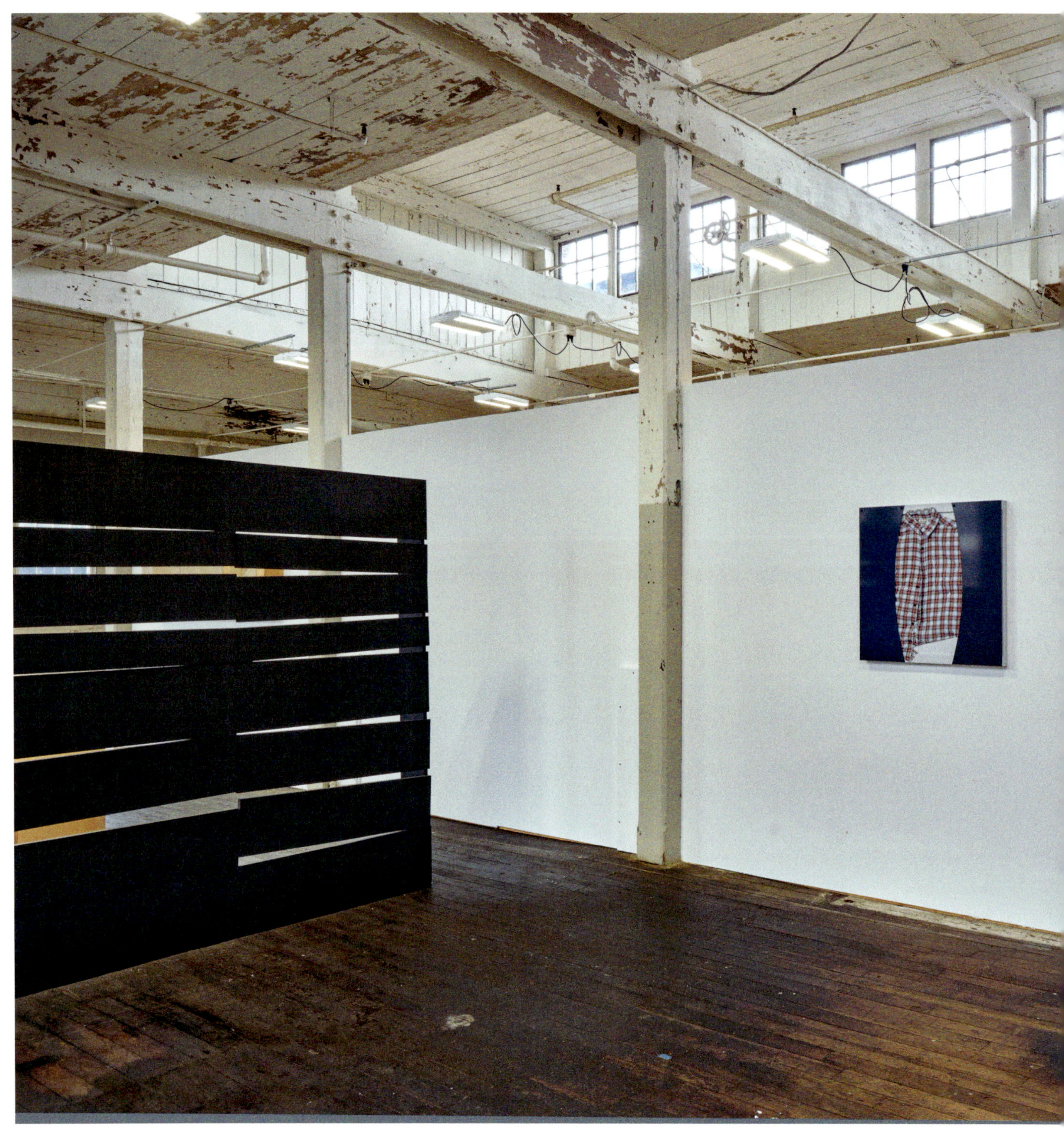

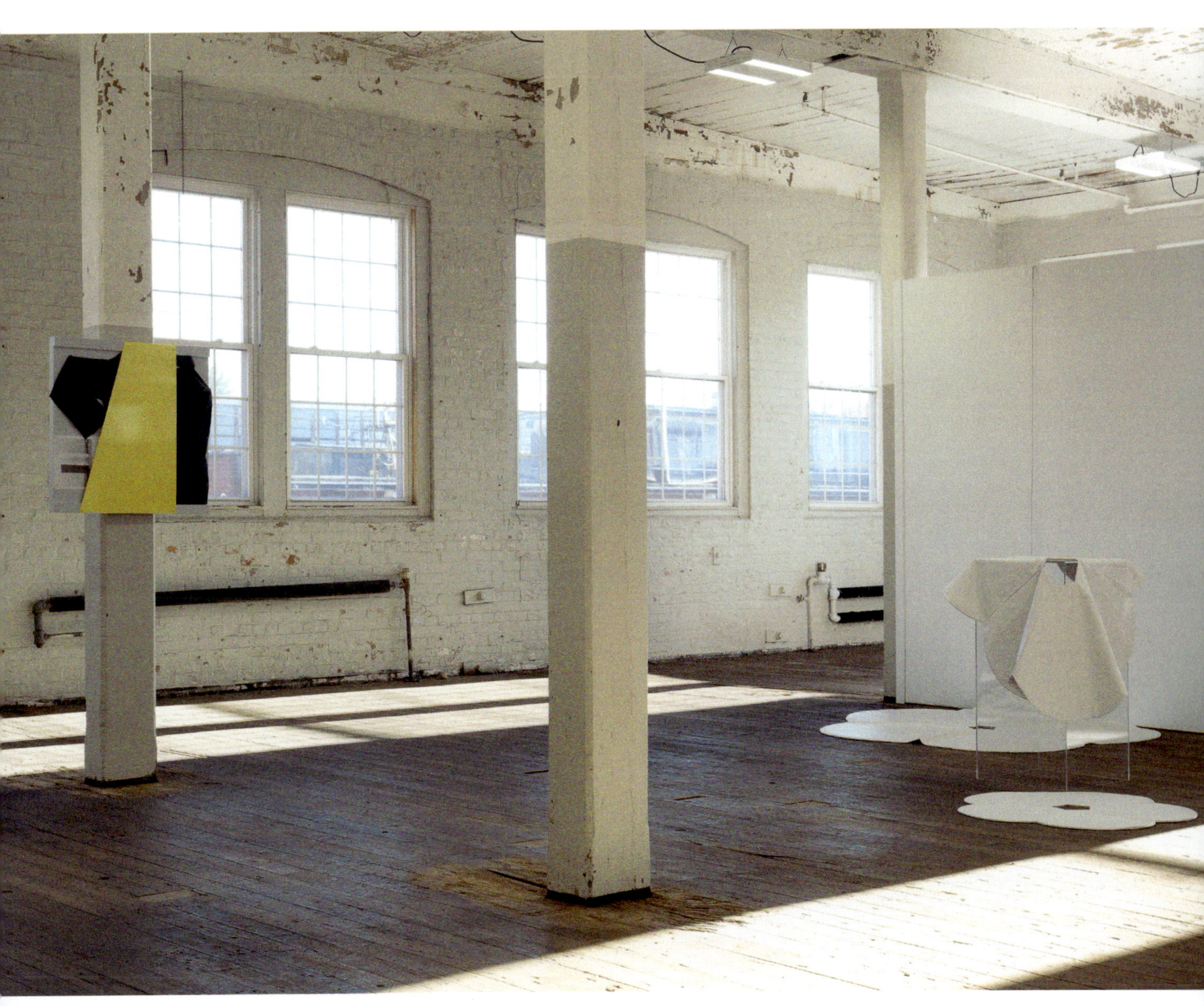

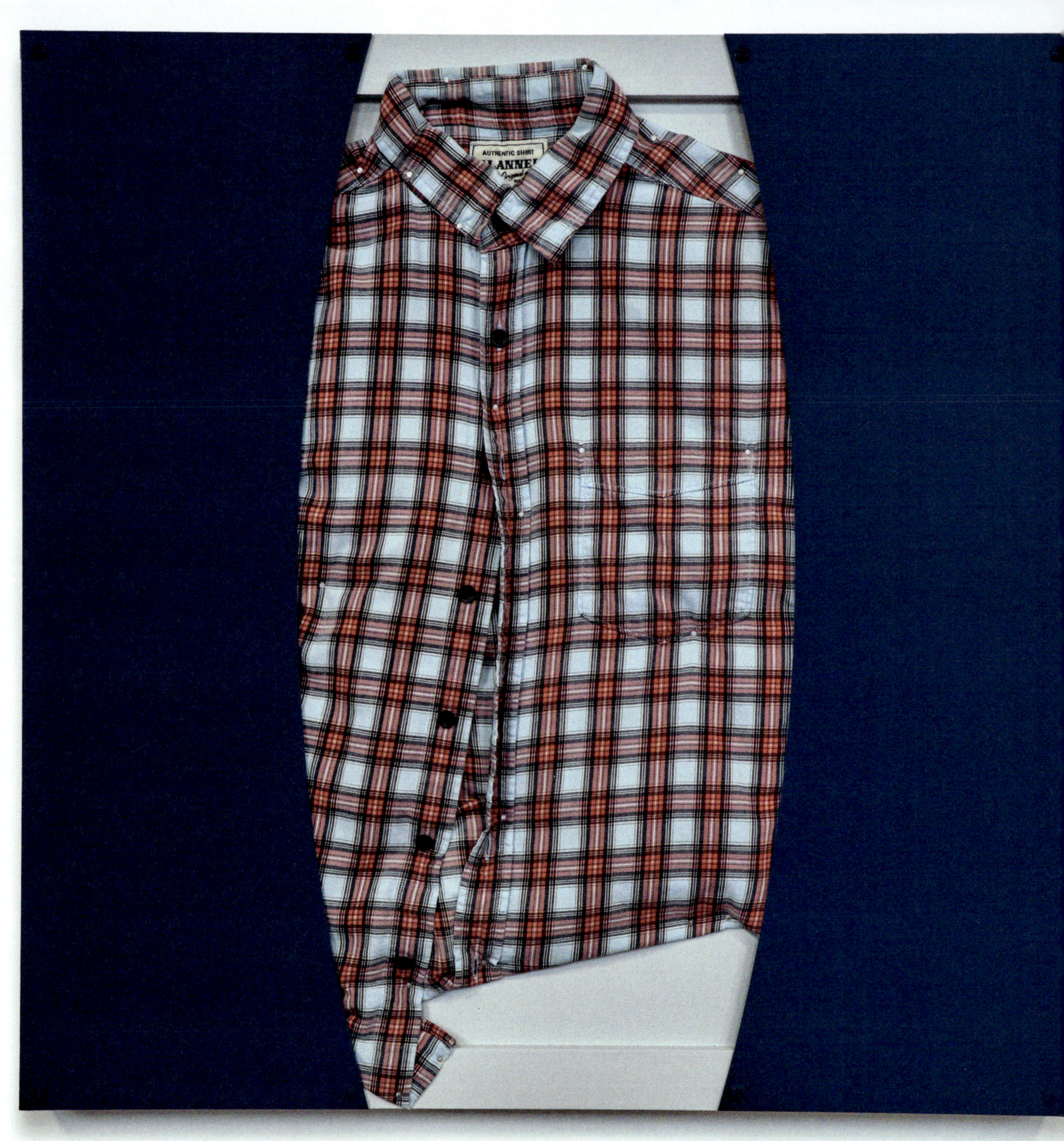

AUTHENTIC SHIRT
FLANNEL
Original

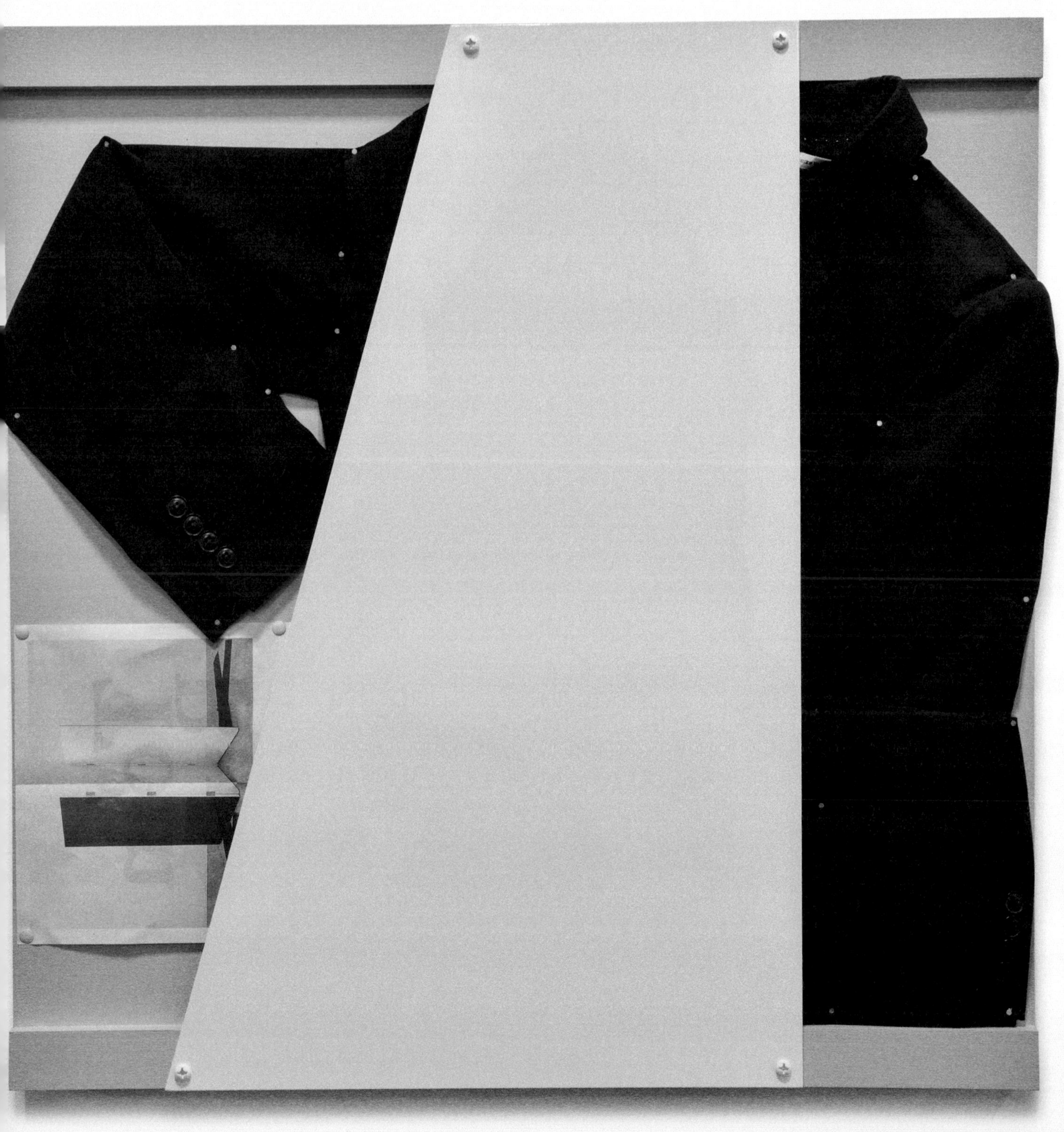

291

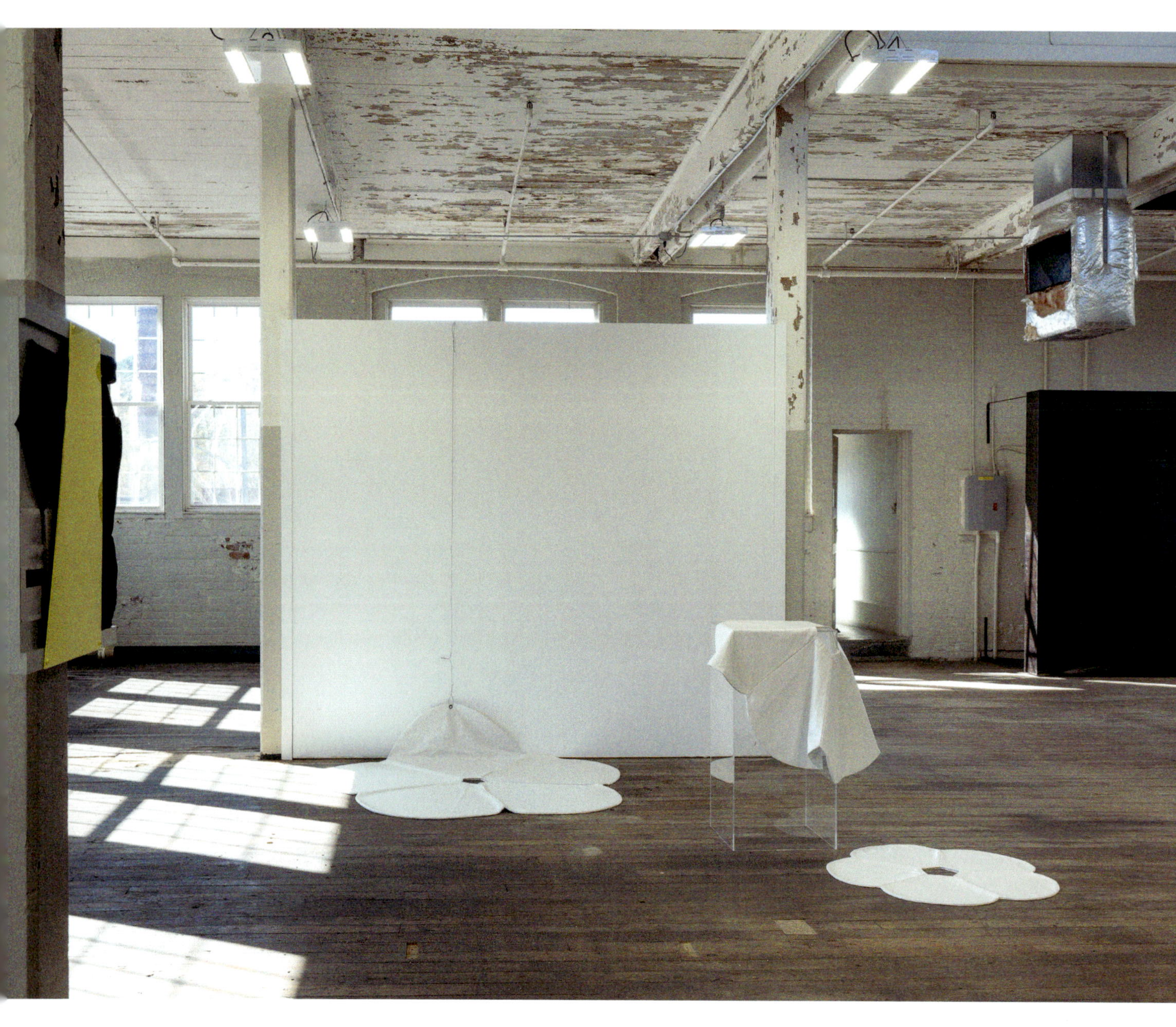

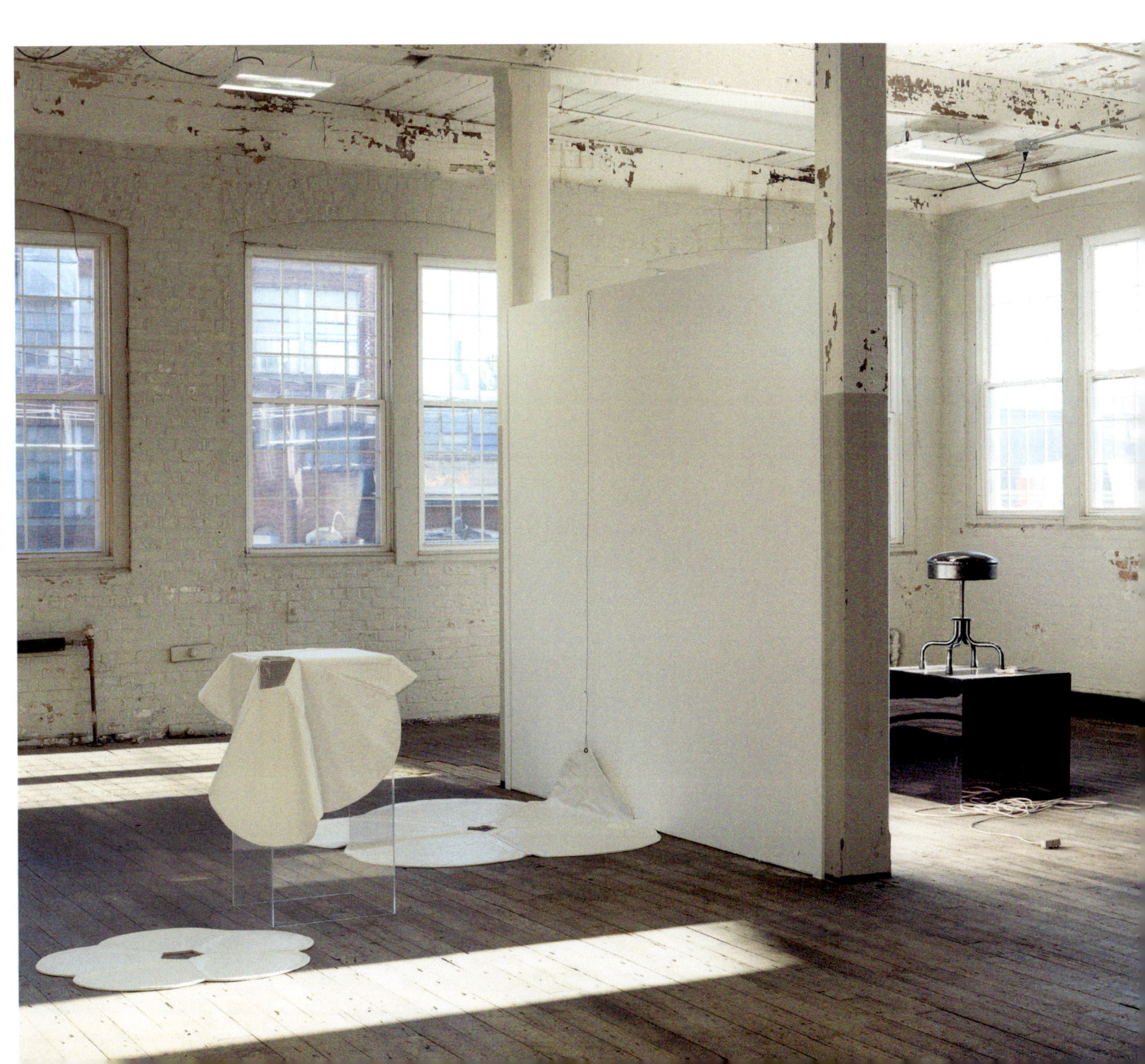

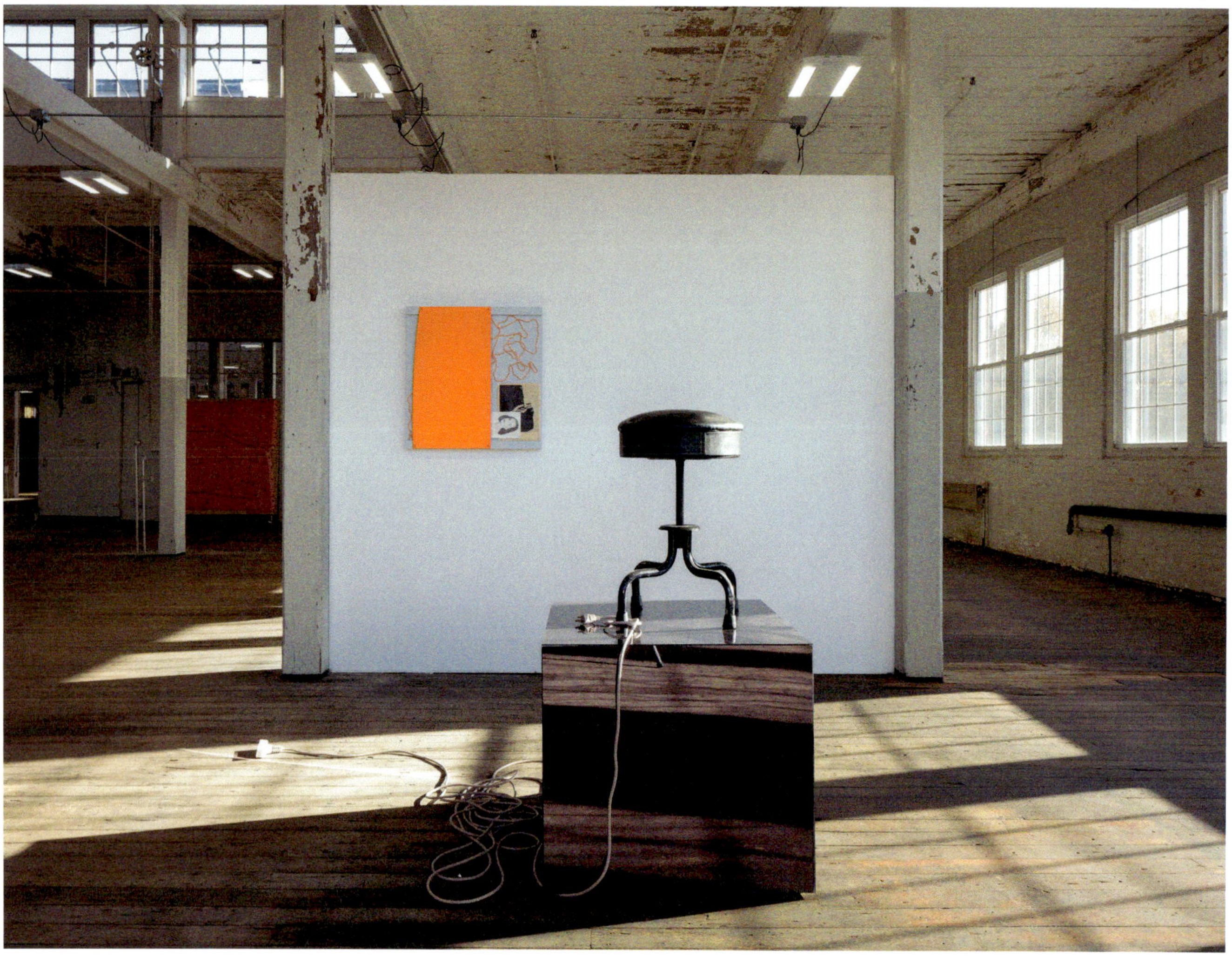

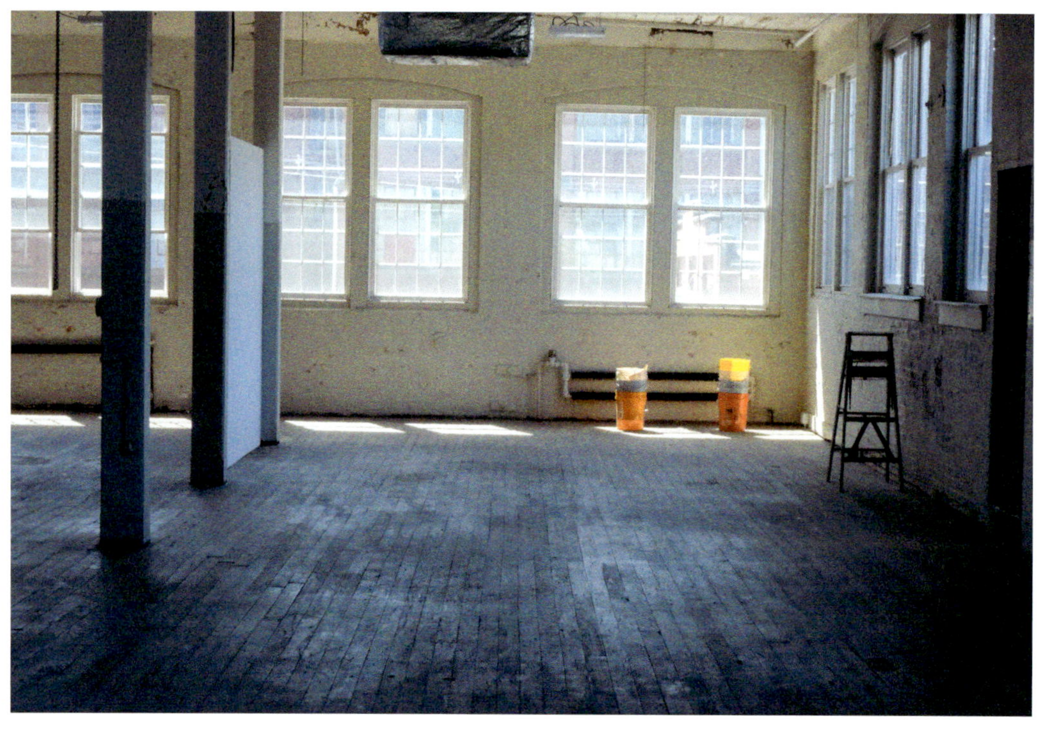

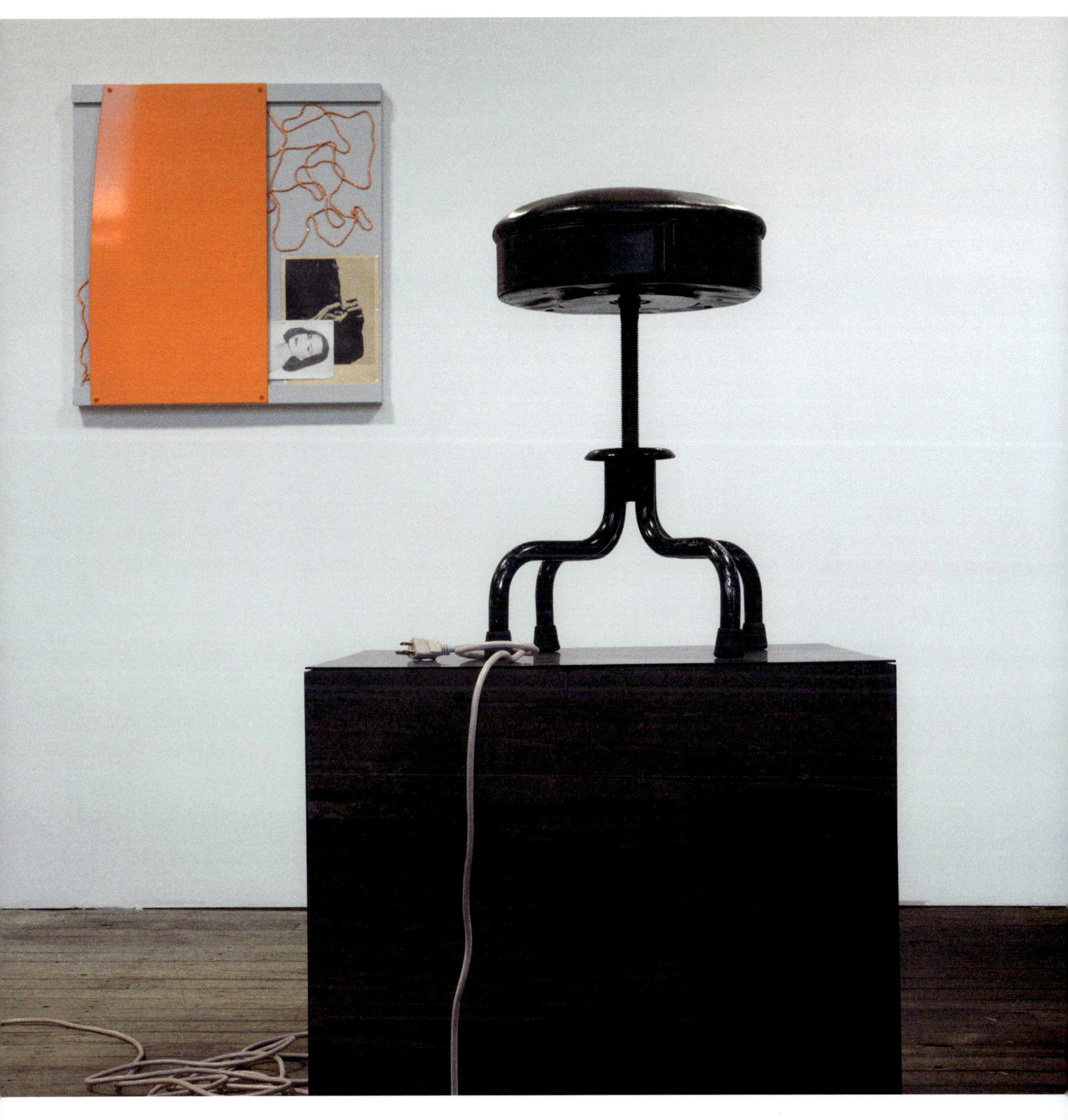

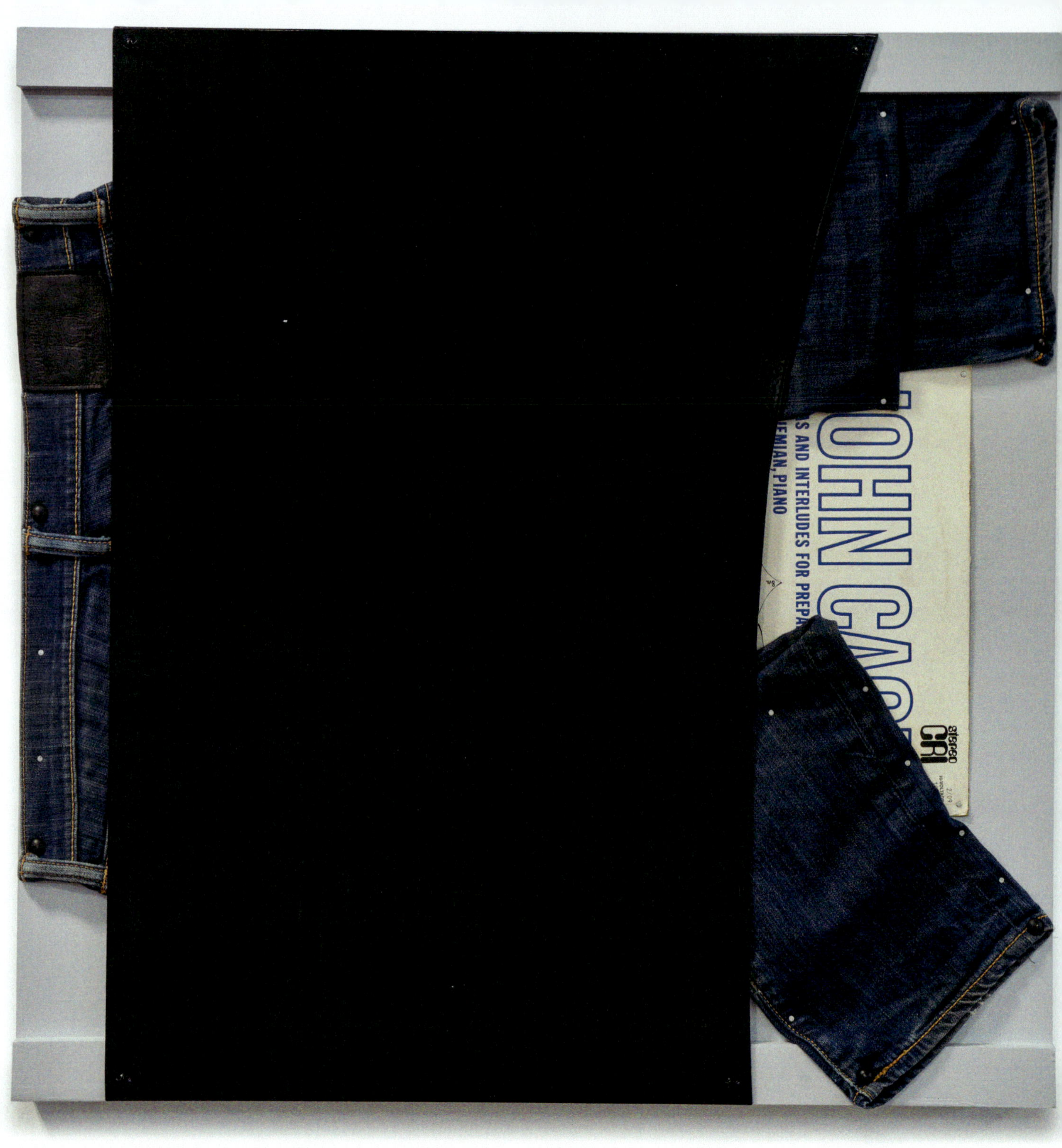
JOHN CAGE
S AND INTERLUDES FOR PREPA
EMIAN PIANO
stereo
CRI

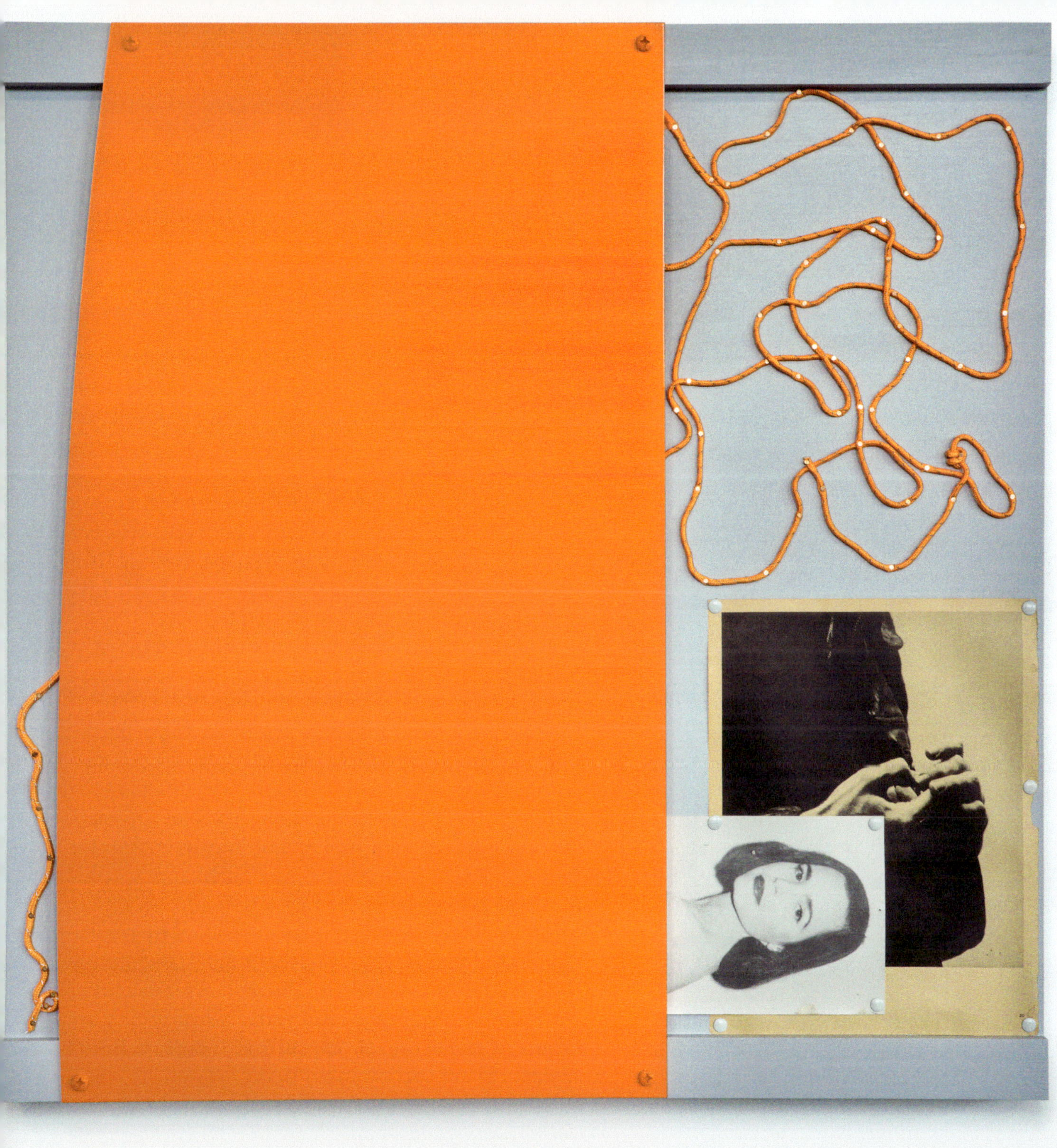

1   See Sara Ahmed, *Queer Phenomenology: Orientations, Objects, Others* (Duke University Press, 2006).

Clothing
Photographs
Walls

These are the building blocks of Tom Burr's recent work. Clothing is our first defense against exposure to the elements and embarrassment in public; it's a membrane that not only keeps people warm and "decent," but projects their image. Photographs make their subjects alienable by enabling their likeness—or "surface"—to circulate anywhere, but walls regulate mobility, sometimes affording a welcome refuge from it, sometimes imprisoning us in a closet, or a cell. Like clothing, the enclosures articulated by walls create spaces that bodies may extend into or be blocked from physically as well as imaginatively. As Sara Ahmed argues, there can be "white" spaces and "straight" spaces arranged to accommodate only those bodies that claim such identifications.[1]

Burr's art invites queer extensions in space. Although his sculptures are not mimetic of human anatomies, they do create *figurations*, like anthropomorphic postures evoked by hinged panels—walls becoming recumbent nudes, sometimes decorated by photographs that act as traps for queer desire. His sculpture is built from the outside in, through assemblages of clothing, photographs, and walls, all of which are means of enclosing, or "capturing," a person. Burr's sculptures are recombinant beings: They are *clothingphotographswalls*, or *wallsphotographsclothing*, or *clothingwalls*, and so on.

Pins and hinges are two of the mechanisms by which these compound figures are held together. Clothing is folded, flattened, and pinned to surfaces; photographs are tacked up too. Walls adopt postures by bending at hinges. Pins are familiar affordances, but sharp and

     David Joselit

implicitly dangerous: In Burr's practice, their use can suggest anarchic upholstery. Folding is the objective of both devices: Hinges allow hardened surfaces to turn; pins hold soft surfaces in place. Pinning and folding are the actions by which *clothing, photographs,* and *walls* touch.

If there is an "interiority" that haunts these abstract figurations, it is not tied to individual identity, but rather to the citation of gay forefathers—like Jean Genet, Gregory Battcock, Andy Warhol, or Cristóbal Balenciaga—whose images are fastened to the works. These "icons" open portals onto complex queer lives that belie any reductive definition of a "gay identity." An example: In *Our Lady of the Flowers* (1943), Jean Genet, the author and narrator, whose body is confined to a cell, extends into a world of Parisian "queens" and "pimps" by gazing at a motley array of photographs he's put up (pinned?) on his prison wall. His body is incarcerated, but his imagination is whoring around Paris. And, importantly, the qualities of queerness in his rendering combine macho and femme stylings in delirious configurations that refuse any gender binary, and whose instability may at any time flip one position into another. When Burr pins Genet's picture to a board, he summons the queer vertigo attached to the name of the author: *Genet.*

Folding/Holding

When I visited Tom's studio in Torrington, Connecticut, I was delighted to see, in one iteration of a series of recent works collectively titled *Journal,* a picture of the art critic Gregory Battcock dressed in what appears to be a brown velvet suit on the Queen Elizabeth 2 (his preferred mode of transportation to Europe was the ocean liner). It was 1975, and a woman in a smart print dress, seated to Battcock's left, holds a cigarette

Ellsworth, Gregory, and Tom

while serving up a hefty dose of side-eye to the grinning gay dandy. As an art history major in college, I regarded Battcock's many anthologies on such topics as Minimalism, video art, and idea art as a kind of road map to contemporary art, my chosen vocation. So it was shocking to come across an obituary in the *SoHo Weekly News* in December 1980 describing Battcock's grisly murder in Puerto Rico, presumably by a trick. I imagined him slumped lifeless in a bloody heap on a Caribbean balcony. The shock has remained with me for forty-five years. This was just before the onset of AIDS, at a time when exuberant, anonymous sexuality still maintained a kind of bawdy innocence. Battcock appeared in Warhol movies; he wrote a gossip column in *Gay* magazine; he kept a diary explicitly recounting his cruising adventures on Manhattan's Upper West Side, all while writing authoritatively about art.

Battcock's photograph, along with the detached front and back covers of Rainer Crone's 1970 monograph on Andy Warhol and a picture of a pink Balenciaga jacket, is held within a sculptural envelope derived from a 1956–57 Ellsworth Kelly work; this is Tom's *Nineteen (Faded Orange Cover)* (2024). Kelly's work, *Sculpture for a Large Wall*, includes 104 anodized aluminum panels suspended on an armature of two rows of rails or rods. These elements, all painted yellow, red, blue, black, or left unpainted, give a nod to Piet Mondrian, but they nevertheless produce a rather queer geometry. Roughly rectangular, the panels are skewed or curved on one side, giving a jittery impression of shivering movement, which is enhanced by the shadows the suspended panels throw onto the wall behind them. The work was commissioned for the Penn Center Transportation Building in Philadelphia, but subsequently came into the collection of the Museum of Modern Art in New York. It appeared on the cover of *Architectural Record* in May 1957. Though it is a

     David Joselit

2   James Meyer, "Art for the City: Sculpture for a Large Wall, 1957," in *Ellsworth Kelly: Sculpture for a Large Wall, 1957* (Matthew Marks Gallery, 1998), 9.

3   Quoted in Ibid., 5.

sculpture *for* a wall, art historian James Meyer has argued that it may also be understood as an allegory *of* the wall. He writes, "The wall is also a metaphor for the work's making. Laying down scraps of paper one by one in his grid collages, attaching monochrome canvases to one another, Kelly emulated the anonymous techniques of the mason: 'The work of an ordinary brick layer,' he believed, 'is more valid than the artwork of all but a few artists.'"[2]

I may have just claimed that Kelly's geometry is queer, but his own words about *Sculpture for a Large Wall*, from 1957, leave a different impression: "Today there is very little collaboration of the plastic arts with architecture producing anything of real value. Perhaps the reason for this is that most contemporary painting is too personal for large wall spaces and the easel painting artist is more involved in his painting as an end in itself.... The monochrome buildings demand color, and the spaces demand an image on a large scale—powerful statements which are very much alive."[3] Tom adapted Ellsworth's impersonal wall as a support for memorabilia of the flamboyant troika of Gregory, Andy, and Cristóbal. For once, gayness is not figured against a ground of heterosexuality. Instead, different modalities of queer aesthetics are folded together in their richness and contradictions, some impersonal and others quite the opposite. Here the *photoclothingwall* holds the compound figure of *ellsworthandycristóbalgregorytom*.

Travesty

One might conclude that Burr is making a travesty of Kelly's sculpture. For one thing, the panel in the work I have been discussing is orange, which veers off the primary palette of *Sculpture for a Large Wall*. And for another, Kelly's sober abstraction has been demoted to a kind of album—or journal—to hold tokens of queer

Ellsworth, Gregory, and Tom

4   See Charles Baudelaire, "The Painter of
    Modern Life," in *The Painter of Modern Life
    and Other Essays*, trans. and ed. Jonathan
    Mayne (Da Capo, 1964), especially part 11,
    "In Praise of Cosmetics," 31–34.

5   Tom Burr, "Some Elements of Some Styles" in
    Anthology: Writings 1991–2015, ed. Florence
    Derieux (FRAC Champagne-Ardenne; Sternberg
    Press, 2015), 108. Previously published as "Tom
    Burr," *Artforum*, September 2010, 267.

style. For me, however, "travesty" is a positive valuation, and it recalls Burr's incorporation of his own "decommissioned" clothing in many works. After all, travesty has everything to do with a kind of sartorial exaggeration, masking, or disguise. And let's not forget that Charles Baudelaire, in his founding essay on modernism, took the cosmetic very seriously.[4] With regard to his use of clothing, Burr has stated: "I'm not a hoarder, but I keep my clothes around for a while after I stop wearing them. I keep them and put them away until their age, or aura, or their almost but not quite outmodedness makes them twitch again and begin to describe the space between objects and bodies, between specificity and abstraction."[5]

It is precisely from the space "between objects and bodies, between specificity and abstraction" that a "queer phenomenology" arises (the term is Ahmed's). In Burr's art, many genres of gay life fold into one another. They need not be in competition, nor must they conform to a single identity. Holding together is more than enough. ◊

David Joselit

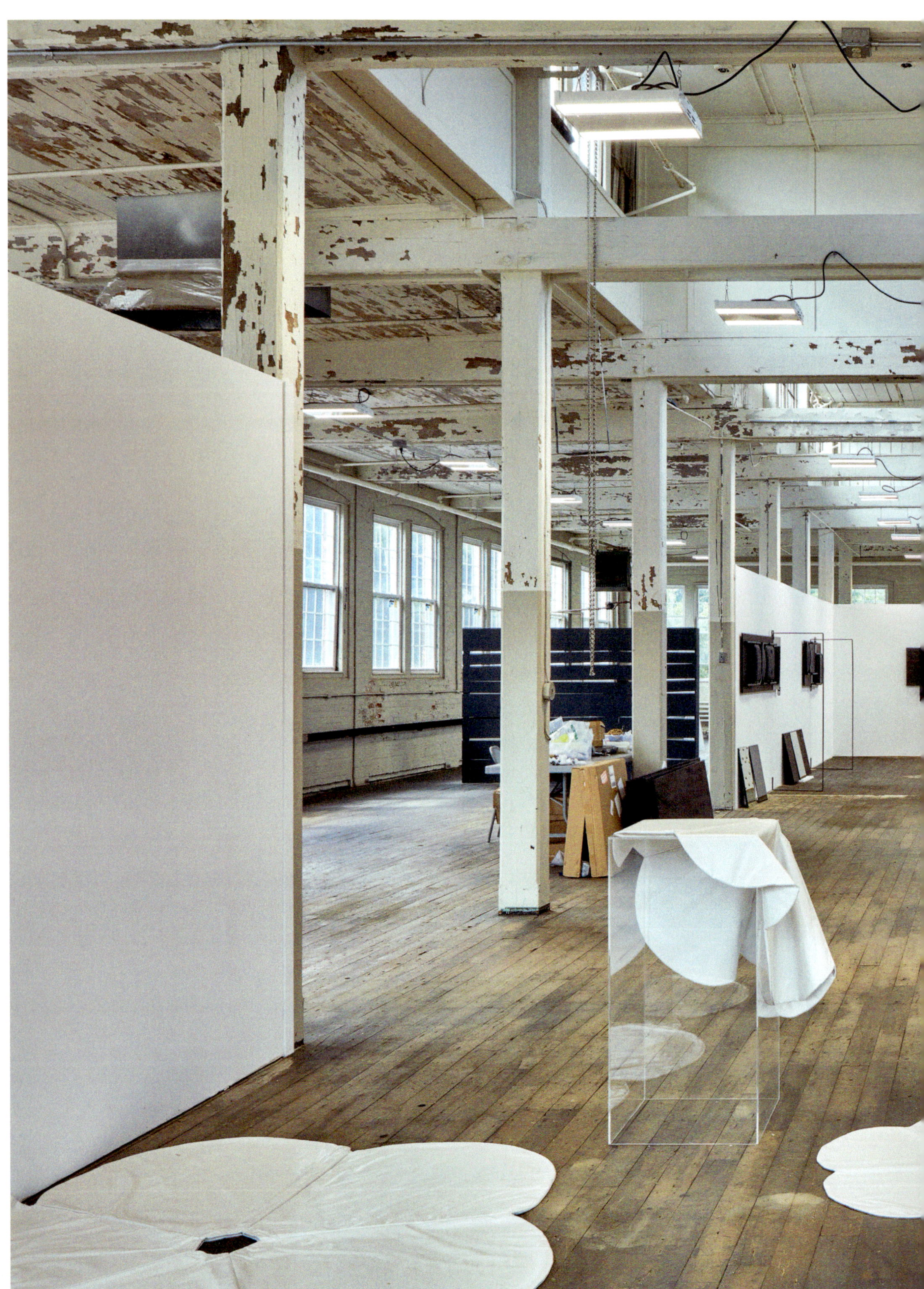

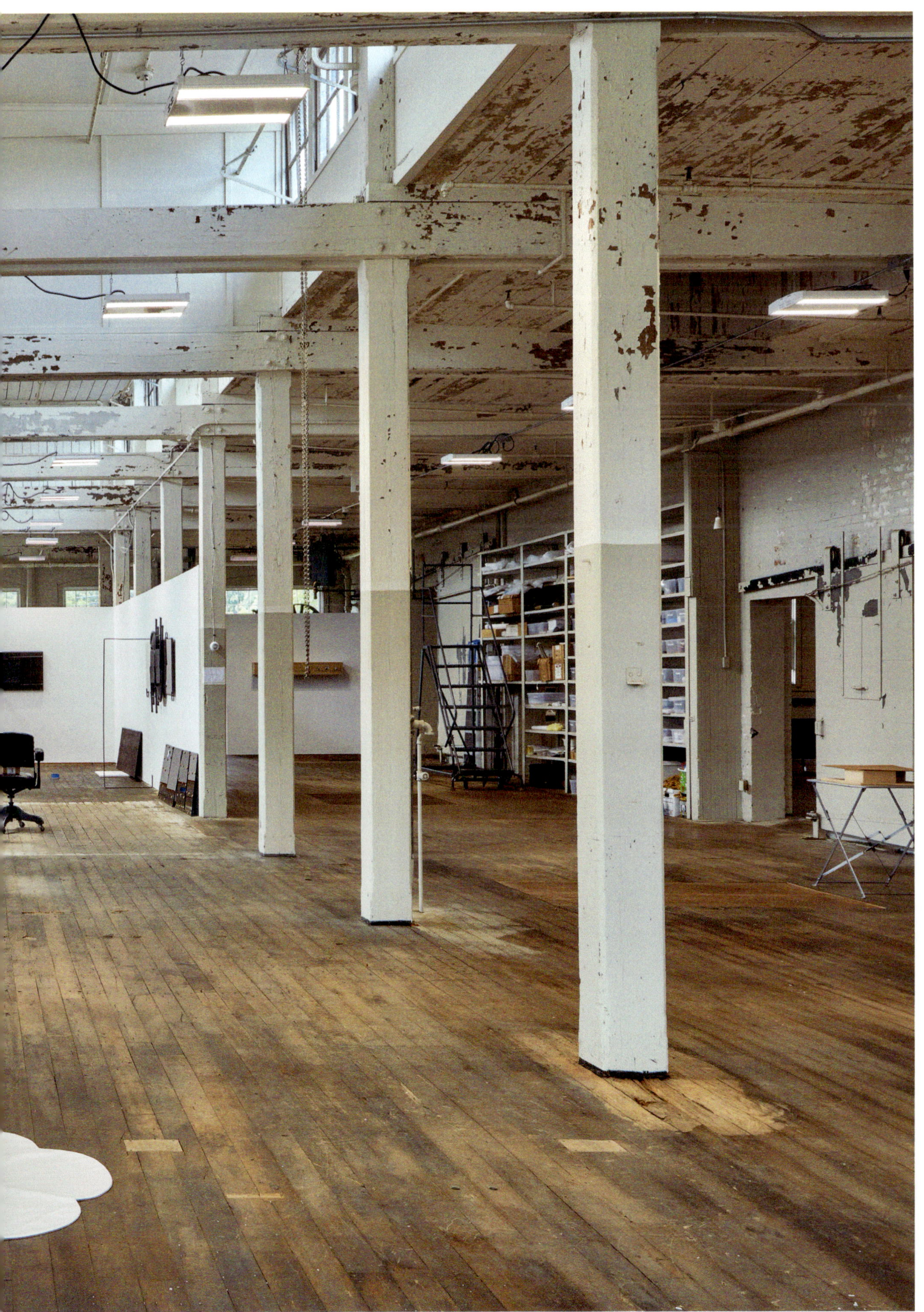

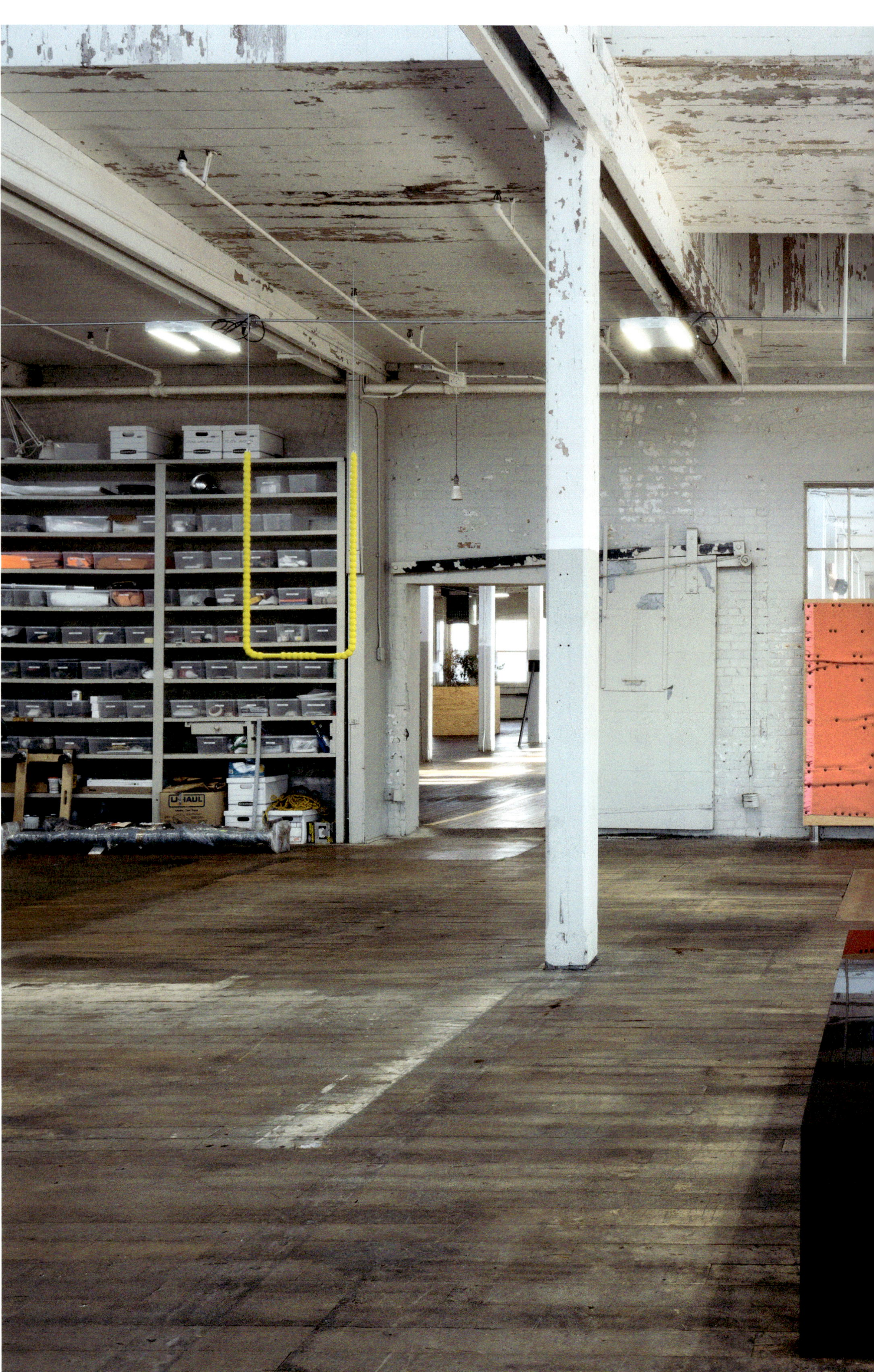

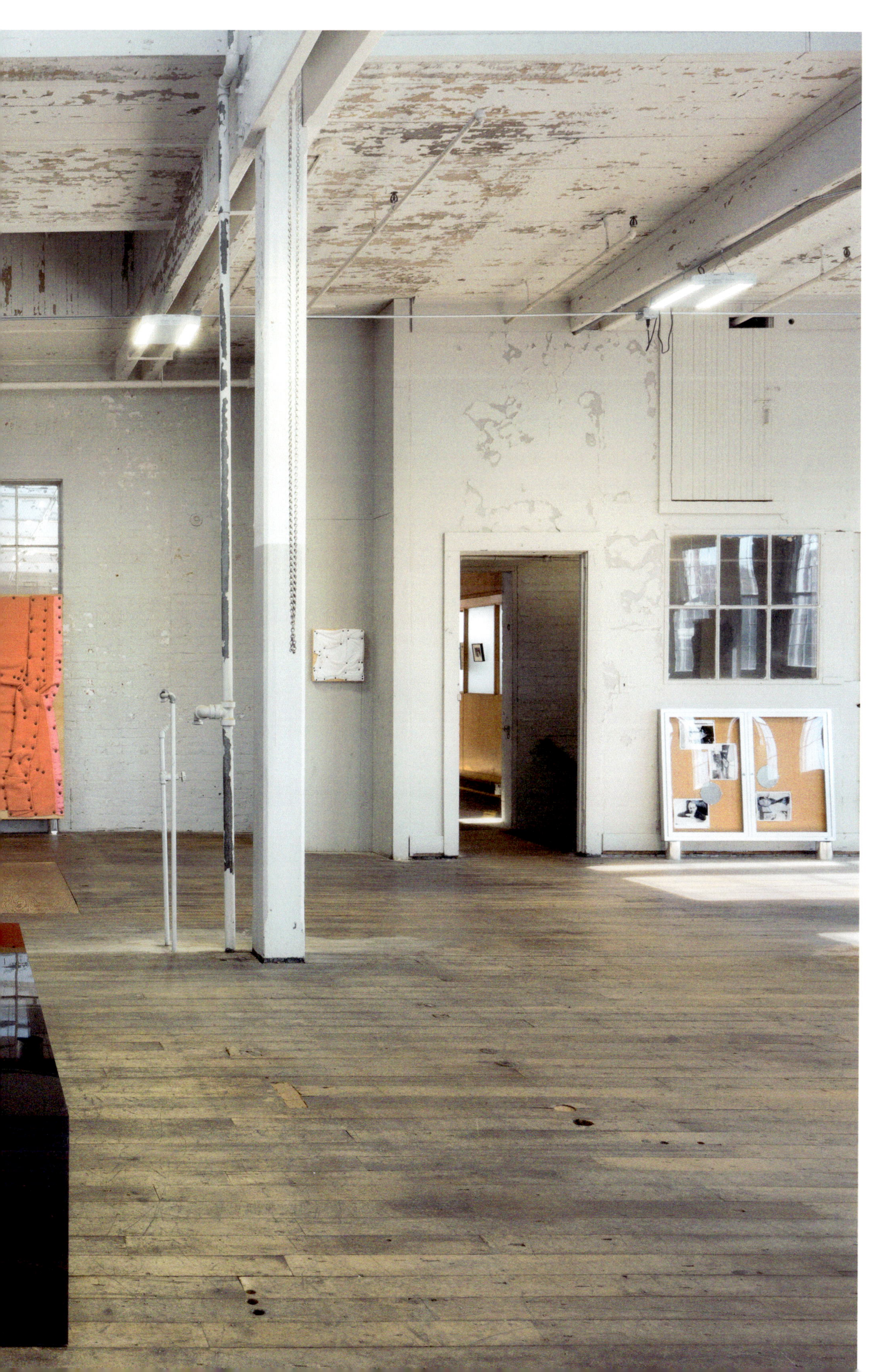

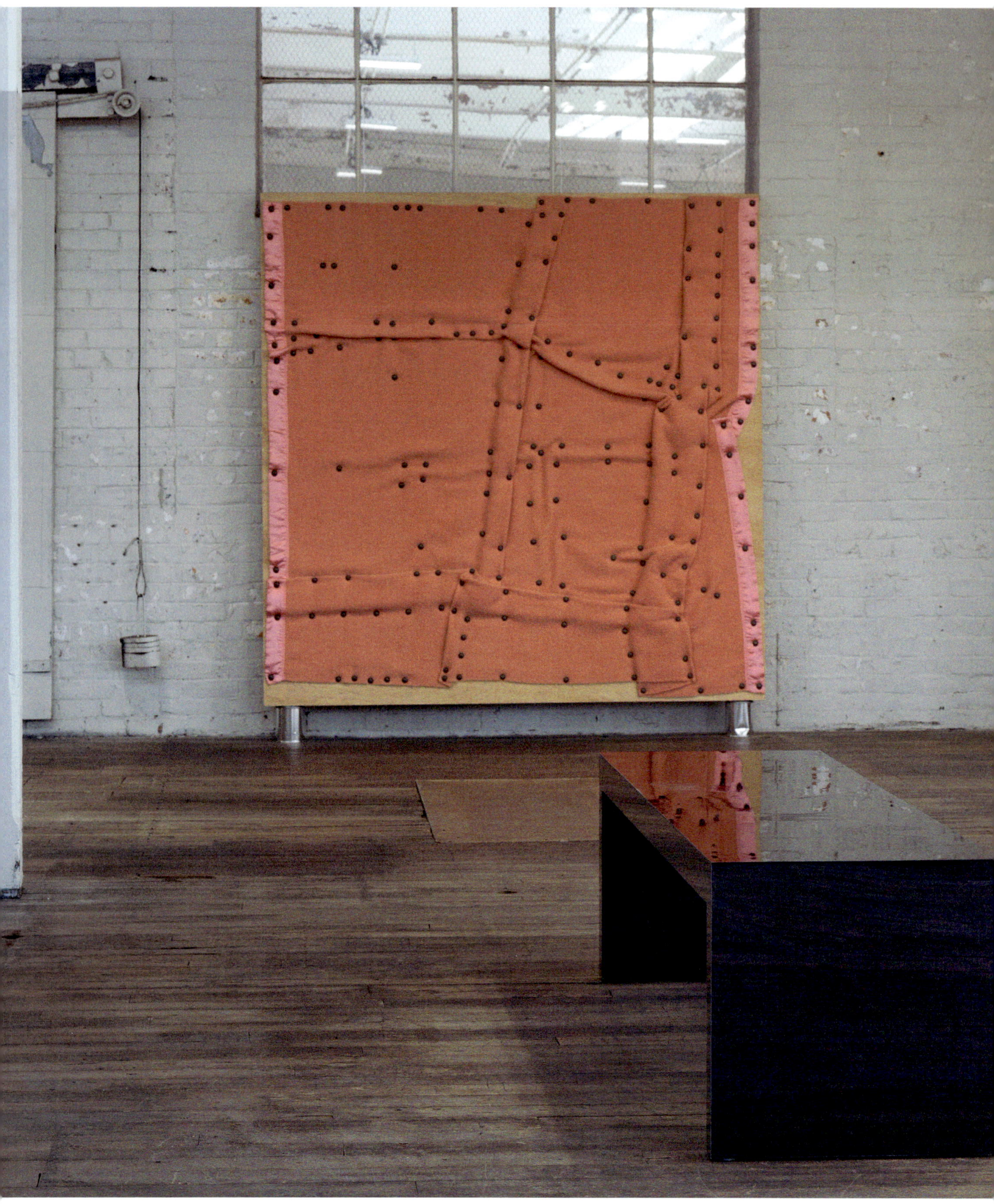

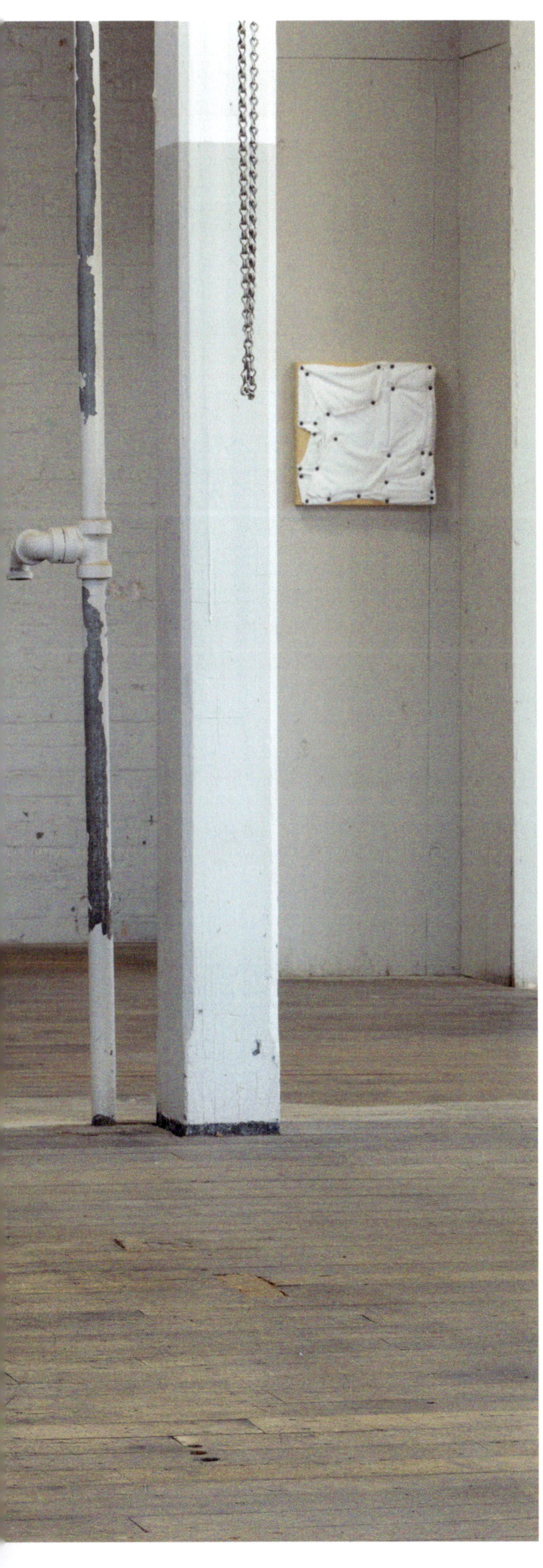

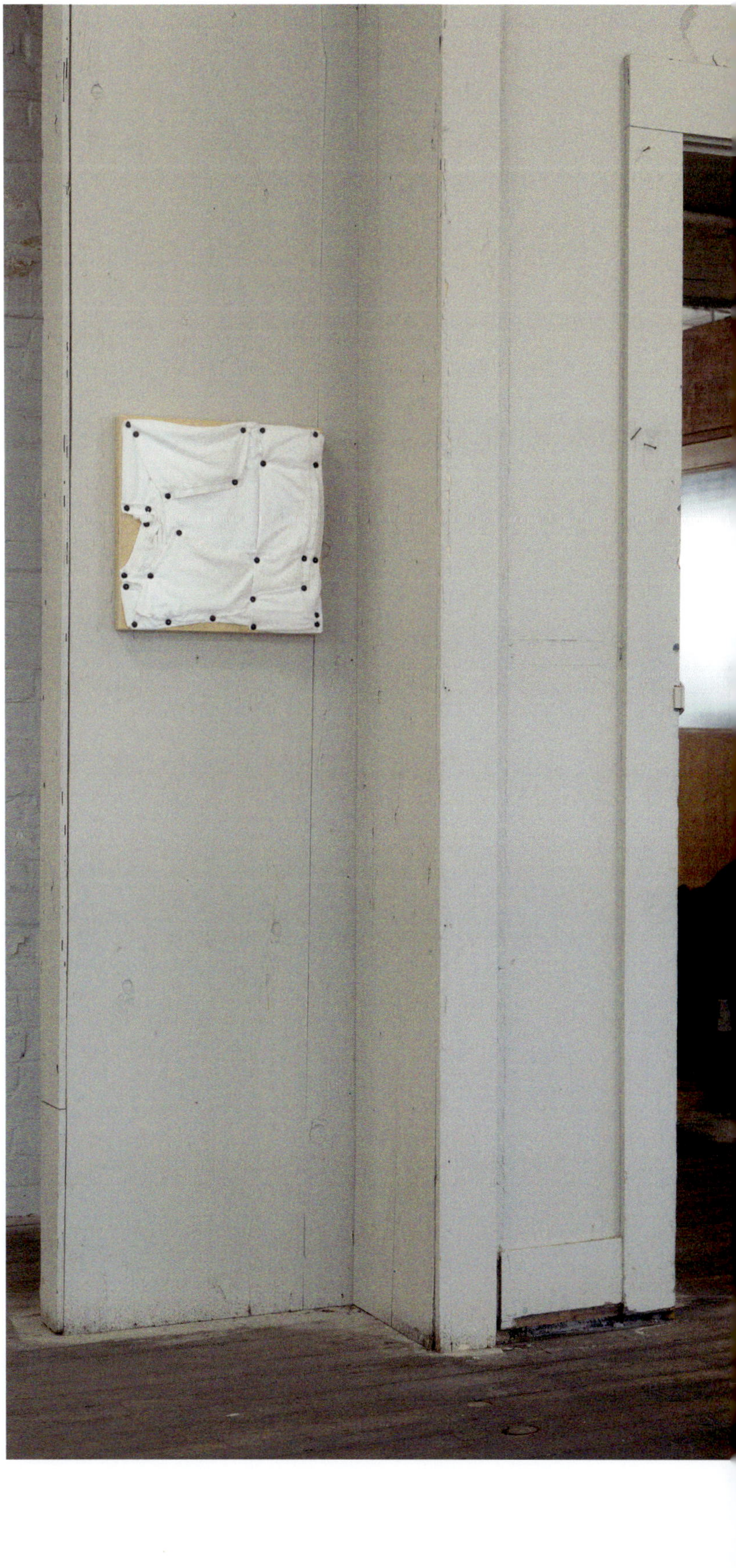

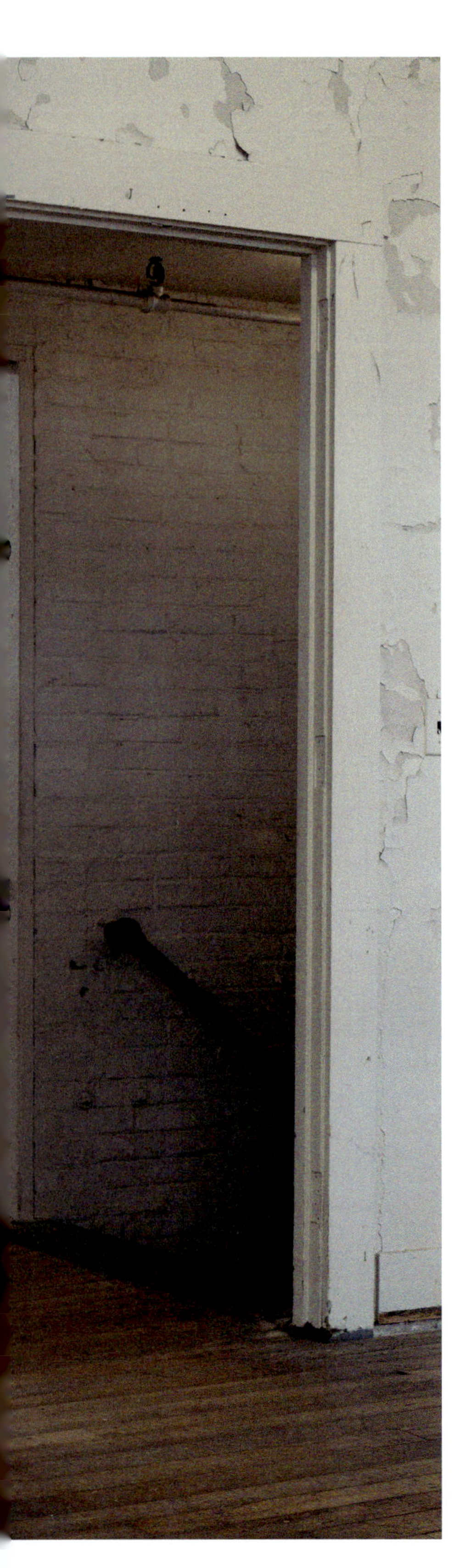

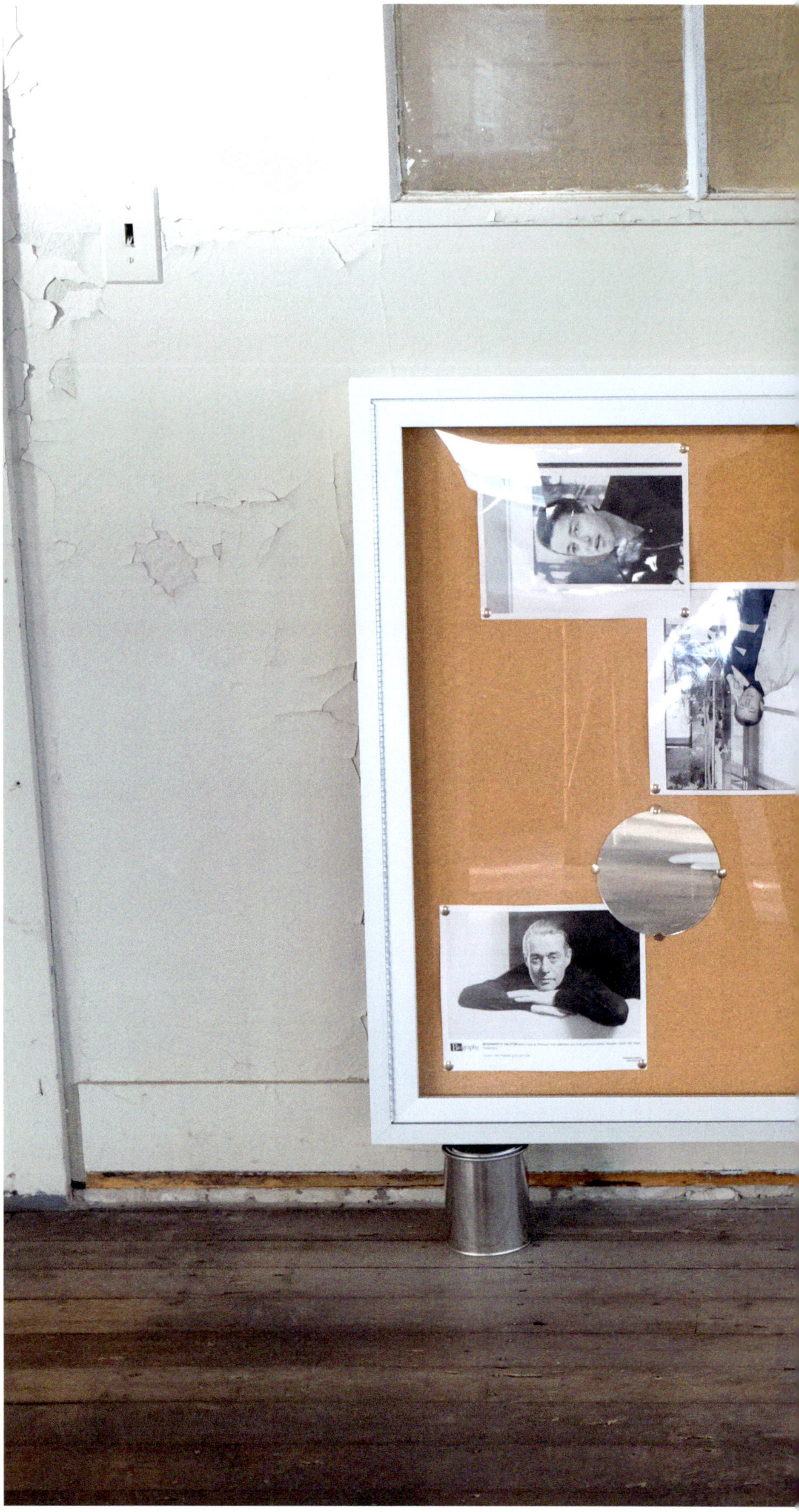

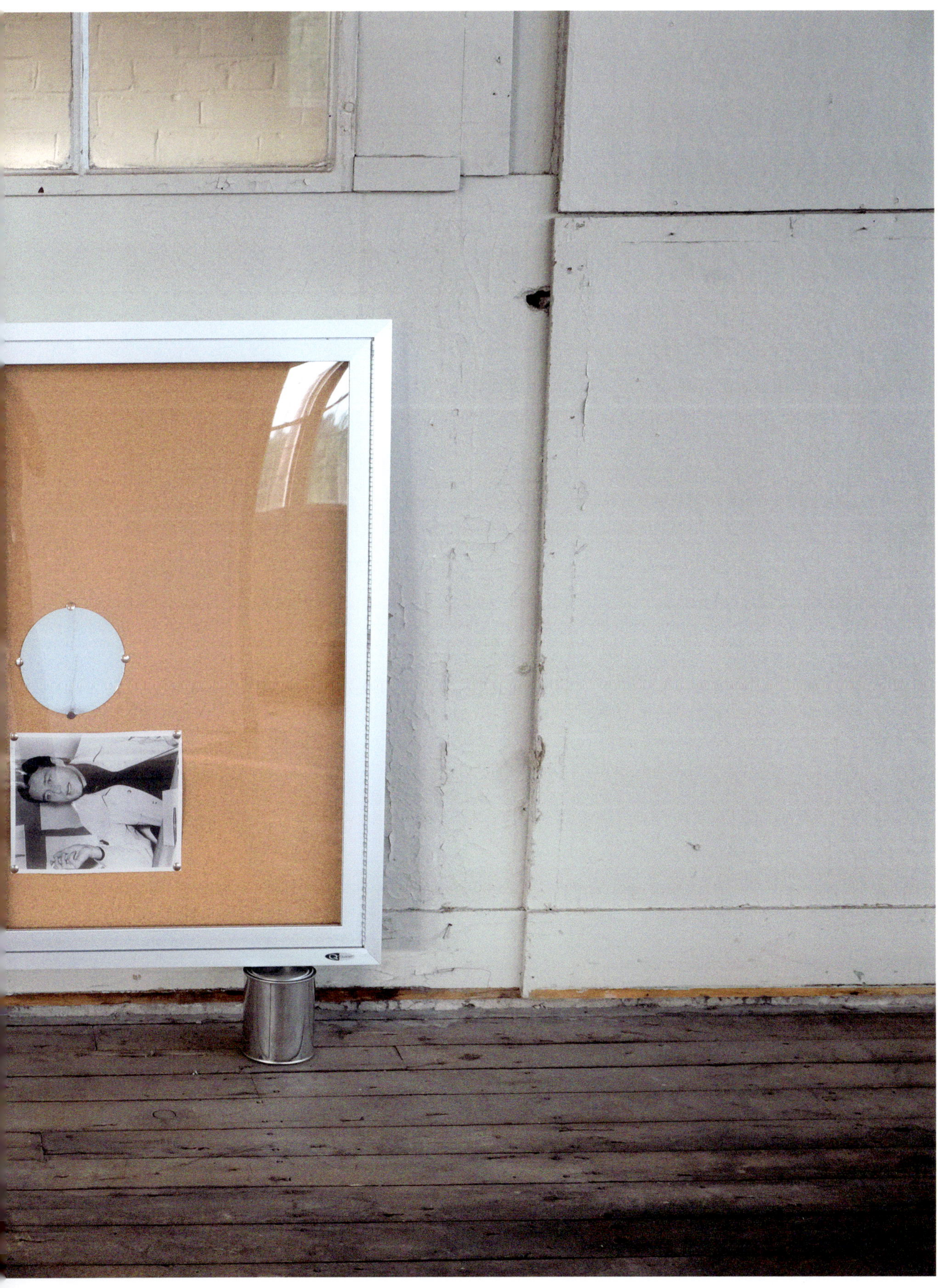

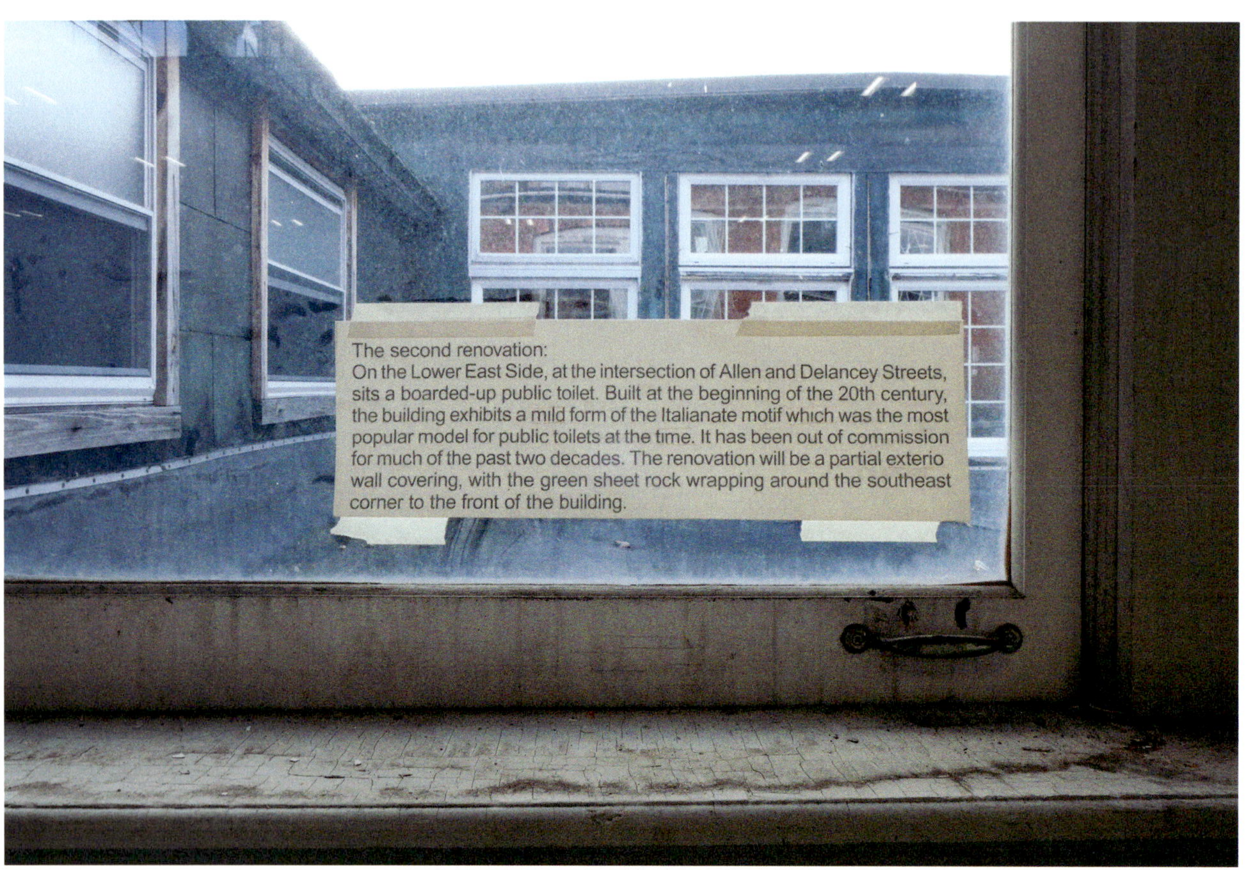

The second renovation:
On the Lower East Side, at the intersection of Allen and Delancey Streets, sits a boarded-up public toilet. Built at the beginning of the 20th century, the building exhibits a mild form of the Italianate motif which was the most popular model for public toilets at the time. It has been out of commission for much of the past two decades. The renovation will be a partial exterio wall covering, with the green sheet rock wrapping around the southeast corner to the front of the building.

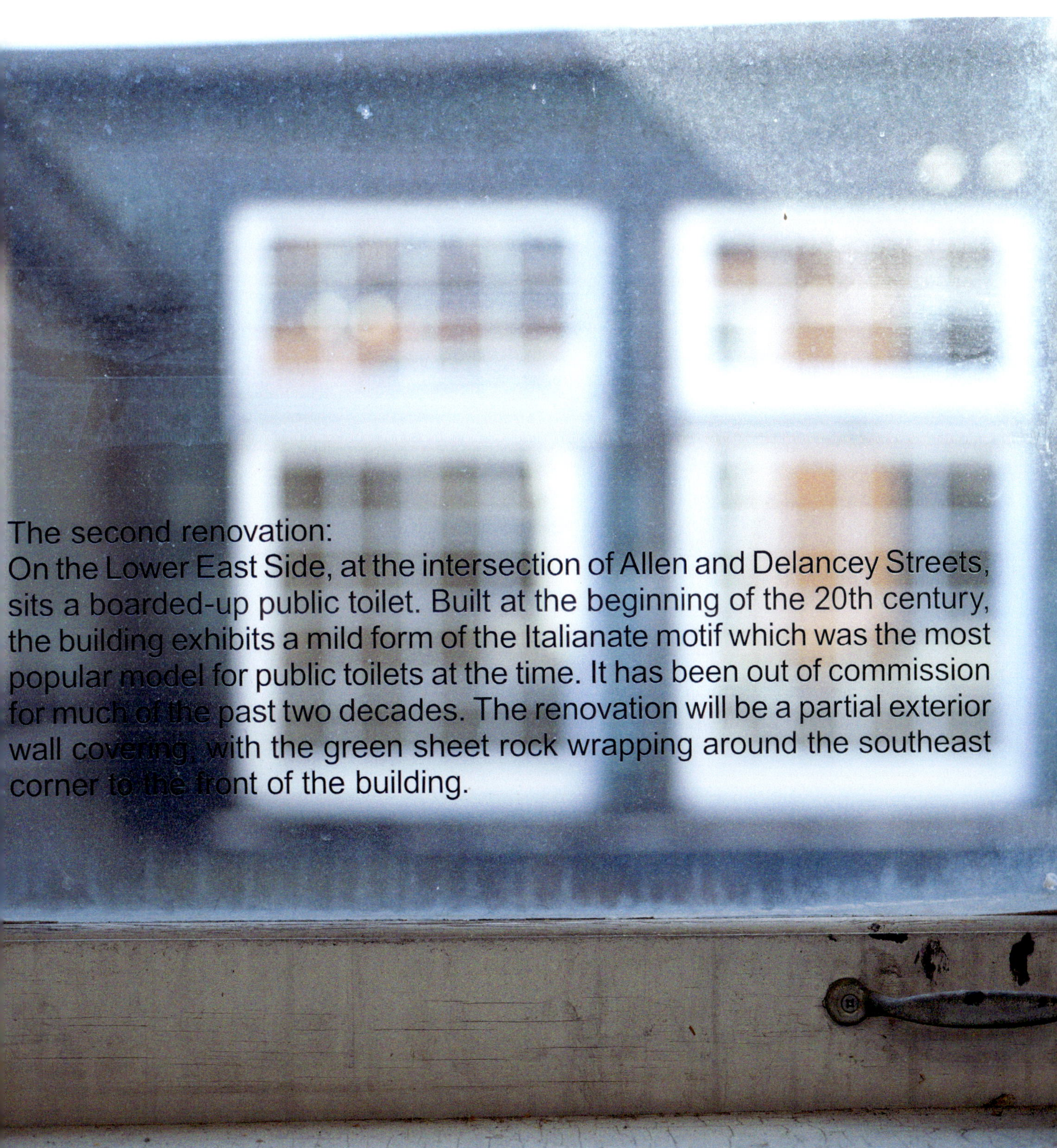

The second renovation:
On the Lower East Side, at the intersection of Allen and Delancey Streets, sits a boarded-up public toilet. Built at the beginning of the 20th century, the building exhibits a mild form of the Italianate motif which was the most popular model for public toilets at the time. It has been out of commission for much of the past two decades. The renovation will be a partial exterior wall covering, with the green sheet rock wrapping around the southeast corner to the front of the building.

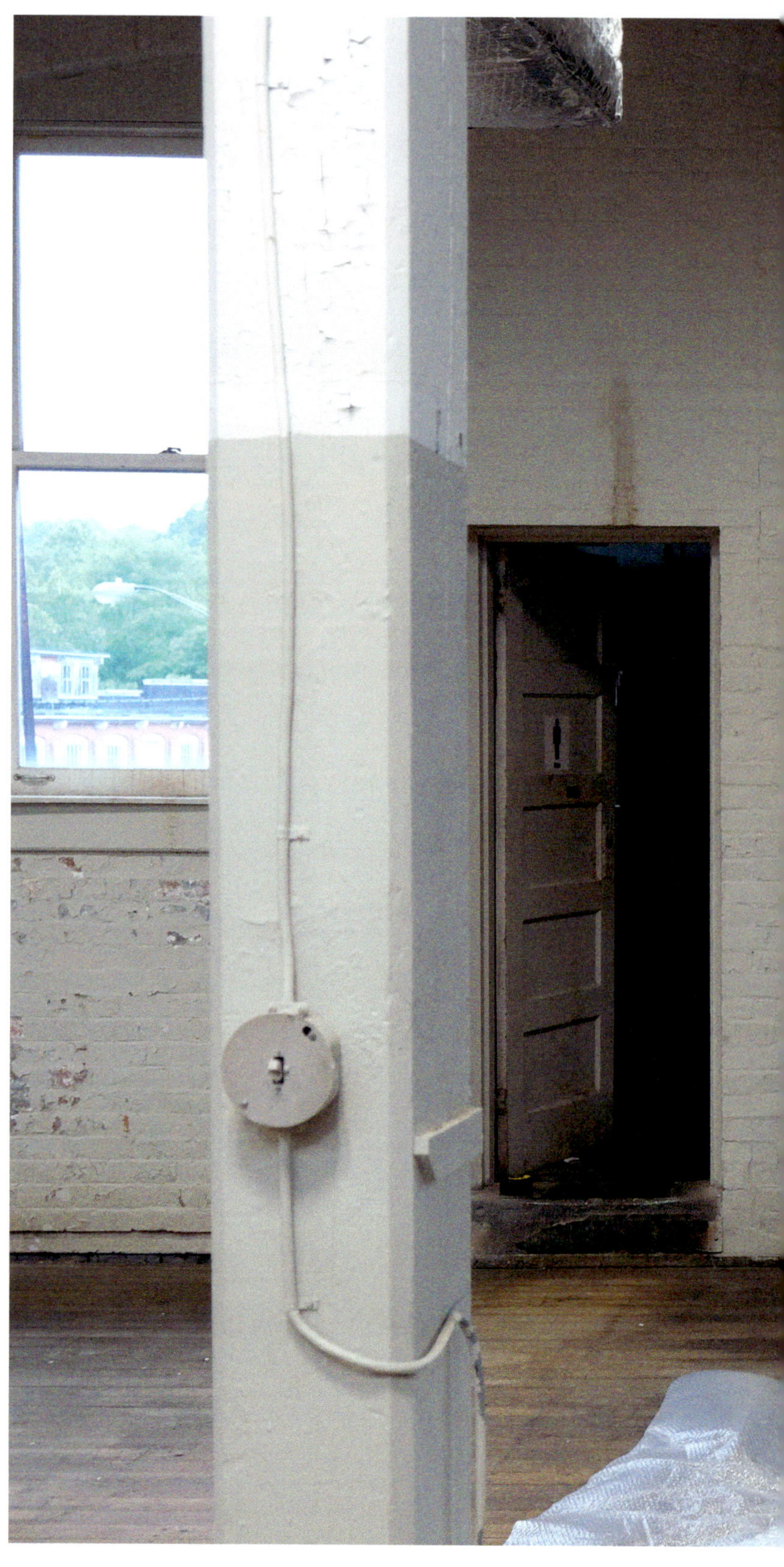

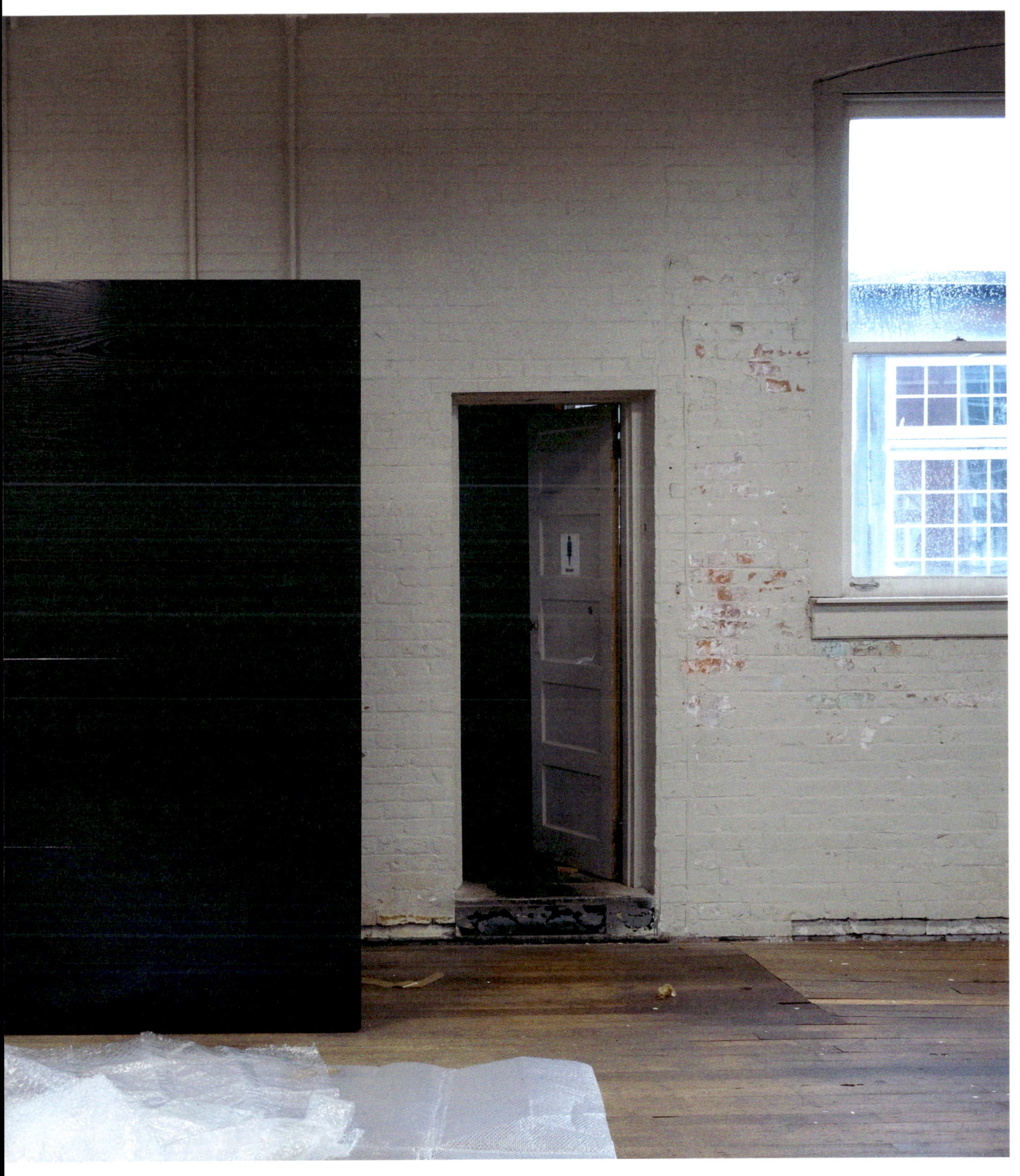

315

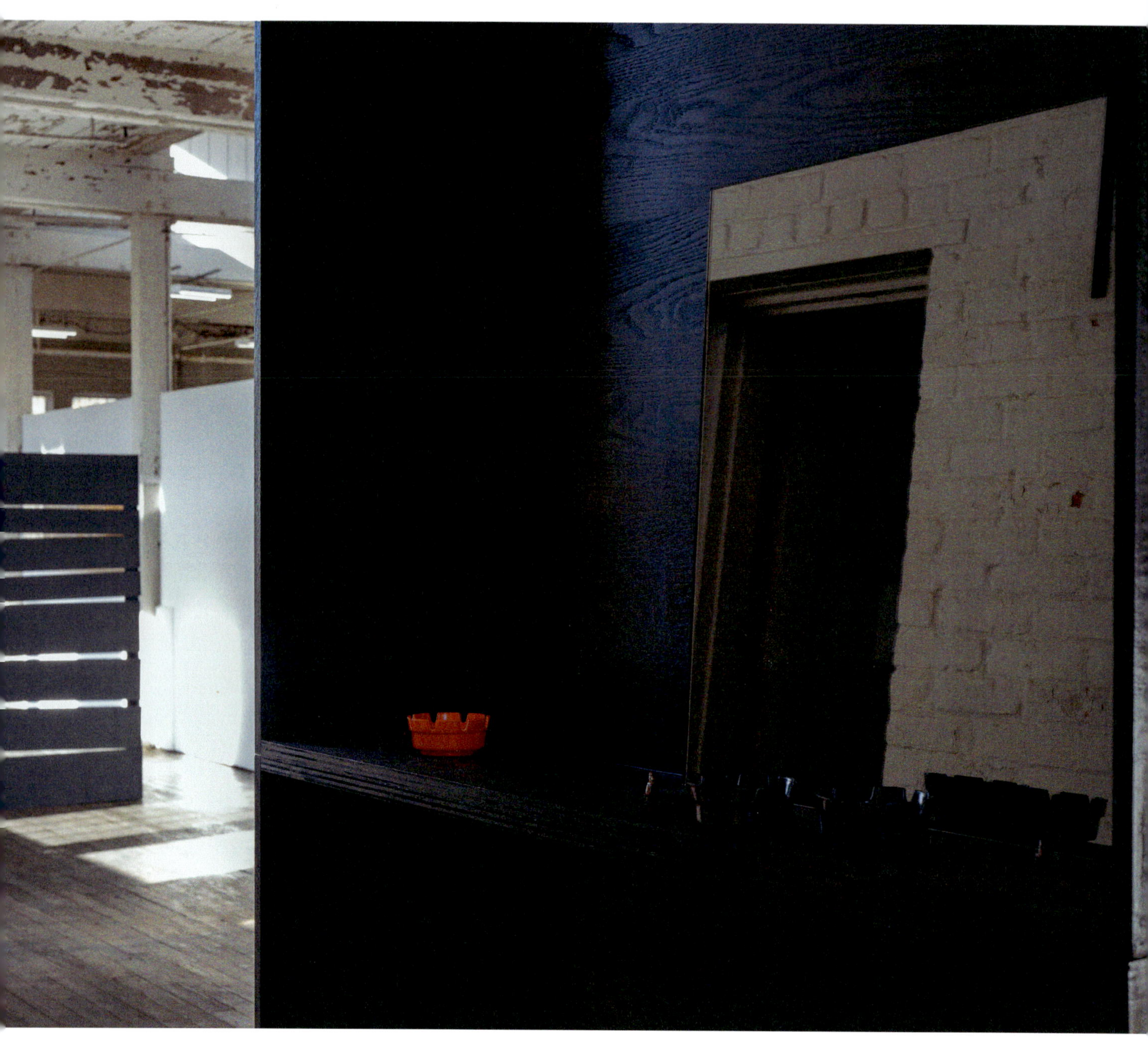

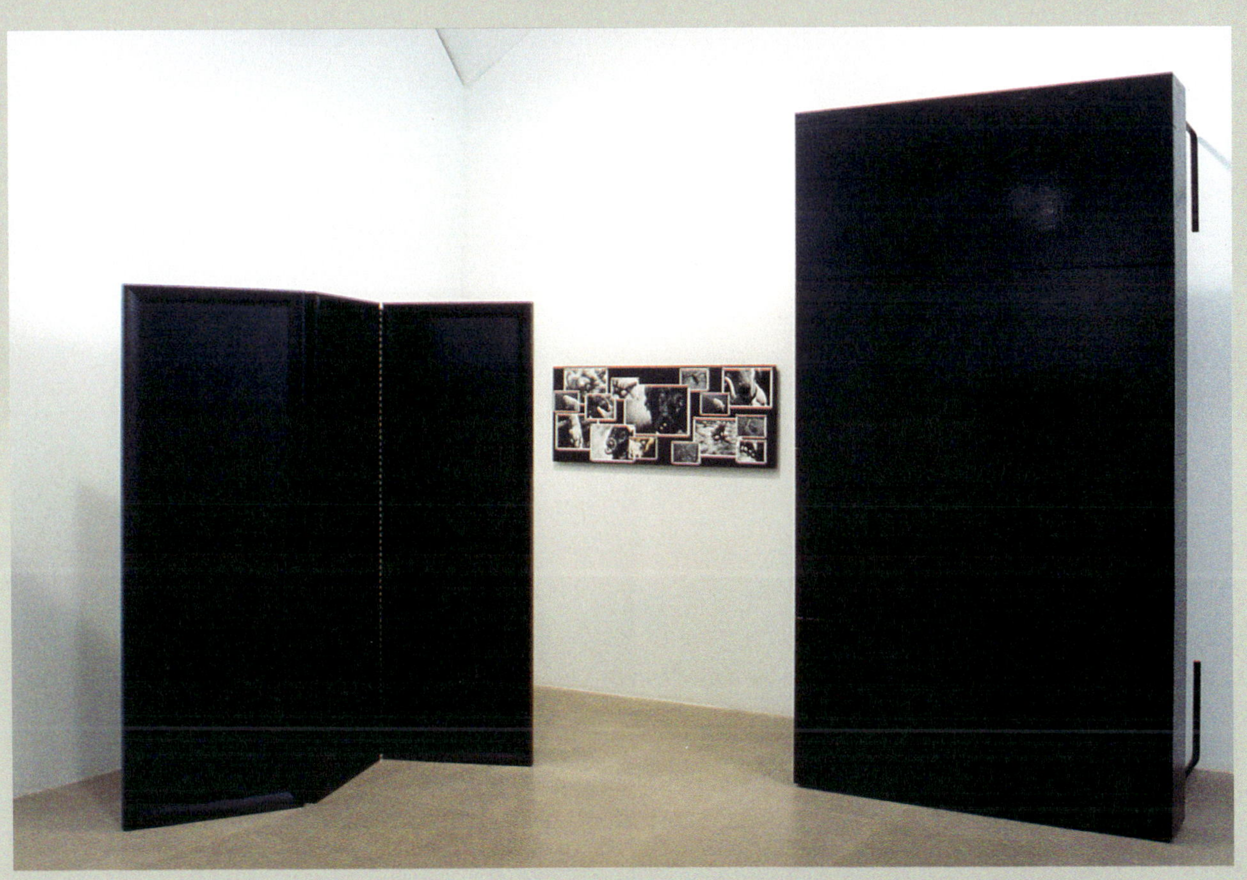

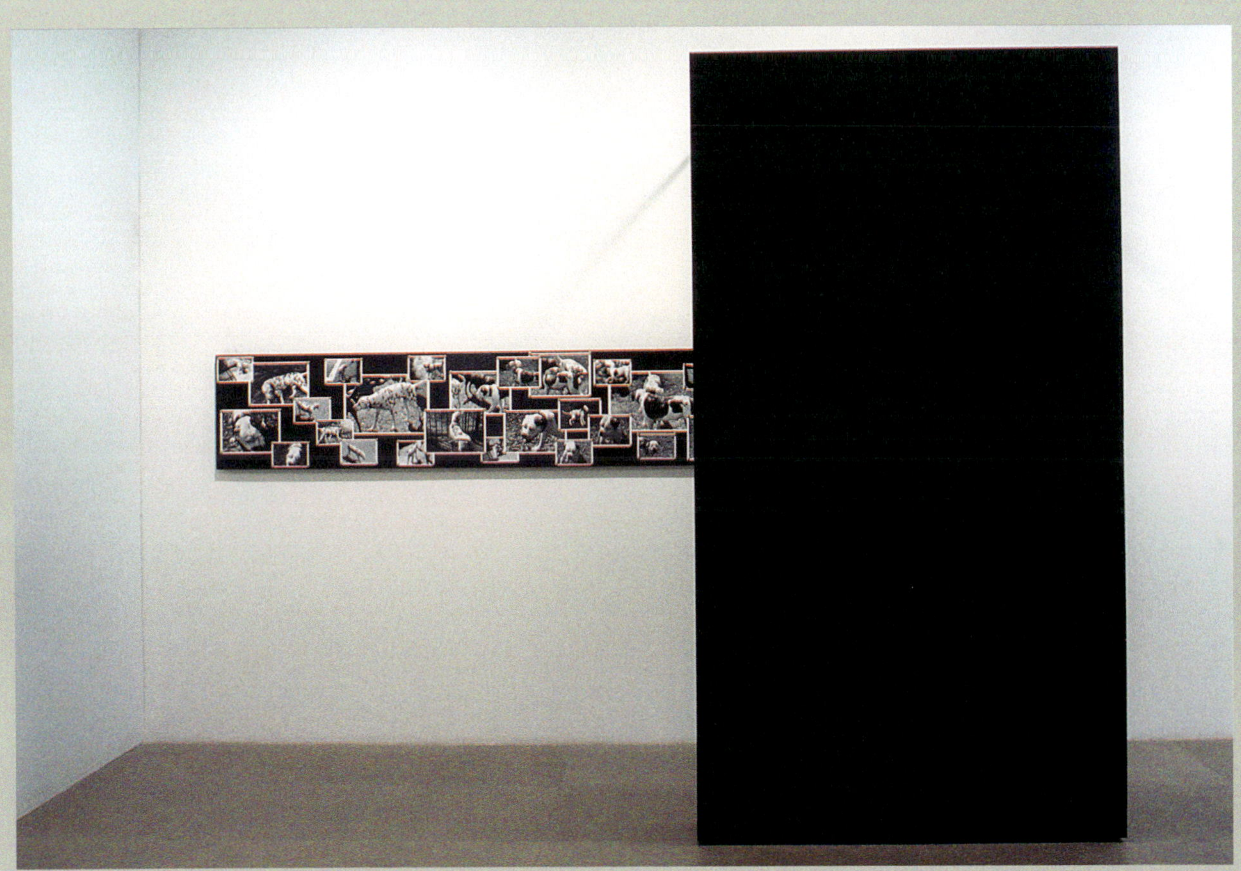

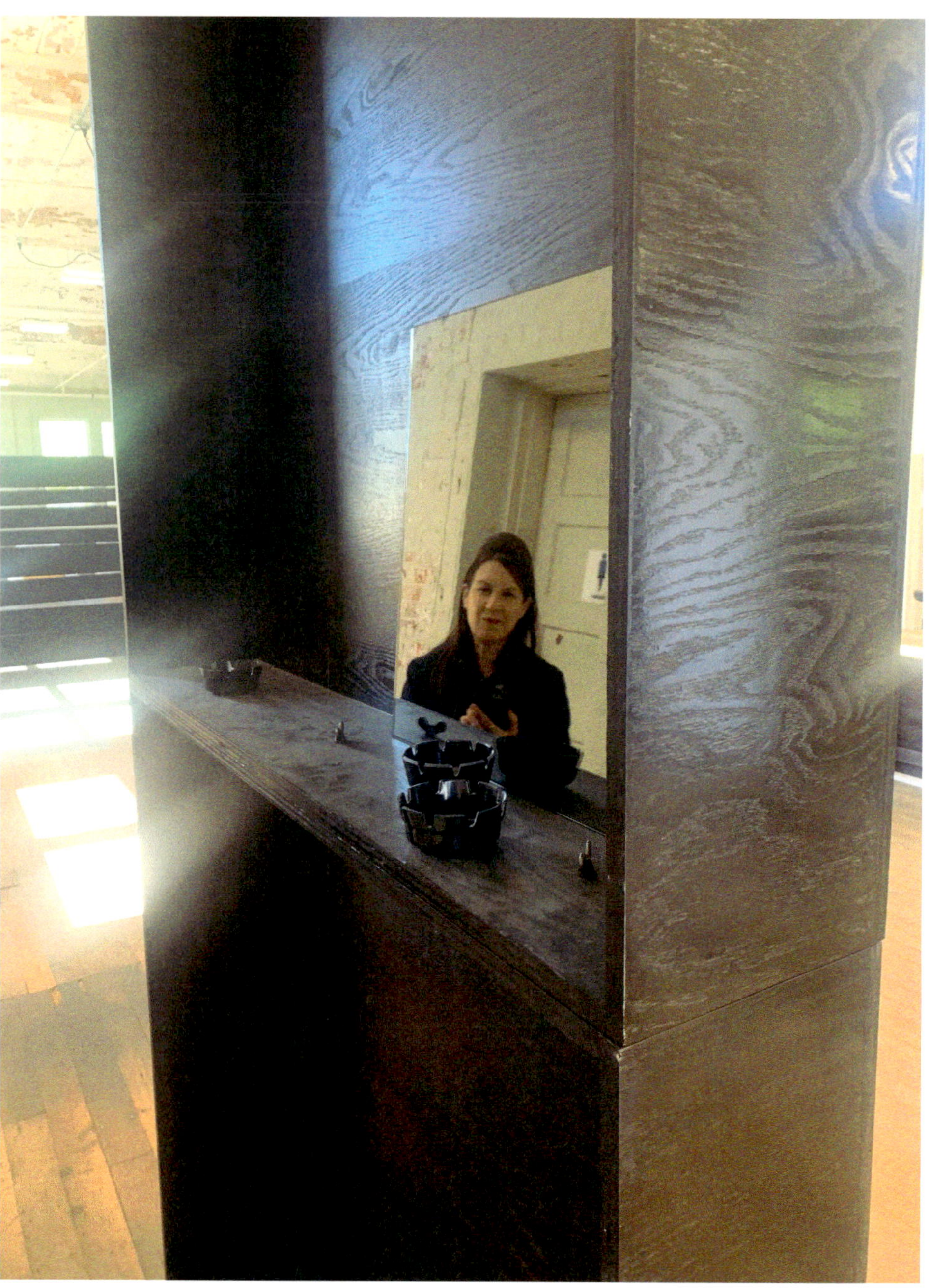

Patrick and I had talked all along about the possibility of works from his collection coming to the space at some point, as another signal of the collaboration that had brought the project into being. With this in mind, Patrick acquired a group of Ull Hohn works, which I was later allowed to select from, as well as five Alvin Baltrop photographs that I wanted to hang suspended on the glass panels of the small compact office space in the corner of the main room, some of them looking in, some looking out. Four of the Baltrop works are from the *Warehouse* series, and the conflation of those spaces on Manhattan's West Side piers in the 1970s with the Torrington space in the present produced something extraordinarily beautiful. The fifth image was of a hand holding a lit cigarette, and it hung in line with Ull's works on the far side of the room, encircled by the excess fabric of *Wide Wall Wound* falling across the floor.

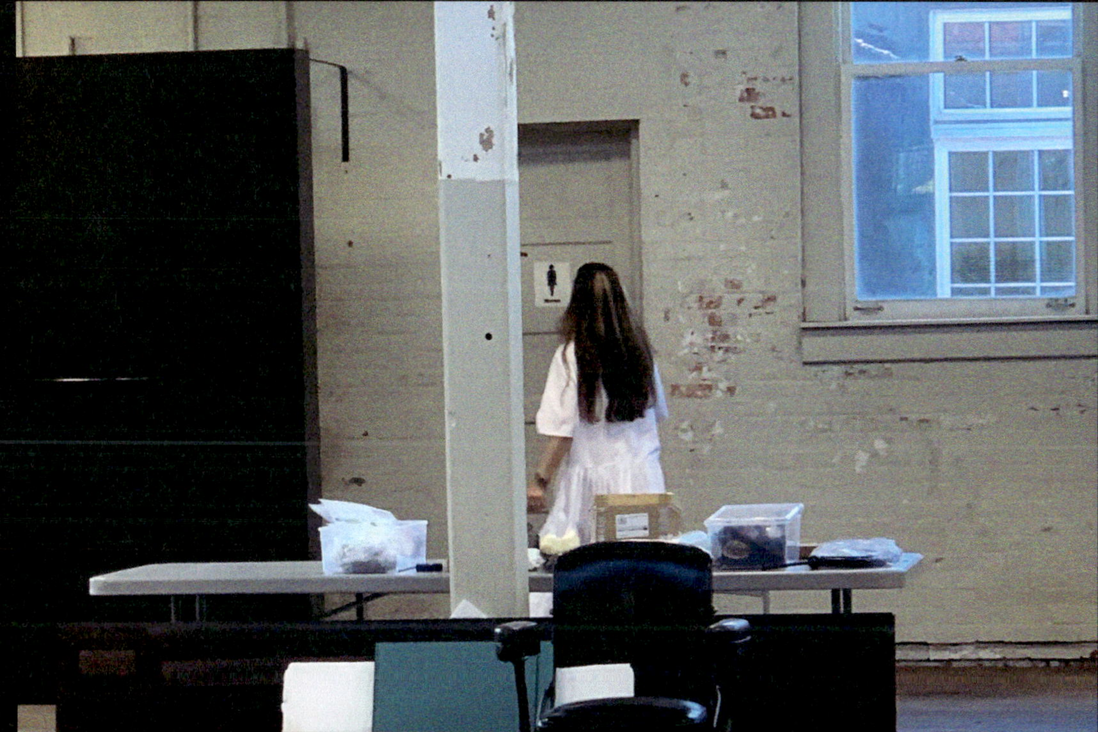

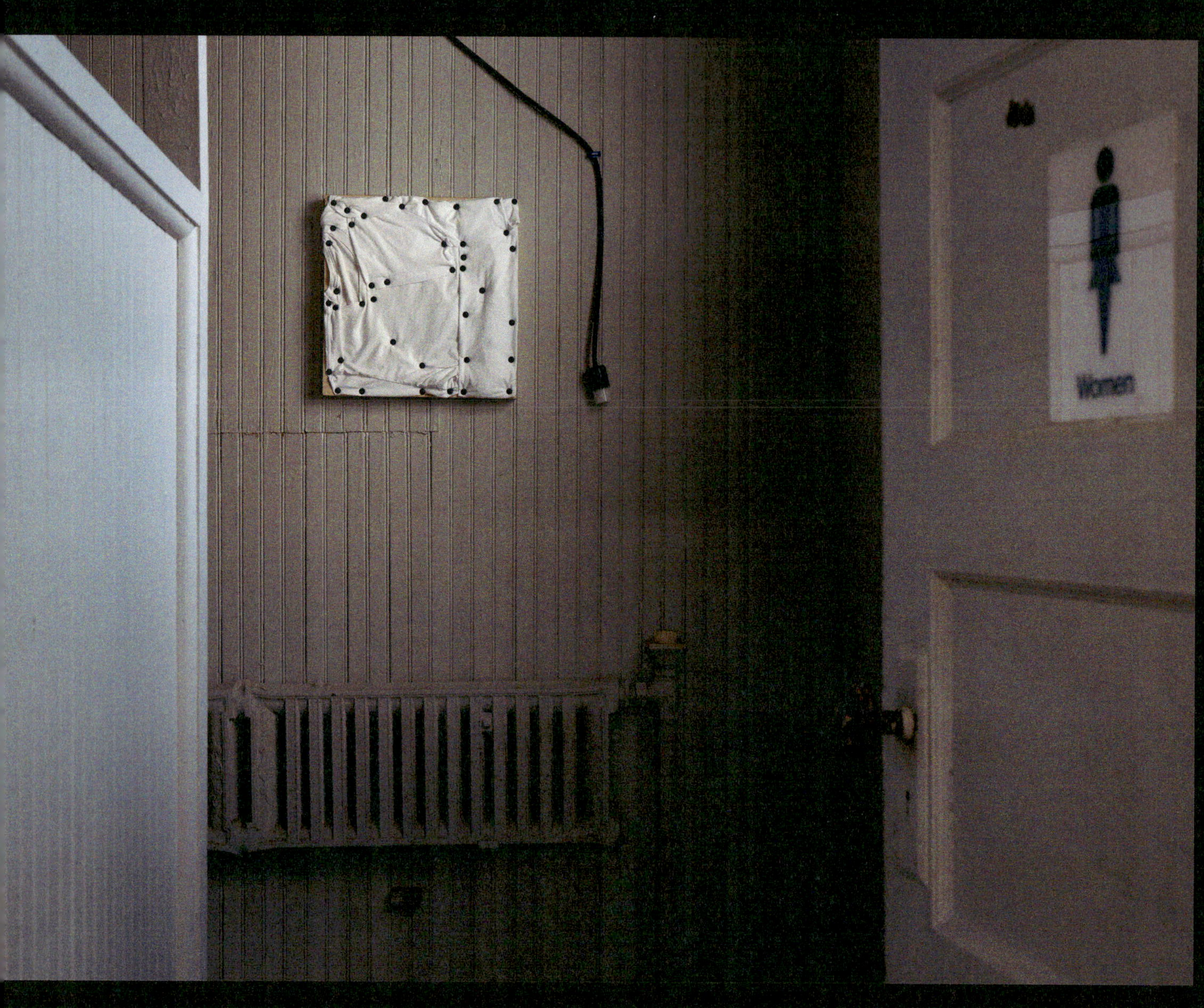

Women

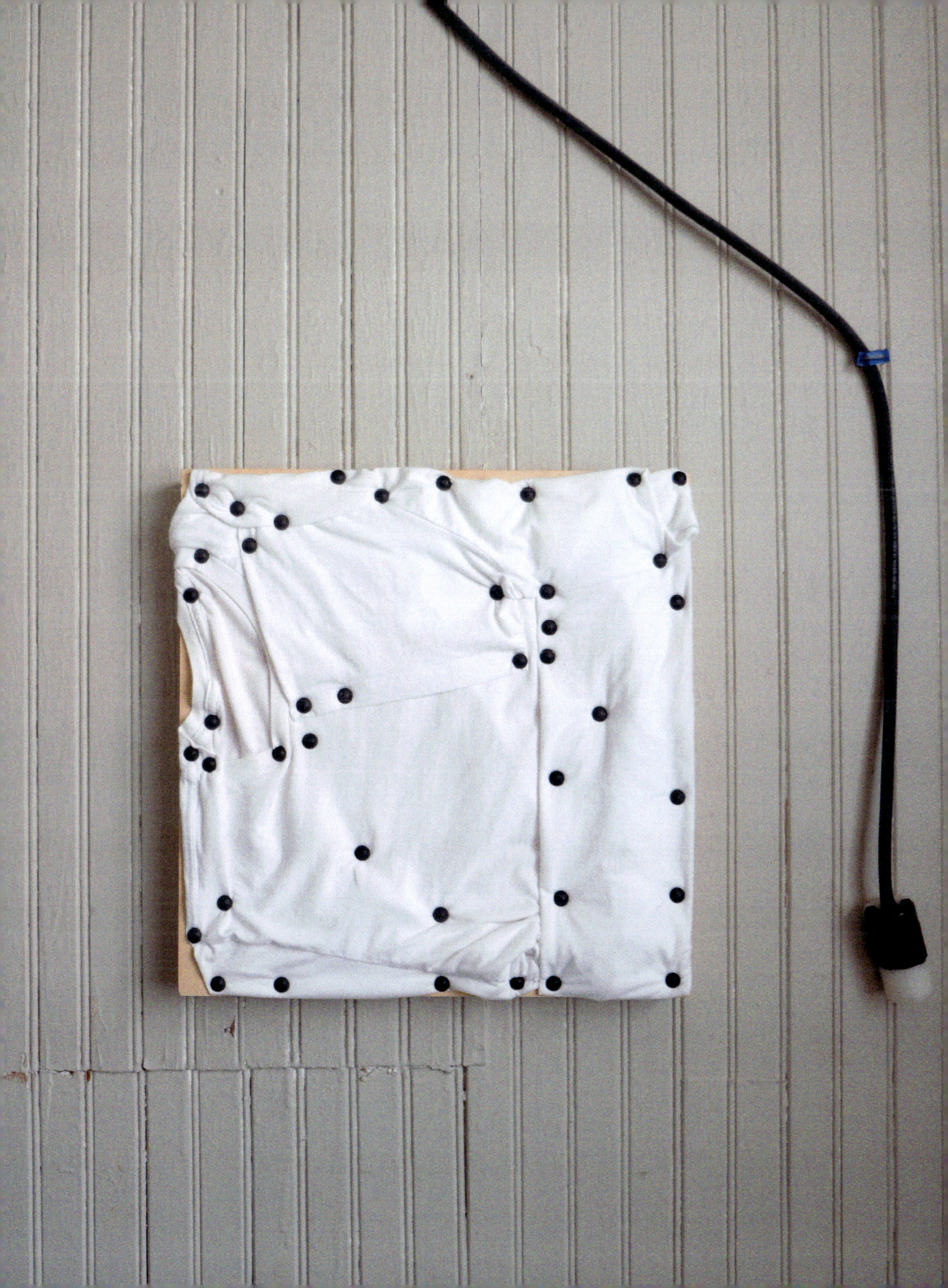

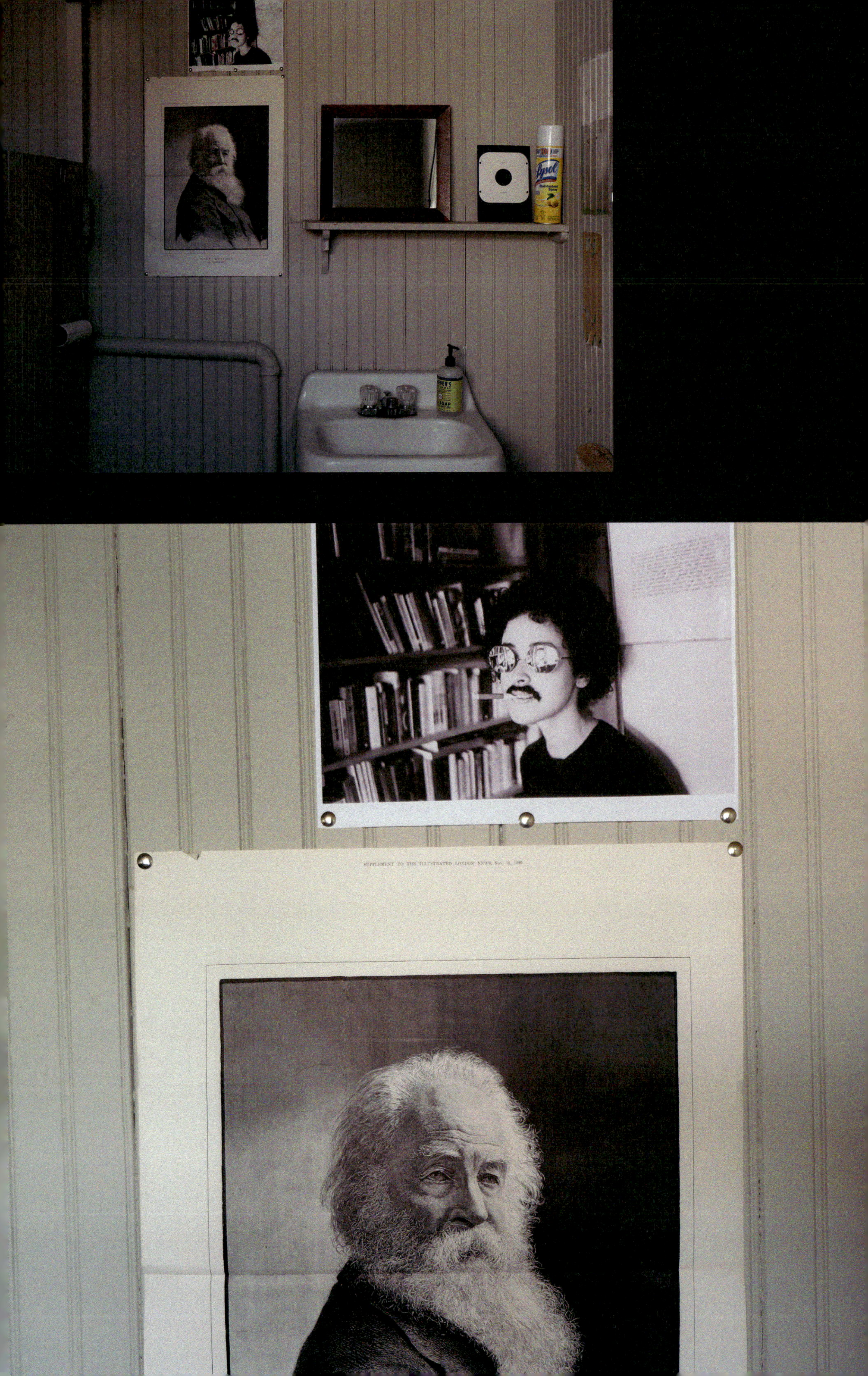

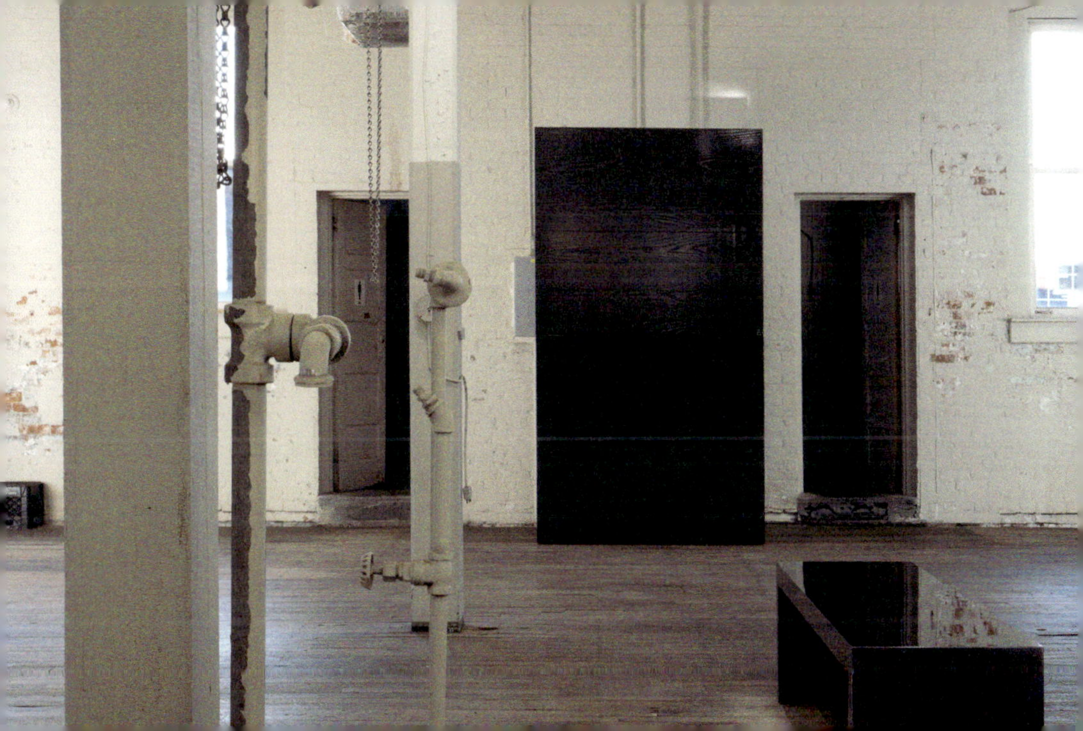

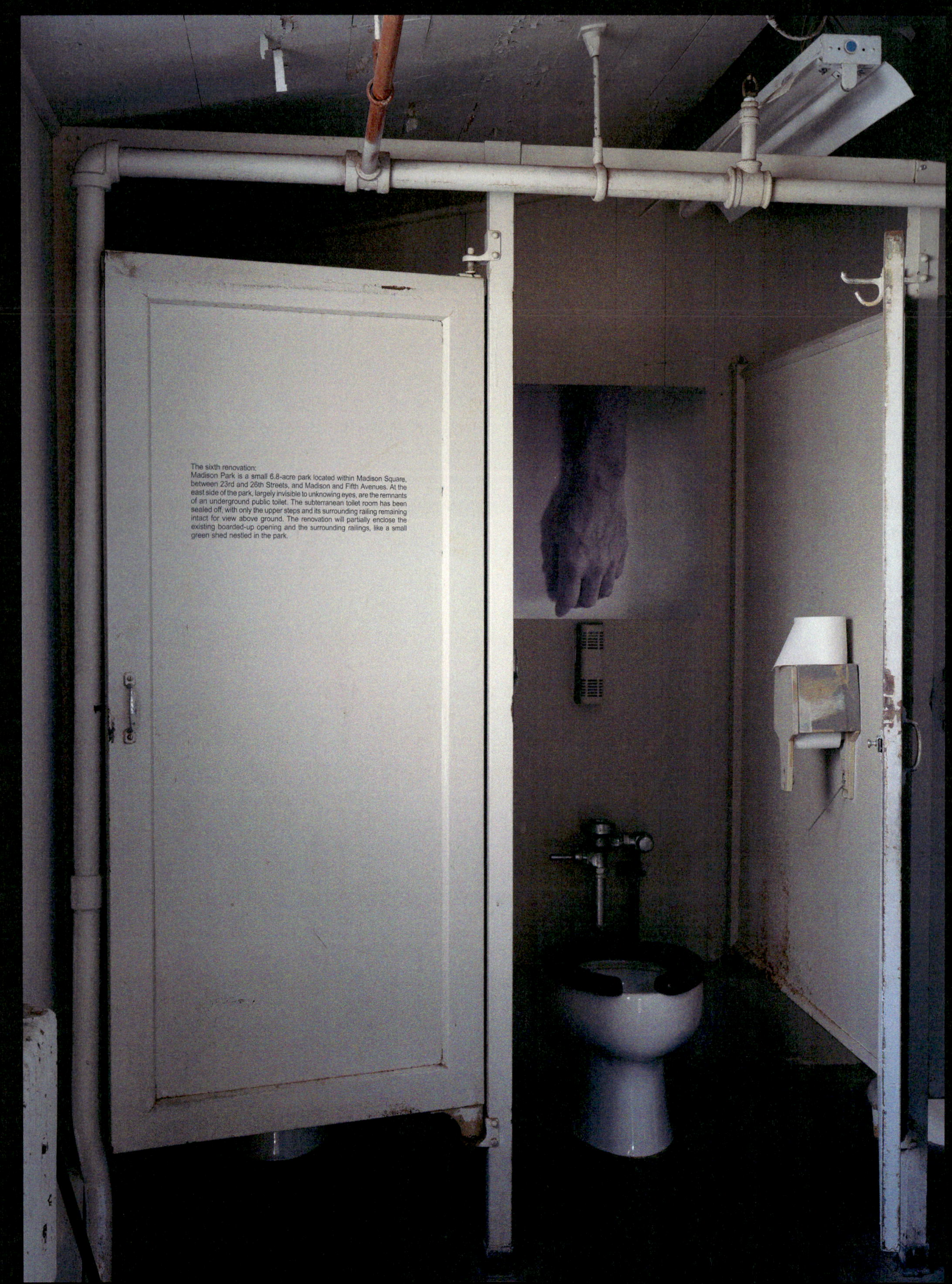

The sixth renovation:
Madison Park is a small 6.8-acre park located within Madison Square, between 23rd and 26th Streets, and Madison and Fifth Avenues. At the east side of the park, largely invisible to unknowing eyes, are the remnants of an underground public toilet. The subterranean toilet room has been sealed off, with only the upper steps and its surrounding railing remaining intact for view above ground. The renovation will partially enclose the existing boarded-up opening and the surrounding railings, like a small green shed nestled in the park.

The sixth renovation:
Madison Park is a small 6.8-acre park located within Madison Square,
between 23rd and 26th Streets, and Madison and Fifth Avenues. At the
east side of the park, largely invisible to unknowing eyes, are the remnants
of an underground public toilet. The subterranean toilet room has been
sealed off, with only the upper steps and its surrounding railing remaining
intact for view above ground. The renovation will partially enclose the
existing boarded-up opening and the surrounding railings, like a small
green shed nestled in the park.

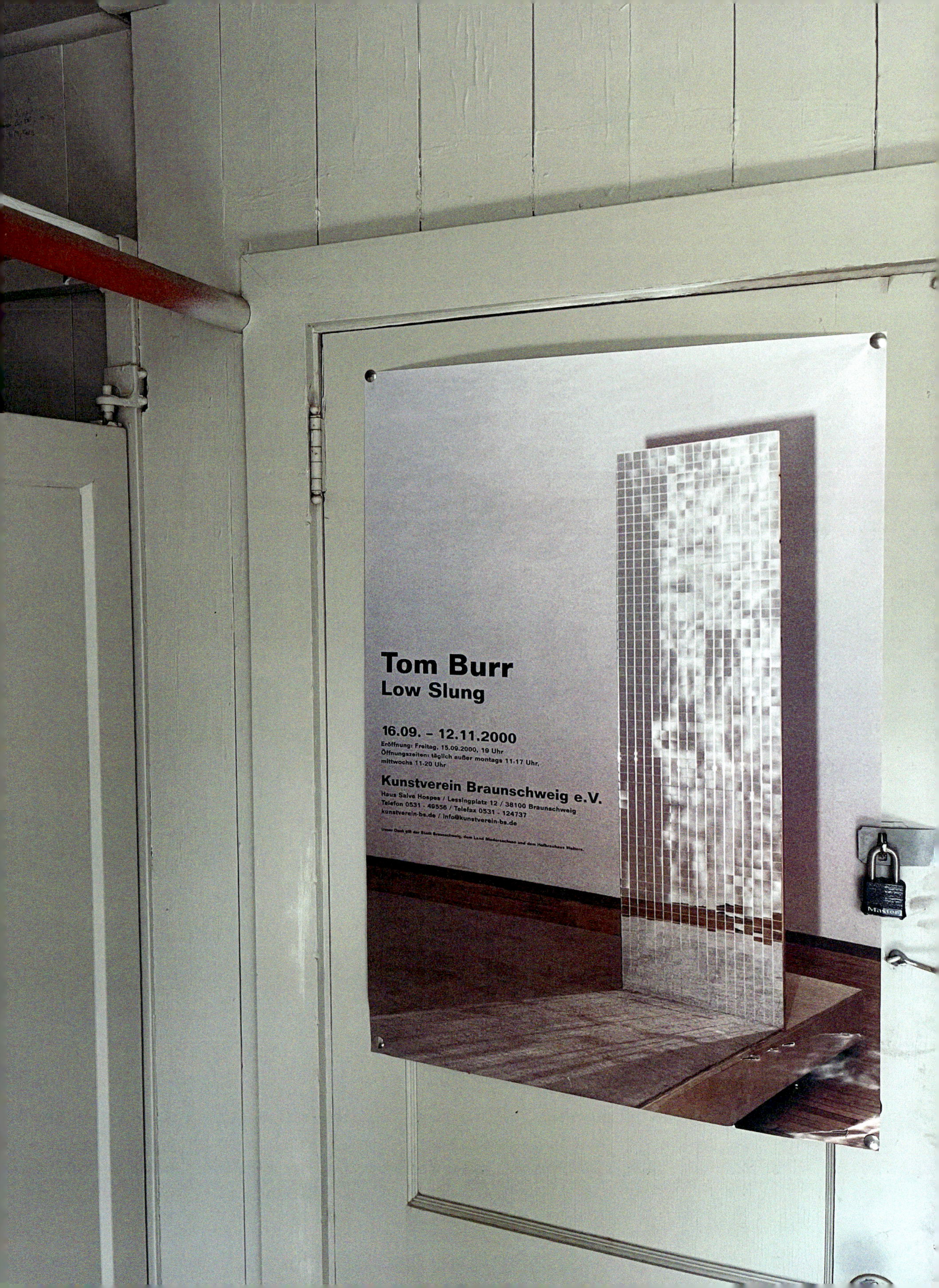

Tom Burr
Low Slung
16.09. – 12.11.2000
Eröffnung: Freitag, 15.09.2000, 19 Uhr
Öffnungszeiten: täglich außer montags 11-17 Uhr,
mittwochs 11-20 Uhr
Kunstverein Braunschweig e.V.
Haus Salve Hospes / Lessingplatz 12 / 38100 Braunschweig
Telefon 0531 - 49556 / Telefax 0531 - 124737
kunstverein-bs.de / info@kunstverein-bs.de
Unser Dank gilt der Stadt Braunschweig, dem Land Niedersachsen und dem Hofbrauhaus Wolters.

T   IN   THE ASS!

TAKES

Bet u dont
Have the Balls to say
it to My Face

13

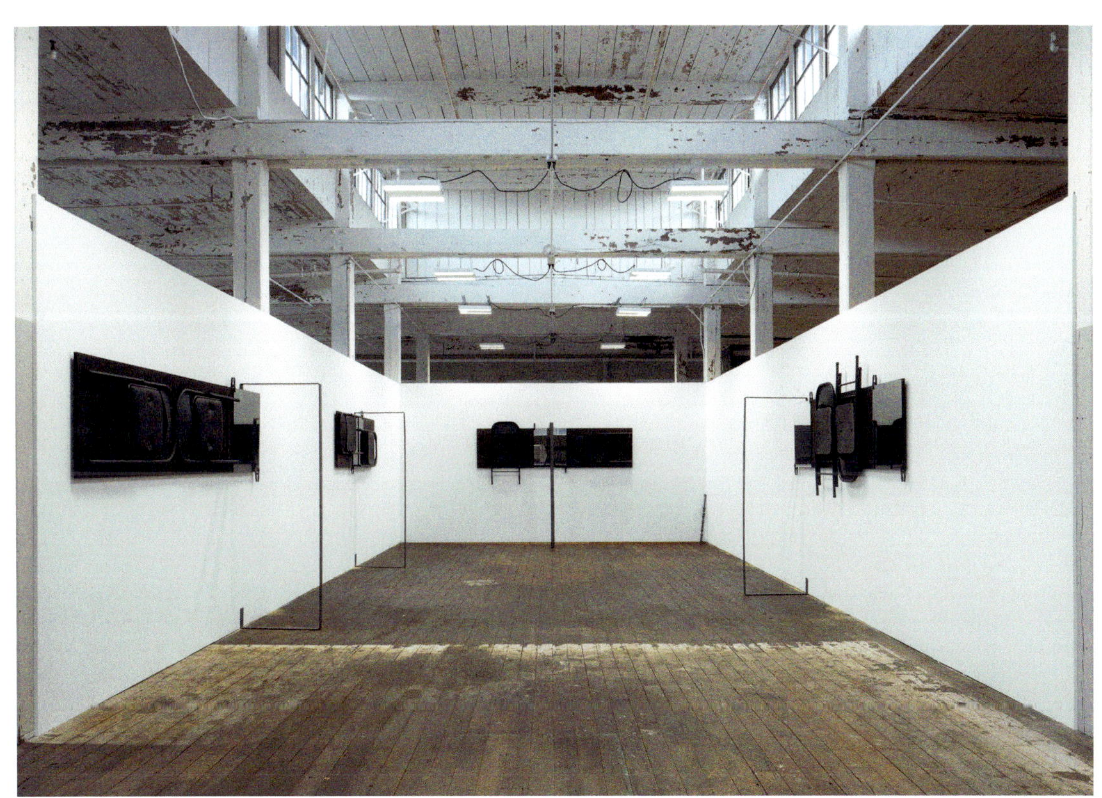

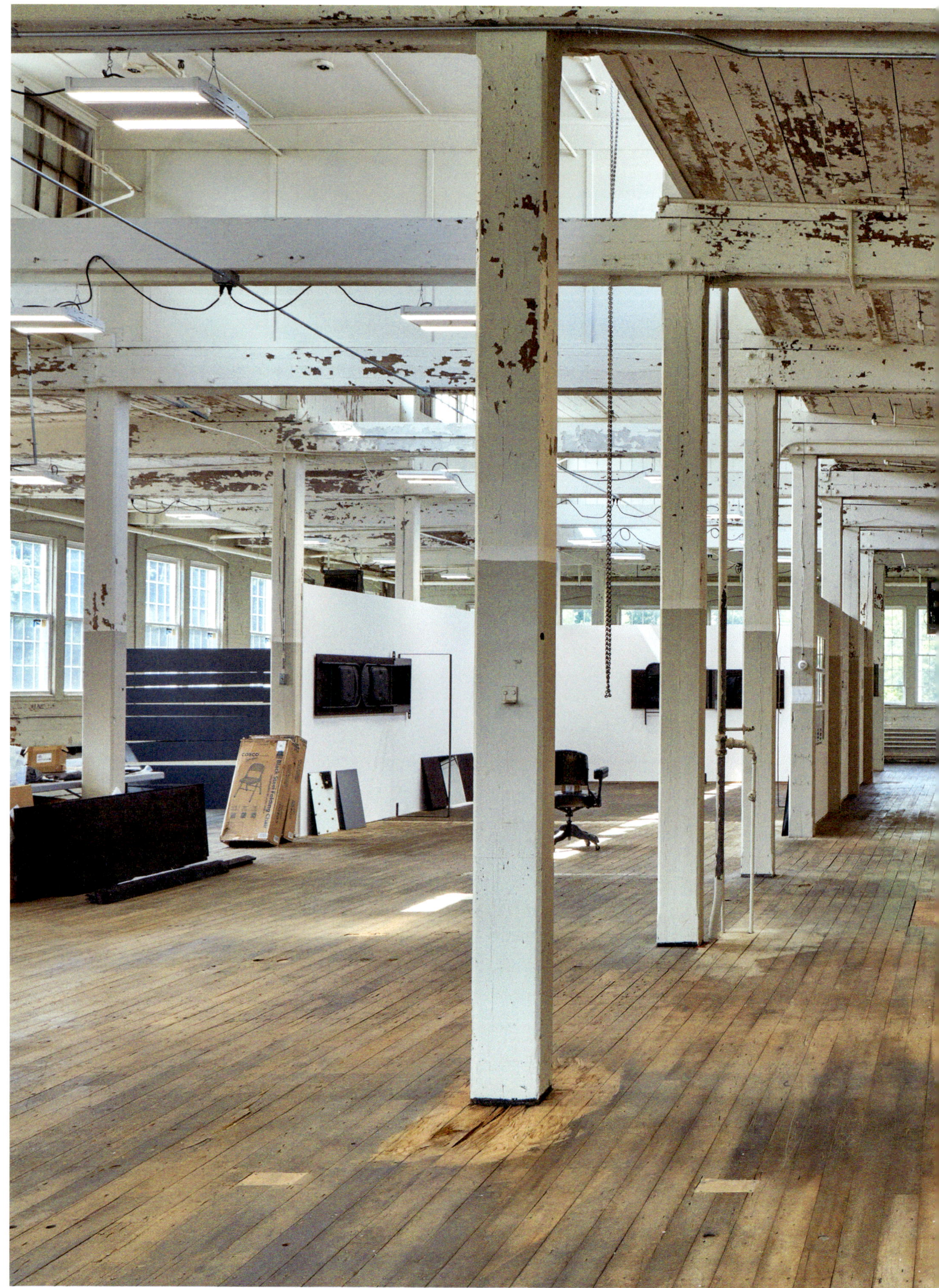

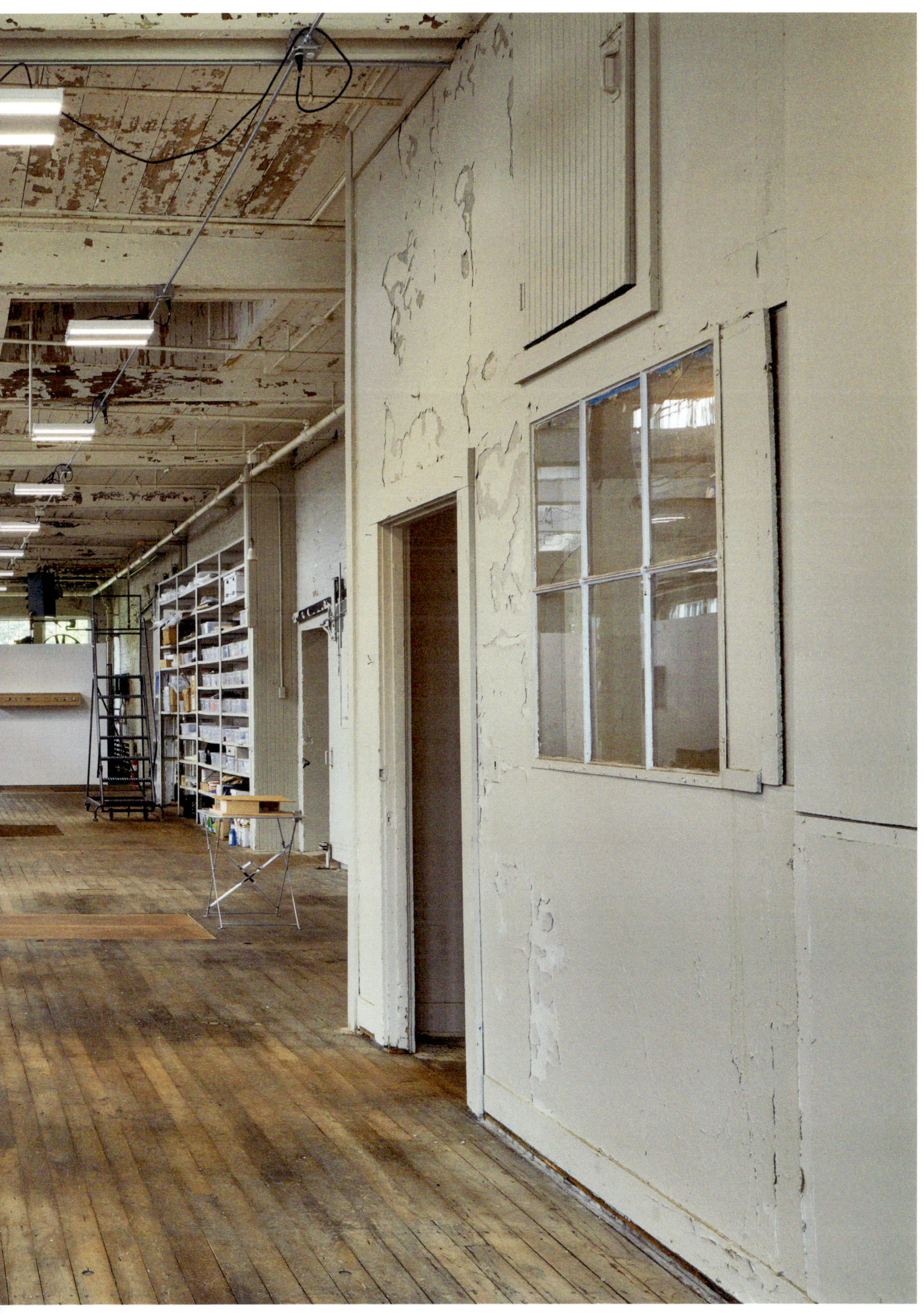

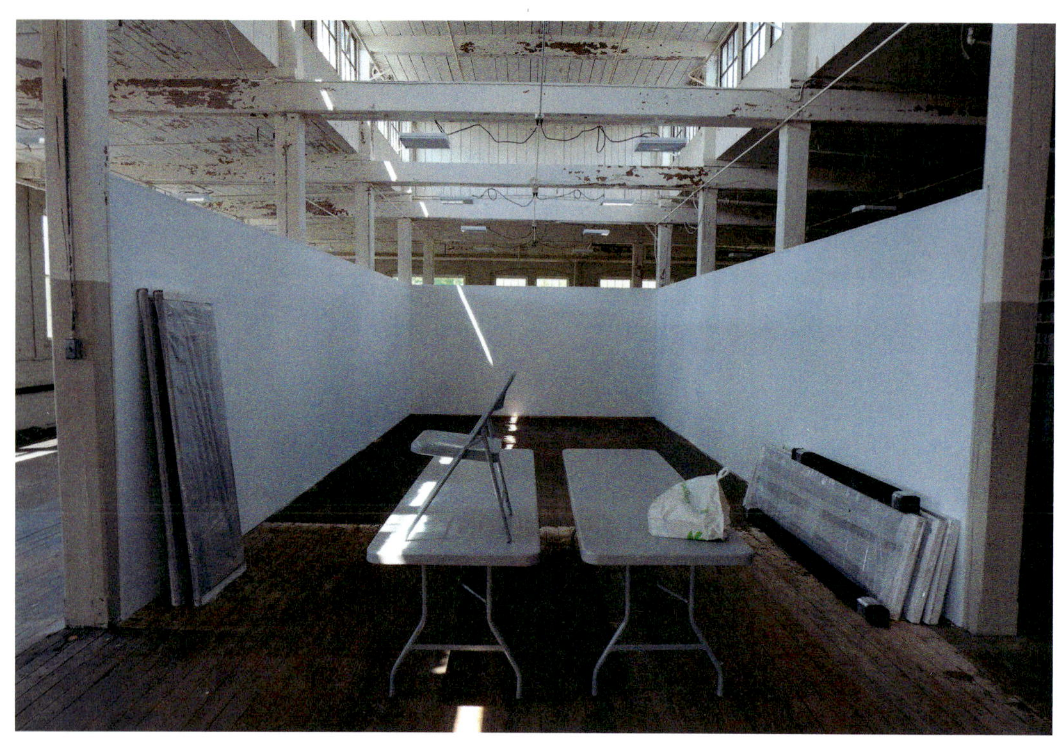

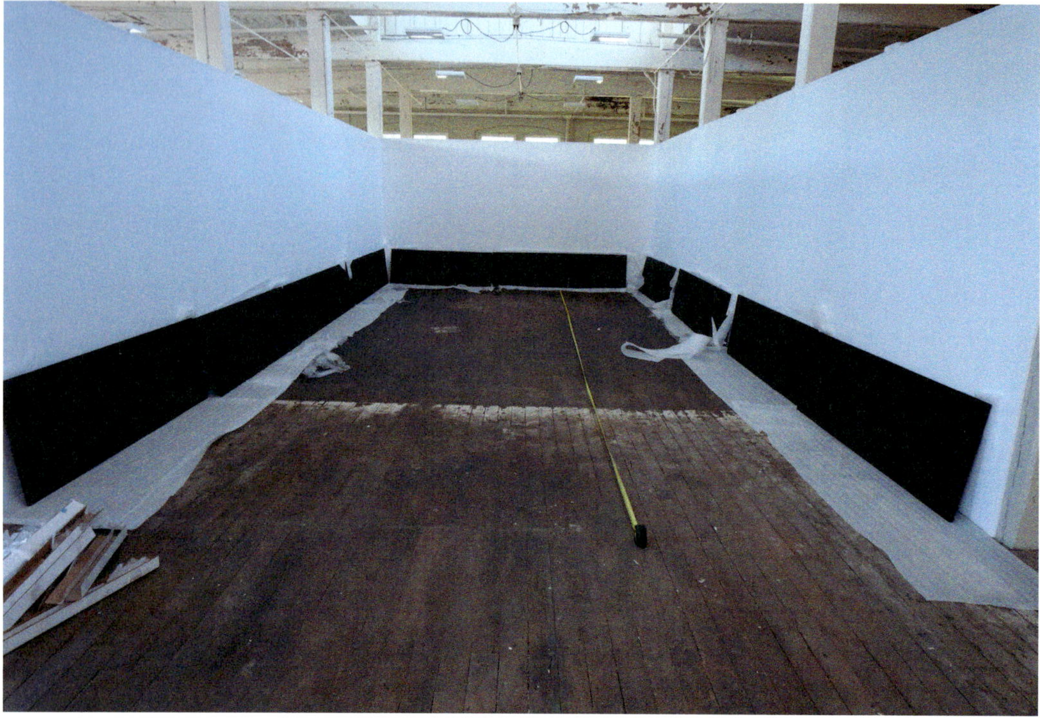

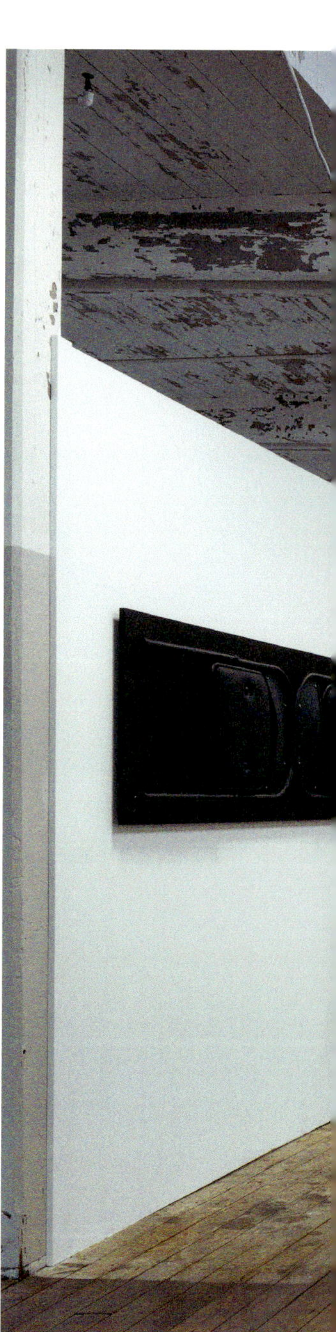

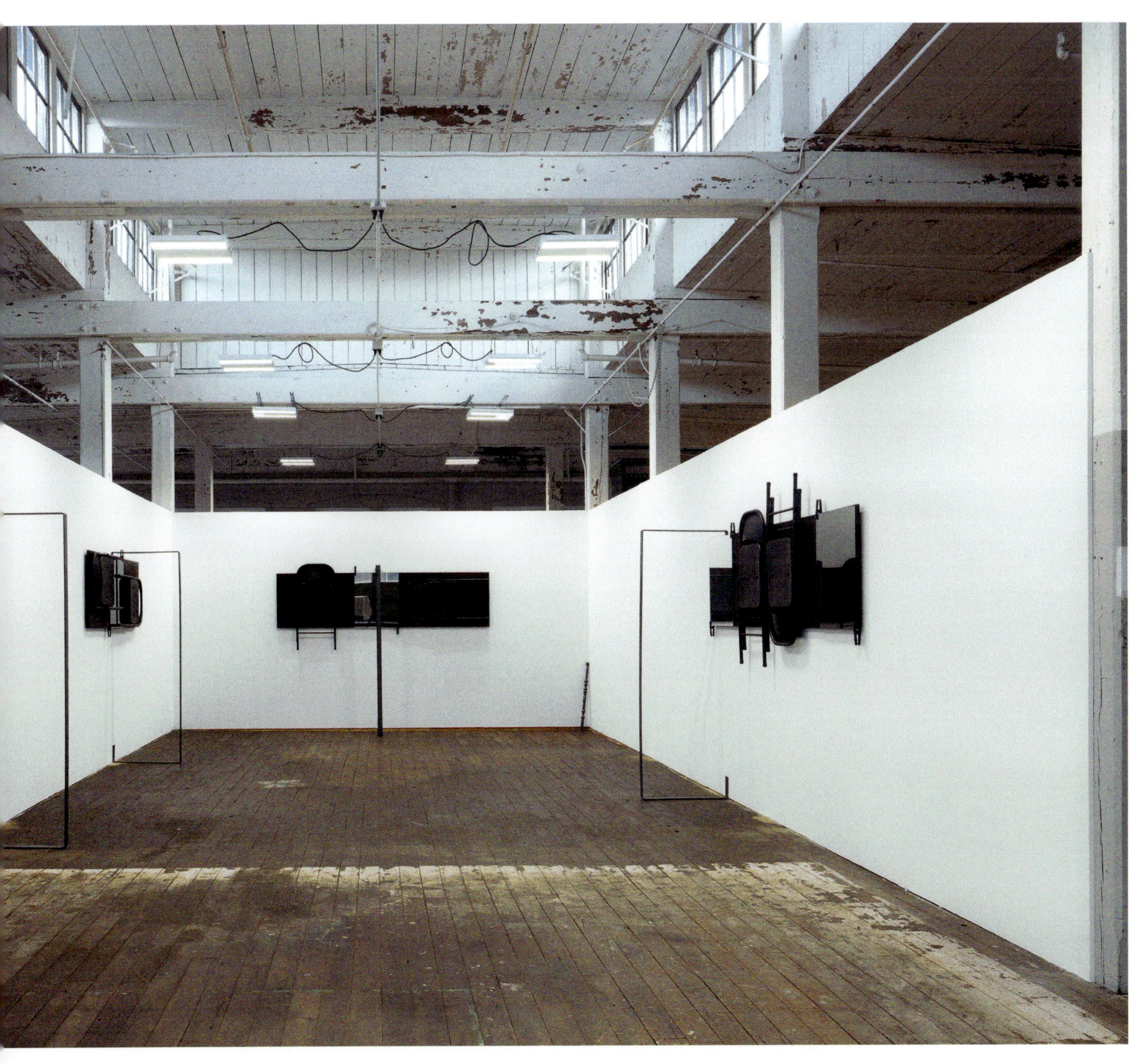

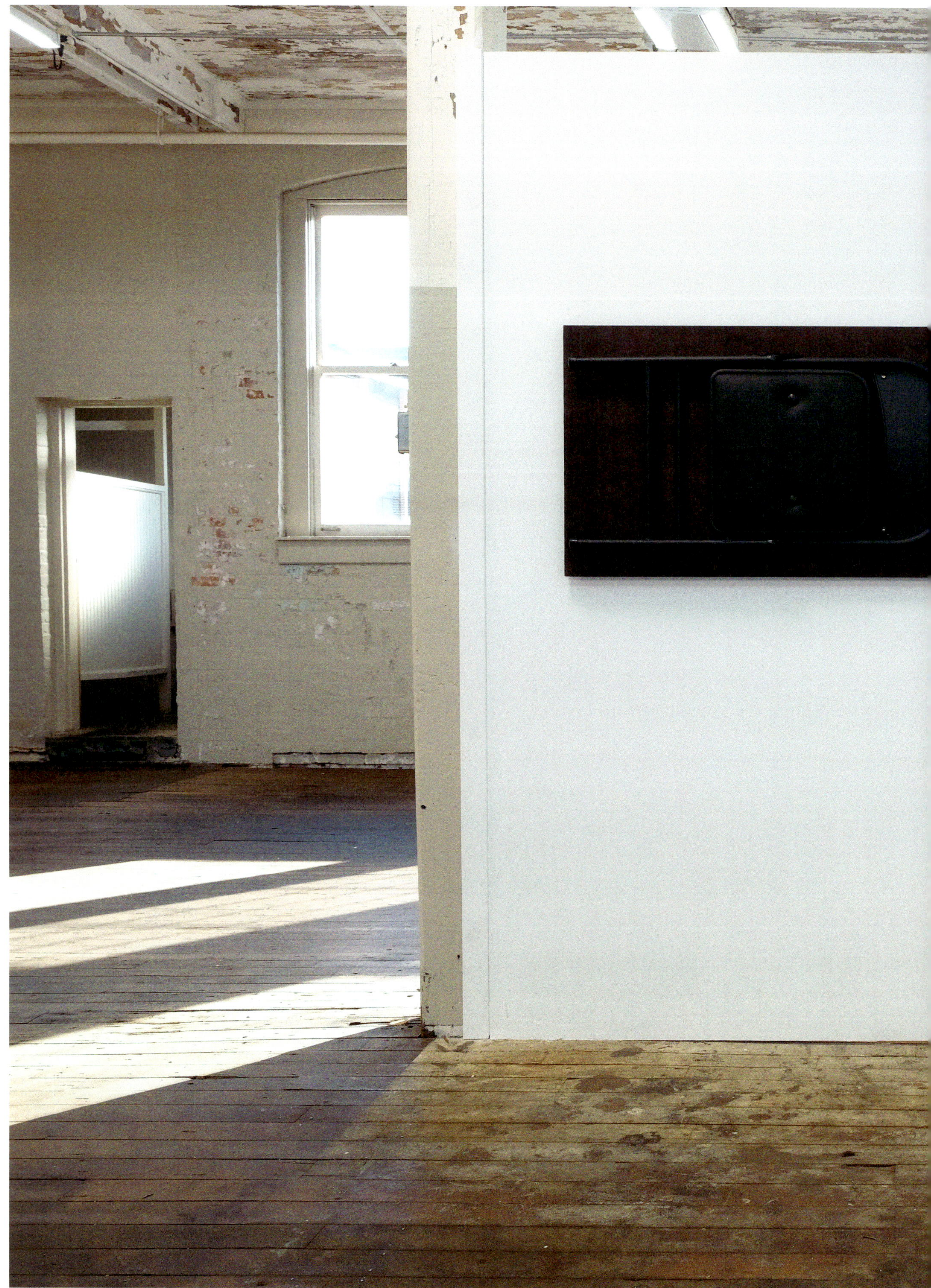

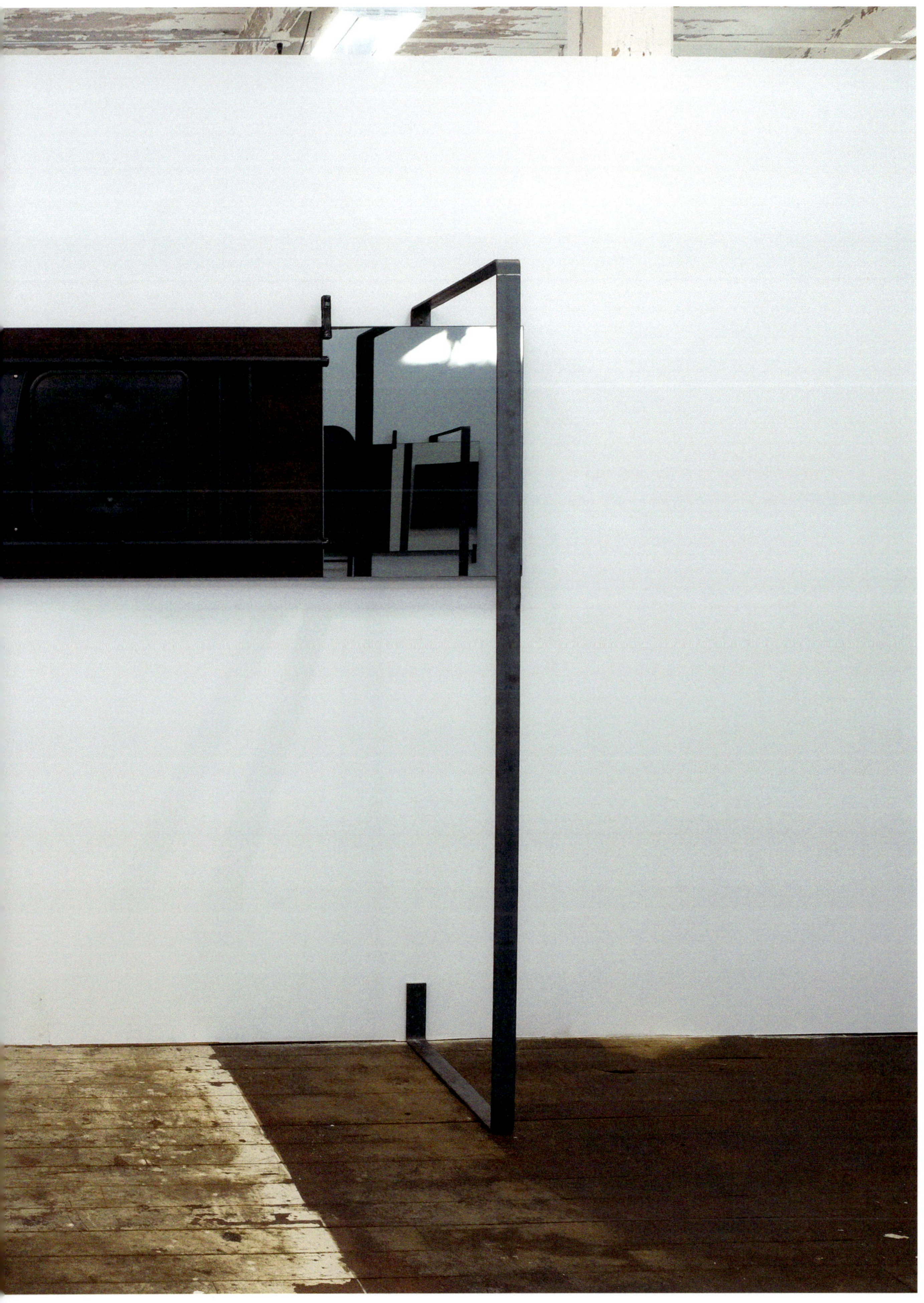

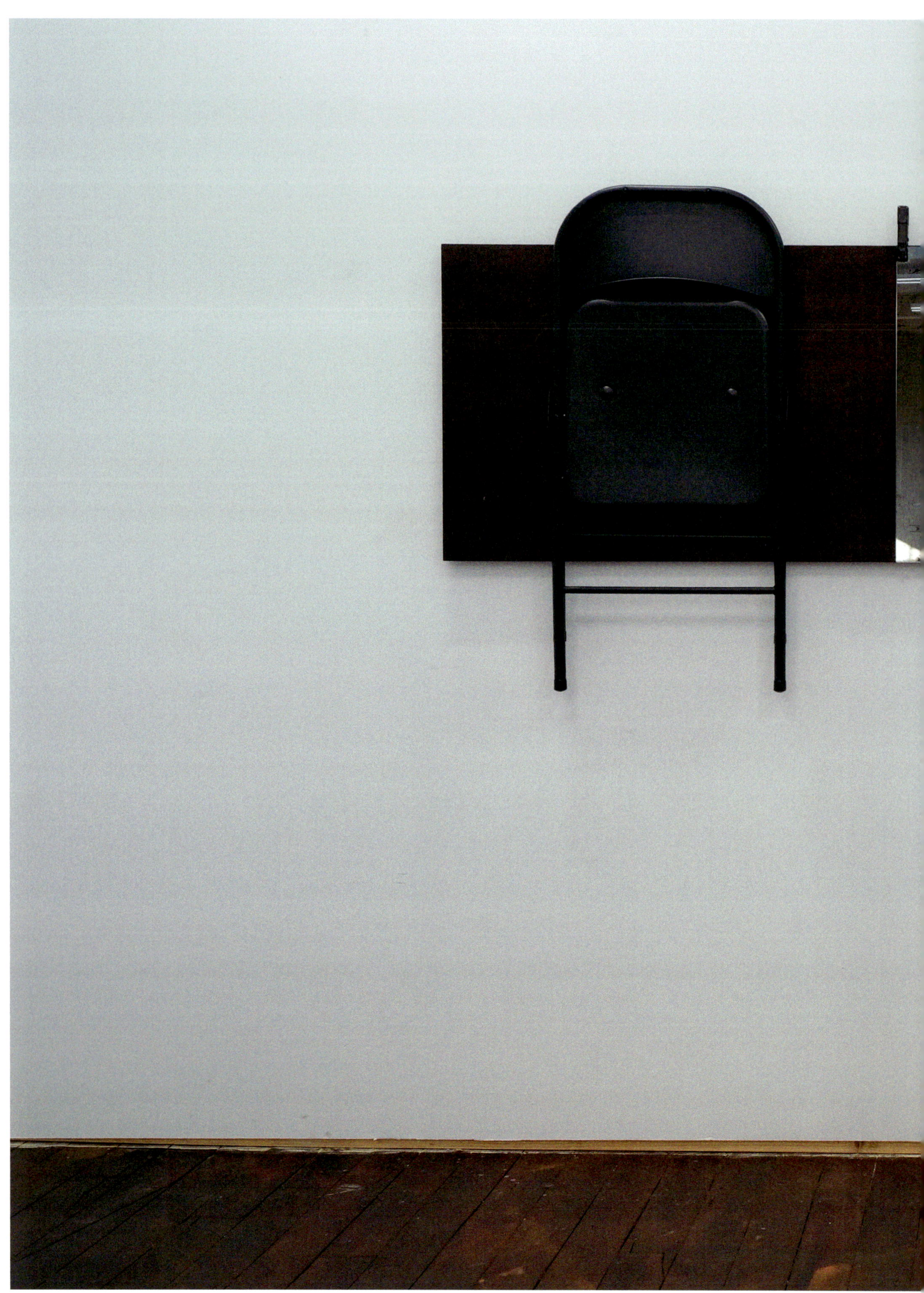

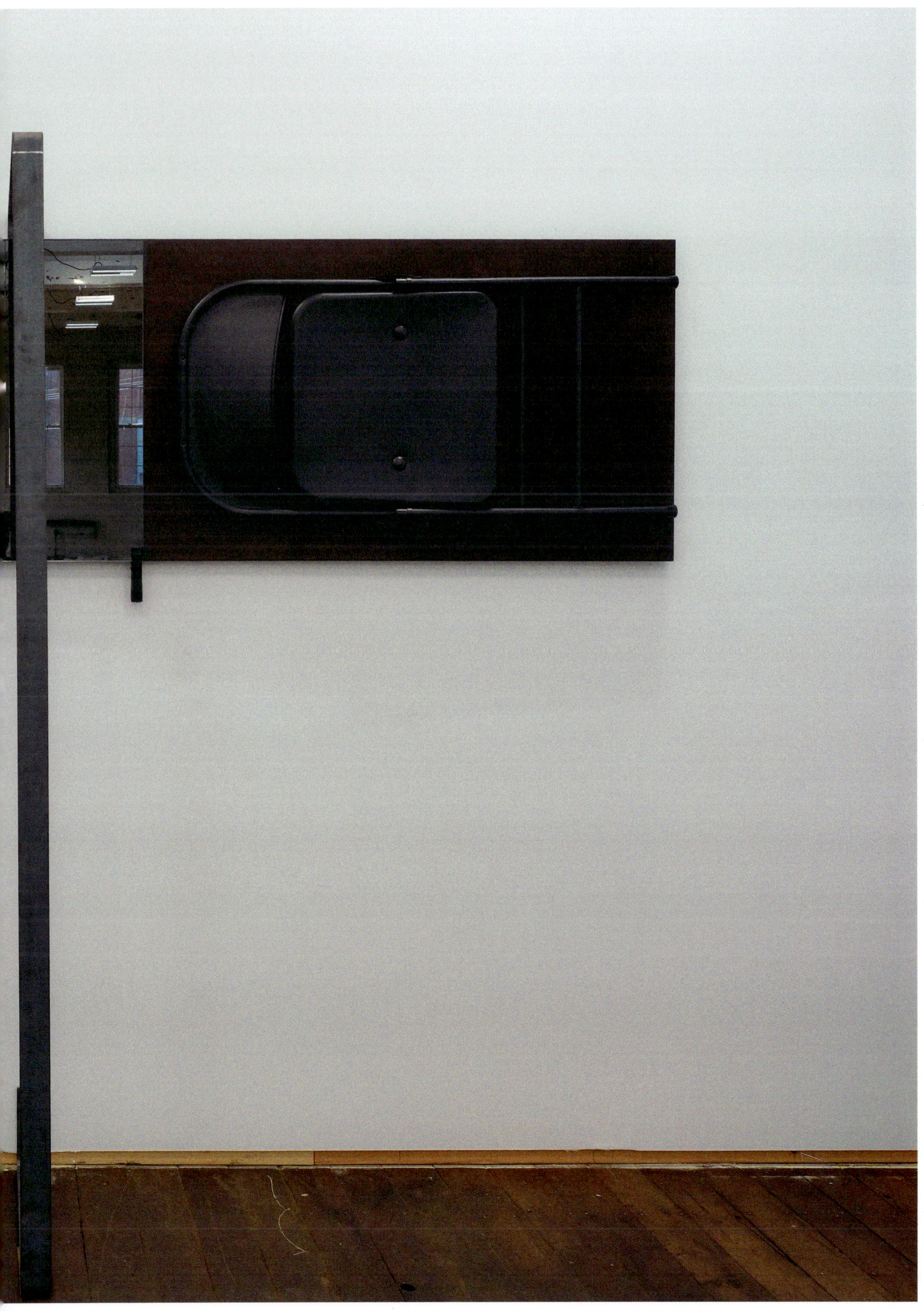

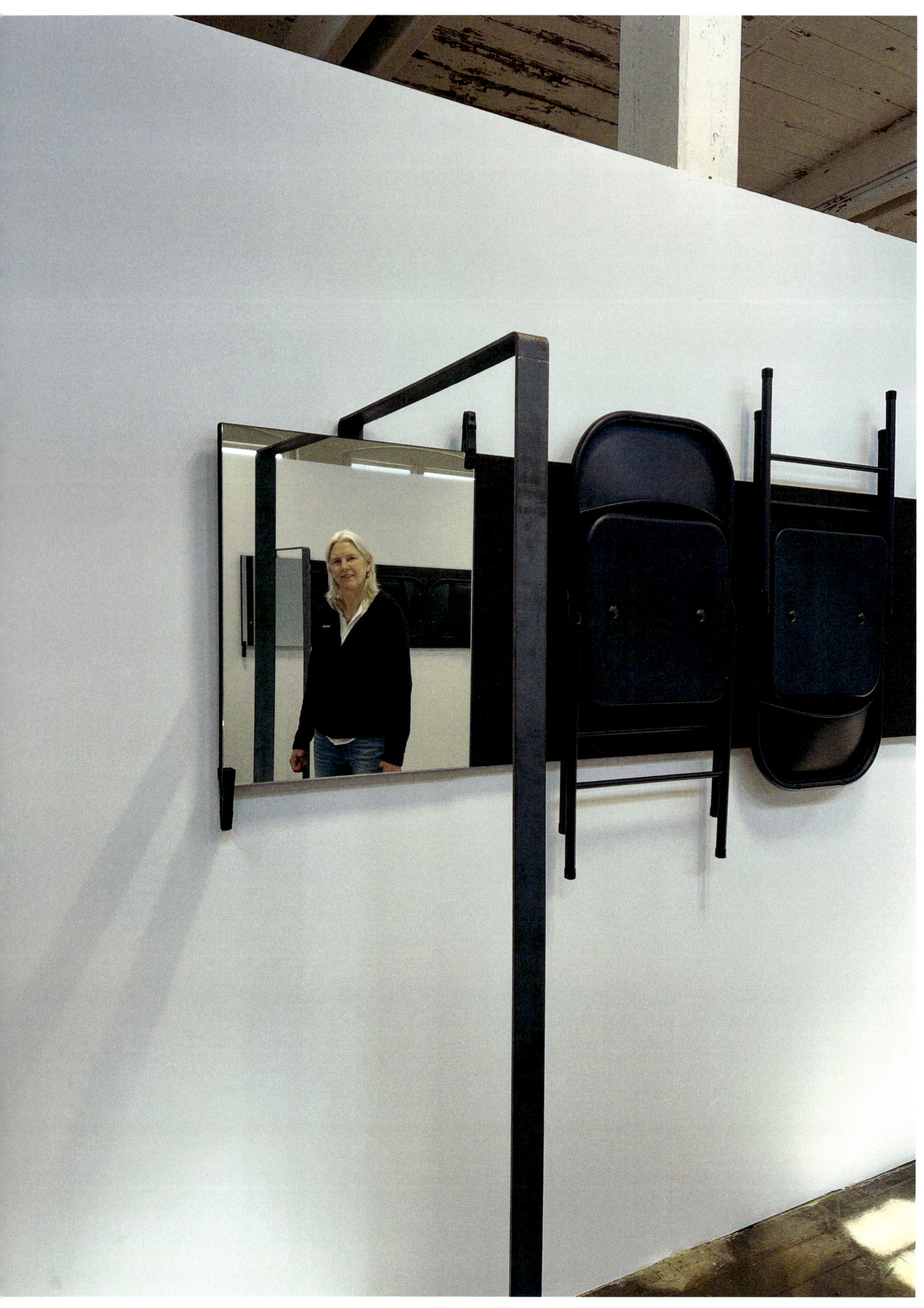

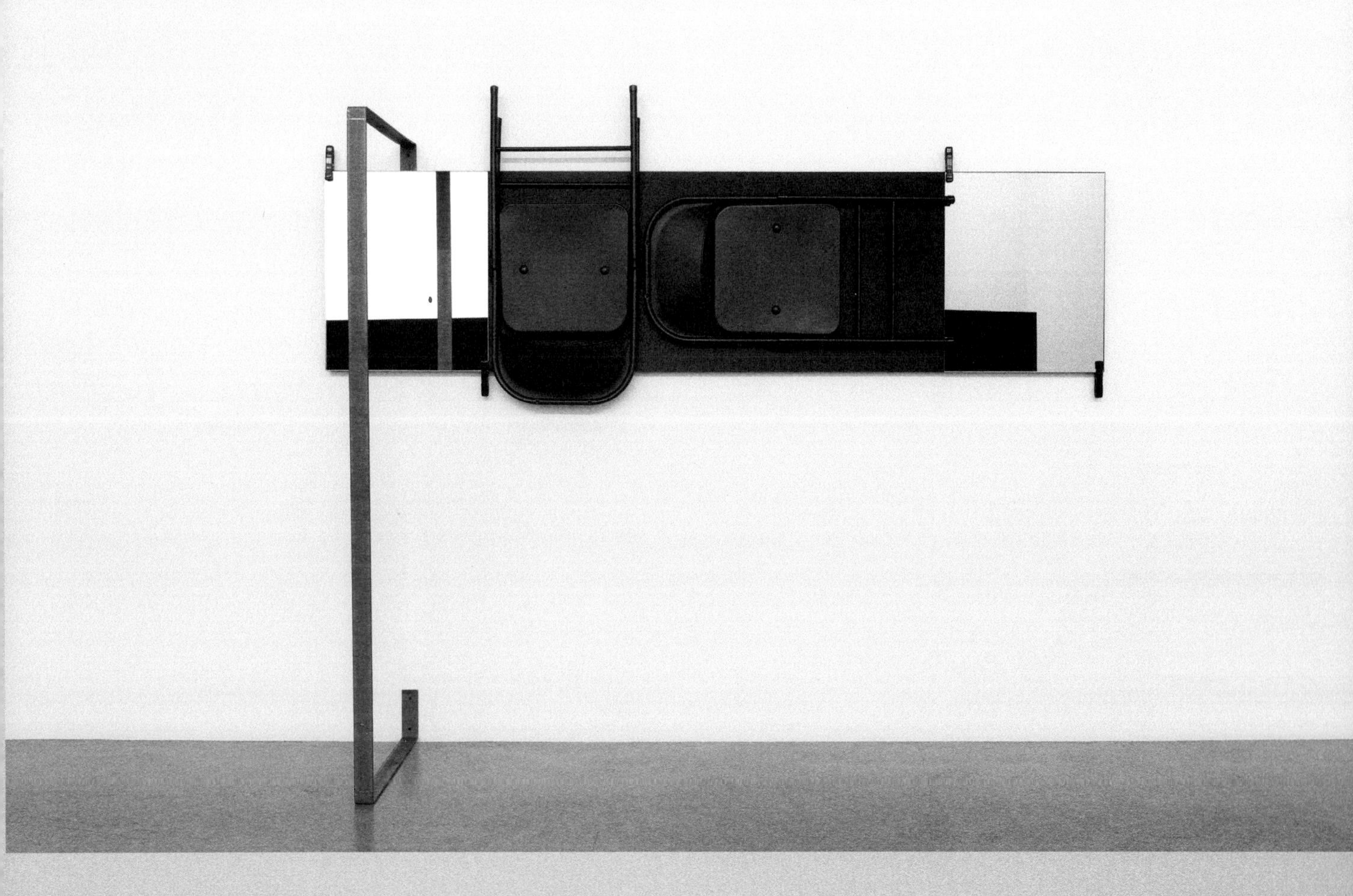

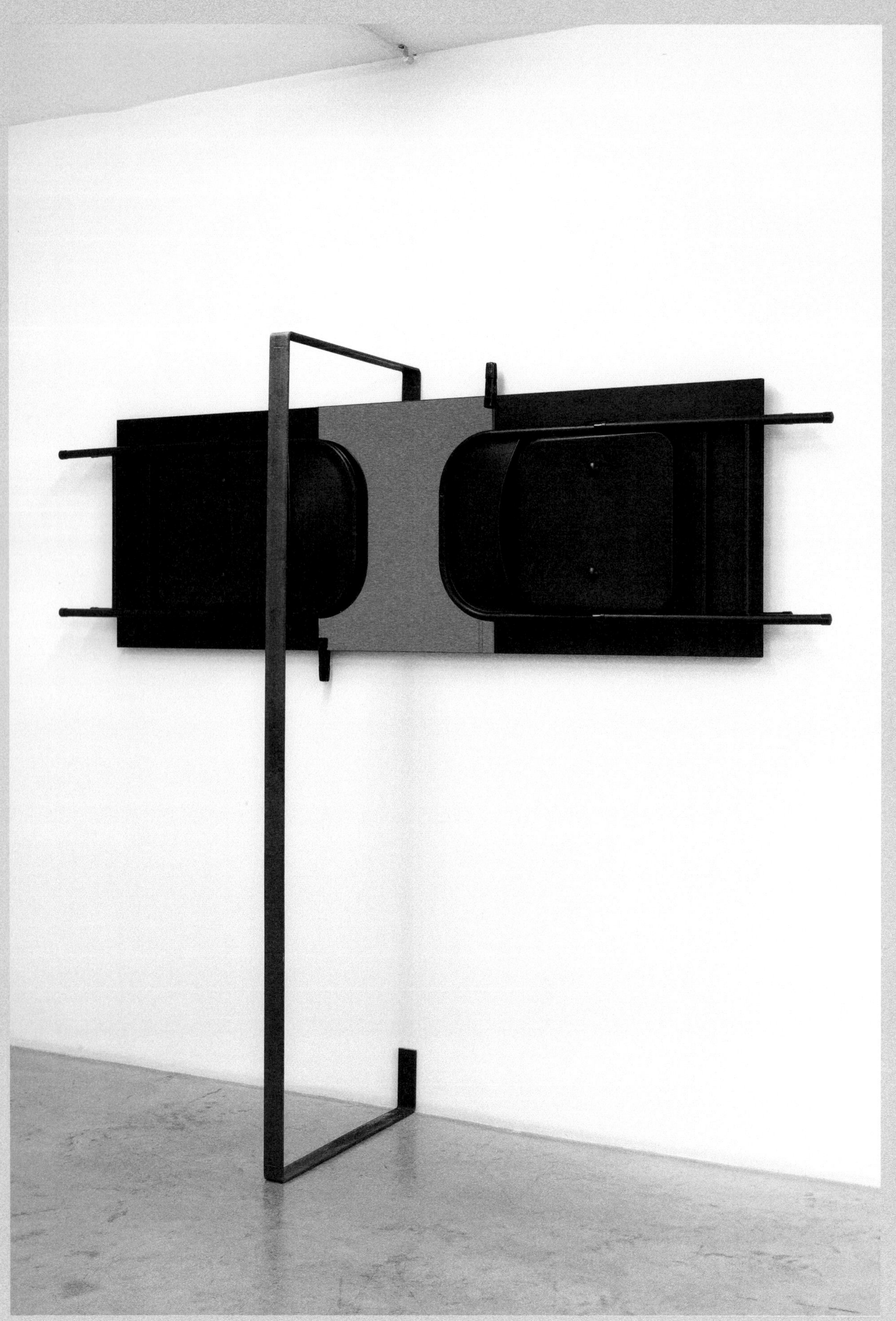

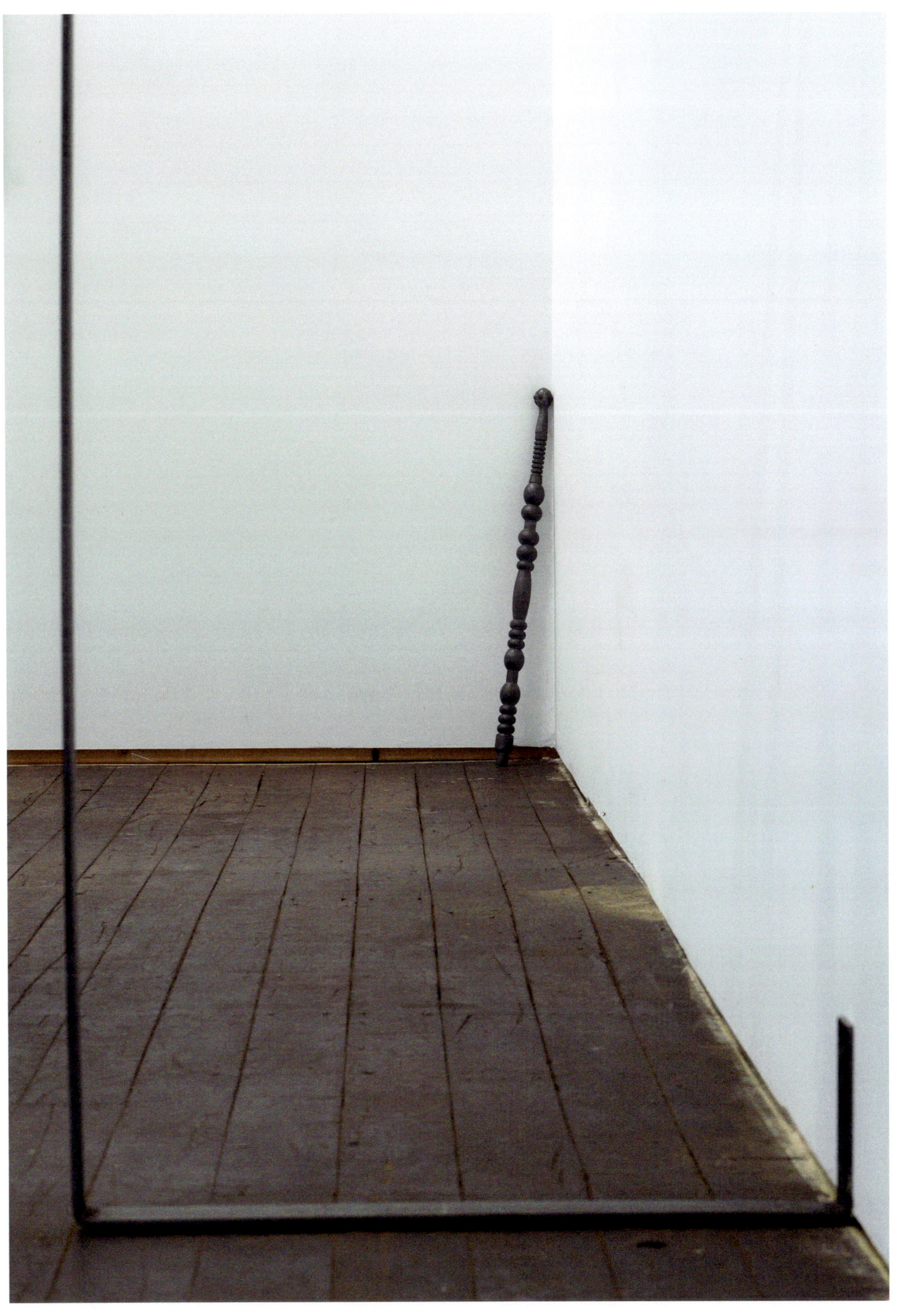

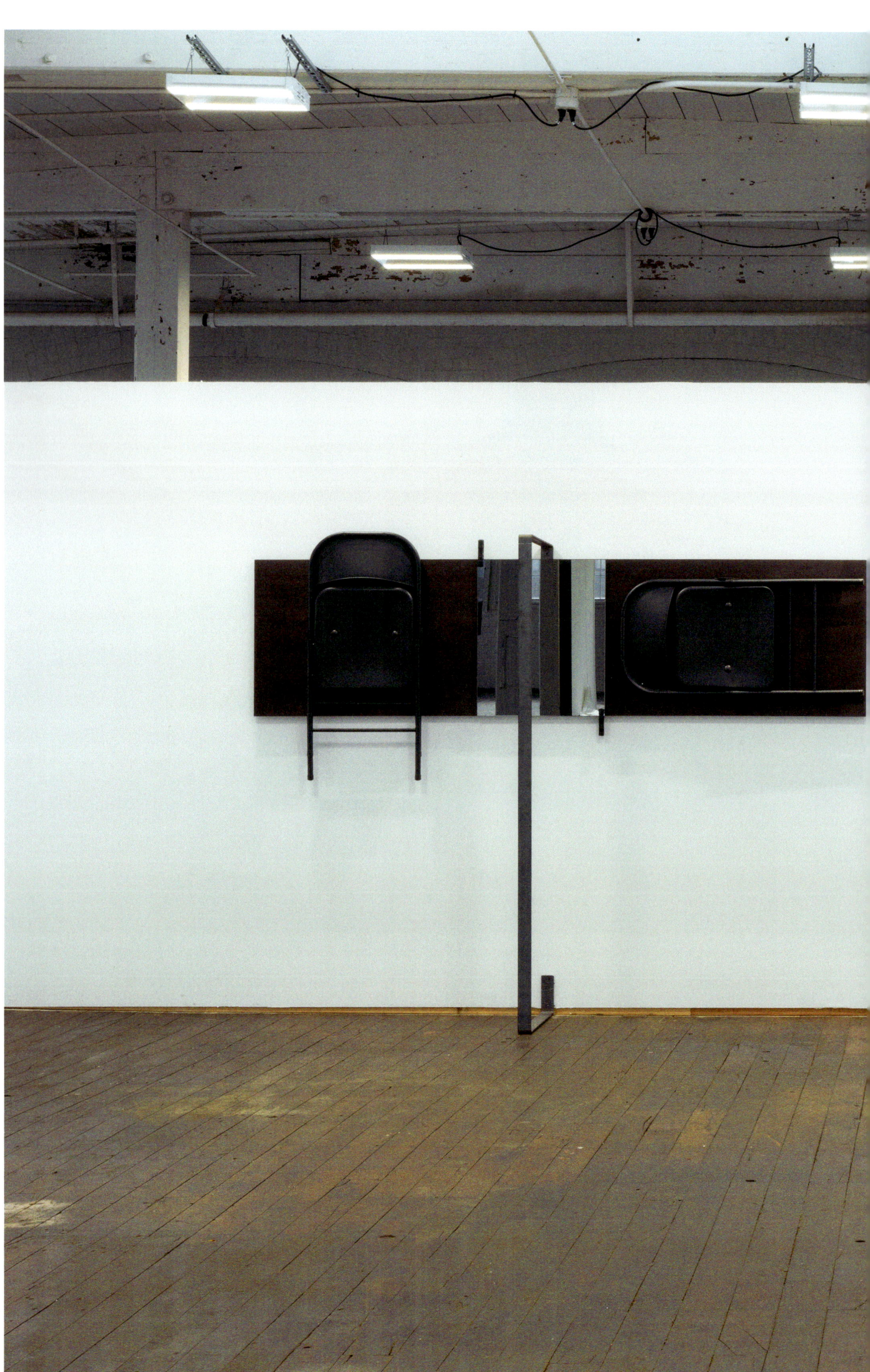

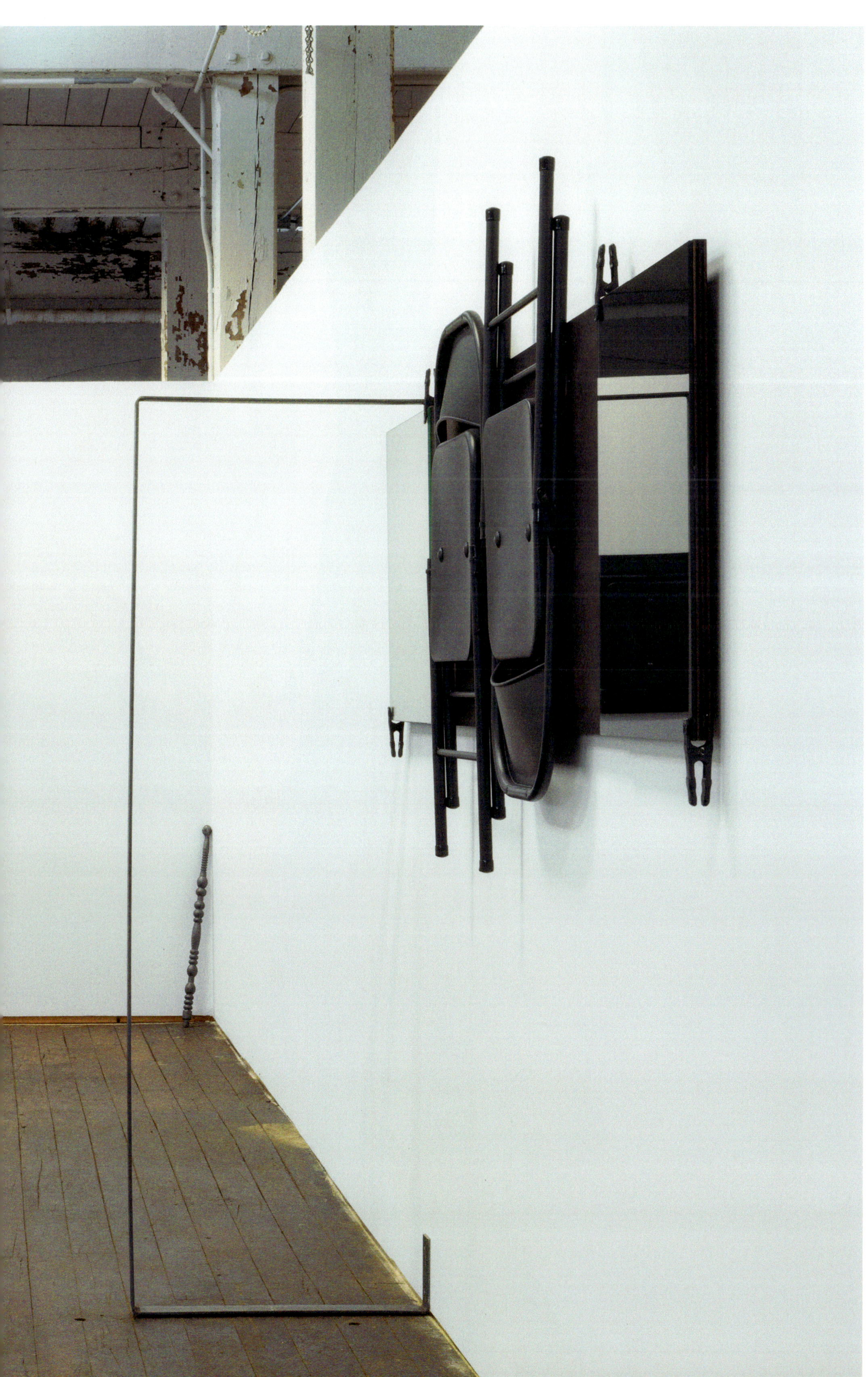

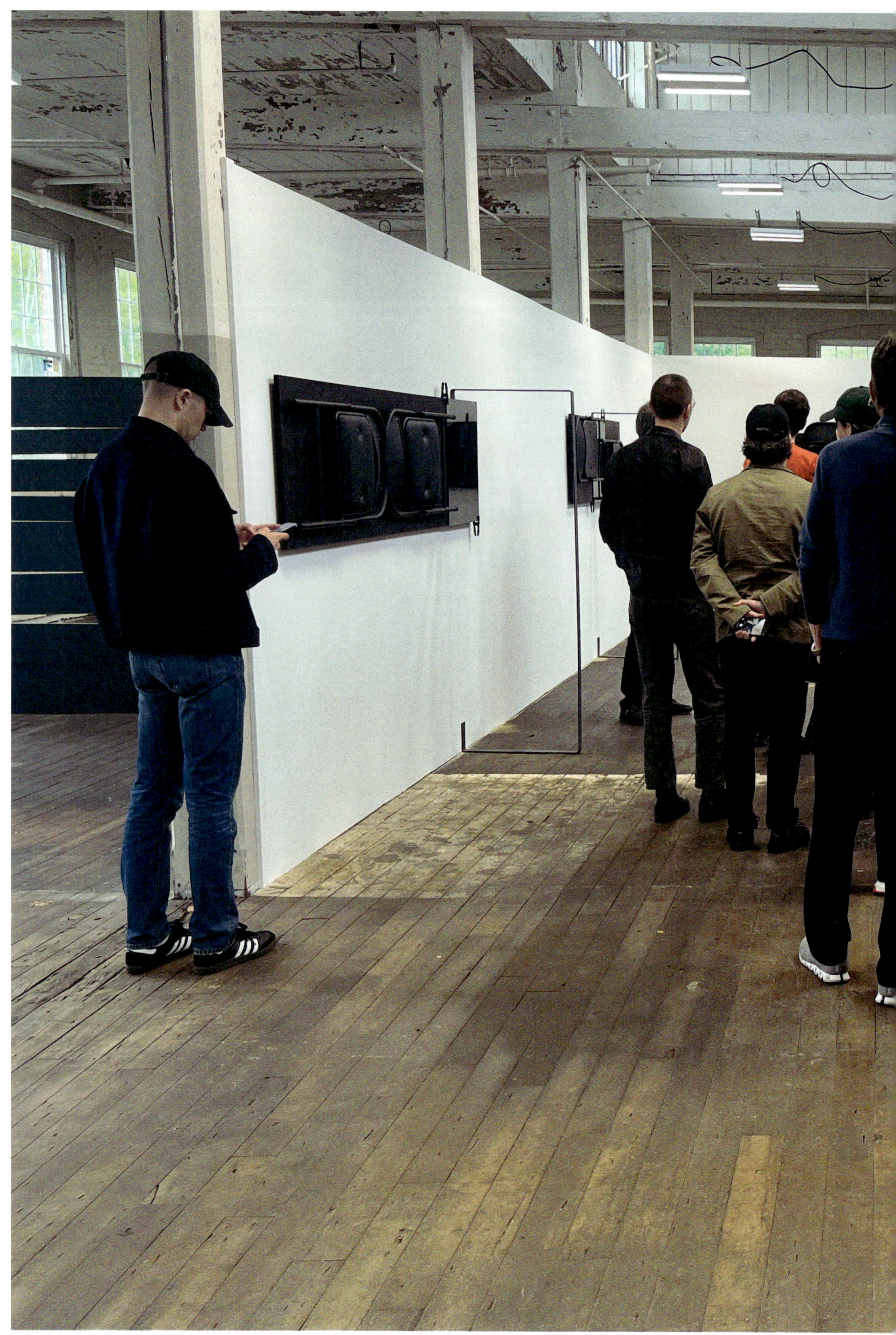

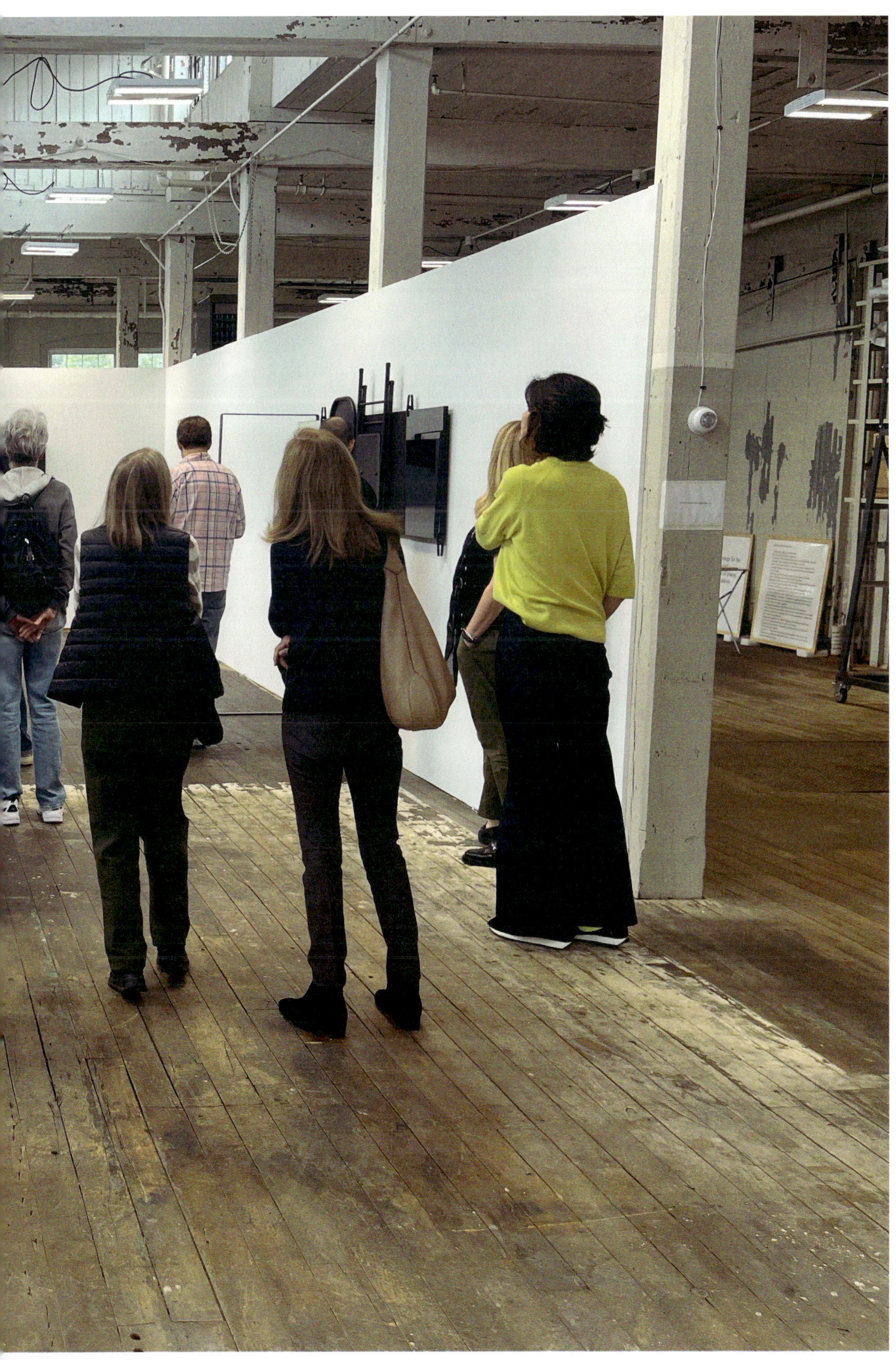

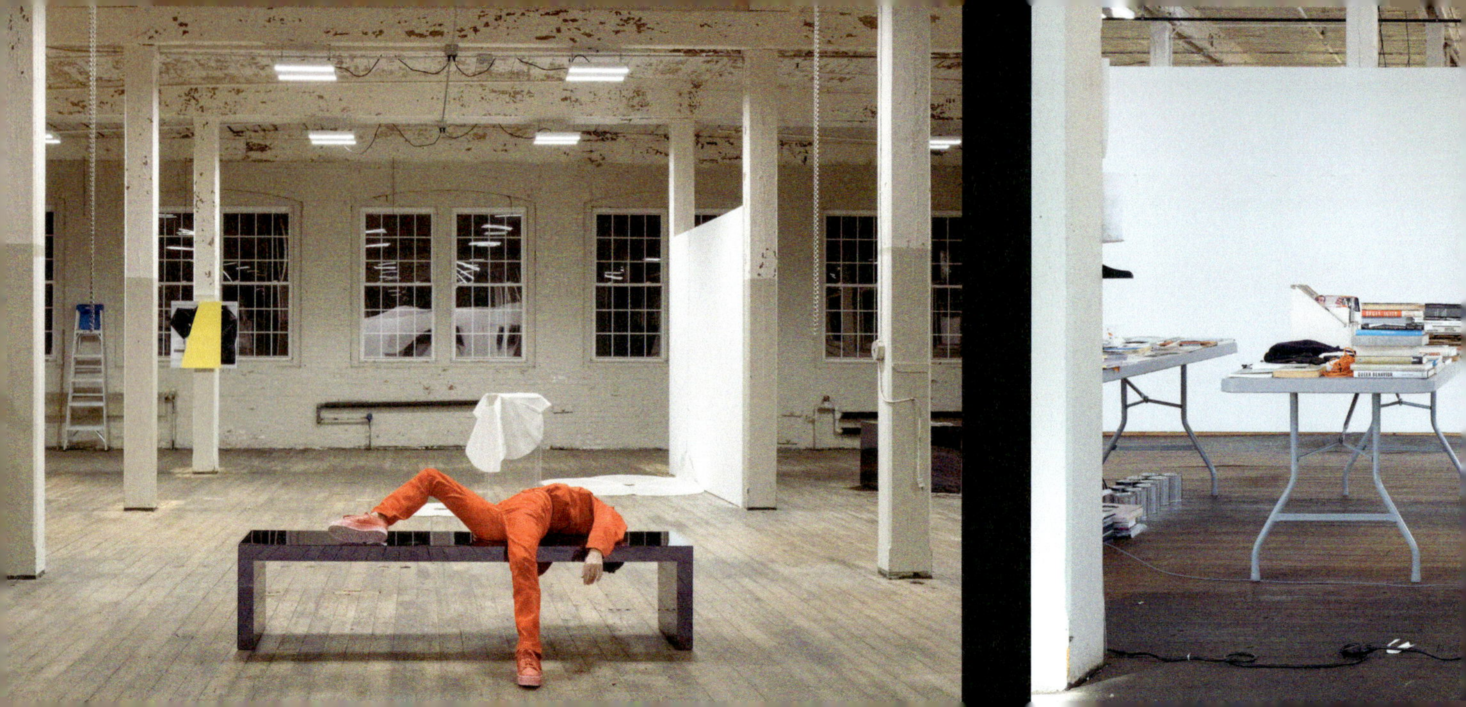

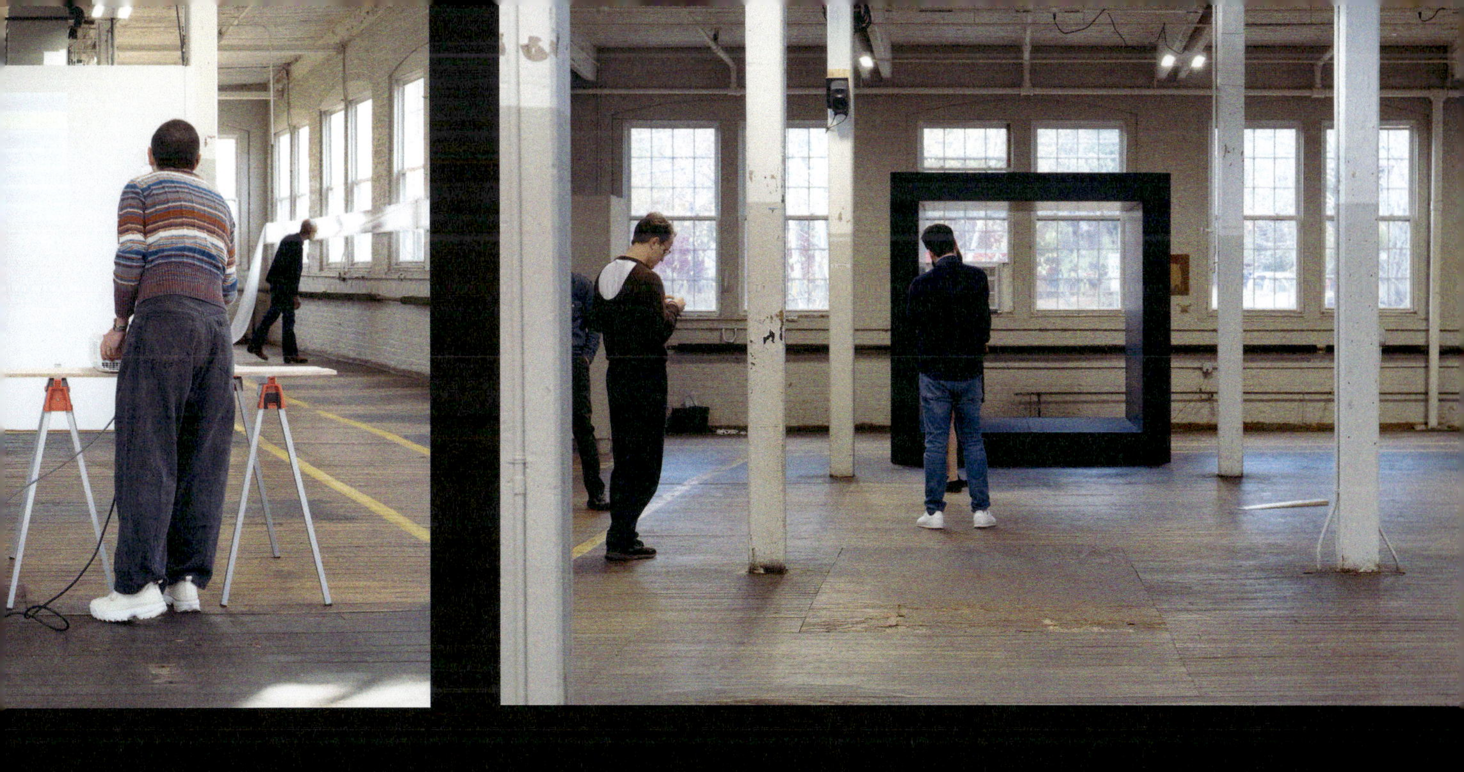

At the end of *Torrington Project*, Maria Hassabi, Gordon Hall, and Nick Mauss were invited to stage performances that responded to the conceptual and physical dimensions of the space. On October 26, 2024, they showcased their work to a small audience. The night before, Hassabi practiced her

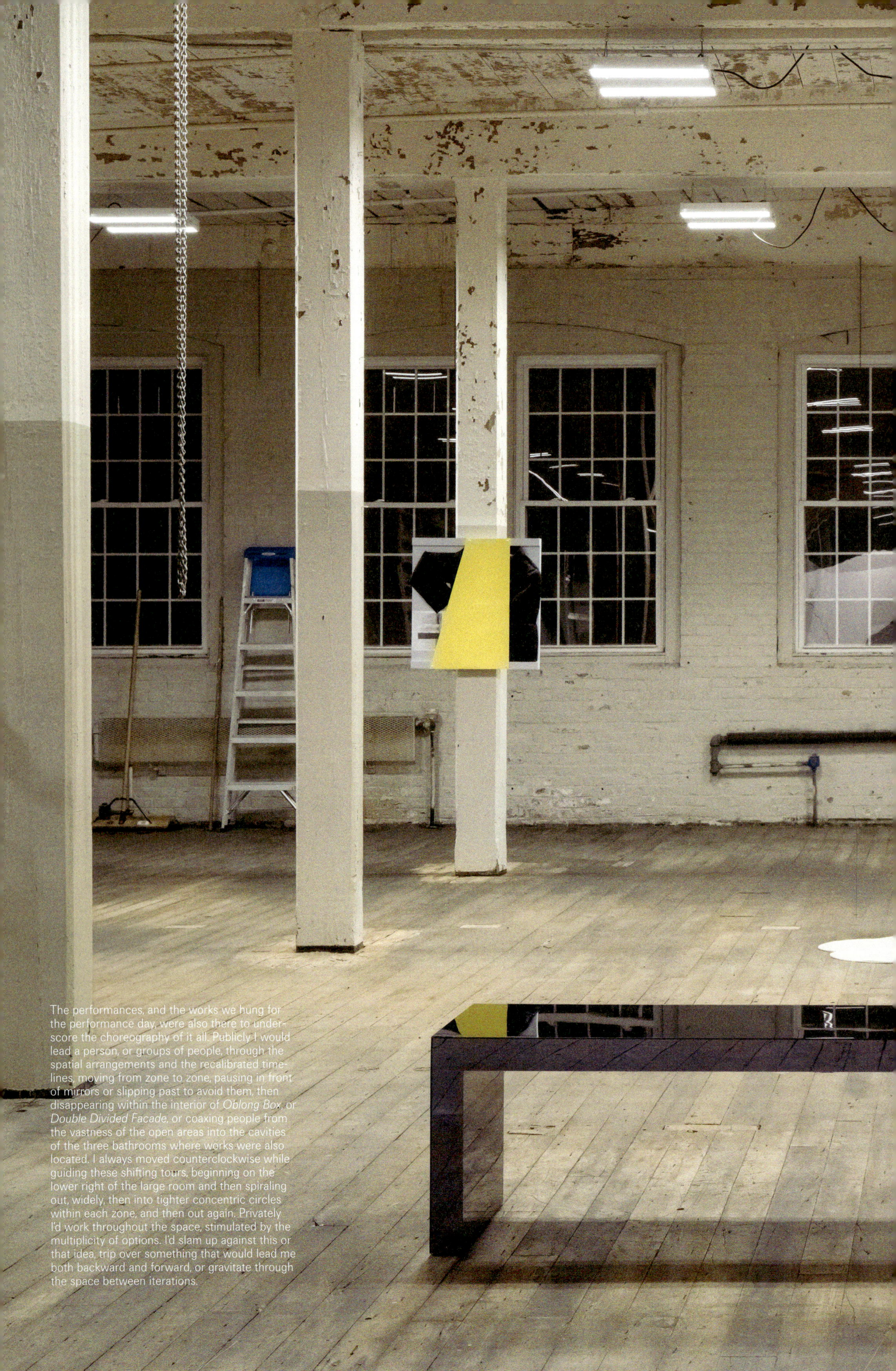

The performances, and the works we hung for the performance day, were also there to underscore the choreography of it all. Publicly I would lead a person, or groups of people, through the spatial arrangements and the recalibrated timelines, moving from zone to zone, pausing in front of mirrors or slipping past to avoid them, then disappearing within the interior of *Oblong Box*, or *Double Divided Facade*, or coaxing people from the vastness of the open areas into the cavities of the three bathrooms where works were also located. I always moved counterclockwise while guiding these shifting tours, beginning on the lower right of the large room and then spiraling out, widely, then into tighter concentric circles within each zone, and then out again. Privately I'd work throughout the space, stimulated by the multiplicity of options. I'd slam up against this or that idea, trip over something that would lead me both backward and forward, or gravitate through the space between iterations.

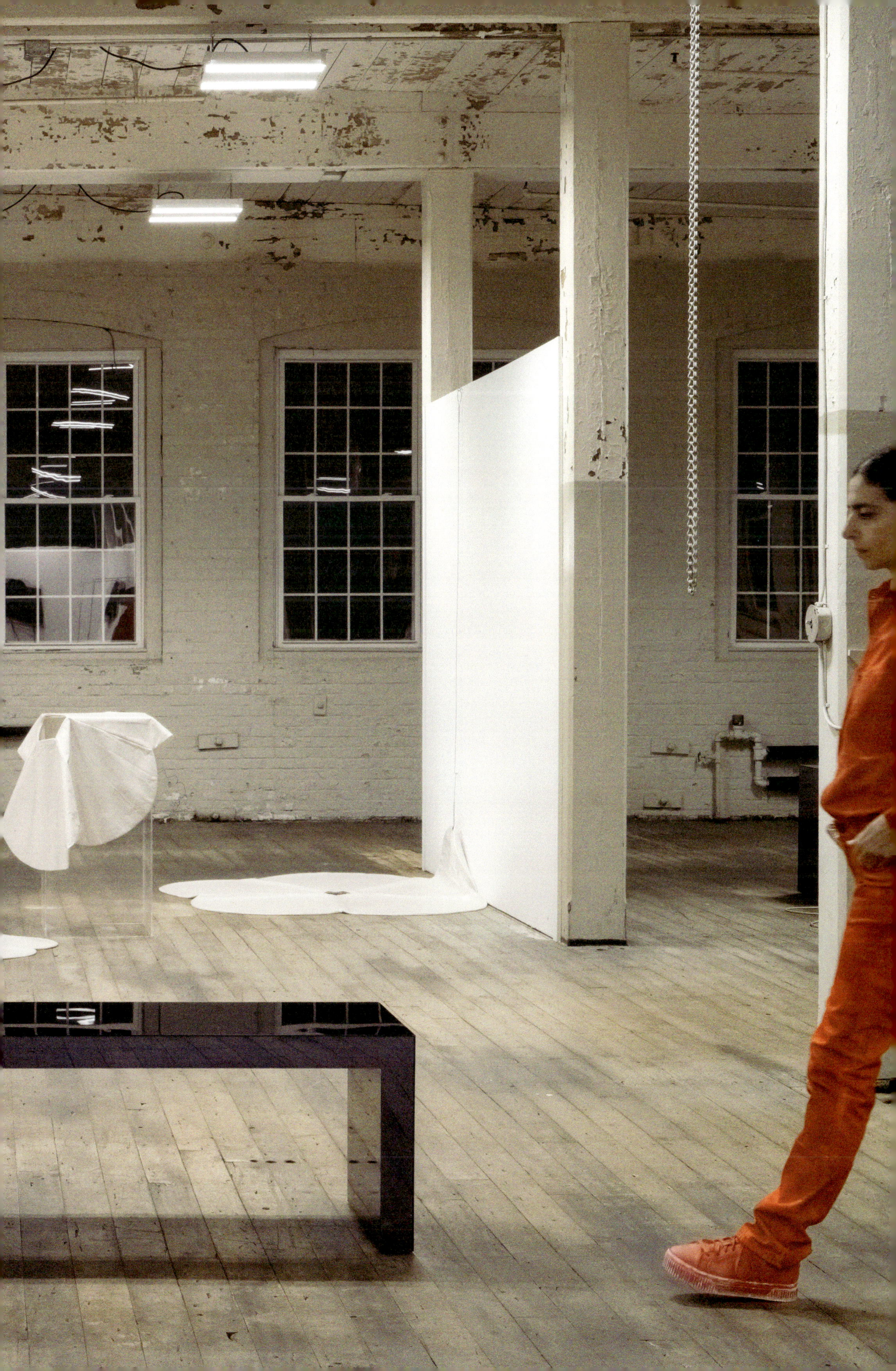

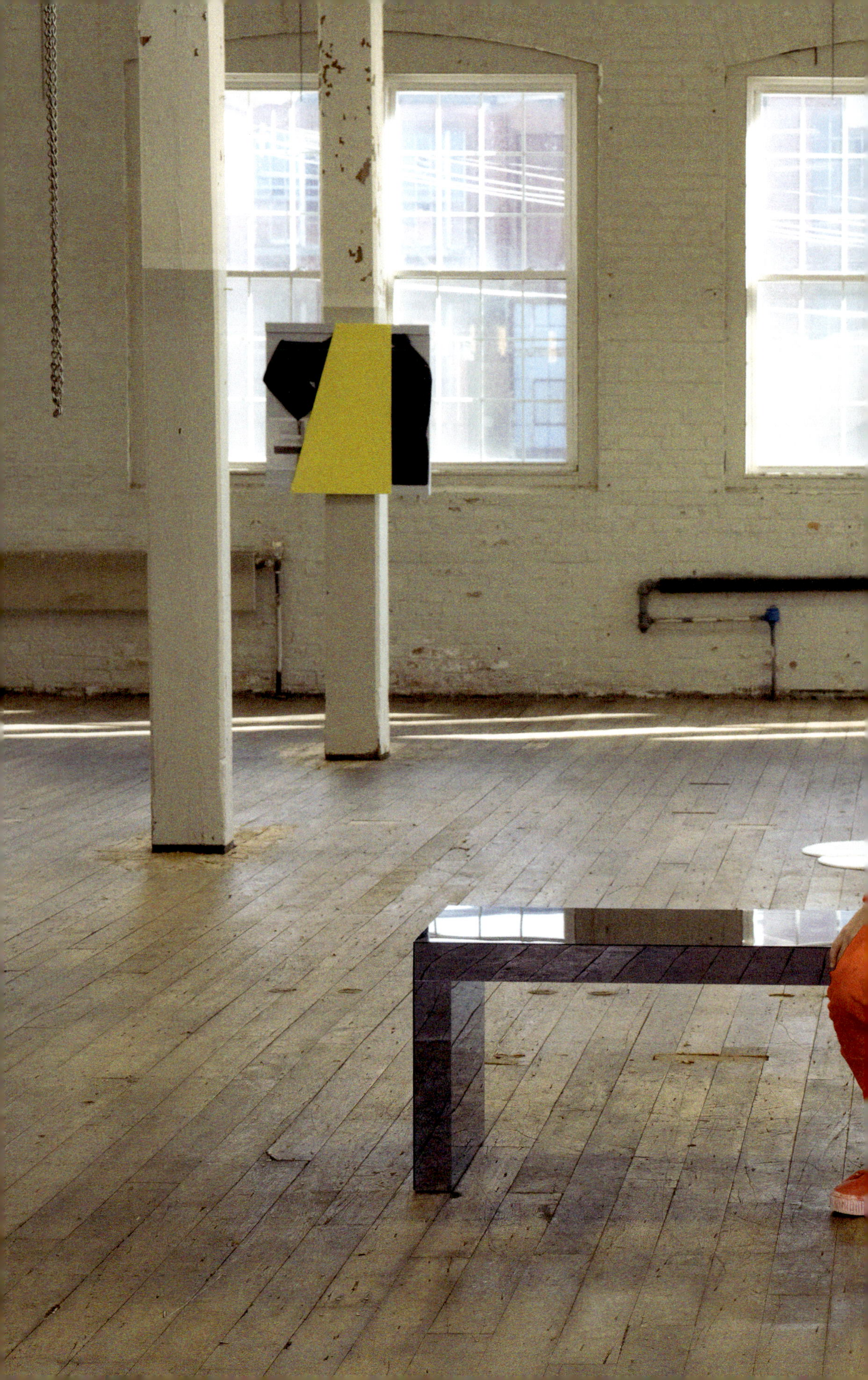

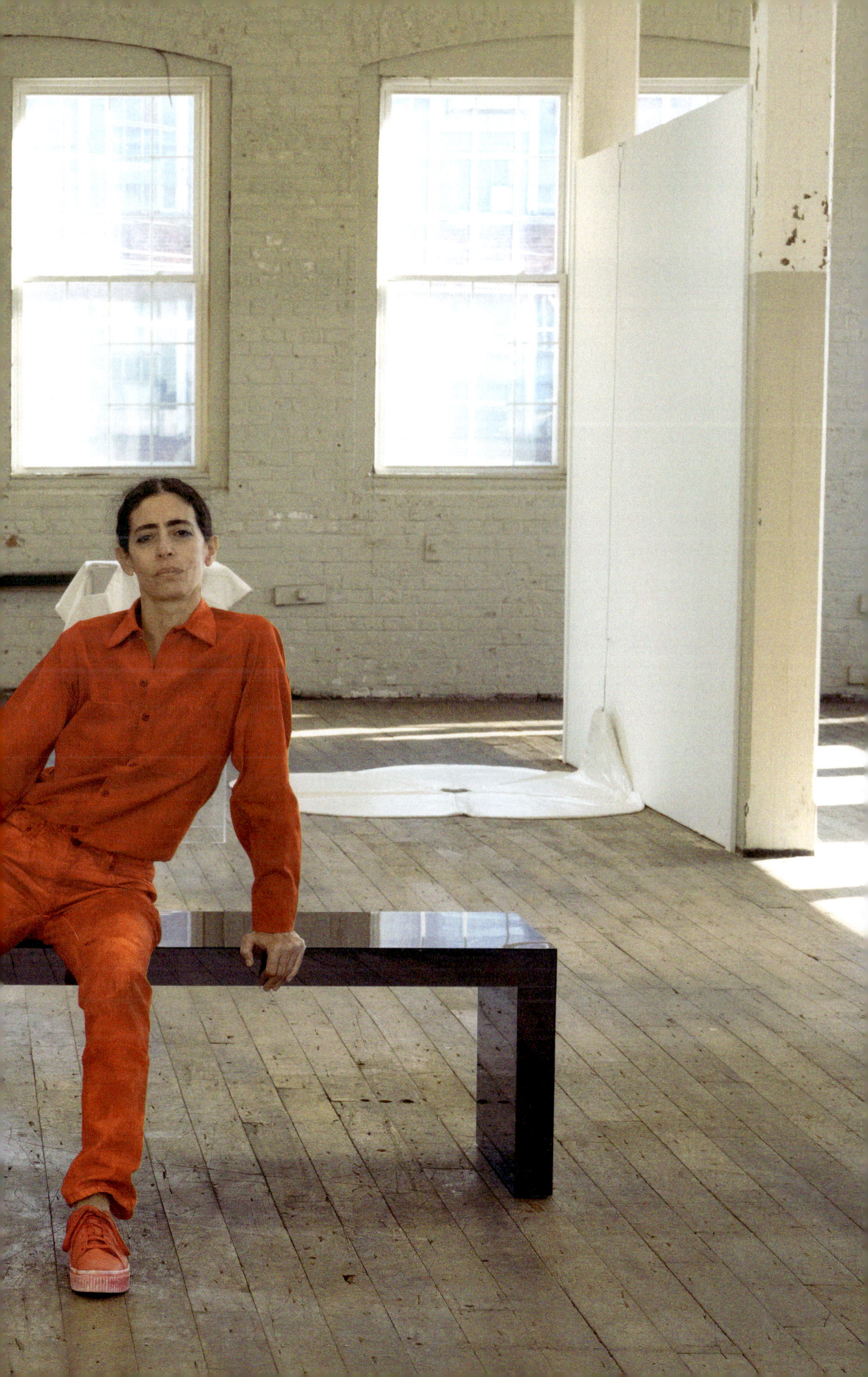

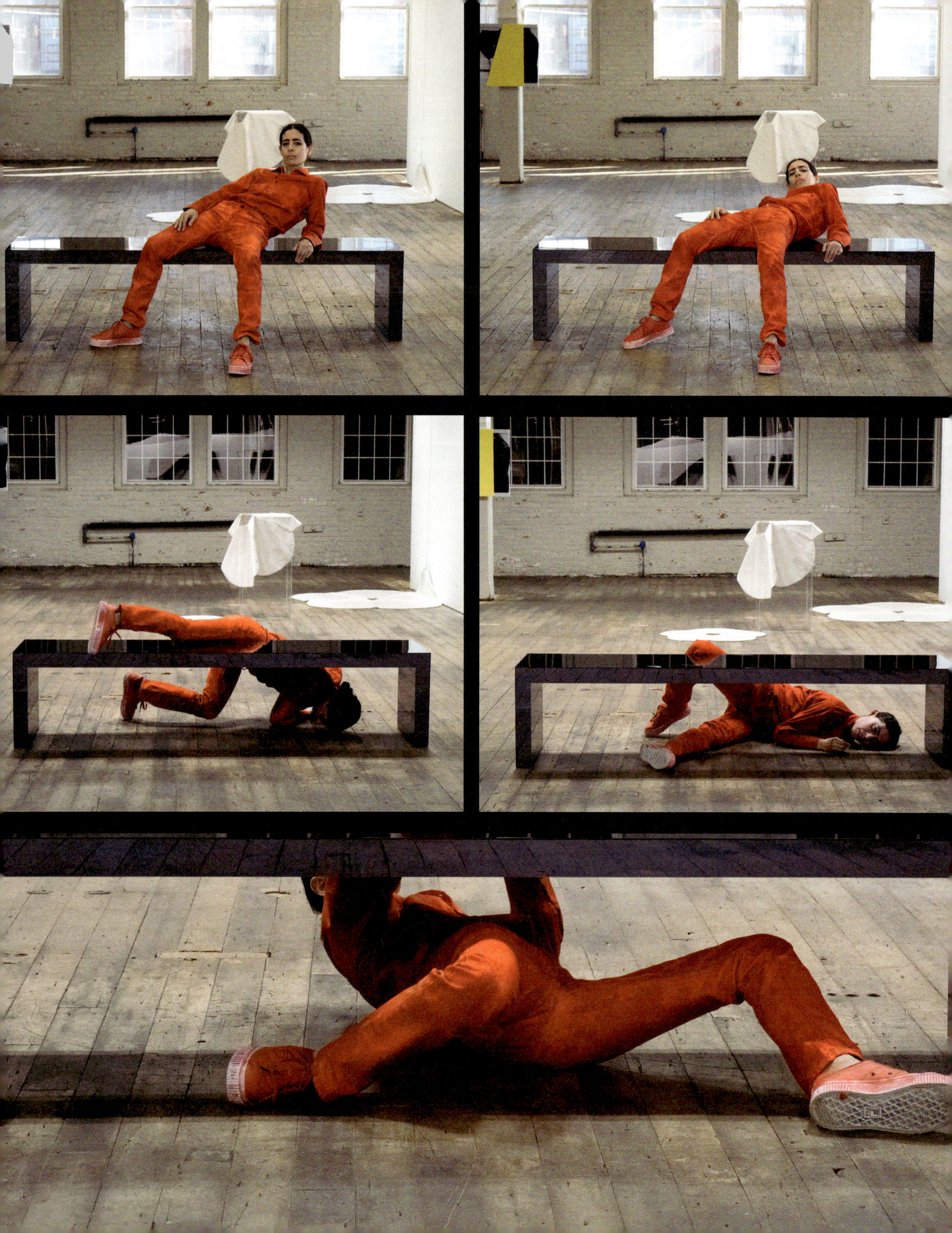

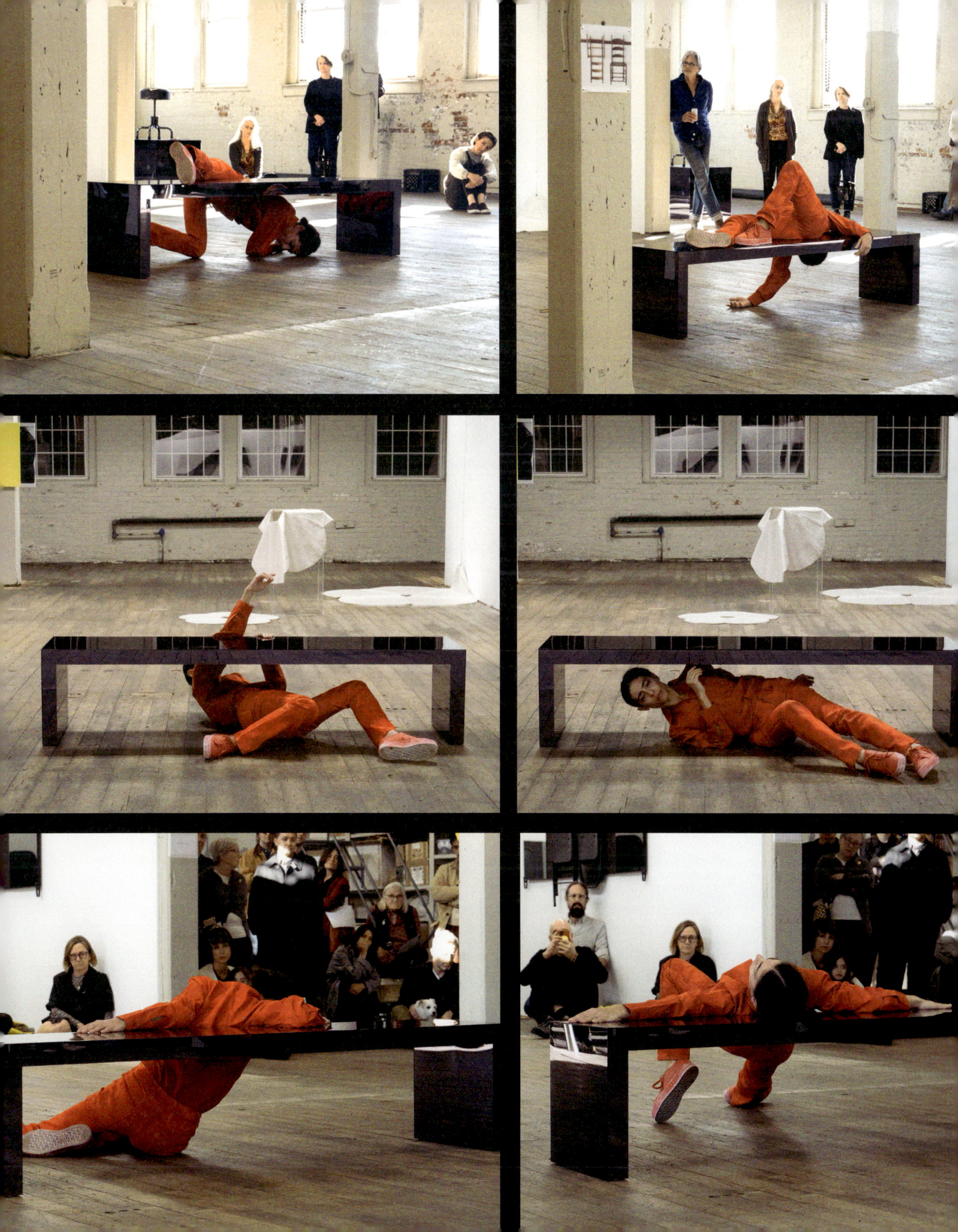

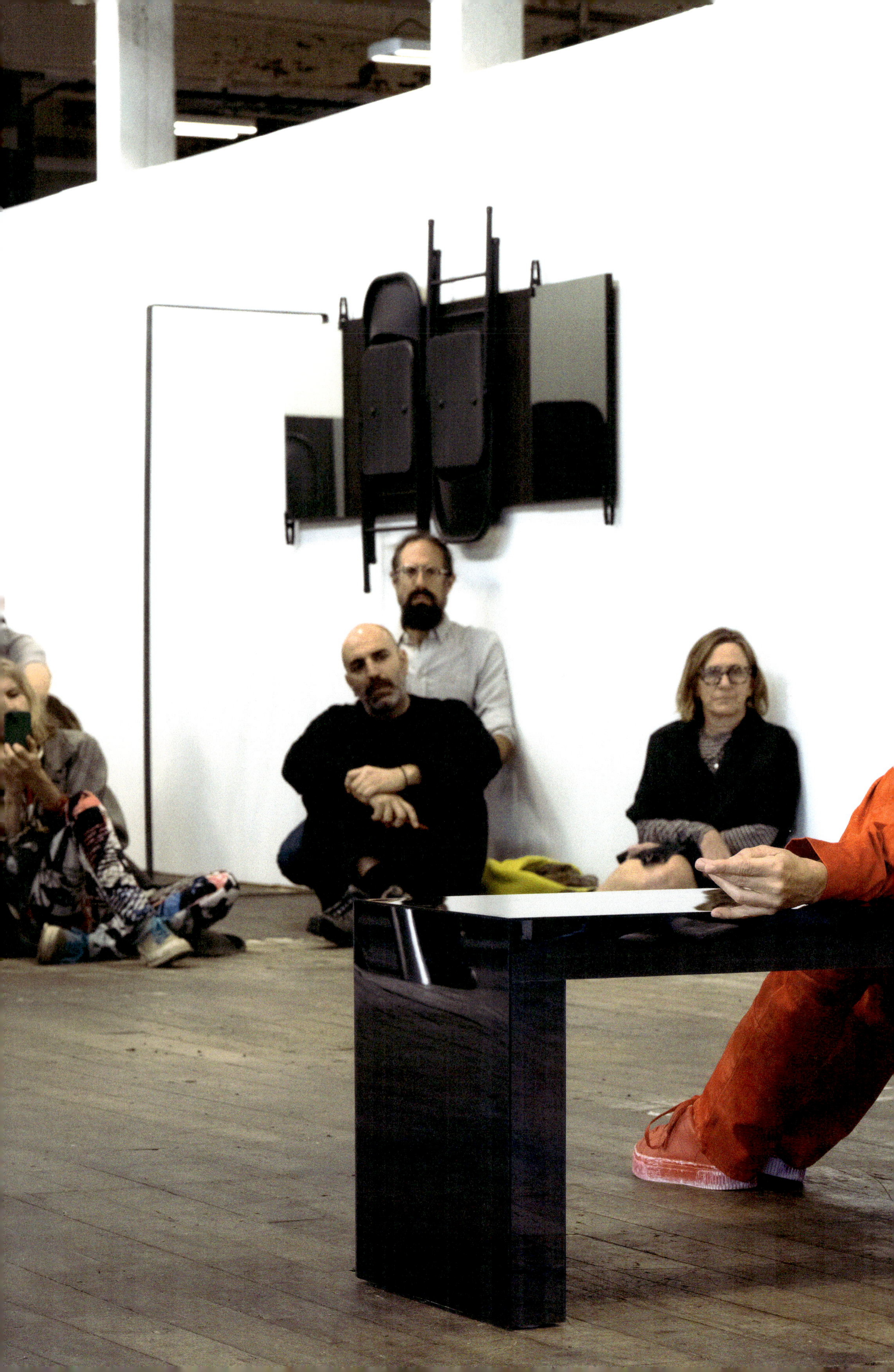

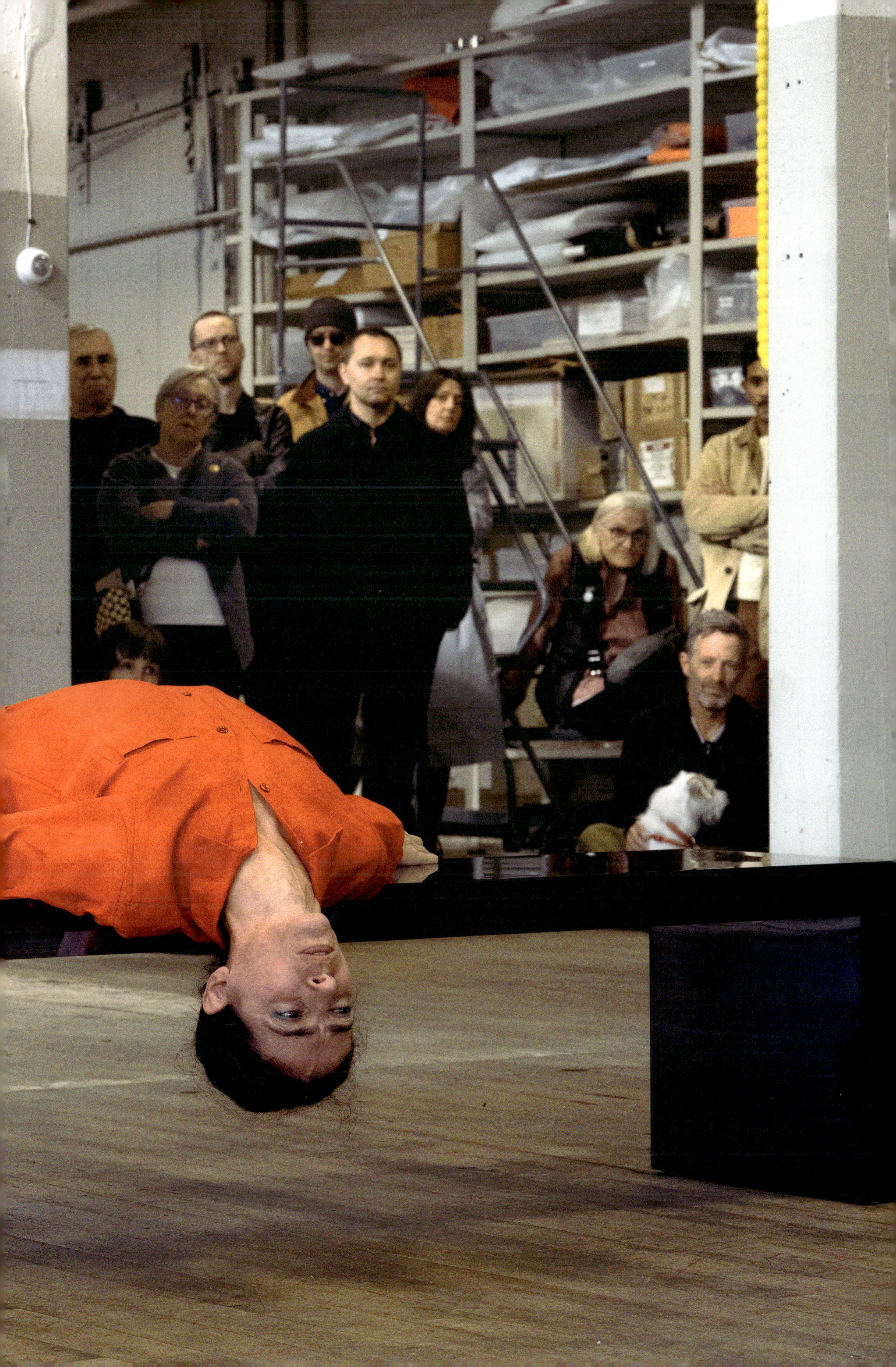

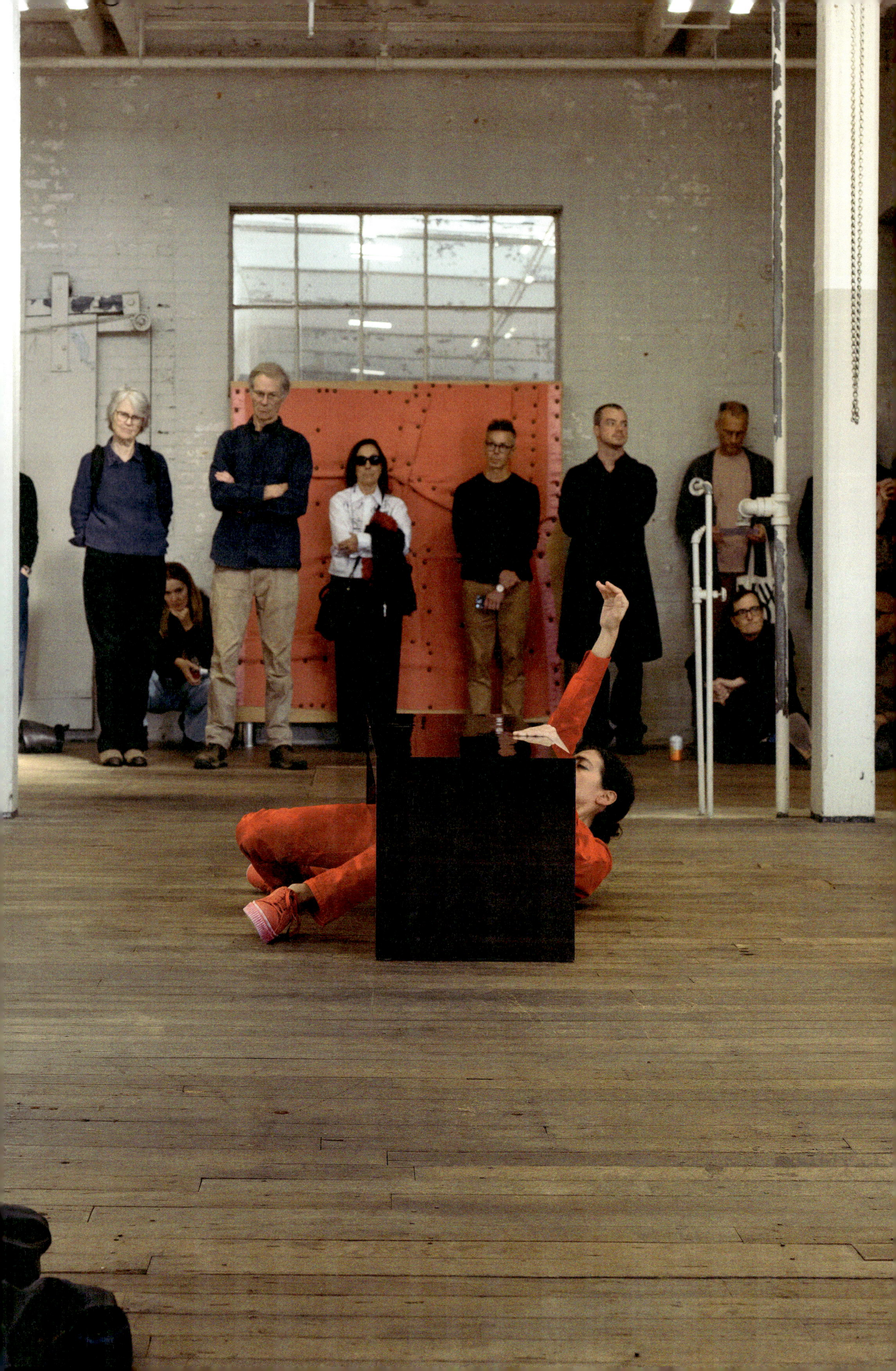

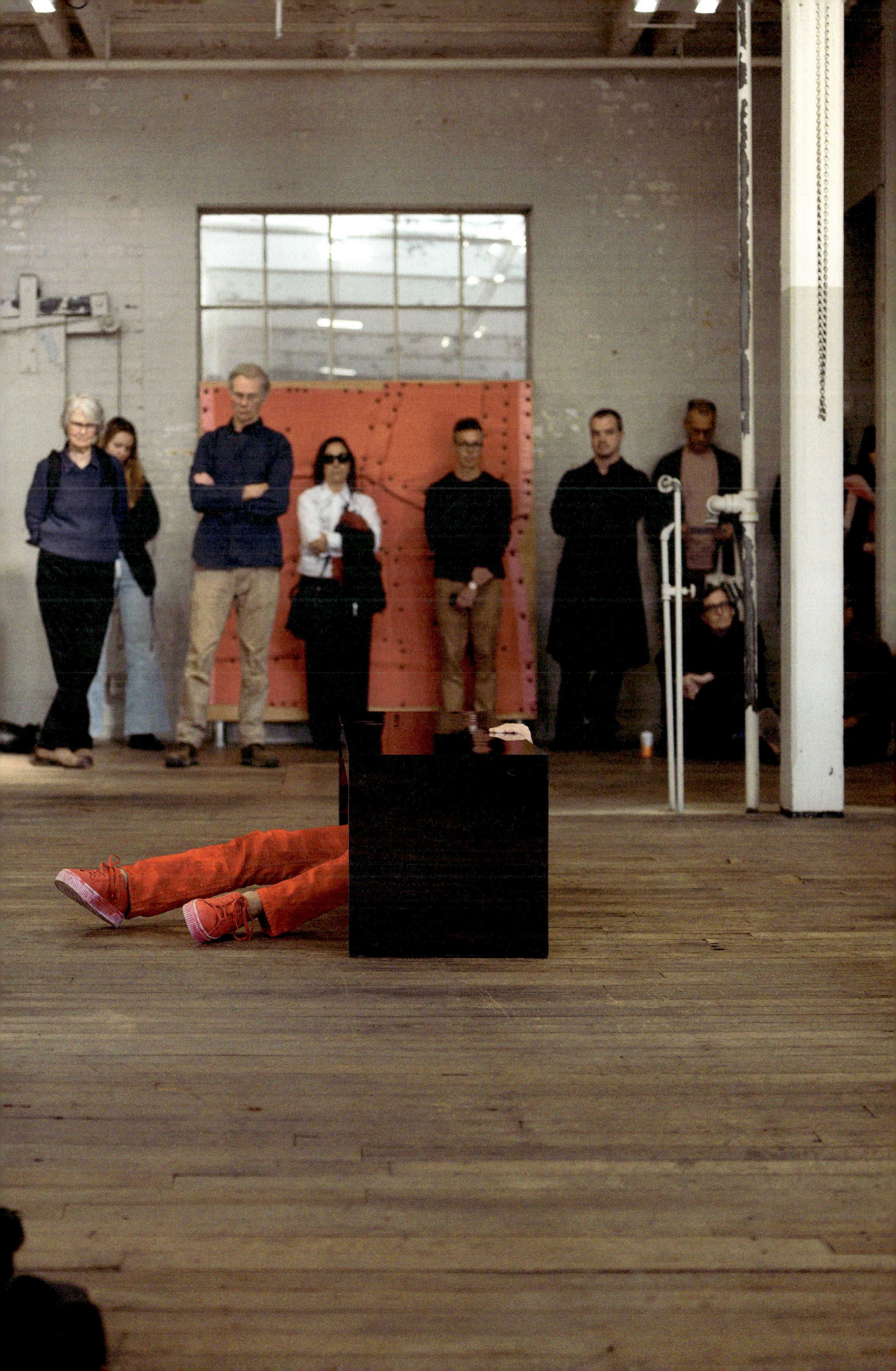

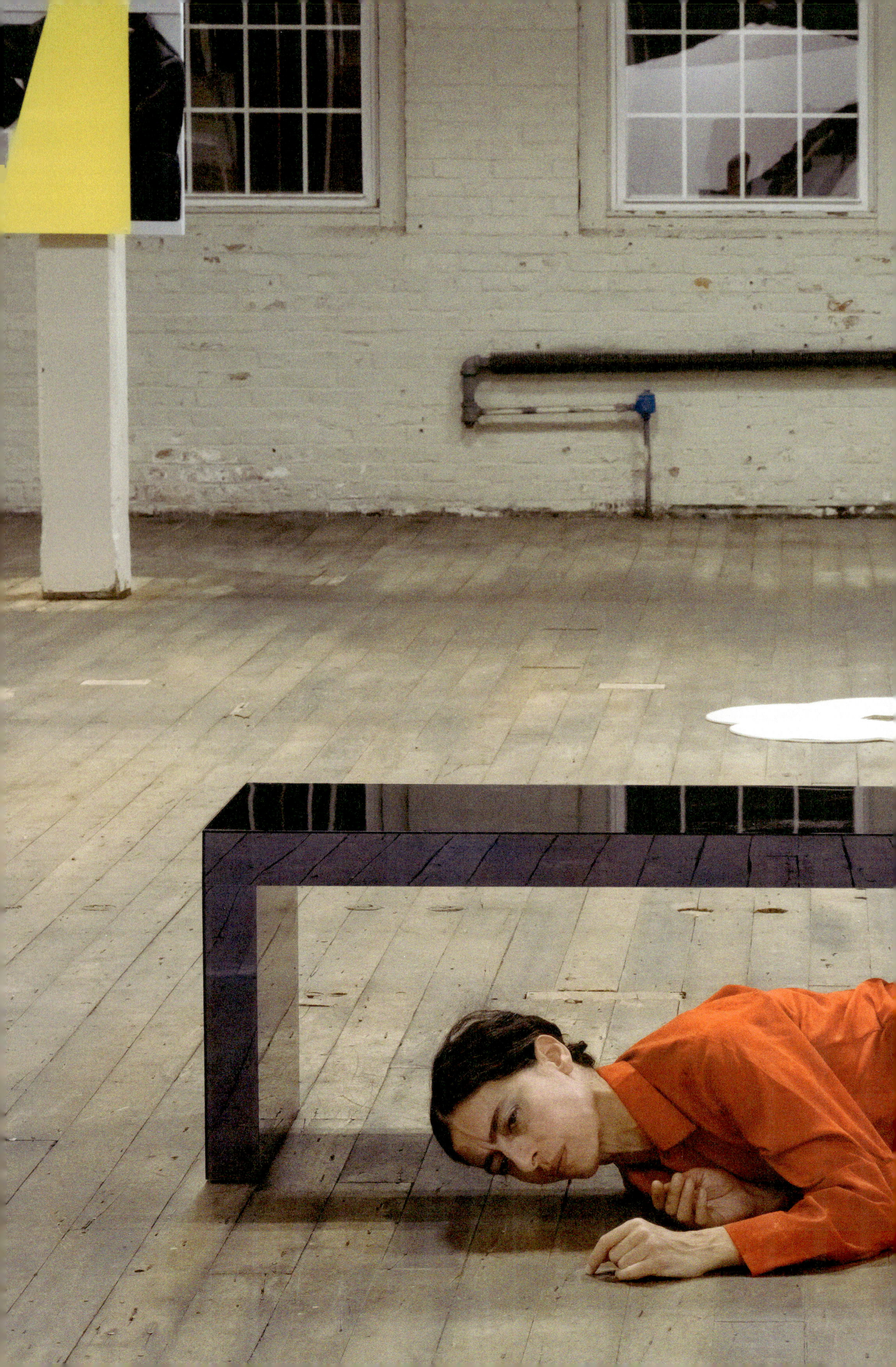

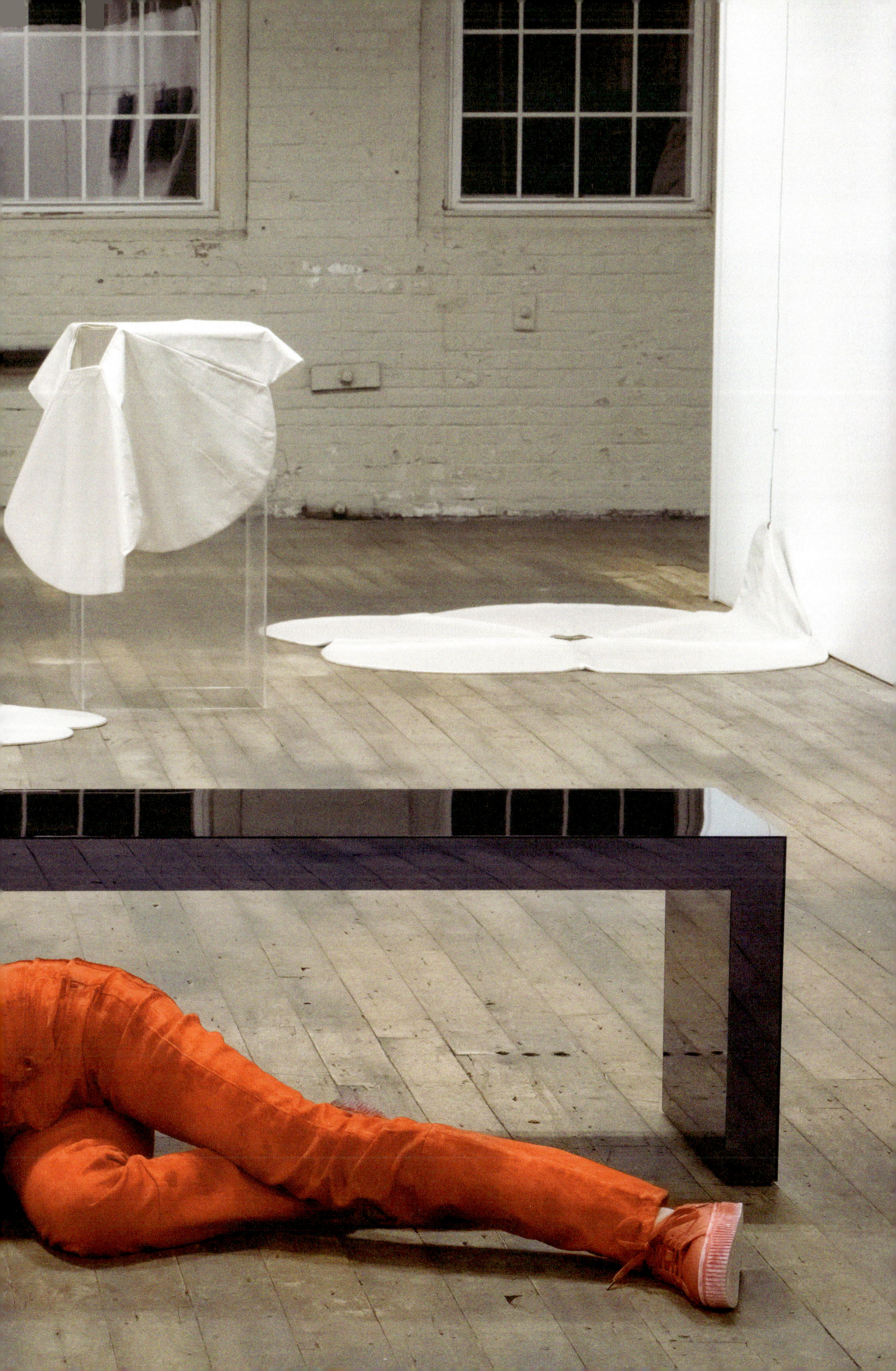

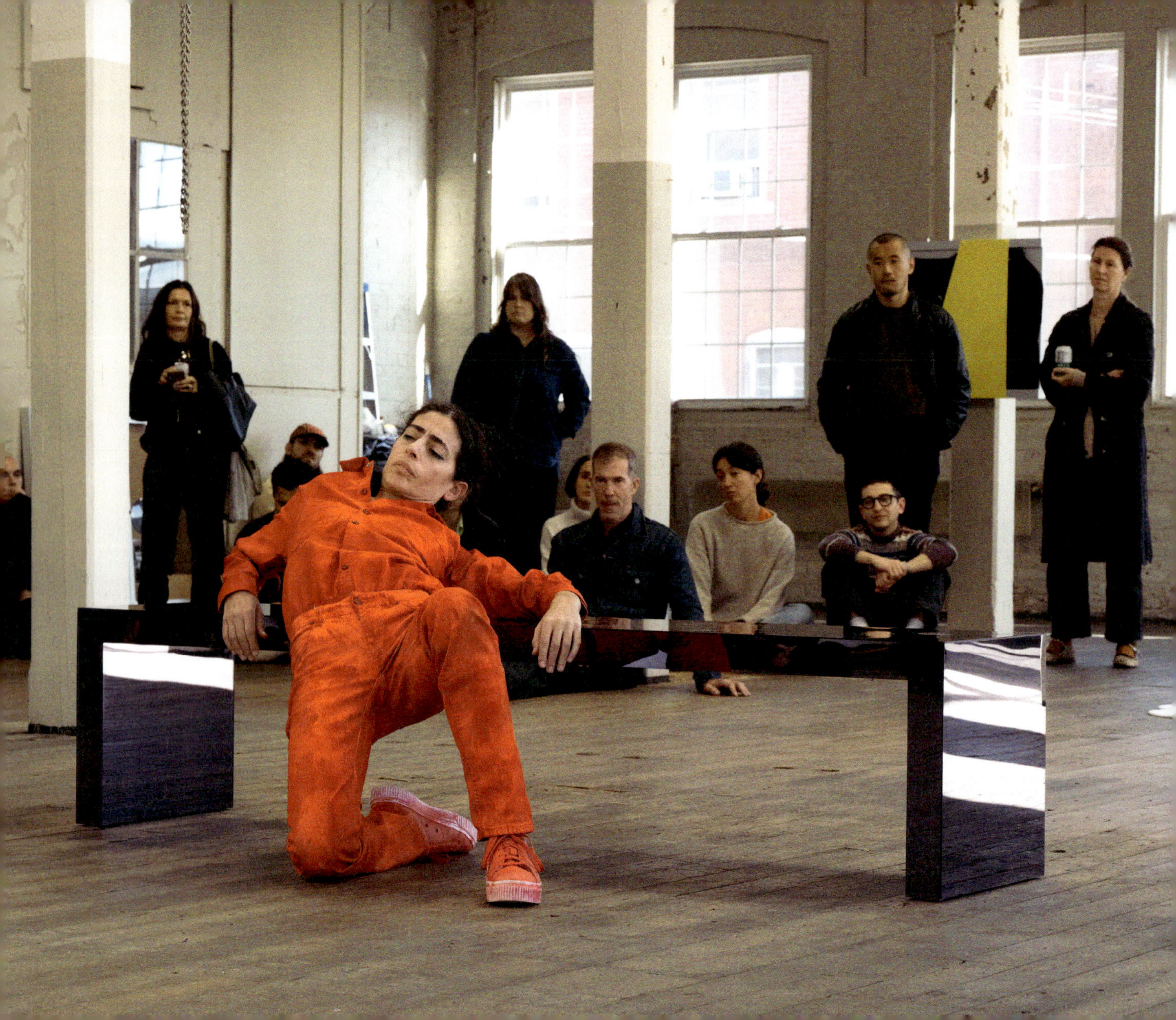

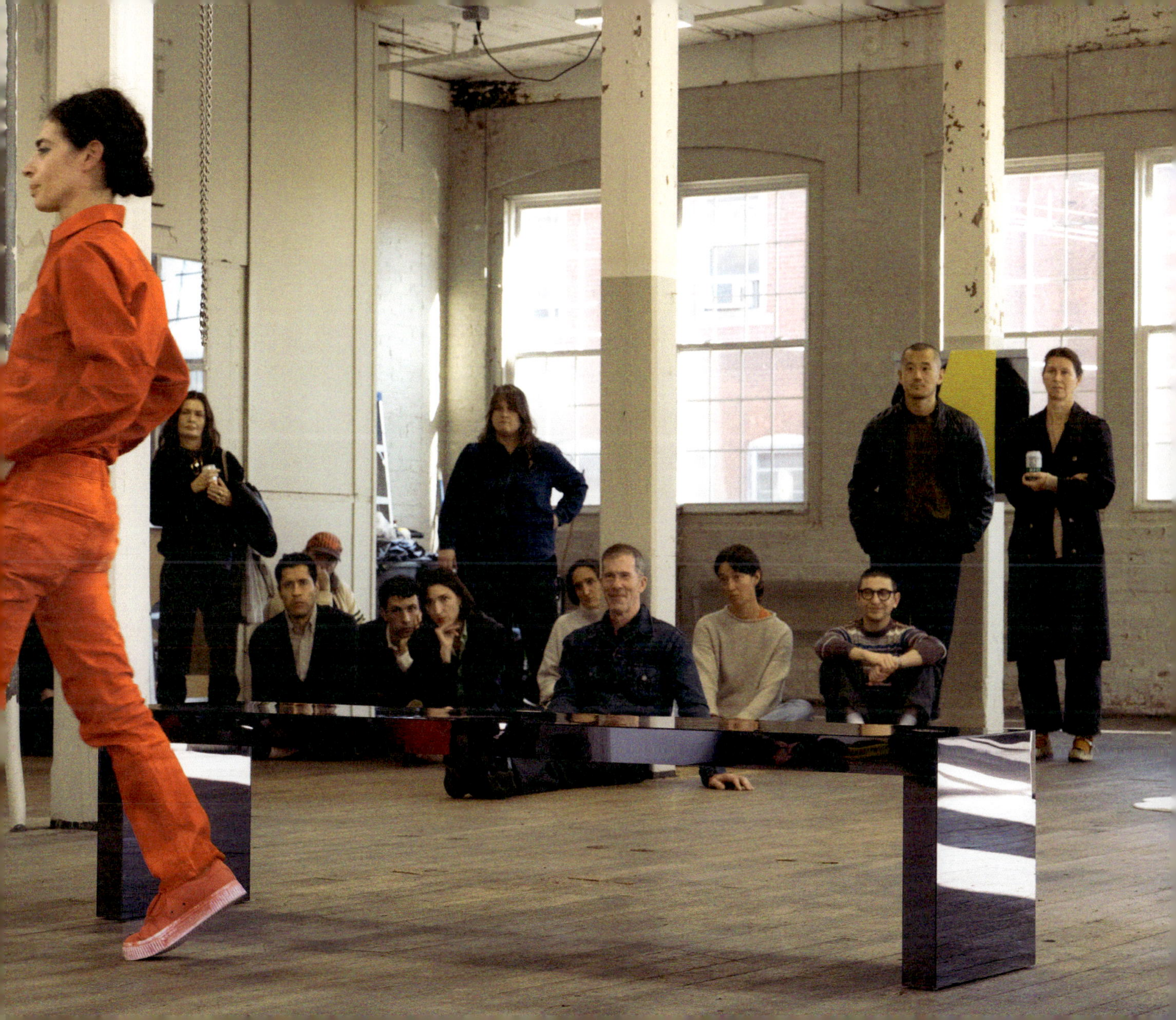

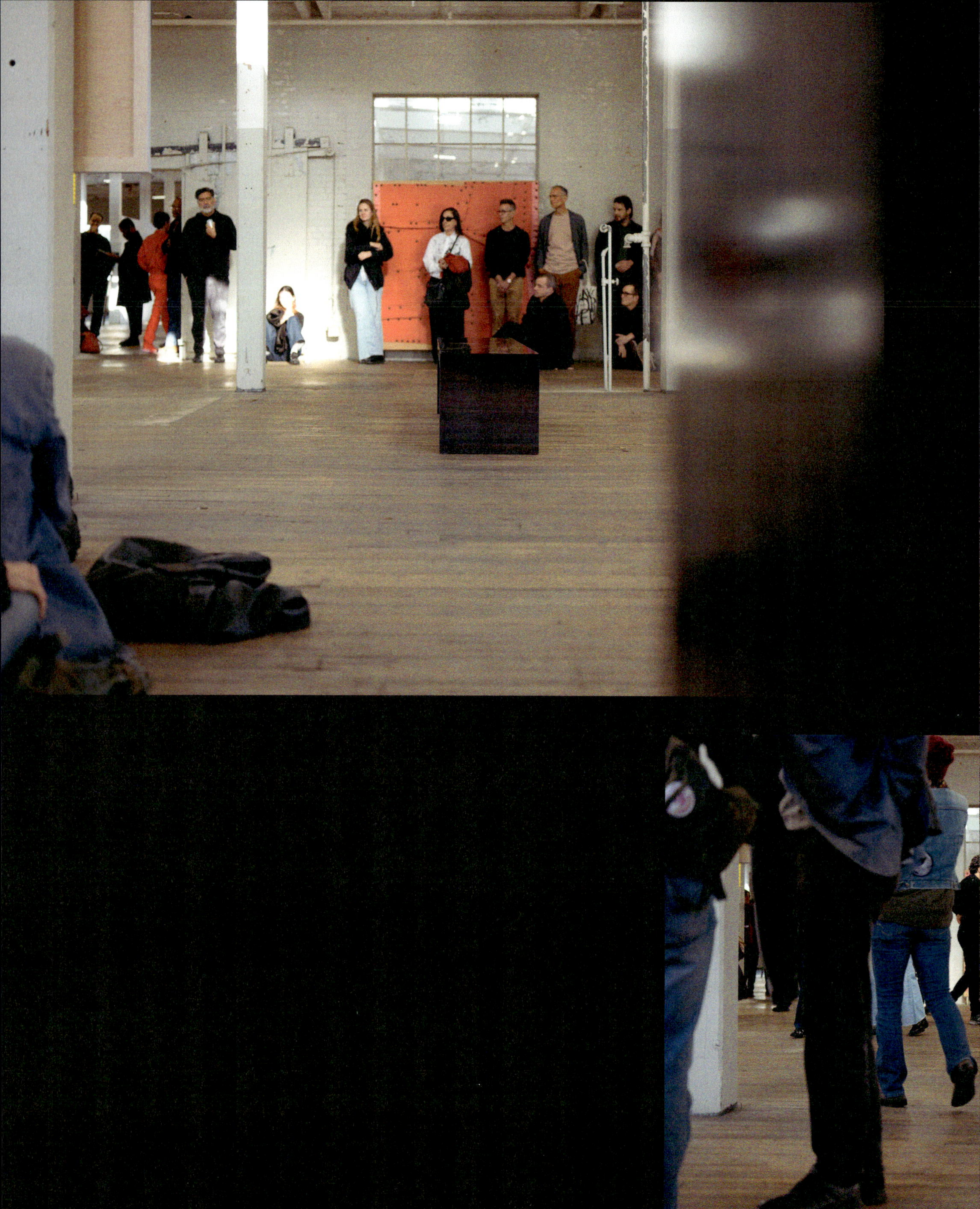

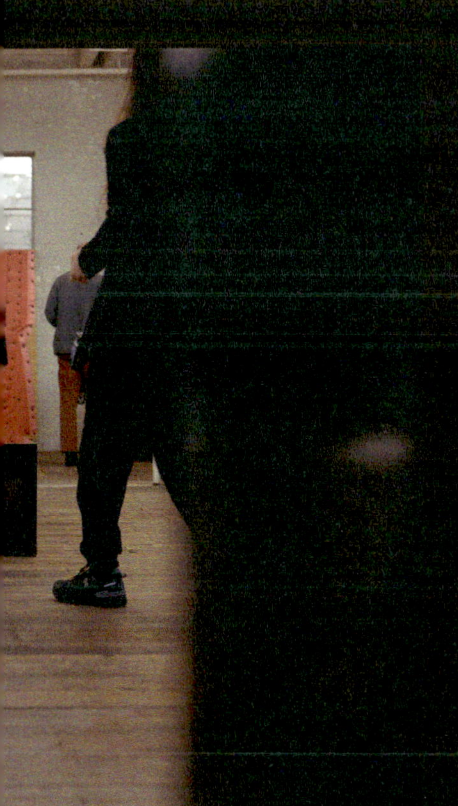
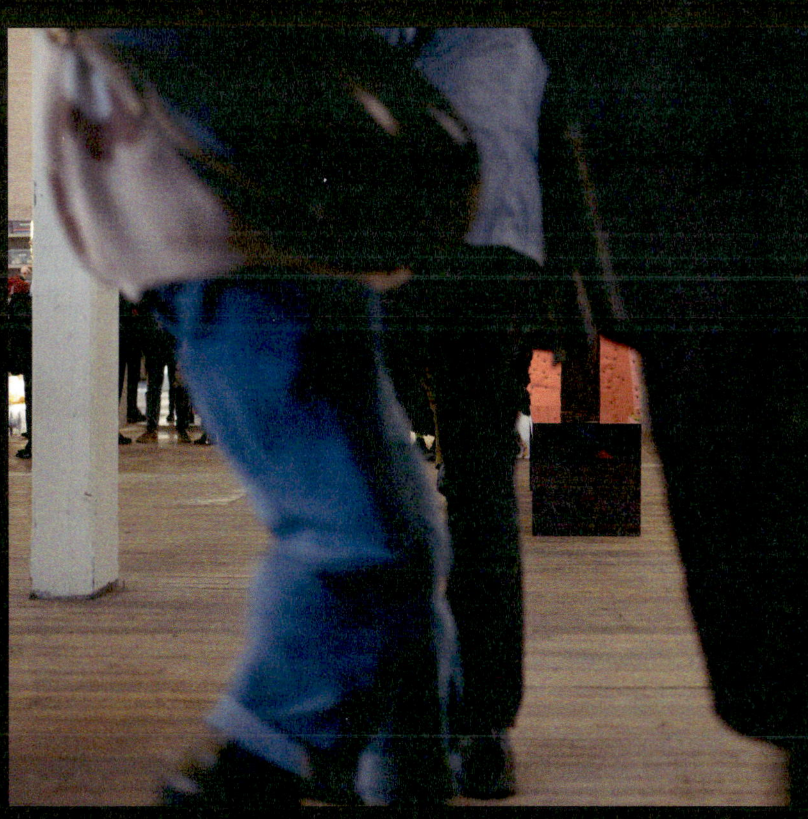

White Out

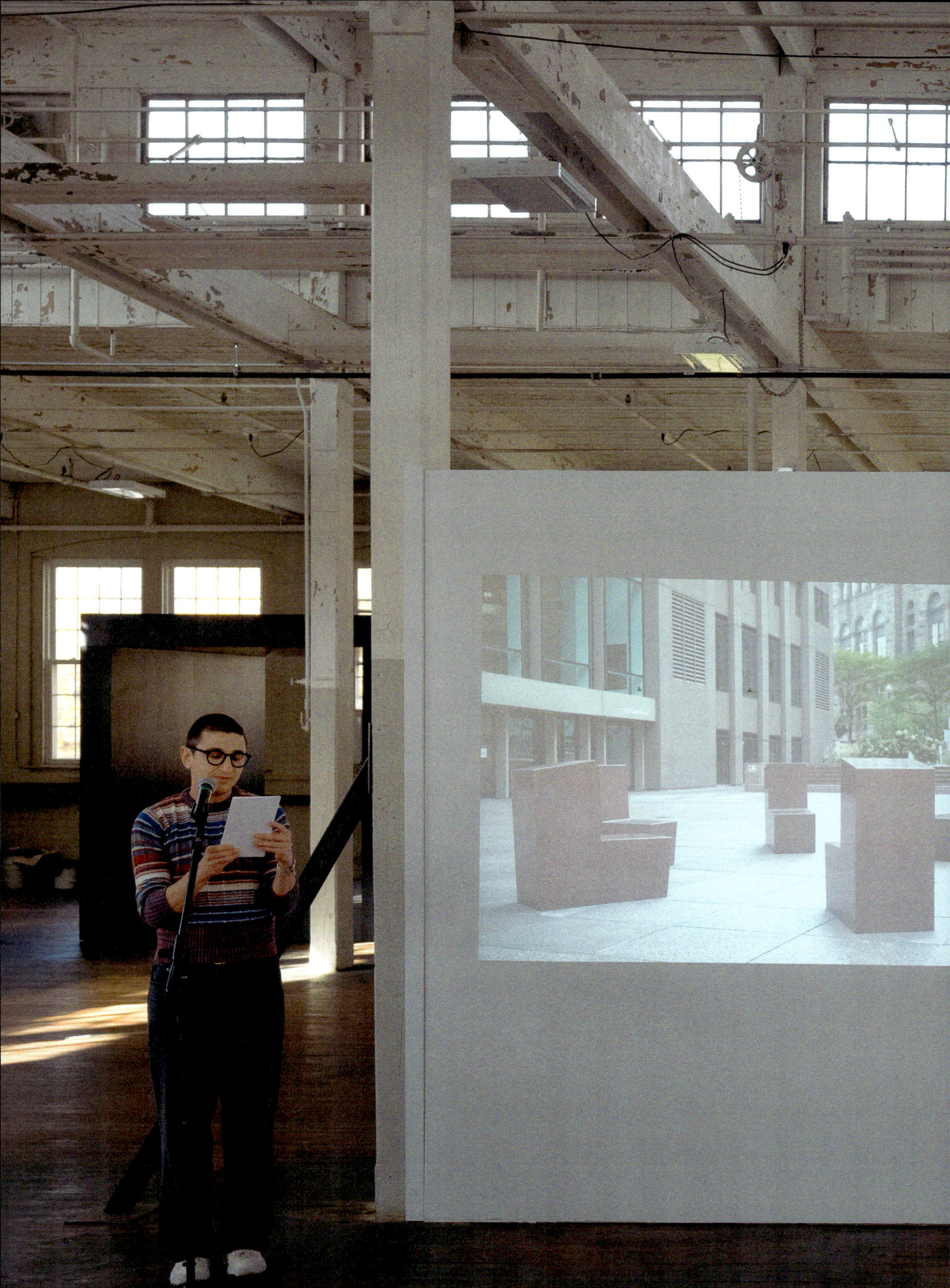

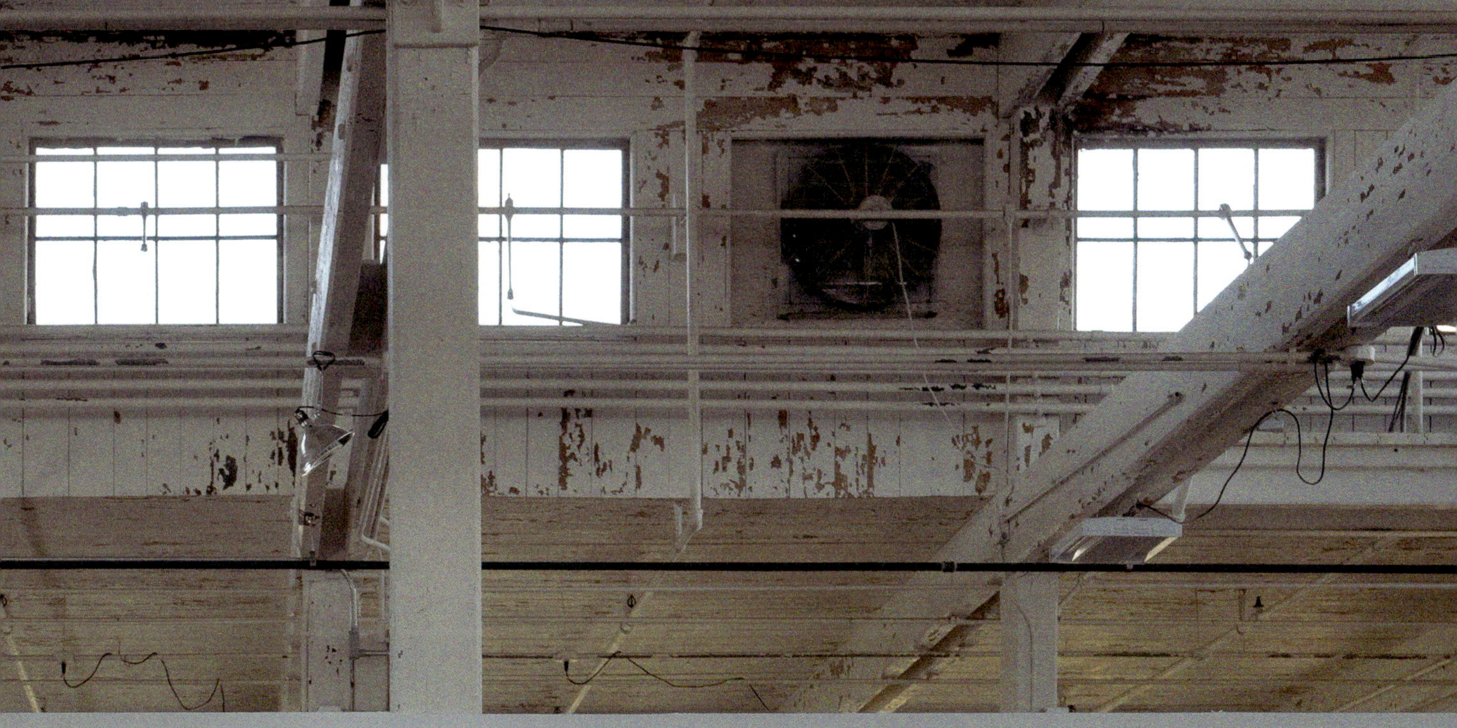

Concerning the Nature of Time 265

novelty. They will be part of the universal weave of things, given at one stroke. We do not introduce them into the world; it is the world that introduces them ready-made into us, into our consciousness, as we reach them. Yes, it is we who are passing when we say time passes; it is the motion before our eyes which, moment by moment, actualises a complete history given virtually.' Such is the metaphysic immanent in the spatial representation of time. It is inevitable. Clear or confused, it was always the natural metaphysic of the mind speculating upon becoming. We need not discuss it here, still less replace it by another. We have explained elsewhere why we see in duration the very stuff of our existence and of all things, and why, in our eyes, the universe

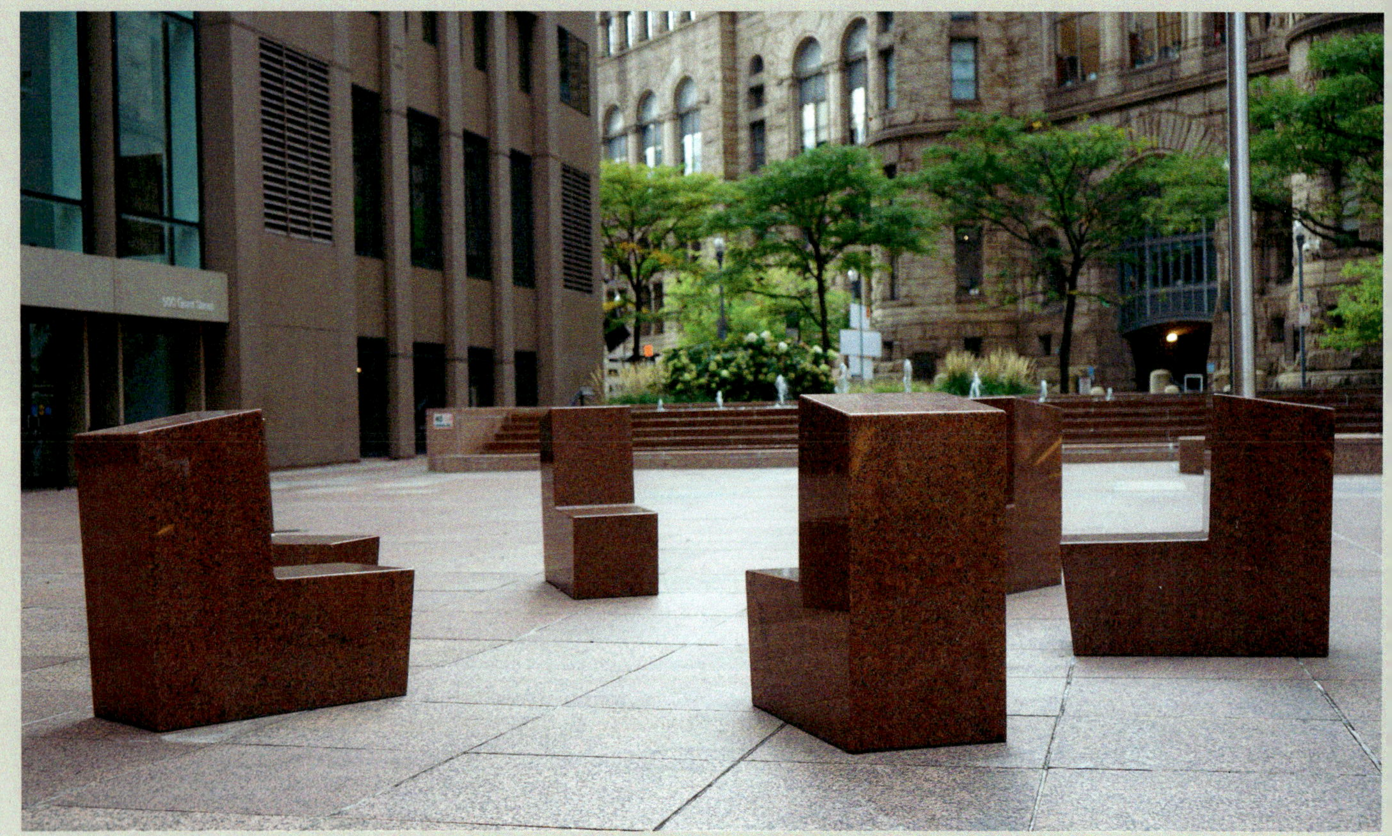

Good afternoon, and thank you all for joining me here today. I love being in the audience waiting for a performance to start. Anticipating what will happen next … attuned to every sound and change of light. Is it starting? Has it already begun? Sitting in a crowd, all pointing our attention in the same direction, oriented away from ourselves, anonymous and together, here for a purpose. Waiting.

I usually enjoy this part more than what happens once it begins, but anticipation requires an object, something that comes next, an after to the before. So here we are, and eventually it must begin.

I'll start with a memory: I'm on a train heading south through New York State toward Manhattan, somewhere between Beacon and Yonkers. The train tracks run parallel to the Hudson River, which is glistening blue and orange outside the western windows. It's May 12, 2023, and at 4:56 p.m. the sun is low in the sky over the river. The sun's yellow light passes through the train car window and hits the phone screen of a young woman sitting across the aisle. On the ceiling darts a glowing rectangle, punctuated by the crisp shadows of her thumbs as they move

          Gordon Hall

about the bottom of her phone screen. Fixated, I pull out my phone and capture a video of this refracted ceiling broadcast. She shifts her position and the bouncing light vanishes.

Over the next several months, I made an artwork from this experience, a digital animation which I titled *May 12, 4:56 pm*. When I make my sculptures out of wood, concrete, fabric, or paper, I'm often painstakingly remaking objects I find in the world, seeking the intimate connection with a thing I find through carefully studied replication. Only here, instead of concrete or wood, I have light bouncing through a lens dictated by a digital file. It's a portrait of this fleeting interstitial conversation between the sun, the train, and this stranger's phone. I was seeing the form, but not the content, of another's solitude as we waited to arrive at our destinations, together, side by side, each absorbed in our own private realms.

May 1986: Scott Burton stands near his recently completed public artwork, titled *Modular Six-Unit Seating*, in downtown Pittsburgh. Six polished red granite L-shaped forms gather in a circle, facing in toward each other. Burton gestures toward a group of women standing nearby and remarks, "That's my audience—people waiting for people."[1]

Most people do not like to wait. When we wait, we are held captive in time by forces we don't control. Oriented toward

1 Patricia Lowry, "Artist Pulls Up Chairs at One Mellon Plaza," *Pittsburgh Press*, May 15, 1986.

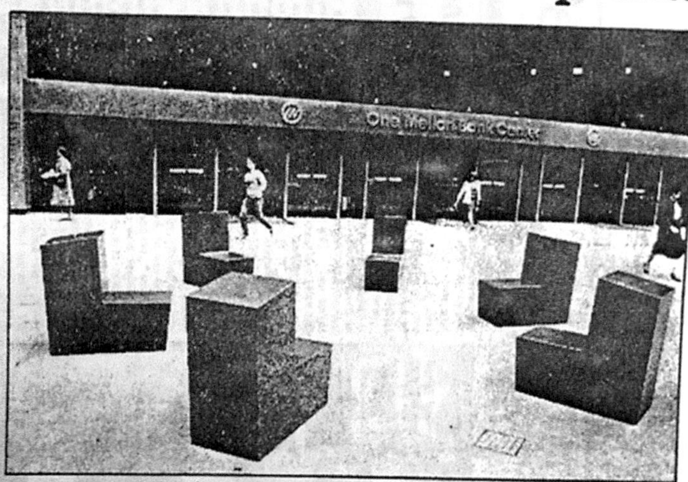

an unknowable future, we lose our agency as we feel trapped in a perpetual present that we can only hope to endure. Do I sound hyperbolic? Waiting, from what I can tell, is one of the most universally reviled human experiences, whether one waits for a subway, a meal, a paycheck, a package, or a text message.

The philosopher Henri Bergson offers an analysis that articulates the particular discontent of waiting. Bergson's phenomenology makes a crucial distinction between time as it is measured and time as it is lived—the time of clocks as opposed to our inconsistent first-person experience of time. Bergson points out that when we are absorbed in activities, we do not viscerally register the passage of time. But when time fails to conform to our needs, when time is not doing what we want it to do, we become aware of its existence. And painfully so. "It is we," he writes, "who are passing when we

370   Gordon Hall

2   Henri Bergson, "Duration and Simultaneity," in *Henri Bergson: Key Writings*, ed. Keith Ansell-Pearson and John Ó Maoilearca (Continuum, 2002), 265. Also see Harold Schweizer, "A Brief Theory of Waiting: Henri Bergson's Lump of Sugar," in *On Waiting* (Routledge, 2008), 14–35.

3   Helmut Puff, "Waiting in the Antechamber," in *Timescapes of Waiting: Spaces of Stasis, Delay and Deferral*, ed. Christoph Singer, Robert Wirth, and Olaf Berwald (Brill, 2019), 19, quoted in Helmut Puff and Bernardo Zacka, "The Architectures of Waiting: Helmut Puff and Bernardo Zacka in Conversation," *Contemporary Political Theory* 22, no. 2 (June 2023): 266.

4   For an extended discussion on waiting and smartphones, see Ellie Anderson and David Peña-Guzmán, hosts, *Overthink*, episode 57, "Waiting," August 2, 2022, https://overthink-podcast.com/episodes/episode-57.

5   Manpreet K. Janeja and Andreas Bandak, eds., "Introduction: Worth the Wait," in *Ethnographies of Waiting: Doubt, Hope and Uncertainty* (Bloomsbury Academic, 2018), 3.

6   Ibid., 3.

7   James J. Gibson, *The Ecological Approach to Visual Perception* (Houghton Mifflin, 1979).

say time passes."[2] Waiting, for Bergson, is agonizing because it thrusts us, without our consent, into a palpable awareness of our own troubled relationship to time. "Impatience" is what we call this agitation.

How, then, can we describe what waiting is? In a recent interview between the historian Helmut Puff and the political theorist Bernardo Zacka, they explore what they call "the architectures of waiting" as spaces in which we assemble in expectant idleness, offering this working definition of waiting: Waiting is a "temporally bounded condition in which time becomes experiential."[3] Now, it is plausible that mobile technologies, specifically our phones, have minimized the amount of time we all wait, unoccupied, insofar as they offer infinite ways to engage and entertain ourselves. We live in the era of mobility and immediacy, and one could argue that the situations in which we purely wait, without anything else to occupy us, are becoming an endangered species of experience.[4] Perhaps this diminishment of waiting is a nonevent, or even a desirable development. Who will miss waiting? Is the disappearance of unoccupied time a loss worth grieving?

Simultaneously, the large-scale power differentials between groups of people express themselves in the language of waiting. Whether one needs government support, medical benefits, asylum, passage through a checkpoint, or permission to leave prison, millions of people around the world wait for conditions needed to sustain life. Who waits, for what, for how long, and from whom is a map of domination and subjugation.

This global topography of waiting has been described by anthropologists Andreas Bandak and Manpreet K. Janeja as "the politics of waiting"—defined as "the structural and institutional conditions that compel people to wait."[5] Here, they distinguish the politics of waiting from what they describe as "the poetics of waiting"—"the existential affordances of being placed in temporal relations, gaps and intervals where the outcome is uncertain."[6]

If we define "affordance" in the tradition of James J. Gibson's theory of affordances as an object's possible range of uses in a given situation, we can ask ourselves: What are these "existential affordances" that waiting offers?[7] In other words, what happens in these gaps?

We often experience waiting as a suspension of time—we are at odds with time, and this misalignment casts us outside the

1–2 pm

shared temporal world we usually inhabit without friction. Theorist Lisa Baraitser describes her book *Enduring Time* as "an unfinishable book about time's suspension—modes of waiting, staying, delaying, enduring, persisting, repeating, maintaining, preserving, and remaining—that produce felt experiences of time *not passing*."[8] For Baraitser, it is specifically these contexts of time's suspension to which we must direct our attention. She goes on to explain the value and meaning of these experiences of suspended time, despite the fact that they are often "arduous, boring, and mundane, or simply unbearable."[9]

Waiting is an insult to capitalism's temporality that links time and usefulness. It is a waste of time; a rebuke to the internalized demand to make the most of our time. Time's standardization makes it a resource that can be used well or used poorly, and waiting is widely believed to be a poor use of our time.

But waiting is more than just an obstacle to productivity. These intervals of wasted time can exceed the distaste we have for them. Beyond the discomfort of waiting lies an orientation toward an uncertain future. In this uncertainty, the agony of waiting sometimes gives way to other sensations: A drifting contemplation arises in these temporal gaps, a curiosity birthed by these states of expectant idleness, and a visceral awareness of our own porosity to the world around us. The agitation of waiting sometimes feels like a door. Estranged from my regular momentum, I walk through, and I find myself in a new orientation to my surroundings.

Thinking about this array of waiting's capacities, it is unsurprising to discover that waiting plays a central, yet overlooked, role in creative work. I sit in a chair in my studio and look at my sculptures and wait to know what to do next. I sit in front of my computer writing this lecture and wait for the right word to come to me. There is no way to rush it; all I can do is position myself to meet what arrives, *if* anything ever arrives. There is risk in waiting, as we use up our time with the hope—*but never the assurance*—that something useful will come from it. In creative work, we *always* may be wasting our time.

This refusal to guarantee anything of value draws me to waiting as a method and an object of inquiry, despite—or perhaps because of—waiting's inefficiency and uncertainty.

Scott Burton's interest in waiting began long before his public sculptures offered people places to wait. His *Behavior Tableaux*

8 Lisa Baraitser, *Enduring Time* (Bloomsbury Academic, 2017), 2.

9 Ibid., 2.

     Gordon Hall

performances of the 1970s used waiting as a primary method, asking—or forcing—his audiences to endure long periods of silent expectation in close proximity to one another. Burton seated his audience in two tightly packed rows of chairs arranged some fifty to seventy-five feet away from the glacially slow and silent movements of the distant performers.

This arrangement divided the audience's attention between the performance itself and the proximity of the hands, thighs,

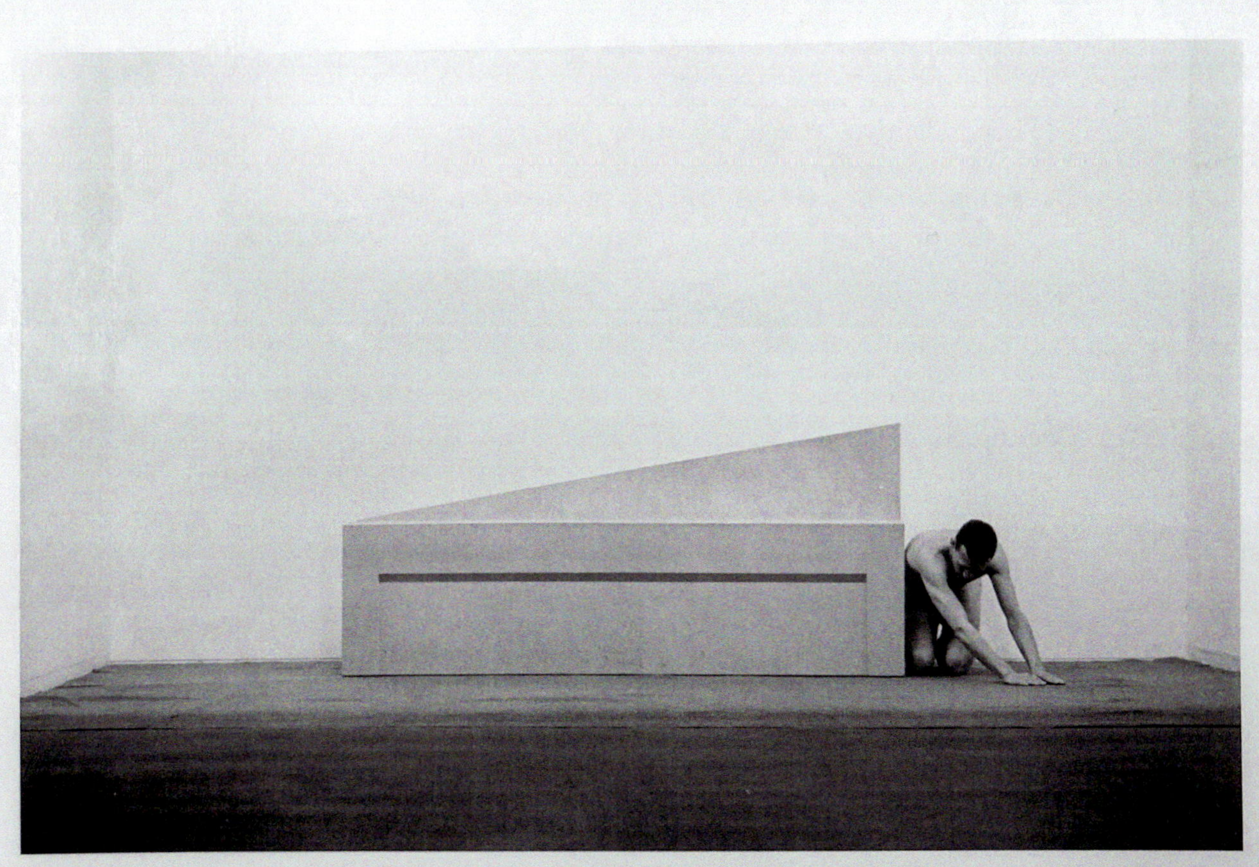

1-2 pm

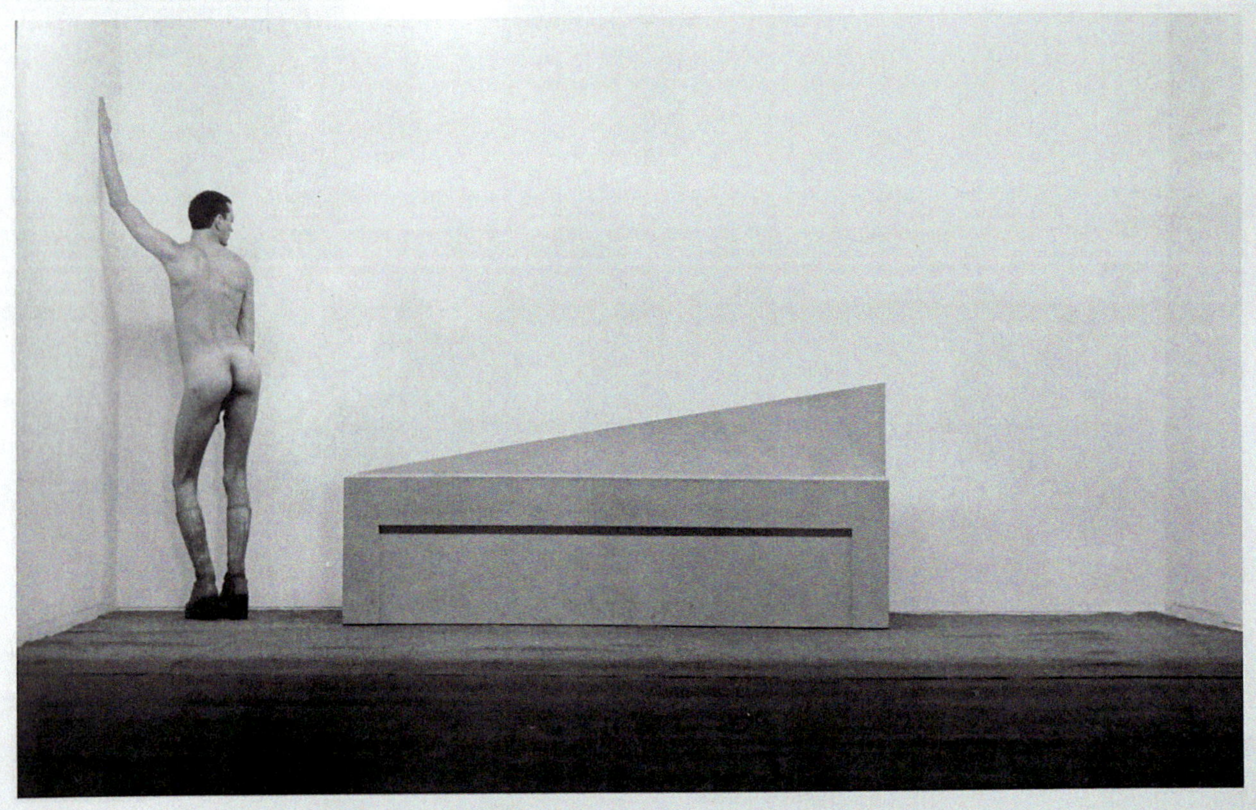

and breathing of the strangers sitting on either side. Audience members became increasingly aware of one another as the minutes passed. The audience watched but also waited—together, side by side, in the dark. Scott Burton's friend Jane Kaufman recalled that "Scott always said: 'On the other side of boredom is creativity.'"[10]

By the 1980s, Burton had stopped making performances and shifted toward his public seating sculptures. Gone were the lithe

10 For a beautiful account of the audience experience of the *Behavior Tableaux* performances, see David J. Getsy, "The Emotional Nature of the Number of Inches Between Them: *Behavior Tableaux*, 1972–80," in *Queer Behavior: Scott Burton and Performance Art* (University of Chicago Press, 2022), 118–30.

naked men in platform shoes, the slow-motion movements modeled on the poses he knew from gay bars and bathhouses. Now, everyday people sat on his sculptures, often with no knowledge that they were artworks. By design, the overtness of Burton's performances of the '70s transformed into the anonymity of his public sculptures. The audiences of the *Behavior Tableaux* performances transformed to become the public itself, Burton's ideal audience: "people waiting for people."[11] While on the surface this shift could be seen as a rupture in his practice, Burton's public sculptures of the 1980s were in fact a continuation of his performances' investigations into the power relations between bodies, objects, and architecture in public space.

We could say that Burton's public seating sculptures offer more interesting places to wait—the sculptural equivalent of

11 Lowry, "Artist Pulls Up Chairs at One Mellon Plaza," *Pittsburgh Press*.

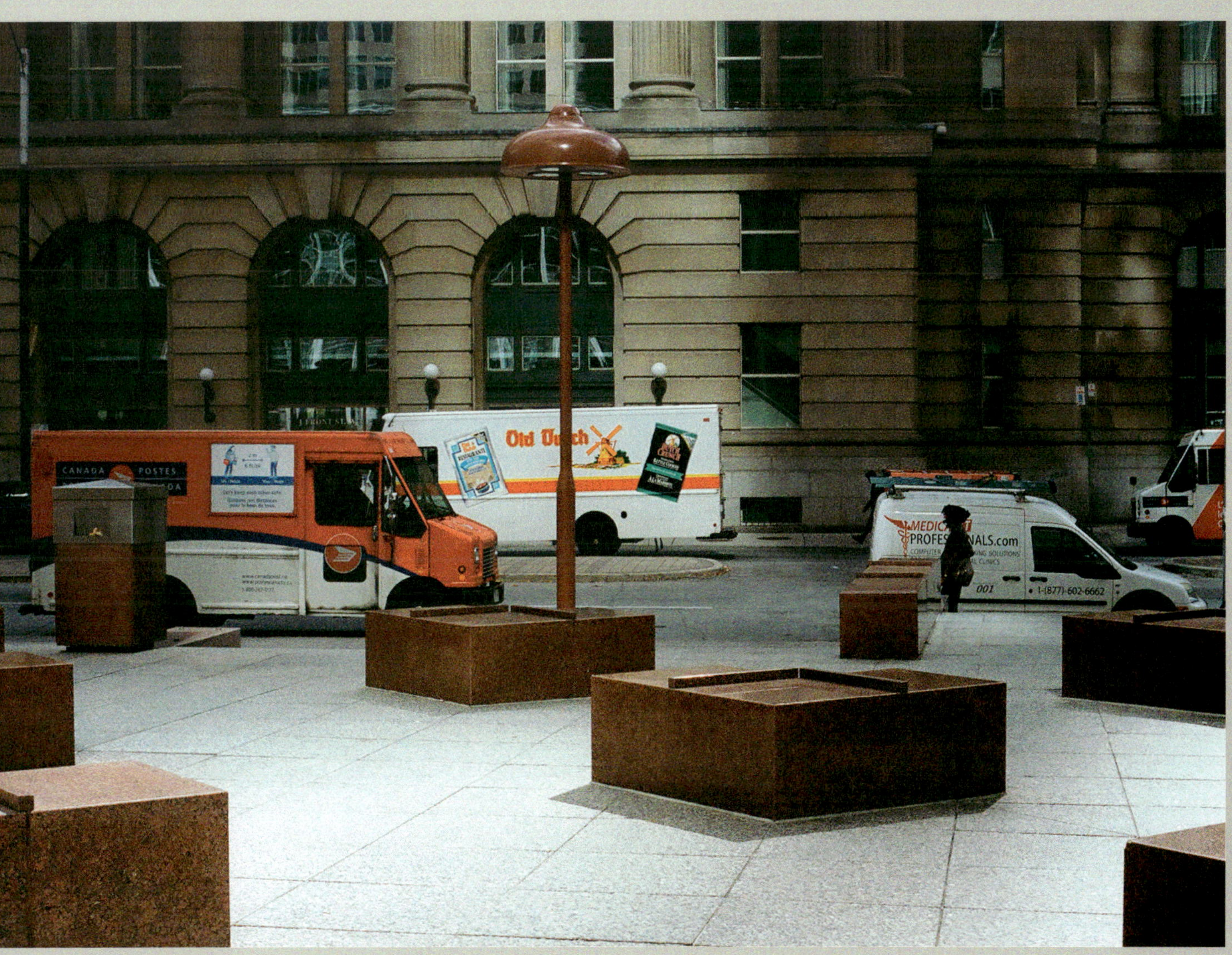

1–2 pm

12 This criticism of Burton's work as complicit in the exploitation of workers in late-capitalist urban environments was articulated by Rosalyn Deutsche and Benjamin Buchloh. For an account of this critique, see David J. Getsy, "On Being a Public Artist with AIDS in 80s America: Scott Burton and Conformational Masking," lecture at the *Art AIDS America* conference, University of Chicago, March 11, 2017, https://vimeo.com/208840307.

13 Sometimes referred to as "hostile architecture," this approach to urban space reduces public seating to combat loitering and homelessness. New York's Grand Central Station, in particular, the destination of the train mentioned at the opening of this essay, no longer has any seating that is not for paying customers. For more information about hostile architecture, see "'Hostile Architecture': How Public Spaces Keep the Public Out," *New York Times*, November 8, 2019, https://www.nytimes.com/2019/11/08/nyregion/hostile-architecture-nyc.html.

14 Scott Burton, "My Brancusi," *Art in America*, March 1990, 150. The exhibition *Artist's Choice: Burton on Brancusi* was presented at MoMA from April 7 to June 28, 1989. Burton passed away in December 1989, and "My Brancusi" was published posthumously in *Art in America* in March 1990. For more information, see "Artist's Choice: Burton on Brancusi," MoMA, https://www.moma.org/calendar/exhibitions/2133.

15 Scott Burton, interview by Edward Brooks DeCelle, March 1980, quoted in David J. Getsy, *Queer Behavior*, 272.

beautiful, well-designed public waiting rooms.[12] Seen through the lens of today's cities' deeply ableist and anti-homeless relationship with sitting, exemplified here in what is known as "hostile architecture," there is radicality in providing an accessible place for people to sit, rest, or sleep.[13]

But this is just the first layer of Burton's engagement with both the politics and poetics of support. One of Burton's last projects was his MoMA *Artist's Choice* exhibition, in which he exhibited only the bases of Brancusi's sculptures. Brancusi's bases were, to Burton, "*sculptures of tables*": "The object as object but with a (supportive) role the *nonfunctional* works do not have." Burton described the pedestal-table that holds up a Brancusi sculpture as a "*usable* meditation on utilitarian form."[14]

Similarly, his public seating sculptures are both places to wait and places to consider waiting in all of its permeability. Rather than distracting us from our waiting, Burton's public seating sculptures frame waiting itself as meriting our attention.

His sculptures operate as he describes Brancusi's pedestals—as objects of both function and contemplation of the meaning of their supportive use. They wait for us to use them to wait for others.

In numerous contexts, Burton described art as a venue for radical politics and a "moral example": "Any chair is useful but a very striking looking chair—something that isn't like a usual chair—can make people perhaps more flexible in their attitudes to accept more things—to become more democratic about what a chair is. They may even become more democratic about what a person is. Art can be a moral example."[15] Burton's many chairs, seats, benches, and stools attest to the promise of the chair itself as a *moral example* that privileges anticipation, subordination, need, and an erotics of receptiveness. His description of art as a moral example is distinct from art that moralizes, telling us what to think and feel. Instead, he offers us objects that invite us into modes of relating that reflect values that differ from those with which we may be familiar.

Burton's focus on seating in its generosity and openness to the bodies of strangers cannot be unwound from the context of the early years of the HIV/AIDS crisis and his own diagnosis around 1983. During a time when bodily contact was pathologized and stigmatized, he made sculptures that welcomed the bodies of strangers, supporting anyone who arrived in need of

          Gordon Hall

16 Waiting recurs as a theme across theories and accounts of disability. For two recent examples, see Carolyn Lazard and Jesse Cohen, *Notes for the Waiting Room*, 2017, and Taraneh Fazeli, "Time After Time," in *Waiting*, ed. Avram Alpert and Sreshta Rit Premnath, *Shifter* 25 (2021): 29–33.

17 Getsy, "On Being a Public Artist."

18 Ibid.

19 As Burton said, "What office workers do in their lunch-time hour is more important than my pushing the limits of my self-expression." Quoted in Rui Mateus Amaral, "Garden Court," in *Garden Court, Scott Burton* (Amaral & P., 2022), 8.

20 David J. Getsy, ed., "Literalist Theater (1970)," in *Scott Burton: Collected Writings on Art and Performance, 1965–1975* (Soberscove Press, 2012), 219.

rest. Burton's engagement with waiting as a category of experience mirrored the role that waiting played in the HIV/AIDS crisis itself, and in many experiences of illness and disability.[16] Waiting for your test results, for assistance, for a friend to visit, for new treatments to become available, to live, to die, in hope, doubt, fear, and anticipation. Might Burton have wanted us to consider the experience of waiting itself as a form of living nonetheless, under the most precarious circumstances?

As the art historian David J. Getsy has compellingly argued, those that couldn't see, or actively rejected, Burton's embrace of objects of support "did not appreciate the resilience, the fortitude, the control, and the generosity that it takes to be the support, to be the bottom."[17]

Getsy describes this mode of valuing the work of supporting and receiving as "critical passivity."[18] This critical passivity is at the core of the politics of Burton's work, manifested across his performances, sculptures, and public art, and, ultimately, extending to what he came to understand as the artist's relationship to the public: to serve.[19] When we consider waiting through the lens of Burton's work, we find that waiting's devaluation originates from our discomfort with the receptiveness and lack of control that defines it. We revile waiting as a scene of interdependence and need. When we wait we are beholden to one another and to the world, open to *what might happen*. Scott Burton welcomes us into this critical passivity, pointing us toward the value and erotics of experiences of waiting.

In 1970, some sixteen years before Burton describes his audience as "people waiting for people," he writes a one-sentence performance score that reads as follows:

> Standing on a corner, waiting for someone, who does not come.[20]

Can we accept Burton's invitation to orient ourselves toward waiting itself? In hope and fear, we loiter, linger, tarry, daydream, wait for someone who might not come. We find ourselves on the outskirts of usefulness, adrift in the mirrored pool of suspended time. The sun is setting in the west, inching ever so slowly across a pair of hands in an adjacent lap. We submit, and to our surprise, we find that we enjoy it. ◊

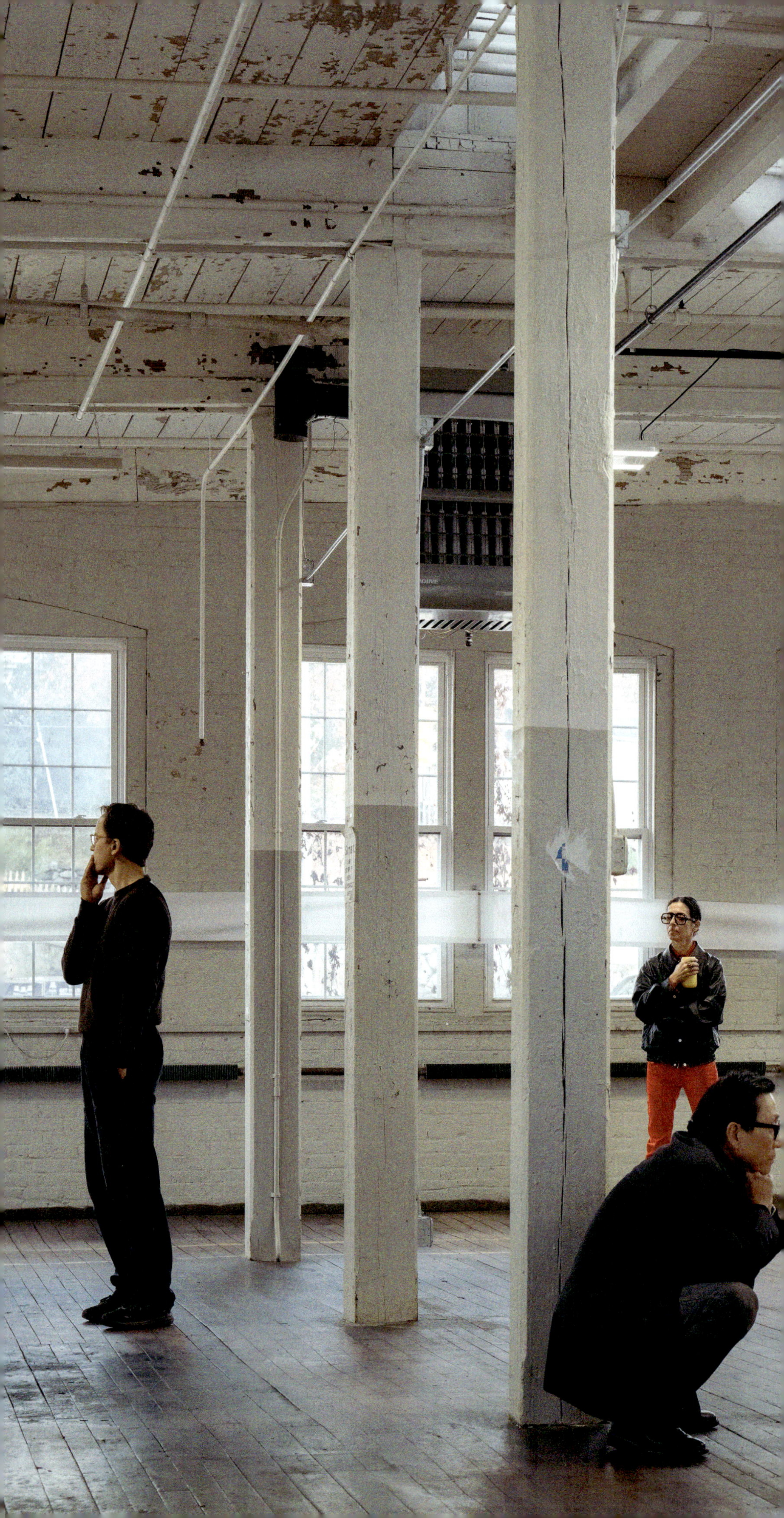

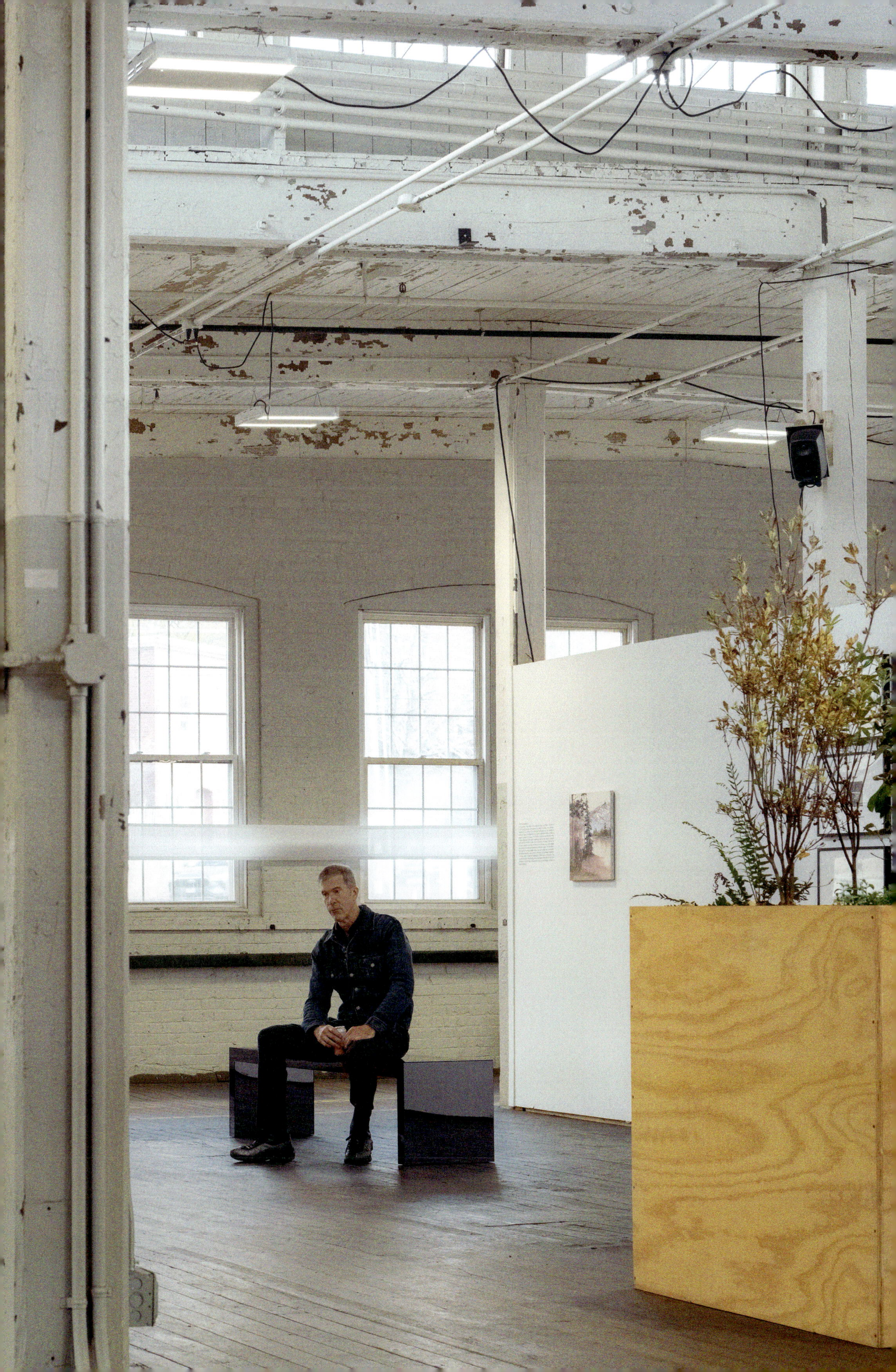

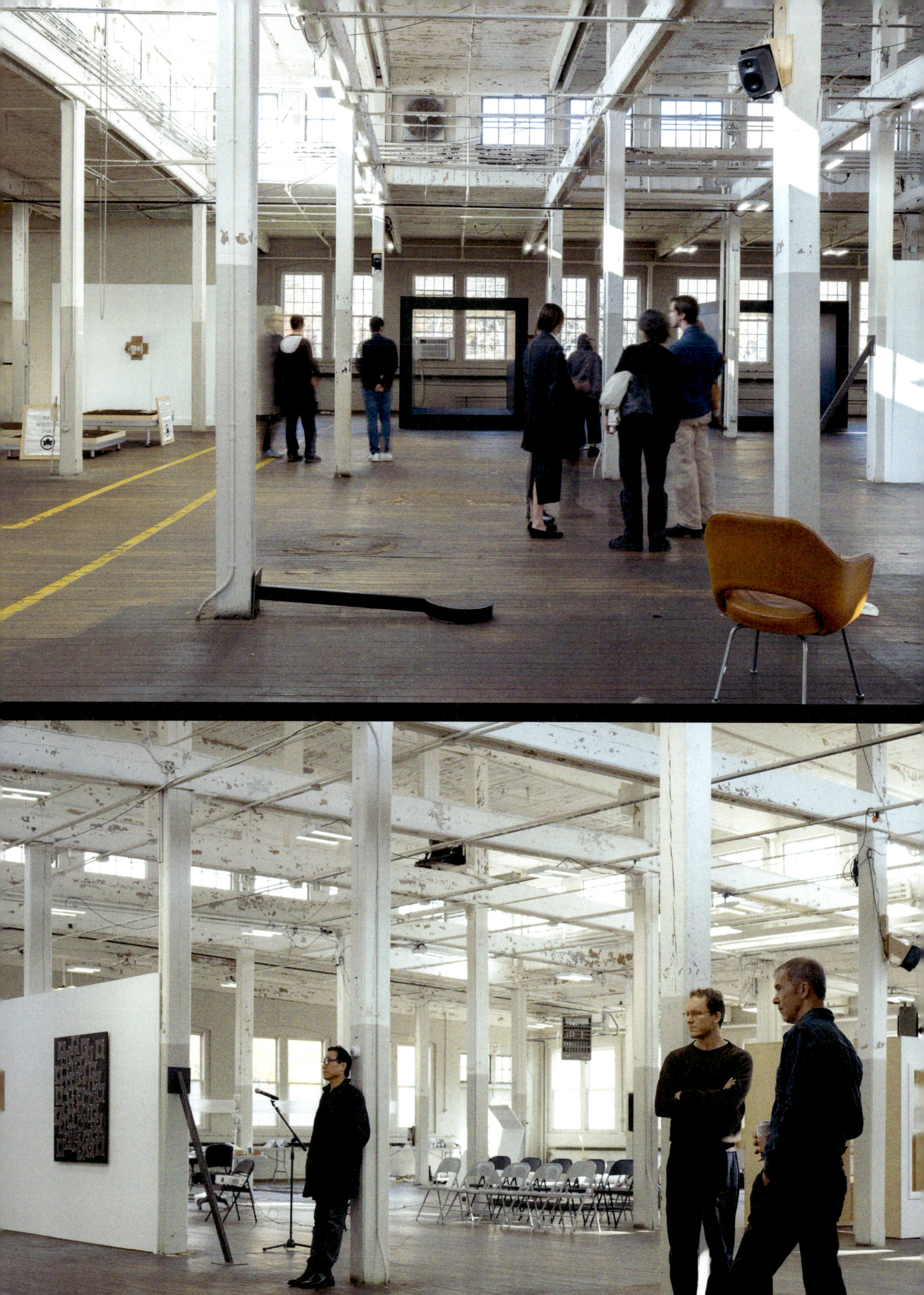

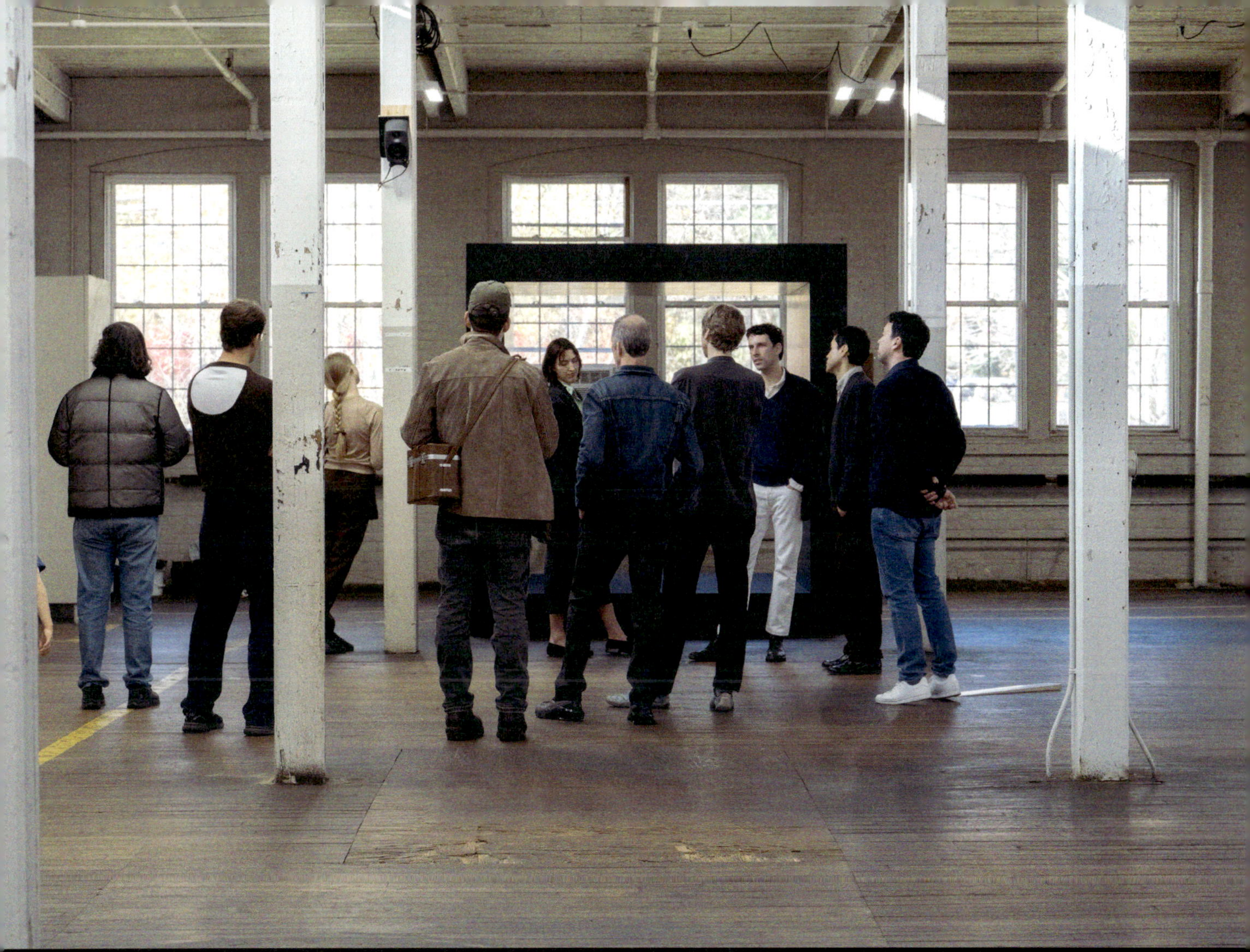

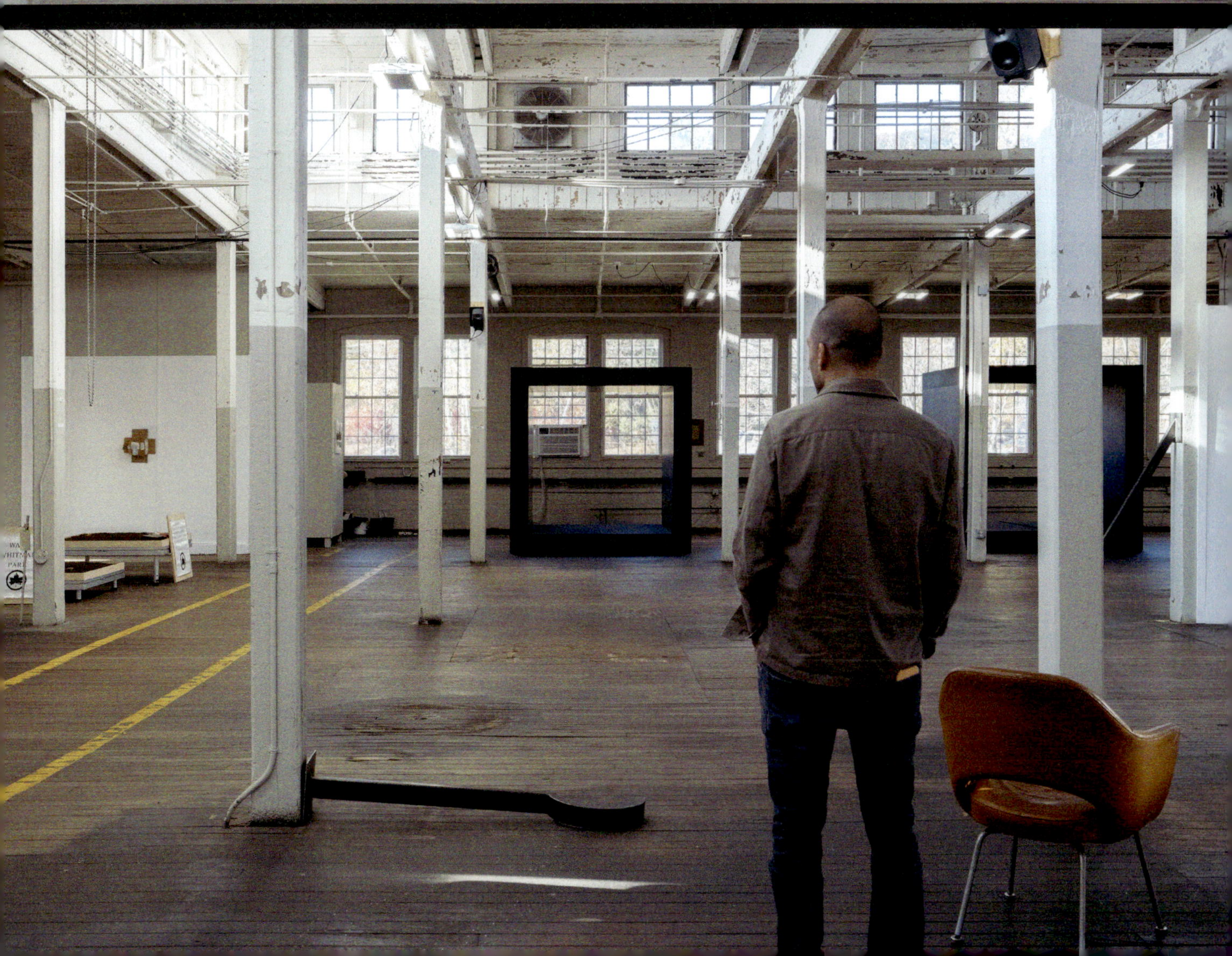

Première publication :
'adame Miroir
Édition musicale, Heugel, 1948.
L'Enfant criminel & 'adame Miroir,
Édition Paul Morihien, février 1949, Paris.

Création le 31 mai 1948, au Théâtre Marigny, à Paris. Ballets Roland Petit, musique de Darius Milhaud, décors de Paul Delvaux, chorégraphie de Janine Charrat.

*Description d'un ballet
dansé par Messieurs*
ROLAND PETIT, SERGE PERRAULT
et SKOURATOFF
sur une musique de
DARIUS MILHAUD

LE DÉCOR. - Il représente l'intérieur d'un palais extrêmement somptueux, dont les corridors sont recouverts de miroirs biseautés. Le lieu où sera dansé le ballet est une sorte de carrefour où aboutissent ces avenues très éclairées. Au plafond, des lustres riches et lourds. Aucune étoffe aux murs, mais de l'or, du marbre, du verre.

LE TITRE. - Je ne veux que signaler cette amusante particularité : quand, à peine ayant achevé le drame, j'eus trouvé ce titre : « Madame Miroir »,

l'idée d'un tel carnaval, et grotesque, m'empêcha de l'énoncer sérieusement. Comme par plaisanterie, je le prononçai pour moi-même avec l'accent faubourien, traînant sur les « a » et le « oir » final, et comme à Belleville, j'élidai le « M » initial. Il me parut facétieux de l'écrire ainsi, or j'obtins une déformation du mot madame qui donnait « adam » où cependant un passé et un possible féminins se laissaient lire : « adam » était, dans un miroir un peu brouillé, l'image estompée, déformée, d'un objet ayant certaines qualités.

LE PERSONNAGE. - C'est un matelot qui n'a pas de passé. Sa vie commence avec la chorégraphie, qui la contient tout à fait. Il est jeune et beau. Ses cheveux sont bouclés. Ses muscles durs et souples : bref c'est pour nous l'idéal amant. Il est vêtu du costume d'été des matelots de la Marine nationale : blanc. Souliers noirs vernis, à semelle très souple. Une rose, par sa tige, est passée dans sa ceinture de cuir.

LE DOMINO. - Il serait trop facile d'y voir la Mort. Ce n'est pas elle. Mais qui? L'auteur l'ignore. C'est un domino de soie violette, ganté de noir, et dont l'accessoire essentiel est un éventail de crêpe noir.

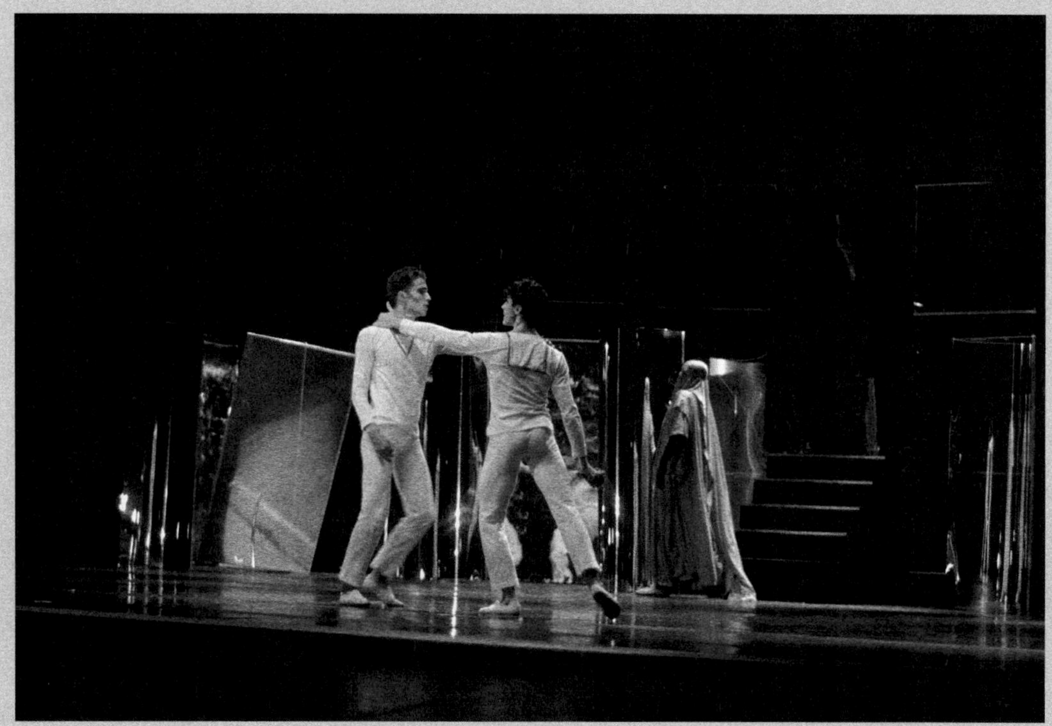

          Nick Mauss

LA CHORÉGRAPHIE. - Le domino sort d'un corridor de droite. Une main en visière au-dessus des yeux (l'autre tient l'éventail de crêpe), il inspecte la salle, puis il lui tourne le dos, et traverse la scène, examinant chaque miroir *où son Image n'apparaît pas*, allant jusqu'au fond, à gauche, où, par une amorce de corridor, il disparaîtra.

La démarche de ce personnage doit être lente et très souple. Il donne l'impression d'être porté par un tapis roulant. Ses gestes avec l'éventail, en direction des miroirs, sont très familiers. Il semble avec, parfois, épousseter une plinthe, une cariatide.

Le domino sorti, la lumière inonde la scène qui reste vide quelques secondes.

La musique joue alors une valse très légère, une sorte de java.

Par où est sorti le domino apparaît, mégot aux lèvres, un matelot.

Pendant toute la danse, le visage du matelot restera impassible *(il serait plus beau qu'il dansât d'abord les yeux clos)* mais en apparaissant *(à reculons)*, ses gestes indiquent l'effroi. Il recule à tout petits pas; et bute contre un miroir. Il se retourne et voit son image. Il court à une autre glace où il voit encore son image. *(Il est entendu qu'un danseur, placé derrière un praticable en forme de miroir – et*

voilé de tulle –, tient le rôle du reflet, copiant à l'envers les attitudes du matelot.)

D'un miroir à l'autre, éperdu, le matelot va buter, se cognant toujours à son Image. Affolé il danse seul, sur un rythme de plus en plus rapide jusqu'à ce qu'épuisé, perdant son béret, il tombe à terre où il continue une sorte de reptation malheureuse. Ensuite il redresse un peu le buste, et regarde un des miroirs.

Dans ce miroir *(celui qui est à droite, près de la scène)* les gestes de l'Image ne semblent pas répondre exactement à ceux du matelot. Celui-ci s'en inquiète. Comme en rampant d'abord il s'en approche, visiblement méfiant. Alors qu'il est encore accroupi, l'Image est déjà debout, au bord du miroir. Le matelot se redresse tout à fait et, avec une sorte de résignation tendre, il va vers elle. L'Image recopie alors ses derniers gestes. Le matelot passe une main sur le miroir, comme pour effacer la buée qu'il vient de faire avec sa bouche. L'Image fait le même geste. Enfin le matelot donne un coup de poing en direction du miroir mais la main, au lieu de rencontrer la glace, heurte le menton de l'Image dont la tête vacillait. Le matelot porte les deux mains en avant, l'Image fait de même, le matelot recule, l'Image recule; le matelot se rapproche encore, l'Image se rapproche; le matelot

recule, mais cette fois l'Image avance et sort du miroir.

Commence une danse *(poursuite d'abord)* du matelot avec son Image, pendant laquelle les miroirs cesseront de réfléchir.

LA POURSUITE. - L'Image, en dansant, essaye d'approcher le matelot qui se sauve, effrayé. Mais, au bout d'un moment, le matelot, manquant de souffle, est forcé dans un angle de miroir *(très visible du public)*. Courageusement, et un peu intrigué, il fait front à son Image et va au-devant d'elle. À son tour l'Image s'enfuit. Enfin, peu à peu, en se tournant mutuellement le dos, ils se touchent, se retournent, et s'enlacent. Se baisent sur la bouche. L'Image, entre ses lèvres, reprend le mégot du matelot.

LA DANSE. - Ils dansent. La même valse très légère du début, qu'ils font à petits pas, comme les marins des musettes : valse très stylisée.

Les deux danseurs tentent d'évoquer une course amoureuse. Ils se prennent par le cou, puis se

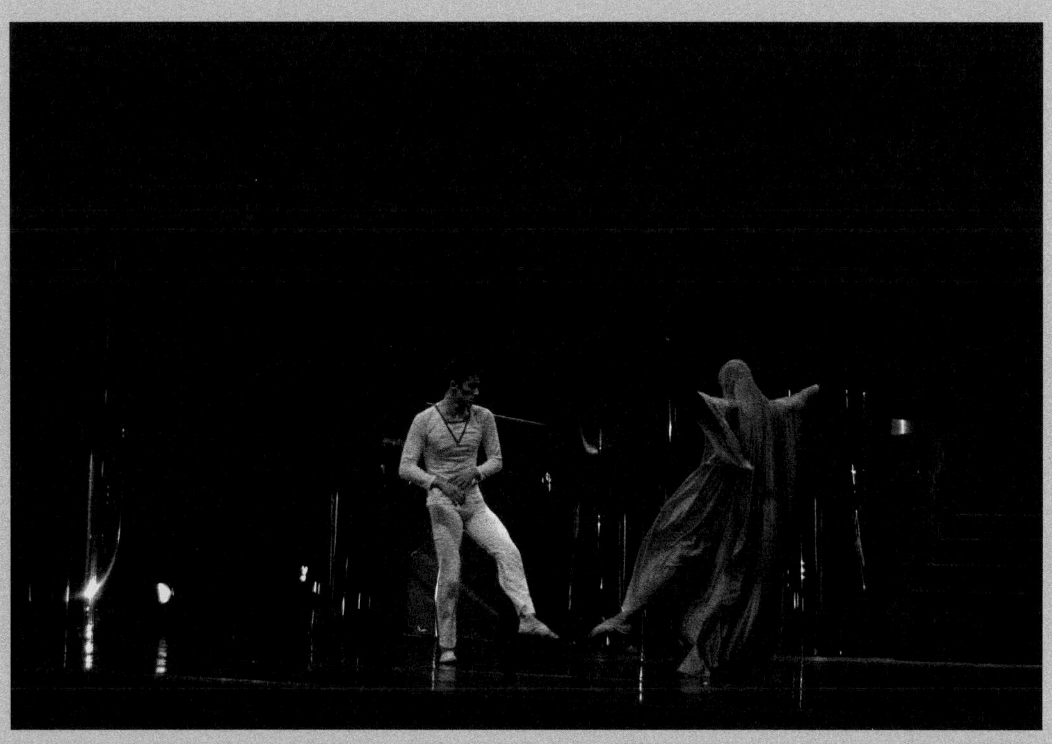

The Image Runs Away

délivrent, dansent joue contre joue. En fait, ils se lâchent très peu.

Dans la chorégraphie dessinée par elle, Mlle Janine Charrat faisait l'Image élever le matelot *(dos à ventre)* et le laisser redescendre, puis continuer la danse. Je conserve cette idée, avec celle-ci : couché sur le plancher, le matelot se roule, traversant ainsi la scène de droite à gauche. Debout devant lui, le regardant *(et face au public)*, l'Image se déplace avec lui, lentement, les quatre pieds s'accordant dans ces mouvements verticaux et horizontaux.

Le reste de la danse doit être extrêmement lascif. Érotique. Les deux danseurs font délicatement les gestes familiers aux marins : remonter leur pantalon avec le plat de la main, passer les pouces dans la ceinture de cuir, en tournant présenter brusquement le profil, s'étirer, faire valoir les muscles des cuisses et des bras, les mains dans les poches tendre l'étoffe de la braguette, s'accrocher par le bras, etc [1].

Les danseurs sont sur le point de s'unir quand, par le praticable où il avait disparu, entre le domino.

1. Épisode de la Rose. L'Image n'a pas de rose à sa ceinture. D'un coup de dent, le danseur jouant le rôle de l'Image arrache cette rose, se sauve et la garde à sa bouche.

LA MORT. - Dès son entrée *(marche toujours souple et lente)*, les danseurs s'inquiètent. Avec nonchalance le domino s'avance. Il semble plutôt les négliger. Il s'attarde *(l'éventail devant son visage)* aux miroirs, mais sûrement il s'approche du couple défait qui s'écarte. Le domino enfin sépare le matelot et son Image *(attitudes aussi familières que possible du domino)*. Le matelot et son Image dansent enfin avec le domino. Une valse très échevelée, de plus en plus turbulente. Le domino est porté tour à tour par le matelot et l'Image, quelquefois par tous les deux.

Enfin le domino se décide, et choisit le matelot. Il le poursuit un moment, puis il le poignarde avec le manche de l'éventail. Durant la mise à mort l'Image est accoudée à un portant et examine la scène sans montrer d'émotion. Enfin le domino prend par les cheveux le matelot couché, et il le tire dans la coulisse où ils disparaissent.

Pendant quelques secondes, l'Image danse seule, un pas qui indique sa solitude et son affolement. Plus précisément, elle danse en reculant.

LA MÉTAMORPHOSE. - Rentre le domino. Il poursuit l'Image qui s'échappe. Enfin il la rattrape et danse avec elle, une danse extrêmement violente. Le domino paraît de plus en plus menaçant. Il essaye de faire entrer l'Image dans un des miroirs du fond. L'Image se débat et s'enfuit. Vers le milieu de la scène, le domino la rejoint. Non pour les spectateurs mais pour l'Image seule, le domino, déplaçant l'éventail, montre son visage. Les deux danseurs s'examinent. On sent par la nervosité de leurs jarrets, des attitudes, qu'ils se toisent, s'affrontent. Enfin l'Image fléchit. Le domino lui prend la main et, face au public, fait glisser son long gant noir sur la main de l'Image *(choisir un gant de jersey de soie)*. Une main gantée, l'Image s'échappe et danse seule, mais à peine a-t-elle fait quelques pas, elle revient, sans qu'ait bougé le domino, auprès de celui-ci. Le domino prend l'autre main du matelot et lui passe le deuxième gant, puis, par un double mouvement de giration inverse, à mesure que le domino se défait de sa robe, l'Image s'en revêt. *(La robe n'est qu'une longue bande de tissu violet.)* Quand l'Image est revêtue de la robe, elle dissimule, sauf la tête, le personnage du domino placé derrière elle. Enfin, un bras *(habillé de blanc)* de ce qu'était le domino, tend, de derrière l'Image *(à l'Image ainsi revêtue de violet)*, l'éventail. Puis le personnage *(ex-domino)* se découvre tout à fait : c'était le matelot de tout à l'heure. *(Quand le domino l'a traîné dans*

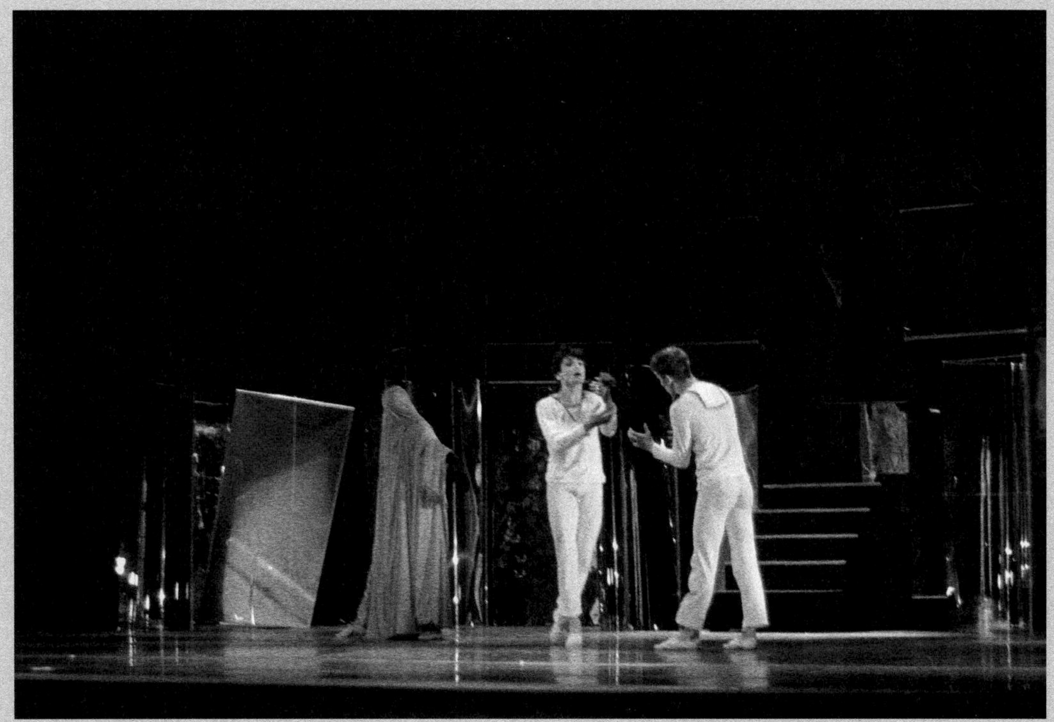

Nick Mauss

la coulisse, une habilleuse l'a très vite revêtu de la robe violette, et c'est lui qui est entré en scène pour échanger son costume avec l'Image.)

Le domino poursuit le matelot. Le matelot se sauve. Il essaie de rentrer dans un miroir, sans jamais s'y réfléchir. Les miroirs résistent. Enfin il est rejoint par le domino avec qui il danse. Le matelot s'échappe encore. Le domino s'acharne dans sa poursuite. Le matelot essaie encore un dernier miroir *(celui par où l'Image est sortie)* et, lentement, à reculons, il pénètre dans le miroir.

Le domino veut l'y poursuivre. Séparés par le cadre du miroir, les deux danseurs se livrent une lutte légère. Enfin, comme pour mieux sauter, le domino se recule. Avec les mêmes attitudes le matelot recule, disparaissant aux yeux du public *(comme le reflet recule de son objet, si l'on éloigne celui-ci).* Le domino fait un bond qui le projette contre le miroir, mais au lieu d'y rencontrer le matelot, d'un bond pareil, c'est à son propre reflet *(un domino violet)* qu'il se cogne. Étonné, il se recule. Son reflet recule. La musique cesse. Le domino, alors, avec les mêmes gestes qu'il avait au début du spectacle *(une main en visière au-dessus des yeux)* examine la salle, puis la scène, le décor, le palais. Il voit le béret du matelot, seul signe de ce qui a dû se passer. Il se baisse et le ramasse, puis il continue

sa route vers le fond de la scène, mais alors chacun des miroirs lui renvoie l'Image d'un domino semblable.

Enfin, la toile de fond étant un praticable représentant un double miroir, sans intervention apparente, cette porte s'ouvre à mesure, et selon son rythme, que s'approche le domino. Il a la démarche décrite plus haut et, la porte franchie le plancher étant incliné, son corps disparaît comme le mât d'un navire à l'horizon. Le rideau descend.

QUELQUES DÉTAILS D'EXÉCUTION. - Les danseurs doivent danser à ras du sol. Jamais ils ne bondissent. Leurs gestes sont exagérément lourds.

Quand l'Image sort du miroir, elle n'enjambe pas le cadre mais un plan incliné doit lui permettre de *descendre* du miroir sans lever les pieds.

Les trois danseurs travaillent assez longtemps pour obtenir une sorte d'identité des gestes.

Tout ce mélodrame doit donner l'impression d'un jeu. Pour cela les danseurs chargent leurs attitudes d'intentions outrées : obscènes, crapuleuses, criminelles.

Aucune ironie. C'est un ballet pour le Grand-Guignol. Le domino sera une bande de tissu qui s'enroule comme un sari. Il porte des chaussures à talons assez hauts. Même quand il danse et tue le matelot, il doit donner l'impression de dormir.

LA MUSIQUE. - Une suite de valses musettes ou de javas populaires habilement stylisées, où l'accordéon et l'harmonica ont une grande importance. Musique dite nostalgique.

Ce ballet fut dansé par M. Roland Petit sur une chorégraphie de Mlle Charrat.

L'idée m'en vint à la foire de Montmartre, devant une sorte de Palais des miroirs où semblaient emprisonnés des badauds se cognant à leur propre image, et incapables de découvrir la sortie. Je me remémorai une scène semblable dont j'avais été le témoin peiné, à Anvers, autrefois. En se superposant dans mon esprit les deux épisodes me troublèrent et, en quelques minutes, j'élaborai le ballet que je viens de décrire.

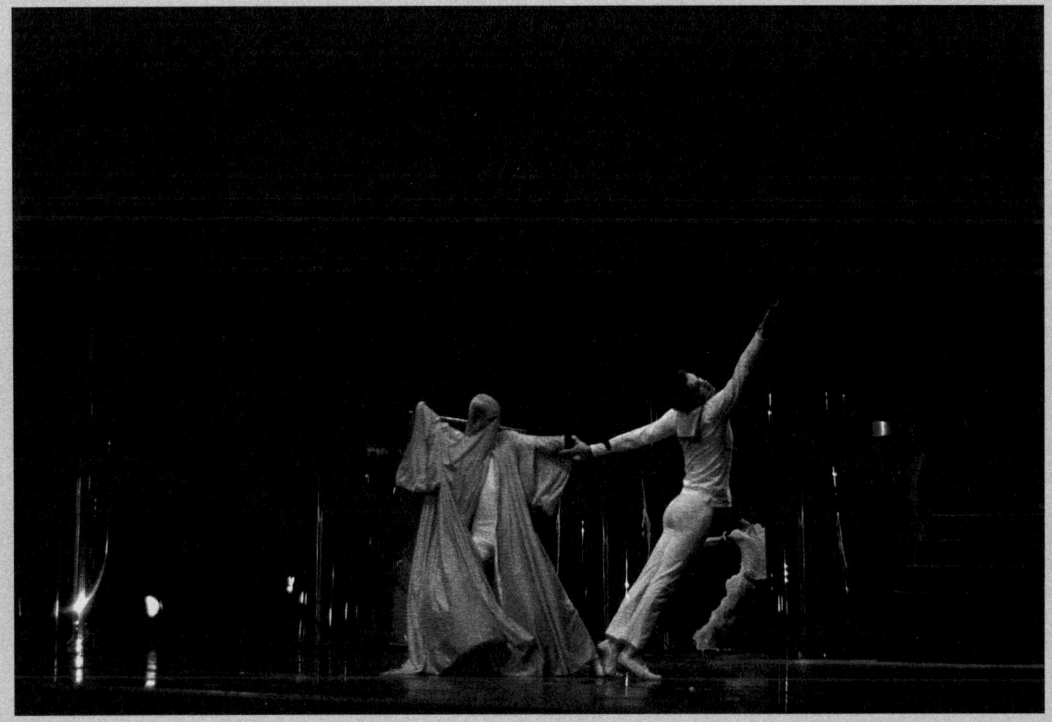

The Image Runs Away

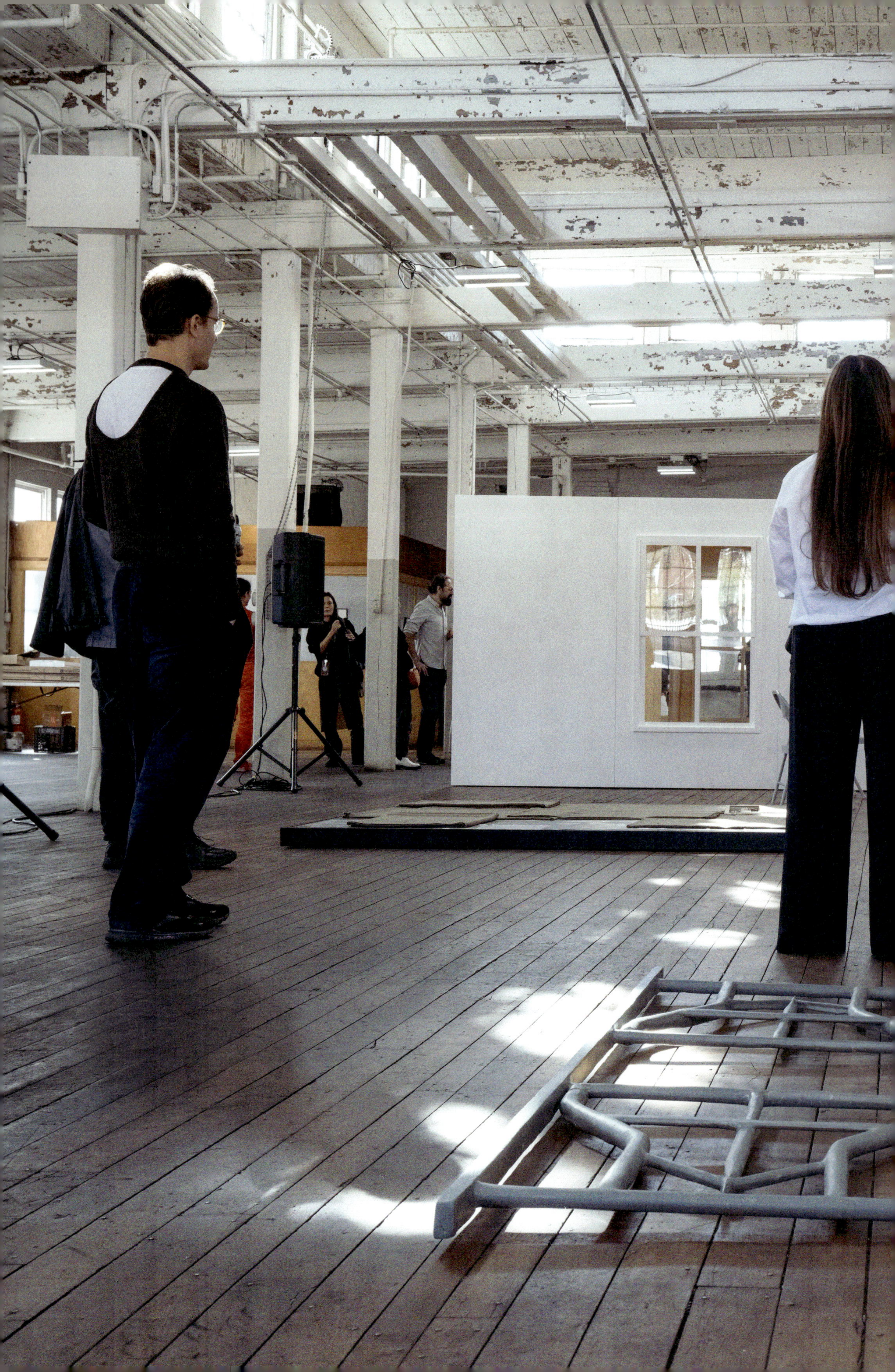

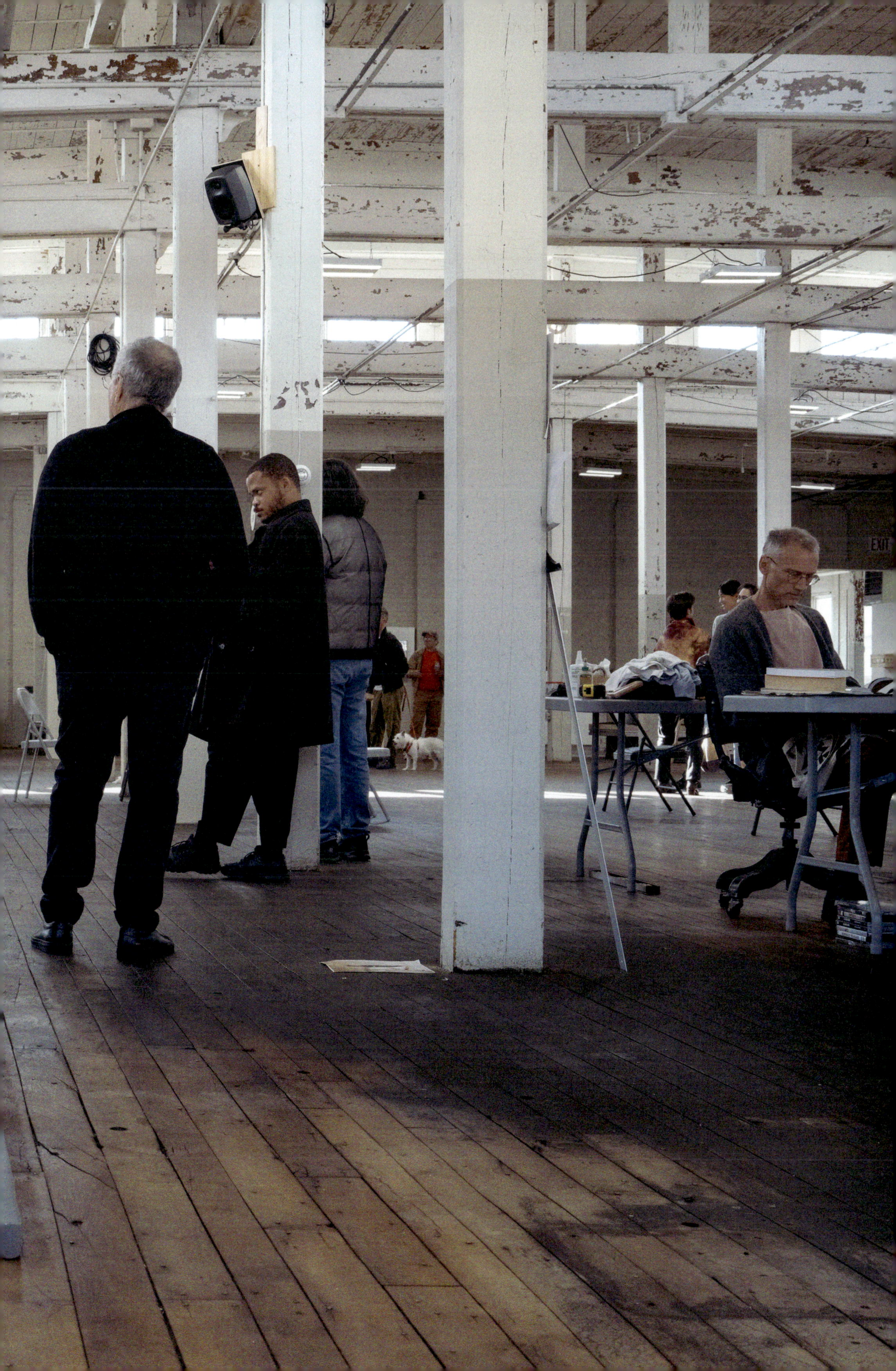

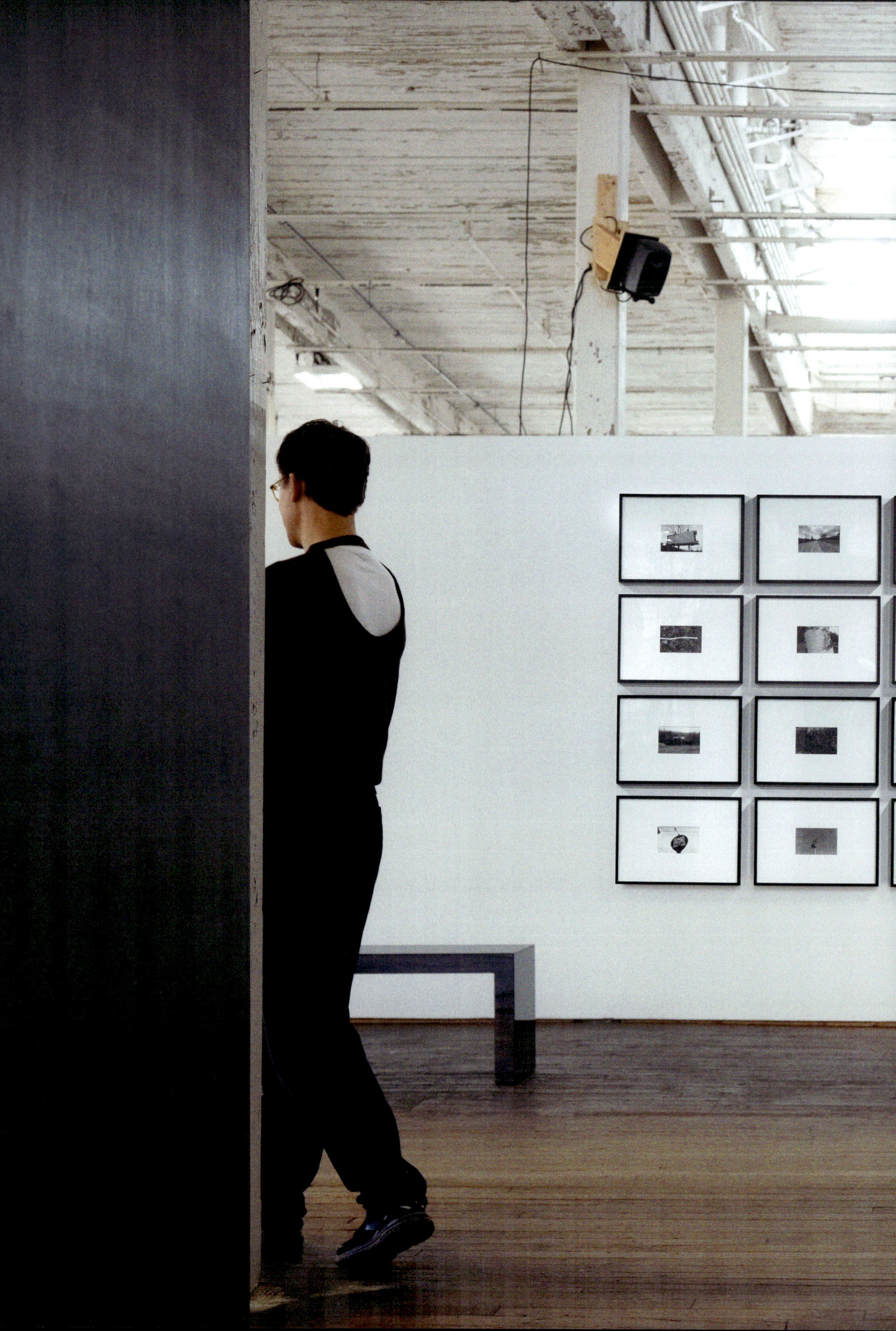

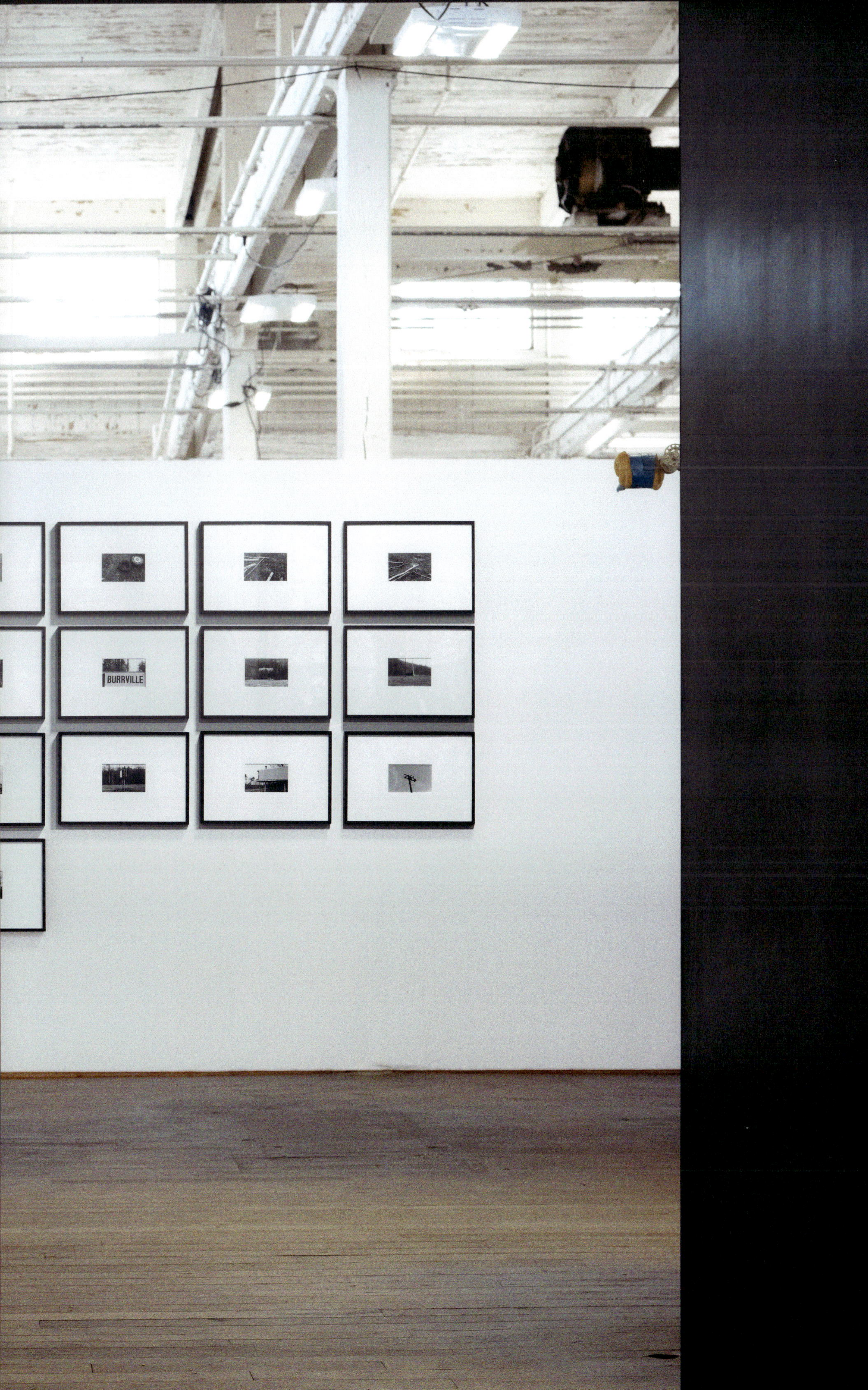

BURRVILLE

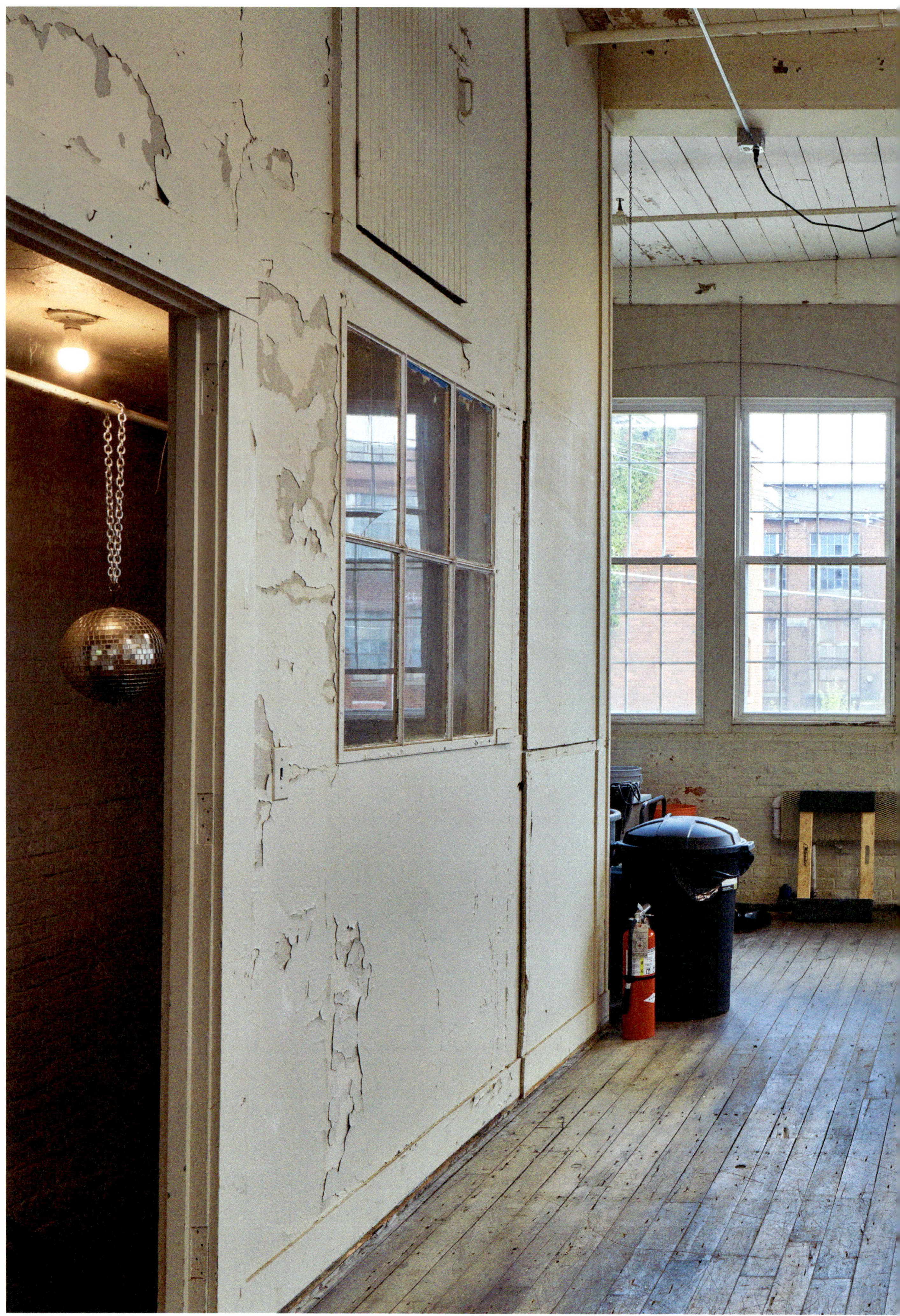

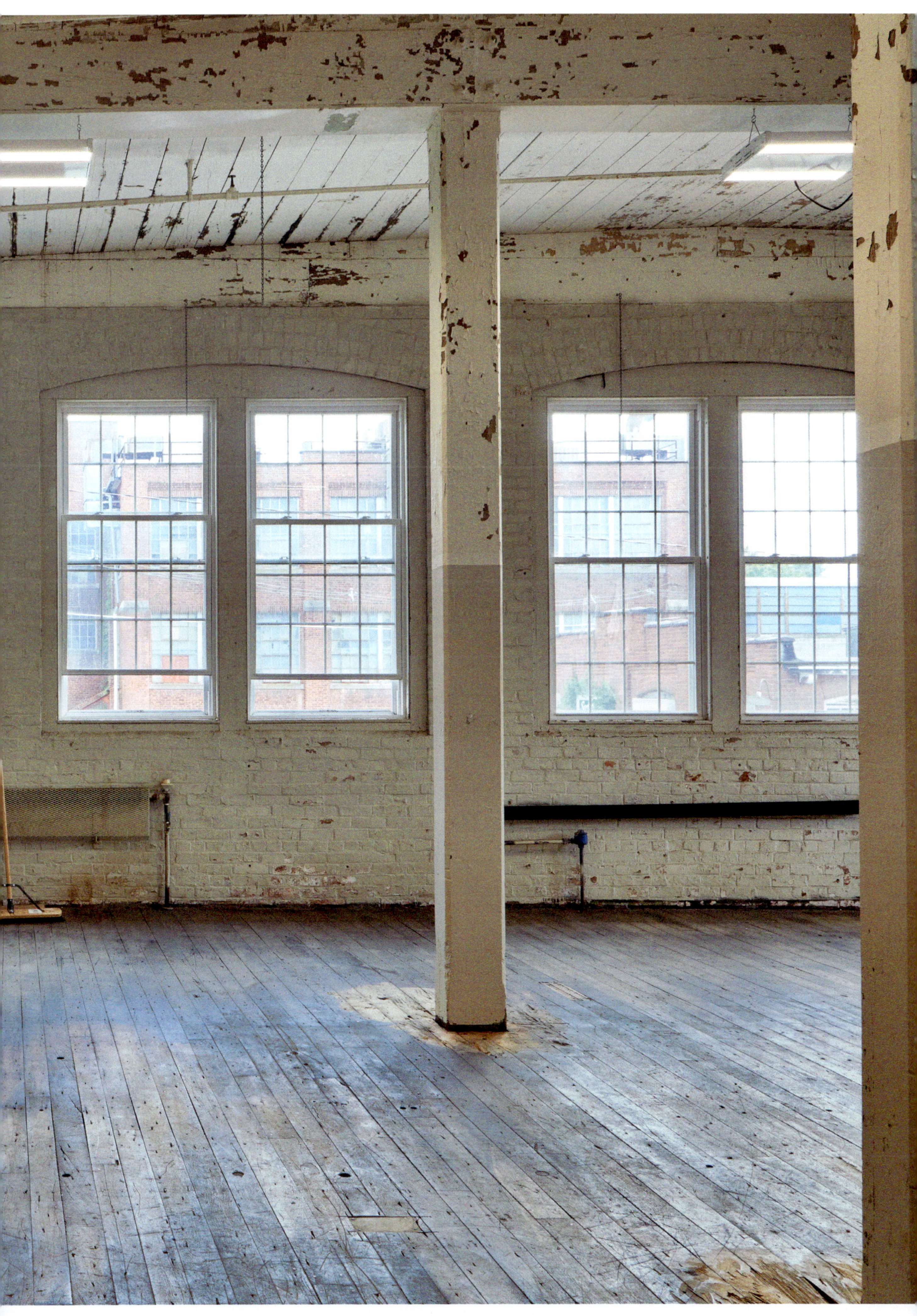

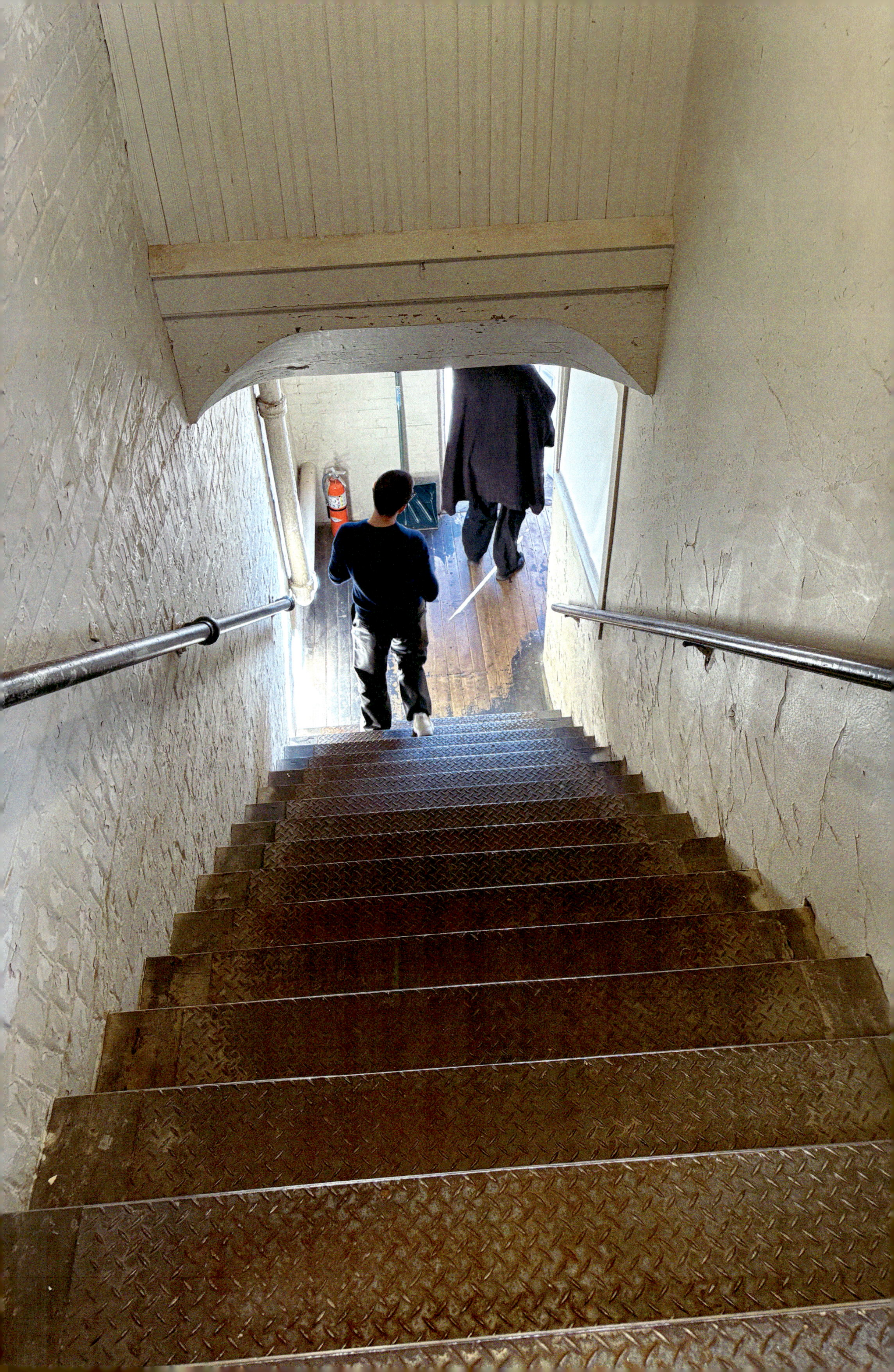

I was always taken with Prospect Cottage, Derek
Jarman's final home in Dungeness, on the south
coast of England. I admire the inscriptions he
made across the exterior clapboards, marking
the conceptual and the poetic, the physical and
the material. I appreciate the gardens he had
there, his pharmacopoeia, as he called it during
his illness there, and the recuperative elements
of that, and the ever-present maintenance
required. And of course I love the pitch-black
paint on the compact, chunky form of the house,
with the contrasting bright Hélio-esque yellow
trim. Prospect Cottage, and Jarman, were among
the dense web of inspirations for Torrington,
transhistorical blueprints for what could happen
there, at the intersection of all these scattered
points. A practice about space that is not strictly
installation, not merely sculptural, not only relational, but about other tendencies, other criteria.

I wanted to find space—to find a physical place
to make and arrange work that had a vastness
to it, a sort of boundlessness, yet still with clear
boundaries in place—physical, architectural
boundaries, but also temporal limitations. I didn't
want this to go on indefinitely.

2, left: Exterior of *Torrington Project* at 535 Migeon Avenue, Torrington, CT. Photo: Tom Burr

7, right: Plaque featuring an excerpt of Tom Burr's poem "Untitled," 2010, enameled plaque, 8 × 11 in. © Tom Burr. Photo: Jackie Furtado

19: Tom Burr, floor plan of 535 Migeon Avenue, Torrington, CT

21–24: Interior views of *Torrington Project*. © Tom Burr. Photos: Guang Xu

25: Tom Burr, *Another thought (for Arthur Russell)*, 2022, paper record sleeves, steel pushpins, stained plywood, 15 × 15 × 1½ in. © Tom Burr. Photo: Elijah Jaquez-Starks

26: Tom Burr, *Ashtray (Smoke)*, 2000, wood, paint, mirrored Plexiglas, Plexiglas, black plastic ashtray, 5½ × 10½ × 10½ in. Shown here alongside other works by the artist: *Untitled*, 1998, 24 Polaroids mounted on cardboard, 20½ × 24½ in.; and *Nightstand*, 1993, MDF, 27½ × 12 × 15¾ in. © Tom Burr. Photo: Blake Oetting

27: Installation view of Tom Burr, *The Storage Project*, 1993, MDF sculptures, dimensions variable. Included in *Project Unité*, Unité d'Habitation, Firminy, France, 1993. © Tom Burr. Photo courtesy Bortolami Gallery, New York.

27: Tom Burr, page from an untitled text, printed in the second volume of the exhibition catalog for *Project Unité*, curated by Yves Aupetitallot in 1993 at the Unité d'Habitation in Firminy, France. © Tom Burr. Scan courtesy Bortolami Gallery, New York

28–29, left: Ull Hohn, *Untitled*, 1988, oil on canvas, 18 × 18 in.; right: Ull Hohn, *Untitled*, 1988, oil on canvas, 18 × 18 in. © Ull Hohn. Photo: Guang Xu

30: Interior view of *Torrington Project*, featuring the ashtray from Tom Burr, *Smoke Me*, 2020, silver permanent marker on black melamine ashtray, mirrored base. © Tom Burr. Photo: Tom Burr

31, top: Tom Burr, *Pulse*, 2023, black faux leather and chrome couch, chrome floor lamp, vintage disco ball, blue wool blanket, 29½ × 82¾ × 27½ in. Included in *Tom Burr*, Bortolami Gallery, New York, 2023. © Tom Burr. Photo: Guang Xu

31, bottom: Tom Burr, *A Pair of Black Chairs*, 2023, two black faux leather and wood chairs, a copy of Leo Bersani's book *Caravaggio's Secrets*, a pair of leather boots, 28½ × 64⅜ × 26½ in. Included in *Tom Burr*, Bortolami Gallery, New York, 2023. © Tom Burr. Photo: Guang Xu

32–33: Interior view of *Torrington Project*. © Tom Burr. Photo: Jackie Furtado

33: Tom Burr, *Mahogany Door (May Day Speech)*, 2021, wooden door from the executive office at the Pirelli Building in New Haven, CT, designed by Marcel Breuer, direct-to-surface print on aluminum panel, iron C-clamp, 84 × 29⅞ in. © Tom Burr. Photo: Jessica Tang

34, top, left: Tom Burr, *Body/Building*, 2017, installation, featuring a superimposed image of Jean Genet on the façade of the Pirelli Building in New Haven, CT, designed by Marcel Breuer. © Tom Burr. Courtesy Bortolami Gallery. Photo: Jessica Smolinski

34, top, right: Tom Burr, *Mahogany Door (the maids)*, 2017, wooden door from the executive office at the Pirelli Building in New Haven, CT, designed by Marcel Breuer, 84 × 29⅞ in. Included in *Body/Building*, Pirelli Building, New Haven, CT, 2017. © Tom Burr. Photo: Jessica Smolinski

34, bottom: Tom Burr, *The Railings (May, 1970)*, 2017, blackened steel, polished steel etched with Jean Genet's 1970 "May Day Speech," tempered glass, 42 × 540 × 300 in. Included in *Body/Building*, Pirelli Building, New Haven, CT, 2017. © Tom Burr. Photo: Jessica Smolinski

35: Tom Burr, *Dark Hang*, 2012, cast bronze, 8½ × 16 in. © Tom Burr. Installed with Gordon Hall, *Belt (Torrington)*, 2024, colored pencil on paper, wood peg, hung on a bronze coat hanger by Tom Burr, 40¾ × 2¼ in. (flat). © Gordon Hall. Photo: Jackie Furtado

36: Gordon Hall, *Three-Part Stool (Corrugated)*, 2023, pigmented cast concrete, 14 × 14 × 19¼ in. © Gordon Hall. In the background: Alvin Baltrop, *The Piers (warehouse interior)*, n.d. (1975–86), silver gelatin print, 6½ × 9¾ in. © 2025 Estate of Alvin Baltrop / Artists Rights Society (ARS), New York. Loaned to Tom Burr by Patrick Collins and Liv Barrett for a one-day exhibition and performance program. Photo: Jackie Furtado

37: Alvin Baltrop, *The Piers (warehouse interior)*, n.d (1975–86). © 2025 Estate of Alvin Baltrop / Artists Rights Society (ARS), New York. Photo: Jackie Furtado

38–39: Tom Burr, documentation of *Circa '77*, 1995, 5 silver gelatin prints, 6⅛ × 9⅜ in. each. © Tom Burr. In the background: Gordon Hall, *Turned Hanging Bar*, 2024, cast concrete, enamel, 27½ × 48 × 1½ in. © Gordon Hall. Photo: Jackie Furtado

40, top: Tom Burr, *Circa '77*, 1995, plywood, soil, plants, debris, 23⅝ × 157½ × 157½ in. Included in *Platzwechsel*, Kunsthalle Zürich and Schweizerisches Landesmuseum, Zurich, 1995, curated by Christian Philipp Müller. © Tom Burr

40, bottom: Tom Burr, *Circa '77* (detail), 1995. Included in *Platzwechsel*, Kunsthalle Zürich and Schweizerisches Landesmuseum, Zurich, 1995, curated by Christian Philipp Müller. © Tom Burr

41–42: Tom Burr, "Trash," in *Platzwechsel*, exhibition catalog (Kunsthalle Zürich, 1995), p. 69, 83. Scan courtesy Bortolami Gallery, New York

43–47: Debris from Tom Burr, *Circa '77*, 1995. © Tom Burr. Photos: Elijah Jaquez-Starks

52–53: Interior view of *Torrington Project*. © Tom Burr. Photo: Jessica Tang

54, top: Tom Burr, *Walt Whitman Park, Brooklyn*, 1996/2023, aluminum stages, plywood, topsoil, photocopies, cardboard box, debris, 19⅝ × 130 × 123 in. Photo: Guang Xu

54, bottom, left: Tom Burr, *Walt Whitman Park, Brooklyn* (detail), 1996/2023. Photo: Guang Xu

54, bottom right: Wrapped elements from Tom Burr, *Walt Whitman Park, Brooklyn*, 1996/2023. © Tom Burr. Photo: Elijah Jaquez-Starks

55, top: Tom Burr, *Walt Whitman Park, Brooklyn*, 1996/2023. Included in *John Knight, Brandon Ndife, Tom Burr, Diamond Stingily*, Greene Naftali, New York, 2023. © Tom Burr. Photo: Zeshan Ahmed

55, bottom: Tom Burr, *Walt Whitman Park, Brooklyn* (detail), 1996/2023. Included in *John Knight, Brandon Ndife, Tom Burr, Diamond Stingily*, Greene Naftali, New York, 2023. © Tom Burr. Photo: Zeshan Ahmed

56, left: Tom Burr, *Walt Whitman Park, Brooklyn* (detail), 1996/2023. © Tom Burr; right: Ull Hohn, *Untitled*, 1988. © Ull Hohn. Photo: Jackie Furtado

57: Ull Hohn, *Untitled*, 1988. © Ull Hohn. Photo: Jackie Furtado

58, top: Ull Hohn, *Untitled*, 1994–95, pencil on paper, 14 × 11 in. © Ull Hohn. Photo: Elijah Jaquez-Starks

58, bottom: Ull Hohn, *Untitled*, 1988. © Ull Hohn. Photo: Jackie Furtado

59, top: Tom Burr, *The Eighth Renovation*, from *Eight Renovations: A constellation of sites across Manhattan*, 1997, vinyl lettering, dimensions variable. © Tom Burr. Photo: Elijah Jaquez-Starks

59, bottom: Tom Burr, *The Eighth Renovation*, 1997. © Tom Burr. Photo: Jackie Furtado

60: Tom Burr, *Dark Hang*, 2012. © Tom Burr. Photo: Guang Xu

61: Tom Burr, *Room Four*, 2012, patinated bronze, electrical cord, lightbulb, 184⅓ × 152¾ × 98⅔ in. © Tom Burr. Photo courtesy Galerie Neu, Berlin. Photo: Stefan Korte

62: Plants used as part of the refabrication of Tom Burr, *Construction of an American Garden*, 1993. Photo: Elijah Jaquez-Starks

63: Graffiti found in the bathroom at 535 Migeon Avenue, Torrington, CT. Photo: Elijah Jaquez-Starks

64: Tom Burr's childhood handprint, 1968. Photo: Jackie Furtado

65: Plaques featuring Tom Burr's poem "Untitled," 2010, enameled plaques, 8 × 11 in. © Tom Burr. Photo: Elijah Jaquez-Starks

66, top: Interior view of *Torrington Project*. © Tom Burr. Photo: Elijah Jaquez-Starks

66, bottom: Tom Burr, *Edge of Seventeen*, 2017, laser print, 11 × 8½ in. © Tom Burr. Photo: Elijah Jaquez-Starks

67: Tom Burr, *The Seventh Renovation*, from *Eight Renovations: A constellation of sites across Manhattan*, 1997, vinyl lettering, dimensions variable. © Tom Burr. Photo: Jackie Furtado

68: Tom Burr, *Put Down*, 2019, silkscreen print on blueback paper 120 gr., 26¾ × 37 in. © Tom Burr. Photo: Elijah Jaquez-Starks

69, top: Left: Tom Burr, *Capricornus IV*, 2023, pigment print, 7 × 10 in.; right: Tom Burr, *Capricornus I*, 2023, 9 pigment prints, 7 × 10 in. each. Included in *Tom Burr*, Bortolami Gallery, New York, 2023. © Tom Burr. Photo: Guang Xu

69, bottom: Tom Burr, *Capricornus IV*, 2023. © Tom Burr. Photo: Guang Xu

70–71, top: Tom Burr, *Capricornus III*, 2023, 9 pigment prints, 7 × 10 in. each.; middle: Tom Burr, *Capricornus II*, 2023, 9

pigment prints, 7 × 10 in. each.; bottom: Tom Burr, *Capricornus I*, 2023. © Tom Burr. Photos: Guang Xu

73: Interior view of *Torrington Project*. © Tom Burr. Photo: Jackie Furtado

74–75: Tom Burr, *Container (1–3)* (detail), 2001, stained plywood, rubber, 98⅜ × 98⅜ × 98⅜ in. each. © Tom Burr. Photo: Guang Xu

76–77: Left: Tom Burr, *Black Sleeves*, 2009, plywood, black stain, paper record sleeves, steel pushpins, 48 × 48 × 2 in.; middle: Tom Burr, one of the braces used in *Tom Burr*, Bortolami Gallery, New York, 2023, steel, 9 × 9 × 72 in. © Tom Burr. Right: Gordon Hall, *Shim (Tom)*, 2024, cast brass, 28 × 1 × 4 in. © Gordon Hall

78, top: Tom Burr, *The First Renovation*, from *Eight Renovations: A constellation of sites across Manhattan*, 1997, vinyl lettering, dimensions variable. © Tom Burr. Photo: Tom Burr

78, bottom: Ull Hohn, *Untitled*, 1988. © Ull Hohn. Photo: Jackie Furtado

78–79: Interior view of *Torrington Project* featuring Maria Hassabi, *Bench*, 2024, wood, acrylic mirrors, steel, 17¾ × 78¾ × 17¾ in. © Tom Burr and Maria Hassabi. Photo: Jackie Furtado

80–81: Tom Burr, *Burrville*, 2006, 21 black-and-white photographs, 4½ × 7 in. each. © Tom Burr. Photo: Guang Xu

81: Tom Burr, *Burrville*, 2006, installed alongside *Abstract Lausanne I* and *Abstract Lausanne II*, both 2006. Included in *Tom Burr: Extrospective: Works 1994–2006*, Musée cantonal des Beaux-Arts, Lausanne, Switzerland, 2006. © Tom Burr and Musée cantonal des Beaux-Arts de Lausanne. Photo: Jean-Claude Durcet

82: Tom Burr, *Burlesque*, 2024, plywood, aluminum, glass mirror, silver paint, aluminum hardware, cotton shirt, 72 × 72 in. © Tom Burr. Photo: Guang Xu

83, top: Left: Tom Burr, *Untitled (Private Property) #5*, 1999, collage and ink on board, 16⅛ × 20½ in.; right: Tom Burr, *Untitled (Private Property) #3*, 1999, collage and ink on board, 16⅛ × 20½ in. © Tom Burr. Photo: Guang Xu

83, bottom: Tom Burr, *Untitled*, 1998. © Tom Burr. Photo: Guang Xu

84: Reconstruction of Tom Burr, *Container (1–3)*, 2001. © Tom Burr. Photos: Elijah Jaquez-Starks

85, top, left: Wrapped elements of Tom Burr, *Container (1–3)*, 2001. © Tom Burr. Photo: Tom Burr

85, top right: Reconstruction of Tom Burr, *Container (1–3)*, 2001. © Tom Burr. Photos: Elijah Jaquez-Starks

85, bottom: Tom Burr, *Container (1–3)* (detail), 2001. © Tom Burr. Photo: Elijah Jaquez-Starks

86: Tom Burr, *Container (1–3)* (detail), 2001. © Tom Burr. Photo: Guang Xu

87, top: Left: Tom Burr, *Container (1–3)* (detail), 2001; right: Tom Burr, *Construction of an American Garden*, 1993, plywood, soil, plants, stamp, base: 48 × 48 × 48 in. © Tom Burr. Photo: Guang Xu

87, bottom: Tom Burr, *Wide Wall Wound* (detail), 2017, white polyester fabric, dimensions variable. © Tom Burr. Photo: Tom Burr

92: Left: Tom Burr, *Container (1–3)* (detail), 2001; right: Tom Burr, *Wide Wall Wound* (detail), 2017. © Tom Burr. Photo: Guang Xu

93, top: Tom Burr, *Container (1–3)*, 2001. Included in the Galerie Neu booth at the 2001 Art Forum fair, Berlin. © Tom Burr. Photo courtesy Galerie Neu. Photo: Thomas Michalak

93, bottom: Tom Burr, *Container (1–3)*, 2001, installed alongside paintings by Ull Hohn. Included in *Partnerschaften: Unterbrochene Karrieren*, nGbK, Berlin, 2001. © Tom Burr and Ull Hohn. Photo courtesy Galerie Neu. Photo: Thomas Michalak

94: Tom Burr, *Container (1–3)*, 2001, installed alongside paintings by Ull Hohn. Included in *Partnerschaften: Unterbrochene Karrieren*, nGbK, Berlin, 2001. © Tom Burr and Ull Hohn. Photo courtesy Galerie Neu. Photo: Thomas Michalak

95: Tom Burr, *Wide Wall Wound* (detail), 2017. © Tom Burr. Photo: Guang Xu

96: Tom Burr, *Wide Wall Wound* (detail), 2017. © Tom Burr. Included in the background: Alvin Baltrop, *Hand holding cigarette*, n.d., silver gelatin print, 7⅜ × 4⅞ in. © 2025 Estate of Alvin Baltrop / Artists Rights Society (ARS), New York. Photo: Jackie Furtado

97: Alvin Baltrop, *Hand holding cigarette*, n.d. © 2025 Estate of Alvin Baltrop / Artists Rights Society (ARS), New York. Photo: Jackie Furtado

98: Tom Burr, *Construction of an American Garden*, 1993. © Tom Burr. Photo: Elijah Jaquez-Starks

99: Tom Burr, *Construction of an American Garden*, 1993, detail of Tom Burr's American Fine Arts, Co. stamp. © Tom Burr. Photo: Guang Xu

100–1: Interior view of *Torrington Project*. © Tom Burr. Photo: Guang Xu

102: Tom Burr, *Construction of an American Garden* (details), 1993. © Tom Burr. Photos: Elijah Jaquez-Starks

103: Tom Burr, *Construction of an American Garden*, 1993. Included in *What Happened to the Institutional Critique?*, American Fine Arts, Co., New York, 1993, curated by James Meyer. © Tom Burr. Photo courtesy Bortolami Gallery, New York

104–5: Tom Burr's proposal for Sonsbeek 93, printed in *Sonsbeek 93*, edited by Valerie Smith (Snoeck-Ducaju & Zoon, 1993), pp. 107–8. Scan courtesy Bortolami Gallery, New York

106: Fax from Valerie Smith, curator of Sonsbeek 93, to Tom Burr regarding his de-installation plans for *An American Garden*. Scan courtesy Valerie Smith and Bortolami Gallery, New York

107: Tom Burr, *An American Garden*, 1993, bricks, soil, plants, placards, dimensions variable. Included in Sonsbeek 93, Arnhem, the Netherlands, 1993, curated by Valerie Smith. © Tom Burr. Photo: Tom Burr

108: Production of Tom Burr, *An American Garden*, 1993. © Tom Burr. Photos: Tom Burr

109: Mark left after the removal of Tom Burr, *Construction of an American Garden*, 1993, from 535 Migeon Avenue. Photo: Tom Burr

116, top: Ull Hohn, *Untitled*, 1988, oil on canvas, 16 × 18 in., installed alongside Tom Burr, *Container (1–3)* (detail), 2001. © Ull Hohn and Tom Burr. Loaned to Tom Burr by Patrick Collins and Liv Barrett for a one-day exhibition and performance program. Photo: Jackie Furtado

116, bottom: Ull Hohn, *Untitled*, 1988. © Ull Hohn. Photo: Jackie Furtado

117, top: Ull Hohn, *Untitled*, 1989–90, oil and varnish on wood, 14 1/8 × 14 in. © Ull Hohn. Loaned to Tom Burr by Patrick Collins and Liv Barrett for a one-day exhibition and performance program. Photo: Jackie Furtado

117, bottom: Ull Hohn, *Untitled*, 1989–90, installed alongside Tom Burr, *Container (1–3)*, 2001, and Tom Burr, *Wide Wall Wound* (details), 2017. © Ull Hohn and Tom Burr. Photo: Jackie Furtado

118–19: Interior view of *Torrington Project*. © Tom Burr. Photo: Jackie Furtado

121: Interior view of *Torrington Project*. © Tom Burr. Photo: Guang Xu

122–23: Interior view of *Torrington Project* featuring Tom Burr's *Atlas* series, 2022. © Tom Burr. Photo: Guang Xu

124: Verso of one of the works in Tom Burr's *Atlas* series, 2022. © Tom Burr. Photo: Tom Burr

125: Production of Tom Burr's *Atlas* series, 2022. © Tom Burr. Photos: Elijah Jaquez-Starks

126, top: Tom Burr's *Atlas* series and *CONFIGURATION (NEXT) GENERATION*, both 2022. Included in *Compressions*, Galerie Neu, Berlin, 2022. © Tom Burr. Courtesy Galerie Neu, Berlin. Photo: Stefan Korte

126, bottom: Tom Burr, *Atlas I*, 2022, plywood and aluminum panel, black-and-white photographs, orange safety fabric, plastic sleeves, steel pushpins, tacks, 72 × 72 × 1 3/8 in. Included in *Compressions*, Galerie Neu, Berlin, 2022. © Tom Burr. Courtesy Galerie Neu, Berlin. Photo: Stefan Korte

127, top: Tom Burr, *CONFIGURATION (NEXT) GENERATION* (detail), 2022, stained plywood, Plexiglas, metal bed frames, blankets, pillow, DVDs, magazines, books, clamps, straps, 55 7/8 × 217 3/8 × 217 3/8 in. Included in *Compressions*, Galerie Neu, Berlin, 2022. © Tom Burr. Courtesy Galerie Neu, Berlin. Photo: Stefan Korte

127, bottom, left: Tom Burr, *Atlas II*, 2022, plywood and aluminum panel, black-and-white photographs, orange safety fabric, plastic sleeves, steel pushpins, tacks, 72 × 72 × 1 3/8 in.; right: Tom Burr, *CONFIGURATION (NEXT) GENERATION* (detail), 2022. Included in *Compressions*, Galerie Neu, Berlin, 2022. © Tom Burr. Courtesy Galerie Neu, Berlin. Photo: Stefan Korte

128–29: Tom Burr, *Atlas II* (detail), 2022. © Tom Burr. Courtesy Galerie Neu, Berlin. Photo: Stefan Korte

130: Tom Burr, *CONFIGURATION (NEXT) GENERATION*, 2022. Included in *Compressions*, Galerie Neu, Berlin, 2022. © Tom Burr. Courtesy Galerie Neu, Berlin. Photo: Stefan Korte

131, top: Tom Burr, *Atlas III*, 2022, plywood and aluminum panel, black-and-white photographs, orange safety fabric, plastic sleeves, tacks, 72 × 72 × 1 3/8 in., installed alongside Tom Burr, *CONFIGURATION (NEXT) GENERATION*, 2022. Included in *Compressions*, Galerie Neu, Berlin, 2022. © Tom Burr. Courtesy Galerie Neu, Berlin. Photo: Stefan Korte

131, bottom: Floor plan of Tom Burr's 2022 exhibition *Compressions* at Galerie Neu, Berlin. © Tom Burr. Photo: Tom Burr

138–39: Production of Tom Burr, *Double Disco*, 2023, plywood, acrylic paint, Plexiglas, direct-to-surface print on stainless steel, 72 × 120 × 3 3/4 in. © Tom Burr. Photo: Elijah Jaquez-Starks

140, top: Production of Tom Burr, *Opening Sequence (blue)*, 2023, plywood, acrylic paint, Plexiglas, direct-to-surface print on stainless steel, 72 × 120 × 3 3/4 in. © Tom Burr. Photo: Elijah Jaquez-Starks

140, bottom: Floor model for *Tom Burr*, Bortolami Gallery, New York, 2023. © Tom Burr. Photo: Tom Burr

141, top: Tom Burr, *Johns (my father's chest)* (detail), 2023, painted wood chest of drawers, steel garment box, set of long underwear, handkerchief, stained plywood, 51 × 96 × 27 in. © Tom Burr. Photo: Elijah Jaquez-Starks

141, bottom: Production of Tom Burr, *Stage*, 2023, plywood, acrylic paint, Plexiglas, direct-to-surface print on stainless steel, 72 × 120 × 3 3/4 in. © Tom Burr. Photo: Elijah Jaquez-Starks

142–43: Installation view of *Tom Burr*, Bortolami Gallery, New York, 2023. © Tom Burr. Photo: Guang Xu

144–45: Tom Burr, *Johns (my father's chest)*, and Tom Burr, *Stage*, both 2023. Included in *Tom Burr*, Bortolami Gallery, New York, 2023. © Tom Burr. Photo: Guang Xu

146: Tom Burr, one of the braces used in *Tom Burr*, Bortolami Gallery, New York, 2023, steel, 9 × 9 × 51 in. © Tom Burr. Photo: Guang Xu

147–48: Installation views of *Tom Burr*, Bortolami Gallery, 2023. © Tom Burr. Photos: Guang Xu

149: Tom Burr, one of the braces used in *Tom Burr*, Bortolami Gallery, New York, 2023. © Tom Burr. Photo: Guang Xu

150: Interior view of *Torrington Project* featuring Tom Burr's *Journal* series, 2024. © Tom Burr. Photo: Jackie Furtado

151: Tom Burr, *Twelve (Skin Deep – Blue)*, 2024, painted wood panel, powder-coated aluminum panel and hardware, blue cotton shirt, psoriasis drug brochure, thumbtacks, nails, 27 × 27 × 2 1/8 in. © Tom Burr. Photo: Guang Xu

152: Tom Burr, *Nineteen (Faded Orange Cover)*, 2024, painted wood panel, powder-coated aluminum panel and hardware, front and back cover of Rainer Crone's catalogue raisonné of *Andy Warhol* (1970), book page with Balenciaga jacket, page from Joseph Grigely's *Oceans of Love: The Uncontainable Gregory Battcock*, thumbtacks, nails, 27 × 27 × 2 1/8 in. © Tom Burr. Photo: Guang Xu

153–55: Interior views of *Torrington Project* featuring Tom Burr's *Journal* series, 2024. © Tom Burr. Photos: Guang Xu

156: Tom Burr, *Thirteen (Brutal Purple)*, 2024, painted wood panel, powder-coated aluminum panel and hardware, pages from *Riots and Disturbances in Correctional Institutions* (1981), postcards from Burr's *Deep Purple* exhibition at the Whitney Museum of American Art, October 30, 2002–January 4, 2003, photograph of *Deep Purple* in the Whitney Museum's Marcel Breuer courtyard, thumbtacks, nails, 27 × 27 × 2 1/8 in. © Tom Burr. Photo: Guang Xu

157: Tom Burr, *Sixteen (Blue / Scott)*, 2024, painted wood panel, powder-coated aluminum panel and hardware, pages from the exhibition catalog *Scott Burton Chairs* (1983), blue vinyl sleeve, thumbtacks, nails, 27 × 27 × 2 1/8 in. © Tom Burr. Photo: Guang Xu

158: Tom Burr, *Fourteen (I see you face to face!)*, 2024, painted wood panel, powder-coated aluminum panel and hardware, pages from Walt Whitman's *Leaves of Grass*, photograph ca. late 1990s, clear Plexiglas, cotton shirt, thumbtacks, nails, 27 × 27 × 2 1/8 in. © Tom Burr. Photo: Guang Xu

159: Tom Burr, *Nine (Jewel Box)*, 2024, painted wood panel, powder coated aluminum panel and hardware, pages of photographs by Howard Sooley from the book *Derek Jarman's Garden* (1995), page from "Rescue, Response, and Resilience: A Critical Incident Review of the Orlando Public Safety Response to the Attack on the Pulse Nightclub" (2017–2023), two photographs c. 2000, clear Plexiglas, thumbtacks, nails, 27 × 27 × 2 1/8 in. © Tom Burr. Photo courtesy Galerie Neu, Berlin. Photo: Joerg Lohse

160: Tom Burr, *Six (Where Angels Tread)*, 2024, painted wood panel, powder coated aluminum panel and hardware, pages from *Art In America* (Summer 1983), pages from *Numbers* magazine (1979), blue plastic sleeve, thumbtacks, nails, 27 × 27 × 2 1/8 in. © Tom Burr. Courtesy of Galerie Neu, Berlin. Photo: Joerg Lohse.

161: Tom Burr, *Eight (Hotel Bathroom Doorframe)*, 2024, painted wood panel, powder coated aluminum panel and hardware, clear plastic sleeves, cardboard, cardboard box lid, page from Rainer Crone's *Andy Warhol* (1970), photograph c. 2000, thumbtacks, nails, 27 × 27 × 2 1/8 in. © Tom Burr. Courtesy of Galerie Neu, Berlin. Photo: Joerg Lohse.

162: Tom Burr, *Ten (Soleil Privé)*, 2024, painted wood panel, powder coated aluminum panel and hardware, black bomber jacket, photograph from *Palm Beach Views* (1999), used as an announcement card for the exhibition at the Ludwig Museum, Cologne, *Family Ties: The Schroeder Donation* (2019), thumbtacks, nails, 27 × 27 × 2 1/8 in. © Tom Burr. Courtesy of Galerie Neu, Berlin. Photo: Joerg Lohse.

163: Tom Burr, *Seven (Clear Orange Camo)*, 2024, painted wood panel, powder coated aluminum panel and hardware, page from E.C. Goossen, ed., *Ellsworth Kelly* (1973), pages from *Mandate* magazine (1982), clear Plexiglas, thumbtacks, nails, 27 × 27 × 2 1/8 in. © Tom Burr. Courtesy of Galerie Neu, Berlin. Photo: Joerg Lohse.

164: Tom Burr, *Constricted Edition*, 2006, white painted wood, printed cardboard, tape, hinges, screws, nails, tracing paper, folded: 9 3/4 × 8 1/4 × 2 3/8 in., unfolded: 4 × 37 3/8 × 9 3/4 in. © Tom Burr. Photo: Elijah Jaquez-Starks

165: Bortolami Gallery photoshoot of Tom Burr's *Visit* collages, 2023. © Tom Burr. Photo: Tom Burr

166, top: Tom Burr, *The Visit II*, 2023, photographic collage and paint on wood panel, LED light strip, 2 panels, 24 × 24 in. each. © Tom Burr. Photo: Guang Xu

166, bottom: Tom Burr, *The Visit III*, 2023, photographic collage and paint on wood panel, LED light strip, 2 panels, 24 × 24 in. each. © Tom Burr. Photo: Guang Xu

167, top: Tom Burr, *The Visit I*, 2023, photographic collage and paint on wood panel, LED light strip, 2 panels, 24 × 24 in. each. © Tom Burr. Photo: Guang Xu

167, bottom: Bortolami Gallery documentation of Tom Burr, *The Visit I*, 2023. © Tom Burr. Photo: Guang Xu

168–69: Interior view of *Torrington Project* featuring Tom Burr's research tables. Photo: Guang Xu

170–75: Tom Burr's research tables (details). Photos: Guang Xu

176–77: A detail of Tom Burr's research tables, featuring the stamp he made of American Fine Arts, Co.'s original letterhead. Photo: Guang Xu

178–79: Interior view of *Torrington Project*. © Tom Burr. Photo: Jackie Furtado

181: Interior view of *Torrington Project*. © Tom Burr. Photo: Guang Xu

182–83: Interior view of *Torrington Project* featuring Gordon Hall, *Table Support Structure (Laying)*, 2024, sculpting epoxy, steel, 94 × 27 × 2 in. © Tom Burr and Gordon Hall. Photo: Jackie Furtado

184: Gordon Hall, *Table Support Structure (Laying)*, 2024, and Gordon Hall, *Table Support Structure (Standing)*, 2024, sculpting epoxy, steel, 94 × 27 × 2 in. © Gordon Hall. Photo: Jackie Furtado

185, top: Gordon Hall, *Table Support Structure (Laying)*, 2024. © Gordon Hall. Photo: Jackie Furtado

185, bottom: Gordon Hall, *Table Support Structure (Standing)* (detail), 2024. © Gordon Hall. Photo: Jackie Furtado

186: Tom Burr, *Bent, Bandaged, Beat Up, Beat Up Again and Bewildered*, 2008, painted wood, bandage, metallic chain, 64 5/8 × 59 × 23 5/8 in. © Tom Burr. Photo: Elijah Jaquez-Starks

187: Tom Burr, *An Abstract Orange*, 2022, birch plywood, paint, glass mirror, fabric, *abstracts* journal (1986), spring clamps, C-clamps, cabinet hinges, wire rope, 80 3/8 × 18 × 64 1/8 in. Included in *detention/suspension/expulsion*, Maureen Paley, Studio M, London, 2022. © Tom Burr. Courtesy Maureen Paley, London. Photo: Mark Blower

188, top: Tom Burr, *Neurotica Etcetera*, 2022, birch plywood, paint, glass mirror, issues of *Neurotica Magazine* (1948–51), rubber gloves, spring clamps, C-clamps, cabinet hinges, carpet, 30 1/2 × 24 1/8 × 87 7/8 in. Included in *detention/suspension/expulsion*, Maureen Paley, Studio M, London, 2022. © Tom Burr. Courtesy Maureen Paley, London. Photo: Mark Blower

188, bottom: Tom Burr, *Bent, Bandaged, Beat Up, Beat Up Again and Bewildered*, 2008. Included in *Tom Burr / Matrix 182: Hinged Figures*, Wadsworth Atheneum, Hartford, CT, 2019. © Tom Burr. Photo: Tom Burr

189: Production of Tom Burr, *An Abstract Orange*, 2022. © Tom Burr. Photos: Tom Burr

190: Tom Burr, *Sexual Soft Target*, 2017, green military-style blankets, black upholstery tacks, direct-to-surface print, clear plastic photographic sleeves, steel pushpins, paperback copy of *Funeral Rites* by Jean Genet (1948), powder-coated aluminum, painted plywood, 3 ½ × 94 ½ × 94 ½ in. Installed in front of Tom Burr, *Bent, Bandaged, Beat Up, Beat Up Again and Bewildered*, 2008, and Tom Burr, *Wide Wall Wound*, 2017. © Tom Burr. Photo: Jackie Furtado

191, top: Tom Burr, *Sexual Soft Target*, 2017, installed in front of Tom Burr, *Double Divided Façade*, 2014, Perspex, plywood, steel, paint, 84 ⅜ × 144 ⅛ × 84 ⅝ in. © Tom Burr. Photo: Elijah Jaquez-Starks

191, bottom: Tom Burr, *Sexual Soft Target* (detail), 2017. © Tom Burr. Photo: Elijah Jaquez-Starks

196–97: Production of Tom Burr, *Double Divided Façade*, 2014. © Tom Burr. Photos: Elijah Jaquez-Starks

198–99: Tom Burr, *Double Divided Façade*, 2014. © Tom Burr. Photo: Elijah Jaquez-Starks

200–1: Interior view of *Torrington Project*. © Tom Burr. Photo: Guang Xu

202: A selection of work from Tom Burr's *Floor Model* series, all 2022. © Tom Burr. Photo: Guang Xu

203: Production of the linoleum panels that make up Tom Burr's *Floor Model* series, all 2022. © Photos: Elijah Jaquez-Starks

204: Tom Burr, *Floor Model (Adolescent)*, 2022, T-shirt, men's sneakers, copy of Louis Dupré's *The Philosophical Foundations of Marxism*, vintage linoleum tiles, MDF, Plexiglas, 18 × 36 × 36 in. © Tom Burr. Photo: Tom Burr

205: Tom Burr, *Floor Model (Adolescent)*, 2022. Included in *Tom Burr*, Bortolami Gallery, New York, 2023. © Tom Burr. Photo: Guang Xu

206: Tom Burr, *Floor Model (Convalescent)*, 2022, MDF, Plexiglas, linoleum tiles, sneakers, bandaged, 18 × 36 × 36 in. © Tom Burr. Courtesy of Galerie Neu, Berlin. Photo: Stefan Korte

207: Installation instructions for Tom Burr, *Floor Model (Convalescent)*, 2022. © Tom Burr. Photos: Elijah Jaquez-Starks

208: Installation instructions for Tom Burr, *Floor Model (Obsolescent)*, 2022. © Tom Burr. Photos: Elijah Jaquez-Starks

209: Tom Burr, *Floor Model (Obsolescent)*, 2022, MDF, Plexiglas, linoleum tiles, sneakers, jeans, book, 18 × 36 × 36 in. © Tom Burr. Courtesy of Galerie Neu, Berlin. Photo: Stefan Korte

210: Tom Burr, *Insomnia*, 2007, painted plywood, steel braces, clothes hanger, pajamas, bedsheets, pillow, book, 78 ¾ × 78 ¾ × 35 ⅜ in. Included in The Campus's inaugural exhibition, Hudson, NY, 2024. © Tom Burr. Photo: Guang Xu

211: Tom Burr, *Insomnia*, 2007. © Tom Burr. Photo: Elijah Jaquez-Starks

212–13: Interior view of *Torrington Project*. In the background: Maria Hassabi, *Bench*, 2024. © Tom Burr and Maria Hassabi. Photo: Jackie Furtado

214: Extra panels left over from the production of *Tom Burr*, Bortolami Gallery, New York, 2023. © Tom Burr. Photo: Jackie Furtado

214–15: Tom Burr, *Blatantly Bronze Landscape*, 2012, aluminum, steel, glass mirror, 70 ⅞ × 141 ¾ × 2 ½ in. © Tom Burr. Photo: Guang Xu

216: Tom Burr, *Blatantly Bronze Landscape*, 2012. © Tom Burr. Photo: Guang Xu

217: Tom Burr, *Blatantly Bronze Landscape*, 2012. Included in Foire internationale d'art contemporain, Paris, 2012. © Tom Burr. Photos courtesy Almine Rech Gallery, Paris

219: Interior view of *Torrington Project*. © Tom Burr. Photo: Guang Xu

220: Interior view of *Torrington Project*. © Tom Burr. Photo: Elijah Jaquez-Starks

220–22: Interior views of *Torrington Project*. © Tom Burr. Photos: Guang Xu

222, bottom: Interior view of *Torrington Project* featuring Tom Burr, *Surplus Edition*, 2017, plastic film and upholstery nails on wood, 15 × 15 × 1 ¼ in., and Tom Burr, *Flag, No. 5*, 2016, acrylic paint on Sailtex, aluminum eyelets, 41 ⅓ × 41 ⅓ in. © Tom Burr. Photo: Elijah Jaquez-Starks

223: Tom Burr, *Green Bomber Jacket (New Haven, CT)*, 2019, silkscreen on bomber jacket, approx. 28 ⅜ × 47 ¼ in. © Tom Burr. Photo: Elijah Jaquez-Starks

224, top: Alvin Baltrop, *The Piers (two containers on dock)*, n.d. (1975–86), silver gelatin print, 4 ⅜ × 6 ⅝ in. © 2025 Estate of Alvin Baltrop / Artists Rights Society (ARS), New York. Loaned to Tom Burr by Patrick Collins and Liv Barrett for a one-day exhibition and performance program. Photo: Jackie Furtado

224, bottom: Alvin Baltrop, *The Piers (warehouse interior)*, n.d. (1975–86), silver gelatin print, 6 × 9 ½ in. © 2025 Estate of Alvin Baltrop / Artists Rights Society (ARS), New York. Loaned to Tom Burr by Patrick Collins and Liv Barrett for a one-day exhibition and performance program. Photo: Jackie Furtado

225, top: Alvin Baltrop, *Untitled (The Piers: two men sitting)*, n.d. (1975–86), silver gelatin print, 7 ¾ × 9 ¾ in. © 2025 Estate of Alvin Baltrop / Artists Rights Society (ARS), New York. Loaned to Tom Burr by Patrick Collins and Liv Barrett for a one-day exhibition and performance program. Photo: Jackie Furtado

225, bottom: Alvin Baltrop, *The Piers (two containers on dock)*, n.d. (1975–86). © 2025 Estate of Alvin Baltrop / Artists Rights Society (ARS), New York. Loaned to Tom Burr by Patrick Collins and Liv Barrett for a one-day exhibition and performance program. Photo: Jackie Furtado

226–27: Tom Burr, *Third Renovation*, from *Eight Renovations: A constellation of sites across Manhattan*, 1997, vinyl lettering, dimensions variable. © Tom Burr. Photo: Jackie Furtado

229: Interior view of *Torrington Project*. © Tom Burr. Photo: Elijah Jaquez-Starks

230–31, top: The "Elijah Shelves" at *Torrington Project*, where installation materials, tech, and artworks were stored. Photo: Elijah Jaquez-Starks

230–31, bottom: The "Elijah Shelves." Photo: Jackie Furtado

232–33: Interior view of *Torrington Project*. © Tom Burr. Photo: Jessica Tang

234–35: Tom Burr, *Twelve Grays*, 2021, suite of 12 photos, archival pigment print on Canson Rag Photographique 310 gsm 100% cotton rag fine art paper, 13 ¾ × 10 ¾ × 1 ½ in. each. © Tom Burr. Photo: Elijah Jaquez-Starks

236–37: Interior view of *Torrington Project* featuring a wall of preparatory drawings made by Tom Burr over the course of his career. © Tom Burr. Photo: Jackie Furtado

238: A selection of preparatory drawings made by Tom Burr over the course of his career. © Tom Burr. Photo: Guang Xu

239, top: Preparatory drawing for Tom Burr's participation in the 2007 exhibition *Wieder und Wider* at Mumok, Vienna. © Tom Burr. Photo: Tom Burr

239, bottom: A selection of preparatory drawings made by Tom Burr over the course of his career, installed alongside Tom Burr, *Untitled (Private Property) #3*, and Tom Burr, *Untitled (Private Property) #5*, both 1999. © Tom Burr. Photo: Guang Xu

240–41: A selection of preparatory drawings made by Tom Burr over the course of his career. © Tom Burr. Photos: Tom Burr

242: A selection of preparatory drawings made by Tom Burr over the course of his career, alongside Tom Burr, *Fourth Renovation*, and Tom Burr, *Fifth Renovation*, both 1997. © Tom Burr. Photo: Guang Xu

243, top: Tom Burr, *Fourth Renovation*, from *Eight Renovations: A constellation of sites across Manhattan*, 1997, vinyl lettering, dimensions variable; bottom: Tom Burr, *Fifth Renovation*, from *Eight Renovations: A constellation of sites across Manhattan*, 1997, vinyl lettering, dimensions variable. © Tom Burr. Photo: Jackie Furtado

244–45: A selection of preparatory drawings made by Tom Burr over the course of his career. © Tom Burr. Photos: Tom Burr

246–49: Tom Burr, *Eight Orange Boxes*, 1989, 8 elements, painted wood, Plexiglas, photographs, 8 × 8 × 7 in. each. Included as part of *Divine*, Galerie Neu, Berlin, 2021. © Tom Burr. Courtesy of Galerie Neu, Berlin. Photos: Stefan Korte

255: Interior view of *Torrington Project*. © Tom Burr. Photo: Guang Xu

256–57: Interior view of *Torrington Project*. © Tom Burr. Photo: Jessica Tang

258, top: Tom Burr, *An Ambient Lounge*, 1996, steel folding table, wood, model-building materials, laminated text, steel pushpins, plywood, dimensions variable. © Tom Burr. Photo: Jessica Tang

258, bottom: Tom Burr, *An Ambient Lounge* (detail), 1996. © Tom Burr. Photo: Jackie Furtado

258–59: Tom Burr, *An Ambient Lounge* (detail), 1996. © Tom Burr. Photo: Elijah Jaquez-Starks

260: Tom Burr, *An Ambient Lounge*, 1996. Included in the American Fine Arts, Co. booth at the Gramercy Art Fair, New York, 1996. © Tom Burr. Photo courtesy Bortolami Gallery, New York

261: Tom Burr, *An Ambient Lounge* (detail), 1996. © Tom Burr. Photo: Jackie Furtado

262, top: Initial construction on *Torrington Project*. © Tom Burr. Photo: Elijah Jaquez-Starks

262, bottom: Works undergoing repair in *Torrington Project*. © Tom Burr. Photo: Elijah Jaquez-Starks

263: Preparatory drawings for Tom Burr's series *Prospect Park: a documentary in four parts*, 1989. © Tom Burr. Photo: Blake Oetting

264, top: Tom Burr, *Prospect Park: a documentary in four parts (part 3)* (detail), 1989, enamel, wood, steel, aluminum, photographic inserts, 8 × 60 × 9 ½ in. © Tom Burr. Photo: Elijah Jaquez-Starks

264, bottom: Tom Burr, *Prospect Park: a documentary in four parts (part 4)* (detail), 1989, enamel, wood, steel, aluminum, photographic inserts, 8 × 60 × 9 ½ in. © Tom Burr. Photo: Elijah Jaquez-Starks

265, top: Two works from Tom Burr's series *Prospect Park: a documentary in four parts*, 1989. © Tom Burr. Photo: Elijah Jaquez-Starks

265, bottom: Tom Burr, *Prospect Park: a documentary in four parts (part 1)* (detail), 1989, enamel, wood, steel, aluminum, photographic inserts, 8 × 60 × 9 ½ in. © Tom Burr. Photo: Elijah Jaquez-Starks

266–67: Interior view of *Torrington Project*. © Tom Burr. Photo: Guang Xu

268, top: Left: Tom Burr, *A Ramble in Central Park (two)*, 1992, wood, model-building materials, Plexiglas, pedestal: 24 × 24 × 24 in., overall: 24 × 24 × 27 ⅝ in.; right: Tom Burr, *A Ramble in Central Park (one)*, 1992, wood, model-building materials, Plexiglas, pedestal: 22 × 22 × 22 in., overall: 22 × 22 × 25 ⅜ in. © Tom Burr. Photo: Jackie Furtado

268, bottom: Tom Burr, *Central Park*, 1989, plywood, paint, Plexiglas, acetate on steel, 22 × 72 × 6 ½ in., installed with the work's original label. © Tom Burr. Photo: Jackie Furtado

269: Script accompanying Tom Burr's 1992 exhibition at White Columns, New York. Scan courtesy White Columns, New York

270, top: Tom Burr, *Hazy View*, 1992, gelatin silver print on wood frame, 28 × 34 in. © Tom Burr. Photo courtesy Bortolami Gallery, New York. Photo: Kristian Laudrup

270, bottom: Tom Burr, *A Ramble in Central Park (two)*, 1992. Included in *Central Park Visitor Center. Focus: "The Ramble,"* White Columns, New York, 1992. © Tom Burr. Photo courtesy White Columns, New York

271, top: Tom Burr, *Untitled*, 1989, plywood, paint, Plexiglas, acetate on steel, 22 × 72 × 6 ½ in. Included in a group show at American Fine Arts, Co. in Summer 1994. © Tom Burr.

271, bottom: Tom Burr, *A Ramble in Central Park (one)*, 1992. © Tom Burr. Installation view of *Life Between Buildings*, MoMA PS1, June 2, 2022–January 16, 2023. Courtesy MoMA PS1. Photo: Steven Paneccasio

278, top: Tom Burr, *A Ramble in Central Park (one)*, and Tom Burr, *A Ramble in Central Park (two)*, both 1992, installed in front of Tom Burr, *Hélio-Screen New York*, 2021, poplar, black matte paint, 76 × 118 × 18 in. © Tom Burr. Photo: Jackie Furtado

278, bottom: Left: Tom Burr, *Oblong Box (Torrington)*, 2002/ 2022, wood, paint, steel, 96 × 53 ⅞ × 50 in.; right: Tom Burr, *Hélio-Screen New York*, 2021. © Tom Burr. Photo: Elijah Jaquez-Starks

279, top: Tom Burr, *Hélio-Screen New York*, 2021. Included in *Hélio-centricities (New York)*, Bortolami Gallery, New York, 2021. © Tom Burr. Photo courtesy Bortolami Gallery, New York. Photo: Kristian Laudrup

279, bottom: Tom Burr, *Hélio-Screen New York*, 2021. Included in *Hélio-Centricities, auroras*, São Paulo, 2019. © Tom Burr. Courtesy Ricardo Kugelmas. Photo: Ding Musa

280–81: Interior view of *Torrington Project*. © Tom Burr. Photo: Guang Xu

282–83: Tom Burr, *Jones Beach State Park*, 1989, plywood, acrylic paint, Plexiglas, steel hardware, steel plates, printed acetate sheets, installed with the work's original label, 22 × 96 × 6 ½ in. © Tom Burr. Photo: Guang Xu

283, top: Tom Burr, *Jones Beach State Park (model)* (detail), 1992. © Tom Burr. Photo: Elijah Jaquez-Starks

283, bottom: Tom Burr, *Jones Beach State Park (model)*, 1992, lamp, sand, mixed media on table, 30 × 60 × 28 in. © Tom Burr. Photo: Elijah Jaquez-Starks

284: Tom Burr, *Jones Beach State Park*, 1989. © Tom Burr. Photo: Elijah Jaquez-Starks

285: Tom Burr, *Jones Beach State Park (model)*, 1992. Included in a 1992 group show at American Fine Arts, Co., New York. © Tom Burr. Photos courtesy Bortolami Gallery, New York

287: Interior view of *Torrington Project* featuring Maria Hassabi, *Bench*, 2024. © Tom Burr and Maria Hassabi. Photo: Jackie Furtado

288: Left: Tom Burr, *Hélio-Screen New York*, 2021; right: Tom Burr, *Eighteen (Red Grid)*, 2024, painted wood panel, powder-coated aluminum panel and hardware, flannel shirt, thumbtacks, nails, 27 × 27 × 2⅛ in. © Tom Burr. Photo: Guang Xu

289: Left: Tom Burr, *Seventeen (Dries Sleeve)*, 2024, painted wood panel, powder-coated aluminum panel and hardware, Dries Van Noten blazer, paper announcement for *Tom Burr: Moods* (Secession, 2008), thumbtacks, nails, 27 × 27 × 2⅛ in.; right: Tom Burr, *Our Lady of the Flowers*, 2010, vinyl, Plexiglas, steel cable, 96 × 120 × 96 in. © Tom Burr. Photo: Jackie Furtado

290: Tom Burr, *Eighteen (Red Grid)*, 2024. © Tom Burr. Photo: Guang Xu

291: Tom Burr, *Seventeen (Dries Sleeve)*, 2024. © Tom Burr. Photo: Guang Xu

292–93: Tom Burr, *Our Lady of the Flowers*, 2010. © Tom Burr. Photos: Jackie Furtado

294, top: Tom Burr, *I Am My Mother*, 2013, stool, extension cord, plywood, acrylic, 48 × 53⅛ × 53⅛ in., installed in front of Tom Burr, *Eleven (Andy's Pat)*, 2024, painted wood panel, powder-coated aluminum panel and hardware, photograph of Pat Hearn by Andy Warhol on postcard used for "Emergency art sale to benefit Pat Hearn Gallery, New York, February 26–March 9, 1997," page from Rainer Crone's catalogue raisonné of *Andy Warhol* (1970) with photograph of Warhol's hands, fabric cord, thumbtacks, nails, mixed media, 27 × 27 × 2⅛ in. © Tom Burr. Photo: Jessica Tang

294, bottom: Interior view of *Torrington Project*. © Tom Burr. Photo: Elijah Jaquez-Starks

295: Tom Burr, *I Am My Mother*, 2013, installed in front of Tom Burr, *Eleven (Andy's Pat)*, 2024. © Tom Burr. Photo: Jackie Furtado

296: Tom Burr, *Fifteen (Interlude)*, 2024, painted wood panel, powder-coated aluminum panel and hardware, dark blue Levis, vinyl record in album cover: John Cage, *Sonatas and Interludes for Prepared Piano (1946–48)*, thumbtacks, nails, 27 × 27 × 2⅛ in. © Tom Burr. Photo: Guang Xu

297: Tom Burr, *Eleven (Andy's Pat)*, 2024. © Tom Burr. Photo: Guang Xu

304–05: Interior view of *Torrington Project*. © Tom Burr. Photo: Guang Xu

306–07: Interior view of *Torrington Project*. © Tom Burr. Photo: Jessica Tang

308–09: Maria Hassabi, *Bench*, 2024, installed in front of Tom Burr, *Early Childhood Development*, 2018, wool blanket and upholstery tacks on plywood, 72 × 72 in. © Maria Hassabi and Tom Burr. Photo: Jessica Tang

309–10: Tom Burr, *White T-Shirt 2 (Torrington Project)*, 2017, plywood, cotton t-shirt, steel pushpins, 15 × 15 in. © Tom Burr. Photo: Jackie Furtado

310–11: Tom Burr, *Halston Make-Up Mirror*, 2012, aluminum, photographs, steel pushpins, bulletin board, 36 × 48 in. © Tom Burr. Photo: Elijah Jaquez-Starks

312: Tom Burr, *The Second Renovation*, from *Eight Renovations: A constellation of sites across Manhattan*, 1997, vinyl lettering, dimensions variable. © Tom Burr. Photo: Elijah Jaquez-Starks

313: Tom Burr, *The Second Renovation*, 1997. © Tom Burr. Photo: Jackie Furtado

314–15: Tom Burr, *Oblong Box (Torrington)*, 2002/2022. © Tom Burr. Photo: Elijah Jaquez-Starks

316: Tom Burr, *Oblong Box (Torrington)* (detail), 2002/2022. © Tom Burr. Photo: Jackie Furtado

317: Tom Burr, *Oblong Box (Torrington)*, 2002/2022, formerly titled *Oblong Box #4*. Installation view of *Dog Days*, Greene Naftali, New York, 2002. © Tom Burr. Courtesy Greene Naftali. Photos: Oren Slor

318: Maureen Paley reflected in the mirror on the verso of Tom Burr, *Oblong Box (Torrington)*, 2002/2022. © Tom Burr. Photo: Tom Burr

319: Interior view of *Torrington Project*. © Tom Burr. Photo: Tom Burr

320: Tom Burr, *White T-Shirt 1 (Torrington Project)*, 2017, plywood, cotton t-shirt, steel pushpins, 15 × 15 in. © Tom Burr. Photo: Jackie Furtado

321: Tom Burr, *White T-Shirt 1 (Torrington Project)*, 2017. © Tom Burr. Photo: Elijah Jaquez-Starks

322, top: Interior view of *Torrington Project* featuring posters and photos of Adrian Piper and Walt Whitman, top to bottom, and an invitation to Tom Burr's 2011 exhibition at FRAC Champagne-Ardenne, *Gravity Moves Me*. © Tom Burr. Photo: Elijah Jaquez-Starks

322, bottom: Interior view of *Torrington Project* featuring posters and photos of Adrian Piper and Walt Whitman, top to bottom. © Tom Burr. Photo: Jackie Furtado

323: Maria Hassabi, *Bench*, 2024, installed in front of Tom Burr, *Oblong Box (Torrington)*, 2002/2022. © Tom Burr. Photo: Jackie Furtado

324: Interior view of *Torrington Project*. © Tom Burr. Photo: Jackie Furtado

325: Tom Burr, *The Sixth Renovation*, from *Eight Renovations: A constellation of sites across Manhattan*, 1997, vinyl lettering, dimensions variable. © Tom Burr. Photo: Jackie Furtado

326: Interior view of *Torrington Project* featuring a poster from Tom Burr's 2000 exhibition *Low Slung* at Kunstverein Braunschweig, Germany. © Tom Burr. Photo: Blake Oetting

327: Graffiti found in the men's bathroom at 535 Migeon Avenue, Torrington, CT. Photo: Blake Oetting

329: Interior view of *Torrington Project* featuring Tom Burr, *Studio Contortion Sequence I–IV*, 2022. © Tom Burr. Photo: Jessica Tang

330–31: Interior view of *Torrington Project*. © Tom Burr. Photo: Guang Xu

332: Production of Tom Burr, *Studio Contortion Sequence I–IV*, 2022. © Tom Burr. Photos: Elijah Jaquez-Starks

332–33: Tom Burr, *Studio Contortion Sequence I–IV*, 2022. © Tom Burr. Photos: Jackie Furtado

334–35: Tom Burr, *Studio Contortion Sequence I*, 2022, stained plywood, glass mirror, metal folding chairs, steel clamps, steel brace, 72 × 96 × 24 in. © Tom Burr. Photo: Elijah Jaquez-Starks

336–37: Tom Burr, *Studio Contortion Sequence III*, 2022, stained plywood, glass mirror, metal folding chairs, steel clamps, steel brace, 72 × 96 × 24 in. © Tom Burr. Photo: Elijah Jaquez-Starks

338–39: Tom Burr, *Studio Contortion Sequence II*, 2022, stained plywood, glass mirror, metal folding chairs, steel clamps, steel brace, 72 × 96 × 24 in. © Tom Burr. Photo: Elijah Jaquez-Starks

340: Tom Burr, *Studio Contortion Sequence IV* (detail), 2022. © Tom Burr. Photo: Quincy Childs

341: Tom Burr, *Studio Contortion Sequence VI*, 2022, stained plywood, glass mirror, metal folding chairs, steel clamps, steel brace, 72 × 85 × 24½ in. © Tom Burr. Courtesy of Galerie Neu, Berlin. Photo: Stefan Korte

342: Tom Burr, *Studio Contortion Sequence V*, 2022, stained plywood, glass mirror, metal folding chairs, steel clamps, steel brace, 72 × 72 × 24 in. © Tom Burr. Courtesy of Galerie Neu, Berlin. Photo: Stefan Korte

343: Gordon Hall, *Graphite Covered Leg (Turned)*, 2024, cast concrete, graphite, 30¾ × 1¾ × 1¾ in. © Gordon Hall. Photo: Jackie Furtado

344–45, from left: Tom Burr, *Studio Contortion Sequence III*, 2022; Gordon Hall, *Graphite Covered Leg (Turned)*, 2024; Tom Burr, *Studio Contortion Sequence IV*, 2022. © Tom Burr and Gordon Hall. Photo: Jessica Tang

346–47: Interior view of *Torrington Project* featuring Tom Burr, *Studio Contortion Sequence I–IV*, 2022, during a visit organized by the Whitney Museum of American Art, New York. © Tom Burr. Photo: Blake Oetting

348–49, from left: Maria Hassabi, *White Out*, 2024, performance; Gordon Hall, *1–2 pm*, 2024, lecture performance; Nick Mauss, *The Image Runs Away*, 2024, audio, four speakers. © Maria Hassabi, Gordon Hall, and Nick Mauss. Photos: Jackie Furtado

350–57: Maria Hassabi, *White Out*, 2024. © Maria Hassabi. Photos: Jackie Furtado

358–59: Maria Hassabi, *White Out*, 2024. © Maria Hassabi. Photos: Jessica Tang

360–63: Maria Hassabi, *White Out*, 2024. © Maria Hassabi. Photos: Jackie Furtado

364–65: Maria Hassabi, *White Out*, 2024. © Maria Hassabi. Photos: Jessica Tang

366–67: Gordon Hall, *1–2 pm*, 2024. © Gordon Hall. Photo: Jackie Furtado

368: Scott Burton, *Modular Six-Unit Seating*, 1986, polished rosso imperiale red and black granite, 6 pieces, 37½ × 17½ × 39½ in. each. © Scott Burton. Photo: Olivia Cunnally, courtesy Gordon Hall

369: Reflected light from a phone screen on the ceiling of a train. Photo: Gordon Hall

370: Scott Burton, *Modular Six-Unit Seating*, 1986, published in the *Pittsburgh Press* on May 15, 1986. © Pittsburgh Post-Gazette, 2025, all rights reserved. Reprinted with permission. Photo courtesy Gordon Hall

373: Scott Burton, *Individual Behavior Tableaux*, as performed by Kent Hines, 1980. © Estate of Scott Burton / Artist Rights Society (ARS), New York. © The Museum of Modern Art / Licensed by SCALA / Art Resource, New York. Photo courtesy Jess Wilcox and Gordon Hall

374: Scott Burton, *Individual Behavior Tableaux*, as performed by Kent Hines, 1980. © Estate of Scott Burton / Artist Rights Society (ARS), New York. © The Museum of Modern Art / Licensed by SCALA / Art Resource, New York. Photo courtesy Jess Wilcox and Gordon Hall

375: Scott Treleaven, *Scott Burton's Garden Court*, 2021, analog photograph. © Scott Treleaven and the Estate of Scott Burton. Photo courtesy the artist

378–81: Interior views of *Torrington Project* featuring the audience for Nick Mauss, *The Image Runs Away*, 2024. © Nick Mauss and Tom Burr. Photos: Jackie Furtado

382–85, top: Jean Genet, "'Adame Miroir" as presented in *Fragments…et autres textes*, collected in *Théâtre complet*. Bibliothèque de la Pléiade (Paris: Gallimard, 1990), pp. 32–43 © Gallimard. Scan courtesy of Bortolami Gallery, New York

382–85, bottom: Documentation of a performance of *'adame Miroir* on September 20, 1988, at the Casino de Paris, choreography by Janine Charrat. Photos courtesy Médiathèque du Centre national de la danse –Fonds Jean-Marie Gourreau

386–89: Interior views of *Torrington Project* featuring the audience for Nick Mauss, *The Image Runs Away*, 2024. © Nick Mauss and Tom Burr. Photos: Jackie Furtado

390–91: Interior view of *Torrington Project*. © Tom Burr. Photo: Guang Xu

392: Interior view of *Torrington Project*. © Tom Burr. Photo: Tom Burr

Works exhibited, but not pictured:

Tom Burr, *Untitled (August Collage)*, 2007, cardboard and collage, 18 × 24 in.

Tom Burr, *Untitled (August Collage)*, 2007, cardboard and collage, 18 × 24 in.

Tom Burr, *Untitled (August Collage)*, 2007, cardboard and collage, 18 × 24 in.

Tom Burr, *Untitled (Beard Boards)*, 2011, wood and paper framed in Plexiglas, 19 × 19 in.

Tom Burr, *Untitled (Beard Boards)*, 2011, wood and paper framed in Plexiglas, 19 × 19 in.

Tom Burr, *Untitled (Beard Boards)*, 2011, wood and paper framed in Plexiglas, 19 × 19 in.

Tom Burr, *Torrington Project (Northwest Corner)*, 2023, digital print, 8⅜ × 11⅝ in.

Torrington Project
© 2025 Tom Burr and Primary Information

ISBN: 979-8-9910367-4-0

"Foreword Backward" © 2025 Blake Oetting
"Containers" © 2025 George Baker
"Distributing Desire Lines" © 2025 Jordan Carter
"factuals" © 2025 Aria Dean
"Shadow Play" © 2025 Jody Graf
"Matter and Memory" © 2025 Renée Green
"1–2 pm" © 2025 Gordon Hall
"White Out" © 2025 Maria Hassabi
"Ellsworth, Gregory, and Tom" © 2025 David Joselit
"The Image Runs Away" © 2025 Nick Mauss
"Treaded" © 2025 Christine Messineo
"Forms of Stasis" © 2025 Humberto Moro

"Artist pulls up chairs at One Mellon Plaza." © 2025 *Pittsburgh Post-Gazette*. All rights reserved. Reprinted with permission. Jean Genet, "'Adame Miroir" as presented in *Fragments...et autres textes*, collected in *Théâtre complet*. Bibliothèque de la Pléiade (Paris: Gallimard, 1990). © Gallimard. Valerie Smith, fax, March 22, 1993. © 2025 Valerie Smith. Published by permission of the author.

The rights to the work remain the sole property of the author(s). All rights reserved. No part of this publication may be reproduced, stored in retrieval systems, or transmitted in any form or by any means, electronic, mechanical, photocopying, recording, or otherwise, without prior permission from the copyright holder.

Editor: Blake Oetting
Managing Editors: James Hoff and Sam Korman
Designer: Garrick Gott
Copy Editor: Allison Dubinsky

Primary Information
232 3rd Street, #A113
Brooklyn, NY 11215
www.primaryinformation.org

Printed by Grafiche Veneziane, Italy

The artist would like to thank Billy Dobbins; Bortolami Gallery, New York; Bryan Savitz; Center for Curatorial Studies, Bard College, Annandale-on-Hudson, New York; Charilaos Meletiou; Charles Asprey; Galerie Almine Rech, Paris; Galerie Neu, Berlin; Galleria Franco Noero, Turin; Greene Naftali, New York; John DeShazo; Magnus Schaefer; Matilde Guidelli-Guidi; Maureen Paley, London; Michael Sanchez; MoMA PS1; Musée cantonal des Beaux-Arts de Lausanne; Nick Hochstetler; Octavius Neveaux; Parker Field; Stand and Build, New York; and White Columns, New York.

This publication is made possible with lead support from Patrick Collins and Liv Barrett. Major support is provided by Philip Aarons and Shelley Fox Aarons and the National Endowment for the Arts. Contributing support is provided by Carol and David Aronowitz, James Crump and Ronnie Sassoon, Ricardo Kugelmas, and Will Paley.

Performances staged by Gordon Hall, Maria Hassabi, and Nick Mauss as part of *Torrington Project* were made possible by support from Jane Hait and Justin Beal, Stephen and Ruth Melville, and Barbara and Howard Morse.

Primary Information is a 501(c)(3) non-profit organization founded in 2006 to publish artists' books and writings. The organization's programming advances the often-intertwined relationship between artists' books and arts activism, creating a platform for historically marginalized artistic communities and practices. The organization receives generous support through grants from the Michael Asher Foundation, Galerie Buchholz, the Patrick and Aimee Butler Family Foundation, The Cowles Charitable Trust, Empty Gallery, The Ford Foundation, The Fox Aarons Foundation, the Helen Frankenthaler Foundation, Furthermore: a program of the J. M. Kaplan Fund, the Graham Foundation for Advanced Studies in the Fine Arts, Greene Naftali, the Greenwich Collection Ltd, the John W. and Clara C. Higgins Foundation, Metabolic Studio, the New York City Department of Cultural Affairs in partnership with the City Council, the New York State Council on the Arts with the support of the Office of the Governor and the New York State Legislature, the Orbit Fund, the Robert Rauschenberg Foundation, the Stichting Egress Foundation, VIA Art Fund, The Jacques Louis Vidal Charitable Fund, Wagner Foundation, The Andy Warhol Foundation for the Visual Arts, the Wilhelm Family Foundation, and individuals worldwide. Primary Information receives support from the Arison Arts Foundation, The Willem de Kooning Foundation, the Marian Goodman Foundation, the Henry Luce Foundation, the Mellon Foundation, and Teiger Foundation through the Coalition of Small Arts NYC.